Monstrosity and Philosophy
Radical Otherness in Greek and Latin Culture

Filippo Del Lucchese

EDINBURGH
University Press

Edinburgh University Press is one of the leading university presses in the UK. We publish academic books and journals in our selected subject areas across the humanities and social sciences, combining cutting-edge scholarship with high editorial and production values to produce academic works of lasting importance. For more information visit our website: edinburghuniversitypress.com

© Filippo Del Lucchese, 2019, 2021

Edinburgh University Press Ltd
The Tun – Holyrood Road
12(2f) Jackson's Entry
Edinburgh EH8 8PJ

First published in hardback by Edinburgh University Press 2019

Typeset in 10.5/13 Goudy Old Style by
IDSUK (DataConnection) Ltd

A CIP record for this book is available from the British Library

ISBN 978 1 4744 5620 3 (hardback)
ISBN 978 1 4744 5621 0 (paperback)
ISBN 978 1 4744 5623 4 (webready PDF)
ISBN 978 1 4744 5622 7 (epub)

The right of Filippo Del Lucchese to be identified as the author of this work has been asserted in accordance with the Copyright, Designs and Patents Act 1988, and the Copyright and Related Rights Regulations 2003 (SI No. 2498).

Contents

Acknowledgements	v
Introduction	1
1. The Myth and the Logos	8
Order and Chaos	13
Mythical Battlefields: Monstrosity as a Weapon	19
Causality and Monstrosity: Challenging Zeus	35
2. The Pre-Platonic Philosophers	56
Anaxagoras: A Material Origin for Life and Monstrosity	56
Empedocles: Wonders to Behold	63
Democritus: Agonism within Matter	70
3. Plato	78
4. Aristotle	93
5. Epicurus and Lucretius	130
An Immanent Causality for an Infinite Universe	130
Zoogony, Monstrosity and Nature's Normativity	140
Concourses of Nature	153
Lucretius's Impact on the Augustan Age	161
6. Stoicism	170
Nominalism	172
Good and Evil, Beauty and Ugliness	181
Providence, God and Teleology	205
7. Scepticism	223
The Tropes and the Critique of Essentialism	228
To What Purpose?	239

8. Middle and Neoplatonism — 248
    The Material World and the Rediscovery of Transcendence — 249
    Demons — 278
    The World Order — 287

Bibliography — 326
Index Locorum — 394
Index Verborum — 408
Index Rerum — 415
Index Nominum — 417

Acknowledgements

I am grateful to Brunel University, London, which granted me two semesters of research leave, an increasingly rare luxury and one that was sorely needed to accomplish a task of this magnitude. I am particularly grateful to Mark Neocleous, who has not only followed my research since its inception, but also wrote one of the first books I encountered on monstrosity, and to Justin Fisher, who provided me with me the institutional flexibility I needed to accomplish this research. I am also grateful to my colleagues and students in the Master in *Teoria critica della società* at the University of Milano Bicocca and the Collège International de Philosophie, who hosted me as a *Directeur de programme* from 2012 to 2019, and where I presented my work as it progressed.

I began working on monstrosity as a recipient of a Marie Curie fellowship that allowed me to spend two years at Occidental College, Los Angeles and one at the Université de Picardie, Amiens. During that time, I benefited immensely from my connection with Warren Montag and Laurent Bove, who offered not only academic supervision, but friendship and human and political solidarity beyond the boundaries of academic work.

At different stages and in different measures I have received support and invaluable criticism from several colleagues: Andrea Bardin, Luca Basso, Laura Cremonesi, Oliver Feltham, Marco Fioravanti, Alain Gigandet, Augusto Illuminati, Susanna Mezzadri, Vittorio Morfino, Gabriele Pedullà, Fabio Raimondi, Tania Rispoli, Hasana Sharp, Martha Shulman, Bruce Tindall, Oreste Trabucco, Dimitris Vardoulakis, Stefano Visentin, Elia Zaru.

With their questions and curiosity, Djalal and Rahma helped me think about monstrosity in ways I could not have imagined before meeting them. Without them, this book's writing would have been . . . much faster, but also much sadder! I am most grateful for their challenging presence in my life.

This book is dedicated to Kady, who supported me in times of wrestling with worse monsters. She has been the shield without which I could have not faced them, and I will never forget.

Un commencement de monstres est possible.
                                   Victor Hugo, *Les Misérables*

Introduction

Monsters abounded in the ancient world. They proliferated on and around Phidias's lost sculpture of Athena Parthenos, one of the most renowned cult images of ancient Greece:[1] amazons and giants were depicted on her shield, which hid the snake Erichthonius, centaurs adorned her sandals; Medusa was represented on her peplos, and the Gorgoneion decorated the aegis. Finally, a Sphinx and two winged gryphons stood on her crest. Athena, endowed with skilful wisdom and warrior virtue, subjugated the monsters who had tried to subvert the Olympian order and who are shown here tamed, thus confirming her might. The Greeks praise the gods, celebrating their final victory over chaos and monstrosity.

Today's prevailing cosmological theories on the birth and evolution of the universe teach that chaos will indeed, ultimately, swallow it. Theoretical physics explains that the universe has two possible destinies, monstrously necessary in their remote and yet eternal presence: the final catastrophic collapse of the universe on the one hand or its slow exhaustion in an unstoppable increase of entropy on the other. I wonder whether the widespread interest in monstrosity that characterises scholarship today is dictated by the intriguing yet unconscious feeling that, in some way, the ancient monsters of chaos have never been fully defeated and, contrary to the Greeks' belief, will ultimately win the fight.

The specific interest in monstrosity in this book, however, derives not so much from its hypothetically eschatological sense, but rather from its concretely ontologico-political meaning. I am interested in monstrosity as radical otherness, as the provoking alterity that challenges – sometimes by its mere

---

[1] Paus. I.24.5–7. With few exceptions, abbreviations of classical works follow those in the *Diccionario griego-español* (DGE): <dge.cchs.csic.es> or the *Oxford Latin Dictionary* (OLD) and, when the DGE or the OLD does not provide them, I have used the abbreviations conventionally adopted.

presence, sometimes with open defiance – the norm's power to signify.[2] In exploring the history of ancient thought, I have tried to show how monstrosity's challenge often comes in the form of a scandalous ontological project, immanent and material. This project is *both* ontological and political, since every metaphysical framework is at the same time determined by, and has implications for, the concept of the human and her role in the world. Equally, every vision of social, economic and political relations, like every idea of the self and the *other*, is grounded on and determines, explicitly or implicitly, a certain notion of being. Every ontology is produced by and produces, in the last instance, a politics; every politics conceives itself and is conceived, in the last instance, through an ontology.

My aim in this book is to reconstruct the concept of monstrosity in classical thought from its earliest beginnings, through pre-Platonic and Attic philosophy to the Hellenistic systems, arriving finally at Neoplatonism. I want to follow the discourse about monstrosity – mostly but not entirely – as it appeared in philosophy, and show how an apparently peripheral concept is in fact central to understanding how each of the above systems explains nature, its functioning and its anomalies.

Although monsters have attracted their fair share of attention in the past, no attempt has been made to analyse the topic extensively throughout antiquity. Articles and monographs on similar topics exist in recent scholarship, such as Morgan's unpublished PhD thesis (1984), the essays in Atherton (1992) or the enquiry on Roman monsters by Cuny-Le Callet (2005), the studies of Jones (1993) and Morfino (2013) on Lucretius, of Johnson (1987) on Lucan, of Louis (1975) and Yartz (1997) on Aristotle, and I have benefited greatly from them. A more comprehensive reconstruction, however, seems to me indispensable for a better understanding of ancient thought as a whole. Furthermore, it is crucial for the study of more recent historical periods in which the heritage of antiquity becomes a battlefield that mirrors modern and – albeit more indirectly – contemporary philosophical debates on the questions of nature, the divine, the relation between normality and abnormality, and, perhaps most importantly, the construction of identity and otherness. In this sense, this book, devoted to the ancient world, is self-contained and autonomous, yet it can also be read as a necessary introduction to the study of monstrosity in the middle ages, the Renaissance and modernity.

It is easier to say what this book is not and what it does not aim to be than to say what it is and what I hope it can do: it is not an exhaustive handbook on a specific topic, such as the classic monograph on fate by Chase Green (1944),

---

[2] See Foucault (1999).

Cotter's work on miracles (1999), the seminal study on Hermetism by Festugière (1949–54), Jaeger's seminal study on *Paideia* (1934–47), or the less well known but exhaustive enquiries on destiny by Magris (1984) and the concept of nature by Naddaf (1992), all of which I have learnt from. My book intends to show the diverse aspects of reflections on monstrosity and the problems related to its interpretation, always conscious of the provisional and incomplete character such a study must have. I make no claim to completeness: fortune and time do not permit the book to extend beyond geographic, linguistic and chronological boundaries that may appear artificial. I try, however, to consider the principal sources that, in my view, speak meaningfully about, shape and are shaped by the development of the concept of monstrosity.

My most serious difficulty has come from an attempt to keep together texts and ideas shaped throughout the centuries, and to follow their development without imposing on them a sense of continuity that emanates from the observer's eye rather than the coherency of the object observed. The multiplicity of such ideas and interpretations, of the problems and their attempted responses across the ancient period, would suggest the necessity to speak about a plurality of monstrosities rather than *one* concept of monstrosity. I have resisted this solution. Although plurality does offer an escape from the challenges of considering a complex set of problems and questions, it fails to acknowledge that this multiplicity challenged classical thought in similar ways. Thus this book grapples with *the* concept of monstrosity and the questions that this monstrosity poses to philosophy and thought.

Monstrosity is not one concept in the sense that different authors in different schools and different periods address it explicitly as a unified theoretical object. Neither philosophers nor poets speak of it as if it were an entity that passes from one thinker to another, ready for analysis across time. Nonetheless, I consider it one concept because whenever it is addressed, however differently, it touches upon the same questions, suggests recurring forms of analysis, and requires similar theoretical tools, though it is not called by the same name or necessarily recognised as a single object. Despite the diversity of the monsters, again and again monstrosity compels philosophers to answer the same questions, to respond to the same set of problems.

Whether it insinuates itself as an uninvited guest or is explicitly evoked and placed at the centre of enquiry, monstrosity insists on raising questions that philosophers can neither dismiss nor fully solve. It is this powerful force that acts across time and systems of thought that I follow in this book. My methodological approach is to look for traces and hints of monstrosity even when it is not mentioned explicitly, and to consider it as one and the same concept despite the apparent multiplicity of its treatment and expression.

Does order come from, and put an end to, chaos – or is chaos the monstrous destiny of any supposed order? Is monstrosity a positive sign of the divine, or is it its negation and perversion? Does everything in nature have a meaning and a purpose, and if so, what is the purpose of monsters? Is monstrosity what we call the lowest level of nature's reassuring hierarchy or does it, more threateningly, speak about the absence of such a hierarchy and the illusion of axiology? These are only some of the questions that ancient authors discussed across the centuries. I am interested both in the answers and in their diversity, as well as the questions that are given. Why are they asked? Why in that form, and what preoccupations and anxieties do these questions reveal? In a word, what is, for ancient thought and for us, a monster?

Of all these questions, the latter is possibly the most difficult one, insofar as, for the most part, the authors studied in this book rarely define monstrosity precisely. What many see as monstrous does not appear that way to other authors with whom they are in dialogue, whether explicitly or implicitly. Thus I prefer to follow their attitude and avoid circumscribing the present study with a precise definition of the monstrous. Instead, I extend this study to all aspects and phenomena of the scientific and philosophical reflection influenced by the monstrous. To be more precise, I focus on all aspects and phenomena that ancient authors considered monstrous without feeling the need to offer a precise definition. In a field of enquiry like this one, to expect or require absolutely clear boundary lines would do more harm than good.

My aim has not been to reify monstrosity or to depict it as the concept that positively resists appropriation, and consequently neutralisation, by metaphysics. I carefully avoid building a Manichaean history of thought around the opposition between good monstrosity and bad normality. Instead, I attempt to consider monstrosity as an unavoidable element that every system must confront, a concept that resurfaces in every system, often beyond and against the role and status that authors explicitly assign to it. In this way, monstrosity reveals all its theoretical potentiality, against the peripheral status that comes when it is designated as the exception, the anomaly, the deviation, or the special case that confirms the normality that deserves centre stage.

A concrete example of what monstrosity reveals when it is considered an object worthy of analysis relates to the classic opposition between materialism and idealism. While this opposition deserves to be maintained in many respects, monstrosity puts it to the test, revealing internal divisions within materialism, as it is revealed by the struggle over finalism between Epicureans on one hand and Stoics on the other. It is not just in the opposition between materialism and idealism that one recognises the ontological fracture caused by monstrosity, but within materialism itself. There the monster's challenge produces different results, eventually leading to the absorption of some Stoic elements within Christian thought, while relegating materialism to the side of monstrous atheism for many centuries to come.

Conceptually, monstrosity appears strictly related to several major problems in the history of philosophy, including the origin of order, the physiology and the pathology of nature, the idea of providence, and the nature and status of evil in the world. Though its presence in these domains is often implicit, it is always central for their analysis. It has been necessary, thus, to look for monsters even where they are not, i.e. where the language of monstrosity is absent, and yet monsters turn out to lurk below the surface of common problematics. Without this kind of analysis, it would not have been possible to study the central argument of these books when it does directly relate to monstrosity.

Since this is how I have attempted to think about monstrosity and what it offers the study of ancient thought, I have assigned both a positive and a negative role to it. I have considered it as an *object* within philosophical systems, but also as a paradoxical *subject*, or rather as an active mover of those systems. I have sought, in other words, to determine how the reflection on the monstrous engages philosophy and forces it to respond to certain questions, how it prevents philosophy from underestimating or even avoiding questions that would otherwise be unsettling, inconvenient or seemingly inexplicable. Their monstrosity consists in rising within a philosophical system and obliging it to hesitate in front of what appears threateningly imperfect, incomplete and incoherent.

The major risk, especially in an enquiry so extensive from a chronological point of view, is to assign to monstrosity the status of a *passepartout* or litmus test against which everything else in a philosophical discourse must be tested. I have tried to avoid that risk by bringing to the forefront of a philosophical system or an author's thought only the elements that are essential to comprehend how that system or thought deals with monstrosity, and whether and how monstrosity has influenced its formation and development, even in doctrinal points in which monstrosity as such does not appear.

I begin with Greek mythical thought. This means I have avoided the non-Greek origins and relations with other civilisations, in part because of lack of linguistic competence. But the other reason is that philosophy does not begin when it begins to call itself 'philosophy'. Rather it begins when humans begin to question the origin of their civilisation, its status and its values through specific questions, and when they offer answers, no matter the form or discourse in which they are presented, be it mythological, poetical, tragic, visual or specifically philosophical.

In each chapter, I explore the many ways in which monstrosity emerges in a set of authors and theories. In Chapter 1, monsters rise as the challenging adversaries of the new gods of the early cosmogonies, but also as the powerful productive forces that support the building of the new order. Similarly, monsters are often the ambiguous characters that catalyse the unfolding of the tragic universe. Among the Pre-Platonic philosophers, the systems of Anaxagoras, Empedocles and Democritus, analysed in Chapter 2, pave the way for the recognition of the philosophical status of monstrosity. This status becomes central in Attic philosophy, first with Plato's philosophical use of mythological monstrosities, then with the construction of a hierarchical structure of the universe, which I take up in Chapter 3. Chapter 4 focuses on Aristotle's study of physical monstrosity and its role within his metaphysical and aetiological framework. Chapters 5 to 7 deal with the extraordinarily elaborate responses to Attic philosophy by the three major Hellenistic systems: Epicureanism, Stoicism and Scepticism. The final chapter looks at the Middle and Neoplatonist response to Hellenism and explores the richness of late antiquity's reflection on monstrosity up to its absorption and reworking by early Christian thought.

I deal with similar questions in each chapter, looking at the prominent role monstrosity plays in shaping an author's thought or a philosophical movement's beliefs. I have tried to focus my discussions on texts and authors that, although not always widely known, offer an original understanding of the concept of monstrosity, especially when situated in a wider debate either within the philosophical tradition they belong to or in the general context of their own epoch. I have spent time on texts that might seem to have little or no appeal for students or readers outside the discipline of classics itself whenever I thought they could throw light on the interpretation of major authors that no reader would ignore.

Oversights, whether conscious or unintentional, necessarily happen in a work of such scope and extension. I believe, however, that such a comprehensive analysis is valuable insofar as it reveals original connections and unexpected dialogues between authors who, although writing many centuries apart, are self-consciously participating in the same philosophical struggle as their masters, allies and opponents. A wide-ranging analysis such as this makes visible the strategical choices these thinkers made – sometimes guided by profound theoretical beliefs, other times by more immediate tactics and the cultural and political struggles of their own epoch.

I have thus modestly tried to follow in the steps of some great scholars of the twentieth century whose works – comprehensive but not exhaustive – indelibly marked my formation. I need not mention these works by name, since their presence is manifest throughout this book. However, since my background is in early modernity, I have also found inspiration in some comprehensive analyses of monstrosity, and more widely on the idea of nature, in the seventeenth and eighteenth centuries. Since they are not mentioned in the following pages, I would like to mention at least three of them: Jean Céard's accomplished study of prodigies in the Renaissance, Bernard Tocanne's monograph on the idea of nature in France in the second half of the seventeenth century, and Jacques Roger's exhaustive analysis of the life sciences between Descartes and the *Encyclopédie*. Each has taught me, in different ways, how to listen to the text and insist on rigorous analysis and clear interpretation. Whether I have learned this lesson, the reader will judge.

1

The Myth and the Logos

Classical mythology is a domain full of monsters. Its analysis is of paramount importance to the comprehension of the role played by monstrosity not only in philosophy but in classical culture as a whole. The ancient mythologems largely predate the early philosophical systems, and continue to be transformed in the Attic and Hellenistic periods and eventually in the Latin world, in the Republican and Imperial ages. Mythology divulges the origin of some philosophical ideas, but is also influenced by them, without a clear or linear evolution from one to the other.

Myth could be seen as an early attempt to make sense of nature, to explain its origin and its functioning, while philosophy could be read as rising above this primitive attempt into a more advanced and rational form of thought.[1] Reale, for example, underlines how the treatment of monstrosity, in Homer, is already different from the primitive and chaotic presentation of the ancients: whereas the old versions lack limits, measure and proportion, a certain eurythmic appears in the Homeric poems. The taming of the primitive and mythical concept of monstrosity, in Reale's view, would progressively coincide with the advent of the problem of causality as the philosophical question *par excellence*.

Such a linear reading, however, would mask the complexity of mythical thought (and philosophical, to some extent), as well as its power to transform and adapt to different historical, social and religious contexts.[2] Together with morality and theology, physics is indeed one of the main domains covered

---

[1] See Nestle (1942, 2. ed.), Gigon (1945), Jaeger (1947), Cornford (1952 and 1957, 2nd ed.), Pépin (1958), Lämmli (1962), Detienne (1962), Fränkel (1962, 2. ed.), Bollack (1971), among the classics and, more recently, Dijck (1997), Morgan (2000) and Bottici (2007).

[2] Finley (1954), p. 24 and *passim*. See also Veyne (1983) and C. Ginzburg, Mito, in Settis a cura di (1996–2002), I.1, pp. 197–237.

by mythology.³ Philosophy and mythology share the claim to account for the origins of the cosmos and its laws and to explain its functioning. However, like philosophy itself, myth is far from having a linear evolution that unfolds via the taming of its most primitive modes of thinking. Myth does not in any manner lose its vitality across the centuries, and evidences a complex development that interacts with, rather than precedes, philosophy itself. Rather than the evolution from mythology to philosophy, thus, I believe it is more correct to speak about the non-linear transition of ideas between myth and logos.

Aristotle already recognises the proximity of mythologists and philosophers, and in particular the continuity between Hesiod's thought and some early naturalists.⁴ A 'thin partition' separates mythical poetry from early cosmogonic philosophy.⁵ Some scholars think that such a membrane makes the whole difference between a fantastic and chaotic account of the universe on the one hand and its rational and ordered explanation on the other.⁶ Others believe, on the contrary, that early mythical thought, e.g. the genealogies of gods, is already a coherent form of philosophical thought.⁷

The complex stratification of rationalising and mythical thought appears in early historiography as well as the extant works of geographers, and logographers like Akousilaos, Pherecydes of Syros, Hellanikos of Lesbos, Hecataeus of Miletus, Palaephatus and, of course, Herodotus. They share – in different degrees – a sensibility. Building their own domain of enquiry, they all indulge in curiosity about marginal, weird and unbelievable facts *and* bring these facts back within the boundaries of a rational explanation that reflects the rational character of nature itself.

The wonders of nature appear constantly in Herodotus's geographically extensive and ontologically inclusive enquiry across continents and natural realms. His θῶμα are often contiguous with the domain of the divine, and for him the τέρας is often religious.⁸ Yet he refuses the idea of an unnatural teratology, consistently supporting his interpretation rationally.⁹ These two aspects should not be seen as in tension with each other, but rather as cooperating to strengthen Herodotus's passionate construction of – in François Hartog's words – a rhetoric of alterity.¹⁰

---

³ Buffière (1956), p. 2 and *passim*.
⁴ Arist. *Metaph*. I.2. 982 a 4, 983 a 23. See Untersteiner (1972, 2a ed.), p. 181.
⁵ Cornford (1952), pp. 198 and *passim*.
⁶ Reale (1975–80).
⁷ Jaeger (1947).
⁸ See Giannini (1963), pp. 254–5, Lachenaud (1978) and Morgan (1984).
⁹ See e.g. Hdt. II.156, III.116, IV.23 and 105.
¹⁰ Hartog (1991, 2e ed.), p. 245 and *passim*. See also Thomas (2000), esp. ch. V.

Herodotus helps establish long-lasting belief in the geographical remoteness of natural monstrosities. One of the most significant examples is represented by the winged snakes of Arabia. In Herodotus's words:

> [. . .] the spice-bearing trees are guarded by small winged snakes of varied colour, many round each tree [. . .]. The Arabians also say that the whole country would be full of these snakes were it not with them as I have heard that it is with vipers. It would seem that the wisdom of divine Providence (as is but reasonable) has made all creatures prolific that are timid and fit to eat, that they be not minished from off the earth by being eaten up, whereas but few young are born to creatures cruel and baneful. [. . .] were [the winged serpents of Arabia] born in the natural manner of serpents no life were possible for men; but as it is, when they pair, and the male is in the very act of generation, the female seizes him by the neck, nor lets go her grip till she has bitten the neck through.[11]

Underlining the importance of Herodotus's explanation for the survival of certain species, Thomas suggests that such a causal principle can be seen as related to Darwin's evolutionism. Accustomed to debates on the prolificacy of different species, Herodotus reads the phenomenon in terms of divine providence, which prevents the excessive reproduction of obnoxious and dangerous species. In other words, though he starts with the exotic tale of fantastic creatures, he is interested in discovering their causes, and intends to intervene in the biological and scientific culture of his time.[12] Equally interesting, in my view, is the function Herodotus assigns to monstrosity in this causal explanation, suggesting indirectly that, through the critical threat represented by monstrosity, one can see and praise the divine and its providence in helping nature self-regulate and avoid self-destruction.

The aetiological intent also reveals the proximity between early historiography and paradoxography – an apparently minor yet influential and persistent literary genre. Palaephatus, one of the most influential Greek paradoxographers, reveals his interest in the traditional marvellous and monstrous phenomena by connecting them to a rational explanation. Behind the mythical event, rationalism tries to unveil the historical and rationally grounded event that, misunderstood or not fully comprehended, gave rise to the myth. Palaephatus builds the opposition between truth (ἀληθής) and a series of terms that are

---

[11] Hdt. III.107–9. See also Romm (1992) and *infra*.

[12] Thomas (2000), pp. 141–9. For both the winged snakes and the hornless cattle of IV.29–30, Thomas sees a parallel in Democritus, Empedocles, as well as the Hippocratic author of *Nat.Puer.* and *Aër*. On the winged snakes, see also Bianchi (1981), who has, however, too broad a concept of the monstrous.

closely linked to the lexicon of monstrosity such as the incredible (δύσπιστος or ἀπίθανος) and the impossible (ἀδύνατος or ἀμήχανος). He sets out his methodological approach in the introduction of *On unbelievable tales*:

> As for the many forms and monstrous shapes which have been described as once having existed, but which now do not exist – these, I believe, did not exist in the past either. For anything which ever existed in the past exists now in the present and will exist hereafter.[13]

The constancy and consistency of nature recalls the Epicurean approach. Yet Palaephatus does not deny the active omnipotence of the Gods. Precisely because of that, however, things would not and could not have happened in the unbelievable or impossible ways seen in mythical tales: through their omnipotence, the Gods would have found a less marvellous and more rational way of making these events happen. These tales must therefore be rationalised to make the principle of the constancy and consistency of natural laws more evident.[14] Whatever has not existed in the past will never be able to exist and thus whatever does not exist in the present has never existed. Nature, for Palaephatus, has one face, which it always reveals in its entirety. Whatever monstrosity is part of, it can and must be explained in a way that removes its incredible character and brings it back to the truthfulness of life. Whereas paradoxographers often expunge the causal explanation from their account of unbelievable tales, Palaephatus's rationalising methodology remains aetiological in principle, and thus closer to the early historiography.[15]

This complexity becomes more explicit when one does not limit the enquiry to mythographic works whose relation with philosophy appears more clearly, such as Homer's and especially Hesiod's *Theogony*, the only consistent source on the origin of gods that we have.[16] The analysis should be extended to other domains, such as tragedy, historiography, paradoxography, novel and of course the visual arts. Myth and logos thus reveal their complicated connection. There are major implications for ideas concerning the creation of the cosmos, the origin and maintenance of the order of nature, divine and human justice, the principle of causality, as well as several other questions that constitute the core of both philosophy *and* mythology for centuries.

---

[13] Palaeph, *Introduction*.

[14] See J. Stern, *introduction* in Palaephatus (1996), A. Santoni, *introduzione* in Palefato (2000), Payón Leyra (2011), p. 165, and Hawes (2014), *passim*. See also Buffière (1956), p. 229, who underlines the proximity between paradoxography and the rationalising exegesis of early historiography, in particular in Strabo and Polybius.

[15] C. Jacob, 'De l'art de compiler à la fabrication du merveilleux. Sur la paradoxographie grecque', in AA. VV. (1983), pp. 121–40 and Payón Leyra (2011), p. 31.

[16] Gantz (1993), p. 3.

Monstrosity in myth fully reveals this complexity and the stratification of cosmogonic ideas. Of course, examples of a linear evolution could be made, especially in the field under scrutiny here. Hershbell, for example, has philologically reconstructed similarities that point to a direct influence of Hesiod's monsters on Empedocles' creatures spontaneously generated from the earth.[17] Empedocles employs the same language that the poet of the *Theogony* uses to describe giants, from whose shoulders a hundred limbs sprout.

The complexity and sometimes ambivalence of early philosophical systems, though, suggest that the advent of philosophy is not simply the progress of order and its affirmation over the capricious and disordered vision of nature, as could be observed, for example, in moving from Homer to Hesiod, from myth to philosophy.[18] Monstrosity powerfully reveals the tension within both the mythical account and the philosophical reflection on nature and its order. Often, for example, one clearly recognises the influence in the opposite direction, from philosophy to tragic myth, such as that of Empedocles' idea on Sophocles' cosmogony.[19]

Ancient and modern ideas clash and are superimposed on each other, especially in domains that, like tragedy, are both influenced from the mythical substratum and oriented toward the elaboration of a new vision of the world. Both Pohlenz and Untersteiner have masterfully described the conflict between old and new religiosity at the core of classical tragedy.[20] This conflict makes tragedy not only a domain full of monsters, but also a monstrous domain itself. In Attic

---

[17] Hershbell (1970), pp 150–2 and *passim*. Hesiod's influence has been recognised on Pre-Socratic philosophers by Diller (1946). More specifically, Stokes (1962 and 1963) has analysed his influence on the Milesians, and Muñoz Valle (1969) on the whole development of the idea of nature's legality. Krafft (1971) has analysed the proximity of Anaximander's and Hesiod's ideas on several philosophical issues. Anaxagoras has been placed at the centre of the early dialectic between logos and myth, because of Homer's influence on his system (Warden (1971)), and of his own influence on the great tragics, such as Aeschylus (Rössler (1970)) and Euripides (Guthrie (1957)). Homer's proto-phylosophical ideas have also been underlined, e.g. by Buffière (1957) and Detienne (1962).

[18] G. Lloyd, *Images et modèles du monde* in Brunschwig and Lloyd (1996), pp. 57–76.

[19] Mugler (1970). On the concept of order, see Krings (1982, 2. ed.).

[20] Pohlenz (1954, 2. ed.) and Untersteiner (1955, 2nd ed.). I do not discuss in this work the political and historiograpical questions that arise from Max Pohlenz's proximity to the Nazi regime and, more broadly, his nationalism. However, this political dimension, as Bossina (2012) has masterfully illustrated, affects Pohlenz's work. Many of his conclusions are not only politically naive, but also ethically unacceptable and historiographically wrong. While careful archival research has shown Pohlenz's efforts to protect his Jewish colleagues from the imposition of racist laws, his ideas were coherent with the regime's ideology and his works reflect its ideas. It is useful, in this context, to reread the criticism by Codino (1963), Mondolfo (1963) and Momigliano (1968). As his critics acknowledge, however, it is possible to find useful conclusions in his work, particularly given its length and scope. I have found some of these conclusions useful for the present analysis.

tragedy, values collide and collapse, norms are continuously challenged and boundaries blurred. Tragic being is δεινός, incomprehensible and disconcerting.[21]

Monstrosity thus reveals the ambivalent and non-linear relation between myth and logos that classical tragedy grasps and represents with so much intensity. Mythology reflects the conflictual relation between chaos and order. The latter's shaping out of the former is everything but a linear and pacific process, as the uncanny presence of monsters suggests at different levels and in different manners throughout classical culture.

Order and Chaos

Every building of a new order must include the account of the defeat of the old order. Every order is the passage from the old to the new and, in Greece, the birth of the new order openly bears the mark of the old, in the form of the coexistence and transformation of ancient deities into the new Olympian pantheon. The antinomy between old and new, reflected for example in the opposition between Dionysus and Zeus, seems to be well integrated in the Greek mentality.[22] Yet the metamorphosis of the old into the new is far from being a peaceful and progressive process. On the contrary, the opposition between old chaos and new order survives with a striking vitality throughout the centuries to show the ambivalent and non-linear progress from one to the other.

Monsters are only old fictions, yet Xenophanes says that it would be better to forget them and their stories, since their battles are shameful reminders of the violent rebellion against the gods who, as guarantors of the cosmic order, deserve only our love and respect. But despite Xenophanes' sharp judgement, the role of monstrosity cannot be identified with certainty as being aligned with the old chaos against the new order.[23] Strauss Clay underlines how Hesiod's monsters are reminiscent of Empedocles' creatures, spontaneously generated from the earth and doomed to extinction, messengers of a world that is not, and that could have not come into being.[24] Hesiod does not often name monsters. He deprives them of an individual identity and a definite place in the cosmic hierarchy. Monsters are failed experiments and negative exemplars. Yet they are not only so. The world of monsters is not in any way separate from the divine in ancient theogonies. It is not *doomed* to failure and extinction because of a pre-existing design. On the contrary, it is defeated after a fierce struggle whose outcome is deeply aleatory. The clash reveals an ambivalent role for monstrosity, which is not only negative, but also

---

[21] Vernant and Vidal-Naquet (1972), p. 24.
[22] Pohlenz (1954, 2. ed.), p. 27 and *passim*.
[23] *Vorsokr.* 21 B 1. (= Ath. *Deipnosophistae* XI.462C).
[24] Strauss-Clay (2003), pp. 160–1.

productive and positive, precisely like the creatures sprung from the earth in Empedocles' cosmogony. Several literary examples illustrate this ambivalence, and the positive role played by monstrosity in building the new cosmic order.

Let us begin with the powerful account of Heracles' dressing, in the pseudo-Hesiodic *Shield of Heracles*. The poet of the *Shield* sings Heracles' expedition against Kyknos, son of Ares. Kyknos is depicted as a bloodthirsty brigand, who attacks and kills travellers and offers his prey's spoils to his father. Stesichoros knows that with the heads of his victims, Kyknos wanted to build a temple to Apollo.[25] The poem imitates Homer's description of Achilles' shield in *Iliad* XVIII, whose philosophical and cosmogonic relevance did not escape Heraclitus and Eustathius. In the *Iliad*, where Homer gives one of the earliest personifications of the death-bringing Ker, monstrosity makes a fleeting appearance, with the Ker almost serving as a foil to the bucolic scenes.[26] In the *Shield*, on the contrary, monstrosity conquers the centre of the stage and dominates almost the entirety of the weapon's surface. The poet has the shield itself as a θαῦμα ἰδέσθαι, a wonder to behold, a lively enough depiction of horror with which Heracles fights a real psychological warfare against Kyknos:

> In the middle was Fear, made of adamant, unspeakable, glaring backwards with eyes shining like fire. His mouth was full of white teeth, terrible, dreadful; and over his grim forehead flew terrible Strife, preparing for the battle-rout of men – cruel one, she took away the mind and sense of any men who waged open war against Zeus' son. [. . .]
>
> Upon it were wrought Pursuit and Rally; upon it burned Tumult and Murder and Slaughter; upon it was Strife, upon it Battle-Din, upon it deadly Fate [Κήρ] was dragging men by the feet through the battle, holding one who was alive but freshly wounded, another who was unwounded, another who had died. Around her shoulders she wore a cloak, purple with the blood of men, and she glared terribly and bellowed with a clanging sound.
>
> Upon it were the heads of terrible snakes, unspeakable, twelve of them: they frightened the tribes of any men upon the earth who waged war against Zeus' son. There was a grinding of their teeth whenever Amphitryon's son fought. They were burning, these marvellous works: spots like marks were visible to see on the terrible serpents, dark along their backs, and their jaws were black.[27]

Against Kyknos, Heracles is the defender of humanity. He fights with Apollo on his side, the good force and protector of true religion, against blind

---

[25] Stesich. 30 (= PMG 207). On the duel see also Janko (1986).
[26] Il. XVIII.535.
[27] Hes. Sc. 144–67. For a commentary, here and below, see C. F. Russo, in [Hesiod] (1965, 2nd ed.).

violence and monstrosity. As Apollodoros notes, though, he is also a violent man.[28] On his side, Heracles enrols monstrosity and employs it as a tool to smash the enemy. Through the shield, the frightful Gorgons fight with him, together with the black Keres, creatures of destruction (close to κηραίνω, harm or destroy) and even more terrifying goddesses of death:

> gnashing their white teeth, terrible-faced, grim, blood-red, dreadful [. . .]. They were all eager to drink black blood. Whomever they caught first, lying there or falling freshly wounded, she clenched around him her great claws, and his soul went down to Hades to chilling Tartarus. When they had satisfied their spirits with human blood, they would hurl him backwards, and going forward they would rush once again into the battle din and melee. [. . .] Beside them stood Death-Mist, gloomy and dread, pallid, parched, cowering in hunger, thick-kneed; long claws were under her hands. From her nostrils flowed mucus, from her cheeks blood was dripping down onto the ground. She stood there, grinning dreadfully, and much dust, wet with tears, lay upon her shoulders.[29]

The impact of the shield in the duel's iconography is mixed. Heracles is mostly represented on the left side, holding the shield with the left arm, and thus hiding its threatening image. Sometimes he also fights without the shield. However, in some versions, it is precisely the shield that Zeus grabs when he intervenes to divide Herakles from Ares, who intends to avenge his son, as if holding back the monsters meant to control and put an end to the fight.[30]

Thus justice, together with the true Delphic religion, defeats monstrosity by making use of monstrosity. Heracles, fighter for a new order, enters the struggle showing on his shield the most horrific monstrosities that the tradition is able to offer. As a tool, or a weapon, monstrosity is thus opposed to the enemy, chaos, and enrolled under the flag of order. Chaos here has a double status. It is the confused and unordered matter that represents the antithesis of the ordered universe, the chaotic horror of nothingness expressed by Medusa's face.[31] Chaos is also the primordial abyss, or non-being, preceding the ordered universe. One can see the nuances of these interpretations comparing, for example, Hesiod's with later cosmogonic accounts, such as Hyginus's, Cicero's or Ovid's.[32]

---

[28] Apollod. II.7.7 (155).
[29] Hes. Sc. 249–69. On the κήρ's iconography see LIMC VI, *sub voce*, Chantraine, *sub voce*.
[30] LIMC *sub voce*. See also Vian (1945).
[31] Frontisi-Ducroux (1995), pp. 65 ff. See also Clair (1989).
[32] Hyg. *Fab.* prologue, Cic. *ND* III.44, Ou. *Met.* I.5–9. See also G. Guidorizzi, in Igino (2000), pp. 167–9. Tannery (1898–9), who underlines Ovid's originality, is still useful. See also Solmsen (1950).

Tragedy is also a domain in which the ambivalence of monstrosity clearly exhibits itself. Several metaphors, especially in Aeschylus, show the conflict between chaos and order as one of the main themes, with a prominent dimension assigned to violent conflict between opposed forces, inspired by Hesiod's early cosmogonic account.[33] Theogony, Moreau claims, is transgression and excess, from which monstrosity emerges. It is a transgression, though, highly creative and powerfully productive, without which humans and the world as we know them would not exist. Paradoxically, order defines itself against excess, but also comes into being through excessive transgression itself.[34]

Whereas order slowly but steadily establishes itself, especially in Aeschylus's later works, his metaphors reveal a powerfully ambivalent role assigned to chaotic forces. Like Hesiod's chaos, this obscure domain cannot be interpreted only as a passive and almost absolute emptiness, plunged in the darkest night of indetermination in which everything is indistinct and undifferentiated. It can also be thought of as a threatening stock of active forces, an abyssal confusion that bewilders the newly established order and challenges identities with an aggressive movement that blurs boundaries.

Aeschylus makes wide use of terms that speak about the indistinct confusion between elements: μείγνυμι, mix or join or bring together, often in a hostile sense and in a context of violent hubris, and φύρω, confound and confuse, mix and mingle. This confusion is of course reminiscent of men's primitive life, e.g. in Pr. 449–50, and more widely of ancient primitive chaos. It also puts forward, however, the threat that ancient chaos represents when, far from disappearing once and for all with the early cosmogonic generation,[35] it resurfaces in and through tragic crimes, such as in Agamemnon's killing or in the monstrous feast of Glaucus's mares.[36]

Many mythological monsters share an interesting genealogical element. They descend from Gaia or the Earth and belong to a pre-Olympic generation. They bring with them the ancient forces of chaos that the new order must defeat in order to establish itself.[37] Although Gaia does not play a prominent role in Homer, it has a fundamental function in Hesiod. Interestingly for us, it embodies the ambivalence implicit in the early concept of monstrosity. Gaia is first and foremost a possibility, a substratum that makes possible the birth of every kind of being: from it, terrible monsters are generated and yet also noble and beautiful

---

[33] Moreau (1985), p. 9 and *passim*.
[34] Moreau (2006). See also G. E. R. Lloyd, 'Images et modèles du monde', in Brunschwig and Lloyd eds. (1996), pp. 57–76.
[35] See *contra* Jellamo (2005).
[36] A. A. 996–7 and Fr. 38. See Moreau (1985).
[37] Moreau (1985), p. 182 ff. and *passim*.

creatures, such as Aphrodite and the nymphs Meliae.[38] Increasingly, the Earth appears as an autonomous and fathomless power that transfers her force to her stock. Iconography, and Hellenistic sculpture in particular, powerfully reflects this overflowing force, such as in the Pergamon Altar.[39]

Through Phorcys 'the monstrous', and the mighty Keto, Gaia's progeny includes Medusa and Gorgo, generated to help the giants, according to Euripides.[40] Medusa is among the most ambivalent of the monstrous creatures. She generates Pegasus, a positive heroic character. Gaia's fecundity, which is both malignant and benign, appears in Medusa, and mythologists stress either of the two sides, depending on the different genealogies assigned to her.[41] Her face is forbidden, not only to mortal gaze, but also to speech. Medusa is always described with vague and imprecise words, like a taboo, as if not only could the eyes not see her image, but also the mind could not bear its verbal description.[42] Because of her nature, face-to-face contact with her is both necessary and impossible. She is always represented as a fully frontal figure, a visual ἀποστροφή.[43] In the fifth century, though, her image is humanised and paradoxically transformed into the image of the virulent beauty made monstrous because of Athena's envy. Ovid still has it as the prodigious transformation of the deepest beauty into its opposite, the most frightful monstrosity. In Perseus's words:

> She was once most beautiful – for so I learned from one who said he had seen her. 'Tis said that in Minerva's temple Neptune, lord of the Ocean, ravished her. Jove's daughter turned away and hid her chaste eyes behind her aegis. And, that the deed might be punished as was due, she changed the Gorgon's locks to ugly snakes. And now to frighten her fear-numbed foes, she still wears upon her breast the snakes which she has made.[44]

Gaia animates the movement of the universe throughout Ouranos's, Cronos's and finally Zeus's age. It is thus in Gaia that the forces which fight against chaos and towards order find their origin and strength. Once again, though, if Gaia's monstrous progeny represents the heritage of a universe still deprived of harmony, it also embodies a tool toward that same harmony and order.

---

[38] See Finazzo (1971), *passim*.
[39] Moreno (1994), pp. 12–13.
[40] E. *Io* 987–97.
[41] A. Moreau, 'Sur la race de méduse: forces de vie contre forces de mort (Hésiode, Théogonie, v. 270–336)', in Jouan éd. (1986), pp. 1–15. On Medusa see Clair (1989).
[42] Frontisi-Ducroux (1995), ch. 5.
[43] Frontisi-Ducroux (1995).
[44] Ou. *Met.* IV.794–803. See also Apollod. II.4.3.

The monstrous forces that Gaia generates, passing across the epochs, do not perish or vanish forever.[45] Ouranos, Cronos, the titans, the hecatoncheires, the Kyklops, the giants and many others: they are all earth's creatures, and they are all tamed and constrained under the rule of a new universal order. Although they cease to act and impose their rules, they somehow remain incorrupted and survive beneath the new order. The latter reveals its always precarious nature that can be shaken by monstrosity every time its harmony is threatened by monstrous forces. These same forces, however, have also contributed to the order's establishment. Here lies the productive ambiguity. Monstrosity is both the manifestation of the threat and the instrument to overcome it. If it is true that the whole theogonic process ends up with Zeus's kingship, it is also true that neither is his reign uncontested nor is the process towards it teleological.[46] Whereas one can say that monstrous forces are pre-harmonic and they are progressively overcome in the path towards order, I believe that such a path must not be interpreted with any teleology or providential scheme in mind.[47]

The ancients already project a providential intention onto Hesiod. Proclus, for example, claims that 'the *Theogony* was composed by worthy Hesiod [...] because he wanted to hand down to later generations the principles of the entire providence of the gods towards the cosmic order as the ancestral tradition of the Greeks presents it. He thus composed that work on the basis of the myths that were told in the sanctuaries.'[48] Such a projection, however, better serves Proclus's providentialist argument than the interpretation of Hesiod itself, since the conflictual dialectic of mythical forces laboriously stabilises itself before the existence of anything that can be called providence.

Gaia pushes for a new order. It does not have in mind, however, a precise design for it. Evil, conflict, disorder, are the effects of necessary forces put into motion by Gaia through the generation of several terrifying monsters. They ambivalently destabilise and build order out of chaos, without any end in view. The new divine order, of Cronos vis-à-vis Ouranos, and of Zeus vis-à-vis Cronos, does not have the characteristic of a τέλος for the universe. The cosmos, throughout its stages, is the outcome of conflicts, of triumphs and defeats, of births and deaths to which divine and monstrous forces contribute together.

Mythical forces reflect the relations between the pre-Hellenic and the Hellenic worlds. The latter overcomes the former, but does not completely

---

[45] Solmsen (1949), p. 72.
[46] See *contra* Strauss-Clay (2003), p. 153.
[47] *Contra*, see also Jellamo (2005).
[48] Procl. *ad.Hes.Op. Prolegomena* I.1 (= Marzillo (2010), p. 3, en tr. Van den Berg (2014), p. 388).

obliterate it. The theogony is the affirmation of the Olympic gods over the pre-Hellenic divinities. Through theogony, Being is located in time and the birth of nature's order is explained as the progressive stabilisation, through conflict, of the primeval forces represented by monstrosity.[49] Ambiguously, though, the νόμος manifests itself in the φύσις with the support of monstrosity, largely embodied by Gaia's progeny. Rationality does not overcome irrationality. Rather they coexist and remain in an antithetical and non-dialectic relation, without any idea of teleology.[50]

Through Gaia's prominent and ambivalent role, early Greek thought has exploited in a powerful way the concept of monstrosity. Order is achieved through monstrosity itself, that is to say through the fundamental help of Gaia's progeny in progressing towards, and finally establishing, the justice of Zeus. Zeus, the greatest god of the Pantheon, king of gods and men, is in charge of maintaining order and justice in the cosmos. However, his rising to power has been achieved through, and supported by, the very same forces of chaos. Through the theomachies, a veritable work of construction of the cosmos, monsters fight on different sides, and without their help, order would not have been established.[51]

Mythical Battlefields: Monstrosity as a Weapon

When Zeus reaches adulthood and decides to seize Cronos's power, he first demands Metis's help. Thanks to a drug, Cronos is forced to vomit the sons and daughters that he had previously swallowed to prevent their development. Supported by his brothers and sisters, the future Olympian gods, Zeus makes war against Cronos and the titans. The titans represent unruliness (πλημμέλεια) and disorder (ἀταξία). However, in the beginning of *Theogony*, gods and titans already appear as two equivalent poles, both of divine nature: givers of good (δωτῆρες) the former, illustrious and nobles (ἀγαυοί) the latter. The fight is ten years long, and the balance is broken only by Gaia's and the monsters' intervention in favour of the Olympians.

To obtain victory over the titans, Zeus follows Gaia's advice[52] and sets the Centimanes free from Tartarus, in which Cronos had imprisoned them. Far from being unambiguously on the side of order, Zeus employs a monstrosity against

---

[49] Untersteiner (1972, 2nd ed.), p. 114 and *passim*.
[50] See Nestle (1930–4) and Lo Schiavo (1983) for the specific contribution of Homeric works in this sense.
[51] Such ambivalence has suggested the intrinsic difficulty in interpreting the whole meaning of Zeus's myth vis-à-vis titans and giants. See for example Cornford (1952), p. 203.
[52] Possibly, and alternatively, Prometheus's advice, as one can understand through A. *Pr.* 219–21.

another monstrosity. Among them, a real contract is established: in exchange for the use of their force on behalf of Zeus, the hecatoncheires recover their lost freedom.[53] The contractual nature of the exchange suggests, to some extent, the equivalence of the subjects. The dialectic between Zeus and Kottos is thus even more striking. Zeus imperatively calls the monsters to their duty to show their invincible force, '[. . .] how after so many sufferings you have come up to the light once again out from under a deadly bond, by our plans, out from under the murky gloom'.[54] Although he knows that the monsters' force is his only solution to win the war, Zeus puts himself on a plane of arrogant superiority. Excellent or blameless (ἀμύμων) Kottos, though, responds by reversing the order of Zeus's argument, and promising fidelity before and outside any plan of subordination. Kottos brings the conversation back onto a plane of equality of pride, suggesting awareness of the role that his stock is about to play in the mythical struggle.[55]

A second intervention of monstrosity in favour of the new Olympian order is represented by the Kyklopes. Another contract is agreed to with these monstrous forces, which this time provide their skilful inventiveness (μηχανή):

> And [Zeus] freed from their deadly bonds his father's brothers, Sky's sons, whom their father had bound in his folly. And they repaid him in gratitude for his kind deed, giving him the thunder and the blazing thunderbolt and the lightning, which huge Earth had concealed before. Relying on these, he rules over mortals and immortals.[56]

Zeus and the Olympians win their war and gain supremacy thanks to the Kyklopes' weapons.[57] They punish the titans by throwing them to the bottom of Tartarus, a place as far from the earth as the earth itself is far from the sky. What was mixed and confused is thus separated and now the new order clearly distinguishes not so much the divine from the non-divine, but rather the winning gods from the defeated ones. The triumphant divinity, however, appears in an ambiguous light, since for its victory it had to employ the same measureless and monstrous force that its enemy represents. Rather than being dominated and obliterated,[58] the monstrous power is negotiated and employed against the old order and in favour of the new one.

---

[53] Calame (1985).
[54] Hes. *Th.* 652–3.
[55] Mazzocchini (2003). See also M. L. West in Hesiod (1966) *ad loc.*
[56] Hes. *Th.* 501–6. On the pact between Zeus and the monsters see Solmsen (1949), pp. 17–18.
[57] A.R. 730 ff.
[58] Calame (1985).

One can follow the multifarious nature of monstrosity in the specific figure of the Kyklopes, who enjoy a great fortune in mythology and art. The ambiguity lies first and foremost in the borderline nature of their character, caught in the grey area between savagery and civilisation. The former is implicit in their nature:

> [They] have very violent hearts (ὑπέρβιος ἦτορ), Brontes (Thunder) and Steropes (Lightning) and strong-spirited Arges (Bright), those who gave thunder to Zeus and fashioned the thunderbolt. These were like the gods in other regards, but only one eye was set in the middle of their foreheads; and they were called Kyklops (Circle-eyed) by name, since a single circle-shaped eye was set in their foreheads. Strength and force and contrivances (ἰσχύς, βίη, μηχαναί) were in their works.[59]

Here, Hesiod is the first author to mention their single eye, a feature that remains remarkably rare in iconography. Together with the three gods mentioned by the poet of the *Theogony*, Hellanikos accounts for two more groups of Kyklopes: the builders of mythical walls, and the comrades of Polyphemus.[60]

Their connection to civilisation, however, is also problematically asserted by their skilful mastery of metallurgy and, more generally, the controlled use of fire. Not only do they endow Zeus with the use of lightning and thunderbolt but, according to Apollodorus, they also provide Hades with his helmet and Poseidon with his trident.[61] Their skills make their subsequent role as Hephaestus's workers natural, notably in the forge under Mount Etna.[62] This idea develops in the vision of the Kyklopes as great builders of mythical defensive walls, like those of Mycenae and Tyrins.

Homer's account of Odysseus in the Kyklopes' land builds the image of a savage race, ἄγριοι ἄνθρωποι according to the *Suda*, who violate the sacred duty of hospitality and descend to cannibalism.[63] Although in Homer, as in Hesiod, the Kyklopes are to some extent civilised, since they perform pastoral activities, they are the anarchists of the *Odyssey* and they live in a kind of

---

[59] Hes. *Th.* 139–46.
[60] Hellanic. in *FGH* IV F 88.
[61] Apollod. I.2.1.
[62] Calame (1985) speaks about the Kyklopes' mediating function between the untamed forces of the underworld and the higher domain of civilisation, of men and gods above them. See also Glenn (1978), Mondi (1983), Morgan (1984), pp. 242 ff., J. A. López Ferez, 'Les Cyclopes et leur pays dans la littérature grecque', in Jouan and Deforge éds (1988), pp. 57–71, I. Aurenty, 'Des cyclopes à Rome', in Bianchi, Thévenez eds (2004), pp. 35–52.
[63] See e.g. Finley (1954), p. 101 and Guthrie (1957), pp. 95 ff.

anomie that is eventually preached by Cynicists, and in particular by Antisthenes.[64] Heraclitus understands the 'Kylops' as the name of the brutal lack of consciousness, which rationality – notably Odysseus's – must overcome.[65] Further scrutiny, though, suggests that they draw their features from their life apart from civilisation. They live in a remote part of the world. They are alien, both geographically and ontologically, and they inhabit the margins of civilised space.[66] For this reason, and this reason only, they do not honour hospitality as a Greek would expect. Hospitality does not belong to their culture. They show more ignorance than lack of respect for the customs of Greek civilisation.[67]

The tension that emerges from the description of the Kyklopes' race reflects perhaps the narrative exigency of the poem. Polyphemus becomes in fact the only evil character, misunderstood and then ignored by the other Kyklopes, once he is fooled about Odysseus's name. His fellows respond to Polyphemus's cry for help that 'sickness which comes from Zeus there is no way you can escape; you must pray to our father the lord Poseidon'.[68] Not only do the Kyklopes recognise divine authority, but they also respect their own genealogy. Polyphemus is left alone. Blind, he cannot reach Odysseus with his stones, but only with his curse.

Polyphemus represents the solitude and powerlessness of monstrosity. In other versions of the myth, these characteristics are explored in different directions. Homer's tale inspires Euripides' satyr play. Here, the Kyklopes are not uncivilised shepherds, but savage and bloody barbarians that feed themselves with men and beasts, rather than milk and cheese as in Homer. It is as if the whole race had become Polyphemus, bloodthirsty and vicious. A marble statue at the Capitoline Museum in Rome represents a sitting Polyphemus with the corpse of a Greek in his left hand.[69] Interestingly, the

---

[64] Buffière (1956), pp. 359 ff. See [Antisthenes of Athens] (2015) and SSR V A. Together with the Lestrygons's, the Kyklops's cannibalism is still an indirect proof, for Pliny, of the existence of practices that, had they not existed in the past, reason would typically rule out. See Pliny NH VII.9: 'I have mentioned that there are Scythian tribes, a good number in fact, which eat human flesh. This might well seem unbelievable were we not to bear in mind that in the centre of the world and in Sicily there once existed peoples equally bizarre, the Cycloped and the Laestrygones [. . .].'

[65] Heraclit. All. 70.

[66] The traditional association of fearsome otherness with remote geographical spaces and foreign lands lasts well beyond the classical age. See Delumeau (1978), pp. 62–5.

[67] Brown (1996).

[68] Od. IX.411–12.

[69] LIMC, Kylops, Catalogue 31. On the representation of Polyphemus, especially in the Sperlonga's group, see Andreae (1982). On Andreae's interpretation, with a special focus on the aesthetic of monstrosity, see 'Ulisse, i mostri e gli imperatori di Roma', in Perutelli (2006), pp. 73–8. See also Garland (1995), pp. 91–6 and R. J. Clare, 'Representing monstrosity: Polyphemus in the Odyssey', in Atherton ed. (1998), pp. 1–17.

iconography has not preserved any collective representation of the Kyklopes as a group.

Euripides imagines Silenus and the satyrs shipwrecked on Sicily, the Kyklopes' island, and enslaved by them.[70] Polyphemus claims a crass and impious materialism, unconditionally deserving the epithets of αἰσχρός by the satyrs and of θήρειος by Odysseus, which unambiguously set him in the domain of deformed and wild monstrosity.[71] This impiety is also reflected in Polyphemus's challenge of Zeus's omnipotence, even after being blinded by Odysseus. The Kyklops, unrepentant, threatens the king of Ithaca with the prophecy according to which he would wander many years before arriving at home.

A different picture emerges in poetry, in which the Kyklops reveals unexpected features of grotesque humanity and even inspires sympathy. Imagined first by Philoxenus of Cythera, the Kyklops of Theocritus's *Idyll* XI has lost his monstrous aspects and reveals rather his clumsiness than his wickedness. Polyphemus finds solace in song for his unrequited love for sea-nymph Galatea. Monstrosity is transformed into grotesque, no longer threatening, but rather suggesting tender feelings because of the monster's ingenuity.[72] On a wall painting, in Livia's house in Rome, Eros makes fun of the Kyklops, bridling him while he offers an unhappy gaze to the naked Galatea. Elsewhere, the two are embracing, and Galatea responds with sympathy to the monster's love.

A wholly different pictures emerges in Ovid, for whom Galatea's disgust for the Kyklops is fully justified by the monster's wickedness, mirrored by his revolting aspect: '[. . .] savage creature, whom the very woods shudder to look upon, whom no stranger has ever seen save to his own hurt, who despises great Olympus and its gods [. . .].'[73] Polyphemus pronounces a long monologue, trying to justify his simple way of life, close to nature more than uncivilised, and attempting to make it – and himself – appealing to Galatea:

> And now, Galatea, do but raise your glistening head from the blue sea. Now come and don't despise my gifts. Surely I know myself; lately I saw my reflection in a clear pool, and I liked my features when I saw them. Just look, how big I am! Jupiter himself up there in the sky has no bigger body; for you are always talking of some Jove or other as ruling there. A wealth of hair overhangs my manly face and it shades my shoulders like a grove. And don't think it ugly that my whole body is covered with thick, bristling hair. A tree is ugly without its leaves and a horse is ugly if a thick mane does

---

[70] See their presence at Polyphemus's blinding, on a Lucanian crater at the British Museum, LIMC, *Kyklops*, Catalogue 27.
[71] E. *Cyc.* 625 and 670.
[72] Phylox.Cit. 2–11 (= PMG 815–24) and Theoc. XI.
[73] Ou. *Met.* XIII.760–2.

not clothe his sorrell neck; feathers clothe the birds, and their own wool is becoming to sheep; so a beard and shaggy hair on his body well become a man. True, I have but one eye in the middle of my forehead, but it is as big as a good-sized shield. And what of that? Doesn't the great sun see everything here on earth from his heavens? And the sun has but one eye.[74]

This seemingly human attitude of the Kyklops is however suddenly turned upside down by Ovid, when the monster discovers his beloved with Acis and unleashes his murderous passion.

Eventually, Callimachus takes a different stance and depicts a tender Kyklops in his *Hymn to Artemis*. The young goddess visits the island of Lipari and encounters the Kyklopes intent on building a watering-place for Poseidon's horses. The nymphs that accompany the young Artemis are scared, not so much by the monsters' aspect, but by the entire sight of their sooty, windy and noisy workshop. Artemis, on the contrary, boldly asks for the weapons she came for, and they immediately make the mythical bow for her. The poet evokes the goddess's youthfulness, through a sweet image of tenderness that makes the monster deeply human:

> [. . .] thou, Maiden, even earlier, while yet but three years old, when Leto came bearing thee in her arms at the bidding of Hephaestus that he might give thee handsel and Brontes set thee on his stout knees – thou didst pluck the shaggy hair of his great breast and tear it out by force. And even unto this day the mid part of his breast remains hairless, even as when mange settles on a man's temples and eats away the hair.[75]

Gentle or brutal, civilised or savage, skilled workers or simple shepherds: the ambivalence of the Kyklops's monstrosity makes him a character able to embody very different roles and perform diverse functions, contributing to enrich the mythological economy of monstrosity.

The ambiguously productive role played by monstrosity also emerges in the gigantomachy, the second great conflict that Zeus must face on his way towards the establishment of the Olympian power. The giants are similar to the Kyklopes but their original representation is quite different. Giants are born out of the blood spilled by Ouranos's castration on earth. Whereas the enemies of the Olympians are initially presented as an ordered hoplitic phalanx, by the fifth century they become a horde of monstrous and savage beings,[76] with γιγαντικός

---

[74] Ou. *Met.* XIII.840–53.
[75] Call. *Dian.* 72–9, evoked on the *frons scenae* of the Hierapolis's theatre. See LIMC, *Artemis*, Catalogue 1262.
[76] Vian (1952), *passim* and Moreau (1985), pp. 133 ff.

felt to be a synonym of monstrous. Through their attack, Gaia's sons intend to subvert the precarious domain of reason and civilisation.

The first poet to offer an account of gigantomachy is Pindar, who intends to glorify the divine race. Pindar contrasts the giants' ὕβρις with the gods' βία (force), and introduces the theme of Heracles who, according to a version of the myth, supports the Olympians and makes their victory possible. Apollodorus describes their appearance:

> [. . .] unsurpassable in size, unassailable in their strength and fearful to behold because of the thick hair hanging down from their head and cheeks; and their feet were formed from dragons' scales. According to some accounts, they were born at Phlegrai, or according to others, at Pallene. And they hurled rocks and flaming oak trees at the heavens.[77]

Aeschylus also makes use of the evocative power of giants. He writes at the time of the metamorphosis of giants from hoplites into monsters, and contributes to this transformation through the powerful image of the Argive attack against Thebes in the *Seven*. The attackers, whose revolt assumes a cosmic dimension, are still warriors and yet limitless and monstrous, excessive to the point of blind folly. They are giants, because of their great size, and because they are enemies of the gods:

> [Kapaneus] is a giant, bigger than the man previously mentioned, and his boasts show a pride beyond human limits [. . .]. As his device he bears a naked man carrying fire: the torch with which he is armed blazes in his hands, and in golden letters he declares 'I will burn the city.' Against such a man you must send – but who can stand against him? Who will await without panic the onset of this braggart man?[78]

Giants are initially anthropomorphic figures. By the sixth century, they become anguipede (snake-legged) figures, deriving from, and confused with, Typhoeus. Their monstrosity becomes thus more physically apparent, underlining the opposition between the anthropomorphic gods and the horrible creatures that threaten Olympus.

The most striking representation of gigantomachy in antiquity is in the fourteen east metopes of the Parthenon. The composition is polycentric and multidimensional. The viewer is pushed through the threatening space of the fight, whose physical impact – as Moreno puts it – counts more than the visual one. Corporeal masses lean out from the sides in a crescendo of

---

[77] Apollod. I.6.1–2.
[78] A. *Th.* 423–36. See also E. *Ba.* 538–44 on Pentheus, and Moreau (1985).

amazement.[79] An original element of the Parthenon Frieze is the introduction of all the monstrous creatures supporting the Olympians in their fight. Excluding Kronos, Koios, Krios and Japetus, the four rebels, the artist of the Parthenon includes the titans that are integrated into the Olympic order.

The Hellenistic artists of the Parthenon inform the composition with a sensibility drawn from recent historical events, collapsing the myth of the Olympian origins with the reality of the consolidation of the power of Rome and its allies, the Pergamenian princes. The giants' defeat echoes the real debacle of the Galatians in 189 BC. Like the giants, the barbarians are guilty of ὕβρις and παρανομία. Like Xerxes in Aeschylus's interpretation, they attempt to violate the order of nature and, for this, they receive the ultimate punishment by the Olympians.

Together with the gods, the giants reveal a careful and innovative study of anatomy, visible in the astonishing details that survive in some of the Parthenon's figures. The giants alone, however, have been used to explore the edge of nature's possibilities and the boundaries of normality, abnormality and monstrosity. The bull-man, the lion-man, the butterfly-man challenge the viable form in a hybrid composition of animal and human features. Moreno defines the atmosphere of the battle as metaphysical, surreal and dreamlike. Its physical materialisation, though, seems to prevail over its psychic suggestions. With and beyond Aristotelian physics of monstrosity, the Altar plunges the viewer into an aleatory cosmogony reminiscent of Empedocles' primeval creatures. Beyond Empedocles, however, these monsters are not doomed to extinction, but rather destined to conquer the sky. Only a stronger fate prevents their bold attempt by establishing at the same time the boundaries of the normal and the monstrous. The monsters that entered the battlefield could have been the new gods, our gods. Only an aleatory outcome makes them monstrously hybrid. Nature, as Moreno puts it, is still entropic and the human shape – as much as the divine – does not pre-exist the monstrous forms, but is rather educed from them, and it is what remains of that cosmic fight.[80]

Although giants are the chaotic opponents of the Olympian order, they strikingly preserve a link with positive forces that come from the earth for the affirmation and defence of national culture. Γηγενής is the epithet applied to both the giants and the earthborn warriors, the Σπαρτοί or sowmen generated by Kadmos, founder and first king of Thebes.[81] After slaying the dragon, Kadmos, the presumed son of Agenor and brother of Europa, follows Ares' instruction and sows the ground with the monster's teeth. Out

---

[79] Moreno (1994), p. 14. My reading is greatly indebted to Moreno's interpretation.
[80] Moreno (1994), p. 476 and *passim*.
[81] Guthrie (1957). pp. 21 ff.

of the earth, armed men spring up and, after a deadly fight with each other in some version of the myth, they become the ancestors of the Theban aristocracy, while Kadmos, after a marriage with Harmonia, is consecrated as the founder and first king of the mythical city.[82] The Thebans, also called the Kadmeioi, are thus the offspring of a monstrous generation, or rather of an autochthonous generation whose seeds are the teeth of a monster defeated and tamed.[83]

The dragon's role itself is ambiguous. It is sacred to Ares, in some versions of the myth, possibly because a descendant of the god himself, and its killing sparks Ares' anger.[84] The earth-born warriors represent the mythical defence of the country, for example in Sophocles' *Antigone*, in which the serpent is the symbol of Thebes against the Argives' eagle, which flies away.[85] The idea of autochthony and resistance is reworked in the context of the struggle against the Persian invaders, with reference to Kekrops, mythical founder and first king of Athens.[86] A peaceful and wise king, he is also a monstrous hybrid, half man and half snake, because of his chthonian origin.[87] After the fight between Poseidon and Athena for influence over the city, this monster is the author of enormous progression in civilisation, like the invention of writing, the building of cities and the burial of the dead.

The ambivalence of the link between the earth-born warriors and monstrosity is once again brought onto the negative side by Euripides, who makes Pentheus, the new king of Thebes in the *Bacchae*, the son of Echion, one of the Spartoi. The Bacchae's chorus unambiguously puts forward Pentheus's monstrosity:

> [What anger]/He shows his earthborn/origin, that he was born from a dragon,/does Pentheus, son/of earthborn Echion,/a monster with visage wild [ἀγριωπός τέρας], no man of mortal frame/but one of the murderous Giants who opposed the gods.[88]

Vomited by the earth, Pentheus and his genealogy are entirely pushed, once again, onto the side of a negative, arrogant and limitless monstrosity.[89]

---

[82] See Vian (1963).
[83] See also the myth's rational explanation in Palaeph. 3 (= Festa et al. eds. (1894–1902), III.II. pp. 8–10)
[84] E. *Ph.* follows this version.
[85] S. *Ant.* 125.
[86] See Loraux (1993, 2nd ed and 1996).
[87] LIMC, esp. Catalogue 2, 9, 11 and 16.
[88] E. *Ba.* 536–44.
[89] On Pentheus, see also Ou. *Met.* III.511 ff.

From a similar stock comes also Typhoeus, the fiercest of Zeus's enemies. Typhoeus appears in the third and last major moment of theomachy and represents the ultimate and most dangerous fight against the Olympian order. After the attack of titans and giants, the most subversive power is now embodied by an individual enemy. Although his force emerges from ancient chaos, Typhoeus's victory would not have caused the fall of the cosmos back into the original abyss of nothingness. Typhoeus's intention is clear in this sense: he fights for a new and alternative order and to seize Zeus's power: 'si vellet ... de regno certare', in Hyginus's words.[90] Hesiod sets the tone for the cosmic dimension of the struggle:

> The violet-dark sea was enveloped by a conflagration from both of them – of thunder and lightning, and fire from that monster of typhoons and winds, and the blazing thunder-bolt. And all the earth seethed, and the sky and sea; and long waves raged around the shores, around and about, under the rush of the immortals, and an inextinguishable shuddering arose. And Hades, who rules over the dead below, was afraid, and the Titans under Tartarus, gathered around Cronos, at the inextinguishable din and dread battle-strife.[91]

The cosmic dimension of the fight is also underlined by Apollodorus's description of the monster as a creature superior to all Earth's offspring, 'of human shape and of such prodigious bulk that he out-topped all the mountains, and his head often brushed the stars. One of his hands reached out to the west and the other to the east, and from them projected a hundred dragons' heads.'[92] Like a rising dark sun, the monster embraces the whole creation, occupying the space from the West to the East and from the bottom of the earth up to the sky.

Differently from the titanomachy, Zeus is here alone and engages individually in this combat. It is for him the ultimate occasion to prove his own superiority, and only after Typhoeus's defeat is Zeus able to distribute honours and provinces to the other gods, and finally inaugurate the Olympian order on a more stable ground.

Typhoeus is a son of the Earth and Tartarus. Interestingly, he is generated after Tartarus has received the titans for their perpetual punishment. After being defeated, monstrosity resurfaces once again, even more powerful and threatening. It literally germinates from Tartarus and the prodigious fecundity of Gaia, against the new victorious and yet precarious order. Even more dreadful is an alternative version that makes Typhoeus the son of Hera by parthenogenesis. Offended by Zeus's autonomous generation of Athena, Hera implores the

---

[90] Hyg. *Fab.* 152. See also Ant.Lib. 28.2, as well as Seippel (1939) and Ballabriga (1990).
[91] Hes. *Th.* 844–52.
[92] Apollod. I.6.3.

Earth, the sky and the titans for revenge. The *Hymn to Apollo* mentions twice her terrible gesture:

> Eyes dark and wide as a cow's, Queen Hera prayed and with down-turned palm struck the earth: 'Now hear me Earth and wide Heaven above, and Titans, gods beneath the earth, dwelling around great Tartaros, from whom men and gods derive: all hear me and grant me a child apart from Zeus, in no way weaker in strength than he, a child greater than Zeus by as much as Zeus is greater than Kronos.' And she struck the earth with her massive hand. Then life-bearing Earth shifted; Hera rejoiced in the sight, believing her prayer would be fulfilled.[93]

Hera demands a son who excels among gods and humans. Yet the Earth gives her a terrible creature, dissimilar from both. The monster's image explored by the poet of the *Theogony* is conceptually dense. The poet makes use not only of visually horrible features, as expected, but also of sound-related characteristics:

> His hands †are holding deeds upon strength,† and tireless the strong god's feet; and from his shoulders there were a hundred heads of a snake, a terrible dragon's, licking with their dark tongues; and on his prodigious heads fire sparkled from his eyes under the eyebrows, and from all of his heads fire burned as he glared. And there were voices in all his terrible heads, sending forth all kinds of sounds, inconceivable: for sometimes they would utter sounds as though for the gods to understand, and at other times the sound of a loud-bellowing, majestic bull, unstoppable in its strength, at other times that of a lion, with a ruthless spirit, at other times like young dogs, a wonder to hear, and at other times he hissed, and the high mountains echoed from below.[94]

Surprisingly, both the myth's iconographic and textual versions set Typhoeus and Zeus on the same level. The monster and the god sometimes seem to reflect each other, bringing to its last consequences the individualisation of the clash between good and evil in the last episode of titanomachy. In Aeschylus, for example, the evil eye of the monster seems to reflect in Zeus's vigilant guard:

> [Typhoeus] once rose up against the gods, hissing terror from his formidable jaws while a fierce radiance flashed from his eyes, with the intention of overthrowing the autocracy of Zeus by force. But there came against him the unsleeping weapon of Zeus, the downrushing thunderbolt breathing out

---

[93] *h.Ap.* 332–43. For this method of invoking chthonian deities or ghosts, see T. W. Allen et al., in T. W. Allen et al. (1936, 2nd ed.) *ad loc.*
[94] Hes. *Th.* 820–35. See Goslin (2010).

flame, which struck him out of his haughty boasts – for he was hit right in the centre of his body, and his strength was thundered out of him and reduced to ashes.[95]

The iconography of Typhoeus, writes Touchefeu-Meynier, is surprisingly not impressive, compared to the verbal description and the daring sense conveyed by mythographers, persuaded that he really represents the ultimate danger to Zeus.[96] Representations of the monster show quite traditional attributes of hybridity. A bearded character with snake's tail and wings, armed only with snakes, Typhoeus lacks the savagery and violence that the tradition ascribes to him. Although sometimes bigger than Zeus, Typhoeus never seems to really threaten the king of the Olympians. It is in the two characters' mirroring of each other, however, that the seriousness of the threat must be read, as if they were equivalent in strength, as if the title of king of gods were not to be recovered, but rather to be newly established, after this ultimate combat.

Typhoeus is indeed defeated. According to Hyginus, once hit in the chest by Zeus's lightning, the monster is enveloped with fire.[97] Less reassuring is the *Theogony*'s version, in which an immense fire is generated from the monster's corpse and spread around, melting everything on earth. The poet compares the effect of the fire generated by Typhoeus's mutilated corpse with Hephaestus's skilful art in melting metals, suggesting once again that while the furious forces of nature are tamed by the metallurgical technique, they nonetheless survive and cannot be definitively obliterated. Mount Etna, for Hyginus, covers the monster's remains and still reveals a trace of that original fire.[98] Zeus finally throws Typhoeus's remains back into Tartarus. Even from there, however, the monster keeps producing his horrendous effects in the form of terrible winds and storms that afflict men on both sea and earth.[99]

Zeus's victory, however, is not so easily obtained in all versions of the myth. Apollodorus's account is far less reassuring for the Olympians, and testifies to the level of the threat posed by Typhoeus's attempt. When the monster attacks, the gods evacuate Olympus and find refuge in Egypt. Attempting a pursuit, Typhoeus forces them to metamorphosise into beasts. Zeus counterattacks but, according to Apollodorus, the monstrous creature overcomes the king of gods:

[. . .] seeing the monster sore wounded, [Zeus] grappled with him. But Typhon twined about him and gripped him in his coils, and wrestling the

---

[95] A. Pr. 354–62. See Moreau (1976–7), pp. 62–3.
[96] LIMC, *sub voce*.
[97] Hyg. Fab. 152.
[98] See also Pindar's powerful and colourful account in P. I.18–26.
[99] Hes. Th. 855–80.

sickle from him severed the sinews of his hands and feet, and lifting him on his shoulders carried him through the sea to Cilicia and deposited him on arrival in the Corycian cave. Likewise he put away the sinews there also, hidden in a bearskin, and he set to guard them the she-dragon Delphyne, who was a half-bestial maiden.[100]

Only with Hermes' and Aegipan's help does the fight take a positive turn for Zeus. The two gods find Zeus's tendons and make possible a new counterattack, finally victorious. The *Library*, thus, amplifies the danger incurred by Zeus and shows how close the Olympian order came to actually ending.

In a classic study, Vian shows how the concept of a subversive character that threatens order, like a force of the past threatening the present order, belongs to Eastern cultures.[101] The Eastern influence must have been clear to the Greek mentality. Vian explains, however, that the contact with Eastern elements occurred quite late in the process, and not *ab origine*. The Greek vision of the monster is thus influenced by exogenous factors but its origin is fully within Hellenic mythologems. The anguipede figure that characterises Zeus's adversary is thus assigned a mythical function that it does not originally possess, in order to unfold the last and final clash with the Olympian ruler.

Eastern influences are also revealed by the proximity of Typhoeus with Xerxes, a powerful tragic figure of otherness. His gaze is that of a dragon, which reflects the ruinous hubris of barbarous nature.[102] Xerxes is a monster that, like Typhoeus, defies the order of the cosmos. His expedition against Greece is unnatural.[103] It is contrary to nature's order. Xerxes' body becomes indistinguishable from the body of his army, terrifyingly multifarious:

> The city-sacking army of the King has now passed over to the neighbour land on the other side of the water, crossing the strait of Helle, daughter of Athamas [i.e. the Hellespont], by means of a boat-bridge tied together with flaxen cables, placing a roadway, fastened with many bolts, as a yoke on the neck of the sea. [...] With the dark glance of a deadly serpent in his eyes, with many hands and many ships, driving a swift Syrian chariot, [Xerxes] leads a war-host that slays with the bow against men renowned for spear-fighting.[104]

---

[100] Apollod. I.6.3.
[101] F. Vian, 'Le mythe de Typhée et le problème de ses origines orientales', in AA. VV. (1960), pp. 17–37. See also Burkert (1984) and G. Guidorizzi in Igino (2000), p. 427.
[102] Pohlenz (1954, 2. ed.), p. 54.
[103] Untersteiner (1955, 2nd ed.), p. 187.
[104] A. *Pers.* 65–86.

The yoke on the sea testifies to the unnaturalness of the Persian enterprise. To the dark army that defies nature, nature opposes its luminous force. As Typheous had many heads, Xerxes has many hands and many ships. The inordinate and savage barbarians lack unity and cohesion. For this reason, they need one name – Xerxes – to keep together the multitude of otherwise heteroclite individualities, each of them named as to underlie their impossible cohesion. The Greeks, on the contrary, are never named individually. They act like Greeks, they exist like Greeks. To their war paean, the Persian responds with a roar or a murmur, a ρόθος which reminds once again of Typhoeus's thousand voices.[105] Aeschylus's Xerxes and Typhoeus physically and morally resemble each other, since they embody the same destructive forces against the universe's order.[106]

The fight between Typhoeus and Zeus is the battle between order and chaos, the neverending clash between chaos and cosmos. Aeschylus clearly perceives the meaning of this when he prolongs the fight under the walls of Thebes. The titanic warrior Hippomedon gives the assault to the fourth door, with Hyperbius in charge of its defence. Not only do they seem to be personal enemies, but they fight with the emblems of enemy deities on their shields. In the scout's words:

> I shuddered, I won't deny it, to see [Hippomedon] brandish his great round threshing-floor of a shield. And it can't have been a cheap artist who gave him that device on the shield, Typhon emitting dark smoke, the many-coloured sister of flame, from his fire-breathing lips; the round circle of the hollow-bellied shield is floored with coiling snakes. The man himself raised a great war-cry; he is possessed by Ares, and he rages for a fight like a maenad, with a fearsome look in his eye.[107]

And Eteocles' response:

> [. . .] a man has been chosen to face this man, Hyperbius [. . .]. And Hermes has brought them together appropriately: the man is an enemy of the man he will face, and on their shields they will bring together two antagonistic gods. One of them has the fire-breathing Typhon and on Hyperbius' shield resides Father Zeus, standing with his flaming bolt in his hand. Such are their alliances with gods; and we are on the side of the winners, they of

---

[105] A. Pers. 406. Sommerstein has it as 'a surge of Persian speech', which neutralises Aeschylus's reference to animality and monstrosity.
[106] Moreau (1985), pp. 112 and 147–50.
[107] A. Th. 489–99.

the losers, that is if Zeus is Typhon's superior in battle. It is to be expected that the human opponents will fare likewise, and by the logic of Hyperbius' emblem the Zeus he has on his shield should become his Saviour.[108]

Eteocles' appeal to the past outcome of the fight between Zeus and Typoheus, as a warranty of his future victory, does not mitigate the sense of a specular confrontation that echoes the larger dimension of the war surrounding the city at its seven doors. Not only does Aeschylus umambiguously speak about the divinity of both mythical contenders, Zeus and Typhoeus, but also other deities are summoned around the imminent clash of the monstrous weapons: Ares and Dionysus with Hippomedon, Hermes and Zeus on Hyperbius's side.

Monsters do not intervene in Zeus's favour solely in exogenous conflicts, such as in the titanomachy. They are also summoned in support of Zeus when serious trouble *within* the Olympian order manifests itself, such as at the time of the threat posed by Hera, Poseidon and Athena's secret plot described by the poet of the *Iliad*. Thetis offers providential help to save Zeus and thus legitimate his reign and his order. Without monstrosity, once again, Zeus would have been tied up and have succumbed to the three deities, all of them related to the pre-Olympian dimension. Achilles to Thetis:

> Often I have heard you boasting in the halls of my father, and declaring that you alone among the immortals warded off loathsome destruction from the son of Cronos, lord of the dark clouds, on the day when the other Olympians were minded to put him in bonds, Hera and Poseidon and Pallas Athene. But you came, goddess, and freed him from his bonds, when you had quickly called to high Olympus him of the hundred hands, whom the gods call Briareus, but all men Aegaeon; for he is mightier than his father [sc. Poseidon]. He sat down by the side of the son of Cronos, exulting in his glory, and the blessed gods were seized with fear of him, and did not bind Zeus.[109]

Besides the central role played by this myth for the *Iliad*, Thetis's intervention clearly reveals that divinity and the good order cannot survive without the active help of monstrosity. The myth has been interestingly connected to meteorological phenomena, and the winter's chill overcome by the warm spring.[110] Even more interesting, though, is the later exegesis by the Stoic Cornutus and Heraclitus allegorista, who explain the myth through a cosmogonic

---

[108] A. *Th.* 504–20.
[109] *Il.* I.396–406.
[110] Buffière (1956), pp. 173 ff.

fight between the current order and the previous one that constantly threatens to resurface. With similar suggestions, both Cornutus and Heraclitus recognise providence's active intervention in support of Zeus. Heraclitus notes that 'Zeus's rescue was more disgraceful to him than the conspiracy, for it was Thetis and Briareus who freed him from his bonds, and hopes of rescue that depend on such allies are disgraceful.'[111] Cornutus finds a sophisticated interpretation and a providential function for Briareus:

> [...] Thetis, *disposing* everything in due order, set 'Briareos' with his hundred hands against the gods that were mentioned – perhaps because the exhalations of the earth are distributed everywhere, as it is through many hands that *division* into all the various forms occur. Or consider whether he is named 'Briareos' from *raising up nourishment* (so to speak) for the parts of the cosmos.[112]

In both cases, Thetis's providence acts and saves Zeus through Briareos's monstrosity and his capacity to scare the other gods, including Poseidon.

Divinity itself carries with it ambiguous traits, in particular in the figure of Dionysus, the Eastern god that makes peace and merges with Apollo in the Hellenic spirit. Since the origin, though, Dionysus embodies ambivalence and contradiction, as the god of folly, which he transmits to his followers, the Bacchae.[113]

Dionysus's ambivalence has never been forgotten. It seems, on the contrary, to affect his counterpart as well, namely the king of the Olympian gods. Aeschylus powerfully evokes the topic in *The Eumenides*. When Orestes and Apollo appeal to Zeus, the Erinyes' chorus responds by accusing the king of gods himself:

> On your account [sc. Apollo], Zeus sets a higher value on the death of a father. Yet he himself imprisoned his old father, Cronus. Isn't your statement in contradiction with that? [*To the judges*] I call you to witness that you have heard these words.[114]

---

[111] Heraclit. *All.* 21 ff.

[112] Corn. *ND* 17. See also Palaeph. 19 (= Festa et al. eds. (1894–1902), p. 27) for whom Briareus and Cottus are only 'Hundredarmers' because they came from a city called Hundredarm, in Chaonia).

[113] Untersteiner (1955, 2nd ed.), p. 90. On Dionysus's ambivalence see mostly the classic literature: Rohde (1894), Otto (1933), Guthrie (1950), Dodds (1951) and, on this literature, McGinty (1978). See also Colli (2010).

[114] A. *Eu.* 640–3. See also Pohlenz (1954, 2. ed.), p. 78 and *passim*, and E. *HF* 345–7 on Zeus's injustice in Amphitryion's words. On the Bacchae's iconography see Philippart (1930).

Interestingly, early texts speak little of Zeus's justice and more of his prudence and cunning.[115] The cosmos is ordered not through justice, but through force, and this force, once victorious, is called justice.[116] It is also ordered by promises, as when Zeus summons the Olympians and builds his army by literally buying the gods' support in his fight against Titans.[117]

Scholars have correctly stressed that Greek gods, and Zeus in particular, are subject to necessity.[118] One can also see why Aeschylus's Erinyes dare to challenge Zeus's name: the necessity that rules even the gods is *their* necessity, which they summon as a universal and exceptionless principle. This is also Prometheus's cry against Zeus's κράτος.[119] Nietzsche underlines that, for this reason, the problem of theodicy is not really a Greek problem, and the Apollonean harmony of the Pantheon hides the Dionysian horror of this insurmountable truth.[120] Festugière reads this dialectic as the transformation of the old inflexible destiny, presiding over the Furies' universe and based on crime and revenge, into the new and more human justice, based on correction, learning and the pedagogy of guilt.[121] I believe, however, that rather than a peaceful transformation, Aeschylus puts forward the endless and possibly unresolved conflict between primitive forces, with justice not as the aim but as what is at stake.

This divine submission to necessity might be the cause of the ambivalence under discussion. The Greek divinity is not miraculously omnipotent. Because he is submitted to necessity, he is thus the cause of everything, including what is contradictory to him.[122] Divinity bears contradiction in its own nature, revealing the duplicity of Apollonian and Dionysian, and the constant resurfacing of the dark side of their union. The contradiction also reveals the nature of the new order established against the old.

Causality and Monstrosity: Challenging Zeus

Causality, as discussed, is one of the ontological principles elaborated in early mythologems. Theogonies describe the affirmation of a principle of causality

---

[115] G. S. Kirk, 'The Structure and Aim of the Theogony', in AA. VV. (1962), pp. 61–107.
[116] On Zeus's justice, Lloyd-Jones (1983, 2nd ed.) and, on Zeus's despotism, Moreau (1985), pp. 205 ff.
[117] Hes. *Th.* 390 ff.
[118] See for example Pohlenz (1954, 2. ed.), pp. 73 and 78–9.
[119] A. *Pr.* 516–9. See Untersteiner (1955, 2nd ed.), p. 418 and *passim*.
[120] F. W. Nietzsche, 'Die dionysische Weltanschauung', in Nietzsche (1967–), III.2, pp. 43–69. On a different ground, see also Gigante (1956), p. 90.
[121] A. J. Festugière, 'Réflexions sur le problème du mal chez Eschyle et Platon', in Festugière (1971), pp. 8–37. See also Pohlenz (1954, 2. ed.), p. 74.
[122] Untersteiner (1955, 2nd ed.), p. 465 and *passim*.

that at the same time explains and justifies Being as it is, opposed to Being as it was or as it could have been. The concept of cause, αἰτία, has a juridical origin, meaning imputation or even indictment or retribution. The whole semantic area is linked to the legal idea of claiming (αἰτεῖν), of the accusation (αἰτιᾶσθαι) and the accused (αἴτιος). The juridical origin of the cause could be related to the act or action whose actor is or should be responsible for it. When projected on the mythological background of the philosophical and legal Greek culture, though, it should rather be interpreted, I believe, as the strenuous and laborious process of construction and interpretation of the idea of responsibility itself. The meaning of αἰτία is very ambiguous.[123] There is no responsibility before the legal order is built, in the same way that there is no physical causality before the cosmogonic order comes into being, and there is no transgression before order itself can be named as such.

Philosophers eventually consider the cause as a synonym of principle (ἀρχή), namely that without which reality itself cannot be, or the ontological foundation of things themselves. Αἰτία and ἀρχή eventually go hand in hand, in the physical domain and beyond, to represent the causality that explains nature's behaviour. Before the name itself, however, the principle already exists. Better, the mythologems contribute to the elaboration of the principle, and go through several transformations in order to become the causality that philosophers eventually exploit. Anaximander's principle of universal justice is reminiscent of the cause's original meaning of guilt. From the human domain, in particular the ethical and the legal, the concept is thus transposed onto the cosmic domain.

The divine principle struggles against the old order to produce the new one, which responds to, and reveals, a principle of causality. Elements are thus manipulated and composed to form new ontological realities. This is the wrong, or injustice, that is done to elements, or that elements reciprocally do to each other and that eventually finds a philosophical configuration in Anaximander and Heraclitus. Because of a separation of elements, the cosmos's formation is an ἀδικία, an offence and a damage, or an unjust violation.[124] Whereas the Greek αἰτία preserves, through the etymology, its constitutive ambivalence, the translation suggests a justice that is violated or a law that is broken. However, no justice pre-exists the new order and no law is given before its causality is established by the new divinity. Attic tragedy represents this idea by the αἰτία θεοῦ, with the divine being at the same time *cause* of a success and *guilty* of a failure, as in Eteocles' words in the *Seven*. As a survival of the old concept of

---

[123] Untersteiner (1955, 2nd ed.), p. 451.

[124] Untersteiner (1972, 2nd ed.). See also Jaeger (1934–47), I, p. 220.

the divine in the new one, of the old demonic moment into the Olympic one, the conflict is inside god itself, cause of good as well as of evil.

Monstrosity is a failure, a disorder, a violation, and yet a kind of otherness that is threatening as much as it is constitutive. It is *Being* that *becomes* something else, and so transforms itself into what it has to be, the target or goal. Transgression, for example in the tragic domain, denounces the instability of the current metaphysical and ontological balance, laboriously reached and still precarious. The same transgression, however, through the many monstrous creatures of the mythological tradition, helps build the new order, beyond and against the old one.[125] The ambiguity is already in Dionysus and, through him, it also extends to Zeus. Zeus remains dual. His justice, for example in Aeschylus, is both a blessing and a fault. Δίκη, justice, is double and ambiguous. Legal vocabulary in mythology, Vernant and Vidal-Naquet suggest, is used not to obtain precision and consistency, but rather incertitude, incompleteness, incoherence and slippery meaning.[126] Zeus τέλειος always catches the target, not because his act is always ethically right but, quite the opposite, because he is the cause of everything, of the good as much as of the bad. His justice resists the transparency of the new Logos, and this is what makes for the power and richness of the tragic. From the cosmogonic point of view, Zeus's target is the union with Hera, the chthonic part of the divine. Only when he integrates the chthonian part, through that union, Zeus becomes τέλειος.

The order that emerges is certainly above Zeus himself. He would not transgress it without causing the other gods' anger, in the same way that he could not transgress a principle of causality. Yet in Homer, Hesiod and the tragedians, this order is precarious. Beginning with Ouranos's violence on Gaia and his castration by Chronos, the affirmation and maintenance of order, through long and painful conflicts, demand the use of violence.[127] Zeus's justice is nothing more (and nothing less) than Zeus's order and, as such, the outcome of a conflict among forces: a conflict that Zeus could not win without the help of monstrous creatures.[128]

Δίκη is first and foremost what it has to be, with the normative or rather imperative meaning being prominent. For the Greeks, it progressively becomes more and more important to define the essence of what is human and define themselves as humans.[129] As Allan suggests, following Benveniste, 'order'

---

[125] See Moreau (2006), pp. 188 ff.
[126] Vernant and Vidal-Naquet (1972), p. 31. See also Stanford (1939).
[127] See Girard (1972).
[128] See Allan (2006), p. 8, 14 and *passim*.
[129] Renehan (1992).

would be a better translation for δίκη than justice, so as to leave behind the ethical sense that is foreign to its origin and inception in Greek thought.[130] Following Benveniste's suggestion, thus, it is not the moral transgression but rather the ontological violation that better represents the jolts and the bumps, the conflicts and the resistances on the precarious pattern toward order and stability. Monstrosity is the ontological violation that makes this progress uncertain and constitutively precarious. It is also, however, the force that moves things forward towards that same progress.

As we have seen above, this ambivalence is omnipresent in early Greek culture. The order of Zeus is painfully reached through force and cunning, using several tools, including monstrosity, to achieve the goal. Possibly for this reason, such an order remains precarious and constantly challenged in mythological and tragic material. Several monstrous figures attack and destabilise cosmic order, revealing the precarity on which it is grounded.

One of the most serious attempts on Zeus's authority is made by Prometheus. Son of Japetus and Klymene, Prometheus is a titan of the second generation in Hesiod's *Theogony*. Although his role in the titanomachy is unknown, he survives the cataclysmal event and finds himself next to Zeus once the Olympian order is established. Instead of patiently serving Zeus, as he is supposed to, Prometheus twice betrays the king of gods, first deceiving him in the episode of the distribution of meat and bones, and then with the theft of fire, which he brings back to men who had been deprived of it by Zeus.[131] As a result, Zeus inflicts the famous punishment on Prometheus: he is chained to a column, where an eagle devours his liver, which grows again each night, rendering the painful punishment endless. Heracles eventually kills the eagle and, according to some readings, sets Prometheus free.

The clash that follows Prometheus's treacherous attempt does not reach the magnitude of the earlier conflicts of the theomachy. It testifies, however, to the fact that the struggle is not over for the king of the Olympians. His order is not seriously threatened, yet it is challenged, and this is enough to raise questions about the solidity of his victory and of the values that he has been trying to establish. Furthermore, if Prometheus's attitude is not entirely clear in Hesiod's account, in which the titan appears as a cheater and a thief, a whole different picture emerges from Aeschylus's version of the myth, or at least from what has survived of a trilogy whose history, date and arrangement are far from clear to scholars.

---

[130] Renehan (1992), pp. 10–11. See Benveniste (1969), II, p. 97 ff. See also Jones (1956), Gagarin (1973 and 1974), D'Agostino (1979) and Severino (2015).
[131] Hes. *Th.* 507 ff.

To begin with, as Reinhardt points out, Prometheus is not the son, but the brother of the titans in Aeschylus.[132] He is the brother of the monsters who have shaken the very foundations of the Olympian regime and whose defeat is still recent. The titans do not forget him in Cratinus' comedy *The Gods of Wealth*: after Zeus is dethroned by the people, the titans set Prometheus, by now weakened, free from his bonds.[133]

Prometheus is the worthy brother of Gaia, mother of archetypical monstrosities. He is thus close to Typhoeus, for whom he feels pity and whose struggle he understands, since the anguipede villain, in Prometheus's words, intended to overthrow the autocracy of Zeus (Διὸς τυραννίς) by force.[134] The term τύραννος initially designates nothing more than the holder of power, the one that embodies the absolute authority, conceived on the model of Eastern kingdoms. In this sense, it has a neutral sense and does not necessarily carry with it the negative meaning of 'tyrant' that involves an ethical judgement on the nature or even the legitimacy of power.[135]

In the *Prometheus*, however, Zeus does not establish his tyranny by replacing a legal void. He crushes the old authority and usurps power. He punishes Prometheus because he dares to disclose the possibility of an alternative order. Zeus is indeed an autocratic ruler, who does not recognise any other law besides his own. God acts ἀθέτως or ἀθέσμως, lawlessly and despotically, and it is precisely this attitude that the titan denounces without ambiguity.

Prometheus is also close to the primeval forces that resist the establishment of Zeus's reign.[136] The titanomachy that Aeschylus refers to, through Prometheus's voice (195 ff.), was probably quite different from Hesiod's. Aeschylus knows an alternative background story for the clash between Zeus and Prometheus, one that could have further reinforced the sympathetic attitude toward the punished titan.

Prometheus's story reveals once again the conflict between the old and new worlds, which both have their legitimacy and values to oppose to each other.[137] As underlined above, dissension and conflict are within the divine itself. The whole trilogy probably showed a movement of Zeus, the victorious god, toward pardon and reconciliation, choosing wisdom and moderation over

---

[132] Reinhardt (1949). See also Solmsen (1949), ch. 2.
[133] PCG IV, fr. 171–9.
[134] A. Pr. 350–76.
[135] See Berve (1967), Mossé (1969) and Di Benedetto (1978), who at least sees a negative meaning in A. Pr. 224–5.
[136] Moreau (1985), *passim*.
[137] Untersteiner (1955, 2nd ed.).

force and violence.[138] The *Prometheus Bound* itself, however, offers the clear picture of an arrogant monarch who punishes a subjugated god whose motivations appear not only understandable, but also reasonable. If one considers the lost material of the trilogy, it might be true that, accompanied by κράτος and βία, Zeus moved away from the latter toward the former in order to establish, on a more compassionate and reasonable basis, the new δίκη, the Olympian legality. The opposite, however, can also be claimed, to avoid watering down Aeschylus's powerful accusation of the present order: even if moral and compassionate, the Zeus of the lost plays was irredeemably stained by the harsh image explicitly presented in the *Prometheus Bound*.

Κράτος and βία, upon which Zeus's power ultimately rests, make a theatrical entrance on stage, and are presented as monstrous figures themselves.[139] Their exterior aspects are frightening, and Hephaestus, who receives harsh and hateful orders from Power, underlines the similitude between the latter's words and his appearance. Zeus's violence can be εὐμενής, benevolent and directed toward the realisation of the good end, the true justice. Nonetheless, it remains βία and, as such, struggles with the image of a compassionate god. Violence is not in the hands of Zeus because it is just, but it is made just because it is exercised by Zeus, and by nobody else.[140]

The pre-Hellenic god Prometheus is often accompanied by Hephaestus, who also comes from the East.[141] Hephaestus is monstrous in his own way and so is his progeny: he is the father of the mortal Palaimonius, one of the Argonauts, who is also lame, and of the monstrous Erichthonius or Erechtheus, sprung from the earth after Hephaestus's semen was spread on Gaia by Athena. Athenians feel themselves to be sons of the earth-born Erechtheus, and thus generated by the lame god and Gaia.[142] Hephaestus is far from happy to obey Zeus's orders in the *Prometheus Bound*, and feels pain for the titan's harsh destiny.[143]

The twisted creatures are united by their antipathy for the absolute sovereign of the universe. Aeschylus's tragic plot intends to challenge the undisputed rule of the king of gods. To do so, it provides Prometheus with a strong weapon. Neither force nor violence anymore, but rather a fate which is older and mightier than Zeus himself. This fate has been revealed to Prometheus by

---

[138] See P. Mazon, in Eschyle (1920–5) and Solmsen (1949), p. 147 and *passim*.

[139] Solmsen (1949), p. 134. Βία is often represented as a monstrous Erinys. See the winged figure in LIMC, *sub voce*.

[140] See *contra* Gigante (1956), pp. 196–201. On violence and justice in early Greek thought see also Agamben (1995).

[141] Pohlenz (1954, 2. ed.).

[142] Loraux (1996).

[143] A. Pr. 12–81.

Themis, here identified with Gaia herself: the mother of monsters reveals the identity of the female who is destined to bear a son stronger than his father and with whom, thus, Zeus cannot mate. Prometheus reveals his knowledge of the secret, without unveiling its content, notwithstanding the threat of harsher punishment. The prophecy is a weapon that keeps Zeus under threat and contributes to maintain the precarity of his order. Zeus can chain the last of the titans but is himself chained by his fate and by the prophecy: the titan resists and, with his knowledge and his undaunted character, opposes the unconditioned and unbridled rule of the cosmos's tyrant.[144]

The Homeric Hymns remind us that Zeus takes power by subjugating feminine divinities.[145] Several figures of the ancient myths associate monstrosity and femininity, as well as the establishment of the Olympian order with their defeat. As elsewhere, however, feminine monstrosity has a status and a function which establishes it as a constitutive force that is indispensable to the new order.

The Erinyes, for example, embody a feature of justice and law that reveals the problematic character of the transition from the old and pre-Hellenic values to the new Olympian world. The Ἐρινύες are born from the drops of blood spilled by Cronos's castration of Ouranos. They are among the oldest divinities. Initially indeterminate, they progressively become three in number: Megaera, Tisiphone and Alecto.[146] With their horrible aspect, they resist the instauration of the gods of the younger generation. They are often represented as winged demons, with snakes on their heads, holding torches or whips in their hands.[147] Aeschylus powerfully conveys the image of this feminine monstrosity in the opening of the *Eumenides*:

> [...] an extraordinary band of women, asleep, sitting in chairs – no, I won't call them women, but Gorgons; but then I can't liken their form to that of Gorgons either. I did once see before now, in a painting, a female creature robbing Phineus of his dinner; these ones, though, it is plain to see, don't have wings, and they're black and utterly nauseating. They are pumping out snores that one doesn't dare come near, and dripping a loathsome drip from their eyes. And their attire is one that it's not proper

---

[144] On the meaning of Prometheus's struggle see also the classic work of Nestle (1934), and Trousson (1964).
[145] See *h.Cer.* and *h.Ven.* as well as Allen (2006), p. 29 and *passim*.
[146] Verg, *Aen.* VI.570–2 and VII.325–6, Apollod. I.1.4.
[147] See Sancassano (1997) and, on the snake, Küster (1913). Patera (2015) studies other feminine figures such as Lamia, Mormo, Empousa and Gello.

to bring either before the images of the gods or under the roofs of men. I have never seen the tribe to which this company belongs, nor do I know what country boasts that it has reared this race without harm to itself and does not regret the labour of doing so.[148]

The Erinyes are creatures of the night and of the earth, and emerge from the underworld's darkness to avenge the victims of crimes, and especially of consanguineous homicides, by torturing their victims and making them descend into a painful madness. Demons usually lack a genealogy, while the Erinyes have one, and a noble one: they are noble *and* monstrous. This contributes to increase the violent force of their tragic role.[149]

Whereas the older generations of gods are progressively diminished and dispossessed by the Olympians, the Erinyes are able to maintain, thanks to their nature, a strong degree of autonomy and independence from the newer generations and from Zeus himself. Their force is the earth's force in which they live and that once again reveals all its ambivalence as a generator of monstrous but also of powerful creatures, mother of death but also of life.[150] Like the Moirai, the Erinyes know only their own laws, and they are subject to them alone. To the Moirai they offer their faculties, and they execute their will.[151] Even more interestingly, Zeus and the Olympians are also subject to them and cannot derogate their implacable decrees. A monstrous divinity, thus, resurfaces from the ancient mythological strata and resists the legality of the new beautiful and harmonious order created by Zeus.

The Erinyes, also called Furies, are primitive forces, often compared to the Keres, who devastate everything they touch, bringing war and death.[152] Hesiod names them the Κῆρες Ἐρινύες, νηλεόποινος or ruthless avengers.[153] The animal or savage side enters into the picture and overthrows values, roles and hierarchies. The nightmarish and infernal hunt of Orestes depicts a hero reduced to a beast, hunted and pursued by the monstrous creatures. Erinyes manage retribution. They incite vengeance, and then punish for the same acts that they have inspired, in an endless spiral. Every sign of a divine or benevolent order has disappeared from this gloomy picture, in which the only implacable law is the law of monstrous revenge.[154]

---

[148] A. *Eu.* 46–59. See Rohde (1894), Krappe (1932), J. Toutain, 'L'évolution de la conception des Erinyes dans le mythe d'Oreste d'Eschyle à Euripide', in AA. VV. (1936), I, pp. 449–53, Brown (1983), Junge (1983), Heubeck (1986) and Zerhoch (2015).
[149] Moreau (1985), p. 159 ff.
[150] Pohlenz (1954, 2. ed.), pp. 120–1.
[151] Dodds (1951), pp. 6–8.
[152] Reinhardt (1949), pp. 154 ff.
[153] Hes. *Th.* 1055 and 217.
[154] Moreau (1985), p. 83 ff. See also p. 101 ff. and Di Benedetto (1978), pp. 230–87.

Aeschylus is the first playwright who brings monstrous masks onto the stage. The Erinyes are the natural candidates for the introduction of this prodigious scenical innovation. The apparition of the gruesome chorus of the Erinyes, the tradition reports, is so shocking that causes audience members to faint and pregnant women to miscarry.[155]

The inflexibility of the Erinyes' punishing nature has been related to the cosmic dimension. In this sense, the monstrous creatures represent the physical necessity that characterises natural processes and is again connected to the Moirai and the most ancient layer of the concept of fate.[156] As fate allocates to everyone what is due, Erinyes administer the punishment that comes with revenge. The monstrous creatures, thus, survive in the early cosmogonic reflections, for example in Heraclitus, for whom they become the keeper of cosmic order, and thus a synonym of φύσις itself: 'The Sun will not transgress his bounds, else the Erinyes, ministers of Justice, will find him out.'[157]

The Erinyes are Δίκη's ministers, and testify to the transposition of the human concept of justice into the physical universe. Interestingly, the justice that Heraclitus mentions is on the threshold between the pre-Hellenic and the Olympian worlds. Far from representing the complete achievement of this process, the Erinyes rather represent the inextinguishable nature of the primitive clash, and bring the conflict into the new order and at the heart of its legal and cosmic structure. Φύσις can be grasped here in all its ambiguity, just like the mythical Earth, symbol of fertility but also of death. In the same way the wind, with which the Erinyes are associated, is both a vital element that helps life and a destructive element that brings death and havoc.

Justice and the Erinyes are often invoked together, making the ambivalence come to light.[158] The nature of the tragic contributes to blur the boundaries, since the monstrous and the divine intertwine in the hard path that leads from revenge as the only form of recognised retribution to its distinction from, and opposition to, justice. Justice cannot but make use of the monstrous female characters for the retribution without which both cosmic and natural order would collapse. Pohlenz suggests that Plato's mentality, for which the divine cannot be the origin of evil, is already at work in the Erinyes' development.[159] The Erinyes' vengeance is not only for specific violations against men but also, and more importantly, for the general wrong made by men against the divine sphere.[160]

---

[155] *TrGF* III.A1 30–2. See also Frontisi-Ducroux (1995), p. 97.

[156] Magris (1984). p. 16 ff.

[157] *Vorsokr.* 22 B 94 (= LM [9] HER. D89c = Plu. *De exilio* 604 A). See also Untersteiner (1972, 2nd ed.), pp. 195 ff. and Gagarin (1974).

[158] See e.g. S. *El.* 480, *Ant.* 1075, E. *Med.* 1389. See aldo Di Benedetto (1978), pp. 253–9.

[159] Pohlenz (1954, 2. ed.), p. 125.

[160] Reinhardt (1933), *passim*.

Such wrong is a monstrosity, to which the divine opposes another monstrosity, that of the avenging Furies.

Inevitably, thus, this feature of divine justice also appears as a dissension or a tension within the divine itself. The Erinyes reveal the fluid status of Justice's being, its lack of univocity that dramatically anticipates the δισσοὶ λόγοι, the contrasting discourses of the Sophists.[161] Antithesis, which appears first in tragedy and then in philosophy, dominates the reasoning. Orestes' formulation in the *Coephore* is the clearest and most impressive: 'War-god shall encounter War-god, Right shall encounter right (Ἄρης Ἄρει ξυμβαλεῖ, Δίκᾳ Δίκα).'[162] As Untersteiner claims, Aeschylus's great and tragic discovery is that in order to achieve justice, justice itself must be violated.[163] I would add that, in order to overcome monstrosity, monstrosity itself must be enrolled. The Olympian god and the demonic numen go hand in hand, but so do the divine and the monstrous, whose function is precisely to restore order and yet constantly reopen the battle *for* it, with aleatory and uncertain results.

The *Oresteia* attempts a composition of the conflict between the ancient and the new concept of retribution through the invention of the Areopagus and the transformation of the Erinyes into Eumenides, or benevolent ones.[164] A composition, however, that is not a solution, because the ancient forces of revenge and retaliation are not overcome but rather integrated within the new law. Several elements confirm this reading. Firstly, the new law of the Areopagus is limited to the city.[165] Outside of the city's walls, the Erinyes continue to operate. The fear

---

[161] See Untersteiner (1949) and Cassin (1995).

[162] A. Ch. 461.

[163] Untersteiner (1972, 2nd ed.), p. 289 and *passim*, especially p. 521 ff. Mario Untersteiner's point about Greek thought's ambivalence about embracing every aspect of the real is particularly relevant for this study. Untersteiner's reading, especially in the late 30s and early 40s when he clashes with and is practically ostracised by the Fascist government, is deeply influenced by his personal intellectual movement toward a strong laicism as a methodology with which to approach the classics. This approach shapes his conviction that, from its inception to the classical age, Greek thought reveals the effort of the *logos* to embrace even those aspects of human experience that appear irrational and difficult to grasp through reason. Although this thesis might appear reductive today, I believe that Untersteiner's approach still offers an invaluable contribution to the reading of the monstrous I am trying to develop. In particular, his notion of the tragic as revealing the irreconcilable contrast between reason and that which appears absurd, contradictory and irrational offers an interesting characterisation of the ambiguous role of the monstrous in early Greek thought. On Untersteiner's intellectual profile, see Battegazzore and Decleva Caizzi a cura di (1989). Moreau (1985) reads Aeschylus's extant fragments as a confirmation that the same scheme is repeated in the lost works. On the origin and meaning of the δισσοὶ λόγοι, see Cassin (1995).

[164] P. Mazon, *Introduction*, in Eschyle (1920–5).

[165] See Solmsen (1949), p. 202, Vernant and Vidal-Naquet (1972), pp. 156–8, Lloyd-Jones (1989).

of them, moreover, is not obliterated. It is rather embodied by the feelings that law itself must inspire. In Athena's words:

> Neither anarchy nor tyranny – this I counsel my burghers to maintain and hold in reverence, nor quite to banish fear from out the city. For who among mortal men is righteous that hath no fear of aught? Stand then in just awe of such majesty and ye shall possess a bulwark to safeguard your country and your government, such as none of mankind hath either among the Scythians or in Pelops' realm.[166]

Fear, or even terror (δεινόν), is useful to hold the citizens' hearths. The good fear of the laws might not be the same as the old fear of the Furies. Yet it is the same feeling that must help prevent, for example, disasters like the civil war. The Erinyes abandon their complete autonomy and independence vis-à-vis the law. Yet they do so by being integrated into the law.[167] The monster is not expelled by the norm but rather conquers it and finds itself at its heart. It is precisely the monstrous πρόσωπον of the Erinyes that must keep, according to Athena, the city in awe: 'From these fearsome faces I see great benefit coming to these citizens.'[168]

It is not surprising, moreover, that Euripides develops a testimony of Pherekydes of Athens in an interesting way.[169] The tragic element, for Euripides, is not dialectically sublimated or overcome in any way. In *Iphigenia in Tauris*, the tension within the divine is brought to a new stage, and within the multiple body of the Furies itself. Only some of them, Euripides imagines, follow Athena's decrees, while others do not accept the outcome and the metamorphosis imposed upon them and continue to pursue Orestes. His fearful words give a sense of the abominable nature of the monstrous, and now also recalcitrant, goddesses:

> They which consented to the judgement, chose nigh the tribunal for themselves a shrine: but of the Erinyes some consented not, and hounded me with homeless chasing eye, until, to Phoebus' hallowed soil returned, fasting before his shrine I cast me down, and swore to snap my life-thread, dying there, except Apollo saved me, who destroyed.[170]

Reinhardt points out that the transformation of Erinyes into Eumenides is everything but natural. Their opposition is complete and only a real 'miracle'

---

[166] A. *Eu.* 696–703. On this passage see Reinhardt (1949).
[167] Following Axelos (1962), Moreau (1985), p. 290 ff. reads once again a convergence between this movement and the dialectic philosophy of Heraclitus.
[168] A. *Eu.* 990–1.
[169] See Pherecyd. in *FGH*.
[170] E. *IT* 969–75.

performed by Athena can accomplish it. Not without irony, Reinhardt also notes that the metamorphosis accompanies a judgement that appears as a masterpiece of partiality and injustice. Like Zeus's acts in the previous establishment of the cosmic order, Athena's decision is built solely on her authority and does not have any other force than force itself.[171]

The Erinyes do not have a father and are on the mother's, Clytemnestra's, side. They come to clash with Apollo, who represents the father's side and Olympian justice, administered by Athena, the motherless goddess.[172] The relevance of the feminine character of monstrosity has been underlined, especially in the *Oresteia*. Only female monsters could have such an ambivalent power in the mythologems accounting for the birth of justice. They have this role, though, beyond the birth of Δίκη. In Greek mythology, and in tragedy in particular, femininity embodies monstrosity in several characters, both collective and individual.[173]

Amazons are of course the first characters that come to mind in this respect. Women warriors who defy all schemes and norms of the gendered division of labour, they enjoy a large success in both literature and art. Amazons are located in an indefinite East and they are assimilated to eastern barbarians, until the celebration of the victory of Marathon against the Persians, on the West metopes of the Parthenon. Although they represent first and foremost the victims of great enterprises of mythical warriors – Heracles, Achilles and Theseus – Amazons develop distinct features that make them rich characters in Greek mythology.[174] According to the epic formula, the Amazon is ἀντιάνειρα, a match for man, equal to but also different from him. Her female body contains a male θυμός, or ardour.[175] When Palaephatus proceeds to rationalise the myth of the Amazons, his approach is simple: *as* women, they could not constitute an army. Such an army has never existed; the so-called amazons were only barbarian men wearing women's clothes that reached their feet. Excellent warriors, to be sure, but men.[176]

Their monstrous otherness is more metaphorical than real. Like Medusa, women are often represented frontally, so as to simultaneously display their

---

[171] Reinhardt (1949), *passim*. See in particular A. *Eu*. 490 ff. Here and *infra*, Reinhardt's position should be read keeping in mind both his connection with Martin Heidegger and Heidegger's relationship to Carl Schmitt.
[172] Moreau (1985), p. 267 ff. More recently, Zeitlin (1996) and McClure (1999), pp. 105–11. See also Bachofen (1861) and Thomson (1941).
[173] See Morgan (1984), pp. 187 ff.
[174] See DuBois (1982), Blok (1995) and Mayor (2014).
[175] Mayor (2014), *passim*. See LM, Glossary, *sub voce*.
[176] Palaeph. 32 (= Festa et al. eds. (1894–1902), pp. 49–50).

grotesque fragility and their closeness to barbarians and monsters, traditionally represented in the same way.[177] Like barbarians and monsters, though, women also embody a threat, especially through their collective aggressiveness. Amazons' otherness speaks less of their appearance than of their customs, which do not reflect fragility but, on the contrary, show their fierce value on the battlefield. They do not have any physical difference from other women besides their weapons and clothing, both variously depicted in a more or less barbarian fashion across the centuries. Blok underlines that their hybrid nature, differently from other kinds of hybridity such as that of the centaur, the hermaphrodite or even the Chimera, is not reflected in their feminine body.[178]

From the artists' interest in the beauty of the feminine body also comes one of the features that contributes to the Amazons' monstrous heritage, namely the breast's ablation. The idea, which was never a traditional mythologem, comes possibly from the depiction of the Amazons on the Parthenon frieze, in which the sculptor chose to extend and apply the pre-existing motif of the uncovered breast in order to stress the violence of the combat and the excitement of the action.[179] Amazons' monstrous or barbarian character remains tangential. Greeks perceive Amazons to be far enough away from them to represent them as associated with people of colour.[180] Yet they are hardly distinguishable from the Greek warriors against whom they fight, often with hoplite armor and in hoplite formation. They often help a wounded comrade, or carry the body of a dead companion. In a word, they are far from the image of savage warriors and reflect another kind of civilisation, the *otherness* in which a female world was thought about, and that clashes with the male supremacy and normality of the Greek world.

Amazons' monstrosity is mainly metaphorical. However, the echo of the otherness coming from their anomalous sexual status can be heard in several other prominent examples of monstrosity, both collective, such as the Danaids, the Lemnian women and the Bacchae, and individual, such as Clytemnestra, Medea and Pandora.

The Danaids enter the scene, in Aeschylus's *Suppliants*, dressed in barbarian fashion. The contrast is immediately visible between the mild appearance that they want to give of themselves, and their threatening and impudent masks. Their dance, performed to implore the gods, is vehement and violent; they tear their dresses apart without masking their savage nature. Nor do

---

[177] Frontisi-Ducroux (1995), p. 248.
[178] Blok (1995), p. 277.
[179] See LIMC, *sub voce*. See also Delcourt (1957).
[180] LIMC, *sub voce*, cat. 650 and 651.

their words hide their nature. With their father Danaus, the Danaids seek refuge and protection in Argos from their cousins, sons of Aegyptus. They feel horror not only at the forced marriage, but also at men and the idea of belonging to one.[181] In short, they rebel against the order of nature and make themselves monstrous against customs and male authority. The king of Argos himself, Pelasgus, struggles to comprehend the fifty maidens among the civilised stock:

> What you say, strangers, is unbelievable for me to hear, that this group of yours is of Argive descent. You bear more resemblance to the women of Lybia – certainly not to those of this country. The Nile, too, might nurture such a crop; and a similar stamp is struck upon the dies of Cyprian womanhood by male artificers. I hear, too, that there are nomad women in India, near neighbours to the Ethiopians, who saddle their way across country on camels that run like horses; and then the man-shunning, meat-eating Amazons – if you were equipped with bows, I'd be very inclined to guess that you were them.[182]

The Danaids appeal to civilisation, and yet their appearance brings them closer to the monstrous and mythical people that live at the edge of the earth and beyond the boundaries of civilisation. This female collective body represents the ancient order that resists the new Olympian religion. Κράτος against κράτος, they resist a different order through their hate for the other sex.[183] 'Unwedded and unsubdued', they want to escape the yoke of men.[184] The tension implicit in the tragic clash emerges through their monstrosity, intended not only as a barbarous appearance but also as a savage stance and resistance to what has to become natural and normal according to the new order.[185] The Danaids are eventually married to their cousins but, with their father's help, they accomplish a bloody vengeance by killing all their husbands. All but one, since Hypermnestra spares her husband Lynceus, because he did not lack respect for her. Once again monstrosity is divided in itself and ambiguously presented in the tragic material.

Because of their nature, and most of all due to their collective murder, the Danaids are often compared to the Lemnian women. Aphrodite (or Medea, according to a different version) curses the women of the island of Lemnos by afflicting them with a bad smell, because of which they are abandoned by their husbands. The women organise themselves and take revenge by killing their

---

[181] A. *Supp.* 9–11. See P. Mazon, *Introduction*, in Eschyle (1920–5), pp. 7–8.
[182] A. *Supp.* 277–88.
[183] Vernant and Vidal-Naquet (1972), pp. 31–2.
[184] A. *Supp.* 141–4.
[185] Untersteiner (1955, 2nd ed.), p. 142 and *passim*.

husbands and taking power on the island.[186] As in the myth of the Danaids, only one of them, Hypsipyle, spares one male, her father and king of the island, Thoas. The Lemnian deed is eventually remembered as the crime of all crimes, generating a powerful mythographic tradition.[187] Once again, women become monsters by revolting against male power and taking the place of men.[188]

A similar picture resurfaces in Euripides' *Bacchae*, in which women embody once again the old Dionysian world that resists the new religious order. The collective body of women appears to repudiate humanity itself, against the Apollonean sense of order and measure.[189] Pentheus, king of Thebes, intends to block and control this collective identity, bringing the ecstatic bodies back to reason. The women, however, claim in a simple way a different knowledge, not necessarily based on reason and yet bringing them toward a kind of wisdom and harmony, both with nature and among them.[190] Because of Pentheus's attitude and claim of superiority, the maenads's response becomes aggressive. With fire and snakes in their hair, the Bacchae show their savage faces and respond violently to the violence that is prepared for them. They become a real prodigy, τὸ δεινὸν, and with hundred hands they fight back and bring an atrocious death to Pentheus:

> They put their countless hands to the fir tree and pulled it out of the earth. Pentheus from his high perch fell to the ground with many a scream and moan: he knew that his end was near.[191]

Like a hundred-armed creature, the god-possessed women kill as a portentous multitude. In another atrocious scene, the countless hands of the feminine monster emerge again, in the darkness of Hecuba's tent. Hecuba, the blessed woman, becomes inhuman, and unleashes the multifarious monstrosity of her women against Polymestor and his sons, to avenge the killing of her son Polydorus. Blinded after the killing of the children, Polymestor himself relates the monstrous attack:

> I sat in the middle of a couch, my legs bent in repose. Many of the daughters of Troy sat near me as if I were their friend, some on the left, others on the

---

[186] Dumézil (1924), Martin (1987). See also Jackson (1995) for Myrsilys of Methymna's exploitation of the story.
[187] In modern times, for example, Bachofen (1861) reads the Lemnian myth in the framework of his monumental reconstruction of Gynecocracy.
[188] Moreau (1985), pp. 190–1. N. Loraux, 'Aristophane, les femmes d'Athènes et le théâtre', in AA. VV. (1993), pp. 203–53, draws an interesting parallel between the Lemnians and Aristophanes' rebel women, but interestingly stresses also the differences among them.
[189] Pohlenz (1954, 2. ed.), p. 25.
[190] E. *Ba.* 395 and 685 ff.
[191] E. *Ba.* 1109–13.

right, and praised the weaving of Edonian hands, examining my clothing against the light. Others looked at my two Thracian javelins and stripped me of this equipment. All those who were mothers admired my children and dandled them in their arms, passing them from one pair of hands to another so that they would be separated from their father. Then after such peaceful talk – you can't imagine – all of a sudden from somewhere in their clothing they produced swords and stabbed the children, while others, seizing me like a captured enemy, held my arms and legs. I wanted to rescue my children, but if I attempted to lift my face, they held me by the hair, and if I tried to move my hands, unhappy man that I was, I could do nothing because of the throng of women. Then as their crowning blow, woe greater than woe, they did a terrible thing: they took brooches and stabbed the pupils of my poor eyes and made them run with blood. Then they fled this way and that in the tent. [. . .] neither sea nor land breeds any creature like them.[192]

Feminine monstrosity reaches the acme of horror in the *Bacchae* and in *Hecuba*. With the image of a collective female body, either possessed by Dionysus or acting for a just vengeance, Euripides enriches the tradition of feminine monstrosity. This monstrosity, however, is also explored, and perhaps with more complexity, through individual mythical and tragic characters.

Several individual female characters present the traits of monstrosity in Greek tragedy. It is not always a physical deformity, nor is it merely a moral or metaphorical monstrosity. In tragedy, individual women often challenge the ethical roles and expected behaviours or redefine the boundaries of normality and abnormality so as to build the complex structure of tragic conflicts, between humans and gods as well as among humans themselves. Pohlenz argues that feminine psychology is one of the great discoveries of tragic theatre and, in particular, of Euripides. The feminine instincts were traditionally relegated to the private sphere but, with Euripides, they violently cross the boundary and take centre stage.[193]

Chained up so as to be conducted in front of Creon, Antigone is called by the chorus a fearful prodigy (δαιμόνιον τέρας).[194] This prodigy translates the struggle between two humans – the man Creon and the woman Antigone – into the opposition between two incommensurable spheres, the divine justice of Zeus and δίκη, and the human justice of Creon, which now appears as ὕβρις. The ambivalence underlined by Heidegger in one of the most famous commentaries of this clash appears to give a cosmic meaning to the monstrous

[192] E. *Hec.* 1151–81.
[193] Pohlenz (1954, 2. ed.), pp. 248–9.
[194] S. *Ant.* 376.

and prodigious nature of the events: there are many fearful and wonderful things, but nothing more strangely wonderful than man (πολλὰ τὰ δεινὰ κοὐδὲν ανθρώπου δεινότερον πέλει).[195] The prodigious act of Antigone has transformed Creon's stubbornness into something monstrous; it has brought into full light its character, limited, falsified, and alienated from itself.[196]

Among the female characters who exhibit the most acute features of monstrosity there is certainly Clytemnestra. She is another figure of retaliation, who plunges into the deepest darkness of inhumanity to seek revenge against her husband Agamemnon, for the immolation of their daughter Iphigenia. In Aeschylus's hands, Clytemnestra becomes a demon in human shape that Cassandra depicts as a monster:

> [Agamemnon] does not know what kind of bite comes after the fawning tongue of that hateful bitch and the cheerful inclination of her ear. Such is the audacity of this female who murders a male; she is – what loathsome beast's name can I call her by, to hit the mark? – an Amphisbaena, or some Scylla dwelling among the rocks, the bane of sailors, a raging, hellish mother, breathing out truceless war against her nearest and dearest. What a cry of triumph she raised, as if an enemy had been routed in battle, this woman who will stop at nothing! – though she pretends to be delighted at his safe return.[197]

Rebel female, Clytemnestra fights back against male power with cunning and duplicity. Comparing her to mythological creatures notoriously famous for their duplicity, Aeschylus invites Clytemnestra to join the monstrous stock and she gladly accepts the invitation. Underlying even further the ambivalence of her monstrosity, so as to seal her tragic nobility, Euripides makes her unrecognisable vis-à-vis her previous evilness in *Iphigenia in Aulis*. The monster is now a compassionate mother and a devout spouse, who certainly does not imagine what she will have to undertake to re-establish her humanity against Agamemnon's violation.

An even more striking and monstrous revenge, because self-destructive as much as destructive of the guilty enemy, is Medea's. Woman *and* barbarian, Medea has twice the characteristics to be the outsider that destroys Greek values. However, it is not like a less-than-human monster, or as an animal,

---

[195] S. Ant. 332–3. See M. Heidegger. *Die Bedeutung des* δεινόν. (*Erläuterung des Anfangs des Chorliedes*), in *Hölderlins Hymne "Der Ister"*, in Heidegger (1975–), LIII, pp. 74–8.
[196] Reinhardt (1933), pp. 75–105, but see also Paduano (1975) on Reinhardt's *Sophocles* and, in particular, on the Hegelian influence on his interpretation of the *Antigone*.
[197] A. A. 1228–39.

that she strikes her enemy, Jason. Reason never abandons her, terrible and efficacious until the conclusion that tradition has transmitted to us in many different forms. She is a monster, first and foremost, because fearful and dangerous.[198] Like Hecuba and Clytemnestra, the blessed woman becomes bloodthirsty[199] and, because of her origin and customs, she does not hesitate to invoke Hecate and the obscure forces of evil for help, and to support her vengeance. Here monstrosity comes forward, since Medea's is a terrible act (τὸ δεινόν).[200]

Euripides' Medea openly acknowledges the feminine aspects upon which she builds her vengeance. She calls the Corinthian women for solidarity, for 'of all creatures that have breath and sensation, we women are the most unfortunate'.[201] Yet a proud awareness of her status is thrown against the pale arguments of men, who 'say that we live a life free from danger at home while *they* fight with the spear. How wrong they are! I would rather stand three times with a shield in battle than give birth once.'[202] Jason's response that it would be better to have sons without women appears as the veritable hubris of this tragic clash.[203] Hateful creature (μῖσος), Jason calls her, and more savage than Skylla. But again, after the monstrous and necessary deed,[204] Medea fully embraces her monstrosity, gladly accepting to be called Skylla and she-lion, since she has finally hit Jason in the heart's vital spot.[205]

Pohlenz suggests that Euripides has felt the positive value of instinct, although, once again, Medea's monstrosity is perhaps instinctual, but never ceases to be rational and lucid until the very end.[206] He uses the term μεγαλόσπλαγχνος, namely with strong internal organs, with a big abdomen. Before being called ἄλογον, irrationality was associated with physical features, and thus connected to a deformation that, in Medea's case, hides within her body and only appears to the nurses' eyes. The theatre of the tragic is displaced by Euripides to within the human's interior, and opens up to the psychological drama. For this reason, Pohlenz claims, we understand and sympathise with Medea, who is not a monster.[207] What if, however, we sympathised precisely

---

[198] E. *Med.* 44.
[199] E. *Med.* 264.
[200] E. *Med.* 395 ff.
[201] E. *Med.* 230.
[202] E. *Med.* 248–51.
[203] E. *Med.* 574.
[204] E. *Med.* 1244.
[205] E. *Med.* 1358.
[206] Pohlenz (1954, 2. ed.), pp. 424–5.
[207] Pohlenz (1954, 2. ed.), pp. 252 ff.

with her monstrosity, namely with her fierce resistance, rational and instinctive at once, against a destiny of exploitation and unjust alienation?

The rational explanation of the myth is not at stake here, nor is its historical development. It is not by chance, however, that the most ancient layer of the myth, as Pohlenz himself recognises, tells a different story: Medea's children are not killed by their mother in an act of indirect revenge. They are killed by the Corinthian, to avoid a progeny of barbarian stock.[208] The conflict between the Dionysian and the Apollonean strikes back once again, as Pohlenz suggests: whereas for Socrates the knowledge of goodness is already an ethical virtue, Medea claims precisely the opposite. In Ovid's words: *video meliora proboque, deteriora sequor*.[209]

Together with other characters, human and non-human, I believe that Clytemnestra and Medea epitomise particularly well the monstrous feminine. If one looked for its archetype, however, it is probably Pandora who should carry off the palm of monstrosity.[210] Zeus's poisoned gift to humanity, after Prometheus's theft, she is the first woman, and she brings evil to mankind. Pandora is given to Epimetheus, Prometheus's brother, who falls in love with her, since she had been made with the beauty of the immortal goddesses. Once on earth, Pandora falls into the trap (Hesiod does not give full details on this part) and opens the jar in which all evils had been encased, spreading them on the earth for humanity's misery.[211]

Pandora is an artificial being. Every Olympian gives her one quality, to hide her poisoned heart. She is modelled, out of clay, by Hephaestus, the lame god and protector of the artisan. A monster creates another monster and makes it available for all the other gods to add something to her.[212] Hephaestus also forges a crown representing all monstrous animals, and when Zeus brings her in front of the other gods, the result is astonishing:

> [...] wonder gripped the immortal gods and the mortal human beings when they saw the steep deception, intractable for human beings. For from her comes the race of female women: for of her is the deadly race and tribe of women, a great woe for mortals, dwelling with men, no companions of baneful poverty but only of luxury. As when bees in vaulted beehives nourish the drones, partners in evil works – all day long until the sun goes down, every day, the bees hasten and set up the white honeycombs, while

---

[208] Pohlenz (1954, 2. ed.), pp. 262–2. See e.g. a late account by Ael. *VH* V.21.
[209] Ou. *Met.* VII.20–21.
[210] Solmsen (1949), p. 47.
[211] Hes. *Op.* 55 ff. and *Th.* 571 ff.
[212] Delcourt (1957), p. 145. On Hephaestus see also Garland (1995), pp. 61–3.

the drones remain inside among the vaulted beehives and gather into their own stomachs the labour of others – in just the same way high-thundering Zeus set up women as an evil for mortal men, as partners in distressful works.[213]

Symbol of all women, Pandora is the punishment, both necessary and inevitable, for the attempted violation of Zeus's absolute authority. The ancient scholia underline how Pandora is a real simulacrum, who hides her nature behind a somatic appearance of beauty, a demonic aspect that falsely embodies human power, middle way between humanity and divinity.[214] However, as usual, the myth's elements bring with them a strong ambivalence. Because of her origin, Pandora is closely linked with Gaia, and thus also is a symbol of fertility and reproduction, which comes to her through Hephaestus's fire. The woman poisons humanity, but also brings life to it, revealing once again the ambiguity ingrained in mythical thinking.

This brief excursus in ancient myth has revealed the whole complexity and richness of the theme of monstrosity. Lying at the foundation of many ancient mythologems, monstrosity reveals at least three main characteristics of both early Greek thought and its heritage across antiquity. First, monstrosity speaks about ambiguity. Monsters are ambiguous characters, often rejected on the negative side and yet holding a position, in a story or a tradition, that is not only destructive, detrimental, pernicious or baleful. Monsters often play a constructive, foundational, valuable and even necessary role. Without them and the disorder that they bring, order and normality would not or could not exist. Second, and often due to its ambiguous nature, monstrosity can be both implicit and explicit. It can lie where one least expects to find it. Not only frightening creatures or wicked villains, but also gods and heroes can be monstrous, or present monstrosity as their feature, or use it as their weapon. Third, although mythology is largely an account of the construction, establishment and stabilisation of order, out of chaos and against disorder, such a pattern is far from being a linear and progressive annihilation, or even simply a domestication of monstrosity. Order is not a fatal necessity or a necessary outcome of the Greek cosmos. It is rather a precarious balance, aleatorily established through the fire of countless battles, in which monstrosity constantly resurfaces and not always or necessarily on the same side.

Whatever relationship one wants to read between the myth and the logos, the latter brings in it the mark of this threefold role played by monstrosity at

---

[213] Hes. *Th.* 588–602.
[214] Procl. *ad.Hes.Op.* 60 ff. (= Marzillo (2010), pp. 37 ff.).

the inception of Greek philosophy. Monstrosity's ambiguous nature, its sometimes implicit position, its aleatory essence mark the philosophical discourse whenever it tackles the question of normality and abnormality. As in the mythological discourse, then, we will see in the next chapters how the philosophical treatment of monstrosity bears the mark of its origin. In other words, philosophy also reveals the ambiguity of the concept of monstrosity, sometimes on the side of the negative, but often and unexpectedly playing a productive, explicative and foundational role. We will see how monstrosity appears also, and sometimes more interestingly, when philosophers do not explicitly deal with it, when they explore not the margins but the centre and the core of their system, such as when they speak about God, and perfection or providence, when they enquire into nature and life in all its beauty. Finally, we will see how the foundation of an ontological order remains almost invariably exposed to its contrary, to chaos and disorder, or rather to the aleatory nature of its threatening origin, not fully explained and always resurfacing. The struggle between materialism and idealism, for example, counts monstrosity as one of the most powerful weapons employed by both sides. Through such a weapon, one can support the foundation of the whole system, by explaining it and fully integrating it in a coherent science of nature. Through such a weapon, though, one can also destroy the enemy's system, by showing its incapacty to explain or account for it.

2

The Pre-Platonic Philosophers

Anaxagoras: A Material Origin for Life and Monstrosity

Our enquiry begins with Anaxagoras of Clazomenae, whose surviving fragments and testimonies bring us some grounding principles through which the concept of monstrosity can be interpreted, and to which other pre-Platonic philosophers, and eventually Socrates, Plato and Aristotle, directly respond. Together with Empedocles and Democritus, Anaxagoras's thought represents one of the strongest and most influential early attempts to explain the origin of cosmic order and, in particular, of life and its abnormal exceptions.

The two aspects, in fact, converge in Anaxagoras's philosophy. One of his most original moves consists in thinking about the generation of animate and inanimate things according to the same principle. The core ideas of this principle are explained in *Vorsokr.* 4, a composite of two extant fragments from different parts of the commentary to Aristotle's *Physics* by Simplicius, one of the most important sources for our knowledge of Anaxagoras.[1] Anaxagoras claims, according to Simplicius, that there are many different things, that is to say, many seeds, in all things, both living and non-living, which are thus natural compounds.[2] All is thus in all things, no matter their individual differences. These mixed things come from an original μεῖγμα or compound that, before the separation, was homogeneous and prevented any individual qualitative difference. Not only is all in all but, in another way, all has always been in all.[3]

The true innovation of Anaxagoras's language is the use of σπέρμα, seed or germ, as Gregory Vlastos has underlined in a highly influential article.[4]

---

[1] See P. Curd in Anaxagoras of Clazomenae (2007), *ad loc.*
[2] Anaxag. B4a (= Simp. *in Ph.* 34.18–20).
[3] Anaxag. B4b (= Simp. *in Ph.* 34.20–7).
[4] Vlastos (1950), *passim.*

Anaxagoras employs the seed not only for organic reality, but also for any other thing conceivable in nature. Whereas Parmenides and Empedocles after him think of a small number of immutable (and thus divine) principles, whose combination produces nature's diversity, Anaxagoras withdraws any special status from the seeds and makes them a mutable entity like any other entity, since they are contained in everything that was as well as in everything that will be.[5]

This concept is crucial in understanding future ideas about monstrosity, since it is the implicit ground of both preformationist and panspermist theories of being. Since everything comes from everything and is in everything, the original and qualitatively homogeneous compound is no different, from an ontological point of view, from the subsequent realities, which are qualitatively differentiated from each other and have in them the dynamically and potentially changing nature of matter. The infinite variety of being, in infinitely diverse proportions, is present in everything as seed, which thus becomes synonymous with transformative power (δύναμις).[6]

An active principle, called νοῦς, operates on this homogeneous material, informing it and dynamically causing the splitting off of the different elements composing things. Differently from everything else, the νοῦς stands above other things, ontologically, if not chronologically:

> The other things have a share of everything, but *Nous* is unlimited [ἄπειρος] and self-ruling [αὐτοκράτωρ] and has been mixed with no thing, but is alone itself and by itself [μόνος αὐτὸς ἐφ' ἑαυτοῦ ἐστιν]. For if it were not by itself, but had been mixed with anything else, then it would partake of all things, if it has been mixed with anything (for there is a share of everything just as I said before); and the things mixed together with it would thwart it, so that it would control none of the things in the way that in fact does, being alone by itself. For it is the finest [λεπτότης] of all things and the purest, and indeed it maintains all discernment [γνώμη] about everything and has the greatest strength. And *Nous* has control over all things that have soul, both the larger and the smaller.[7]

Αὐτοκρατής means not only self-governed, but also the source of its own power. However, Anaxagoras does not present the Intellect as separated from

---

[5] A mindful analysis of the different historiographical interpretations about the meaning of this theory is in Bailey (1928), pp. 537–56.
[6] See also Tannery (1930, 2e ed.).
[7] Anaxag. B4b (= Simp. *in Ph.* 156.13).

or transcending the material mass of things or the cosmos. The Intellect is in itself, and it is this that makes it able to control and inform anything else. The Intellect can thus be interpreted as a cosmogonic principle; it resembles a divine force, theological and even teleological in principle, because of its knowing power.[8] It can also be interpreted as a cosmological principle that resembles a natural force, impersonal and not teleological, because of its rational nature. Though different, the interpretations are coherent, as they both contain the idea that the Intellect dominates both nature as a whole and every compound within it. Both readings leave open the question of either the responsibility for or the cause of nature's imperfection, disorder and monstrosity, and therefore they have been scrutinised not only by modern scholars, but also by ancient philosophers interested in the question of normality and abnormality.[9]

Aristotle, for example, agrees with Anaxagoras on the νοῦς's purity and unity, with an open reference to his unmoved mover,[10] because only one principle of generation must exist.[11] Eventually, Cicero is even more explicit, claiming that Anaxagoras is the first philosopher to understand natural order as the result of the rational force of an infinite intellect.[12] Others, however, have denounced Anaxagoras's ambiguity about the divine and transcendent nature of the Intellect, claiming that the obscurity of the doctrine reveals a poor understanding of nature and its becoming. Socrates' dissatisfaction with Anaxagoras is possibly the most influential of these denunciations, which Plato uses to put order in the genealogy of true philosophy, namely Platonism itself. In *Phaedo* 97 b–98 c, Plato's Socrates declares his initial satisfaction with Anaxagoras's promising theory of an Intellect that 'arranges everything and establishes each thing as it is best for it to be'. The best and most excellent is, in Socrates' view, the key to understanding nature and every part of it, vis-à-vis its ultimate end. Anaxagoras, however, ultimately reveals himself to be a bad teacher: after reading his books, Socrates confesses his deception, since he

> [. . .] never imagined that, when he said they were ordered by intelligence, he would introduce any other cause for these things than that it is best for them to be as they are. So I [*scil*. Socrates] thought when he assigned the cause of each thing and of all things in common he would go on and explain what is best for each and what is good for all in common [but]

[8] See Theiler (1924).
[9] See Furley, Allen eds. (1970–5).
[10] Anaxag. A56 (= Arist. *Ph.* 256 b 24).
[11] Anaxag. A45 (= Arist. *Ph.* 203 a 19).
[12] Anaxag. A48 (= Cic. *ND* I.11).

I saw that the man made no use of intelligence, and did not assign any real causes for the ordering of things, but mentioned as causes air and ether and water and many other absurdities.[13]

Physical explanation is nothing more than an absurdity if it is not subordinated or functional to the real understanding of nature, namely what makes the difference between the best in it and the worst, imperfection, waste, all that is inferior.[14]

Indeed, Anaxagoras seems to be remembered for two different philosophical ideas, i.e. the purity and unity of the Intellect vis-à-vis natural reality, and the Intellect's immanence to the same reality, as a sort of norm or *ratio* of its functioning: the two principles are not easily consistent with each other. The lack of consistency, however, emerges less from Anaxagoras's attempt to explain nature's origin and its diversity, and more in his followers' systems, which need to relegate one of the two ideas to the margin in order to reinforce the other and support either an idealist or materialist reading of cosmogony.

When one focuses on monstrosity, the materialist reading comes to the fore. Anaxagoras is deeply concerned with the origin of life, and the testimonies offer something close to a materialist reading of it. Diogenes Laertius reports that, for Anaxagoras, 'animals first came to be from moist, hot, and earthy stuffs, but later from one another; and males from the right side and females from the left side [of the uterus]'.[15] The material origin of life, with no other mention of any superior informing agent, is already remarkable. Equally striking, however, is the double stage of life's formation: animals first spring from the earth and then later, presumably after a selection, begin to procreate through sexual reproduction. Such a two-stage process is eventually at the heart of materialist oriented systems, and is very reminiscent of Empedocles' and the atomists' theory.[16] Kucharski also stresses the proximity of Anaxagoras's argument to some of the most explicitly quantitative and materialist layers of the Hippocratic corpus, particularly in the attempt to explain quality through quantity and the formation of organic tissues and membranes through different proportions of earth and heat.[17]

---

[13] Anaxag. A47 (= Pl. *Phd.* 97 b–98 c). Nietzsche is particularly impressed by Plato's criticism of Anaxagoras. See 'Die Philosophie im tragischen Zeitalter der Griechen', esp. par. 19, in Nietzsche (1967–), III.2, pp. 293–366. See also Warden (1971), p. 14. Plato's criticism is eventually shared by Ar. *Metaph.* 985 a 18 and Simp. *in Ph.* 327.26 (= Anaxag. A47).

[14] See also Josephus's critique in Anaxag. A19 (= I. *Ap.* II.265).

[15] Anaxag. A1 (D.L. II.9). Hippolytus still knows this argument, in Hippol. *Haer.* I.8.12.

[16] Aristotle, on the contrary, reads Anaxagoras against Empedocles. See Anaxag. A43 (= Ar. *Cael.* 302 a 28).

[17] Kucharski (1964), *passim*. See also Reeve (1980–1).

The most important testimony on Anaxagoras, for the present enquiry into monstrosity, also associates Anaxagoras with a materialist epistemology and contrasts it with an idealist and religiously grounded approach. This testimony reported by Plutarch narrates the discovery of a monstrous ram in the time of Pericles, who is traditionally associated with Anaxagoras. The Athenian general, Plutarch claims, was driven out of ignorance and superstition by Anaxagoras's materialist approach to the study and interpretation of nature, especially of those phenomena that, because of their unknown nature, traditionally drive people into fear and amazement. In Plutarch's words:

> It is said that once the head of a one-horned ram was brought to Pericles from the country; Lampon the soothsayer, when he saw that the horn had grown strong and firm from the middle of the forehead, said that, whereas there were two factions in the city, those of Thucydides and Pericles, sovereignty would pass to the one to whom the omen came. But when the skull was cut in two, Anaxagoras demonstrated that the brain had not filled out its space, but was pointed, like an egg, and had pulled away from the skull to the very spot from where the root of the horn had its starting place. Then Anaxagoras was admired by all who were present. But a little later, when Thucydides had been overthrown and Pericles had taken charge of public affairs, it was Lampon who was admired. Nevertheless, there was nothing, I suppose, that prevented both the physical scientist and the soothsayer from being right; for the one rightly understood the cause and the other the purpose of the event.[18]

I shall analyse later Plutarch's interesting approach to monstrosity and the materialist attitude. It is interesting, however, that Plutarch, not without irony, follows Socrates' and Plato's reproach to Anaxagoras, and situates him on the side of a materialist, if not an atheist, explanation of nature's monstrous manifestation. For Anaxagoras, although not for Plutarch, monstrosity is not caused by an immaterial force as a sign or a symptom of a higher, more anthropocentric reality. Instead, it is a spontaneous anomaly in the organisation of matter, possibly due to the abnormal composition and proportion of hot and earthy stuff in the ram's body.

The cause and meaning of monstrosity and, more generally, of nature's diversity in its full extent, lies at the heart of Anaxagoras's ontology of homoeomeries. The difference between a normal and a monstrous ram, the

---

[18] Anaxag. A16 (= Plu. Per. 6).

difference between normality, abnormality and monstrosity is only quantitative. The difference reveals the organisation of homogeneous matter. It is not a qualitative difference due to extrinsic norms or criteria or boundaries that are set in order to differentiate matter and distinguish within it shapes that more or less resemble forms or paradigms. Normal or monstrous shapes manifest themselves, Lucretius explains, by making more visible what is prominent among matter's qualities, and making inconspicuous what is inferior and in smaller quantity: 'Anaxagoras [supposes] that all things are hidden mingled in all things, but that alone appears which preponderates in the mixture and is more to be seen and placed right in the front.'[19] Lucretius disagrees with Anaxagoras because, he claims, not all things but rather the seeds common to all things are in all things. Otherwise – this is Lucretius's famous argument – fire would burn even before rubbing the wood, and not after it.

More important than the disagreement, though, is that both Anaxagoras and Lucretius underline that it is the concept of similarity that explains the transformation of all things. Only the similar can produce the similar and, in this sense, all monstrously organised matter, of any degree, must be similar to the matter it originally came from. Aetius reads this principle in an anti-materialist sense, grounding it in Anaxagoras's hypothesis of an ordering Intellect: 'the homogeneous stuffs are the matter, and mind is the creative cause setting all things in order. He begins like this: "all *chrēmata* were together, and *Nous* arrived and set them in order"; (by *chrēmata*, he means "things"). He is worthy of tribute then, because he linked the maker to the matter.'[20] Simplicius too stresses the order and the ordering principle that applies itself to matter so as to make *everything* possible, but only *according* to a reason or a rule: 'he saw that everything comes to be from everything, if not immediately then in order (for air comes from fire, and water from air, earth from water, stone from earth, and fire comes once again from stone) and [...] like is augmented by like'.[21] Monstrosity comes from normality or, better, from the homogeneous matter that contains different proportions of stuffs that make the monstrous and the normal equally possible, according to one and the same ordering principle.

Vlastos once again masterfully comments upon this passage, underlining that it is the concept of the infinitesimally small that allows Anaxagoras to explain the difference between species as well as between individuals of the same species. Varying the proportions of stuffs, even infinitesimally, causes the outcome and the offspring also to vary, so as to fall, one can add, either

---

[19] Anaxag. A44 (= Lucr. I.830 ff.). See also B12 (= Simp. *in Ph.* 156.13).
[20] Anaxag. A46 (= *Placit.* I.3.5).
[21] Anaxag. A45 (Simp. *in Ph.* 460.4)

within the domain of normality or the realm of monstrosity, whereby the latter is only a variation of the former, possibly an infinitesimally small one.[22] Vlastos argues that Lucretius has misinterpreted Anaxagoras and confused the variety of the proportions of the mix of powers in things with the variety of seeds themselves in order to explain the differences among things. Building on Vlastos's interpretation, one can say that things do not differ because they have more of something (e.g. bones) or less of something else (e.g. blood) in them. They differ because of the different proportions of powers that lie below bones and blood. If one extends this argument to monstrosity, one can properly understand the argument of the origin of the similar from the similar. This interpretation explains not only why and how normality comes from normality and monstrosity springs out of monstrosity, it also reveals how, in the same framework, monstrosity can originate in normality, or normality in monstrosity. It makes it possible, in other words, to see how, according to the Anaxagorean ontology, everything comes from everything, and everything is possible, although – as Simplicius says and Lucretius eventually claims – only according to a certain order and norm, the norm of νοῦς.

What then is the difference between normality and monstrosity? If one adheres coherently to the Anaxagorean hypothesis, it is only a difference of quantity, of proportion, of organisation, a difference within homogeneity and in accordance to the same ordering principle, immanent and material. This principle is not only the efficient cause of both normality and abnormality, it is also their only cause. It does not require much effort for subsequent materialist authors to use this idea and clarify the ambiguities caused by obscure (because original) language. Within an idealist ontology, however, these ambiguities open the door to much more serious allegations. Commentators who build the unity and purity of the principle on a more religious and anthropomorphic ground, a Platonic and Christian framework, for example, put more emphasis on the ontologic difference between normality and abnormality, thus weakening the power of Anaxagoras's Intellect. Clement of Alexandria's comment is revealing in this sense: 'Yet even if Anaxagoras were the first to set *Nous* over things, not even he preserved the making cause; rather, he depicts some unintelligent whirls together with the inactivity and thoughtlessness of *Nous*.'[23] Anaxagoras's Intellect, for Clement, does not reach everywhere: the lower layers of reality remain untouched by it, and this is where monstrosity manifests itself.

Aristotle also gives an interesting perspective, from the point of view of his own theory, by claiming that Anaxagoras's system would result in an unintelligible muddle. Were everything in everything, Aristotle argues, not only actually

---

[22] Vlastos (1950), p. 45.
[23] Anaxag. A57 (= Clem.Al. *Strom.* II.14).

but also potentially, as Anaxagoras maintains, nothing could be distinguished from anything else. In matters of life generation and animal forms, for example, the normal individual could not be distinguished from the monstrous one, and the diversity of nature, which Aristotle sees as necessary and praiseworthy, could not be accounted for.[24]

Anaxagoras introduces powerful philosophical innovations that necessarily remain ambiguous for early readers as well as for modern scholars. Through such ambiguities, monstrosity makes its appearance within philosophy, creating room for radically different alternatives in the interpretation of nature and life within it, as will be seen in Empedocles and Democritus.

Empedocles: Wonders to Behold

A Sophist like Protagoras and a democrat like Pericles,[25] Empedocles develops, in his poem Περὶ Φύσεως (On nature),[26] one of the most striking pre-Platonic cosmogonies, to respond to some of the most urgent problems raised by thinkers such as Parmenides and Melissus. Empedocles' initial concern is to respond to the Eleatic aporia on the permanent and immutable nature of *Being* vis-à-vis the changing and unstable reality of its *Becoming*, as it is experienced by men in the real world. For the unique matter of Ionian naturalism, he substitutes multiple elementary determinations, that he calls the *roots of all things*,[27] and to which he assigns divine names (Zeus, Hera, Aidoneus and Nestis), prolonging Homer's personification of the cosmic elements.[28] These roots are infinite in number, immutable in time and space, and eternal. The universe is continuous and full, i.e. emptiness does not exist and therefore nothing is born from nothing, since nothingness does not exist in the first place. Death and birth – the Becoming of things – consist of the composition and dissolution of the composites of eternal roots, fire, water, air and earth, that, as substances, always remain themselves. Thus, Empedocles connects the older mythical dimension of Greek cosmogony with a new interest in physical explanation of the phenomenal world.[29]

The unchangeability of the four roots makes Empedocles' philosophy an early version of atomism, despite its differences with Democritus's atomism.

---

[24] Anaxag. A61 (= Arist. *Metaph.* 1069 b 15 ff.).
[25] See Bollack (2009), p. 8. On the democratic character of Empedocles' theogony see also Jaeger (1947), p. 139 ff.
[26] Although Empedocles' second poem, *The Purifications* (Καθαρμοί), has to be read together with the Περὶ Φύσεως (see Bignone (1916)), I will deal with it only insofar as it is directly relevant to the discussion on the idea of monstrosity.
[27] *Vorsokr.* 31 B 6 (= LM [22] EMP. D57 = Inwood 12, p. 209).
[28] Buffière (1956), pp. 81–2.
[29] See *supra*, as well as Schuhl (1947, 2e ed.), Cornford (1952), Hershbell (1970), Mugler (1970).

Empedocles' roots are uncreated and do not change qualitatively. Becoming and change in the universe happen only by means of changes in the combinations of different quantities of different roots, following processes of mechanical composition and dissolution within a homogeneous space; Empedocles thus paves the way for a purely mechanical explanation of the physical world. More importantly, rather than regarding the One as the *fundamental* element,[30] Empedocles considers the multiplicy of the roots ontologically and physically prior to the One and, as Bollack beautifully puts it, as 'l'origine de leur propre origine'.[31]

In order to conceive movement within this universe without emptiness, Empedocles needs a further principle of explanation. He describes this principle in anthropomorphic terms, as the reciprocal and opposite work of two forces, νεῖκος (Strife or Discord) and φιλότης (Love or Friendship). The latter pushes multiplicity toward unity, while the former works toward reality's disjunction and toward plurality.[32] Between the two extremes of absolute unity and immobility and absolute plurality and chaotic movement, the two forces incessantly unfold their action and manifest their power in the world: one on the other, one *against* the other.

Fragment 27 describes Love's victory, when harmony is at its apex in what Empedocles calls the *Sphere*, the perfect unity of all things.[33] But then Discord attacks it from the edges, dissolving the Sphere's purity. The movement is infinite and necessary. No individual thing, no world as we experience it, can possibly exist at either extreme – in the perfect immobility of the Sphere or in the perfectly formless chaos of the cosmos. Creation and destruction take place *between* the extremes, and our world is part of this process, our time a tiny portion of the Strife-governed part of the cycle.

The richness – or the essential ambiguity – of Empedocles' thought is visible in the distinct natures of his two masterpieces: the Περὶ Φύσεως, more scientifically oriented and compatible with a mechanist explanation of the universe, and the Καθαρμοί, more religious and compatible with a magic and orphic vision of nature. This rich ambiguity is perhaps even clearer in the role that

---

[30] Τὸ ἓν στοιχεῖον: see Arist. GC 315 a 23. Empedocles' relationship between the One and the Many implies a contradiction with Aristotle's view, as, for Empedocles, 'the Many are more "elementary" than the One and by nature prior to it'. (315 a 3–25).

[31] Bollack (1965–9), I, p. 33.

[32] *Vorsokr.* 31 B 17 (= LM [22] EMP. D73, R68 = Inwood 25, pp. 215–17).

[33] Daughter of Ares and Aphrodite, i.e. war and beauty, Harmony symbolises the unity of antitheses. Zeus gives her as a wife to Kadmos for his role in fighting the monster Typhoeus, representing the primordial chaos. On harmony see Lalande, p. 401, Auroux, pp. 1116–17, Ritter, Gründer hrsg. (1971–2007), III, c. 1001, RAC XIII, pp. 593–618 (*Harmonie des Sphären*), HRW, III, cc. 1297–1304, NDHI III, pp. 960–4. See also Nietzsche, 'Die dionysische Weltanschauung', in Nietzsche (1967–), III.2, pp. 43–69, Buffière (1956), pp. 467–81, Spitzer (1963) and Caye et al. a cura di (2011).

he assigns to necessity (ἀνάγκη) and chance (τύχη). Empedocles' cosmic cycle operates under strict necessity. Within it, however, it is the stringent logic of chance that rules.

Empedocles seems to have made a huge effort to keep together aspects of his thought that were (and will be) traditionally seen as incompatible. Thinkers such as Anaxagoras or Hippocrates, for example, disapprove of his ideas regarding necessity and chance and the mechanical vs magical interpretation of nature. The most influential and authoritative denunciation of Empedocles' thought, however, is certainly Aristotle's, and it is largely based on Empedocles' treatment of monstrosity.

Monstrosity comes into the picture with Empedocles' zoogony. There is hardly any other Greek philosopher for whom monstrosity occupies such an important place in the process of formation and development of life. Chance, as I said, rules the inner development of the cosmic cycle, and this is particularly clear when Strife prevails, as it does in the time that precedes our age. Developing in four stages, as recorded by Aetius, the origin of life appears to Empedocles as 'a wonder to behold' (θαῦμα ἰδέσθαι).[34] Initially, isolated members appear, rising from the earth:

> as many heads without necks sprouted up
> and arms wandered naked, bereft of shoulders,
> and eyes roamed alone, impoverished of foreheads.[35]

These members randomly wander around, and fortuitously encounter each other, joining with one another to form all sorts of monstrous beings, such as the βουγενῆ ἀνδρόπρωρα, the man-headed oxen.[36] Separate limbs and monsters

---

[34] *Vorsokr.* 31 B 35 (= LM [22] EMP. D75, R70 = Inwood 61, p. 236). See Bollack (1965–9), II, p. 69: 'La chose *merveilleuse à voir* [. . .] qu'est l'homme, ou le soleil se levant au matin, fut d'abord un exploit.' On Empedocles' zoogony see also Morgan (1984), pp. 90 ff., D. Sedley, *Empedocles Life Cycles*, in Pierris ed. (2005), pp. 331–71 and M. L. Gemelli Marciano, *Empedocles' Zoogony and Embriology*, in Pierris ed. (2005), pp. 373–404.

[35] *Vorsokr.* 31 B 57 (= LM [22] EMP. D154, R75 = Inwood 64, p. 245).

[36] *Vorsokr.* 31 B 61 (= LM [22] EMP. D152, D156 = Inwood 66, p. 247). Man-headed quadrupeds eventually constitute one of the paradigmatic forms of hybrid monstrosity in classical culture and beyond. See N. Icard-Gianolio, A.-V. Szabados, *Monstra*, LIMC, *Supplementum* 2009, 1, pp. 339–59. See also J. König, *Bestiarium*, HRW, I, pp. 1513–23. At the dawn of modernity, Piero di Cosimo evokes them in the astonishing panel *The Forest Fire*, at the Ashmolean Museum of Oxford. Modern scholarship, following Erwin Panofsky's seminal interpretation, has associated it with Lucretian reminiscence. See 'The Early History of Man in Two Cycles of Paintings by Piero di Cosimo' in Panofsky (1939), pp. 33–67. Lucretius, however, denies the existence of such creatures precisely in opposing these Empedoclean phantasies. What Piero seems to have in mind, although vaguely, seems to be closer to the Empedoclean oxen. See Bacci (1976) and Whistler, Bomford (1999), who also suggest the name of Empedocles. See below on Empedocles' influence on Lucretius.

are thus the first creatures to appear on earth, driven by the increasing force of Love, but with Strife being more powerful than it is now. Monstrous creatures – but of a whole different monstrosity – also characterise the other part of the cycle, when homogeneous and undifferentiated (οὐλοφυής) creatures appear from the earth, driven by the increasing force of Strife, but with Love being still more powerful than it is now.

Empedocles' zoogony of Love, according to O'Brien, is paradoxical, because monsters are less harmonious creatures than men and women, but they are also 'put together' by Love's force, when Love's power is increasing.[37] This is paradoxical, however, only if the creatures' harmony is seen as depending absolutely on which force (Strife or Love) is currently increasing in power, and if the ultimate destination of this part of the cycle (chaos or unity) is seen as already dominating the zoogonic process. I would argue, however, that the increasing harmony of creatures can be seen only by comparing successive generations of creatures: Love or Strife controls the direction of change, rather than imposing absolute harmony or chaos on every creature that develops during the cycle.[38]

The ἀνάγκη to which any part of the cycle responds works as an end or τέλος only at a general level. At a particular level, on the contrary, i.e. at the level of each creature's production, only τύχη operates. That is why the οὐλοφυής creature is to be described as *homogeneous* in itself, depending on the way it *happened*, and also *undifferentiated*, vis-à-vis the process of differentiation which will only be visible in the subsequent production of creatures from the earth. When O'Brien says that 'monsters are an advance upon separate limbs, even though they are a decline compared with men and women or οὐλοφυῆ',[39] this is true from a global point of view, but certainly not from the point of view of the individual creature, whose monstrosity is perfectly *normal* and in fact constitutive of the zoogonic cycle itself: no zoogony and no cycle would be conceivable without monstrosities.[40]

Men and women are born from both kinds of monstrosities and during both segments of the cycle: after the existence of separate limbs in the cosmic cycle, and resulting from the separation of οὐλοφυῆ in the period which begins in the Sphere. The relevant point for the present discussion is that the

---

[37] O'Brien (1969), pp. 205–6.
[38] See also J. Wilcox, '"Whole-Natured Forms" in Empedocles' Cosmic Cycle', in Preus (2001), pp. 109–22.
[39] J. Wilcox, '"Whole-Natured Forms" in Empedocles' Cosmic Cycle', in Preus (2001), p. 207.
[40] My reading does not contradict O'Brien's main thesis, which is to demonstrate that not every kind of monstrosity is born at every stage, but rather that separate limbs rise under Love's increasing power, while homogeneous and undifferentiated creatures rise under Strife's increasing power.

two sequences are symmetric and that normal and viable creatures are generated *from* monsters with increasing or decreasing success, depending on the relative chronological position within the cycle. There is nothing that specifically keeps humans apart from monstrosities (despite the readings of Eduard Zeller and many other scholars).[41]

Monstrosity inhabits both sequences of the cycle, and humans and animals as we know them are related to both kinds of monstrosities considered by Empedocles – separated limbs on the one hand, and homogeneous and undifferentiated creatures on the other. Οὐλοφυῆ, precisely for this reason, must be considered a kind of monstrosity and, *at the same time*, a kind of perfection.[42] Again, this is not a paradox if we are able to grasp the simultaneously teleological *and* mechanical nature of the cycle.

O'Brien gives a thoughtful account of this productive ambiguity. Nonetheless, when he wants to clarify its meaning, he associates Empedocles' system with the holistic approach of Teilhard de Chardin and his concept of the □ point as the point of convergence of all of humanity in God.[43] Elsewhere, O'Brien stresses the anti-materialist character of Empedocles' philosophy, suggesting a convergence with the later emanatist thought of Neoplatonism.[44] I believe that both conclusions betray the productive ambiguity and richness of Empedocles' visionary cosmogony and that in fact, the philosopher's zoogony offers a strong ground for future generations of philosophers to criticise finalism.[45]

Finalism and providence are indeed ruled out by Empedocles' system. Nature, as Bollack has underlined, does not accomplish forms that pre-exist the individuals and determine their development.[46] Although generation

---

[41] Zeller (1856), I, pp. 537–8. For a complete literature review, see O'Brien (1969), pp. 196 ff.
[42] As O'Brien (1969) does, opposing though the idea of monstrosity and the idea of perfection.
[43] O'Brien (1969), pp. 199–200: 'It is indeed only in the most recent times, so far as I am aware, that Empedocles has found those who would to some extent agree with him, notably the late Teilhard de Chardin.'
[44] O'Brien, *Empédocle*, in Brunschwig, Lloyd eds. (1996), p. 643.
[45] Empedocles' theory of monstrosity, in this sense, is far from being 'ridiculous'. See *contra* Schadewaldt (1978), p. 452. See also Girard's interpretation in terms of double monstrosity in Gerard (1972).
[46] Bollack (1965–9), II, p. 63. See also Solmsen (1963), pp. 478–9 and, *contra*, Cuny-Le Callet (2005), p. 215, who argues that the whole argument of the generation from the earth, which later appeals to Lucretius, is in fact teleological and theological: '[. . .] contrairement à Lucrèce qui s'oppose à tout finalisme, Empédocle développe une vision téléologique de l'origine des êtres: il affirme que chaque détail de l'organisme a été créé par la divinité – appelé Aphrodite ou Cypris – selon un projet préconçu, pour remplir une fonction précise'. Cuny-Le Callet grounds her claim on *Vorsokr.* 31 B 73, 75, 86 and 87 (= LM [22] EMP. D199, R70, D200, R70, D213, R70 and D214, R70). I do not see in these texts anything that could support her conclusion concerning 'chaque détail de l'organisme', the 'projet préconçu' and the 'fonction précise'.

from the earth might seem quite an extravagant account of the formation of beings,[47] it in fact opens up the space for a mechanical and anti-teleological process of generation of life based on chance encounters and endless transformation of beings: a conception that will echo in atomism. Becoming is, for Empedocles, a ceaseless and multifarious series of attempts. Perfection is not a τέλος, but rather the aleatory outcome of encounters generating individuals of all shapes. Some of them are non-viable and perish, some of them are viable and live. The former are more numerous in the beginning, and then give place to the latter, which become prevalent as the cycle continues.

Franz Lämmli has argued that some form of order *must* be found in every beginning, in order for it to be the beginning of *something*.[48] Yet this is not Empedocles' hypothesis, in which order is born from chaos, in the same non-teleological manner in which viable beings follow monsters. The very concepts of order and disorder, like normality and monstrosity, exist only *ex-post* and not as aims, or ends, or criteria guiding action or evolution towards any order.

Being is not accomplished at once, but incrementally, as a result of innumerable encounters. In Empedocles' philosophy and its heritage, the word *encounter* (τυχεῖν), Bollack claims, does not have the meaning that Aristotle gives to it. Far from expressing the accident and the exception, it means *the success*.[49] Harmony and perfection are not the adequacy of a pre-existing form. They *are* this particular form, or rather this particular shape in which the eternal movement of composition and decomposition of roots has stabilised itself in a viable being.

Monstrosity thus becomes the key to moving beyond the aporias of those philosophers who had been looking for a unique and unifying principle, *beyond* and *above* worldy phenomena. Being, for Empedocles, is neither beyond nor above Becoming. It is not simpler or richer than what exists or has existed or will exist at the various stages of the cycle: monstrosity is not less than normality, it is not different from it:

> But come! Gaze on this witness to my previous words,
> if anything was in my previous [remarks] left wanting in form:

---

[47] With the limbs born ready to be assembled. See Bollack (1965–9), II, p. 69. The Berlin red-figure vase mentioned by Bollack, however, narrates mythical events, thus taking place in a highly civilised setting. See Beazley (1963, 2nd ed.), p. 400 and G. Zimmer, 'Trinkschale. Namensgebendes Werk des Erzgießerei-Malers', in Scholl, Platz-Horster hrsg.(2007), pp. 68–9. See also Guthrie (1957), pp. 44–5.

[48] Lämmli (1962).

[49] Bollack (1965–9), I, p. 68. Chantraine, p. 1142: τυγχάνω, aor. τυχεῖν, for 'atteindre, toucher, rencontrer' and 'reussir [opposé à σφάλλειν], se trouver, se produire par hasard, se rencontrer'. Fontanier, p. 704: τυγχάνω = *adsequor*.

the sun, bright to look on and hot in every respect,
and the immortals which are drenched in heat and shining light,
and rain, in all things dark and cold;
and there flow from the earth things dense and solid.
And in wrath all are distinct in form and separate,
and they come together in love and are desired by each other.
From these all things that were, that are, and will be in the future
have sprung: trees and men and women
and beasts and birds and water-nourished fish,
and long-lived gods first in their prerogatives.
For these very things are, and running through each other
they become different in appearance. For the blending changes them.[50]

Jackie Pigeaud has stressed how Empedocles' attitude depends on a wider convergence between natural and artistic thinking in the Greek world.[51] Early philosophers and artists – and Empedocles among them – are interested in, and aim at, defining the concept of norm and normativity. The norm, Pigeaud powerfully argues, is nothing but the outcome of the essays incessantly made by Aphrodite 'the Lifegiving' in her workshop,[52] whereby life is created according to a logic and a vocabulary both biological and aesthetical – by painting, fixing, riveting, gripping or cooking.[53] The result is the astonishing role that monstrosity plays in defining the norm, at once biologically and aesthetically: the monster is *not* defined by the norm, 'the monster is the norm'.[54]

---

[50] *Vorsokr.* 31 B 21 (= LM [22] EMP. D58b, D77a, R68 = Inwood 26, p. 219).

[51] Pigeaud (1988), p. 197: le 'rapports entre la pensée de la *physis*, ou pensée de la production spontanée, et la pensée de l'art, ou pensée de l'artefact'.

[52] *Vorsokr.* 31 B 151 (= LM [22] EMP. D64 = Inwood CTXT–64, p. 120): 'ζείδωρον ['Αφροδίτην].'

[53] Pigeaud points to *Vorsokr.* 31 B 19, 32–4, 73, 75, 87 (= LM EMP. D62, R93, D259, D72, D71, D199, R70, D200, R70, D214, R70).

[54] Pigeaud (1988), p. 203: 'Le beau n'est pas autre chose que l'effort des éléments pour se rencontrer; le beau constitué c'est le chevillage de ce rencontre. L'artiste colle, cheville, durcit ce qu'il pense fait pour aller ensemble. Mais le monstre guette l'artiste. Ou plutôt, le monstre précède la forme définitive. Il est l'ébauche, et l'ébauche précède l'œuvre comme un tâtonnement. Des ces essais naîtra l'œuvre. En quelque sorte, pour Empédocle, *le monstre est la norme*, il est même la seule norme; puisque c'est à le voir que l'artiste jugera de son travail. Il n'est pas d'œuvre sans monstre préalable; et il arrive parfois à l'artiste de sanctionner le monstre, c'est-à-dire de prendre la norme pour le normal.' One can hardly guess the effects that such an ontology would produce when coherently applied to political and legal thought. Given Empedocles' explicit engagement with politics, it is a matter for enquiry. On monstrosity in early Greek art, see Winkler-Horaček (2015).

Although the metaphor of nature as an artist is powerfully evocative, Pigeaud probably pushes it too far, even if only because of the risk of anthropomorphisation and teleologisation. Empedocles' teratogeny – Pigeaud argues – is antithetical to both Aristotle's and Lucretius's theories, which would be allied against the idea that *every* kind of monstrosity, without limit, could happen during the zoogonic process. The opposition, in my view, is rather between Aristotle's finalist approach, in which such limits are of transcendent and external origin, and the anti-teleological approach, with immanent limits arising internally, on which, I believe, Empedocles and Lucretius converge, as I will show later on.[55]

Monstrosity is of paramount importance in Empedocles' philosophy. Through the monstrous creatures, Empedocles is able to coordinate the necessary movement of the cycle of Love and Strife in *one* specific course with the necessary movement of life's expansion in *multiple* and undetermined directions. Monstrosity thus allows the coexistence of mechanism and teleology at different ontological levels, thus connecting Empedocles' philosophy with the more genuine materialism of the early atomists.

In the next paragraph, I present the position of the leading figure of early atomism, Democritus of Abdera. As we will see, if early atomism has a connection with the attitude of the physicist Empedocles, Democritus's contribution implies a thorough and unconditional rejection of any and every form of teleology, and it is his ideas about monstrosity that reveal the paramount importance of this shift.

Democritus: Agonism within Matter

Is the idea of monstrosity, as described in Empedocles' zoogony, a powerful conceptual tool to help overcome the Ionian aporias on the relation between the One and the Many, as well as Being and Becoming? Or is monstrosity actually neutralised by Empedocles, by introducing it *within* a cycle governed by necessity, and necessarily unfolding in the cosmic movement from and towards the One? By imagining a plurality of elements, Empedocles responds to Parmenides' One. Nevertheless, atomists argue, it is still unclear how multiplicity can be explained. The plurality of στοιχεῖα, they claim, does not resolve in itself the aporias of the relation between the One and the Many. It does not matter whether the elements are two or four. What counts, for atomists, is that these elements are rigorously composed of homogeneous, eternal, uncreated particles, and thus still unfit to explain multiplicity. A real multiplicity

---

[55] See, *contra*, Warden (1971), p. 14.

must be the origin and the beginning of everything. It must not be based *on*, but rather moving *against* the unity of the Parmenidean Being-One.[56]

Multiplicity is thus the starting point of Democritus and his master Leucippus, and this starting point is made possible by the concept of atom. I will not distinguish the doctrines of atomism's father, Leucippus of Miletus (or Elea), and his brilliant scholar Democritus of Abdera.[57] It is of paramount importance, though, to remember that Democritus is *not* a pre-Socratic philosopher, as the historiographical tradition, already created by Aristotle, has too often presented him.[58] He is on the contrary Socrates' contemporary. Like Empedocles, he is linked to the origins of democratic thinking.[59] He outlives Socrates by at least three decades, and he offers an alternative system that strongly counters Socratism on many vital points. It is indeed for this reason that Plato, as well as many ancient and modern scholars after him, is interested in presenting atomism as a *pre*-Socratic system, when not as an *anti*-Socratic one. Democritus is, for Plato, only one of the many old philosophers whose systems have been once and for all surpassed by Socratism. Didn't Plato himself, according to Aristoxenus's anecdote, try to burn all of Democritus's works?[60]

His system is too dangerous for Plato's idealism. The whole cosmos, for the atomists, is based on the concurring and dialectic presence of a Being, which is full (πλήρης) and something (δέν), and the non-Being, which is void (κενός) and nothing (μηδέν). These two principles are immutable and correspond to an infinite number of not furtherly divisible bodies (ἄτομα), on the one hand, and the vacuum on the other hand.[61]

The indivisible bodies differ from one another in three characteristics: shape (ῥυσμός or σχῆμα), position (τροπή or θέσις) and order or arrangement (τάξις or διαθιγή). Joined together, they form atomic masses whose qualitative

---

[56] Salem (1996a), p. 47.
[57] In this I follow Aristotle as well as Robin (1923). On Leucippus's early development of a principle of causal explanation, see Klowski (1966).
[58] See D. O'Brien, *Démocrite d'Abdère*, in Goulet, éd. (1989–) II, pp. 655–77 and Salem (1996a).
[59] See Ferguson (1965) and Farrar (1988).
[60] See D.L. II.9.40, and Wehrli (1967–9, 2. ed.).
[61] Discussing Karl Marx's *Doktordissertation* and his early reading of Democritus, Mehring (1923), p. 31, summarises the fundamental thesis of atomistic physics as follows: 'Out of nothing nothing can come. Nothing that is can be destroyed. All change is nothing but the joining and separation of parts. Nothing happens fortuitously and everything that happens happens with reason and necessity. Nothing exists but the atoms and empty space, everything else is opinion. The atoms are endless in number and of an infinite variety in form. Falling eternally through infinite space, the larger atoms, which fall more quickly, collide with the smaller atoms and the material movements and rotations which result are the beginning of the formation of worlds. Innumerable worlds form and pass away co-existently and successively.' See also Salem (1996a), p. 31.

differences are only secondary and subjective, or by convention, depending on the primary and objective differences of shape, position and order. Against eleatism, atomists maintain that movement can happen only in the void, which is thus its condition, rather than its cause.[62]

Democritus's atomism is the first coherent and consistent form of materialism: a principle of explanation of the whole purely based on the primary ontological reality of atomic matter. In this sense, its character emerges as a powerful alternative to a philosophical explanation of nature based on abstract and ideal principles, an alternative that Plato eventually fights with all his strength. The very nature of nature, as well as the possibility of its philosophical and scientific investigation, is at stake and depends on the conception of Being, of matter and of atom itself. No surprise, then, that philosophers, ancient and modern, have tried to neutralise the revolutionary doctrine of Leucippus and Democritus, trying to claim that a universe conceived exclusively as atoms in motion is in fact an unthinkable monstrosity, because it dispenses with a norm to imitate and end to pursue.[63]

One might object that Democritus himself has ultimately framed his naturalistic explanation of the origin and life of the cosmos idealistically: does not Democritus, after all, employ the word ἰδέα to describe the indivisible material substances of his universe?[64] Since Homer, though, and through Anaxagoras and the Hippocratic Corpus, the 'idea' has been nothing more (and nothing less) than shape, or form in its morphological and exterior appearance. The original

---

[62] Aristotle, on the contrary, will object that vacuum would make motion impossible. See Arist. *Ph.* IV.8.

[63] H. Wismann, *Realité et matière dans l'atomisme démocritéen*, in Romano (1980), pp. 61–74, for example, has argued that only the form is, properly speaking, a characteristic of the atom itself, while order and position make sense only once atoms are combined together with other atoms. See also Wiśniewski (1973). More acutely, J. Bollack, *La cosmogonie des anciens Atomistes*, in Romano (1980), pp. 11–59, develops the idea that the atom acquires its weight only when it enters into relations with other atoms, and not before. Atoms, Bollack maintains, do not *possess*, but rather *acquire* their physical characteristics once they enter the cosmogonic vortex, collide with each other and form the bodies. Salem (1996) has convincingly criticised Wismann's and Bollack's conclusions, arguing that their consequences imply the de-materialisation of atoms, and thus the negation of the physical reality of matter itself.

[64] We do not have any surviving definition, by Democritus, of the εἶδος or the ἰδέα. It might of course be lost. Even if he did not give one at all, however, can one blame him, knowing that not even Plato himself ever bothers to define ideas? Lur'e argues that since the idea is one of its distinctive features, Democritus sometimes calls the atoms themselves *ideai*. See Lur'e (1970), also quoted by Salem (1996a). Interestingly, Clement of Alexandria associates Democritus and Plato in their common interest for a higher divine reality. See Clem.Al. *Prot.* VI.59P.

concept of 'idea' is altogether material, and it will only be bent and transformed by Plato in order to distinguish the superior from the inferior, the higher reality of forms from the lower reality of bodies, particularly in *Timaeus*. Democritus's idea resists, however, such idealistic appropriation and diversion of the concept. His 'idea' is the physical shape of the atom, a real characteristic upon which a materialist universe can be conceived, without transcendence, and in a necessary way. And this is where the concept of monstrosity comes to the fore, related to the major question that Democritus leaves to us as a legacy, namely the question of necessity and chance.

Democritus's theory is the first to be able to describe nature, its formation and its phenomena without requiring any transcendental, external or superior principle of explanation.[65] For example, Empedocles, after having introduced the four elements in a full universe, needs the forces of Love and Strife to put them in motion. In Democritus's universe, the void provides the same result. The void is the condition, necessary and sufficient, that allows the atoms' motion with no external and, even more importantly, no anthropomorphic force acting upon them. The scandal of such a bold approach to the explanation of φύσις vibrates through the wonderful parody of Aristophanes' *The Clouds*, in which 'Vortex reigns, and he has turned out Zeus.'[66]

If no anthropomorphic force operates throughout the universe, then how do things happen? How can order, the order that we experience every day in the world, be explained? How do things happen the way they happen, if no law is established and no authority is there to impose them from above, but everything is left to itself and happens randomly? This is precisely what Democritus is accused of. Democritus, 'who assigns the world to chance',[67] inaugurates atheism, since it reduces the universe to a self-moving machine, which does not need a machine-maker to be formed and to continue functioning.[68]

At the same time, it is known all too well that Leucippus and Democritus have been accused of submitting everything to an absolute and unconditional necessity. The allegation comes not only from the atom's opponents but also, as I will show later, from inside the atomistic field as well: Epicurus and Lucretius eventually introduce substantial innovations in the atomic system precisely to avoid the consequences of a too strict necessity. If this is the case, however,

---

[65] *Contra* Reale (1975–80), I, p. 181.
[66] Ar. *Nu.* 828 ff.
[67] Dante Alighieri (1996), *Inferno*, IV.136, p. 77.
[68] See Berryman (2009), especially pp. 37–8, who, *contra*, underlines how *little* use of the machine analogy ancient atomists made, because of the necessity of implying a machine designer. On the idea of atheism see Drachmann (1922), Ley (1966–89), vol. I for Greek and Roman atheism, Fahr (1969) and Winiarczyk (2013).

how can necessity (ἀνάγκη) and chance (τύχη) be *both* and *at the same time* the pillars of Democritean physical and cosmic causality? The question is highly relevant to monstrosity. In fact, within a universe governed by chance, order appears either inexplicable, or constantly threatened by its opposite, disorder: monstrosity reveals itself as the always-possible threat to an ever-too-precarious normality. In a universe of strict necessity, however, what then is the meaning of monstrosity which must also be, in its own manner, necessary?

The term employed by Democritus is αὐτόματον, ambiguously translated either as 'chance' or as 'spontaneity'. Spontaneous things happen, according to Democritus, by themselves and by virtue of their own causal development, without any external influence. The spontaneous happens, in a word, by its own nature, which *also* means necessarily. Corresponding to the Latin *sponte*, the idea of spontaneity is particularly relevant here, because it rules out not only external forces that might compel an event to be produced or to happen in a specific way (e.g. the water of the river to be constrained to flow within the riverbanks), but also any kind of external or transcendent principle, like the one implied by the Aristotelian 'cause for the sake of which' (τὸ οὗ ἕνεκα).

The coexistence of necessity and chance appears paradoxical only from a teleological point of view, endorsed by Aristotle. In fact, as Salem and other modern scholars explain (against many ancient and modern scholars who have perpetuated this conceptual confusion), the paradox is non-existent: chance is nothing else than necessity, under a different name.[69] Everything happens spontaneously in Democritus's universe, according to the immanent causality that is opposed to every kind of teleology as well as to its monotheistic version, providence.[70] Eventually, Plato strongly clashes with this vision, subordinating the αὐτόματον to the intelligent cause.

On this ground, one can easily understand why Democritus's universe, ordered by unconditional necessity, is absolutely without εἱμαρμένη (fate or destiny), whether in its ontological, ethical or religious sense. Monte Ransome

---

[69] See Salem (1996a), p. 77 ff.: the *hasard* is nothing but 'a nickname for universal Necessity'.
[70] See Zeller (1856), II, p. 1078, n. 3: 'not the accidental [Zufällige], but what is necessary by nature', and Salem (1996a), p. 81: '[. . .] *automaton* – the Greek word that we translate with "chance" – does not mean the "accidental" (*das Zufällige*) for Democritus. It rather means "what produces itself," that is to say "what is necessary by nature" (*das Naturnotwendige*). This is because [. . .] the school of Abdera denied the existence of chance, but it also made use of the concept and the word *automaton*. Differently from Aristotle's use, the school of Abdera does not consider the *automaton* as opposed, but rather as essentially identical to the *ananke*.'

On Aristotle's concept of chance see below, and Johnson (2005 and 2009). See also Morel (1996), pp. 71–2. On the origin of the concept of teleology see Theiler (1924), Festugière (1949–54) vol. II, and *infra*.

Johnson has underlined the ethical consequences of such a vision, explaining how Democritus's conception of spontaneity and necessity is not only compatible with, but also fosters, ethical freedom and individual responsibility.[71] Far from being a universe of resignation and passive acceptance of necessity, Democritus's human world is based on the accomplishment of individual freedom and responsibility. Determinism, Johnson argues, is not a threat, but rather a condition for moral responsibility. One could say that the space left empty by the gods is now available for human freedom, and filled by individual responsibility.

What happens to monsters? When gods are withdrawn from the world, how are order, disorder and monstrosity to be explained? Except for Empedocles, Democritus is the only philosopher before Plato whose opinion on physical monstrosity has reached us: *pangenesis* explains monsters' formation and development.[72] Democritus is committed to a pangenetical theory, namely the belief in the production of the seed (σπέρμα or γονή) not by one single organ, but by the whole body and its most important parts (ἀπὸ παντὸς τοῦ σώματος).[73]

Herman De Ley has interpreted the difference between Democritus's pangenesis and Aristotle's panspermia (πανσπερμία) in terms of preformationist vs epigenetic theory.[74] Aristotle's commitment toward epigenesis is well known. What is at stake, for him, is the possibility of denying the 'ambospermatic' theory (which holds that both parents' semen contribute to the fetus's formation) as well as explaining the regularity in the succession of generations (i.e. why humans come from humans, and apples from apple trees). Democritus, on the contrary, develops the theory of ἐπικράτεια, distinctly illustrated in three different and closely related Hippocratic texts: *Generation*, *Nature of the Child* and *Diseases IV*.[75] According to this theory, the seed comes from the whole body of *both* parents, weak from the weaker parts and strong from the stronger parts. The mother's and father's seeds thus mix together, and from the mix, the offspring results.

---

[71] Johnson (2009).

[72] Pangenesis is a word coined by Charles Darwin and eventually employed to describe several different theories of heredity. See especially the *Variation of Animals and Plants under Domestication* [1875, second edition], in Darwin (1986–9), vols XIX and XX. The preformationist theory holds that the seed already contains a miniature version of the mature organism; epigenetic theory, that the mature organism develops from a simple, undifferentiated seed.

[73] See *Vorsokr.* 68 A 141 (= LM [27] ATOM. D165 = *Placit.* V.3.6), and *Vorsokr.* 68 B 124 (= LM [27] ATOM. D164 = Gal. *d. defin med.* 439).

[74] De Ley (1980).

[75] See Hippocrates (2012). On Democritus's influence on this specific section of the Corpus Hippocraticum see Salem (1996a).

The word ἐπικράτεια has political and military senses, referring to dominion, empire, sovereignty; in Democritus's usage, it refers to the competition in which either the female or the male seed dominates to produce a specific hereditary characteristic in the offspring. Democritus and the Hippocratic authors put forward a strictly mechanical theory, perfectly compatible with the atomistic paradigm. It explains the offspring's diversity of sex (which depends on the relative strength of the mother's or the father's seed), as well as all other kinds of diversity (e.g. colour, shape, etc., that is to say all secondary qualities). Every characteristic of the offspring results from a strictly *immanent process* of production, epigenetic rather than preformationist.

The ἐπικράτεια also explains physical monstrosity and abnormality, as a result of the process of composition of the fetus from the mix of male and female seed. *Vorsokr.* 68 A 146 reads as follows:

> Democritus said that monsters [τέρατα] are produced by the confluence of two successive discharges of semen. The later one is also emitted and flows into the uterus, so that the parts are fused and interlocked. And since in birds copulation occurs quickly, he says that eggs and their colours always get interlocked and confused.[76]

Mixing, confusion, disorder, heterogeneity, excess: Democritus's teratology is based on these concepts. The union of different seeds is always a struggle, whose outcome is uncertain and precarious.[77] Monstrosity is a *fundamental threat* to normality: the difference between the two is only one of degree, and not of nature; the difference is contingent and not essential, since both result from the *normal* mixture of male and female seed, in and through the conflictual process of generation (i.e. the only one conceivable). It is also a *fundamental* threat because, without conflict and without the resulting ἐπικράτεια, there would not be any generation at all, and thus no normality. As I will show later, Aristotle is also committed to an agonistic process of formation, which is also the necessary condition of Being's development. For him, however, the agonism is between form and matter. For Democritus, on the contrary, only matter exists, and the conflict is all internal to it. Monstrosity, as a specific case of diversity and differentiation in nature, allows Democritus to banish all teleology from nature.

The importance of this theory and of these different approaches to life's generation will appear in the following chapters. The vitality and originality

---

[76] Taylor (1999), 140, p. 130 (= LM, ATOM D.168 = Arist. GA IV. 4, 769 b 30–6).
[77] Salem (1996a), p. 242: '*un combat douteux*'.

provided by the theory of ἐπικράτεια, for example, can imply an infinity of atomistic production in the universe,[78] which in turn suggests the existence of an innumerable number of κόσμοι springing out of the atomic components. Metrodorus of Chios puts it blatantly: when the causes are infinite, infinite are also the effects.[79] Aristotle draws the same consequences:

> There can be no absolute limit, for nothing can be limited except by something else beyond its limit. [...] the imagination can always conceive a 'beyond' reaching out from any limit, so that the series of numerals seems to have no limit, nor mathematical magnitudes, nor the 'beyond the heavens'. Moreover, it seems to follow from the 'beyond' being unlimited, that 'body' must be unlimited, and that there must be unlimited worlds.[80]

Democritus's thought, together with that of Empedocles, is the most powerful attempt to coherently explain nature and the world on a mechanical basis, without any transcendent principle guiding it from above. The production of monstrous life, put on the same ground as normal life, plays a fundamental role in Empedocles' and Democritus's system. Monstrosity is a powerful conceptual tool that strengthens ancient materialism vis-à-vis the alternative idealistic discourse put forward by the 'defining figures' in the subsequent development of Greek thought, Plato and Aristotle, which I will explore in the following chapters.

---

[78] See Mondolfo (1956).
[79] *Vorsokr.* 70 A 6 (= *Placit.* I.5.4).
[80] Arist. *Ph.* III.4, 203 b 20 ff.

3

Plato

Plato does not develop a consistent study of physical monstrosities. Plato is, nevertheless, interested in the problem, so much so that one could explain the absence of a *specific* discourse on monstrosity in his philosophy by saying that the *general* problem is disseminated throughout the entire system. Besides the explicit mention of monstrosity in some passages of his works, the question of evil, corruption, degradation, anomaly, disorder is at the core of the myths that he presents. Such myths are the foundation for the rational explanation that Plato gives to build his idealism – the most powerful reaction against the naturalism of the Ionian philosophers, and Democritus's materialism.

Plato represents the philosophical ideas he intends to fight as monstrosities, and, through his Socrates, condemns such irrational monstrosities in the name of a normal and rational philosophy. But he also actively uses the monster as an ideological tool that supports, illustrates and explains his philosophy. Monstrosity emerges as the unavoidable problem of philosophy, one which even the authors who intend to ban it, at least from the core of their systems, are forced to address. The concept of monstrosity is at the heart of Plato's philosophy, through the question of matter and form, the soul and its parts (in particular the human soul and its relation to the body on the one hand, and to the cosmic order on the other hand), the meaning of providence and the role of the demiurge.

Matter (ὕλη), in *Timaeus*, is used in its original sense of wood, 'ready for the joiner' (*Ti.* 69 a), rather than in the Aristotelian sense of raw material of any process of construction.[1] In Democritus's account, matter was the only

---

[1] It is worthy to note that Plato often prefers the ὑποδοχή, the receptacle or space in which things are created (e.g. *Ti.* 49 a, 51 a), and that the full identification of ὑποδοχή with ὕλη is only Aristotelian. See *Ph.* 209 b 11–12 or *Cael.* 306 b 17–19. See also Taylor (1928), p. 493.

existing material, self-ordering; Plato introduces it in a theological framework as the passive object upon which the divine craftsman acts.² As a cause, matter is called necessary (ἀναγκαῖος) and posited as secondary to the divine cause (θεῖος);³ matter and necessity itself are thus subordinated, and not only inferior but also recalcitrant and dangerous to the order and harmony of the universe. The necessary cause is the πλανωμένη αἰτία or the errant (Bury, Cherniss), rumbling, and aimless (Taylor) cause, the kind of cause from which monstrosity could rise.

Plato explicitly associates the errant cause with anomalous, singular and irregular phenomena. In this sense, as a cause, it has an active role, but a threatening one, associated in Plato with ταραχή (trouble, disorder and confusion), as well as with ἄνοια (derision, folly and unintelligence), in turn related to ὕβρις (violence and insolence) and opposed to φρόνησις (wisdom and intention). Plato is thus setting the stage for the opposition of what is good and positive to what is bad and negative, namely the monstrous anomaly, the exception.⁴

Plato's necessity, though, must not be seen exclusively as what is evil or irrational. His attitude towards it is more an ambivalence, and a fruitful one after all, since matter is indeed a cause, required by the craftsman to perform his work and organise the world. Such a powerful ambiguity surfaces through the concept of χώρα, the spatiality or place and receptacle where things are. Necessity is truly opposed to reason,⁵ but it also participates, as χώρα, in the intelligible.⁶ Necessity is required: it makes possible both the teleological cosmogonic movement, and the purposiveness ascribed to the craftsman's

---

² On the demiurge as a craftsman see Auroux, pp. 577–8, Lalande, pp. 214–15, Ritter, Gründer hrsg. (1971–2007), II, cc. 49–50, BNP IV, PP. 262–63, RAC III, PP. 694–711, Solmsen (1963), Reydams-Schils (1999) and O'Brien (2015).
³ Pl. Ti. 68 e–69 a.
⁴ See Ast (1835–8) and des Places (1989), *passim*. See also D. Frede, 'Grund', in Schäfer (2013, 2. ed.), pp. 141–5. Taylor (1928), p. 300, convincingly argues that 'it is not the "necessary" but the "contingent," the things for which we do not see any sufficient reason, the *apparently* arbitrary "collocations" in nature which are the contribution of that which Plato calls here ἀνάγκη. [. . .] There is in the world a good deal of what we may call "brute" fact. We know it is there but we do not see "what the good of it" is, though, if we think with Timaeus and Plato, we feel satisfied that it subserves *some* good end. Take for instance the apparent anomalies of the planets. [. . .] what Timaeus means to put down to the score of ἀνάγκη [. . .] is specifically those "conjunctions" for which we can see no justification in the form of a valuable result, and have to accept simply as "given fact".' A similar and coherent example would be that of monstrosities.
⁵ Pl. Ti. 47 e–48 a.
⁶ Pl. Ti. 52 b. See also Festugière (1949–54), II, pp. 110–16 and *Réflexions sur le problème du mal chez Eschyle et Platon*, in Festugière (1971), pp. 8–37.

work itself. Within this theist vision,[7] ἀνάγκη is opposed to νοῦς, and thus it becomes a tool to undermine Ionian naturalism and atomistic mechanicism. Socrates leads the charge in *Phaedo* 97 d–99 b, with his ironically bitter disappointment for Anaxagoras, whom he believed to be a true philosopher but who in fact 'made no use of intelligence, and did not assign any real causes for the ordering of things'.[8] The Athenian Stranger in *The Laws* follows up, rebuffing those who believe that νοῦς, θεός and τέχνη (design) do not play any role in the cosmogony.[9]

Heraclitus had already recognised that guilt, injustice, contradiction and pain exist only from the limited point of view of men, but from the divine point of view of the whole they result in the ultimate harmony. Plato appropriates Anaxagoras's concept and turns it upside down, making it a principle of transcendence. Plato's universe becomes entirely theological and thoroughly teleological.[10] Its craftsman purposively works to produce it with a τέλος in mind:

> All things are ordered systematically by Him who cares for the World-all with a view to the preservation and excellence of the Whole, whereof also each part, so far as it can, does and suffers what is proper to it. To each of these parts, down to the smallest fraction, rulers of their action and passion are appointed to bring fulfilment even to the uttermost fraction; whereof thy portion also, O perverse man, is one, and tends therefore always in its striving towards the All, tiny though it be. But thou failest to perceive that all partial generation is for the sake of the Whole, in order that for the life of the World-all blissful existence may be secured, – it not being generated for thy sake, but thou for its sake.[11]

Every part or individual in the universe, no matter how minute or imperfect, is thus thought of as a part of the universal and divine teleology.

Plato's theological and teleological cosmogony has important implications for the nature of the body, in particular the human body, and its relation with the soul. Because perfection and divinity are above, and act from above,

---

[7] Taylor (1928), p. 299: 'Henceforth νοῦς and ἀνάγκη are the regular names used for what have hitherto been distinguished as the true αἰτία or the αἰτία which is an ἔμφρων φύσις and its "accessory" or "accomplice".'
[8] See Warden (1971), p. 14.
[9] Pl. *Lg.* X.889 b–d.
[10] See Festugière (1949–54), II, pp. 100–32 on *Timaeus*'s teleology. See also J. Müller, 'Ziel/Zweck', in Schäfer (2013, 2. ed.), pp. 340–3.
[11] Pl. *Lg.* X.903 b. E. B. England, in Plato (1976), II, p. 49 thinks of this passage in connection with *Ti.* 41 a ff.

all the universe's parts are hierarchically and vertically ordered, disposed from the more to the less perfect as in a great chain of being.[12] The further down this chain one moves, the more disorder and evil one finds. Evil, in Plato's view, depends precisely on the distance that separates it from the superior sphere. Everything material is confined below, while everything ideal and immaterial is raised above. Being, in its bodily nature and existence, is thus inferior and subordinated to its psychic essence. What is, though, the relation between the two?

The ψυχή, ungenerated and indestructible, moves itself (*Phdr.* 245 c); it is the cause of life (*Cra.* 399 d) and, equally important, it is first in order of Becoming and has superior authority over bodies.[13] Despite its priority, though, the soul actually inhabits the body, as if imprisoned in it, in order to expiate its faults. 'I once heard one of our sages say,' Socrates says in *Grg.* 493 a, 'that we are now dead, and the body is our tomb [σῆμα],' and he also explains in *Cra.* 400 c 1 that 'the Orphic poets gave this name [σῆμα] with the idea that the soul is undergoing punishment for something; they think it has the body as an enclosure to keep it safe, like a prison, and this is, as the name [σῶμα, body] itself denotes, the safe [σῶμα] for the soul, until the penalty is paid, and not even a letter needs to be changed.'[14] Thus, Plato suggests that evil, undeniably present in the phenomenal world, must be explained through the relation between the soul, or the incorporeal, and the body, or the material.[15]

On the one hand, only ideas are perfect and perfectly real entities (*Ti.* 52 a–c), thus constituting the model and paradigm, whereas everything that inhabits the phenomenal world is by definition less perfect, a copy or a reflection. Ideas and objects thus face each other, like the Same and the Other, the positive and the negative, good and evil. On the other hand, nothing corporeal can be the cause of its own motion, but rather needs to be moved by the soul, which also exclusively exhibits reason and purposiveness (*Ti.* 46 d 5 – e 2).[16] The soul is therefore the origin and the cause of every motion *including* the one that produces imperfect or evil or monstrous things.

---

[12] See Lovejoy (1942).
[13] Pl. *Lg.* X.892 b and *Ti.* 34 d–35 a. Taylor (1928), p. 105 explains that '"first in order of becoming" need not mean first in order of time; it means first in the ontological order, the order of dependence'. See also W. Brinker, 'Seele', in Schäfer (2013, 2. ed.), pp. 253–8.
[14] See also *Grg.* 525 a. On the theme of the body as a tomb and the false etymology σῶμα-σῆμα see Courcelle (1966) and A. J. Festugière, 'Réflexions sur le problème du mal chez Eschyle et Platon', in Festugière (1971), pp. 8–37. On the non-Orphic origin of this idea, see Dodds (1951), ch. V. For its influence on Middle and Neoplatonic thought see below.
[15] See C. Schäfer, 'Böse', in Schäfer (2013, 2. ed.), pp. 63–7.
[16] See Taylor (1928), pp. 292–3.

This ambiguity surfaces once again in the *Laws* (book X), where Plato explicitly holds that evil too, no differently from good, has its origin in the soul – or souls:

> ATH. Must we not necessarily agree, in the next place, that soul is the cause of things good and bad, fair and foul, just and unjust, and all the opposites, if we are to assume it to be the cause of all things? [...] One soul, is it, or several? I will answer for you – 'several'. Anyhow, let us assume not less than two – the beneficent (εὐεργετικός) soul and that which is capable of effecting results of the opposite kind. [...] Soul drives all things in Heaven and earth and sea by its own motion [...] both when, in conjunction with reason, it runs aright and always governs all things rightly and happily, and when, in converse with unreason, it produces results which are in all respects the opposite.[17]

Scholars have extensively debated the possible Oriental influences on Plato's theory of the soul. This text is extremely influential for the dualist interpretation of Platonism, claimed by several Middle and Neoplatonic authors in the following centuries.[18] The origin of evil and imperfection comes threateningly close to the same principle that generates goodness and order. Plato must have felt this problem less intensely than his Platonic followers who would eventually have to face Gnosticism. He must have been well aware, though, of the alternative at stake, as well as of all its nuances: discharging the demiurge from the responsibility of generating evil ends up making the principle of evil itself dangerously autonomous. Conversely, recognising only one principle at the origin of everything means making it responsible for both good and evil.

The ψυχή seems thus to be assigned an ambiguous status,[19] being at the same time the victim as well as the artificer of evil, to some extent related to the ὕλη and, more in general, to everything that is visible (ὁρατός), corporeal (σωματοειδής) or tangible (ἁπτός). This ambiguous status is of primary importance to Plato's heritage in the interpretation, understanding and justification of monstrosity both in the world and in the soul. The monist and the dualist interpretations of Plato have confronted each other on this ground. Insofar as

---

[17] Pl. *Lg.* 896 d 3–897 b 4. E. B. England, in Plato (1976), II, p. 476: '[effects] are orderly and happy if νοῦς is ψυχή's guide, and quite the reverse if it allies itself with ἄνοια.'

[18] See *infra*.

[19] The classical opposition in scholarship is between Festugière (1947), who locates the evil's source in matter, and Cherniss (1954), who maintains that evil has a plurality of sources in Plato's thought, claiming that matter is passive and that evil is a necessary consequence of the action of soul upon the body. See also Hager (1962) and Sambursky (1956 and 1962).

the soul is considered as victim, monstrosity is seen as otherness, threatening the soul and its order from outside. When the soul, on the contrary, is considered as the only mover acting upon matter, Being itself is dangerously polluted by a sort of inner monstrosity at every level of its expression, including its highest and divine dimension.

Plato insists on keeping together the ethico-political, aesthetical and ontological aspects of this analysis, denouncing the deleterious consequences of an evil soul in the *Sophist*: 'We must say that there are two kinds of evil in the soul. [. . .] The one is comparable to a disease in the body, the other to a deformity. [. . .] we must regard a foolish soul as deformed and ill-proportioned.'[20] Ignorance and foolishness are analysed through the category of deformity (αἶσχος) and disproportion (ἀμετρία), and thus linked to monstrosity. This deformity can be normalised and corrected through a gymnastic – that is, the proper way of reasoning – after which the monstrous sophist will have been ultimately defeated.

One of the most striking metaphors in Plato's works speaks openly of the dangerous implications of the soul's multiple nature: the image by which Socrates describes the soul. It occurs in book IX of the *Republic*, where Plato deals with injustice, contrasting Thrasymachus's and Glaucon's infamous position on the utility of injustice for the unjust human. Plato wants the sophists to see what the implications of such a position are. In order to do so, Socrates forges an 'image of the soul', linking together the city and the individual (that is, politics and morality) in the most monstrous vision in all of Plato's work:

> One of those like the creatures whose nature is recorded in ancient myth [. . .] such as Chimera, Scylla, and Cerberus, and the numerous other cases where many forms are said to have grown into one. [. . .] put together a single form of a complex many-headed animal, but with a circle of heads of both tame and wild beasts, capable of changing and growing all these parts out of itself.[21]

---

[20] Pl. *Sph.* 227 d 5–228 d 2.

[21] Pl. *R.* 588 c. Note the active and growing character of this beast's monstrosity. It is in fact able to multiply and produce new heads, like the Lernaean Hydra, which will become the paradigmatic symbol of rebellion and revolt in modernity. Plato humorously explores the theme of the hydra, which he compares to a female sophist, in *Euthd.* 297 c: by cutting off one of the sophist's arguments, new ones proliferate threateningly. On Plato's image see also Cherniss (1944), I, p. 254, n. 262 and Walter Leszl's commentary in Aristotele (1975), pp. 139 ff. On the hydra μυριόκρανος RE IX.1, pp. 44–52, BNP VI, pp. 598–99, RAC XVI, pp. 904–15, Roscher (1884–90), Grimal (1951), Grimal (1965) and Gantz (1993). On the enormous iconographic success of this subject see LIMC IV–V, Reid (1993), I, pp. 553–4. See also Oriol-Boyer (1975).

Plato finds inspiration, of course, in the traditional image of the chimera. In the *Iliad*, it has the head of a lion, the body of a goat, and a serpent for a tail. Hesiod also speaks about a three-headed creature in the shape of lion, goat and snake.[22] Plato's monster seems closer to Homer's than to Hesiod's. It is, however, stunningly original, since Plato not only refers to a tradition but also reshapes it in view of the precise and detailed moral meaning that he intends to assign to the allegory. Socrates does not simply describe an existing monster but, as if the monstrous animals of the tradition were insufficient to convey a philosophical meaning, actually forges an image under the reader's eyes, as if the constructive process were more effective and rhetorically powerful.[23] He continues:

> Now put together another in the shape of a lion, and one in the shape of a human being: let the first one be by far the biggest and the second one second in size. [. . .] now join these three into one so that they are somehow fused together. [. . .] now put the figure of a single creature on the outside of them, the image of a human being so that to someone who can't see what's on the inside, only the covering on the outside, it looks like a single creature – a human being [. . .].[24]

Traditional chimeras did not have any human part. Not only does Plato innovate the human part of the monster; he also sets the human in contrast to the monstrous within the same body. The balance of the individual parts of the soul is carefully described by Plato, underlining that the monstrous part is bigger than the animal one, which is bigger than the veritable human part of it, precisely as workers are more numerous than warriors, which in turn are more numerous than philosophers in Plato's best city.[25] The stage is thus ready for the ultimate conflict between humanity and monstrosity, whose function is to rebuke the sophist's claim about justice.

Plato's deployment of the mythical chimera is striking, considering that he openly condemns myths and their allegorical use. He blames Homer and Hesiod in particular, since myths cannot be used to educate or convey truth.[26] The myth corrupts the mind, especially the young minds, and cannot reflect the higher truth that only philosophical speculation can attain. *Phaedrus*'s

---

[22] *Il.* VI.180–3. Hes. *Th.* 321–2. See also *supra*.
[23] See Louis (1945).
[24] Pl. *R.* 588 d–e. J. Adams, in Plato (1963, 2nd ed.), II, p. 363: '[. . .] according to Plato, the true unity of the individual is realised only through the subjection of the two lower "parts" of the soul to the highest [. . .].' On the conflict within the soul in Plato see Dodds (1951), ch. VII.
[25] See Marignac (1951), pp. 111–15.
[26] Pl. *R.* 376 e–377 c.

Socrates blames the chimera explicitly: giving a rational explanation for Oreithyia's rape by Boreas, he censures the false images that corrupt the spirit, such as 'Centaurs, [. . .] Chimaera, [and] the whole crowd of such creatures, Gorgons and Pegas, and multitudes of strange, inconceivable, portentous natures.'[27] Once used, such images should be corrected, amended, improved and restored to their correct meaning, for which Plato uses ἐπανορθόω: with a medical, ethical and political sense, it is a veritable remedy (φάρμακον), which would be needed against the perversion of such imaginary monsters to bring them back to what is knowable, likeable and plausible (the εἰκός). It is better, thus, to avoid them and turn to the philosophical enquiry about the true nature of things. Beyond and against the rationalisation of myths, which produces solely a plausible knowledge, Plato offers the only true philosophical enquiry.[28]

Poets and artists are capable of creating only ghosts and appearances, and their work never approaches reality. Every representation is condemned to such a destiny because of the necessary distance from the highest ontological reality, that of ideas, as explained in R. 595 a–608 b. Plato himself, however, paradoxically makes use of a plethora of such images, myths and allegories throughout his work.[29] Their strategic role is essential to Plato's argumentation and they cannot be dismissed as pure rhetorical ornaments. The image of the tripartite soul is of this kind, and Plato establishes this monstrous image at the core of his theory of the soul:

> Let's say [. . .] to the speaker who argues that it's profitable for this person to do wrong and there's no advantage in doing just deeds, that he means nothing more than that it's profitable for him to feed the compound creature well and make it strong, as well as the lion and what's related to it, but to starve the man and make him weak, so that he's dragged about wherever either of them leads him, and not to get either of them used to each other and become friends, but leave them to bite each other, fight, and eat each other [. . .][30]

---

[27] Pl. *Phdr.* 229 d. See Reinhardt (1927), Jaeger (1947), Buffière (1956), C. Ginzburg, *Mito*, in Settis a cura di (1996–2002), I, pp. 197–237, Morgan (2000), Janka, Schäfer hrsg. (2014).

[28] Following Nestle (1942, 2. ed.), Untersteiner (1955, 2a ed.), p. 352 suggests that Plato is criticising Palaephatus here, since the list of mythical monstrosities appears in the paradoxographer's work. On paradoxography see Giannini (1963 and 1964).

[29] See e.g. Brochard (1926, 2e ed.), *Les mythes dans la philosophie de Platon*, pp. 46–54, Frutiger (1930), Schuhl (1947a), Pépin (1957), Bollack (1971), Morgan (2000), Moreau (2006), pp. 65–100, Collobert, Destrée, Gonzalez eds. (2012) and Destrée, Edmonds III eds.(2017).

[30] Pl. *R.* 588 e–589 a.

The mythical image is prodigiously set in motion, and it starts living its life, made of the conflictual dynamic among the soul's different parts. It is a veritable dialectic, in which the exclusively human part of the soul must make use of its affective dimension, while at the same time taming the monstrous part and preventing its growth. Who or what is the real human? And if it has to make the νοῦς prevail over the other faculties, how would it overcome its own irrational components?

> And on the other hand does this mean that he who claims that justice is profitable would say that one must do and say those things from which the man within the man will be the strongest and will look after the many-headed beast, like a farmer, by feeding and domesticating the tame animals and preventing the wild ones from breeding, and, making an ally of the lion's nature, and, caring for them all in common, will bring them up in such a way as to make them friendly to each other and himself?[31]

The 'man within the man' personifying reason and logic has, in particular, puzzled interpreters. Is this man also only a human shape, enveloping in turn a monstrous creature? A human form (ἰδέα ἀνθρώπου) represents the intelligence (λογιστικόν). However, it hides, in an ambiguous manner, the potentially monstrous reality of an untamed passionality. This reveals Plato's difficulty in representing human psychology, since only reason seems to be really human but, at the same time, reason needs affectivity, which is indeed part of the human. Even worse, reason itself possibly hides something impure, precisely as the human does.[32]

Notwithstanding Plato's effort to hide the savage beast inside the soul, and tame it with the force of reason, the outcome is nonetheless deformed, even though wrecked by a different kind of monstrosity. This is Friedrich Nietzsche's reading of Socrates and his hyper-intellectualism. Socrates becomes

---

[31] Pl. *R.* IX.588 b–c. See S. Gastaldi, 'L'immagine dell'anima e la felicità del giusto', in Vegetti (1998–2007), VI, pp. 593–633.

[32] Annas (1981), p. 145: 'The more Plato insists that reason is responsible for the welfare of the soul as a whole, the more he expands its capacities until it threatens to become not just a homunculus but a bogeyman.' Rosen (2005), p. 349, has also noticed the ambiguity, without however underlining the difficulty that might arise from it: 'We see at once that the human being inside the outer shell is supposed to stand for the intellect, whereas the lion represents spiritedness and the remaining bestial heads are the various desires of the part of the soul that loves gain. There is of course no point-by-point analogy; to mention only the obvious, the inner human being presumably has a soul with three parts of its own. But the soul is more like a fantastic mélange of human and nonhuman loves and desires than it is like a ratio of numbers and geometrical forms.'

in Nietzsche's reading an atrophic being, or rather a monstrous *defectus*.³³ Nietzsche identifies the rationalist response to instinctivity as a monstrosity opposed to another monstrosity in Greek culture. Whereas, though, the monstrosity of irrational instinct is openly named, the monstrosity of the hypertrophic reason is hidden under the surface of the new Greek man.

Socrates develops – one should rather say *invents* – a moral psychology, in order to claim the happiness of the just. Justice, however, needs to be defined vis-à-vis injustice, which in turn reveals its monstrously unobliterable presence. The sudden and chimeric appearance of the monstrous creature, the θηρίον, testifies not only to Plato's great inventiveness in forging powerful metaphors, but also to his serious concern in explaining and dealing with the conflict between the superior and the inferior, between good and evil, between the perfection and the imperfection that inhabit the world.³⁴

The θηρίον is the savage beast, the lion, the bear or the boar, and has been used as a legendary monster by Homer, Aeschylus and Herodotus.³⁵ It is not irrelevant that Plato chooses a rare term, as well as one around which, as Chantraine underlines, a whole family of Greek words has arisen related to hunting, fishing and, in a more figurative sense, chasing.³⁶

---

³³ Nietzsche, *Die Geburt der Tragödie. Oder: Griechenthum und Pessimismus*, in Nietzsche (1967–), III.1, par. 13, p. 86: 'Einen monstrosen defectus jeder mystischen Anlage [. . .], so dass Sokrates als der specifische *Nicht-Mystiker* zu bezeichnen wäre, in dem die logische Natur durch eine Superflötation eben so excessiv entwickelt ist wie im Mystiker jene instinctive Weisheit [a monstrous defect of every mystical talent, so that Socrates can be considered a specific case of the *non-mystical* man, in whom the logical nature has become simply too massive through an excessive use, just like instinctive wisdom in the mystic].' Socrates was harshly ridiculed even in his own time, for example by Aristophanes. The mask representing him was intended to be close to his actual appearance, thus collapsing the distance between the physical reality and the grotesque caricature that would be expected. Ael. VH II.13 reports how fiercely Socrates responds to this public attack – he stands up in the theatre to draw attention away from the scene being presented and toward him, confronting the play's authors and actors and claiming his reality in the face of the play's caricature.
³⁴ See Heidegger (1961 [1942/7]), p. 226 and *passim*, Bernhardt (1971), *passim*, K. A. Morgan, 'Theriomorphism and the Composite Soul in Plato', in Collobert, Destrée, Gonzalez eds. (2012), pp. 323–42, Tsagdis (2016), and D. Cairn, *The Tripartite Soul as Metaphor*, in Destrée, Edmonds III, eds. (2017), pp. 219–38. On the θηρίον see Chantraine, p. 435.
³⁵ TGL *sub voce*.
³⁶ Chantraine, p. 435. Plato also employs the image of the yoke of the idea, whose explicit violence should not be undermined. See R. VI, 507 e 5–508 a 2: 'It is by no insignificant notion that the sense of sight and the ability to be seen have been yoked together by a more valuable yoke [ζυγόν] than all other combination, unless light has no value' [translation modified].

The allusion to hunting and fishing brings the reader to the struggle against the sophist once again, as Umberto Curi has suggested.[37] The term διαιρέω (dividing) in Plato's philosophical method refers to the choice and the distinction between arguments, but is also built on the αἵρεσις, the conquest or the taking of someone else's power and belonging. The αἱρέω ambivalently suggests the grasping of something with the intellect, but also with the hands. It is a polemical notion that leaves little space to the pacific confrontation of opinions. The necessity of catching the monstrous beast of the tripartite soul resonates in Plato's choice of words, especially the θήρα, referring to the monstrous sophist: 'It is now our business not to let the beast get away again, for we have almost got him into a kind of encircling net of the devices we employ in arguments about such subjects, so that he will not now escape the next thing' (*Sph.* 235 a 10 – 236 b 3).[38] Facing the monstrous sophist, the true philosopher must employ the same means one employs with lions and boars: to constrain (βιάζο), and even torture and torment (βασανίζο), to arrive at the truth. The inner conflictual dimension of the soul is thus connected with the external, and equally conflictual, relation between the bearer of knowledge and the malevolent liar.

This conflict also reflects the opposition between the material and ideal which constantly challenge the order of the universe and make it essentially and dangerously precarious. Νοῦς and ἀνάγκη face each other in a never-ending struggle, evidenced by the evil and monstrosities, thus revealing the unstable character of the demiurge's work.

Plato makes a huge effort to depart from the superstitious and vulgar conception of deity.[39] Matter is in God's hands and he necessarily operates for the sake of the good; this is his τέλος:

> God desired that, so far as possible, all things should be good and nothing evil; wherefore, when He took over all that was visible, seeing that it was not in a state of rest but in a state of discordant and disorderly motion, He brought it into order out of disorder, deeming that the former state is in all ways better than the latter. [...] He constructed reason within soul and soul within body as He fashioned the All, that so the work He was executing might be of its nature most fair and most good. Thus, then, in accordance with the likely account, we must declare that this Cosmos has

---

[37] Curi (2000).

[38] See Curi (2000), pp. 61–2. Such a polemical attitude, as well as the conception of the search for truth as a battle, was indeed shared by the Sophists themselves. See Untersteiner (1949), pp. 26–7.

[39] Pl. R. II, 378 e ff. See also Babut (1974).

verily come into existence as a Living Creature endowed with soul and reason owing to the providence of God.[40]

The universe's order, supposedly beautiful (καλός) and good (ἀγαθός) because of the demiurge's action, which is necessarily positive, is continually challenged by everything that is bad and evil (κακός and φαῦλος), defective and perverse (πονηρός), but also monstrous and bestial (θηριώδης, associated with the savage [ἄγριος], irrational [ἄλογος] and unknowable [ἄγνωστος]).[41] The process of ordering of matter, moreover, is far from being peaceful: the demiurge must use violence (βία) to harmonise it.[42] The demiurge's providence (πρόνοια) and care (ἐπιμέλεια) for the universe are thus caught between their foundational role for the entire cosmogonic account and their powerlessness to fully achieve the end of goodness.

Another famous myth perfectly illustrates the absence of linearity in the movement that brings chaos to order. In the *Statesman*, Plato claims that it is not possible to hold a coherent discourse on the origin of the universe, given the ignorance of it to which we are forever condemned.[43] He thus employs once again the myth describing the double origin of the world and the cosmogonic movement. God directly guides the universe for a certain time, keeping it in order and caring about every aspect of life. Once this cycle is accomplished, God leaves the world to itself, and the world revolves back, with no guidance from the divine. The former is the age of Chronos, and the latter the age of Zeus, in which we live and die.

In our (Zeus's) age, we know the reproduction of living beings one from the other, ancestors producing offspring. In Chronos's time, though, generation happened in a completely different way:

> First the age of all animals, whatever it was at the moment, stood still, and every mortal creature stopped growing older in appearance and then reversed its growth and became, as it were, younger and more tender; [. . .]

---

[40] Pl. *Ti.* 29 e 1–30 c 1. See also R. 379 b–c and *Lg.* 900 d 2–3. Does god produce the world out of his will or out of necessity, given that he is necessarily good? This question will deeply affect the early Christian reception of Platonism, and is extremely relevant for every future theodicy, since two very different principles become available to explain the presence of evil, imperfection and monstrosity in the world.

[41] See R. Schönberger, 'Gute, das', in Schäfer (2013, 2. ed.), pp. 145–50. See also W. Mesch, 'Demiurg', in Schäfer (2013, 2. ed.), pp. 74–6. More in general, on the κακός in the ancient world, see Sluiter, Rosen eds. (2008).

[42] Pl. *Ti.* 35 a. See Bernhardt (1971), p. 196 and J. J. Porter, *The Disgrace of Matter in Ancient Aesthetics*, in Sluiter, Rosen eds. (2008), pp. 283–317.

[43] Pl. *Ti.* 29 c–d.

being begotten of one another was no part of the natural order of that time, but the earth-born race which, according to tradition, once existed, was the race which returned at that time out of the earth; and the memory of it was preserved by our earliest ancestors, who were born in the beginning of our period and therefore were next neighbours to the end of the previous period of the world's revolution, with no interval between.[44]

After a short overlapping, then, one age gives place to the other, in an endless succession of cycles. With respect to Chronos's time, Plato tackles the question of spontaneous generation that had been at the heart of ancient cosmogonies, e.g. of Empedocles and Anaximander, in whose work one finds its earliest mention.[45] However, no monster comes out of the earth in Plato's version. On the contrary, in the age of Chronos, such generation from the earth is not spontaneous (αὐτόματος) at all. It is directly guided by God and cared about in its minutest details. There is no attempt to generate different species through monstrosities, but rather, perfection is brought forth, from the earth, at once. Plato can thus turn upside down the mechanist explanation of the ancient cosmogonies and, through the *absence* of monstrosity, build the hypothesis of a caring divinity directly responsible for the production of life.

The *Statesman* is not the only work in which the duality of the creative movement is explored. Another myth, that of the androgyne in the *Symposium*, reinforces the idea of a double process of generation. This time, it happens to a creature which is indeed monstrous, and through a process reminiscent of the trial-and-error development of creatures posited by ancient cosmogonies.

> [O]ur original nature was by no means the same as it is now. In the first place, there were three kinds of human beings, not merely the two sexes, male and female, as at present: there was a third kind as well, which had equal shares of the other two, and whose name survives though the thing itself has vanished. For 'man-woman' [ἀνδρόγυνος, hermaphrodite] was then a unity in form no less than name, composed of both sexes and sharing equally in male and female; [. . .] the form of each person was round all over, with back and sides encompassing it every way; each had four arms, and legs to match these, and two faces perfectly alike on a cylindrical neck. There was one head to the two faces, which looked opposite ways; there were four ears, two privy members, and all the other parts, as may be imagined, in proportion.[46]

---

[44] Pl. *Plt.* 270 e. See Schuhl (1947a).
[45] Kirk, Raven (1960, 2nd ed.), 136–9.
[46] Pl. *Smp.* 189 d–190 c.

These original monsters are once again the opposite of the early creatures of the ancient cosmogonies. Whereas Empedocles' monsters died for their lack of adequacy to the environment, Plato's original androgynes are very nimble and vigorous, to the point that, self-confident enough, they decide to assault the gods, like the giants their predecessors.

The gods are perplexed, since they wish to avoid the same outcome of the gigantomachy and the complete destruction of the androgynes. Zeus thus suggests to only diminish their strength, slicing them in two parts so as to make them weaker and more useful at once. He also promises to keep slicing them in two, should it be needed, to fraction their strength even further. With the help of Apollo, Zeus accomplishes the task. Although the living beings are perfectly functional, the division impacts their behaviour as well. Unexpectedly, they irresistibly tend to reunite with each other and embrace their mate until they starve. Zeus is thus forced to quickly find a remedy, before the whole race becomes extinct. He therefore moves the genitals so as to create men and women as we know them.

The final outcome is far from being the refinement of a coherent project, or the accomplishment of the best shape, guided by a rational design. Men and women, contrarywise, shamefully bear the mark of their genealogy, in the ugliness of their present conformation: 'Each of us, then, is but a tally [σύμβολον, also a "portent" and an "omen"] of a man, since every one shows like a flat-fish the traces of having been sliced in two; and each is ever searching for the tally that will fit him.'[47] The human is tentatively crafted by Zeus, from its original powerful monstrosity, to its current and no less ugly shape. Its weakness reflects its tortuous genealogy, whose beginning and end is equally monstrous.

In this chapter, I have outlined the main areas in which we can discern monstrosity directly and indirectly in Plato's philosophy. Monstrosity surfaces in his account of the world's order and its formation as a testament both to the superiority of ideas over matter and the rational design through which the demiurge has shaped the cosmos. As we have seen, Plato's main target is ancient materialism, particularly Democritus's atomism. Monstrosity also emerges in Plato's psychology as a polemical metaphor whose normative function is to point to the model of a rational creature that has to tame the irrational and instinctual dimension that is dangerously hidden in each and every human. Prodigious myths and monstrous metaphors are thus at the core of the idealist construction that fundamentally shapes Attic Greek thought.

---

[47] Pl. *Smp.* 191 d.

Plato's language and metaphorical approach make it easy to integrate monstrous beings into his philosophical framework. As we will see in the next chapter, however, a different attitude arises in this period – a less metaphorical, more scientific approach to the study of nature developed outside the Academy, initially by Aristotle, Plato's most brilliant pupil, and later by new philosophical systems such as Epicureanism and Stoicism. Platonism, as we have seen, was decisive for the depiction of a vertical and transcendental concept of nature and for its axiological ontology, in which the inferior and monstrous beings are pushed to the bottom of the scale. As we will see in the next chapter, Aristotelianism somehow flattens this ideal concept of the universe without completely renouncing either transcendence or axilogy.

4

Aristotle

Plato's effort to counter the materialism of early natural philosophers in general, and of atomists in particular, is pursued by Aristotle, his most brilliant pupil in the Academy. Far from repeating his master's steps, firmly anchored in the mythical explanation of nature and its origin, Aristotle develops one of the most extraordinary philosophical systems ever conceived. Aristotle's idea of nature and, within it, of normality, abnormality and monstrosity, becomes the reference for generations of scholars and represents, with important variations, the mainstream philosophical and scientific conception for centuries.

In this chapter, I will show how Aristotle's causal theory functions as a framework to interpret monstrosity and rework the conclusions reached by the materialists and idealists who came before him. If monsters deserve scientific analysis, it is because they must be accommodated within the normal regime of production of being in nature. Only a complex causality that subordinates every aspect of being to its end or purpose satisfactorily explains, in Aristotle's view, apparently abnormal phenomena. I will next show how this approach brings Aristotle to completely re-evaluate the notion of chance and necessity, beyond and against ancient materialist theories. Although Aristotle also intends to overcome Plato's radical realism, his main targets are Empedocles and Democritus, whose theories remain potent, nourishing the Hellenistic renaissance of materialism that comes with Epicurus. This struggle, as I will show in the last part of this chapter, is also reflected in the internal debates of the school Aristotle founded, the Lyceum, in which leading figures such as Theophrastus and Strato rework the master's doctrines, including the notion of monstrosity.

Aristotle's is both a philosophical and a scientific enterprise. Not only because no clear distinction is really possible between science and philosophy, but also because, more specifically, Aristotle is interested in developing, within his philosophy, a proper scientific attitude toward the enquiry into natural phenomena, thus developing an approach that many modern investigators of nature, including the anti-Aristotelians, regard with respect. While a few words, sometimes cryptical and hermetic, were often enough for the earlier mythographers and philosophers, and even for Plato, to evoke the basic principles of an entire metaphysics, Aristotle insightfully explores, with rich and original prose, every aspect of reality without sparing details and digressions. He questions every aspect of a problem and tackles issues of all sorts, including the systematical analysis and critique of his sources, within whose works he is capable of recognising not only faults, but also merit.

While the earlier philosophers had aimed, first and foremost, at identifying a founding principle upon which every aspect of reality could be grounded, without necessarily detailing every aspect, Aristotle is on the contrary keen to cover the whole of reality, explicitly developing different scientific discourses for the different parts of the universe, from the highest to the lowest. Thus, the former, i.e. the skies and the celestial bodies, lose their traditional ontological primacy and priority. Or, in other words, this primacy and priority is valid only within the metaphysical discourse, but not absolutely, when one analyses the physics of the universe. Every aspect of reality has its own dignity and its own priority within its specific domain, and especially in the biological one. Every angle of reality is thus worthy to be studied:

> So far as in us lies, we will not leave out any one of them, be it never so mean; for though there are animals which have no attractiveness for the senses, yet for the eye of science, for the student who is naturally of a philosophic spirit and can discern the causes of things, Nature which fashioned them provides joys which cannot be measured. [. . .] Wherefore we must not betake ourselves to the consideration of the meaner animals with a bad grace [ἀτιμοτέρων ζῴων], as though we were children; since in all natural things there is somewhat of the marvellous [ἐν πᾶσι γὰρ τοῖς φυσικοῖς ἔνεστί τι θαυμαστόν].[1]

People, and scientists in particular, speak about the ἄτιμος, what is not honourable or deemed worthy of any esteem and consideration. Nevertheless, no such thing exists in nature for Aristotle, since even the lower beings participate in and convey the marvellous nature of the universe.

I find particularly important here Aristotle's suggestion of joining together the ἄτιμος and the θαυμαστός, the unworthy and the wonderful, admirable and excellent. Aristotle is not only stimulating the reader's attention with a

---

[1] Arist. PA I.5, 645 a 7 ff.

striking paradox. He is also drawing the reader's regard to the fact that what is usually despised and considered as worthless, at least in the physical world, conduces on the contrary toward the highest spheres of knowledge, and in some sense toward the divine.[2]

There is something seminal in this new attitude toward the marvellous character inherent in inferior things. Wonder, for Aristotle, fuels the attitude toward knowledge in general and philosophy in particular, as stated in a famous page of *Metaphysics*, which reiterates a Platonic idea: 'It is through wonder (θαυμάζειν) that men now begin and originally began to philosophise; wondering in the first place at obvious perplexities, and then by gradual progression raising questions about the greater matters too.'[3] Θαυμάζειν leads to curiosity and curiosity awakens the desire to understand. It is not the perfection of the heavenly bodies, Aristotle argues, that leads men toward knowledge, but rather the amazing character of nature as a whole, including (especially) its supposedly unworthy phenomena. That these phenomena occur only in the terrestrial realm and not in the superior world must be taken as an invitation to connect the two domains and focus on the unity of metaphysics, physics and biology.[4] As Heraclitus invites his puzzled guests to join him in his house's less worthy place, since 'there are gods even in the kitchen',[5] similarly, Aristotle invites his reader to join him in the animal world, the authentic 'kitchen' of the universe, worthy of the most honourable visitor, in which one can find both φύσις and καλός.

The presence of the gods in the kitchen goes far beyond the simple anecdote. In the Christian revaluation of Aristotle's thought, everything regarding the divine must be seriously considered as a contention against the enemies of faith. In this sense, Pierre Aubenque correctly underlines the importance of this passage for every future attempt to connect the physical world with the divine domain and, in particular, of every theodicy. Aristotle's gods in the kitchen certainly transfer their divine character to the lower world. However, by doing so, they also present themselves as somehow responsible for the cooking and, beyond the metaphor, for everything that is produced in the world. The divine and the natural are thus intertwined once and for all, and the problem of theodicy has its roots precisely in this revolutionary aspect of Aristotle's attitude.[6]

---

[2] See P. Pinotti, 'Aristotele, Platone e la meraviglia del filosofo', in Lanza and Longo a cura di (1989), pp. 29–55.
[3] Arist. *Metaph*. 982 b 11–983 a 25.
[4] P. Pellegrin, 'Taxinomie, moriologie, division', in Devereux, Pellegrin éds. (1990), pp. 37–48.
[5] Arist. *PA* I.5, 645 a 19–23.
[6] See Aubenque (1962), p. 502.

According to Aubenque, the anecdote of the gods in the kitchen testifies not only to Aristotle's belief that everything is worthy to be studied in nature, but also to the result that, in practice, the knowledge of the lower things paradoxically becomes more certain and desirable that the knowledge of higher beings.[7] Catherine Wilson has suggested that Aristotle expands on Plato's conception and prepares the Stoic's view of the hierarchy of perfection, for which the lower the reality enquired into by the philosopher, the more uncertain and degraded his knowledge.[8] Without underestimating the evolution of Aristotle's thought, I believe on the contrary that Aristotle's effort is increasingly directed toward a revaluation of the knowledge coming from the lower reality, and the realm of inferior bodies and things.

PA's reference to Heraclitus is thus a key text for interpreting Aristotle's evolution toward the more scientific character of his whole philosophical enterprise. The older opposition between what is immutable and pure on the one hand and what is mutable and impure on the other loses its importance. Not only the former, but also the latter fully acquires the status of an object worthy of scientific investigation. As Gotthelf has underlined, although heavenly bodies are worthier than living beings, the latter have the priority within the scientific enterprise because knowledge of them is more solid and complete.[9]

The universal beauty of nature that Aristotle emphasises also suggests how to interpret his conception of abnormality and monstrosity, as well as his position vis-à-vis his predecessors. Geoffrey Lloyd links Aristotle's conception of beauty to what tends to unity, immobility and superiority, as opposed to what is moving and changing.[10] This is the reason why, in Lloyd's view, Aristotle's biology, in modern terms, is fixist and opposed to that of Empedocles, who already holds a transformist view of life. This also suggests why monstrosity holds a central place in Empedocles' process of nature's unending transformation, while it is peripheral to Aristotle's view of a stable and immutable nature. Whereas the monster is part and parcel of the cycle of normality for Empedocles, it is, on the contrary, a tendentially unique event for Aristotle.[11]

---

[7] Aubenque (1962), p. 27.

[8] C. Wilson, 'From Limits to Laws: The Construction of the Nomological Image of Nature in Early Modern Philosophy', in Daston, Stolleis eds. (2008), pp. 13–28, esp. p. 15.

[9] See A. Gotthelf, 'First principles in Aristotle's *Parts of Animals*', in Gotthelf, Lennox eds. (1987), p. 170. See also Johnson (2005), p. 229.

[10] See Lloyd (1996), p. 113.

[11] See also Morgan (1984), pp. 124 ff. and A. Jaulin, 'Aristote et la pathologie politique', in Ibrahim ed. (2005), pp. 29–45.

Beauty is thus the character of *normal* nature, of its ontological as well as its logical status.¹² Beauty offers the scientist not only an aesthetic satisfaction in its contemplation; it also suggests to him nature's order, coherence and consistency. It would be difficult to overestimate the importance of this aspect of Aristotle's reflection. Nature's worthiness and beauty are the key to understanding the deep transformation that Aristotle imposes upon the Greek conception of the relation between the divine and the terrestrial domain. In order to accomplish this, Aristotle needs a powerful new theory of causality, a theory that joins together what is good with what is ordered and beautiful. It is the study of inferior things, of the abnormal and even monstrous ones, that makes us able to grasp nature's unity and consistency.

One of the most remarkable achievements of Aristotle's new philosophy is his theory of causes, developed in particular in book II of the *Physics*. This theory is central to our discussion, since it also involves one of the most impressive reflections about the concept of monstrosity, which Aristotle brings to a new level of cogency and relevance for any future scientific enterprise. Aristotle's point of departure is a sound critique of his predecessors: the idealists on the one hand, and the mechanicists on the other.

The exponents of the philosophy of ideas, in Aristotle's view, fall into error because they do not well enough distinguish mathematical and physical entities. Whereas the former can be abstracted, the latter cannot, at least not in the same way. When the idealist thus considers the idea of physical entities, his abstraction depends on the illegitimate operation of separating the idea of the thing from the thing itself. While Aristotle's aim is to criticise the excessive abstraction involved in Plato's philosophy, as delineated for example in *Prm*. 130 b 2–3 and *Phd*. 74 b–c, one should not read this passage of *Ph*. II.2 as a full commitment to some form of radical realism or nominalism. As Charlton clearly explains, even Aristotelian forms are 'separable in account' from things.¹³ Precisely this separation in account, I believe, is the ground for Aristotle's original treatment of monstrosity as something *formally* separable, distinguished from and subordinated to normality, according to the *Physics*.

---

¹² As Gilson (1971), p. 40, has remarkably noted, for Aristotle, *pulchrum index ueri*. Gilson claims Aristotle's *modernity*, matching his attitude, specifically on the point of nature's beauty, with Darwin's perspective. I believe, on the contrary, that Lloyd's considerations on Aristotle and Empedocles are also true for what concerns Aristotle and Darwin, and that their idea of nature's beauty suggests the opposition rather than the analogy between them.

¹³ Charlton (1970), p. 94: '[...] that is, an account can be given of the form of a thing which is separate from, does not involve, the account of its matter'.

A further proof of Aristotle's interest in the formal possibility of the separation of ideas from things or, in other words, in the identification of something essential and distinguishable from things themselves, is his criticism of the physicists' position. Falling into the opposite error, the physicists' only concern is matter, as is testified by Empedocles or Democritus, who 'have remarkably little to say about kinds of things and what is the constituent essence of them.'[14] The mechanicists consider only matter and its composition, because they lack any interest in what is above it and shapes it according to an essential principle.

Both idealists and physicists thus miss the point, in Aristotle's view, by focusing respectively on too high and abstract a level or on too low and concrete a level of nature. They all lack an appropriate theory of causality because they miss the proper distinction between the different genres of cause and their correct interaction. These genres must *all* be considered by the investigators of nature, without leaving any of them aside.

More importantly, Aristotle introduces a concept that, although recognised by previous philosophers, did not find its proper place as a pillar of the theory of causality, namely the end or goal of things themselves. Things, in fact, must be studied in motion. More precisely, they must be studied according to the systematic and continuous motion that is part of the whole and unending transformation of nature itself. Nature's movement – this is Aristotle's strong point – is directed toward a goal or an end: 'The [. . .] enquiry must embrace both the purpose or end and the means to that end. And the "nature" is the goal for the sake of which the rest exist; for if any systematic and continuous movement is directed to a goal, this goal is an end in the sense of the purpose to which the movement is a means.'[15]

Whereas the idealist erroneously concerns himself with abstract ideas, and the mechanicist fallaciously focuses on matter alone, the physicist who follows the correct method, i.e. the Aristotelian one, finds his middle ground by reintroducing the form within a process of transformation of nature that allows him to grasp every aspect of nature's causality, the multiplicity of its components and, more importantly, the proper priority and hierarchy among them. The philosopher, in fact, '[is concerned] with the form primarily and essentially [. . .], with the material up to a certain point [. . .]. For his main concern is with the goal, which is formal; but he deals only with such forms as are conceptually, but not factually, detachable from the material in which they occur.'[16]

---

[14] Arist. *Ph.* II.2, 194 a 20 ff.
[15] Arist. *Ph.* II.2, 194 a 28.
[16] Arist. *Ph.* II.2, 194 b 11.

Having established the correct ground of a theory of causality, Aristotle can now move to properly define its multiple components which, with little variation, are repeated in other major texts, such as *Metaph.* I.2, 983 a 24 ff. These are the material cause (ὕλη, ὑποκείμενον), the formal cause (οὐσία, τί ἦν εἶναι, εἶδος, παράδειγμα), the efficient cause (ἀρχὴ τῆς κινήσεως) and the final cause (οὗ ἕνεκα καί τἀγαθόν), which the Scholastics eventually call respectively the *causa materialis, formalis, efficiens* and *finalis*. These principles cover, in Aristotle's view, all the many senses in which *because* can be said of all things for which *why* can be asked: to the question of why something is what it is, several answers can be given. This is true of every natural thing. If it is relevant for *normal* things, however, it is even more relevant for abnormal and *monstrous* ones. Moreover, I think that if a new treatment of what is abnormal and monstrous becomes possible in Aristotle's physics, it is precisely on account of his original and powerful approach that he is able to grasp the many *becauses* of monstrosity.

The first dimension of causality to consider is the material one, i.e. 'the existence of *material* for the generating process to start from [. . .].'[17] The ὕλη is an immanent and inherent (ἐνυπάρχω) kind of αἰτία. Aristotle stresses its essentiality and necessity to the phenomenon in question. He also stresses, however, its distinction from another causality, which is *not* inherent but external, and moves the process forward from the outside.[18] The material cause is not sufficient for anything to be what it is.[19] The formal αἰτία brings us closer to the *definition* of the thing, and what is essential for it.

The relation between the material and the formal introduces the dimension of Becoming, which Aristotle had used in particular to criticise his idealist predecessors. Things should not be conceived only for what they are, but rather what they become, how they become what they are, and all this vis-à-vis what they *should* be. The form, thus, speaks of the thing's essence more in the sense of what it *has to be* than what it actually *is*.[20]

This *normative* dimension of the causal principle is, on the contrary, completely absent from the third αἰτία that Aristotle speaks about, namely the efficient one, the moving factor that induces the transformation and acts as an engine toward it.[21] This is the main, possibly the only causal principle recognised by the earlier mechanicists, certainly within atomism, and Aristotle's point is that, although necessary, the efficient agent is far from being sufficient

---

[17] Arist. *Ph.* II.3, 194 b 24–7.
[18] See also *Metaph.* XII.4, 1070 b 22.
[19] Arist. *Ph.* II.3, 194 b 27–9.
[20] Cornford, in Aristotle (1980), p. 128: '[the thing] must have actually "arrived" and realized its "being-what-it-had-to-be"'.
[21] Arist. *Ph.* II.3, 194 b 29–33.

for any thing to become what it has to be, namely what one can call its form or its essence.

To the form and essence, Aristotle adds a last and fourth causal principle, namely the τέλος: 'the *end* or purpose, for the sake of which the process is initiated [...].'[22] Although sometimes difficult to distinguish from the form itself, the τέλος really epitomises Aristotle's pivotal argument in his original theory of causality. The four genres are all essential, and yet the end acts as a unifying principle that gives its ultimate sense to the causal process in its full complexity, a complexity that, once again, was lacking in all previous philosophical accounts: '[T]he goal or *end* in view, [...] animates all the other determinant factors as the best they can attain to; for the attainment of that "for the sake of which" anything exists or is done is its final and best possible achievement (though of course "best" in this connexion means no more than "taken to be the best").'[23]

In this passage a crucial principle surfaces, a principle that is pivotal for our entire discussion on monstrosity. Aristotle explicitly suggests that the becoming-what-something-should-be happens, following the *end*, in the best possible manner, but not always perfectly. After having criticised Plato for the excessive abstraction and the separation between the absolute perfection of ideas and the actual reality of things, Aristotle is somehow forced to reintroduce this hiatus in the ontological structure of reality – not anymore on a transcendent ground, though, but rather on the immanent pattern that brings things to what they are, or rather to what they should be.[24] Perfection in general exists. Yet, individual things in particular are far from being perfect, in their becoming what they are. They *tend* to their perfection, and this is their end or goal. The more they achieve it, the more perfect they are. Yet the complexity and intricacy of the causal factors might interfere with this goal, and make the processs only as effective as the best it can do. Here lies our question: In a system grounded on ends and goals, what is the specific τέλος of monstrosity?

Kept at the margin by Aristotle, monstrosity infiltrates the core of his system in these pages of the *Physics*, setting itself at the very centre of his theory of causality. The notion of τέλος resolves many problems that Aristotle ascribes to predecessors, and in particular to mechanicists. Yet it also raises new questions for him, especially in the field of biology and the generation of

---

[22] Arist. *Ph.* II.3, 194 b 33–5.
[23] Arist. *Ph.* II.3, 195 a 23–6.
[24] Solmsen (1963), p. 487, insists on the immanent character of nature's craftsmanship and its capacity to produce the best.

life. I believe that this is the crucial point of Aristotle's system and that around this point the question of monstrosity will be tackled in future centuries. No surprise, then, that the τέλος has attracted so much attention in scholarship, in recent and less recent times.

In his seminal *Geschichte des Materialismus*, Lange explains the Socratic origin of the reaction against ancient materialism.[25] This reaction is grounded in a radical separation between matter and form, on which both Plato and Aristotle follow Socrates. This origin is religiously based in the desire of seeing the gods present, and actively working, in the world. The religious approach finds an early support in the scientific one, and in particular in the concept of teleology. Anthropomorphic and providential at the same time, the Socratic explanation is fully compatible with the more scientific one of Aristotle. His opposition between the material and the formal principle of causal explanation is, in Lange's view, a development of the Socratic approach, paradigmatically presented in Xenophon's *Memorabilia*, in the conversation between Socrates and Aristodemus:

> Do you [sc. Aristodemus] not think then that he who created man from the beginning had some useful end in view [ὠφέλεια] when he endowed him with his several senses, giving eyes to see visible objects, ears to hear sounds? Would odors again be of any use to us had we not been endowed with nostrils? What perception should we have of sweet and bitter and all things pleasant to the palate had we not tongue in our mouth to discriminate between them? Besides these, are there not other contrivances that look like the results of forethought [πρόνοια]? Thus the eyeballs, being weak, are set behind eyelids, that open like doors when we want to see, and close when we sleep: on the lids grow lashes through which the very winds filter harmlessly: above the eyes is a coping of brows that lets no drop of sweat from the head hurt them. The ears catch all sounds, but are never choked with them. Again, the incisors of all creatures are adapted for cutting, the molars for receiving food from them and grinding it. And again, the mouth, through which the food they want goes in, is set near the eyes and nostrils; but since what goes out is unpleasant, the ducts through which it passes are turned away and removed as far as possible from the organs of sense. With such signs of forethought in these arrangements, can you doubt whether they are the works of chance [τύχη] or design [γνώμη]?[26]

---

[25] Lange (1873–5), ch. III.
[26] X. *Mem.* I.4.5–6. On Xenophon's divine providence as part of the elaboration of the concept of nature as a craftsman, see Solmsen (1963), p. 479.

This text, widely read for centuries, testifies to the strength of Socrates' idea which, without directly addressing biological issues, reverberates through Aristotle's more scientific and less anthropomorphic theory of final causality. When Aristotle criticises his materialist predecessors, in Lange's view, he is merely developing the Socratic and Platonic origin of the theological, teleological and providential view.[27]

Ancient philosophers explain nature by intellectually decomposing it into pure basic and material elements, such as fire, water, etc. This is the right pattern, in their view, to approach the real nature of Being. For Aristotle, on the contrary, such decomposition of nature means moving away from Being and its essential understanding, which lies first and foremost in the formal and teleological reality. Preus goes as far as maintaining that matter itself is intelligible only through form and organisation.[28] Matter would not really exist as absolutely independent from its formal reality, without a given form. Matter is necessarily conditioned to the process of teleological formation, and thus ontologically subordinated to it.

Although a 'mere' development of previous Socratic positions, the core of Aristotle's teleology is nonetheless fundamentally important to his philosophy. Causality as a whole could not be understood, for Aristotle, without a strong idea of teleology. Monte R. Johnson has reconstructed the modern debate around Aristotle's finalism, in particular for authors as important as Hegel, Gomperz and Wieland.[29] Johnson elucidates the proper place, aim and

---

[27] Simplicius already underlines the agreement between Aristotle and Plato's Socrates. See Simp. *in Ph.* 308.25-33: 'For all knowledge which stems from the causes is most appropriate for a proper understanding, but that which stems from the final cause is the most important of all.' Aristotle seems to be agreeing with Socrates in the *Phaedo* when he tells the natural scientist to press his enquiry into cause as far as the final cause. For in the *Phaedo* [*Phd.* 97 c] Socrates says, 'If anyone were to want to find the cause of each thing, how it comes-to-be, is detroyed and exists, he should discover this about it – how it is best for it to exist or to affect something else or to be affected itself – in other words he should discover for the sake of what each thing comes-to-be or exists.'

[28] Preus (1975), pp. 256 ff.

[29] Johnson (2005), pp. 182: 'Some hold that teleological explanations are appropriate only where reduction to so-called mechanical forces (material-efficient causes) is impossible. Kant originally formulated this position in the *Critique of Teleological Judgement*. He distinguished and opposed "mechanism" (efficient causes) and "teleology" (final causes), and argued that mechanical causes should be determined so far as possible, and that it is only when something remains unexplained (which always and only happens in organic contexts) that it is right to invoke "final causes". [. . .] Hegel, but not Kant himself, pointed out the similarity of what Kant was arguing for and Aristotle's teleology.' Johnson refers to section 204 on *Teleologie* of Hegel's *Enzyklopädie der philosophischen Wissenschaften*. See Hegel (1969–71), VIII, pp. 359–61. On Aristotle's teleology see also Berti (1989–90), D. Charles, 'Teleological causation in the *Physics*', in Judson (1991), pp. 101–28.

scope of the teleological argument within Aristotelianism by showing that too often finalism has been undermined by modern historians and interpreters. In particular, Aristotle's teleological argument has been weakened by considering it an additional principle of explanation of phenomena.[30] Only when the efficient principle reveals itself insufficient to explain things, the majority of scholars since Kant have maintained, does Aristotle bring the final cause into the picture. Gotthelf, for example, claims that although Aristotle sincerely believes in ends, he considers them only when material and efficient elements do not exhaust the explanation of phenomena.[31] Johnson is adamant, on the contrary, in explaining that finalism is a pillar of Aristotelianism, and that the final cause should not be subordinated or postponed to other causal principles of explanation.

Teleology, thus, is not an auxiliary principle that fills the gap of the epistemological insufficiency of other explanatory principles. Following Johnson, I believe that the relation between the end and the other causes must be turned upside down: because matter is functional and subordinated to teleology, even the efficient cause cannot be considered separately and independently from the end. The teleological explanation is not reducible to any other explanation, and it is on the contrary the framework within which all other causes acquire their meaning, without being separable from them. The four causes should thus be seen not so much as organic components that add to each other, as parts of a single whole, to define causality. They should be seen as individual and distinct aspects of the causal principle, irreducible to each other and contributing to explain different sides of causality, with different degrees of clarity and cogency depending on the phenomenon under scrutiny.[32]

Johnson, however, claims that not everything is teleologically explicable in nature, as for example rainfall in the meteorological domain or waste as a residue of nutriment's concoction in the animal realm.[33] Although not explicable, I believe that everything is at least teleologically *conceivable*, even if efficient causes alone give us a satisfactory explanation of the phenomenon, e.g. of rainfall, or if, at the opposite end, they fail to do so, because we do not *teleologically* see what something, e.g. waste, is for the sake of. We can certainly say that the end does not have the same explanatory strength in every case or domain. And this is precisely where monstrosity comes to the foreground: monsters and monstrous phenomena challenge the teleological principle and

---

[30] This is the main thesis of Wieland, who argues against scholars such as Zeller and Hartmann. See Wieland (1962), p. 256.
[31] Gotthelf (1976-7), also included, in a slightly revised version, in Gotthelf, Lennox eds. (1987).
[32] See also Quarantotto (2005), esp. p. 342.
[33] Johnson (2005), p. 186.

strain it to its highest degree, assuming a central position in Aristotle's biological works. Aristotle is aware that only by succesfully taming the concept of monstrosity can his system acquire the necessary strength, coherence and consistency.

Let us now take a step back to Xenophon's account of Socrates' praise of teleology. In his dialogue with Aristodemus, as we have seen, Socrates insists on universal purposefulness, which depends on the intelligent design of the creator, whose forethought (πρόνοια) is clearly readable in the works of nature. Can anyone doubt – Socrates ironically asks – whether such a work has to be ascribed to chance (τύχη) or to design (γνώμη)? The opposition between chance and design, as well as the concept of πρόνοια,[34] are crucial for our discussion, not only because Xenophon's Socrates is challenging the ancient mechanicists' theories, and in particular the atomists', but also because Aristotle himself develops the most extraordinary criticism of chance in his age, by introducing it within his theory of causality. It is also crucial because Aristotle explicitly draws his argument on monstrosity from this theory. Are monsters chance *events* in nature?

Ph. II. 4–6, in which Aristotle develops his critique, remained the reference for centuries in the debate on necessity and chance. In these topical chapters, Aristotle sets out to give a full and exhaustive account of whether or not chance exists, and how chance should be understood. Against his predecessors' theories, Aristotle aims at clarifying a traditional discussion by granting the fact that we all regularly ascribe events to fortune or luck (τύχη), and accident (αὐτόματον); that is, we consider luck and accident as real causes of things and events.[35]

Aristotle aims at emphasising the inconsistency of his main polemical targets, namely Leucippus and Democritus, by stressing that, on the one hand, they question the existence of chance by declaring that everything exists for a definite cause. They attribute, on the other hand, 'our Heaven and all the worlds to chance happenings, saying that the vortex and shifting that disentangled the chaos and established the cosmic order came by chance'. Empedocles' cosmogony

---

[34] Which already has the sense, in Xenophon, of *prouidentia* and *cura*, πρόνοιας διuinae ἔργον. See Sturz (1964), III, p. 688. On providence see Auroux, pp. 2098–2900, Di Berardino a cura di (1983), cc. 2942–5, Lalande, pp. 847–8, Ritter, Gründer hrsg. (1971–2007), XI, cc. 1206–18, RE XXIII.1, p. 747 and Suppl. XIV, pp. 562–5, Daremberg, Saglio éds. (1877–1919), IV, pp. 715–16, Betz et al. hrsg. (1988–2005), VIII, cc. 1212–20 (= Betz et al. eds. (2007), X, pp. 477–81), EK III, cc. 1705–10 (= Fahlbusch et al. eds. (1999), IV, pp. 402–4), DTC XIII.1, cc. 935–1023, TRE XXXV, pp. 303–27, Lacoste, pp. 946–52, Fahlbusch et al. eds. (1999), X, cc. 219–24.

[35] Arist. *Ph.* II.4 195 b 30 ff.

is also targeted here, insofar as he says that the members of animals are haphazardly formed: 'τὰ μόρια τῶν ζῴων ἀπὸ τύχης γενέσθαι τὰ πλεῖστά φησιν.'[36] The main inconsistency that Aristotle sees at work here is the distinction between the heavenly bodies and the terrestrial domain, which corresponds – according to this account – to different logics and should thus be treated differently.

It is indeed strange that earlier philosophers, in Aristotle's view, deem that the heavens had a random origin, when they also recognise that 'neither animals nor plants are, or come to be, by chance, but are all caused by Nature or Mind [φύσιν ἢ νοῦν] (for it is not a matter of chance what springs from a given sperm, since an olive comes from such a one, and a man from such another)'. Aristotle here introduces the argument of the regularity of events, which plays a pivotal role in his treatment of monstrosity. The aim is not so much to deny chance, but rather to redefine it and reintroduce it into the new theory of causality. An olive tree gives olives, and humans give a human: no monstrosity, in the ordinary process of natural generation, and thus no chance. Only in the *ordinary* processes though, since Aristotle is too well aware of the existence of monstrosities both in the vegetal and the human realm. Regularly, though – that is to say for the most part – one can observe a Mind acting in nature, precisely as Xenophon's Socrates had taught to Aristodemus.

The regularity of events is the tool that Aristotle employs to narrow down this difficult field of enquiry: when things always or almost always happen in the same way, chance is not concerned in any possible manner.[37] If things repeat themselves with inflexible regularity, there must be a cause, even if that cause is unknown or difficult to grasp. Still, an enormous number of phenomena and events question the philosopher about the existence of chance. There are things that happen exceptionally, or occasionally. There are also things that can be considered recognisable ends for a particular agent, yet were not, however, within the initial plan of action of that same agent, and therefore are

---

[36] Arist. *Ph*. II.4 195 b 30 ff. In Philoponos's view, however, Aristotle blames Democritus more than Empedocles. See Phlp. *in Ph*. 261.26–262.2: '[Empedocles] says the parts of animals, most of them, came to be in this way in accordance with chance as though they had come to be from forethought, the front teeth sharp and suitable for tearing and the molars for grinding. So that [the ancients] are worthy of accusation because they say that some things exist altogether by chance but have specified nothing concerning chance. But Empedocles ascribes [only] certain small-scale things to chance, and if he has given no discussion of it might be worthy of less accusation; but there are some, [Aristotle] says, meaning Democritus and his followers, who thought it to be a cause of this heaven and of the divinest among the things that are manifest, but did not discuss it even slightly.'

[37] Arist. *Ph*. II.5, 196 b 10 ff.

reached *accidentally* (κατὰ συμβεβηκός);[38] they are unintended consequences. Aristotle points out the purposive character of such actions in *Ph.* II. 5, i.e. even if the end is accidentally reached, a purpose must be involved in the initial plan. Furthermore, although the name of τύχη is used, this is *not* a cause, either in the causal or in the final sense of the term. A result reached κατὰ συμβεβηκός is rather an effect of the complex web of causes and effects accumulated in the process or action under scrutiny.

The necessity of the purposive nature of actions, even when we speak about chance or luck, is again underlined in II. 6, in which Aristotle claims that neither inanimate things nor beasts and infants can accomplish anything whatsoever by τύχη, precisely because they do not exercise any deliberate choice, and thus their action is, by definition, not purposive in nature. Aristotle, however, recalls here the category of αὐτόματον, which was central for Democritus. Aristotle also intends to explain once and for all its meaning, a meaning that remains obscure, in his view, in previous authors. The etymology that Aristotle gives is wrong. His mistake, though, makes his argument exceptionally interesting for our present discussion. He claims the term comes from μάτην, i.e. 'for nothing' or 'to no purpose', meaning that the end or purpose is not realised, but only the means to it: 'αὐτόματον, as the form of the word implies, means an occurrence that is in itself (αὐτό) to no purpose (μάτην)'.

Aristotle's false etymology becomes directly relevant for our discussion on monstrosity. It would be inappropriate, Aristotle claims, to speak about τύχη in cases where Nature's production is παρὰ φύσιν (contrary to nature). In this case, we may instead attribute it to αὐτόματον. But then the question resurfaces: what would be monstrosity's purpose in nature? If nature is teleological, although not inflexibly so, how can monsters fit into it?

Aristotle is adamant in explaining that being 'to no purpose', as an αὐτόματος event is, does not mean being without a τέλος. A τέλος always exists, and in this sense a teleological dimension always operates in any and every causal determination, although sharing its place with other kind of causes, as illustrated above. 'To no purpose' *only* means, in this sense, that the τέλος has not been properly reached, that it has not been achieved according to the essential and formal nature of the thing in question.

The failure to reach the proper end is particularly evident in the biological realm, as we will see. Before moving to the analysis of the biological works, however, it is important to highlight something that has remained implicit in

---

[38] This is sometimes translated as *incidental*. Although there is a slight difference, both accidental and incidental depends on *cado* and refers to the same contingent way of happening.

the exposé of the causal theory, namely the conflictual nature of every single causal process, in which different forces act one upon the other, and collide against each other. Within this conflict, Aristotle takes a stand, unambiguously, in favour of teleology as the principal dimension of causality: everything that resists teleology must be deemed abnormal and monstrous. Αὐτόματον and τύχη, Aristotle clarifies, have to be related to efficient causality, for they are always attached to the multiple and complex web of efficient causes. They must also be subordinated, though, to the teleological principle which is now presented as ontologically prior and superior to the others:

> Since there is nothing incidental unless there is something primary for it to be incidental to, it follows that there can be no incidental causation except as incident to direct causation. Chance and fortune, therefore, imply the antecedent activity of mind and Nature [νοῦν καὶ φύσιν] as causes.[39]

Teleology has the priority. The τέλος commands the process, whereas the αὐτόματον sometimes resists it. The random happening of the latter is the failure of the former. This priority is confirmed in *Ph.* II. 7, in which the specific skills required of the natural philosopher are precisely those that make her able to recognise the purposeful character of nature (as well as the reasons of its failure), namely its capacity of constituting each thing's proper end.[40] This is why the natural philosopher needs a specific starting point for the enquiry. Not every beginning would put her on the right track. Here, Aristotle can exploit another original and innovative aspect of his theory, namely the question of potentiality (δύναμις) and actuality (ἐνέργεια).

By decomposing Being into these two different categories, potentiality and actuality, Aristotle is able to account for Becoming, which denotes not a type of creation but rather a passage – a passage from one mode of Being to another; from the conditions that make something possible, i.e. potentiality, to the actual realisation of the thing itself, i.e. its actuality.[41] The δύναμις is

---

[39] Arist. *Ph.* II.6, 198 a 7–10. In other texts, the order seems to be different: how things are, by necessity or by chance, is the starting point, which is later framed in a teleological structure. See PA III.3, 663 b 22, the famous passage on the deer's horns: 'The necessary nature [ἀναγκαίας φύσεως] being what she is, we must now describe how the rational nature [λόγον φύσις] takes advantage from what she finds available to her.' First comes their necessity, and eventually the explanation of how nature takes advantage of them.

[40] Arist. *Ph.* II.7, 198 b 3 ff.

[41] Arist. *Metaph.* V.7, 1017 a 35 ff. On δύναμις and ἐνέργεια see Auroux pp. 2122–7 and 23–4, Lalande, pp. 859–61 and 16–19, Ritter, Gründer hrsg. (1971–2007), I, cc. 134–42, RAC IV, pp. 415–58 and RAC V, pp. 4–51. On the various uses in Aristotle see Bonitz, pp. 206–7 and 251. See also TGL III, cc. 1706–9 and IV, cc. 1064–5.

chronologically prior to the ἐνέργεια, but the ἐνέργεια has the ontological priority, with respect to the question of perfection, and explains the δύναμις, not vice versa. In order to explain how this relation works in the universe, but especially in the terrestrial and biological domain, Aristotle makes use of a comparison that will be extremely influential for centuries, namely the analogy between nature and art.

The physicist needs a starting point to analyse and comprehend Being *qua* Becoming. Depending on it, her enquiry will be correct or faulty:

> We ought surely to begin with things as they are actually observed to be when completed. Even in building the fact is that the particular stages of the process come about because the Form of the house is such and such, rather than that the house is such and such because the process of its formation follows a particular course: the process is for the sake of the actual thing, the thing is not for the sake of the process [γένεσις ἕνεκα τῆς οὐσίας ἐστίν, ἀλλ'οὐκ ἡ οὐσία ἕνεκα τῆς γενέσεως].[42]

That the final result and the outcome should be used as a starting point both to judge the perfection of something and to produce it is self-evident in the domain of art and construction. The same is true in nature, in which things are produced, and should be studied, following the same pattern, from what is ontologically prior to what comes chronologically first.

One may see here how much Aristotle has learned from his predecessors, but also how he chooses his place in the battle between finalism and mechanicism. Whereas Preus claims that Aristotle acknowledges Empedocles' and Democritus's achievements, and prefers them even to Plato, Taylor suggests that, precisely in this introductory passage of *PA*, Aristotle shows where he stands: *against* the mechanicists; he entirely follows Plato's finalism. Although Aristotle is most of the time fair when he presents his predecessors' opinions, I think that here he makes the development of Plato's finalism *against* the mechanicists one of the major pillars of his philosophical system.[43]

Aristotle draws on Plato's presentation of the opposition between γένεσις, production, generation, coming into being, and οὐσία, stable being, immutable reality, substance, essence (also opposed to non-being, τὸ μὴ εἶναι, or to affections, πάθη, or to accidents, συμβεβηκότα). Plato's most relevant text is the *Philebus*, in which Socrates asks Protarchus whether γένεσις should be considered for the sake of οὐσία, or the opposite. Protarchus is puzzled by the apparent naivety of Socrates' question. His ironical answer is used to introduce

---

[42] Arist. *PA* I.1, 640 a 12 ff.
[43] See Preus (1975), pp. 28 ff. *Contra* see Taylor (1928), p. 302, and Wieland (1962), p. 273.

the interesting parallel between nature and art that Aristotle also makes use of. It is like asking – Protarchus responds to Socrates – whether shipbuilding is for the sake of ships, or ships for the sake of shipbuilding! It is true, Socrates confirms, in the same manner that, in general, one can say that 'every instance of generation is for the sake of some being or other, and generation in general is for the sake of being in general'.[44]

Aristotle follows Plato in firmly establishing teleology within nature, as the analogy with art and crafts best reveals. What Aristotle draws from Plato, though, is no less important than what of his he rejects. As we have seen above, Plato's natural teleology has a strongly transcendent character, whereby nature becomes the artefact of a demiurge whose mind, i.e. an exterior and transcendent power, orders elements otherwise left to chaos. The good and the best implied in Aristotle's teleological nature, on the contrary, are intrinsic and inherent to natural beings.[45] As Pierre Aubenque has rightly underlined, similar things serve different purposes in Plato and Aristotle.[46] The scientist and the philosopher, thus, must still look for things' models – but within nature itself, not in the sky of ideas nor in the demiurge's mind – and must, on that model, ground every further enquiry. This is Aristotle's basis for his severe criticism against the mechanicists, in which he makes use once again of what he certainly considers his strongest argument regarding generation, namely the analogy with art and the regularity that one observes in nature:

> So Empedocles was wrong when he said that many of the characteristics which animals have are due to some accident in the process of their formation, as when he accounts for the vertebrae of the backbone by saying 'the fetus gets twisted and so the backbone is broken into pieces':[47] he is unaware (a) that the seed which gives rise to the animal must to begin with have the appropriate specific character; and (b) that the producing agent was pre-existent: it was chronologically earlier as well as logically earlier: in other words, men are begotten by men, and therefore the process of the child's formation is what it is because its parent was a man.[48]

Thus the process of generation depends on the finished and perfect product, and not the other way around. Mechanicists like Empedocles have wasted their time in looking for material causes, because the 'formal' nature is of more

---

[44] Pl. *Phlb.* 54 a–c. See also *supra*.
[45] See D. M. Balme, 'The place of biology in Aristotle's philosophy', in Gotthelf, Lennox eds. (1987), pp. 9–20, who quotes several different texts to support this thesis.
[46] Aubenque (1962), pp. 332–3. See also Johnson (2005), p. 81.
[47] *Vorsokr.* 31 B 97 (= LM [22] EMP. D177, R20).
[48] Arist. PA I.1, 640 a 20 ff.

fundamental importance than every other aspect of individual things (ἡ γὰρ κατὰ τὴν μορφὴν φύσις κυριωτέρα τῆς ὑλικῆς φύσεως).[49] The methodology thus proceeds from above or, if one wants to distinguish between Plato's transcendence and Aristotle's immanence, it proceeds backwards, namely from the end towards the beginning, from the actuality to the potentiality, from the finished to the unfinished, from the cause 'for the sake of which' to every other kind of cause:

> Whenever there is evidently an End towards which a motion goes forward unless something stands in its way, then we always assert that the motion has the End for its purpose. From this it is evident that something of the kind really exists – that, in fact, which we call 'Nature', because in fact we do not find any chance creature being formed from a particular seed, but A comes from a, and B from b; nor does any chance seed come from any chance individual.[50]

In the same way that the actuality comes ontologically before the potentiality, the finished organism comes before its seed. No chance creature exists that is formed by a specific seed whose characteristics we know. This experience rules out chance and the mechanistic encounters of material and efficient causes as a principle of explanation of the cosmos, as in the theories of Empedocles and Democritus. It does not rule out, however, the question of monstrosity. As we have just read, in fact, Aristotle's explanation is that a process reaches its evident end *unless something stands in its way*: ἐμποδίζω, 'to be a hindrance to or interfering with something', and also 'to thwart'. Because the process toward perfection can be hindered, chance and its power within the generating process are reintroduced into the picture.[51] Seeds do not produce randomly. They can, however, produce monsters.

Along the line of monstrosity, once again, Aristotle develops his critique of mechanicism. If one starts from the potentiality, the process is left open to modifications and to every possible outcome. This is Empedocles' transformist solution. If, on the contrary, one starts from the actuality and the end, the process is closed. No random outcome is possible and, most of all, no transformation is going to happen vis-à-vis what one already knows and already sees. The mechanicist conceives of the transformation, because she does not have

---

[49] Arist. PA I.1, 640 b 28–9.
[50] Arist. PA I.1, 641 b 24–9.
[51] Ancient commentators already read the end, i.e. 'that for the sake of which', as being potentially hindered by some obstacle. See for example Phlp. *in Ph.* 235.18–20: 'He has in mind, [it seems] to me, change which goes forward in an unhindered fashion and is limited by itself, with no outside cause bringing it to a halt. For if it is interrupted, that state of stability [which results] from its being interrupted is not an end of the change.'

any perfection to guide the process. The fixist, on the contrary, rules out the transformation, because there is a superior perfection that, although sometimes hindered, guides the whole process. For the mechanicist and the transformist, monstrosity is an essential part of the process. For the formalist and the fixist, on the contrary, it is an anomaly that the system will soon correct by eliminating the less fit to survive, such as the Empedoclean man-headed oxen.[52]

Here, Aristotle firmly establishes the opposition between the mechanicist's and the finalist's methodologies. After Aristotle, 'how and for the sake of what' things are what they are will not be one and the same question anymore. The *how* and the *what for* questions will be perceived, on the contrary, as two different issues, polemically opposed one to the other, corresponding to different logics and methods of enquiry. The consequents will be seen not only as following the antecedents, but also opposed to them. What commands the process, the former or the latter? There is no doubt that, for Aristotle, the consequent – i.e. the end – dominates the antecedent. In terms of anatomy and physiology, for example, the organ perfectly formed explains its function as well as the process of its formation. Animals have eyes and are able to see not because of *how* the eye is, but rather because of *what* the eye *is for*, since sight belongs to and is part of animals' essence.

Although Aristotle is faithful to his grounding principle that nature does not make anything in vain, but everything is in view of some end,[53] his investigation of this principle is particularly pregnant with implications in his *Generation of Animals* in which, together with the *Physics*, he deals with monstrosity. Again, Aristotle makes clear that an accurate theory of causality is essential. Causes are the main theme of the book.[54] Together with their definition, it is fundamentally important to grasp their order, relationship and hierarchy, in order to understand nature's offspring in general, and their perfection in particular. Although all animals are worthy of study, as we have previously seen, not all of them are equally worthy when compared to one another. On the contrary, Aristotle's biology is unfolded as a real science of hierarchical differences, both among and within individuals and species:

> The object which [...] takes shape may be more valuable in kind or less valuable; and the differences herein depend upon the envelope which encloses the soul-principle; and the causes which determine this are the situations where the process takes place and the physical substance which is enclosed.[55]

[52] Darwin's erroneous attribution of this theory to Aristotle is remarkable. See Darwin (1887), III, p. 252, C. Darwin to W. Ogle, 22 February 1882. See also Lerner (1969), p. 87 and *passim*.
[53] See again *de An*. III.12, 434 a 31–2.
[54] Arist. GA I.1.
[55] Arist. GA III.11, 762 a 24–7.

Aristotle employs the concept of τίμιος/ἄτιμος to suggest that things are all distributed on a scale, from the worthiest to the less honorable. The reader is thus brought to the edge of monstrosity, though rigidly within the framework of normality: although of different value, one vis-à-vis the other, animals and plants are never exceptions to nature. As Aristotle says elsewhere, anything can be ἀνάπηρος, lame and mutilated, or πήρωμα, deformed, imperfect, as opposed to τέλειος, fully grown, accomplished, perfect in its kind.[56] He rules out the idea of a break between a normal inside and an abnormal outside of nature, by introducing hierarchy and differences within it. As a result, the concept of monstrosity becomes central to his description. It is now time for him to explain the very meaning of the τέρατα.

Aristotle's argument on monsters follows from his theory of causality and, in particular, from the teleological character of nature developed in his *Metaphysics* and *Physics*, but also – and perhaps especially – visible in the animal world. Monsters exist, and they can be explained by the relationship that the theory of causality has established between matter and form, the material and the formal cause. When matter is not 'mastered', Aristotle argues, the offspring presents monstrous features. The examples that Aristotle uses, e.g. a calf with a child's head or a sheep with an ox's head, unsurprisingly recall Empedocles' monsters.[57] In fact, Aristotle intends to seriously treat and explain the phenomenon of monstrosity, at the same time denying certain kinds of monstrosity, and in particular a kind of causal theory that *could* explain them as Empedocles himself and Democritus had attempted to do:

> In no case are they what they are alleged to be [i.e. *real* calves with *real* children's heads], but resemblances only [. . .]. It is [. . .] impossible for monstrosities of this type to be formed (i.e. one animal within another), as is shown by the gestation-period of man, sheep, dog, and ox, which are widely different, and none of these animals can possibly be formed except in its own period.[58]

---

[56] From τέλος: see Chan., 1063. On this category, see Lloyd (1996), p. 120.

[57] Arist. GA IV.3–4, 769 b 11 ff.

[58] Arist. GA IV.3–4, 769 b 11 ff. The τραγέλαφος also does not exist. For Aristotle, this half goat (τράγος), half deer (ἔσαφος), rooted in a mythical background, is nothing but a word, a composite name that reflects a mental representation of something that does not exist and thus cannot be connected to any substratum. Sillitti (1980) has analysed the treatment of the τραγέλαφος in early Greek commentators on Aristotle, showing the crucial role this concept, because of its coherence, possibility and comprehensibility, whether scientific or conjectural, played in the discussion of being and non-being. However, it is a mistake to consider this through the lens of the monstrous. While modern readers might conceive this animal as a monster because of its composite nature, Greek commentators do not speak about the τραγέλαφος as a τέρας, but instead as a species, some of them an actual one, others only as an imaginary one.

While for Empedocles and Democritus,[59] and because of their mechanical theory of causality, these monsters were *real* possibilities, for Aristotle they only *resemble* the animals whose names are given them to describe their monstrosity. In fact, they are coherent, and yet deformed. They are unachieved and imperfect beings that happen because matter has not been properly mastered by the formal principle.

Aristotle has thus come to the point in which he needs to either acknowledge monsters' naturalness, or rule it out. His explanation is original and groundbreaking, and its importance could hardly be overestimated for future debates:

> A monstrosity [...] belongs to the class of 'things contrary to Nature' [παρὰ φύσιν], although it is contrary not to Nature in her entirety but only to Nature *in the generality of cases* [ὡς ἐπὶ τὸ πολύ]. So far as concerns the Nature which is *always* and is *by necessity* [ἐξ ἀνάγκη], nothing occurs contrary to that; no; unnatural occurrences are found only among those things which occur as they do *in the generality of cases*, but which *may* occur otherwise.[60]

Nature's unity is not questioned here. Nevertheless, the reader learns, nature must now be considered from two different points of view, precisely in order to grasp monstrosity's naturalness: nature in the generality of cases, and nature by necessity. Whereas the latter does not know any monstrosity at all, the former is where monsters are born. I think that one has to resist the idea of treating the two concepts of nature that Aristotle speaks about as distinguished and complementary domains. I think that Aristotle emphasises two different *ways* of considering the natural domain in its unity, and within which things must be considered at the same time monstrous (i.e. when they are grasped vis-à-vis nature in the generality of cases) *and* normal (i.e. when they are considered from the angle of absolute necessity). Aristotle is, once again, trying to embody the peculiar kind of exceptionality that characterises monstrosity within the normality of nature ἐξ ἀνάγκη.

Aristotle's striking and powerful description has a twofold aim: to offer, on the one hand, a scientific description of monstrosity at least as clear as the one previously offered by the (much simpler) mechanicist hypotheses, and

---

[59] Whereas the examples clearly recall Empedocles' monsters, Aristotle is also describing Democritus's explanation. See *Vorsokr.* 68 A 146 (= LM [27] ATOM. D168 = Arist. GA IV.4, 769 b 30): 'Two semens fall into the uterus, one of them having started forth earlier and the other later, and the second when it has gone out goes into the uterus with the result that the parts grow on to one another and get thrown into disorder.'

[60] Arist. GA IV.4, 770 b 10.

to neutralise, on the other hand, the threat that monstrosity presents for the principle of a purposive nature. Aristotle makes it clear in what follows:

> Why, even in those instances of the phenomena we are considering, what occurs is contrary to this particular order, certainly, but it never happens in a merely random fashion [τυχόντως]; and thus it seems less of a monstrosity because even that which is contrary to Nature is, in a way, in accordance with Nature (i.e. whenever the 'formal' nature has not gained control over [κρατέω] the 'material' nature). Hence, people do not call things of this sort monstrosities any more than they do in the other cases where something occurs habitually [. . .][61]

Nature, thus, is sometimes wrong after all. But what is its fault due to? At stake, in the first place, is matter's nature or rather the kind of resistance that matter is capable of opposing to the formal cause. Is this a sort of *action*? In this case monstrosity is an active inner resistance of nature to be what it is supposed to be. Is it *only* a lack of something, i.e. an insufficiency? In this case monstrosity rather falls under the category of incompleteness. Dudley has recently claimed that nowhere does Aristotle suggest an active role played by matter.[62] Dudley can do so, however, only by downplaying the context and, in it, the meaning of κρατέω, which, he claims, does not refer to any struggle or confrontation between the formal and the material cause. However, I believe that Aristotle has precisely in mind Democritus's ἐπικράτεια and, as a consequence, the idea of both an active character of matter[63] in response to its being informed, and of a resistance of one causal principle to the others.[64]

The attempt in *Generation of Animals* to explain monstrosity *within* nature's necessity must not be read in a theoretical vacuum, but rather in connection with other texts, and in particular the *Physics*, whose importance I have already underlined. Here, Aristotle asks how nature can be considered a purposeful cause and how things happen by necessity in it. Would it not be an option, Aristotle rhetorically asks, to recognise only necessary causes and explain everything, even what seems to be purposeful, by necessity and chance, as the mechanists had previously done?

> So why should it not be the same with natural organs like the teeth? Why should it not be a coincidence that the front teeth come up with an edge, suited to dividing the food, and the back ones flat and good for grinding it,

---

[61] Arist. GA IV.4, 770 b 10.
[62] Dudley (2012), p. 165 and *passim*.
[63] Happ (1971), p. 753, underlines the active character of matter. See also Pacchi (1976).
[64] Canguilhem (1981), p. 125.

without there being any design in the matter? And so with all other organs that seem to embody a purpose. In cases where a coincidence brought about such a combination as might have been arranged on purpose, the creatures, it is urged, having been suitably formed by the operation of chance, survived; otherwise they perish, as Empedocles says of his 'man-faced oxen'.[65]

Through this rhetorical question, Aristotle claims that material and mechanical causes alone are not sufficient to explain what we see in nature. The answer can be based, once again, only on the observation of the striking regularity of natural events, which would be inexplicable, in Aristotle's view, without a causal principle above and beyond the mechanical and the fortuitous one.[66]

At stake is Aristotle's interpretation of chance, as well as the one that he ascribes to Empedocles and Democritus. Whereas Gotthelf thinks that Aristotle is clear and consistent in his use of the notion of chance,[67] Cherniss speaks about an 'ambiguous use of the term fortuitous'.[68] I agree with Cherniss's reading, if one intends for 'ambiguous' not so much a voluntarily misguiding or dishonest presentation, but rather an incompatibility of Aristotle's predecessors' theories with his own system. This incompatibility calls for a *redefinition* of chance: a redefinition that Empedocles and Democritus would not have recognised themselves, and would have deemed not only unfair but also incomprehensible.

The distinction between the usual and the exceptional, to use Cherniss's language, or between what happens for the most part and what happens always and by necessity, to use Aristotle's own terms, would have not made any sense

---

[65] See the whole passage, Arist. *Ph.* II.8, 198 b 10–32. See also Phlp. *in Ph.*: '[Empedocles] said that the parts of animals were not ordered for the sake of something, but it happened that they were so related by chance as if they had come to be for the sake of this; and in this way, too, he says, those too [speak] who say that nature does not produce [things] for the sake of something, because all those things that it produces so as to be as if it had produced [them] for the sake of something – these are preserved, but all those that are not [so produced] – these perish, as Empedocles says "the man-prowed oxen-kind" [do]. For these, since they did not come to be as if they had come to be for the sake of some good, because of this are not even preserved. So they take the examples of monsters given by Empedocles, because he himself says that the monsters which came to be in the original state of affairs are not preserved.'

[66] Arist. *Ph.* II.8, 198 b 33–199 a 7: 'All [. . .] phenomena and all natural things are either constant or normal, and this is contrary to the very meaning of luck (τύχη) or chance (αὐτόματον). No one assigns it to chance or to a remarkable coincidence if there is abundant rain in the winter, though he would if there were in the dog-days; and the other way about it, if there were parching heat. [. . .] There is purpose, then, in what is, and in what happens, in Nature.'

[67] A. Gotthelf, 'Aristotle's conception of final causality', in Gotthelf, Lennox eds. (1987), p. 224.

[68] Cherniss (1935), p. 252 and *passim*.

before the new definition of natural teleology that is being offered in book II of the *Physics*. The incompatibility lies in the meaning of mechanical causality. Subordinating mechanism to the teleological principle not only reduces its scope, but changes its nature. As Cherniss suggests, Aristotle's reduction of mechanicism to *only* its material cause brings him to identify necessity and chance, 'under the influence of his own doctrine which traces necessity, as "resistance," and chance, as "indeterminateness," to the material:'[69] a doctrine – Aristotle is adamant – that subordinates every other causality to teleology. As Cherniss brilliantly and clearly concludes:

> Aristotle himself admits that the fortuitous birth of monsters is contrary to nature not in the sense that it does not proceed from natural causes but only because the form fails to master the matter completely; the whole doctrine rests upon a circular argument, for when the variations are frequent they can no longer be called monsters. Consequently, the various forms of the Empedoclean monsters would have to be called natural as proceeding from the same order of cause and effect which produced the variations that managed to survive; and, if on Aristotle's narrower concept of nature they were unnatural because the matter had not been fully shaped by a form as yet indeterminable, they could not be called fortuitous either for they did not fall within the scope of purposive action.[70]

Empedocles and Democritus only recognise *one* order of cause. Aristotle plays against them his quadripartite system, and only as such he is able to consider their monstrosities to be fortuitous and unnatural. I disagree, though, with Cherniss's qualification of Aristotle's concept of nature as 'narrower' vis-à-vis the Empedoclean one. On the contrary, it seems to me at least as wide, rich and complex as Empedocles', and perhaps more complex than any previous one.

I touched already on the analogy between art and nature. Aristotle uses it to strengthen his contention and this also has a strong influence in future centuries. Nature's purposiveness is visible, one can read in the *Physics*, because of art's purposiveness, i.e. because it functions *as* in the artificial productions. Provided that no impediment obstructs the process – this must be reiterated – nature proceeds from stage to stage, like the artisan who produces an artefact:

> If a house were a natural product, the process would pass through the same stages that it in fact passes through when it is produced by art; and if natural products could also be produced by art, they would move along the same

---

[69] Cherniss (1935).
[70] Cherniss (1935). See *contra* Preus (1975), p. 105, who is not convinced by Cherniss's argument on circularity.

line that the natural process actually takes. We may therefore say that the earlier stages are for the purpose of leading to the later. Indeed, as a general proposition, the arts either, on the basis of Nature, carry things further than Nature can, or they imitate Nature. If, then, artificial processes are purposeful, so are natural processes too; for the relation of antecedent to consequent is identical in art and in nature.[71]

Teleological action presupposes a precise relation between the antecedent and the consequent, whereby the former depends on the latter, which commands the process's direction. The final cause is the privileged point of view both for the artisan/artist and for the physicist/scientist. This is why Aristotle's analogy helps build the idea of convergence between beauty and order. Harmony is at the same time an ontological and an aesthetical concept that describes the human and the natural world alike. As Gilson puts it, Aristotle thinks that nature's truth is grasped through its beauty. Not so much the aesthetical beauty, but rather its intelligible one. In the animal realm, admiring nature's beauty and recognising its purposive order are one and the same.[72]

Everything happens with an end in view, namely a form.[73] This principle is clear in animals and plants alike, whose marvellous purposiveness progressively discloses itself to the acute observer of nature, able to focus on it step by step, from the superior to the inferior order that embraces all kinds of Being, monsters included. They are all just nature's attempts at fulfilling the proper end. Most of them are fulfilled, some of them are not: the latter, we call τέρατα:

> If in art there are cases in which the correct procedure serves a purpose, and attempts that fail are aimed at a purpose but miss it, we may take it to be the same in Nature, and monstrosities will be like failures of purpose in Nature. So if, in the primal combinations, such 'ox-creatures' as could not reach an equilibrium and goal should appear, it would be by the miscarriage of some principle, as monstrous births are actually produced now by abortive developments of sperm. Besides, the sperm must precede the formation of the animal, and Empedocles' 'primal all-generative' is no other than such sperm.[74]

Aristotle is so self-confident that now he can even attempt to absorb Empedocles' explanation in his own hypothesis, as if no other theory except his own could really be possible. Midway between the wrongly done (ἀδίκημα) and the misfortune (ἀτύχημα), Aristotle's 'failure and fault' (ἁμάρτημα) draws from

---

[71] Arist. *Ph.* II.8, 199 a 8–21. See also b 15–32.
[72] See again Gilson (1971), pp. 37–8.
[73] Arist. *Ph.* II.8, 199 a 32–3.
[74] Arist. *Ph.* II.8, 199 a 33–b 9.

both ideas, conveying a message that is much more complex than the simple 'mistake'.[75] To do this, however, Aristotle must invent a tradition that does not exist in the texts. Nature's regularities, whose frequency guarantees the possibility of Aristotle's taxonomy by allowing him to attempt the appropriation of Empedocles, do not exist in the Empedoclean hypothesis itself.[76] The Empedoclean monsters, which, unfit, do not survive, could have certainly been more numerous than the individuals who do survive and which, *for this reason and this reason only*, i.e. for nothing that they intrinsically possess, eventually become normal. Moreover, Aristotle's monster can be such only vis-à-vis an actuality, i.e. another group of individuals *already* existing *in fact*, when potentiality is unable to reproduce once again the existing normality. Now, such an actuality simply does not exist in Empedocles. The actual normality does not exist by definition; it becomes such only as a result of a transformation which is not confronted by any pre-existing actuality. Whereas for Empedocles potentiality precedes actuality, for Aristotle the opposite is true.[77]

What kind of necessity, then, is Aristotle able to speak about and use in his argument? Employing again a striking formula, Aristotle develops the concept of accidental necessity. It is the task of *Generation of Animals*, once again, to explain that monstrosities are not necessary as far as the final cause is concerned, but rather *per accidens* (κατὰ συμβεβεκός),[78] for example 'when

---

[75] Louis (1975), p. 283, underlines that, in this sense, the mistake is not and can not ever be complete. No monster denounces nature's total failure.

[76] See Simplicius's hesitation in following Aristotle's attempt to appropriate Empedocles' theory, *in Ph.* 382.2–21: 'Aristotle points out that Empedocles himself appears to mean that the seed is produced before the animals. The phrase spoken by Empedocles, "the whole-natured shape that came first," was the seed, which did not yet display "the desirable form of limbs" because it was liquid in actuality, being fluid, but the form of man in potentiality. But perhaps it was impossible for either the animal to exist before the seed, or the seed before the animal. For just as each plant and animal is born from its own particular seed, so each seed is produced by its own particular animal or plant. Aristotle might have pointed out that Empedocles does not say that the seed *always* exists before the animal. And it is clear that the animal does exist before the seed. He confirms his observation by concluding that "'the whole-natured shape that came first' was the seed," since even Empedocles himself realised that the seed must exist before the birth of the animal. If it is the seed, then it seems to me remarkably suitable to attribute the term "whole-natured" to it. For strictly speaking it is whole-natured because it is that which is, throughout itself, entirely what it is if no differentiation has yet taken place within it. For every part of the seed is all the parts of the body, but no part of the body is the other parts once the differentiation has taken place in them and the whole nature has been dispersed.' See also Thomas Aquinas (1963), book II, lecture 14 (= Sancti Thomae Aquinatis [1954], pp. 128–31).

[77] On the weaknesses of Aristotle's treatment of Empedocles, see also Cherniss (1935), p. 255.

[78] Arist. GA IV.3, 767 b 13–15.

a female is formed instead of a male [...] since it is possible for the male sometimes not to gain the mastery [κρατέω] either on account of youth or age or some other such cause, female offspring must of necessity be produced by animals'.[79] This idea has profound consequences for Aristotle's system. It is, on the one hand, the best solution that Aristotle finds to maintain the naturalness of every event, including monstrosities. It is also, on the other hand, what shakes the whole system from the bottom, casting a shade on the concept of necessity itself and its possible meanings.

Pierre Aubenque has underlined how crucial this passage is in posing the necessity of accident, and the essentiality of contingency. Nature's mistakes are paradoxically constitutive of the material world itself. Without them, the world would collapse into the nothingness of absolute *identity* with its perfection. In order to *really* exist, on the contrary, it must be *different* from its perfection, and this happens thanks to nature's failures: 'a world without failures would be a world in which Being would be everything it can be, where there would not be any matter, or power, or movement, or multiplicity; such a world would melt into its principle: pure act, immaterial, motionless and one like its principle, this world would be, in the end, undistinguishable from it.'[80]

The contingent and the accidental strike back at Aristotle's attempt to tame them. The unintended consequence of Aristotle's endeavour to naturalise monstrosity within a teleological framework is that monsters become necessary not only because of the way they are produced in nature, but also for nature itself to be what it is. Without questioning the consistency, coherency and ultimately the argumentative force of Aristotle's system, what is pivotal for the present discussion is that monstrosity produces the clash and the collapse of terms that are normally taken as opposite to one another, necessity and the accidental.

As Louis has emphasised, παρὰ φύσιν cannot be intended as something fully outside nature. Rather, it occurs at or across nature's edges. This, I think, makes it possible for Aristotle to develop his concept of accidental necessity. The edge, paradoxically, takes centre stage and becomes the terrain on which monstrosities are analysed. Nonetheless, can they really be analysed, i.e. scientifically studied? If one grants absolute pre-eminence to the assumption of the *Metaphysics* that no science of irregularity is possible, then the answer must be negative.[81] This is Dudley's conclusion, for whom

---

[79] Arist. GA IV.3, 767 b 10–13.
[80] Aubenque (1962), pp. 388–90.
[81] Arist. Metaph. VI.2, 1026 a 32 ff. in fact establishes that 'since the simple term "being" is used in various senses, of which we saw that one was *accidental* (κατὰ συμβεβηκός), and another *true* (not-being being used in the sense of "false") [...] it must first be said of what "is" accidentally, that there can be no speculation (θεωρία) about it. [...] no science (ἐπιστήμη), whether practical or speculative, concerns itself with it.'

monsters are natural irregularities, and thus cannot be foreseen or studied.[82] The accidental necessity, however, is still a kind of necessity, and one must acknowledge Aristotle's careful, although striking, choice of terms. It must be possible, thus, to scientifically study objects and phenomena falling under this kind of necessity, as Johnson has argued. Johnson translates τέρας with 'freak'. I wonder whether the term 'monster' better suggests something that is *not* an 'abnormally developed individual': although rare, its development is indeed normal and necessary.[83]

Preus discusses in detail the question of accidental necessity. He claims that monsters must be considered in the same way as the unnecessary by-products of necessary processes, such as the production of bile in the human body. Precisely because of this, they do not survive. Just as part of the matter composing food does not have any use and is discarded,[84] part of the matter produced by copulation is of inferior quality and is discarded by nature, preventing it from reproducing itself and creating a new race.[85] Preus seeks to explain a difficult concept through what is clearer and causes less of a problem in Aristotle's thought. Of course, this methodology has certain advantages, such as avoiding projecting meaning from an outside point of view. Yet it also prevents one from seeing the tensions that might permeate this theory, which can also be productive and rich for future debates. Not only the process of producing monstrosity, I think, but the monster itself as its offspring must be considered as necessary by accident in Aristotle.

Preus calls the monstrous production in Aristotle's system 'dysteleological'.[86] We should consider necessity and *accidental* necessity as two opposed concepts for Aristotle, and we should not attempt to save Aristotle from himself by neutralising his most inconvenient conclusions,[87] as doing so would make it possible to see him as a precursor of modern mechanism. I agree with Preus's view: Aristotle's system is the negation of mechanicism in different ways. Yet it seems to me that Preus himself is trying to save Aristotle's system from the inconsistencies and ambiguities that mechanicists see in it, in particular concerning monsters and accidentally necessary phenomena. The accidental necessity is still a necessity, encompassing all aspects of the phenomenon, and thus qualifying all its causal determinations together. Aristotle himself makes it clear, against the possibility of an interpretation like Preus's, that chance is an accidental cause

---

[82] Dudley (2012), pp. 192–3.
[83] Johnson (2005), pp. 198–9.
[84] Arist. PA III.7, 670 a 30.
[85] Preus (1975), pp. 200 ff.
[86] Preus (1975), pp. 205–6.
[87] As Charlton (1970) does, in Preus's view.

(ἡ γὰρ τύχη τῶν κατὰ συμβεβεκός αἰτίων) opposed to *both* the invariable and the usual necessity of natural phenomena.[88]

These are Aristotle's topical points regarding nature and its accidentally necessary anomalies, such as monsters. Their importance, in future centuries, is proportional to the importance of his system in the history of philosophy overall. The points that Aristotle has made are clear. Both his disciples and opponents show, besides the differences, that they have clearly understood his heritage. The crucial question for them is whether to use and reuse Aristotelianism either as a polemical target to be destroyed to introduce new and revolutionary ideas, or as a tool to give authority and support to old and more traditional views. The history of the idea of monstrosity constantly refers to the Aristotelian attempt of founding, although paradoxically, a new science of monsters.

This is already visible, I believe, in the early history of Peripateticism with Aristotle's immediate successors, Theophrastus of Eresos and Strato of Lampsacus. Scholars have underlined the originality of Theophrastus vis-à-vis Aristotle, in part because of his important contribution to the understanding and acceptance of the teleological principle. Theophrastus carries out his analysis at the same time Aristotle does, and consideration of Theophrastus has focused on the degree of the pupil's faithfulness toward the master's doctrine. Theophrastus's reworking of finalism offers a new understanding of lower and imperfect, or apparently random, phenomena; without discarding Aristotelian teleology, he nevertheless sees it differently than Aristotle. The key text here is book IX of the *Metaphysics*, which is particularly difficult to reconstruct, but which underlines the problems of the idea that everything is in view of something and nothing is in vain (τοῦ πάνθ' ἕνεκά του καὶ μηδὲν μάτην).[89] In considering this, Theophrastus tackles the principle of teleology in its entirety and tests its heuristic power even vis-à-vis phenomena that seem to escape its domain.

He writes:

> With regard to the issue that all things are for the sake of something and nothing is in vain, the delimitation required is not easy anyway [. . .], and

---

[88] In other words, the invariable and the normal achievements of natural events stand on the same side, vis-à-vis what happens by chance. See *Ph.* II.8, 199 b 23–6: 'As we have explained, chance is an incidental cause (ἡ γὰρ τύχη τῶν κατὰ συμβεβεκός αἰτίων). But when the desirable result is effected invariably or normally, it is not an incidental or chance occurrence, and in the course of Nature the result always is achieved either invariably or normally, if nothing hinders.'

[89] Thphr. *Metaph.* IX.10 a 22.

some things in particular <are difficult> because they do not seem to be such; but some of them coincidentally, others by some necessity – as in the case both of the heavenly bodies and of the majority of things on earth.[90]

Theophrastus sounds the alarm about a naive or acritical acceptance of finalism in every domain, since there are phenomena that appear to evade a teleological explanation. Whether Theophrastus is criticising his master's theory or trying to save it from the attacks of its adversaries is not important for the present enquiry. What is more important is that monsters, though generally absent from Theoprastus's extant works, can clearly be conceived as being among these unexplainable phenomena.

In their *notes complémentaires*, Laks and Most explain that, for partisans of teleology, the admission that anything happens without an end wrecks the entire principle.[91] With this in mind, we see that Theophrastus is trying to avoid this problem and save teleology by assigning a less negative status to facts and things that seem to lack any end. However, as Laks and Most add, the expression τοῦ πάνθ' ἕνεκά του καὶ μηδὲν μάτην echoes a panglossian argument that not even Aristotle ever held. Such optimism is more typical of the Stoics. Theophrastus's criticism thus would not be addressed to his master. This is also Luciana Repici's claim; she sees a strong continuity between Theophrastus and Aristotle on the consistency and coherency of the teleological principle.[92]

The question at stake for Theophrastus, as for Aristotle, seems to be not so much whether teleology can unambiguously explain everything, but whether those things that seem inexplicable through ends can still be *conceived* within a teleological framework. As Most and Laks point out, Theophrastus's expression can be seen as an early attempt to separate what is in view *of something* and what is in view *of the better*:

> one should try to grasp some limit [ὅρος], both in nature and in the being of the whole, both of the <explanation of things as being> 'for the sake of something' and of the impulse towards the better. For this is the starting-point of the study of the whole, in what things really consists and how they relate to one another.[93]

The distinction between a purely functional teleology (ἕνεκά του) and an axiological one (εἰς τὸ ἄριστον) can be seen as Theophrastus's contribution

---

[90] Thphr. *Metaph.* IX.10 a 22–8.
[91] Théophraste (1993), p. 74.
[92] Repici (1991). *Contra*, see e.g. J. G. Lennox, who correctly points out that a debate on the legitimacy of Aristotle's teleological explanation already existed in his time.
[93] Thphr. *Metaph.* IX.11 b 25–7.

to establishing a more solid ground for the principle and its scientific cogency. At the same time, however, once teleology needs limitations in order to retain its coherence and usefulness, one can surely ask if it has in fact been supported or undermined. However, one cannot undermine the strength of Theophrastus's idea of a boundary or a limit (ὅρος) that teleology requires to reinforce its cogency.

In this sense, van Raalte concludes that this part of the *Metaphysics* speaks less to a continuity between pupil and master than to teleology's inability to *conceive of*, rather than just explain, phenomena.[94] There are things, Theophrastus seems to argue, that simply are not guided by ends or, more clearly, things that fall outside the boundaries of the dominion of teleology itself:

> [...] the very possibility that [some phenomena] have no explanation is problematic, and especially for those who do not suppose this <to be the case> in other things, prior and more worthy <than these>. This is also why the account that it is by spontaneity and through the rotation of the whole that these things acquire certain forms or differences from one another seems to have some plausibility.[95]

Laks and Most underline that this is a difficult and perhaps corrupted passage. Their reading of it is that even lower and less noble phenomena (indubitably including monstrosities) must be explainable in the superior reality, without that reality being their direct cause. It thus becomes possible to establish an indirect link between the two levels of reality, a link that Theophrastus calls *mechanic* (τῷ αὐτομάτῳ).[96] Laks and Most's interpretation is convincing. However, given the paramount effort Aristotle puts into opposing the mechanist explanation and the intention that seems to guide Theophrastus in devoting so much attention to his master's theory, the reading of the spontaneous as a mere indirect link between a finalist principle and its abnormal and monstrous phenomena seems perplexing, or at least reductive. Theoprastus is certainly aware that the αὐτόματον had been the flag of the mechanist explanation since Democritus, and that Aristotle had built his teleology largely against it as he continued, not without originality and substantial changes, the efforts of Socrates and Plato.

---

[94] See van Raalte's entire commentary to book IX in Theophrastus (1993). On Theophrastus's teleology see also A. Jaulin, 'Le meilleur et les contraires: De la nécessaire limitation à l'impulsion vers le meilleur', in Jaulin, Lefebvre eds (2015), pp. 135–48 and J.-B. Gourinat, 'Les limites du finalisme chez Aristote et Théophraste', in Jaulin, Lefebvre éds (2015), pp. 149–77.

[95] Thphr. *Metaph.* IX.10 b 24–11 a 1.

[96] Laks and Most, 'Notes complémentaires', in Théophraste (1993), *ad loc.*

In this sense, the treatment of monstrosities in Theophrastus's work is significant. Monstrosity was a pillar of Aristotle's analysis of natural phenomena and Theophrastus continues the Aristotelian effort to give monstrosity a fully natural explanation, to free it from religious and superstitious implications. This, I believe, is the meaning of Theophrastus's applications of limits and boundaries to teleology. They are efforts not to limit the conceptual domain of finalism, but rather its potential use to support superstitious explanations of strange or apparently unnatural events.[97] Things always happen with a cause, but often cannot be explained through an end. They happen coincidentally or inevitably, by some kind of necessity, τὰ μὲν συμπτωματικῶς, τὰ δ'ἀνάγκη τινί.[98] In the *Meteorology*, as Mansfeld suggests, Theophrastus goes even further, saying that the divine can only be conceived as the cause of order, never disorder, which arises from the natural movement of the cosmos itself.[99] By extending this coincident and necessary character to celestial bodies, Theophrastus is pushing the boundaries of Aristotle's teleology while limiting its scope and domain.

This is also reflected in Theophrastus's writings on plants, in which the abnormal and the monstrous are not presented as a challenge to the teleological explanation, but rather framed within it so as to exclude amazement or belief in anything besides natural causes. In book V of *De causis plantarum*, Theophrastus explains that every seemingly unreasonable thing can in fact be explained: they are doubtful or poorly accounted for or due to natural causes that an ignorant observer does not recognise as such.[100] Regarding unnatural sprouting, for example, Theophrastus writes that they occur:

> when the generative power collects in [boughs or trunk]: when a starting-point has become fixed, the food that flows to it becomes assimilated, just as in the other parts, to the thing that is to be produced. The formation of such a starting-point is not unreasonable, if the tree has acquired in some part a tempering that is favourable, but is a good deal more reasonable than the formation that occurs in animals, as when a horn grows from the chest or something else of the kind occurs, since here the departure is greater than that in plants to the extent that plants are more undifferentiated than animals.[101]

---

[97] See Mansfeld (1992), who exploits the rediscovery of Theophrastus's *Meteorology* in the fragmentary Syriac version published and translated by Hans Daiber in Fortenbaugh, Gutas eds. (1992), pp. 166–293.
[98] Thphr. *Metaph.* IX.10 a 26–7.
[99] See e.g. Thphr. *Meteorology* 6, on the thunderbolt, in Fortenbaugh, Gutas eds. (1992), pp. 263–6. Mansfeld correctly argues that the same principle can be extended to monstrous births.
[100] Thphr. *CP* V.1.2 ff.
[101] Thphr. *CP* V.2.1.

The vegetal domain appears to be more resistant to monstrosity than the animal one, a fact Theophrastus explicitly evoked with regard to Aristotle's GA.[102] Theophrastus seems less interested, however, in the distinction between the animal and the vegetal domain, but in rationalising the approach that, without fear or superstition, should characterise scientific enquiry in both domains, just as Aristotle taught. When Theophrastus states that 'these cases perhaps fall outside the realm of a natural cause',[103] he is not recognising the existence of supernatural or unnatural causality, but of unusual facts whose origin is external to the inner nature of the plant itself, but certainly not outside nature as a whole, since Theophrastus's last word seems to be that there is hardly anything abnormal in nature.

A similar and perhaps even more ambiguous relationship with Aristotle's position can be found in Theophrastus's successor, the third scholarch of the Lyceum, Strato of Lampsacus. The situation with Strato's works is even more problematic than with Theophrastus's, as only a very limited number of doxographic texts are extant. This, however, has not prevented ancient and modern scholars from seeing in Strato's thought another interesting step in the debate about teleology, a position extremely relevant to the study and conceptualisation of monstrosity in the ancient world.

Partisans of divine providence and, in particular, of Christian providence have seen Strato as an enemy. Lactantius denounces the scandal of those who do not put God at the origin of the universe:

> [They] say either that it was composed of first-principles that came together at random or that it was brought into existence by nature in an unlooked-for way; [they suppose that] nature indeed, as Strato says, has in itself a power of producing generation, growth and decay, but it has no consciousness or shape, so that we may understand that all things have as it were been produced spontaneously, not by any craftsman or originator. Both of these [positions] are idle and impossible.[104]

Strato is thus associated with those who support the random or spontaneous formation of the universe and its parts, namely the mechanicists and Epicureans. They are the most horrible intellectual and human monsters in the history of philosophy, '[. . .] going astray in what they see, deceived by what they hear, castrated in their souls, unreasoning, sterile and barren, like

---

[102] In particular to GA 769 a 10–771 a 14. See also S. Amigues in *Théophraste* (2012–17), ad loc.
[103] Thphr. CP V.4.7.
[104] Lact. *De ira dei* X.1 (= Desclos-Fortenbaugh, fr. 19C).

a lion without courage, a bull without horns or a bird without wings [. . .]', or so says Maximus of Tyrus.[105]

The association of Strato with the Epicureans has also been made by modern scholars including Georges Rodier, who, although claiming a continuity between Aristotle and Strato, reads the only extant fragment that deals with monstrosity, the doxographic testimony of the *Placita*, through an Epicurean lens:

> How do monstrous births occur? . . . Strato [says that they result from] addition or removal or transposition [of certain parts] or inflation by *pneuma*.[106]

Extremely important, as we will see, is the idea of ἐμπνευμάτωσις, or inflation, to explain monstrosity. Grounding his reading on this fragment, Rodier joins the ancient authors who generally see a break between Strato and Aristotle on the fundamental question of teleology and, as a consequence, on a mechanical and materialist explanation of monstrous births. Plutarch, for example, explicitly contrasts Strato and Aristotle on the role of chance:

> Indeed the leader of the rest of the Peripatetics, Strato, in many things disagrees with Aristotle, and holds opposite opinions to Plato concerning motion, mind, soul and generation, and finally he says that the world itself is not a living creature and that what is natural follows from what is according to chance. For what is spontaneous gives the lead, and then each of the natural processes is brought to completion in this way.[107]

The opposition also seems unproblematic to Cicero, who rebukes both Strato and Theophrastus, clarifying, though, their differences:

> Nor is Theophrastus' inconsistency tolerable; at one moment he gives the divine supremacy to mind, at another to the heaven, and then again to the constellations and stars in the sky. Nor should we listen to his pupil Strato, the one who is called 'the naturalist [*physicus*]', who holds the view that all divine power is located in nature, which is responsible for generation, growth and decay, but is without any consciousness and without any shape.[108]

---

[105] Max.Tyr. XI.5 (= Desclos-Fortenbaugh, fr. 21).
[106] *Placit.* V.8.2, 905 F–906 A (= Desclos-Fortenbaugh, fr.74). See Rodier (1890), p. 91 n. 2. Both W. Capelle, *Straton* in RE, 310–11 and Wehrli hrsg. (1967–9, 2. ed.), V, esp. pp. 47, 57–8 and 69, agree on this point. See also Gatzemeier (1970), p. 143 and *passim*. On Strato through a more prudent reading of Rodier see P. Pellegrin, 'La physique de Straton de Lampsaque. Dans la lignée de Georges Rodier', in Desclos, Fortenbaugh eds. (2011), pp. 239–61.
[107] Plu. *Moralia. Adversus Colotem* 14.1114 F–1115 B (= Desclos-Fortenbaugh, fr. 20).
[108] Cic. *ND* I.35 (= Desclos-Fortenbaugh, fr. 19A). See also Minucius Felix 19.8 (= Desclos-Fortenbaugh, fr. 19B).

In the eyes of the ancients, Strato seems to go much further in revising and criticising Aristotle's theory. Teleology is not necessary to explain natural phenomena, and nature is described as a spontaneous force that is not guided by a divine mind or by any end directed toward what is better or most accomplished. In the end, Aristotle's teleology fades away and the fragment on monsters, despite its incompletion, seems to suggest that monsters could well have played a significant role in Strato's reconception of teleology.

Another passage from Cicero, however, clarifies something equally important, namely that in reconsidering the role and status of teleology in nature, Strato does not join the mechanicists and explicitly rejects Democritus's atomism. In Cicero's words:

> You [Stoics] say that nothing can [come to be] without god; look, here unexpectedly is Strato of Lampsacus, who gives this god a release from a great task, indeed; but seeing that the priests of the gods have no holiday, how much fairer is it that the gods themselves [should do so]. He says that he makes no use of work by the gods in constructing the world, and teaches that whatever there is is all brought about by nature, and not in the same way as he who says that all these things are composed of rough and smooth and hooked and barbed bodies interspersed with void; he says that these are the dreams of Democritus, who does not teach but [indulges in] wishful [thinking], while he himself, investigating the individual parts of the world, teaches that whatever is or comes to be is brought about or has been brought about by natural weights and movements.[109]

Cicero's testimony is of great importance in clarifying the ambiguity that several ancient authors have seen in Strato's mechanicist turn. Reappraising Rodier's and Wehrli's interpretation, Repici and Pellegrin have clarified that Strato openly rejects fundamental points of atomism. As with Theophrastus, Strato's exact position vis-à-vis Aristotle is not in itself central to the present enquiry. What is important is that Strato must have had an extensive interest in teratology, and could have used it to clarify his position on finalism, given how important monstrosity is to Aristotle's theory of final causes.

---

[109] Cic. *Acad.* II.121 (= Desclos-Fortenbaugh, fr. 18). Cicero stresses Strato's ethical concerns in line, as we have seen above, with Theophrastus and close, at least in this sense, to the Epicurean and Stoic enterprises. See again *Acad.* II.121: 'To be sure, [Strato] both sets god free from great toil and sets me free from great fear. For who, thinking that he is of concern to god, can fail to shudder at the divine power both by day and by night, and, if something bad has happened (to whom does it not?), can fail to be terrified that it happened justly? However, I do not agree either with Strato or with you; now this [view] seems more worthy of approval, now that.'

This is why the teratological fragment of the *Placita* is of paramount importance. Both Torraca and Repici suggest that the fragment's meaning is that monsters have an addition or removal of parts and that the anomalies can be explained by an excess of air or pneuma.[110] Although pneuma recalls the material nature that the Stoics assign to the principle pervading the whole universe, Strato does not believe it has a teleological and divine nature. The ἐμπνευμάτωσιν, as Repici explains, suggests a non-teleological process of the body's transformation that is connected to the πνεῦμα, a term Aristotle uses precisely in relation to monstrous bodies.[111] Repici thus claims against Rodier, Wehrli and Gatzemeier that one can read Strato's text as the attempt to connect the mechanical with the teleological explanation rather than as a rejection of finalism as a whole. This, Repici adds, is possible if one separates the teleological and the providential or, much as Laks and Most have suggested about Theophrastus, the functional and axiological within teleology itself.

Repici's reading is grounded on the idea that Aristotle's theory is already capable of absorbing a mechanist point of view against the excesses of Platonic or Stoic finalism, the nature and aim of which is more religious than scientific. It seems to me, however, that Strato is trying to build an original position that rejects both Democritus's atomism and Stoic teleology. I believe that our knowledge of Theophrastus and, most of all, of Strato, is too lacunary to establish whether there was a serious challenge to Aristotle's theory from inside the Lyceum.

We have seen in this chapter how, implicitly or explicitly, monstrosity challenges the Aristotelian system. If, on one hand, Aristotle pursues Plato's effort to undermine earlier materialism, on the other, his effort goes beyond what Aristotle perceives as the shortcomings of radical idealism, opening new ways of understanding the norm and its monstrous exception. Monsters exist and deserve the attention of the scientist and the philosopher who, in their attempt to include these monsters in a systematic understanding of the world, must understand their causes and function. This, in turn, requires a new theory of causality. Aristotle's treatment of monstrosity depends on the application of his new theory of the four causes – the material, the formal, the efficient and the final – to events that seem to represent exceptions to nature's normal course.

As we have seen, though monsters are exceptional, their inclusion in the normal scheme of causality is an antidote against their apparent incomprehensibility or lack of meaning: for Aristotle, nothing happens without nature requiring it. The phenomenology of the monstrous, no matter how varied and

---

[110] See Torraca's translation in Diels (1961) and Repici (1988), esp. ch. IV, 'La teratologia: sulle tracce di una teoria'.
[111] Arist. GA IV.4, 772 b 26–31.

diverse, is part of the causal pattern of normal events. Aristotle achieves this by giving a privileged status and encompassing role to the fourth and highest kind of cause, the end or τέλος. The normative achievement of the end – for all natural phenomena, but especially biological ones – becomes the key to define and comprehend monstrosity. The material cause, the only one that counted for physicists, remains important, yet as we have seen, Aristotle sees the material cause as a potential disrupting factor that comes to be considered an obstacle to the full, perfect accomplishment of the individual τέλος of every being.

This innovative approach sees monstrosity as the result of a process that has been hindered by an unfavourable dynamic of the causes that prevents the realisation of a perfect end. Aristotle develops the opposition between normal and abnormal development through the concept of accidental necessity, namely the necessity at stake in processes that do not always happen the same way. Monsters are pivotal here because of their paradoxical ambiguity. They are the sign and symptom of a resistant nature that opposes itself to Aristotle's major ontological invention, the form and the final cause. At the same time, without this hiatus between formal perfection and actual reality, nature would not exist in the way we experience it. In fact, nature would not exist at all: there would be no diversity, no individuality or multiplicity, no better or worse, no similarity or difference, no normal and monstrous. Perfection destroys actuality. Monstrosity is thus necessary because it lets Aristotle explain nature and its ontological structure based on the substitution of dynamic forms and ends for both Plato's static ideas and the atomists' exclusively material reality.

In the last part of this chapter we have seen how the debate is pursued by Aristotle's successors in the Lyceum, particularly Theophrastus and Strato. Although our understanding is limited by the limited and fragmentary nature of the extant works (especially for Strato), it is safe to say that the debate around normality, abnormality and monstrosity must have been one of the main preoccupations during and after Aristotle's life. Aristotelianism was a response to ancient materialism and to the Socratic–Platonic idealism, but as new challenges arose, his followers had to adapt to the Academy's development after Plato's death as well as to the development of other major systems, i.e. Epicureanism, Stoicism and Scepticism, during the Hellenistic period. These are discussed in the next chapters.

5

Epicurus and Lucretius

An Immanent Causality for an Infinite Universe

I will analyse in this chapter Epicurus's and Lucretius's treatment of monstrosity. Not only do they share a great number of theoretical elements, but they have often been read together, and their philosophical systems are considered as constituting, together, the core of the atomist response to Platonism and Aristotelianism. Τέρατα are not part of the Epicurean language, in which one only finds the τερατεία, the wonderful and the amazing that are used to make an impression on common people and strike their imagination.[1] Epicurus seems more interested in the superstitious use that can be made of monsters than in understanding their ontological meaning and biological presence in nature. Monsters are indeed present in the atomist account of the early zoogonies, but not much is available to speculate on, since the only surviving text of Epicurus on zoogony is a fragment mentioned by Censorinus.[2] Most of Epicurus's works have been lost, and in particular the thirty-seven books of his Περὶ φύσεως, together with the very many other books that this prolific author wrote, according to Diogenes Laertius's account.[3] It is thus difficult to believe that Epicurus was not interested in monstrosity, given how important it is for both his polemical targets, such as Plato and Aristotle, and his sources, such as Democritus.[4]

---

[1] See Epicur. *Ep.*[3], 114 (= Usener, *Ep.* 53.114), Arrighetti in Epicuro (1973, 2a ed.) and Usener (1977), pp. 663–4.

[2] Epicur. *Fr.* 333. See Spoerri (1997).

[3] D.L. X.26.

[4] Moreau (1975), p. 475, shows that Democritus and Epicurus share the same principles, even if they understand them differently. It is hardly conceivable that Epicurus, in the now lost parts of his treatise on nature, did not take the chance to discuss a topic so important from a materialist and atomistic point of view. On the early atomists in Epicurus, see P.-M. Morel, 'I primi Atomisti nel II libro "Sulla Natura" di Epicuro', in Guadalupe Masi and Maso a cura di (2015), pp. 55–66.

It is not a surprise, then, that monstrosity occupies a large part of Lucretius's *De rerum natura*, directly inspired by Epicurus. Lucretius probably had access to a larger amount of Epicurean text than we have.[5] Scholarship has proved, however, that the relation between the two authors is quite complex and one cannot immediately use a work taken from a later context to directly supplement an earlier and lost source. Whereas some scholars tend to neglect Lucretius's originality and deem that the Latin poet only repeats the Greek master's theories,[6] others openly recognise the evolution that naturally takes place across centuries within atomist philosophy.[7] This awareness of the historical development, even within the same philosophical school, makes it impossible to immediately use Lucretius to reconstruct Epicurus's theory of nature and, in particular, of monstrosity. In this light, other authors, such as Empedocles, appear as important as Epicurus himself for Lucretius.[8] It is possible, however, to delineate the core arguments of what is perceived over the following centuries as the atomist philosophy, beyond the differences among individual contributions.

The general principles of Epicurean physics are in the *Letter to Herodotus* and in the fragments of the Περὶ φύσεως, later reworked in Latin by Lucretius in the *De rerum natura*. The fundamental ground of the Epicurean theory is that

> nothing is created out of that which does not exist: for if it were, everything would be created out of everything with no need of seeds. And again, if that which disappears were destroyed into that which did not exist, all things would have perished, since that into which they were dissolved would not exist. Furthermore, the universe always was such as it is now, and always will be the same. For there is nothing into which it changes: for outside the universe there is nothing which could come into it and bring about the change.[9]

---

[5] See Arrighetti in Lucrezio (1973, 2a ed.), *contra* Woltjer (1877), for whom Lucretius basically repeats Epicurus and Campbell (2003), p. 101. See also the discussion in Spoerri (1997), 'Appendice: deux excursus sur les sources de Lucrèce'.

[6] Woltjer (1877) and Boyancé (1963).

[7] Usener and De Lacy (1948). See Bollack's reconstruction of this debate in Bollack (1978), pp. 96 ff.

[8] See Arrighetti in Epicuro (1973, 2nd ed.), p. 493, Gale (1994), pp. 59 ff., Sedley (1989, 1998), D. Sedley, 'The Empedoclean Opening', in Gale (2007), pp. 48–87, L. Piazzi, 'Atomismo e polemica filosofica: Lucrezio e i presocratici', in M. Beretta, F. Citti a cura di (2008), pp. 11–25. It is also important that the question of Epicurus's influence on Lucretius assumes a theoretical dimension beyond the merely historiographical one: early Christian authors such as Lactantius and Arnobius, for instance, tend to save Lucretius from the impious influence of the atheist Epicurus. While Lactantius is ready to accept that Lucretius has been influenced by Empedocles, he tries to break the link with Epicurus, on whom the whole blame is to be put. See *De opificio Dei* VI.1 and Bollack (1978), pp. 118–19.

[9] Epicur. *Ep.* [2], 38–9 (= Usener, pp. 5–6).

As Bailey underlines, this first set of principles, already known by Anaxagoras and Democritus, implies immediately the crucial idea that 'every material object has a material cause', and that 'every creation of which we have cognizance implies a previous seed'.[10] The whole treatment of monstrosity by Lucretius and, more generally, within the atomist perspective is developed within this framework, according to which transformation and constancy characterise the whole universe with no exception, offering the possibility of understanding it and ruling out every transcendent and mysterious explanation of natural phenomena, even the most curious, strange or monstrous ones. They too happen according to the principles ruling the universal transformation, but they will be confined within the limits of the absolute constancy of the universe itself, because nothing exists *outside* of the universe that can act *upon* it.

Lucretius powerfully echoes this idea, by making the combat against transcendentalism even more explicit: 'No thing is ever by divine power produced from nothing (*nullam rem e nilo gigni diuinitus umquam*).' Otherwise everything could and indeed would have been produced from all things, and there would be no need of seeds. Moreover, when things perish individually, they do not fall into nothingness, but are rather transformed into their composing elements (*in sua corpora rursum | dissoluat natura neque ad nilum interemat res*).'[11]

The universal constancy and transformation constitute the theatre of the ceaseless activity of the entities composing the whole (πᾶς), namely bodies (σώματα) and space (τόπος), or void (κενός).[12] The atoms or *corpora* are indivisible,[13] they move constantly,[14] and they have many different shapes.[15] Both Epicurus and Lucretius subscribe to Leucippus and Democritus, but they also introduce important modifications and new ideas.

Atoms' features, from which all the composite bodies and their variety depend, are the shape (σχῆμα), the weight (βάρος) and the greatness or magnitude (μέγεθος). With these elements Epicurus, and Lucretius after him, sets out to counter Aristotle's philosophy by thinking together, and in a non-paradoxical way, the permanence and the mutation of phenomena alike. The existence of immutable but microscopic elements of matter's components cannot, of

---

[10] Bailey, in Epicurus (1926), p. 179.
[11] Lucr. I.150, 159–60, and 215–16.
[12] Epicur. *Ep.* [2], 40. Lucretius closely follows the demonstration in Lucr. I.418 ff.
[13] Lucr. I.265 ff. The indivisibility of atoms plays a strong role in denying the anti-materialist consequences of the dialectic developed by the Eleatic school and, in particular, by Zeno, whose infinite divisibility of matter nullifies Being itself. See Plu. *Adversus Colotem* 16.1116C in Usener, p. 202, fr. 282.
[14] Lucr. II.62 ff.
[15] Lucr. II.333 ff.

course, be detected or experienced by our limited senses. Nevertheless, following another basic principle posed by Epicurus, namely the faith in sensation,[16] the immutability of atoms reflects itself at the macro level of composed bodies in many ways. In particular, and this is utterly important for our enquiry, the constancy of living species, their consistency and regularity, are precisely the signs that immutable elements constitute natural reality. In a strategic passage of book I of *De rerum natura*, Lucretius insists that

> since a limit has been fixed for the growth of things after their kind and for their tenure of life, and since it stands decreed what each can do by the *foedera naturae*,[17] and also what each cannot do, and since nothing changes, but all things are constant to such a degree that all the different birds show in succession marks upon their bodies to distinguish their kind, they must also have beyond a doubt a body of immutable matter. For if the first-beginnings of things could be changed, being in any way overmastered [*si primordia rerum commutari aliqua possent ratione reuicta*], it would also now remain uncertain what could arise and what could not, in a word in what way each thing has its power limited [*finita potestas*] and its deep-set boundary mark [*ratione atque alte terminus*], nor could the generations so often repeat after their kind the nature, manners, living, and movements of their parents.[18]

From the constancy and consistency universally experienced at macroscopic level, one can induce the existence of immutable elements at the microscopic one. Such constancy and consistency, however, are far from being universal and without exception, as many inexplicable phenomena such as abnormalities and monstrosities prove. It is thus extremely important for the atomists to frame and interpret them within the boundaries of what is possible and impossible: the very structural understanding of the universe depends on this task.

The *terminus*, or boundary, thus becomes a central concept in the atomist physics. It represents the range within which atoms can vary in shape,

---

[16] See Epicur. *Ep.* [2], 50 (= Usener, p. 12 = Epicurus (1926), p. 29: '[...] every image which we obtain by an act of apprehension on the part of the mind or of the sense-organs, whether of shape or of properties, this image is the shape <or properties> of the concrete object [...]. Falsehood and error always lie in the addition of opinion with regard to <what is waiting> to be confirmed or not contradicted, and then is not confirmed <or is contradicted>.')

[17] I have left this expression untranslated for the time being. I will show below why the translation is crucial for the interpretation and understanding of this central concept of atomist physics.

[18] Lucr. I.584–98.

magnitude and weight. This is why atoms must have parts, in order to differ from each other, and yet parts that are not separable from each other, in order to constitute the material ground for nature's consistency. Epicurus calls this minimal part or minimal possible variation ἐλάχιστον.[19] The boundary also represents the limits of nature's possibilities. These limits have not been posed by a demiurge, nor do they come from outside nature itself. These limits are closely related to the *foedera naturae*. They are the limits that we can observe in nature and that make it a familiar realm that we can study and understand, without fearing the unknown.

The limit or boundary also has a crucial role in the epistemological enterprise. Humans, and philosophers in particular, can successfully overcome their ignorance and understand nature. Their understanding is also subject to all kinds of boundaries, for example those imposed by the limitation of their perceptive faculties. However, nature's theatre and its components, as they have been outlined by Epicurus, make philosophers part of this same spectacle. In other words, their limits do not come from the outside and do not transcend humans' possibilities. The atoms and the void provide everything that is necessary for the philosopher to obtain the knowledge of nature.

Due to its incorporeal nature, the void cannot act or endure anything whatsoever in itself. These are exclusive features of bodily reality. As a consequence, concepts that occupy a central role in different metaphysical systems, such as incorporeal entities, ideas, divine intelligences or incorporeal souls, are wiped out as absurdities, incompatible with the fundamental elements of nature. Atomists read every phenomenon as nothing less and nothing more than a determined configuration of void (*inane*) and bodies (*corpora*), without a third nature ever being conceivable. These configurations of matter and space help us to identify what is essential in things, and what is not. Lucretius translates Epicurus's concepts of συμβεβηκότα and συμπτώματα with *coniuncta* and *euenta*: 'For whatsoever things have a name, either you will find them to be properties [*coniuncta*] [of void and bodies] or you will see them to be accidents [*euenta*] of the same.'[20]

---

[19] See Verde (2013).

[20] Lucr. I.449–50, developing Epicur. *Ep.* [2], 40 and 68–73. Bollack (1978), p. 157, notes the important shift introduced by Lucretius's choice of translation. According to Bollack, Lucretius does not translate the Epicurean concepts of συμβεβηκότα and συμπτώματα with terms having the same prefix. *Coniuncta* translates the qualities strictly attached to the thing (I.449), while *euenta* translates its accidents. Whereas Epicurus brings the two concepts close to each other, Lucretius does not translate the terms, but the ideas, and distinguishes the two orders, that of the solid background (*coniunctum*) on the one hand and that of the punctual and transitory event (*euentum*) on the other. Below I will indicate another important aspect of the idea involved in this choice of translation and, in particular, in the concept of *coniunctum*.

Nature recognises only properties and accidents, necessarily constituted according to the general principles of physics and necessarily contained within physical boundaries (thus alien to any intervention of metaphysical forces). It is curious, however, that the most important innovation introduced by Epicurus in ancient physics has been seen as contrasting with the very same foundation of the atomists' principles. In order to *explain* the actual dynamic of bodies in the void, beyond what he sees as the major limitation of Democritus's and Leucippus's physics, Epicurus introduces the concept of παρέγκλισις, swerve or deviation. And this has been seen as the Achilles' heel of the whole system.

Atoms incessantly move in space. Whereas ancient atomism conceives a chaotic, manifold and multidirectional movement, Epicurus and Lucretius draw the consequences of having introduced weight as one of the atom's basic properties. Weight uniformly drags atoms toward the bottom. The universe, although homogeneous, is thus oriented.[21] Such orientation, however, is in no way an anthropomorphic or merely empirical representation.[22] It rather means the necessity of an ordered movement that atoms pursue. Vis-à-vis the Democritean originally chaotic space, Epicurus has in mind a 'perpendicular' conception of space, within which the formation of composite bodies from indivisible atoms must be explained.[23]

During their fall, atoms encounter other atoms, due to the minimal deviation in their parallel downward motion.[24] The παρέγκλισις or *clinamen* has a double function: to explain the physical contact of atoms, which then aggregate and form composite bodies, but also to avoid the rigid necessity that Epicurus sees in Democritus's account of original cosmogony, whose consequences are for him unacceptable.[25] The *clinamen* should not be seen as a movement – or a cause – without a cause, but rather as a kind of *spontaneous* movement that obliterates every *external* cause in the beginning and at the time of the universe's generation. The fact of a movement being the cause of itself is of course unacceptable only if the causal theory rests on the ontological and chronological primacy of a τέλος, i.e. a direction that supposedly guides, more or less successfully, that same movement. Now, it is precisely to fight against a teleological vision of the origin of the universe that atomists conceive the swerve as an autonomous movement that has its origin in, and produces effects on, matter in the void.

---

[21] See Epicur. *Ep.* [2], 60 (= Usener, p. 18).
[22] See *contra* Alfieri (1953), p. 82, who claims Epicurus's subordination to the Aristotelian idea of an absolute orientation of the space, with its high and low.
[23] DeWitt (1954), p. 168.
[24] Lucr. II.216–24. See Fr. 281 (= Usener, pp. 199–201) in Cic. *Fin.* in particular.
[25] See Epicur. *Ep.* [4], 134. (= Usener, p. 65). See Marx, *Doktordissertation: Differenz der demokritischen und epikureischen Naturphilosophie nebst einem Anhange*, MEW, Ergänzungsband, erster teil, pp. 278 ff.

Cicero's argument against Epicurus is enlightening in this sense. Epicurus invents the swerve *ad libidinem* and *sine causa*.²⁶ Not even if one granted this (wrong) premise to Epicurus, however, would our universe result and, Cicero adds, likewise for Democritus, whose system relied upon the absence of cause. Only causality *rightly intended* can explain 'the ordered beauty of the world we know'.²⁷ The *ornatus mundi* is for Cicero the mark of causality properly intended. Without the former, the latter also disappears. On this point, the difference between Epicurus and Democritus is, for Cicero, irrelevant. The swerve, in fact, corresponds to assign 'to the atoms their different spheres of action [*quasi prouincia atomis dare*]', and thus to reintroduce that autonomous character to matter in motion that also Democritus had postulated, and that so many philosophers had been criticising.

Epicurus and Lucretius are thus brought within the traditional critique of the absence of causality that had already been directed against ancient atomists. Freedom and necessity, as well as spontaneity and causality, go hand in hand in both versions of atomism. Their original sin is to have flattened the universe within an immanent causal and ontological dimension. So, it is true, as Cicero claims, that Epicurus's swerve lacks a cause, but only in the sense of a teleological causality, the only cause that is able to constitute, for Cicero and many others, the ordered beauty of the world, and that the *turbulenta concursio* of atoms, in Cicero's view, would never be able to create.

The swerve, *pace* its detractors, confirms nonetheless the atomists' aim to rule out every form of transcendence, including the one implied in the teleological conception of the universe. The swerve is the autonomous and spontaneous cause that characterises Epicurus's matter in motion. It excludes every final cause and brings all causality on the same plan of immanence. Being without a τέλος, as Epicurus claims, does not mean being without a *ratio*, a state Cicero deplores.

Epicurus and Lucretius also mobilise a theory of the infinite. Atoms have not been completely exhausted, Epicurus explains to Herodotus, for the production of *this* world. Thus, nothing prevents us thinking that the number of *worlds* can be infinite.²⁸ Lucretius makes clear that the world of atoms resists its limitation by a spatial boundary, as much as by an ontological principle of transcendence: 'Nothing can have an extremity unless there is something

---

²⁶ Cic. *Fin.* I.19. See again Marx, *Doktordissertation: Differenz der demokritischen und epikureischen Naturphilosophie nebst einem Anhange*, MEW, Ergänzungsband, erster teil, p. 282 and Usener, p. 200, fr. 281.12–13.

²⁷ Cic. *Fin.* I.19.

²⁸ Epicur. *Ep.* [2], 45.4–11 (= Usener, p. 9). See also Epicurus (2012), the recent edition of the *On Nature*'s book II by G. Leone, coll. 1–7 and Leone's commentary, pp. 497–506.

beyond to bound it.'²⁹ This *nihil ultra* is at the same time physical and ethical. More importantly, it is linked to chance as an autonomous cause of production, a cause that does not exhaust itself in one world: as long as there is matter and space, there will be occasions for swerving atoms to encounter each other and form new composite bodies, and thus new worlds.³⁰

It is not by chance that neither Plato nor Aristotle accept the idea of an infinite world. Rejecting the existence of anything beyond bodies and space, as Epicurus does, has not only physical but also ontological consequences. It means, in fact, the rejection of separate planes of being, the same separation that both Plato and Aristotle, although in different ways, pursue. The Epicurean whole is infinite and unlimited, *thus* nothing exists beyond it. The infinite *takes* everything, and does not leave anything. It becomes, in the hands of Epicurus and Lucretius, a prodigious war machine against transcendence, as Plutarch has correctly remarked.³¹

Next to the quantitative infinity of the Epicurean cosmos, the atomists also develop the idea of a chronological infinity. Not only matter and space are endless, but so is time, which is therefore capable of hosting an infinity of encounters, aggregations and disaggregations of bodies and worlds. Together with matter and space, the idea of infinity of time is of paramount importance for the mechanistic hypothesis, and for the development of non-teleological explanation of natural phenomena. Unlimited time, in fact, means an endless reserve of attempts that nature might have made in order to achieve its present configuration. Nature and its order, Lucretius explains, come *ex infinito*:

> For certainly neither did the first-beginnings [*primordia rerum*] place themselves by design in their own order with keen intelligence, nor assuredly did they make agreement what motions each should produce; but because, being many and shifted in many ways [*multa modis multis mutata*], they are harried and set in motion with blows throughout the universe from infinity, thus by trying every kind of motion and combination, at length they fall into such arrangements as this sum of things consists of.³²

We know today how important this idea is in Darwinist evolutionism. Ancient atomism, however, had already realised its potentiality, to counter the idea of

---

²⁹ Lucr. I.958 ff.
³⁰ Lucr. II.1048 ff.
³¹ Fr. 76 (= Usener, p. 345). See Mondolfo (1956), pp. 497 ff. Although praising the atomist conception of infinity, Mondolfo (p. 507) shares the feeling that the swerve somehow contradicts the Epicurean premise, by introducing an incongruous element.
³² Lucr. I.1021–7. See Moreau (1975), pp. 472–3.

a superior intelligence creating what – providentialists argue – nature alone could never be able to produce without a design, namely order and beauty.

Usener includes, in his collection, an interesting fragment from Jerome's *Commentary on Ecclesiastes*, criticising Epicurus on the infinity of time: signs and prodigies are sent by God – Jerome claims – and one should not believe that they are the simple *repetition* of events that already happened in the past or will happen again in the future, as the impious philosopher claims. These events are indeed exceptional and new, and thus worthy of our astonishment.[33] The believer should never cease to be amazed at the wonders created by God. It is thus clear the social function played by physics in supporting a religious system of beliefs or, as Epicurus and Lucretius put it, superstition.

Atomists' philosophy revolves around the justification of the ethical function of knowledge. Knowledge is always employed to set men free from fear and awe, caused by the ignorance of nature. The observation of nature's regularity and consistency, on the contrary, makes them confident and frees mankind from fear, as Epicurus explains to Pythocles: 'We must not suppose that any other object is to be gained from the knowledge of the phenomena of the sky, whether they are dealt with in connexion with other doctrines or independently, than peace of mind and a sure confidence, just as in all other branches of study.'[34]

The ἀταραξία (imperturbability of the mind), the pillar of Epicurean ethics, can be reached first and foremost by changing one's attitude toward nature and its spectacle. This is the main aim of science. Lucretius often repeats his unlimited gratitude toward Epicurus for this paramount achievement.[35] By opening the gate of knowledge, the science of nature also closes the door to fear:

> As children tremble and fear everything in the blind darkness, so we in the light sometimes fear what is no more to be feared than the things that children in the dark hold in terror and imagine will come true. This terror, therefore, and darkness of the mind must be dispersed, not by rays of the sun nor the bright shafts of daylight, but by the aspect and nature's *ratio*.[36]

The first consequence is a real revolution in the conception of gods. Both Epicurus and Lucretius rule out the superstitious idea of a divinity that acts upon the world as if it were a man.[37] This is not an atheist position, as one

---

[33] Fr. 307 (= Usener, p. 215).
[34] Epicur. *Ep.* [3], 85 (= Usener, p. 36).
[35] Lucr. I.62–79 and *passim*.
[36] Lucr. III.87–93. Munro in Lucretius (1891, 4th ed.) and Rouse in Lucretius (1975) has 'law of nature' for *naturae species ratioque*.
[37] Grant (1952), p. 83.

might think. On the contrary, Epicurus and Lucretius believe in the existence of something that can be called divine. Because nothing exists beyond bodies and space, however, gods too must be of the very same bodily nature, although at its highest degree of perfection. Still, they are not of a different nature, and do not stand *above* nature. Imperturbable, gods live their own perfect existence without ever entering into contact with the human realm.[38] Moreover, they did not produce the world for the sake of men and will not in any possible way be moved by our devotion or prayers.[39] The basis of traditional religious practice and superstition is thus undermined,[40] and a new approach toward the study of nature – and toward a free life – can begin.

Plato and Aristotle, possibly the exoteric Aristotle rather than the one we have access to, as Bignone has maintained,[41] form the polemical target. For the atomists, they form the target for *both* the ethical and the physical arguments upon which their systems are based.[42] The end of physics is to set humankind free from fear and superstition. End and means, however, go hand in hand; one is the symptom and the cause of the other. The largest section of Usener's collection is devoted to these aspects. Epicurus's texts on this doctrine, preserved by its most fierce detractors, speak about the necessary implications of atomist physics on ethics and religion. Lucian honestly praises, through the powerful irony of his work, this attitude.[43] Simplicius, Cicero, Plutarch, Plotinus, Galen and Lactantius fiercely attack him. The ὑλικὴ ἀνάγκη, the material necessity that Epicurus sees working in the universe, wipes out all anthropomorphic images of God.[44] Yet the sin has been committed. Lucretius boldly rehearses the fully immanent origin of everything: nature and the world are explained without providence, without God and without design. The world, infinite, is left to itself and to men's curious exploration of its phenomena, their causes, their effects.[45]

---

[38] Lucr. V.146.

[39] Epicur. *Ep.* [2], 76–7 (= Usener, p. 28).

[40] Epicurus makes clear that the tranquillity of men is the most important aim, and his purpose is not, in this sense, to move men toward rebellion against authority. See Epicur. *Ep.* [2], 77 (= Usener, p. 28).

[41] Bignone's thesis has been criticised too many times and with too many good arguments to be repeated here. See Bignone (1936) and Caratelli (1983). An esoteric Aristotle, however, has existed, and it contained most certainly the kind of arguments that Epicurus and, subsequently, Lucretius, are thinking about.

[42] See *contra* Reale (1995), III, p. 217. Marx explains the strategic role played by the principle of multiple explanations in *Doktordissertation: Differenz der demokritischen und epikureischen Naturphilosophie nebst einem Anhange*, MEW, Ergänzungsband, erster teil, p. 301.

[43] Fr. 368 (= Usener, p. 246).

[44] As Simplicius claims. See Fr. 377 (= Usener, p. 254).

[45] Lucr. V.419–31, which substantially repeats I.1021–7.

Zoogony, Monstrosity and Nature's Normativity

Once the general atomistic principles have been established, the account of the origin of the universe has to be unfolded, so as to give the necessary details that will accomplish the ethical and scientific task that Epicurus and Lucretius are pursuing. Epicurus's traces fade away here, as most of his writings are lost. Lucretius, however, masterfully develops the topic of the world's origin in book V of *De rerum natura*, in which one also finds the account of the role and status of monstrosity.

Verses 772–836 of book V contain the essence of the Lucretian zoogony. Once the earth is formed, according to the composition of atoms described above, it starts producing living beings. The earth is in its youth, and thus it is powerful and abounds in life. Mother of all things, it spontaneously produces larger and smaller animals, initially out of wombs growing from the earth, and eventually nourished by it. That time is now gone and the earth, although still producing small creatures spontaneously, is not mighty enough to produce the bigger ones any more. Nevertheless, life has been born and perpetuates itself autonomously, as Lucretius explains in the following section.[46]

The first striking contention of Lucretius is the total absence of any anthropocentrism. Nature creates all sort of creatures in many ways and following different processes (*multis modis, varia ratione*). No distinction is made between humans and animals, and this is another polemical argument against the traditional accounts of the initial creation, guided by a theological and teleological rationale, centred upon the special status recognised to humans vis-à-vis animals.[47] Lucretius is echoing Empedocles, whose Περὶ φύσεως he

---

[46] Paradoxographer Phlegon of Tralles explicitly connects the earth's force of production in its youth and the progressive exhaustion of this force to monstrosity. In his *Book of Marvels*, XIV and XV, Phlegon relates how, after earthquakes, buried giant bones resurface: 'One should not disbelieve in these bones [. . .], considering that in the beginning when nature was in her prime she reared everything near to gods, but just as time is running down, so also the sizes of creatures have been shrinking (XV.2 (= FGH 257 F 36.XV).' The earth's senescence is a well-known theme in antiquity, employed to explain the present diminution of her vital force. Phlegon, however, goes further, using this theme to explain the appearance of vestiges of monstrously giant creatures. See Lovejoy and Boas (1935), pp. 98–102 and Guthrie (1957), *passim*. Following Mayor (2001), Payón Leyra (2011), pp. 152 ff. reads Phlegon's argument as a confirmation that the Greeks knew about fossils. He uses the argument in his reading of a famous iconographic manifestation of monstrosity, namely the Boston mixing bowl (column krater). The painter shows the Trojan princess Hesione, next to Heracles, throwing stones at a threatening dragon. According to the *Il.* XX.144–8, this is a sea monster (κῆτος), yet the giant head clearly resembles a fossil skull emerging from the earth.

[47] See Schrijvers (1974). See also Casini (1963), pp. 200 ff.

certainly knew.⁴⁸ According to Empedocles, during the epoch of Love, countless types of creatures (ἔθνεα μυρία θνητῶν), which are a wonder to behold (θαῦμα ἰδέσθαι), have been created from the earth.⁴⁹

Gordon Campbell has intelligently remarked on the ethical implications of the plurality of modes of production as well as the communality of the process for animals and humans alike.⁵⁰ Against Plato's demiurge and the Stoics' providence, Lucretius's aim is thus to remove every teleological idea by dissolving the wonder traditionally attached to the early zoogony, including that of Empedocles. Whereas to Empedocles the early creatures were wonders to behold, for him they are *simply* the result of atomic combinations, produced with no design or rationale, but only following their own bodily necessity.

Lucretius's metaphor of the earth as *magna mater* of all creatures seems to contrast with his anti-teleological stance.⁵¹ There is of course a danger in presenting nature as a creative personified entity, amplified by the idea of a 'feminine nurturing force' opposed to the Stoic 'masculine *controlling* universal force'.⁵² However, Lucretius employs here a powerful rhetorical strategy to appropriate the enemy's language and turn it upside down by infusing a purely material process into an apparently teleological idea.⁵³

Terrestrial creatures, Lucretius argues, cannot have fallen from the sky or have come out of the sea. Nature has boundaries according to which not everything can happen in any possible manner. The bodily necessity is first and foremost a necessity, namely something that discriminates between the *impossibilis* and the *possibilis*. Creatures and events falling under our senses depend on their material constitution, and thus respond to what such a constitution allows to happen. It is a fixist argument, widespread in antiquity,

---

⁴⁸ Waszinsk (1954). See also Morgan (1984), pp. 102 ff.
⁴⁹ See *Vorsokr.* 31 B 35 (= LM [22] EMP. D75, R70 = Simp. *in Cael.* 528.30) and *supra*. See also Ernout and Robin (1925–8), I, pp. 146–7, Spoerri (1959 and 1997) and Kranz (1944), p. 44. *Contra* Jones (1993).
⁵⁰ Campbell (2003), pp. 56–7.
⁵¹ Campbell mentions Lovejoy and Boas, 'Some Meanings of Nature', in Lovejoy, Boas eds. (1935), pp. 447–56.
⁵² Campbell (2003), p. 82.
⁵³ See Fowler (2002). It is interesting to note that even Charles Darwin has to defend himself from the accusation of personifying nature, an accusation that often comes from those who believe in a personified entity. See C. Darwin, *The Origin of Species*, IV, in Darwin (1986–9), XVI, on his concept of natural selection: 'Everyone knows what is meant and is implied by such metaphorical expressions; and they are almost necessary for brevity. So again it is difficult to avoid personifying the word Nature; but I meant by Nature, only the aggregate action and product of many natural laws, and by laws the sequence of events as ascertained by us. With a little familiarity such superficial objections will be forgotten.' See also Pievani (2014).

that Lucretius develops along the lines of his *foedera naturae* and *alte terminus* (deep-set boundary mark).[54]

Thus, the earth changes its status. Powerful and young once, it is now weak and incapable of producing the same variety of animals that it once produced. An important idea emerges from verses 828–36, namely the balance between constancy and change. Everything changes ceaselessly but according to a certain regularity. This regularity, expressed by the *foedera* and the *termini*, is neither imposed *on* nature from above, nor established *by* nature in its realm. As I will show later, it is rather the *result* of the flux of events or, better, what humans perceive of it, from their limited point of view. This point of view is limited by the boundaries of our senses, incapable of grasping the exact nature of bodily necessity and, even more importantly, by the boundaries of our mortal existence, vis-à-vis the endless nature of time, that ceaselessly shapes nature's appearance. What are, thus, the regularities that we recognise in nature, in the everlasting change of the balance between different parts of the universe?[55] And, beyond such regularities, what are the anomalies and monstrosities that we both see and imagine?

Verses 837–54 narrate the immediate aftermath of the origin of life:

> Many were the portents [*portenta*] also that the earth then tried to make [*creare conatast*], springing up with wondrous appearance and frame: the hermaphrodite, between man and woman yet neither, different from both; some without feet, others again bereft of hands; some found dumb also without a mouth, some blind without eyes, some bound fast with all their limbs adhering to their bodies, so that they could do nothing and go nowhere, could neither avoid mischief nor take what they might need. So with the rest of like monsters and portents [*monstra ac portenta*] that she made, it was all in vain [*nequiquam*]; since nature banned their growth [*natura absterruit auctum*], and they could not attain the desired flower of age nor find food nor join by the ways of Venus. For we see that living beings need many things in conjunction [*multa rebus concurrere debere*], so that they may be able [*ut . . . possint*] by procreation to forge out the chain of the generations: first there must be food, next there must be a way for the life-giving seeds throughout the frame to flow out from the slackened body; and that male and female be joined, they must both have the means to exchange mutual pleasures.

---

[54] Campbell (2003), p. 59. See *infra* on the *foedera naturae*.

[55] For the relationship between the constant flux of matter and the *foedera naturae* see Long (1977) 81ff.

Monsters and portents are born by the earth in the beginning of the world, in different shapes and constitutions. Some of them are produced in vain (*nequiquam*) because, being unable to find food, or consume it, or copulate, they do not reproduce themselves and do not last. Many things are needed for these early beings to stabilise themselves on earth and produce progeny. Only some of these things are actually available, and only a few fortunate beings are actually able to find them all, and that is how they survive. Without any design or divine providence presiding over the world, this is how certain beings have been able to reproduce, while others simply died out without progeny.[56]

Although *many* things are necessary for the survival of a species, Lucretius lists some qualities that appear to be the proper feature of certain species: courage for lions, cunning for foxes, swiftness for stags. Others had the chance to prove their utility for men, who in turn protect animals such as dogs or sheep, and allow them to survive.[57] However,

> those to which nature gave no such qualities, so that they could neither live by themselves at their own will, nor give us some usefulness for which we might suffer them to feed under our protection and be safe, these certainly lay at the mercy of others for prey and profit, being all hampered by their own fateful chains [*uincla fatales*], until nature brought that race to destruction.[58]

In this passage, much more than when he speaks about the *magna mater*, Lucretius dangerously approaches the anthropocentric language that he so carefully intends to avoid. For this account already places the reader at the time when humans claim superiority over animals, at least a superiority in deeds, if not in principle. Humans are already able to survive, defend themselves and propagate their *genus*. More importantly, they show what appears to be the exclusive ability to protect other *genera*, namely those that they find useful, whose work they can exploit, and that they can use for their purposes. While other creatures are still struggling for survival, on the edge of extinction, humanity has already acquired a special position, although factual and not ontological, in nature.

---

[56] This, Bailey suggests, is the passage from individuals to species. See Bailey, in Lucretius (1947), III, p. 1465: 'When chance has developed an appropriate kind of animal, then that kind is established as a permanent species. Once again contingency establishes natural law (*foedus*).'
[57] Lucr. V.855–70.
[58] Lucr. V.871–7.

What are then the *uincla fatalia* of V.876? Is it nature that guides some animals toward survival, while pushing others toward extinction? Is it destiny? The choices that translators have made are revealing. Ernout, Costa and Flores all stress the role of a quasi-personified fate, acting upon creatures and bringing them to extinction.[59] I believe, however, that one should completely avoid such a personification. Interestingly enough, *fatalia* appears only once in the whole *De rerum natura*.[60] It should be read, I believe, as a disastrous, harmful and deadly limitation, rather than the intervention or even the effect of Fate, which is wholly at odds with the atomist mentality.[61]

Alluding to Empedocles' account of the origin of the world, Lucretius nevertheless moves out of the myth. While Ackermann focuses on the surface of Lucretius's language, thus claiming that the Latin poet is still imbued with an old mythical mentality,[62] Casini claims that beyond the surface of the zoogonic account, Lucretius brings atomism towards what modern philosophers eventually see as a scientific study of nature, or at least find useful for developing it.[63] Lucretius is not only attempting to develop a concept of nature alternative to the Aristotelian one. He is also showing how natural regularities have been shaped and forged, immanently, within nature.

Nature does not receive laws, nor does it implement them. Early living beings are Nature's *attempts* or, even better, *efforts*. The choice of the verb *conari* is extremely important. Lucretius certainly echoes Empedocles' account, as several scholars have already pointed out. Munro suggests that Lucretius at the same time refutes Empedocles' theory, as he would have deemed absurd the idea of wandering limbs, looking for each other.[64] Munro, however, focuses on the outcome of nature's production rather than on the process of production itself. Lucretius is not in line with Aristotle and his commentators here. By seeing the process as a spontaneous series of attempts, or multiple efforts,

---

[59] Ernout in Lucretius (1924): 'chaînes de leur destinée'; Costa in Lucretius (1984): 'chains of fate'; Flores in Lucretius (2002–9): 'ceppi voluti dal fato'.
[60] Paulson (1911) and Wacht (1990).
[61] Bailey in Lucretius (1947) and Rouse and Smith in Lucretius (1975) are closer to this reading, with 'fateful chains'. Munro (1873, 3rd ed.) pertinently avoids all reference to fate with 'death-bringing shackles'. See Campbell (2003), p. 138, for a fair compromise, i.e. Lucretius *does* think about Fate, yet he turns its meaning upside down: 'The "bonds of fate" are perhaps the closest L.'s language sails to the teleological wind in this whole passage (see [also 811]). All such ideas are fair game for L.: not even the hateful notion of predestined doom can escape his remorseless appropriation and recontextualization [. . .].'
[62] Ackermann (1979).
[63] Casini (1963). See the discussion in Spoerri (1997).
[64] Munro (1873, 3rd ed.). Also absurd, for Munro, is the concrete example of the βουγενῆ ἀνδρόπρωρα, the man-headed oxen, which had already been refuted by the champions of the final cause, like Aristotle and his commentators Themistius and Simplicius.

with no end in view, Lucretius moves away from teleology, following precisely Empedocles' intuition.

Bailey recognises Empedocles' influence in Lucretius's account of the *process* of nature's production, not only that of its actual outcomes.[65] Besides moving the account beyond the myth and making it more 'scientific and consistent with the general theory', Bailey regards it as paralleling the account of the creation of the worlds in books I.1021–8 and V.419–31.[66] More importantly, Bailey suggests that laws do not come *before* nature's efforts, but rather they are outcomes of those attempts, once they stabilise themselves and progenies become possible. In this respect, however, I find problematic Bailey's reference to 'perfection'. Only the more 'perfect' creatures, he writes, became viable 'after many failures'. Perfection, in fact, refers to the impossibility of further improvement, full possession of essential characteristics, completion, correspondence to a pre-existing pattern of principle, accurateness in reproducing a model, full development and normality, conformity to laws: all these views, I believe, are alien to Lucretius's concept.

Lucretius is on the contrary ruling out any achievement or *perfection* that must be reached by creatures in order to survive. The *ut . . . possint* of V.850 has a consecutive and not a final sense, as has often and correctly been noted.[67] It is true, as Schrijvers claims, that monsters are found within nature for both Lucretius and Aristotle alike.[68] They are within it, however, in opposite ways for the two philosophers. A convergence between Lucretius and Aristotle has also been urged by Jackie Pigeaud. Pigeaud claims that Aristotle and Lucretius share the necessity of proving the impossibility of mixed monsters, such as centaurs or chimaeras.[69] Following a botanical model, both authors are concerned with the problem of the impossible graft, for example the graft of a human

---

[65] Bailey in Lucretius (1947), III, p. 1461: 'The idea of nature's experiments had already been expressed by Empedocles, though many of his fantastic notions, such as the creation of parts of the body themselves, which went about seeking for union, and the creation of creatures of mixed species, were rightly rejected by Epicurus.'
[66] Bailey in Lucretius (1947), III, p. 1461: 'Here, as there, all sorts of combinations were produced which could survive. Once again what was produced by contingency then acquired the government of "natural law".'
[67] Bailey in Lucretius (1947), III, p. 1464. See also Campbell (2003), p. 115: 'The *portenta* are not variations from a norm, since no norm could exist until sexual reproduction took over from spontaneous generation and fixed creatures into discrete species.'
[68] Schrijvers, *Un chapitre de l'histoire de l'humanité: Lucretius, De rerum natura V 837–854*, in Giannantoni, Gigante a cura di(1984), pp. 841–50. Schrijvers develops his thesis on the similarity between Aristotle's theory that monsters are more frequent in multiparae and Lucretius's idea that the Earth is the multiparous being *par excellence*.
[69] Pigeaud (1988), p. 205: 'C'est lui qui met en péril l'ordre de la nature, en proposant une logique de la tératologie. Il n'y a pas de térato-logie.'

onto a horse, or a snake onto a goat and the goat onto a lion. In his brilliant article, Pigeaud shows how Columella's argument on grafts in *De re rustica* is a direct response, proudly based on his successful grafting, to the authors claiming the impossibility of joining together different and supposedly incompatible plants. Pigeaud suggests that Columella has in mind Aristotle and Lucretius, united by their common aversion towards the composite monster and to the older Empedoclean arguments.[70] I think that Pigeaud's hypothesis dismisses too quickly the striking and clear contrast between Lucretius and Aristotle.

The regularity of forms always pre-exists individual beings for Aristotle, while Lucretius sees regularities *only* as the outcome of individuals' effort to survive their birth.[71] This effort, close to the verb *conari* chosen by Lucretius, must be referred less to nature as a whole and more to the multiplicity of its individual creatures, all striving to survive. Beings are born: some live, others die. The latter are the exception, vis-à-vis the former which become the norm. They do so because they reproduce themselves, because their effort to preserve their life is successful (the success of their effort is *not* due to any adherence to or respect for the norm).[72]

The striving and conflictual dimension of the relation between creatures is not all that Lucretius has in mind, though it is too often emphasised by scholars discussing its similarities with Darwin's theory of natural selection.[73] Just as important as the selection are the cooperation, the concurrence and the agreement between creatures. The regularity of shapes, as Vittorio Morfino puts it, does not pre-exist the encounter between individuals. It is rather the outcome of the encounters and the union of necessary and sufficient conditions. It is a *concurrere multa rebus* that transforms the conjunction into a conjuncture, and a happy one, favourable to the survival of a species.[74] As soon as they are created, one could say, all animals are monstrous (something that Aristotle would have deemed absurd).[75] They do not fight to become

---

[70] On grafts in Virgil see Ross (1987), pp. 104–9, and A. Deremetz, 'The Marvellous in the *Georgics*', in Hardie (2009), pp. 123–5.

[71] See Campbell (2003), p. 114: 'Earth produces random creatures to no avail since *natura*, here "physical necessity" or simply the physical make-up of the creatures, prevents them surviving.' On Lucretius's dialogue with his sources see Spoerri (1997), Appendix.

[72] Nineteenth-century finalism, in some sense, still responds to this question and to the priority to assign to the norm vis-à-vis the exception and the abnormality. See Janet (1876), pp. 184–5 and p. 340 in particular.

[73] See for example Bailey in Lucretius (1947), III, p. 1462. See also *infra* on vv. 855–77; Guthrie (1957), pp. 203 ff.; Casini (1963), who claims that *because* Lucretius follows Empedocles, he cannot be considered evolutionist; Campbell (2003), pp. 101 ff.; Costa in Lucretius (1984), pp. 102–3.

[74] Morfino (2013).

[75] See Campbell (2003), p. 115.

normal. They fight to survive and *thus* they create normality. They need each other more than they need to fight *against* other animals. Monsters, as Michel Serres has beautifully written, are the losers of a competition which is against themselves rather than against the others:

> The earth, recently formed, begins to produce. Wombs grow in the soil, fixed by their roots. Then monsters are born. Their features or limbs are strange. Now, this strangeness is always negative. The androgynous, for example, is not both sexes at the same time. It is neither one, nor the other, and it does not belong to any of them. Teratology constitutes itself by the rule *determinatio est negatio*. The unnamed and innominable monsters are deprived of feet, of hands. They are mute, with no mouth, blind, with no sight, they cannot do anything, neither move nor avoid dangers, nor take care of their needs, nor grow up, nor find food, nor mate through Venus's act. These negative determinations define them as *closed systems*: the monster does not have ways, because it does not have a way out [either literally or figuratively]. It is without doors or windows. Lucretius's monster is Leibniz's monad. Without hole or door, without mouth or vagina. As if, precisely, life was possible only through the capacity of combining oneself, that is to say through the opening. Life is an open system. The monster is in itself and for itself, autistic and dead. Nature eliminates them, it abandons them as prey for animals selected through their positive attributes.[76]

Beyond Serres, however, one could say that *determinatio* is both and at the same time *negatio* and *affirmatio*, because it is only by determining itself, by entwining and intertwining relations with others, more or less similar to itself, that the individual acquires a chance to survive.

This, as I will show more clearly later on, discussing the translation of *foedera naturae*, brings the argument toward the meaning and status of a 'law' of nature, a term that I have carefully avoided so far in order to keep away from the interpretation, common in scholarship, that something like a 'law' is acting in Lucretius's theory. Alain Gigandet, for example, has correctly insisted on Lucretius's anti-teleological stance by focusing on the role played by *concurrere* as the verb that epitomises the many initial attempts made by nature.[77] These attempts clash, for Gigandet, with the boundaries of nature, i.e. the limits of what is possible and impossible. The metaphor of the boundaries might suggest their being external to the phenomena that they would have to prevent and

---

[76] Serres (1977), pp. 175–6.
[77] Gigandet (1998), p. 137: '*multa videmus enim rebus concurrere debere* (v. 849): *concours*, an encounter without any finalist presupposition, and depending on statistic chance'.

select. Boundaries would act as a filter or a net, that let some phenomena pass through, while preventing some other from moving ahead.[78]

It is certainly true that Lucretius is developing here a dialectic between the possible and the impossible.[79] This dialectic, Gigandet claims, is grounded on the structure of nature, obeying three laws of atomic combination: 1) only certain combinations are possible, 2) no combination is unique, and 3) every combination traverses a cycle of creation and destruction that brings it from its origin to its dissolution.[80] As discussed above, however, the atomic combinations at the microscopic level are tuned with the macroscopic combinations that can be seen at the physical level. They are the causes, as much as the effects, of what we experience and observe in nature. In other words, laws of atomic combination certainly exist. Where do they come from, though? Neither from a superior intelligence, nor from an inner intelligence of matter itself. They rather are the regularities that matter has acquired *through*, and not before, nature's attempts. The concept of limits is indeed essential to comprehending nature.[81] Nonetheless, I believe that the limits of variation do not explain nature's Being, but rather they are *explained by*, because they are *shaped through*, nature's Becoming.

As Gigandet has pointed out, chance plays here a fundamentally important role. Not so much, however, within the boundaries of laws, but rather in creating and defining those same boundaries. The initial chance, Gigandet maintains, creates its own necessity.[82] Borrowing Bailey's language, Gigandet speaks about the opposition between the viable organisms' perfection and the unviable monsters' imperfection – a formula that implies an axiological position and a substantial difference between normal beings that will survive and abnormal ones that are doomed to extinction. The former's *only* perfection, in my view, is that they *actually* have survived, nothing more, and nothing less. Gigandet recalls the metaphor of the *iactus veneris*, a winning throw of four dice in which each of them has a different number on its face. This image can, however, be a misleading image of what Lucretius is arguing. For this to be the winning combination, in fact, a *rule* must have been established

---

[78] Gigandet (1998), p. 137: 'In this perspective, Lucretius contrasts earth's *attempts* and nature's *prohibitions* (vv. 845–6) which essentially concern growth and reproduction. Ultimately, the pacts of nature (*foedera naturae*) manifest themselves here in the form of a negative condition, of limits imposed to the profusion of forms effectively accomplishable.'

[79] Gigandet (1998), p. 136. On such a dialectic see also Courtès (1968).

[80] Gigandet (1998), pp. 146–7.

[81] See De Lacy (1969) and *infra*.

[82] Gigandet (1998), p. 143: 'Les monstres primitifs sont indissociables des origines de la vie, c'est-à-dire des "tentatives" de la terre, entendues comme "coups" successifs du hasard, essais aveugles finissant par produire des composés viables, créant leur propre nécessité.'

before the game is played. No configuration of the dice's upper faces, *in itself*, is more or less perfect, more or less probable than any other.[83] Thus, I think that although chance is indeed the ground – and the only ground – for atoms' encounter, the metaphor of the winning throw might be confusing, because I see the rules of the game, in Lucretius's mind, as being perpetually remade.

Let's try to clarify further Lucretius's assumption that not everything can happen in nature, and not in just any possible manner. This is clearly stated, already, in book II.700–29 of *De rerum natura*:

> It must not be thought that all can be conjoined in all ways: for then you would commonly see monstrosities come into being, shapes of men arising that would be half beasts, lofty branches at times sprouting from a living body, parts of terrestrial creatures often conjoined with creatures of the sea, Chimaeras again, breathing flame from noisome throats, pastured by nature over the lands that produce everything. But that none of these things happen is manifest, since we see that all things bred from fixed seeds by a fixed mother [*seminibus certis certa generatrice creata*] are able to conserve their kind as they grow. Assuredly this must come about in a fixed way. For in each thing, its own proper bodies are spread abroad through the frame within from all its foods, and being combined produce the appropriate motions; but contrariwise we see alien elements to be thrown back by nature upon the earth, and many, beaten by blows, escape from the body with their invisible bodies, which were not able to combine with any part nor within the body to feel the life-giving motions with it and imitate them.
>
> But do not think that animals only are held by these laws [*legibus*], for the same principal holds all things apart by their limits [*ratio disterminat omnia*]. For just as all things made are in their whole nature different one from another, so each must consist of first-beginnings differently shaped; I do not say that very few are endowed with the same shape, but that commonly they are not all like all. Since, further, the seeds are different, different must be their intervals, passages, connexions, weights, blows, meetings, motions, which not only separate animal bodies asunder, but keep asunder the earth and the whole sea, and hold back all heaven away from the earth.

---

[83] Gigandet (1998), p. 143. Gigandet mentions Cic. *Div.* I.13 and II.21. Cicero's use of the metaphor, however, shows how problematic its use would be for the atomist. See *Div.* I.23: 'You ask, Carneades, do you, why these things so happen, or by what rules they may be understood? I confess that I do not know, but that they do so fall out I assert that you yourself see. "Mere accidents [*casu*]," you say. Now, really, is that so? Can anything be an "accident" which bears upon itself every mark of truth [*numeros veritatis*]? Four dice are cast and a Venus throw results – that is chance; but do you think it would be chance, too, if in one hundred casts you made one hundred Venus throws?'

Animate and inanimate things respond to the same *leges* and *rationes*. Lucretius seems particularly concerned, here, with explaining why shapes do not monstrously collapse into each other, as well as why elements do not mix together and dissolve in the same undistinguished chaos. We regularly observe the reproduction of animal shapes and the separation of different elements. All this is rooted in the atomic principle of combination that, for animals, takes the form of reproduction by a *certa* mother with *certa* seeds. This is also why we do not see mythical monsters being grown on earth. Unlike the zoogonic account of book V, monsters are here the exception, the *impossibilia* that nature's principles rule out.

We have seen above how Aristotle reflects on the same question of nature's regularities. The difference, however, is striking. Whereas Aristotle explains regularities through forms that also act as causes for the sake of which something is (or is not) what it has to be, Lucretius excludes every end from the process. Lucretius's *leges* and *rationes* are strongly opposed to Aristotle's ἀνάγκη φύσεος. Within a teleological framework, the regularity of forms rules out any atomic explanation, and a τέλος is needed to avoid the undistinguished chaos of forms. Within Lucretius's framework, on the contrary, the regularity of forms confirms the atomist explanation, and speaks against the teleological idea.[84]

Léon Robin reads an inconsistency in Lucretius's thought, as if the same laws and principles that allowed the initial formation of monstrosities, although unviable, were eventually used by Lucretius to deny the possibility of *some* monsters, notably the mythological ones, such as chimeras or centaurs.[85] How to explain this apparent inconsistency? Bailey claims that Lucretius speaks about two different kinds of monstrosity, one possible but extinguished, the other utterly impossible, thus establishing a sort of legal principle of impossibility.[86] Nevertheless, I think that the impossibility is not based on a principle. The legality that Lucretius speaks about, using the terms *lex* and *ratio*, has its origin *in itself*, as its material ground proves, rather than disproves. Without doubling the causes, as well as the kinds of monstrosities, in order to avoid the inconsistency, one can argue that Lucretius is indeed speaking about the same set of causes and the same kind of monstrosities, but in different moments and circumstances.

Time is infinite, and so are space and possible worlds. The initial natural efforts *could* have given birth to different creatures that *could* have found a way of surviving, even if this has not actually happened (i.e. it has proven impossible) in this world. There are not, in other words, two kinds of impossibility. It is indeed impossible, for an animal, to spit fire, because fire and

---

[84] See Moreau (1975), *passim*.
[85] Ernout and Robin (1925–8), III, p. 122 on Lucr. V.878 ff.
[86] Bailey in Lucretius (1947), III, p. 1468. See also Gigandet (1998), pp. 140–1.

animal flesh are incompatible. *In the same way*, it is impossible for a chicken to fly, even if it has wings, or for oxen to have human heads, or for men to have equine bodies, or for a soul to be immortal. It is a physical impossibility that, as such, has a specific origin in time and space and does not contrast with the idea of the changing character of nature: 'Time changes the nature of the whole world, and one state of the earth gives way to another, so that what she bore she cannot, but can bear what she did not bear before.'[87]

When Lucretius fully unfolds the consequences of his cosmogony and zoogony, he once again puts forward the argument that monstrosities are impossible. He explains that 'centaurs never existed, nor at any time can there be creatures of double nature and twofold body combined together of incompatible limbs, such that the powers of the two halves can be fairly balanced'.[88] Different *genera* have different rhythms of growth and maturity. They also have different compatibilities and incompatibilities with foods and thus among themselves. They cannot be joined together because this implies contradiction, both anatomical, or physiological, and behavioural, since they could not even agree in habits.[89]

If mythical creatures such as centaurs and chimeras, which play such a large part in superstitious beliefs, have to be destroyed on a rational and physical basis, then their explanation must be the same, or at least compatible with, the same rational and physical contentions used to explain monstrosities in the earliest age. Munro thus argues that this passage derives from refutation of Empedocles' ideas and, in particular, his man-faced oxen.[90] However, we have already seen how Empedocles' thought is positively present in Lucretius's account of early zoogony. Schrijvers has underlined a possible source of Lucretius's argument in the rationalist critique of myths in Palaephatus.[91] Like

---

[87] Lucr. V.834–6.

[88] Lucr. V.878–82. 881 is uncertain and its interpretation is not without consequences. For a full discussion of this *crux* see Bailey in Lucretius (1947), III, p. 1468.

[89] Lucr. V.833–900.

[90] Munro in Lucretius (1891, 4th ed.), *ad loc.*: 'This passage is extremely well and acutely reasoned out: he covertly refutes Empedocles' notion of the βουγενῆ ἀνδρόπρωρα and the ἀνδροφυῆ βούκρανα which are as impossible as the centaurs Scyllas and chimeras of the poets. The man-woman or hermaphrodite is possible enough, because the natures of man and woman are not incompatible; and doubtless it and other monstrous things tries at first to continue existence; but the creatures here described never could begin to come into being.'

[91] Schrijvers in Caratelli (1983). See Palaeph. 1 (= Festa et al. eds. (1894–1902), III.II, pp. 1–2): 'What is said about the Centaurs is that they were beasts with the overall shape of a horse – except for the head, which was human. But even if there are some people who believe that such a beast once existed, it is impossible. Horse and human natures are not compatible, nor are their foods the same: what a horse eats could not pass through the mouth and throat of a man. And if there ever was such a shape, it would also exist today.' On Palaephatus's historical exegesis see *supra*. See also Grant (1952), pp. 47–8, and Hawes (2014), ch. 1.

Palaephatus, Lucretius has both an interest in the *impossibilia* and the psychological attitude that can be used to rationalise the myth.[92] Against Schrijvers, however, Gigandet argues that it is precisely the psychological attitude that marks the difference between the two authors: whereas Palaephatus believes that the myth can be amended to remove its unbelievable and unacceptable features,[93] Lucretius intends to destroy the myth and substitute for it a physical explanation.[94] It is thus more appropriate, Gigandet suggests, to focus on the nature of the insuperable limits in order to grasp the originality of the physical boundaries that constrain all animals and monsters alike. Lucretius insists:

> [H]e that supposes that such animals could have been born when earth was young and heaven new, depending upon this one empty word 'newness', may with equal reason babble on without end, saying that then rivers of gold used commonly to flow over the earth, that trees used to have jewels for flowers, that man was born with so great expanse of limbs that he could set his stride across the deep sea and with his hands turn the whole sky about him. For although there were many seeds of things in the soil at the time when first the earth poured forth the animals, that is nevertheless no proof (*signi*) that creatures of mixed growth (*mixtas animantum*) could be made, and limbs of various kinds of plants and the corn and the luxuriant trees, which even now spring in abundance from the earth, nevertheless cannot be produced interwoven together, but each thing proceeds after its own fashion, and all by *foedere naturae* preserve their distinctions (*certo discrimina servant*).[95]

Lucretius, Gigandet argues, accepts the Empedoclean theory of nature's attempts, but at the same time he establishes limits to it, and makes it dependent on the possible combinations of atoms, carefully distinguished from the impossible ones. Not everything can happen in nature, not even in its initial stage, because atomic combinations are given *within* a 'cadre délimité (*certus*)'.[96] Lucretius, thus, rules out Empedocles' idea of individual limbs looking for each other. Not so much because earthly wombs produce individuals and not limbs, but because 'looking for each other' implies some form of intentionality and teleology. Individuals do not look for the conditions that will allow them to

---

[92] See also Pigeaud (1988), p. 208.
[93] Palaeph. introduction: '[...] some people are too credulous and believe anything [...] others [...] totally disbelieve that any of these tales ever happened. My own belief is that there is a reality behind all stories. For names alone without stories would hardly have arisen: first there must have been deeds and thereafter stories about them.'
[94] Gigandet (1998), pp. 44–5.
[95] Lucr. V.907–24.
[96] Gigandet (1998), p. 140.

survive, but they survive because they meet those conditions. The *certus discrimen* mentioned by Lucretius, however, does not function, in my view, as a boundary or a net, and far less as a law. The *discrimen* is rather the outcome or effect of the *foedera naturae*, an outcome that is immanently realised rather than being given or determined by any other force.[97] It is *certus* – an adjective repeated more than one hundred times in *De rerum natura* – in the sense of being univocally related to its causes: certain causes produce *certain* effects and no others, as if everything could happen indistinctly.

Bollack calls attention to the similitude between the atoms that compose the world and the letters of the alphabet (the *elementa*) that compose words.[98] Moreau emphasises the same argument, to stress that, as the letters of the alphabet must be different, in order for words to have a sense, so the atoms must be different for the physical beings to differentiate from each other and have their specific and recognisable characteristics.[99] Now, this differentiation must of course be limited, otherwise words would be infinite and language, in a sort of Babylonian and Borgesian scenario, would become unintelligible. Likewise, beings must have regularities and their forms be limited, in the same way that the diversity of their shapes and magnitudes must be limited. The similitude is penetrating, and I suggest extending it to the process of formation of these regularities: words are not fixed; they acquire their meaning through their use, through being spoken by people, or disappear by being abandoned and forgotten. In the same manner, living beings acquire their meaning, i.e. their ontological consistency, not as a *condition*, but as a *consequence* of their existence. Beings exist because they reproduce themselves in the world and because, in some sense, they 'speak' themselves in nature.

Concourses of Nature

The *foedera naturae* is one of the most important expressions used by Lucretius. They have been seen as the archetype of a law of nature,[100] as it is proved by the quasi-overwhelming consensus among translators.[101] In my view, however, the translation 'law of nature' is misleading not only because of the anachronism

---

[97] Morfino (2013).
[98] Bollack (1978), pp. 246–59.
[99] Moreau (1975), p. 477.
[100] On natural laws in the ancient culture see Grant (1952), Chroust (1963), Koester (1968), Martens (2003).
[101] Just a few examples: Munro in Lucretius (1873, 3rd ed.), Ernout in Lucretius (1924), Bailey in Lucretius (1947), Rouse and Smith in Lucretius (1975), Flores in Lucretius (2002–9).

of projecting the early modern idea of *lex naturalis* on Lucretius,[102] but also because Lucretius's argument itself does not suggest the idea of a law that binds or constraints natural phenomena.[103]

The expression appears six times in the meaning under scrutiny: I.586, II.302, VI.906 and three times in book V at verses 57, 310 and 924. I have discussed at length the passage in book I. Here one may discern, perhaps more clearly, that the *foedera naturae* are quite different from 'ordinances of nature',[104] or even 'compact of nature'.[105] The *ordo* that the acute observer discerns in nature is the regularity and the consistency of a series of events over time,[106] and not a superior order imposed on phenomena. The expression, Ernout and Robin argue, seems to come from πλατὺς ὅρκος [broad or firm-based oath] in Empedocles,[107] with its idea of a compact and a strong oath. It is close to the occurrence in III.416, in which Lucretius speaks about the *foedus* between the mind and the soul: no law then, unless one wants to project the hierarchical kind of relation between the soul and the body that is implied, for example, in the Platonic view.[108] Given the atomic nature of *every* natural entity, Lucretius rather suggests the agreement, the conjunction and the union between natural elements. But let us analyse the six occurrences of the term in *De rerum natura*, as each of them reveals a particular aspect of the question of its meaning and relevance for Lucretius's philosophy.

---

[102] In this sense Boyancé (1963), p. 86.
[103] See Reich (1958), p. 126, Milton (1981), pp. 176–7, and C. Wilson, 'From Limits to Law: The Construction of the Nomological Image of Nature in Early Modern Philosophy', in Daston and Stolleis (2008), pp. 13–28.
[104] Rouse and Smith, in Lucretius (1975).
[105] Proposed by Grant (1952), p. 24. Grant suggests considering an important text for the tradition that I have been discussing, namely Minucius Felix's *Octavius*, a dialogue between a pagan sceptic and a Christian. Grant underlines that Minucius makes use of the concept of natural law, the 'compact of nature' that corresponds for him to Lucretius's *foedera naturae*, in the sceptic and Christian argument alike, by giving it an opposite meaning. See also Minucius Felix 17.7–9 e 34.2–3. In contrast, I believe that precisely because this concept does not correspond to the modern idea of *lex naturalis*, it is in fact wide enough to be filled in with both providentialist and anti-providentialist arguments. See also Reich (1958), p. 125.
[106] As suggested by Ernout and Robin, in Lucretius (1925–8), I, p. 129.
[107] Lucretius (1925–8), I, p. 128. See *Vorsokr.* 31 B 30 (= LM [22] EMP. D94, R74 = Inwood 35, p. 225 = Arist. *Metaph.* III.4, 1000 b 12) and *Vorsokr.* 31 B 115 (= LM [22] EMP. D10, D11, R48, R50, R89 = Inwood 11, p. 207 = Hippol. *Haer.* VII.29). See also Boyancé (1963), p. 87 and, *contra*, G. Droz-Vincent, 'Les *foedera naturae* chez Lucrèce', in Levy éd. (1996), pp. 191–211, who claims the Lucretius's philosophy is alien to the anthropomorphic character of the Empedoclean compacts.
[108] On Lucretius's use of *animus/anima* see Bailey, in Lucretius (1947), II, p. 1006.

Let us begin with the last occurrence, in VI.906. When Lucretius explains the *foedera naturae* for which 'it comes about that iron can be attracted by that stone which the Greeks call magnet from the name of its home', the reader is no longer struck by the use of the expression. The *foedera* appear here in their more neutral sense, as synonym of 'reasons' or *rationes*,[109] those that *explain* this phenomenon, traditionally ascribed to nature's strangeness. Notwithstanding the translators' choice, the reasons are here far from being laws that compel the iron and the magnet to attract each other. They are rather the clarification of something traditionally held as obscure and mysterious, the description of a fully natural phenomenon that links two different matters in a peculiar manner.

The first occurrence of the *foedera naturae* is in I.586, in which, as I explained above, Lucretius connects the microscopic level of atomic composition with the macroscopic level of physical phenomena: the latter's constancy and consistency precisely depends on the former's regular dynamic. Thus, certain things are or are not able to behave in certain ways, or produce certain effects. Knowing and observing nature, Lucretius argues, allows humans to understand what things are and are not able to do. De Lacy has pointed out how Lucretius's poem is a direct response to Platonism: knowing nature means grasping the 'formal aspect of the cosmic process, what can happen and what cannot, what the limits are'.[110] The *foedera naturae*, De Lacy argues, are thus laws of nature, and 'to that extent they are the Epicurean equivalent of the eternal and unchanging forms glimpsed by the soaring soul in *Phdr.* 247 c–e.' In line with De Lacy's thesis, however, I would rather say that they are the equivalent insofar as they claim the same role and status within the system, but also that they turn upside down the very nature and meaning of Platonic forms and contrast with them in the strongest possible way. Lucretius's natural phenomena do not draw their reality from above, namely from their participation in forms or norms.

The *foedera naturae*, in this sense, sometimes represent for Lucretius the general and universal principle *within which* every phenomenon takes place, rather than the laws that guide them, as it is the case in II.294–309, in which Lucretius explains that

> nothing increases [the mass of matter] nor does anything perish from it. Wherefore in whatsoever motion the bodies of first-beginnings are now, in that same motion they were in ages gone by, and hereafter they will always

---

[109] One of the most frequent terms in the poem, less frequent only than *corpus*, *terra* and *natura*. See Wacht (1990).

[110] De Lacy, 'Lucretius and Plato', in Caratelli (1983), p. 293.

be carried along in the same way (*simili ratione*), and the things which have been accustomed to be born will be born under the same conditions (*eadem condicione*); they will be and will grow and will be strong with their strength as much as is given[111] to each by the *foedera naturai* (*quantum cuique datum est per foedera naturai*). Nor can any power change the sum total of things; for there is no place without into which any kind of matter could flee away from the all; and there is no place whence a new power could arise to burst into the all, and to change the nature of things (*naturam rerum mutare*) and turn their motions.

Here, once again, one should not personify the *foedera naturae* as anthropomorphic and normative principles that grant or concede or accord something. The *foedera naturae* are rather the manifestation of what things can or cannot be, depending on the features, nature and atomic constitution that they have been capable to reproduce.

That Lucretius is thinking about the general principle that describes all phenomena alike is supported by the reading of Epicurus, whom the Latin poet is here repeating.[112] Even more important, as Ernout and Robin emphasise, is the fact that the *foedera naturae* are here opposed to the *fati foedera*.[113] Nature's *foedera* are not inflexible laws imposed by fate, but *certa ratio* that expresses nature's regularity, in the total absence of a personified lawgiver Fate.

In V.55 one can read one of the most important occurrences of the *foedera*:

I teach in my poem by what *foedere* all things are created, and how they must needs abide by them, strong laws of time that nothing could annul (*nec ualidas ualeant aevi rescindere leges*).

Foedera and *leges* are here close, both relating to the natural domain, and to the conditions[114] and features according to which everything has been created and reproduces itself by confirming the constancy and consistency of nature seen above.

Although the concept of law of nature does not exist in ancient culture, Lucretius makes use of the *lex* for the natural domain. *Lex* appears ten times in the poem,[115] seven times to speak about human laws or laws specifically concerning the legal sphere, and only three times referring to nature and natural

---

[111] Rouse and Smith: 'granted to each of them'.
[112] *Ep.* [2] 39. See Ernout and Robin (1925–8), I, p. 255.
[113] Ernout and Robin (1925–8) and Morfino (2013).
[114] Flores *ad loc.*, translates *foedera* by 'condizioni'.
[115] Vis-à-vis, once again, the 222 occurrences of *ratio*. See Wacht (1990), *ad loc.*

things. In II.719 *lex* is a synonym of *ratio*, and *holds* things apart by their limits.[116] In III.687 Lucretius mentions a specific law that inflexibly applies to all things, namely the 'law of death', or *lex leti*. The occurrence of V.55 should be read, I think, in this light, namely to reflect the constancy of events throughout the ages, with no change possibly appearing within the same given conditions.

It is utterly important, I think, that Lucretius associates here *leges* and *foedera*. Ernout and Robin point to two relevant examples: Virgil's *Georgics* I.60: 'continuo has leges aeternaque foedera certis | imposuit natura locis' and Lucan II.2: 'Iamque irae patuere deum, manifestaque belli signa dedit mundus, legesque et foedera rerum praescia monstrifero vertit natura tumultu indixitque nefas.'[117] Lucan's reference is strikingly important for the present enquiry, for the role played by monstrosity in breaking the *foedera rerum legesque*, and the universe thus showing its being at war.[118] Lucretius, however, takes a very different direction in claiming the unchangeable nature of the *foedera*. Striking, once again, is that this unchangeability does not proceed from above, as if Lucretius were simply turning upside down Lucan's intention: whereas for Lucan the universe's laws can be overturned, Lucretius sees nature's immanent constancy.

De Lacy suggests Polystratus as another Epicurean source for Lucretius's concept of *foedera*.[119] Its meaning, however, is grounded in the Epicurean attempt to give an immanent foundation to nature by setting apart things that are possible (δυνατὰ) and impossible (μὴ [δυ]νατὰ). Salem also agrees with this reading, highlighting the idea that the variation of natural phenomena, the παραλλαγή, can only happen within determinate limits that are physical and unchangeable.[120] Every natural phenomenon can happen only between a minimum and a maximum, beyond which physics is limited by 'bornes ontologiques', or metaphysical impossibilities.[121] An example of possible variation would be the child's resemblance to her parents, either one of them, when the mother's or the father's seed has prevailed, or both of them, *utriusque figurae*, when neither of the seeds has conquered the other.[122]

---

[116] Lucr. II.718–20: 'Do not think that animals only are held by these laws (*legibus*), for the same principle (*ratio*) holds all things apart by their limits.'
[117] Ernout and Robin (1925–8), *ad loc.*
[118] See *infra*.
[119] And in particular the Περὶ ἀλόγου καταφρονήσεως. See Polystratus (1905) and De Lacy (1969), p. 104 and *passim*. The concept of limits is, for the Epicureans, the most powerful tool to contrast transcendency.
[120] Salem (1994), pp. 83 ff. Following De Lacy (1969), p. 107, Salem also quotes Philodemus's Περὶ σημείων καὶ σημειώσεων. See Phld. *Sign*.
[121] See Courtès (1968).
[122] Lucr. IV.1209–17.

The argument of the child's resemblance had also been used by Aristotle as an example of minor monstrosity: within the teleological scheme, the children *should* resemble their parents. Whenever this does not happen, children are to some extent monstrous.[123] The Epicureans, I believe, frame the same contention within a completely different pattern, materially and physically determined by the mechanical dynamics of seeds' mixture, and avoiding all references to teleology. Once again, thus, the limits should not be seen as laws governing from above, or far less metaphysical boundaries, but rather the expression of what nature becomes, following only its mechanical dynamic, and no other normative principle.

De Lacy underlines that these limits also allow a certain freedom of variation within them, that is to say within the maximum and the minimum, and link them to the *clinamen*. 'But even the swerve,' he adds, 'has a limit; it can be no more than the minimum (Lucr. 2.244). Its consequences must not disrupt the fixed limits of natural processes but must only add variety within those limits.'[124] The swerve surely has limits, as everything else in nature. Who set these limits, though? What does it mean that it *must* be in a certain way and not another one? Not a lawgiver Nature, I believe, but matter itself, spontaneously organised in the origin of this world, and *thus* now operating in a certain determinate manner. The word 'laws' does not clarify, but rather confuses, the sense of radical immanence that Lucretius consciously opposes, carefully choosing the *foedus*, to the transcendent normativity of alternative philosophical systems.

This is why even fate can now be transformed in Lucretius's hands: 'Do you not see that even stones are conquered by time, that tall turrets fall and rocks crumble, that the gods' temples and their images wear out and crack, nor can their holy divinity carry forward the boundaries of fate [*fati finis*], or strive against *naturae foedera?*'[125] Fate and *foedera* stand here on the same side, an irresistible boundary against religious superstition: metaphorically, against its claimed *sanctum numen*, and physically, against the material resistance of its temples, whose rocks, like everything else, will one day fall apart.

It is following this pattern that Lucretius brings the reader to the argument of monstrosities in V.907–24. Only some of them, as we know, have been produced by the earth, but not the mixed ones, *inter se complexa*, such as centaurs and chimeras. All animals, even those produced by the earth in the beginning, proceed *suo ritu* and distinguish themselves from the others, according to the *foedera naturae*: immanent principle of distinction, regularity and combination.

---

[123] See Arist. GA IV.3, 767 b 10–13 and *supra*. De Lacy (1969), p. 109.
[124] De Lacy (1969), pp. 108–9.
[125] Lucr. V.310.

The idea of 'law' or 'limit' *imposed* by nature or by fate seems to me too strict for the *foedera naturae*, and the possibility, or rather the necessity, of monstrosities in the beginning of the world testifies to it. The most significant meanings mentioned by the OLD suggest the idea of a criterion defining moral violations, such as the one implied by suicide according to Cicero, following Plato and Pythagoras,[126] or that of a decree voluntarily established by the Parcae in Ovid.[127] Manilius's use of the term *foedus* is also quite interesting: 'I shall sing of God,' he writes, 'silent-minded monarch of nature, who, permeating sky and land and sea, controls with uniform compact [*aequali foedere*] the mighty structure [. . .].'[128] *Foedera* are laws given by nature's monarch. Moreover, Manilius opposes such divine laws to the Epicurean spontaneous organisation of the cosmos: 'Who could believe that such massive structures have been created from tiny atoms without the operation of a divine will, and that the universe is the creature of a blind compact [*caeco foedere*]?'[129] The *foedus* is thus employed by the Stoic Manilius in an explicit teleological polemic against Epicurean chance and the Lucretian idea of the necessary *concourse* of different things, of different conditions, necessary and sufficient for events to happen, or for living beings to survive.

Multa videmus rebus concurrere debere, Lucretius says.[130] These are the *foedera naturae*: not the conditions imposed by nature, but the concourse itself of the *multa rebus*, with its natural effects. The Lucretian concept of *foedera* is thus enlightened by the ideas of agreement, convenience, even cooperation of natural things *from which* the regularities stem. Their origin is in the atomic clashes, their *concursus*. Before these clashes and the possible agreements that come out of them, no law exists, not even in principle, because no lawgiving entity exists. Nature is the outcome of multiple *concursus* and the stabilisation[131] of the multiple agreements and cooperations among things, some of which last, while others do not. If not everything was possible, it is *only* because not everything has *actually* happened. Regularity and natural necessity include rather than exclude chance. They only come *after* chance, they are chance's result.[132] 'Law of nature'

---

[126] Cic. *Scaur.* 5: 'Even these teachers, though they praise death, forbid us to fly from life, asserting that such conduct is a violation of nature [*contra foedus legemque naturae*].'
[127] Ou. *Met.*, V.532. It is often clear, in Ovid, the meaning of a command or an order conveyed by the concept.
[128] Manil. II.62. See also *infra*.
[129] Manil. I.492–3.
[130] Lucr. V.849.
[131] Moreau (1975), p. 474, interestingly speaks about Nature's habit of reproducing itself in a regular way. Nature 'gets used to' something (and gets rid of something else), and this is its only rule.
[132] See also Costa, p. 104.

is thus a misleading translation. I prefer the idea of *concourse/concursus*, the conjunction or concurrence, and even the encounter or the assemblage, closer to the Greek σύνοδος.

Boyancé claims that the *foedera naturae* can be considered natural laws only if one stresses the negative and limitative character of a law, rather than its positive and prescriptive nature. Laws, he claims, allow Lucretius to point toward what the fables' gods *cannot* make, rather than to what they can create out of their arbitrary imagination. The ethico-political character of the *foedera* is indeed present in Lucretius's mind, but it is not necessary, here, to oppose their positive and their negative character. The *foedera* are the actual concourse of things, that both negatively prevents and positively allows them to happen.[133]

Something needs to be added to the role played by the *foedera naturae* in the Epicurean polemics against teleology. Droz-Vincent suggests that the genitive in *foedera naturae* can be intended in a subjective and an objective sense.[134] He rules out the latter, laws that 'govern' or 'control' nature, though, because it is too close to the modern idea of a law of nature. It remains, thus, the former, laws 'belonging to' nature, in the sense of the *rules* that Nature imposes on and prescribes to its phenomena, in order to guarantee their regularity.[135] Droz-Vincent claims[136] that Lucretius is discreetly reintroducing some kind of teleology, precisely through the idea of a rule-giver Nature. Such finalism would also be confirmed by the repeated use of *finis*, with its double meaning of end and scope. I believe, on the contrary, that Lucretius is not reintroducing any kind of finalism here. On the contrary, the *foedera naturae*, intended as the concourse of many several things, are precisely the antidote to any finalism.

Lucretius explicitly obliterates, for example, the subordination of animal organs to their function, which would teleologically act as a shaping principle:

> Do not suppose that the clear light of the eyes was made in order that we might be able to see before us; or that the ends of the calves and thighs were jointed and placed upon the foundation of the feet, only to enable us to march forward with long forward strides; that the forearms again were fitted upon sturdy upper arms, and ministering hands given on either side, only that we might be able to do what should be necessary for life. Such explanations, and all other such that men give, put effect for

---

[133] See Boyancé (1963), *passim*. See also Morgan (1984), p. 110 and *passim*.
[134] G. Droz-Vincent, 'Les *foedera naturae* chez Lucrèce', in Lévy éd. (1996), pp. 191–211.
[135] G. Droz-Vincent, 'Les *foedera naturae* chez Lucrèce', p. 210.
[136] Following Mesnard (1947). *Contra* Casini (1963).

cause and are based on perverted reasoning [*omnia peruersa praepostera sunt ratione*];[137] since nothing is born in us simply in order that we may use it, but that which is born creates the use [*quod natumst id procreat usum*]. There was no sight before the eyes with their light were born, no speaking of words before the tongue was made; but rather the origin of the tongue came long before speech, and the ear was made long before sound was heard, in a word all the members, as I think, existed before their use; they could not then have grown up for the sake of use [*haud igitur potuere utendi crescere causa*][138]

In the same way that order and regularity do not pre-exist the ordered and regulated development of nature, the functions performed by organs do not pre-exist the organic life of individuals within a determinate species.[139] The case of human inventions is different, as they have been created out of experience, and thus invented *for the sake* of their use.[140] *Sensus* and *membra*, however, does not have any teleological origin in the Epicurean system.

Lucretius's Impact on the Augustan Age

The materialist and atomist theories powerfully reworked by Lucretius have a large impact on the literature of the Augustan age as some of the most important authors react to his rationalisation and systematisation of philosophical thought. Virgil, Horace, Vitruvius and Ovid, none of whom is, strictly speaking,

---

[137] Ernout and Robin (1925–8), II, p. 261: 'This is, in fact, the problem with the doctrine of final causes according to its opponents: it turns upside down the relationship between things, *peruersa ratione*, it everywhere puts the effect before the cause, *omnia praepostera*; it makes πρότερον-ὕστερον. The critique is perfectly clear: it is not the need or the usefulness that create the organ (834 sq., 842, 857); the organ has created itself spontaneously, and thus originates the need to use it, in short the usage or the function (835, 840 ff.), by giving us its idea, *notitiam utilitatis* (853 ff.).' *Contra* Bailey in Lucretius (1947), II, p. 1281, for whom: 'Lucr.'s argument in this paragraph is simple-hearted [...]. The argument is not in itself convincing [...].'

[138] Lucr. IV.825–42.

[139] Casini (1963) underlines the anti-Aristotelian nature of this argument, as well as its faithfulness vis-à-vis the core of the doctrine in Diodorus I,7 and *Ep.* [2] 73–6. Insofar as they agree with Aristotelian teleology, Stoics are also targeted by Lucretius. *Contra* Schrijvers, 'L'homme et l'animal in the *De rerum natura*', in Algra, Koenen, Schrivers eds. (1997), pp. 151–61, who thinks that one should see the finalist and anti-finalist explanations alike in Lucretius, insofar as a certain kind of finalism, at least in humans, results from their initial formation by chance. On Lucretius and Diodoros see also Woltjer (1877) and Spoerri (1959).

[140] Lucr. IV.843–57.

a philosopher, feel compelled to tackle philosophical ideas, influenced by, or as a response to, Lucretius's enterprise. Monstrosity, once again, comes to the foreground, as if it were the concept that, though marginal, threatens the whole system from the exterior, or as if only its internal consideration and absorption could make a system of thought strong or appealing enough to establish itself and represent the spirit of the age.

In his *Eclogue* IV, Virgil prophesises a new golden age. To materialist rationalism, as Hardie has underlined, Virgil responds with real *impossibilia* whose existence would overturn the consistency of Lucretius's nature.[141] Virgil's position, however, is far from being a simple opposition to Lucretian rationalism. For Virgil, monsters appear not only in the threatening marginal world of Circe, in which nature's normality has been twisted and subjugated by the obscure force of magic, but also in the enlightening explanation of the souls's incarnation pious Anchises gives to Aeneas.[142] Virgil does not indulge in credulity, but neither does he unconditionally adhere to Lucretius's enterprise of completely rationalising nature to obliterate every and any form of marvellous. Indeed, the marvellous is essential to Virgil's poetry. As Alain Deremetz suggests, Virgil instead elaborates an original conception of the marvellous that is strongly influenced by Lucretius yet open to the rhetorical effect of prodigious monstrosities, such as the *mirabile monstrum* of *Aen.* III.26, the bleeding bush into which Polydorus has been metamorphosised.[143] Such a blend of materialist influence and mythological materials resurfaces powerfully in Silenus's cosmogonic and mythological song in *Eclogue* VI, which clearly reveals the influence of Virgil's teacher, the Epicurean Siron. After the unambiguously Lucretian cosmogonic account, representations of thorny subjects and unhappy passions proliferate.[144]

In the *Aeneid*, Virgil places monsters in the underworld's vestibule, where 'many monstrous forms besides of various beasts are stalled at the doors, Centaurs and double-shaped Scyllas, and the hundredfold Briareus, and the beast of Lerna, hissing horribly, and the Chimaera armed with flame, Gorgons and Harpies, and the shape of the three-bodied shade'.[145] Accompanied by the Cumaean Sibyl, Aeneas has the human reaction of fear and repulsion.

---

[141] Verg. B. IV.37–48. See P. Hardie, 'Cultural and Historical Narratives in Virgil's *Eclogues* and Lucretius', in Fantuzzi, Papanghelis eds. (2006), pp. 275–300.

[142] Verg. Aen. VII.21 and VI.724. See also P. Hardie, 'Virgil: A Paradoxical Poet?' in Hardie (2009), pp. 95–112.

[143] A. Deremetz, 'The Question of the Marvellous in the *Georgics* of Virgil', in Hardie (2009), pp. 113–25.

[144] Verg. B. VI.31 ff.

[145] Verg. Aen. VI.285–9.

He reaches for his sword, but the Sibyl explains that monsters are not real, but only appearances: 'did not his wise companion warn him that these were but faint, bodiless lives, fitting under a hollow semblance of form, he would rush upon them and vainly cleave shadows with steel.'[146] As Lucretius explained, monsters spring out of the traditional thought as illusory images, *simulacra* of reality whose composite nature is possible only in the imagination, not the reality of the physical world. The Cumaean Sibyl offers Aeneas a sketch of Lucretian wisdom, without renouncing the rhetorical power evoked by the mythical creatures. Monstrosity ultimately makes it possible for the poet to present Epicurean arguments favourably. Monsters also allow Virgil to keep the fearful strength of ancient tradition intact, while presenting it in the frame of his highly original poetry.

The ambivalence toward the monstrous also appears in Horace, one of the Augustan poets whose works most explicitly insist that monsters are not real. Nonetheless, at the end of *Ode* II.20, the poet imagines himself transformed into a monstrous swan, thus transgressing Lucretius's opposition to the impossible phenomena of metamorphosis that Horace typically insists on.

The beginning of Horace's *Ars poetica* is famous for the denunciation of the chimaera as a paradigm of impossible monstrosity that ruins not just poetry but all aesthetics:

> If a painter chose to join a human head to the neck of a horse, and to spread feathers of many a hue over limbs picked up now here now there, so that what at the top is a lovely woman ends below in a black and ugly fish, could you, my friends, if favoured with a private view, refrain from laughing? Believe me, dear Pisos, quite like such pictures would be a book, whose idle fancies shall be shaped like a sick man's dreams, so that neither head nor foot can be assigned to a single shape. 'Painters and poets,' you say, 'have always had an equal right in hazarding anything.' We know it: this licence we poets claim and in our turn we grant the like; but not so far that savage should mate with tame, or serpents couple with birds, lambs with tigers.[147]

The *Ars* is one of the most influential classical texts on the writing of poetry and drama. Its opening moulds a monstrous shape whose impact recalls the hybrid compositions of forms in struggle with each other that Plato locates within the soul. This chimaera should be killed and replaced by a correct esthetic canon that avoids all exaggeration, that does not attempt to seduce the reader with images of impossible creatures. The almost Surrealist image of

---

[146] Verg. Aen. VI.292–4.
[147] Hor. Ars poetica 1–13.

the chimaera, Citroni suggests, is refused more for its inconsistency than for its irreality.[148] In this sense, Horace's philosophical approach is inspired both by Lucretius's principle of *nihil admirari* and by Aristotle's appeal to the consistency of parts that explicitly connects the physical and the poetical domain.[149] The diversity of subject is acceptable only if it does not push the boundaries of the impossible or unreal.

Interestingly, Steidle suggests that the *Ars poetica*'s debut does not de-legitimate the composite figures transmitted by tradition such as centaurs or the Sphinx.[150] Although impossible, these characters are solidly legitimised by tradition and transposed into a mythical dimension. The continuity of the tradition grants a certain truth value to the mythical fantasy. In this respect, because he recognises the value of tradition, Horace grants a certain form of existence to the mythical creatures that he explicitly denounces. Its impossibility notwithstanding, the monster becomes true because tradition keeps it alive beyond and against the aesthetic and physical logic that demolishes its ontological reality. The monster thus survives imaginatively at the expense of its ontological possibility.

This radical rejection of the ontological reality of monstrosity echoes the position of another prominent Augustan-age personality – Vitruvius. The opening of *De architectura* is often associated with Horace's denunciation of chimeric monstrosity. In Vitruvius's view, such condemnation extends to all that is grotesque, because the grotesque lacks the ethical sense that is necessarily anchored in a certain proportion, balance and measure. In Vitruvius's words:

> [the] imitations based upon reality are now disdained by the improper taste of the present. On the stucco are monsters rather than definite representations taken from definite things [*imagines certae*]. Instead of columns there rise up stalks; instead of gables, striped panels with curled leaves and colutes. Candelabra uphold pictured shrines and above the summits of these, clusters of thin stalks rise from their roots in tendrils with little figures seated upon them at random [*sine ratione*]. Again, slender stalks with heads of men and of animals attached to half the body. Such things neither are, nor can be, nor have been. [. . .] pictures cannot be approved which do not resemble reality. Even if they have a fine and craftsmanlike finish, they are only to receive commendation if they exhibit their proper subject without transgressing the rules of art.[151]

---

[148] M. Citroni, 'Horace's *Ars Poetica* and the marvellous', in Hardie (2009), pp. 19–40.
[149] Arist. *Po.* 1451 a 1–2.
[150] Steidle (1939), p. 12.
[151] Vitr. VII.V.3–4.

Vitruvius echoes the same principle we have seen in Palaephatus: because such things have never existed, they do not and will not exist. Existing reality stands for Vitruvius as an inflexibly normative principle according to which the artist must not create and represent things that do not exist. The boundaries of artistic creation exclude everything stained by falseness, making them inconvenient and undesirable, even if they are skilfully fashioned: the falseness in fact perverts and diverts the skills from their true end, i.e. representation according to reality.

The monstrous in Vitruvius relates to an unbreakable connection between form and function. Things are condemned because they are *sine ratione* and thus ontologically and aesthetically contradictory.[152] Monsters do not and cannot perform any function; they have no role to play, and for this reason, they must be condemned. When the artist recreates them, he is artificially keeping monsters alive, against the truth of nature. Artistic representation is praised when inspired by the principle of verisimilitude, and condemned when it violates the boundaries of ontological possibility.

Differently from Virgil, Horace and Vitruvius appear little concerned about the ambivalent relation between normality and monstrosity. Such an ambivalence, however, appears again in the last great author of the period: Ovid. The *Metamorphoses*'s impact on literature, arts and the comprehension of mythology at large can hardly be overestimated. Largely conceived as a response to the rationalising and demythologising project of ancient materialism, particularly Lucretius, Ovid aims to rediscover the encyclopedia of mythology inherited from the Greeks, especially Homer and Hesiod.

Scholars are divided on Ovid's intention and attitude. His aetiological method, Myers claims, does not just oppose the scientific approach, but makes use of it by mingling science and myth.[153] Beagon also points out the unphilosophical nature of Ovid's approach to the philosophical material the poem explores.[154] Alfonsi, on the contrary, places the development of Ovid's poetry within the framework of the Stoic enterprise. In this sense, the *Metamorphoses* is not a poem of wonders, but a poetic theology of history philosophically grounded in Posidonius's system.[155] More recently, Nelis has insisted on the philosophical, and in particular Lucretian and Empedoclean, background of

---

[152] V. Platt, 'Where the Wild Things Are: Locating the Marvellous in Augustan Wall Painting', in Hardie (2009), pp. 41–74.
[153] Myers (1994), pp. 25–6.
[154] M. Beagon, 'Ordering Wonderland: Ovid's Pythagoras and the Augustan Vision', in Hardie (2009), pp. 288–309.
[155] L. Alfonsi, 'L'inquadramento filosofico delle Metamorfosi ovidiane', in Herescu (1958), pp. 265–72.

Ovid's discourse.[156] A precise reconstruction of the philosophical and literary background of such a complex poem is a difficult enterprise.[157] Ovid's use of natural science and mythology produces an often original interpretation of classical myths in which monstrosity, which is at the heart of the metamorphic logic that characterises nature as a whole, plays a prominent role.

The cosmogony in book I and Pythagoras's discourse in book XV are two places in which Ovid explicitly touches upon philosophical questions. By no means, however, are they his only use of philosophical material; in fact, it is by exploring Ovid's account of each and every myth that the reader discovers not only the original reworking of scientific theories, but also monstrosity's fundamental role in setting into motion nature's endlessly metamorphic character. Metamorphosis is the affirmation not only of the instability and fluidity of natural laws, but also the imaginative production of what nature was and could be vis-à-vis what it currently is.

Ovid's scientific mythology turns the principle of nature's inflexible constancy, clearly expressed by Palaephatus and resurfacing, for example, in Vitruvius, upside down. Ovid is not searching for a stabilising principle, but rather a destabilising one that challenges the constant predetermination of forms. Nature, for him, is wonderful, not rational; ever-changing, not self-stabilising. The only stability is fluctuation, in which the extraordinary becomes normal, and the monstrous becomes the norm. In Pythagoras's speech, wonder, as Beagon puts it, fills the gap between the reality of what nature is and the reality of what it could be.[158]

Paradoxically, Ovid accomplishes the re-mythologisation of science via Lucretius's materialism and, more generally, the cosmogonic accounts of Empedocles and the Epicureans. Ovid often explicitly contradicts Lucretius, as in XV.153 ff. in which Pythagoras states that the reason one does not have to fear death is not because when we are, death is not and when it is, we are not, but rather because our soul is deathless.[159] Lucretian language, however, comes forward in key moments in which a general cosmogonic account frames and prepares for the exploration of individual metamorphoses. The four Empedoclean elements, as Lucretius calls them, are renamed *semina rerum*, beyond and against Lucretius's explicit opposition to Empedocles. Book I presents the formation of diverse species from the earth:

---

[156] D. Nelis, '*Metamorphoses* 1.416–51: *noua monstra* and the *foedera naturae*', in Hardie (2009), pp. 248–67.

[157] See e.g. A. Barchiesi's commentary in Ovidio (2005–15), *passim*.

[158] See again Beagon, 'Ordering Wonderland', *passim*.

[159] Ou. Met. XV.153–9.

> [. . .] the earth spontaneously produced [forms of life] of divers kinds; after that old moisture remaining from the flood had grown warm from the rays of the sun, the slime of the wet marshes swelled with heat, and the fertile seeds of life, nourished in that life-giving soil, as in a mother's womb, grew and in time took on some special form. So when the seven-mouthed Nile has receded from the drenched fields and has returned again to its former bed, and the fresh slime has been heated by the sun's rays, farmers as they turn over the lumps of earth find many animate things; and among these some, but now begun, are upon the very verge of life, some are unfinished and lacking in their proper parts, and oft-times in the same body one part is alive and the other still nothing but a raw earth. For when the moisture and heat unite, life is conceived, and from these two sources all living things spring. And, though fire and water are naturally at enmity, still heat and moisture produce all things, and this inharmonious harmony [*discors concordia*] is fitted to the growth of life. When, therefore, the earth, covered with mud from the recent flood, became heated up by the hot ethereal rays of the sun, she brought forth innumerable forms of life; in part she restored the ancient shapes, and in part she created creatures new and strange [*noua monstra*].[160]

Without any divine intervention, life mechanically springs from the earth in a variety of forms and shapes. The *concordia discors* of fire and water takes the place of divine providence and leaves the processes to their aleatory metamorphical reproduction of ancient forms and creation of new monsters, just as they did for Empedocles and Lucretius.[161] Ovid's re-mythologisation of materialist science leads to a different outcome than that of Lucretius. Whereas Lucretius had excluded the existence of mythical forms such as the centaur, Ovid presents the formation of all sort of monstrous shapes. According to Nelis, this is the proof that Empedocles' presence in the poem is stronger than Lucretius's. However, as we have seen, it is not so simple to separate the two, especially on the role of the spontaneous generation of life in the early cosmogony. Moreover, the outcome of Ovid's account is, after all, the birth of a mighty monster:

> [The earth], indeed, would have wished not so to do, but thee also she then bore, thou huge Python, thou snake unknown before, who wast a terror to new-created men; so huge a space of mountain-side didst thou fill.

---

[160] Ou. *Met.* I.416–37.
[161] See, for an exhaustive account of this passage, Nelis, '*Metamorphoses* 1.416–51: *noua monstra* and the *foedera naturae*'.

> This monster the god of the bow destroyed with lethal arms never before used except against does and wild she-goats, crushing him with countless darts, well-nigh emptying his quiver, till the creature's poisonous blood flowed from the black wounds.[162]

Python is a strong and threatening monster that would certainly have survived had not the god exterminated it, but both Lucretius and Empedocles would have seen it as spontaneously disappearing from the earth.

Physical and mythical causality coexist in the poem, not always in opposition to each other. As Beagon has underlined, whereas Lucretius (and, to some extent, Empedocles) offers tools to overcome astonishment, Ovid's Pythagoras invites the reader to experience it and enjoy its wonderful outcomes. For Ovid, monstrosity plays a strategic function of both supporting a scientific understanding of nature's fluidity and exploring the mythical account of nature without prejudice. Following Lucretius, Ovid is not interested in finding, through divine providence, a comprehensive explanation for every aspect of life. His intent instead is to obliterate the role of an intelligent providence in order to leave room for the monstrously productive forces of nature. Ovid's Typhon in book V, as Rosati has underlined, is a bold hero who challenges the Olympians and reveals a world in which humans are not frightened of the gods. He reveals the possibility of *another* world, possibly a world to come.[163]

We have seen how Epicurean and Lucretian atomism developed ancient materialism in an original and powerful fashion. I have focused on Epicurus's and Lucretius's treatment of the generation of life, not only its consistency, but its mutability: these two ideas constitute the major challenge facing the atomists as they respond to the Platonic and Aristotelian philosophy of ideas and forms. Only by explaining abnormality and monstrosity can atomists make sense of their immanent ontology that, based solely on matter in motion, rules out every transcendent, divine and providential principle of organisation. Order *does* exist in the universe, and it *does* include monstrosity. This concept must be explained within the limits that nature has to produce its diversity, and the *foedera naturae* that guarantee the stability of this order.

I have attempted in this chapter to develop the thesis that the *foedera* and the limits of nature are neither imposed *on* nature from above nor established *by* nature in its realm. They are the result of spontaneous atomic motion. Within a plane of radical immanency, my suggestion is that not only do the *foedera* discriminate between the possible and impossible monstrosities produced on earth, as much scholarship suggests, but that successful monstrosities

---

[162] Ou. *Met.* I.438–44.
[163] G. Rosati, '*Latrator Anubis*: Alien Divinities in Augustan Rome, and how to Tame Monsters through Aetiology', in Hardie (2009), pp. 268–87.

play a role in determining what those *foedera* are. I have thus argued that the Lucretian expression *foedera naturae* is best understood less as a natural law and more as a *conjuction* or *concourse* of favourable events. This means that Epicureans understand monstrosity's appearance in nature completely differently than Aristotle. Whereas Aristotle speaks about monsters' accidental necessity, Lucretius views them as necessarily contributing to the spontaneous shaping of nature's regularity.

Epicurus's and Lucretius's philosophy allows us to see the emergence of a metaphysics that flattens the universe on a monistic plane of immanence, one whose ontology definitely rules out every transcendent principle or superior normativity. Exceptions, anomalies and monstrosity are essential elements in this system, which is also intended to rule out fear and superstition. Against Plato and Aristotle, as shown in the previous pages, Epicurus and Lucretius think about monstrosity not as the deviant exception, but rather as part of a norm that constantly makes itself, immanently and progressively, out of nature's autonomous effort to reproduce itself.

Atomism thus stands as a viable alternative to Platonic idealism and Aristotelian formalism. The magnitude of the struggle between these philosophical systems cannot be understated. It is echoed in the poetry and aesthetic theory of the Augustan age, as we saw in the last paragraphs of this chapter, in which authors such as Virgil, Horace, Vitruvius and Ovid react in different ways to the atomist system and its reinvigoration by Lucretius.

Materialism is the necessary condition for this philosophical reinvigoration. However, it is not sufficient, as Stoicism, the other powerful materialist system of antiquity (and the subject of the next chapter) shows: metaphysics can be materialist *and* normative and teleological. The treatment of monstrosity, once again, reveals the differences and specificities of philosophical systems, pointing to the radical alternatives found in the history of Western philosphy.

6

Stoicism

A large amount of the writings of Stoic philosophers has been lost. When we are able to reconstruct their thought, it is often through fragments and the testimonies of their opponents. Yet the Stoics' physics, cosmogony and anthropology have been extremely influential since the Hellenistic period, first as a powerful response to both Attic philosophy and Epicureanism, then through its fusion with Platonism, for example in the Hellenised Judaism of Philo of Alexandria, as well as its reception in early Christian theology.

The fragmentary literature by and on Stoics shows little interest in the topic and language of monstrosity. Nevertheless, Stoic physics and ontology originally develop arguments on many, if not all, of the philosophical domains that we have been discussing so far and that are relevant for the comprehension of the concept of monstrosity: the origin and development of life, the meaning of nature and its functioning, the divine and its relationship to the cosmos, necessity and chance, fate and providence. I will show in the following pages how Stoicism thinks about monstrosity in its main fields of interest, as well as the most important heritage that classical Stoicism leaves to the future.

I use the traditional and widely accepted distinction between ancient, middle and late Stoicism.[1] Compared to Epicureanism, in which two names – Epicurus and Lucretius – stand out in importance, Stoicism is much more articulated in different and sometimes opposed positions, developed across several centuries in Greek and Latin culture. The grounding tenets of Stoic physics have been developed by the school's fathers, Zeno, Cleanthes and Chrysippus, in the early stage of Stoicism.[2] Stoics postulate a divine force (πῦρ τεχνικόν) that, reminiscent of Heraclitus's fire, produces, permeates and organises the

---

[1] Against the use of the expression 'middle Stoicism', see Pohlenz (1948), p. 191, who prefers to speak about the hellenisation of Stoicism.
[2] SVF I.98 (= Eus. PE XV.816 d).

universe. God and the world are thus the only two existing realities, sharing a material nature, although active in the former case and passive in the latter. The Stoics derive the idea of a demiurgic force from Plato but, against him, they proclaim its immanence to the world. Stoic ontology is thus based on a strict monism: everything that exists is not only material,[3] but is also somehow divine, being a part of God, organised and directed by its intelligence.[4]

From Empedocles and the early cosmogonies, they draw the idea of an endless cycle of birth and destruction.[5] The cosmos's organisation begins with the transformation of fire into water, which contains seeds (σπέρματα or λόγοι σπερματικοί) whose nature is rational and whose function is to produce the four traditional elements.[6] This rational principle is also a causal principle, universal and absolute, which has operated forever and will operate forever as a normative virtue. Thus, fate (εἱμαρμένη or *fatum*), truth (ἀλήθεια or *ueritas*) and law (νόμος or *lex*) are strongly intertwined and make possible the ontological comprehension of nature. The three principles act necessarily and necessarily produce the best possible outcome, indeed the only possible one.

The active principle that dynamically produces the universe is the πνεῦμα. It is a force that keeps together all the universe's beings with different degrees of tension (τόνος) and through the continuity of matter, since Stoics, against the Epicureans, deny any existence to the void within the universe and imagine matter as infinitely divisible. Beings are thus diversified according to the principle that grounds their consistency, namely λόγος for humans, ψυχή for animals in general, φύσις for all living beings and ἕξις for inanimate objects. The πνεῦμα functions as a unifying principle, according to which the common nature of all things is ensured in the best possible way.

It is utterly important, for the Stoics, to postulate the rational essence of the cosmological unifying force. Working at the same time as a causal principle and a normative virtue, the πνεῦμα ensures the order, constancy and consistency of the universe. Stoics push this concept to its extreme consequences, postulating a rigid determinism which takes also the form of an

---

[3] On the process whereby Stoic philosophy absorbs Plato's cosmology, see Reydams-Schils (1999).
[4] SVF II.1027 (= Athenag. *Leg.* 6). See R. B. Todd, 'Monism and Immanence: The Foundation of Stoic Physics', in Rist (1978), pp. 137–60.
[5] A notable exception is Panaetius, who believes instead in the eternity of the cosmos and rules out the periodical conflagration marking the end of a cycle and the beginning of the following one. See [Panaetius] (1952, 2nd ed.), 69.
[6] Manil. I.149–70, gives an account of the initial process during which fire cools down into water. See also Simon and Simon (1956) and Hahm (1977).

optimistic providentialism. Their effort to mediate this grounding aspect with the actual configuration of nature and the world – which the Epicureans saw as far from perfect – constitutes one of the most powerful explanations of imperfections, evil and monstrosity in classical thought. It forms the core of Hellenistic Judaist theodicy and part of the later Christian theodicy, reverberating throughout future centuries.

Nominalism

The monism and materialism of the Stoics are closely related to their conceptualism or nominalism, namely their critique of ideas. Incorporeals, or ἀσώματα, exist for them beyond the actual material bodies. They are void, space and time, together with sayables and meanings. They do not exist in themselves, but only in our mind, and depend on our capacity of thinking. Not only are they the only incorporeals, but they are also the only universals. They are universal, one can say, because they are not real and existent in themselves, but rather in and through our mental capacity of thinking beyond individuality. In other words, because of the grounding function of materiality, existence is first and foremost individual: materiality and individuality go hand in hand in the Stoic universe.[7]

Stoics generally employ the concept of εἶδος in the sense of σχῆμα, or external appearance. Ideas do not exist for themselves in the technical sense established by Plato. Whereas for Plato they possess the highest degree of reality, Zeno claims that they merely are soul's representations, φαντάσματα, without an autonomous or full existence.[8] Τό λεκτόν, 'something', is different from the 'thing': the name 'Socrates', for example, is different from the real and corporeal man named Socrates. Whereas Socrates has a full existence, Socrates' name *almost* exists.[9]

According to Chrysippus, ideas depend upon and are necessarily embodied in individual things.[10] Isnardi-Parente argues that Chrysippus's generalisation of Zeno's initial theory is aimed at obliterating the character of reality attributed to ideas not only by Plato's transcendentalism, but also by Aristotle's

---

[7] Reale (1975–80), III, p. 336. See also 'Nominalisme', in Lalande and Panaccio eds (2012). The ἀσώματα eventually play a strategic function, beyond and sometimes against their Stoic meaning, in Christian literature, in which they become the incorporeality, opposed to the visible world, the spiritual opposed to the physical. See Lampe, *ad. loc.*

[8] SVF I.65 (= Stob. I.136.21).

[9] See Pohlenz (1948), p. 65.

[10] SVF II.394 (= Alex.Aphr. *de An.*). In themselves, Chrysippus argues, ideas are not determinate: SVF II.278 (= Simp. *in Cat.*). See also the group of fragments regarding Chrysippus's idea that *sola corpora esse, non esse ideas*, SVF II.357–68.

hylemorphism.[11] The ἀνατύπωμα, or mental image, does not have any correspondence in material reality, in the same way that the λεκτά do not have any autonomous existence. They only connect – in thought – material objects, which are fully existent only in the corporeal world. This definition is thus a polemical nominalism, whose function is to attack transcendentalism and universalism.

The Stoics' account of ideas and mental representations is not intended, however, to epitomise only their limitation, or their inferior nature vis-à-vis corporeal things. Imagination and mental activity, *qua* activity, is also a capacity for reasoning; that is, for composing and decomposing concepts that can help formulate hypotheses, thoughts and theories if appropriately employed. This is when the example of monstrosity becomes useful for understanding how the mind works. Diogenes Laertius explains that analogy is, for Chrysippus, one of the possible ways of knowledge: 'Under notions derived from analogy come those which we get (1) by way of enlargement, like that of Tityos or the Cyclops, or (2) by way of diminution, like that of the Pygmy. [. . .] Of notions obtained by transposition creatures with eyes on the chest would be an instance, while the centaur exemplifies those reached by composition [. . .].'[12] The λόγος works upon the physical representation, enabling the mind to imagine monsters that, as the Epicureans claim, do not exist.[13]

This activity of the mind can be seen as a potentiality because it is subject to rational laws that homogeneously characterise all of reality. In other words, imagination can be useful because it is to some extent rational, being an activity of the λόγος. As Sextus explains,

> every thought occurs either owing to sensation or not apart from sensation, and either owing to experience or not without experience. Hence we shall find that not even the so-called false presentations – such as those in dreams or madness – are detached from things known to us by experience through sense. And in fact when the hero in his madness imagines as his Furies 'Maids shaped like dragons and all blood-besprent', he is conceiving a shape compounded of things that have appeared to his senses.[14]

Sensation is the ground of intellection. More importantly, and because of this, both sensation and intellection always rely upon, and are bound to, the actual material reality of things. Nothing is or can be imagined that has not been previously experienced in one way or the other: the Centaur, which has never

---

[11] Isnardi-Parente (1999), pp. 67 ff. Hylemorphism is the claim that Being consists of both matter and form.
[12] SVF II.87 (= D.L. VII.53).
[13] See Pohlenz (1948), pp. 56–7.
[14] SVF II.88 (= S.E. M. VIII.56). The quote is from E. Or. 256.

been seen by anyone, can be imagined because both men and horse belong, on the contrary, to everyone's common experience. Within Stoic ontology and psychology, thus, no monstrosity can be conceived which is absolute, in the sense of not being somehow anchored to an existing reality. Monstrosity, at least in the mental domain, is subject and subordinated to experience and, as such, to the material reality of things.[15]

Stoics, in this way, obliterate the transcendence of ideas and forms by substituting for it the immanent principle of λόγος. The explanation and conception of Becoming and multiplicity is thus obtained neither by way of emanation of superior ideas, nor by way of actualisation of perfect forms. Becoming and multiplicity in the world are the unfolding of the λόγος itself that immanently operates within and upon matter, like a seed in the earth. The idea of *semina rerum* is precisely what the Stoics have in mind as an active, dynamic and vital principle to oppose to ideas and forms.[16]

This dynamic principle, firmly rooted in the physical world and in the vital tension of matters, shaped and informed by the πνεῦμα, helps frame the relation between normality and monstrosity in an original way, especially in the physical and biological domain. Concrete shapes in the physical world do not reflect the superior reality of ideas, nor do they actualise the perfection of forms into matter. They are immanently produced by life itself, vibrating through matter in accordance with the πνεῦμα's tension.

The theory of seminal reasons has an important place in early Stoicism, and it provides an account of zoogony that is coherently opposed to Attic teleology and Epicurean materialism alike. The σπερματικός λόγος is identified with the divine principle that shapes and informs the material world in its actual existence.[17] The material cosmos being changeable and diverse, the seed functions as a principle of stabilisation.[18]

The seminal reason is produced by the fire in the ἐκπύρωσις, the conflagration that marks the end of the old and the beginning of the new world. The

---

[15] See also *SVF* II.332 (= Sen. *Ep.* 58.15): 'Certain of the Stoics regard the primary *genus* [Gummere: 'i.e. the *genus* beyond "that which exists"'] as the "something". I shall add the reasons they give for their belief; they say: "in the order of nature some things exist, and other things do not exist. And even the things that do not exist are really part of the order of nature. What these are will readily occur to the mind, for example centaurs, giants, and all other figments of unsound reasoning, which have begun to have a definite shape, although they have no bodily consistency".' This strategy will be used by Descartes to think about mental images of monsters. See Del Lucchese (2011). On Seneca and early modernity see Marzot (1944) and Chevallier, Poignault eds (1991).

[16] See Reale (1975–80), III, p. 379.

[17] *SVF* II.580 (= D.L. VII.135–7).

[18] *SVF* II.717 (= Procl. *in Prm.* V).

individual λόγοι are fragments of the single λόγος that unfolds itself to give life to the whole. They bear within them, thus, the rational character of the universe and correspond, within the material monism of the Stoic universe, to the Aristotelian views. If the σπερματικοὶ λόγοι have the same active force of ideas, however, they lack their strong teleological character.[19]

The very material nature of the seed, its relationship with the earth and the idea of germination are strongly reminiscent of animals being generated in and sprouting from the earth, as in the early zoogonies. Unlike Empedocles or Lucretius, though, early Stoics do not think about monstrosities as a specific zoogonic stage, at least in the fragments that survived.[20] This is due to the subordination of the entire cosmic cycle, including zoogony, to the divine principle of fate, with its religious providential connotation.

This is particularly clear in middle Stoicism, and especially in Posidonius, who gives a detailed account of early cosmogony, based on the ἐκπύρωσις.[21] Posidonius is interested not only in the physical mechanism of germination of seeds, but also, and more importantly, in its providential unfolding, religiously accomplishing the rational order of the universe. Stoics, however, have different visions on the providential nature of the universal movement. The Latin poet Lucan, for example, develops an opposed vision of it. The ἐκπύρωσις is not for him the accomplishment of the harmonic cycle of the universe. It is rather the movement subverting natural laws and plunging the world into the chaotic end of civilisation:

> When the framework of the world is dissolved and the final hour, closing so many ages, reverts to primeval chaos, then [all the constellations will clash in confusion,] the fiery stars will drop into the sea, and Earth, refusing to spread her shores out flat, will shake off the ocean; the moon will move in opposition to her brother, and claim to rule the day, disdaining to drive her chariot along her slanting orbit; and the whole distracted fabric of the shattered firmament will overthrow its laws [*totaque discors machina diuulsi turbabit foedera mundi*].[22]

---

[19] As explained by Aetius and Athenagoras, this is also the origin of Stoics' pantheism. See SVF II.1027 (= *Placit.* I.7.33 and Athenag. *Leg.* 6). See Pohlenz (1948), pp. 78–9.

[20] See for example SVF II.739 (= Origenes *Cels.* I.37).

[21] Pohlenz (1948), pp. 219–20.

[22] Lucan. I.72–83. Johnson (1987) stresses the importance of the direct attack against the Stoics' idea of the harmonius and divine craft (p. 17): 'To call any machine, particularly this machine, the universe, discordant is to accuse it of failing itself, of being and not being itself simultaneously, of betraying itself, of destroying itself. [. . .] This is not, needless to say, a very Stoical attitude.' On the comparison between civil war and the final conflagration see also Lucan. II.289–91.

Generally, however, Stoics share a positive vision of the cosmic cycle that might contain anomalies, but is nonetheless providential and divine in nature. Within this framework, the Aristotelian idea of monstrosity as an imperfect actualisation of the form becomes untenable. The development of the eternal λόγος is by definition perfect, both at the global and the individual level.[23] Zeno was already able to explain apparently abnormal and anomalous phenomena with very powerful intuitions. Concerning animal beings, for example, he claims the idea of a panspermia, i.e. the origin of the seed from the whole body and, beyond it, from the whole genus. Whereas the lack of resemblance between the child and the parents is a form of monstrosity for Aristotle, for early Stoics, on the contrary, it is perfectly explained by the global origin of the σπερματικοὶ λόγοι in the entire ancestry.[24]

It is important to stress, once again, the pre-eminence of the religious and providentialist argument over the mechanical explanation of matter and its motion. If everything is matter in the Stoic universe, including the spirit, everything is also divine and rationally determined. If, on the one hand, the Stoic conception undermines the Peripatetic explanation of monstrosity as a failure of the actual information of matter by the form, on the other hand Stoicism always places the rational action of the πνεῦμα before and above the mechanical arrangement of matter.

The early Christian reception of Stoicism and its reworking of the concept of *semina rerum* is crucial here. Tertullian, for example, makes use of the Stoic doctrine to clarify the Christian concept of God. God is spirit or πνεῦμα, in the Stoic sense. He pervades the whole universe inasmuch as he is material and corporeal.[25] This element becomes for Tertullian a powerful tool against Gnosticism and its condemnation of matter. Matter cannot be evil and monstrous precisely because it is divine, just as it was for the Stoics.[26]

Grant argues that the originality of the doctrine of *semina* and their strong bond with rationality is transformed by Augustine into the active and original

---

[23] Cic. *ND* II.86–7: 'The government of the world contains nothing that could possibly be censured; given the existing elements, the best that could be produced from them has been produced. Let someone therefore prove that it could have been better. But no one will ever prove this, and anyone who essays to improve some detail will either make it worse or will be demanding an improvement impossible in the nature of things.'

[24] Pohlenz (1948), p. 86.

[25] See Moreschini (2004), pp. 485 ff.

[26] See Tert. *Adu.Marc.* and *Adu.Val. passim.*, as well as *Cult.fem.*, in which the female toilette is condemned as a vain attempt to improve and embellish nature, which is already perfect because divine.

action of God in nature. All events, normal and miraculous, as well as all beings, normal and monstrous, have their origin in the *semina rerum* that God has initially implanted in nature. The immanent nature of Stoic σπερματικοὶ λόγοι is thus transformed in the ordinary course of nature, created and directed *ab aeterno* by the transcendent God.[27] Although the Judeo-Christian idea of creation is alien to Stoicism, Christianity is able to implant it on the philosophical ground inherited from the Greeks. For Christians like Minucius Felix this is the chance to rebuke all the fantasies and superstitious beliefs of the pagans, especially their awful monsters:

> Our ancestors were so ready to believe in fictions, that they accepted on trust all kind of wild and monstrous marvels and miracles: Scylla with serpent coils, a hybrid Chimaera, a Hydra replenishing its life from vivifying wounds, Centaurs half-horse half-man, or any other fiction of folklore fell upon willing ears. Why recall old wives' tales of human beings changed into birds and beasts, or into trees and flowers? Had such things happened in the past, they would happen now; as they cannot happen now, they did not happen then.[28]

Such a strong belief in the divine order of the universe takes the shape of a boundary against the fictions of ancient poetry, so as to recall the regularity of nature's behaviour in a quasi-Epicurean fashion: whatever is not possible now has never been possible before. For Minucius, however, this is due to the active action of the omnipotent God.

The dialectic between laws of nature and the will of a personal God also characterises the philosophy of Lactantius, a Christian who was strongly influenced by Stoicism yet harshly critical of its immanentism. Lactantius believes firmly in the divine nature of the world preached by the Stoics, but this nature is not immanently self-generated, but rather created by a God who is and remains above and beyond his creation:

> since the Stoics are of opinion that all the heavenly bodies are to be considered as among the number of the gods, since they all have fixed and regular motions, by which they most constantly preserve the vicissitudes of the times which succeed them. They do not then possess voluntary motion, since they obey prescribed laws, and plainly not by their own sense, but by

---

[27] See Grant (1952), pp. 218–19.
[28] Minucius Felix 20.

the workmanship of the supreme Creator, who so ordered them that they should complete unerring courses and fixed circuits, by which they might vary the alternations of days and nights, of summer and winter. But if men admire the effects of these, if they admire their courses, their brightness, their regularity, their beauty, they ought to have understood how much more beautiful, more illustrious, and more powerful than these is the maker and contriver Himself, even God.[29]

Lactantius insists on the idea of a normative regularity of natural phenomena, but he sees the danger of worshipping the creature and forgetting the creator, especially because the Stoic God did not create the world. Seeds of divinity have been sown throughout nature, but God is responsible for how they germinate.

The idea that providence extends to the whole of nature, but also exceeds its limits and our comprehension of it, is also developed by John Chrysostom. Notwithstanding his anti-philosophical stance, John's Christian thought reveals an interesting use of Stoic (and Platonic) elements against Aristotelianism. Whereas Aristotle claims that providence does not extend to the sub-lunar realm, Chrysostom follows the Stoics and their praise of the beauty, harmony and order of nature as a whole. Interestingly, however, monsters reveal better than normal phenomena providence's direct action in the world. Providence can act directly to produce phenomena like sea-monsters and reptiles that immediately show God's absolute power over nature.[30] When our reason is challenged by such phenomena, as well as by the evil and imperfection that we struggle to explain, it is better to withhold our judgement, recalling that we are merely the created facing the mysteries of creation.[31]

Pelagius, another theologian strongly influenced by Stoicism, insists instead on the capacity of reason to recognise the Lord and read, in his creations, the magnificent work of the creator. The beauty of the world simply demonstrates God, says Pelagius with a Stoic accent:

> *Since what is known about God.* What can be known by nature about God, that he exists and that he is just. *Is plain to them.* To their consciences. For every creature bears witness that it [is] itself [not] God, [and] shows that it

---

[29] Lact. *Epit.* XXI (= XXVI in AA. VV. (1970), vol. VII).
[30] John Chrysostom, *Homilies on Genesis* VII.12.
[31] See M. A. Schatkin, *St. John Chrysostom's Attitude toward Nature and Science*, in AA. VV. (2007), pp. 259–69.

was made by another, with whose will it ought to comply. [. . .] Furthermore, [the creatures'] changeability, which cannot belong to eternity, proves that they were created.[32]

Although already filtered by many early Christian thinkers,[33] this position clearly exploits Stoic arguments. The *ordo naturae* that allows humans to naturally and spontaneously know God through the creation comes close to the concept of natural laws and legality. This has both a normative and a descriptive function: humans should behave in accordance with this order, which describes the infinite wisdom of the creator and the goodness of His work. Pelagius often employs the expression *reddere rationem*, which points to an objective reality of order and harmony in a Stoic vein, not just to an individual rational faculty.[34]

Back to pagan Stoicism, from his own horrified perspective, Lucan also confirms, by opposition, the divine nature of the seminal origin of things. When the world is on the edge of the catastrophe, nature, 'at variance with itself', produces monsters, 'brought forth from no seed [*nullo semine*]'.[35] Together with ghosts and evil omens, physical anomalies are produced spontaneously, as if they were at the same time within and outside the world and its normal cycle of production and reproduction. Monstrosity plays here the role of a principle antithetic to life as it expresses the divine in the world.

Stoic nominalism has another important consequence concerning the knowledge of individual things. Aristotle's metaphysics of forms explains monstrosity as a fault and a failing of the form's action upon matter. The intelligible reality, no matter how defective its actualisation is, remains intact beyond its individual manifestations. This is also why a proper science, i.e. knowledge and explanation, of individual monstrosities cannot be obtained and should not be the object of scientific research for Aristotelians. For Chrysippus, on the contrary, a science of individual things is not only

---

[32] Pelagius *Exp. Rom.* 1.19. See also 1.20: '*For since the creation of the world his invisible properties, even his eternal power and divinity, are clearly seen, having been understood through the things that were created, so that they are without excuse. His hidden qualities are deduced from things that are manifest. For if he made the things which are visible so splendid that some considered them gods and tried to assert that they are eternal, how much the more were these people able to understand that the one who made these things is everlasting and almighty and boundless.*' See Moreschini (2013), p. 677.
[33] As claimed by Matteoli (2011), pp. 29 and *passim*. See also Spanneut (1957), pp. 162–3.
[34] See Valero (1980), pp. 103 ff.
[35] Lucan. I.589.

possible, but necessary. It is indeed the only science that one can have. By criticising the Aristotelian forms, Stoicism argues for a science of objects that were previously excluded from the domain of scientific explanation and that could only fall under sensation.[36]

Stoics, however, do not intend to recognise the absolute authority of sensations. They know that sensations are often fallacious. For this reason, they must be submitted to the authority of λόγος, which is indeed held as a superior faculty. We have a full comprehension, Zeno claims, only when λόγος assents to the αἴσθησις and the representation is thus verified.[37] This process produces a cataleptic representation, in which the object is directly apprehended, seized and grasped by the mind, as if it was firmly held by one's hand, according to the famous Stoic metaphor. The κατάληψις thus reintroduces a certain hierarchy among principles of knowledge, moving away from the Epicurean theory, which had also taken sensation as a starting point. Whereas for Epicurus only the regularity and repetition of observations can verify the sensation, Stoics postulate the superiority of a rational criterion that must dominate sensation.

This opposition to the Epicurean theory reintroduces a form of transcendence of rationality over material reality. Monstrosities are by definition the individual, unique and irregular manifestations of nature. Whereas nature's regularity is, for Epicureans, the only acceptable and fully immanent criteria with which to analyse and interpret exceptions, Stoics introduce, through the cataleptic representation, a transcendent norm of judgement. The λόγος is the mental authority through which the material and actual existence of individual phenomena must be judged and interpreted. Properly speaking, Stoics recognise the existence of *laws* in the sense of authoritative principles that shape natural individual existences, whereas Epicureans recognise only *generalisations*, stemming from the repeated observations of regularities. Stoics mistrust these generalisations, because they see in them the claim of philosophy to build universal descriptions, while for them only individual phenomena have a real existence.

The presence of transcendence in the Stoic criterion is particularly recognisable in later Christian sources, directly influenced by Stoicism. The individual, unique and irregular phenomena, in this milieu, become God's direct intervention in nature or, in other words, the miracle. The individual, irregular and monstrous phenomenon was undermined by the Epicurean theory of knowledge, with the aim of defusing superstitious beliefs. Stoics, on the

---

[36] Isnardi-Parente (1999). See also Sedley (1982) on the specific problem of individual identity.
[37] SVF I.60 (= Cic. Acad. I.41).

contrary, acknowledge the full reality of individual phenomena, no matter how irregular they are, since regularity is only the vain philosophical attempt to build universals. Christians will appropriate this idea and build on it a theological critique of philosophy, according to which natural laws are only unjustified generalisations. To these generalisations, Christians respond with the faith in God's power of performing miracles, producing monsters and, more in general, establishing or demolishing regularities at his own wish.[38]

Individual, anomalous and monstrous things must be recognised as God's intervention, outside and against any possible generalisation or universalisation. Stoic nominalism thus becomes the ground for the religious belief in individual and exceptional events, beyond and against the attempt to rationalise nature through the recognition of regularities and repetitions.[39] The evolution of this reasoning opens up to the problem of beauty and goodness in the universe, coupled with the question of evil. Stoicism, once again, has much to offer on this ground.

Good and Evil, Beauty and Ugliness

A group of fragments informs us about Chrysippus's belief that everything beautiful (καλός) is also good (ἀγαθός), and everything ugly (αἰσχρός) is also bad (κακός).[40] The link between καλός and ἀγαθός is already established by

---

[38] There is a complex discussion in scholarship regarding the relationship between Stoicism and Christianity. This is connected to the debate about the Semitic origin of Stoicism, already underlined by Nietzsche in 'Nachgelassene Fragmente. Herbst 1887 bis März 1888', in Nietzsche (1970), VIII.2, p. 356 and developed by Pohlenz, whose entire reading is grounded on the Semitic character of Stoic philosophy. The thesis of the Semitic origin of Stoicism has a specific source in the German intellectual milieu of the 1930s and is worth mentioning here more for its relevance to understanding intellectual and academic life under the Nazi regime than for its historiographical strength. See Canfora (1979 and 1980) as well as Bossina (2012). Pohlenz also insists on the unfillable gap between the Stoics' interest in nature and its laws on the one hand, and the Christian doctrine of the creation on the other hand. See Pohlenz (1948), p. 401. Through the *Hellenisierungsprozeß*, Pohlenz argues, the Christian absorption of Stoic philosophy becomes possible only by rejecting the core ideas of the system. See Pohlenz (1948), p. 418 and p. 423. Reacting to Bonhöffer's thesis (1911), according to which Stoicism prepares the way for Christianity, Duncan (1952) also claims their incompatibility, because of the opposition between monism and dualism. More wisely, I believe, Spanneut (1957 and 1970) underlines the Stoic reminiscences in the Christianised concept of natural and divine normativity in the Church's fathers. See also Campenhausen (1955 and 1960) and, more recently, Moreschini (2004 and 2013).

[39] Grant (1952), pp. 194–5.

[40] SVF III.16 (= Stob. II.77.16) and SVF III.29–37.

Plato and is a widespread topos in Greek classical culture. Stoicism, however, puts a stronger emphasis on the correspondence between beauty and goodness, expanding the idea and assigning an ontological and epistemological meaning to the aesthetic and ethical concept, through the pervasive action of reason (λόγος) that informs the whole universe at every level and in every manifestation.

This vision of the universe has a strong religious flavour. The divine permeates the whole world, establishing the uncreated and absolute character of its goodness, which is thus fully natural. A life according to nature, κατὰ φύσιν ζῆν, is human's end according to the Stoics. Through this idea, Stoicism develops several elements already present in Attic philosophy,[41] and opposed to the Epicureans' philosophy, which claims on the contrary the unkind character of nature.[42] God's nature, and thus nature as a whole, is absolutely good. Humans as well as animals are attracted by goodness and beauty,[43] and by following them, they accomplish their nature according to the highest principle of reason and virtue.[44] Humans can of course deviate from such natural virtue, and opt for vice instead. Yet this leaves untouched and uncorrupted, for Stoics, the nature of beauty and goodness, which is absolute in itself. As Marcus Aurelius puts it:

> Everything in any way lovely is lovely of itself and terminates in itself, holding praise to be no part of itself. At all events, in no case does what is praised become better or worse. This I say also of what is commonly called lovely, for instance materials or works of art; and indeed what is there lacking at all to that which is really lovely? no more than to law, no more than to truth, no more than to kindness or reverence of self. Which of these is lovely because it is praised or corrupted because it is blamed? does an emerald become worse than it was, if it be not praised? and what of gold, ivory, purple, a lute, a sword-blade, a flower-bud, a little plant?[45]

---

[41] In particular, the notions of οἰκείωσις, close to that of self-conservation, and ζῆν ὁμολογουμένως, or adaptation to nature. See Spanneut (1970). See also Chroust (1963), p. 285: 'The Greek term which expresses most closely this "according to nature" is the word οἰκείωσις – a term which also denotes "the taking as one's own", "appropriation", or "adaptation". It was liberally used by the Early Stoics, who made it a key term in their philosophy.' See also Wiersma (1937).
[42] See for example Lucr. V.222–34 and *supra*.
[43] SVF III.38 (= S.E. M. XI.99).
[44] SVF III.76 (= D.L. VII.94).
[45] M.Ant. IV.20 (= Farquharson I, pp. 58–9).

Both from the global and the individual point of view, the perfect good consists in a balanced life according to the harmony requested by nature, namely consistent with its order.[46]

Whereas it is true that life in harmony with nature and, more in general, the absolute nature of goodness are not specific to Stoicism, Stoic philosophers develop this idea in a highly original manner. Stoics boldly depart from the Platonic origin of this idea, following a radical monism. Against any idealisation of goodness, Stoics postulate its material nature. An *idea* of goodness does not exist, because ideas are not superior entities, and thus goodness itself unfolds, and can be pursued, within the only existing natural dimension, that of materiality.

The good, Seneca claims, produces effects. It produces happiness in the mind and in the body alike. But everything that *moves* things in a similar fashion must be of the same nature, namely corporeal. Bodies only, in the Stoic universe, can act, and thus, strikingly, Stoics do not hesitate to postulate the material and corporeal nature of goodness: 'the good is active: for it is beneficial; and what is active is corporeal. The good stimulates the mind and, in a way, moulds and embraces that which is essential to the body. The goods of the soul. For the soul, too, is corporeal. *Ergo*, man's good must be corporeal, since man himself is corporeal.'[47]

The immanence of goodness in materiality is a strong and bold stance for Stoics. It is also what opens up several problems and renders them vulnerable to criticism. First of all, if everything is matter, including goodness and divinity, then the origin of evil, imperfection, anomalies and monstrosities must be explained referring to one and the same causal principle. Both Plato and Aristotle, although in different ways, had made use of matter's inferiority as an adjuvant cause of the imperfection of the world. Matter, however, is conceived by Stoics both as the divine principle *and* the world. Where does imperfection

---

[46] SVF III.83 (= D.L. VII.100) and SVF III.13 (= Cic. *Fin.* IV.14). Cleanthes speaks about the harmonic movement of the universe: SVF I.502–3 (= Clem.Al. *Strom.* V.8.48 and Corn. Theologiae Graecae Compendium *ND* 32). See also Manil. I.247–54: 'This fabric which forms the body of the boundless universe, together with its members composed of nature's diverse elements, air and fire, earth and level sea, is ruled by the force of a divine spirit; by sacred dispensation the deity brings harmony and governs with hidden purpose, arranging mutual bonds [*foedera*] between all parts, so that each may furnish and receive another's strength and that the whole may stand fast in kinship despite its variety of forms.' On the concept of harmony, see W. Hirschmann, *Harmonie*, in HRW, III, pp. 1297–1304, and Spitzer (1963), who, however, does not address the Stoic concept at length. See also Spanneut (1970), p. 166 and M.-A. Zagdoun, *L'harmonie chez les stoïciens*, in Caye et al. a cura di (2011).

[47] SVF III.84 (= Sen. *Ep.* 106.2).

come from? Stoics walk on a narrow path when they try to keep together the material nature of God and the material origin of imperfections.[48]

The Stoics' treatment of this issue shows a strong ambivalence. Pohlenz underlines that the debasement of matter constitutes a Platonic and Aristotelian element carried forward by Stoicism.[49] At the same time, as Pohlenz himself recognises, this idea was developed with more and more emphasis during the imperial period in the Academic and Peripatetic culture, *against* Stoicism and, more specifically, against Poseidonius's immanentism, for example in the theological cosmology of the pseudo-Aristotelian Περὶ κόσμου, whose author claims God's transcendence and the unworthiness of lower and imperfect things to be inhabited by the divine principle.[50]

Early Stoicism makes clear that, although the universe's nature is exclusively material, a distinction can be made between an active and a passive principle. As Diogenes Laertius explains, '[Stoics] hold that there are two principles in the universe, the active principle and the passive. The passive principle, then, is a substance without quality, i.e. matter, whereas the active is the reason inherent in this substance, that is God. For he is everlasting and is the artificer of each several things throughout the whole extent of matter.'[51]

The πῦρ τεχνικόν, or creative fire, is an active principle that shapes passive matter. Although it is material itself – the Stoic prerequisite to be a cause[52] – fire acts *upon* something which is indifferently intended as an underlying layer without quality and inert (ἄποιος), pure matter (ὕλη) and a substratum (ὑποκείμενον).[53] Although this theory reproduces the Aristotelian distinction between matter and form,[54] it also develops the Peripatetic principle in a wholly new direction,

[48] As Plutarch, SVF II.1168 (= Plu. *Moralia, De communibus notitiis adversus Stoicos* 34. 1076 C) argues, '[. . .] while they [*scil.* the Stoics] are cross with Menander for his theatrical pronouncement 'Of human ills the chiefest origin/Is things exceeding good' – for this, they say, is at odds with the common conception – yet they do themselves make god, though good, the origin of things evil. For matter has not of itself brought forth what is evil, for matter is without quality and all the variations that it takes on it has got from that which moves and fashions it. That which moves and fashions it, however, is the reason existing in it [i.e. the immanent reason, λόγος ἐνυπάρχων], since its nature is not to move or fashion itself.' On Plutarch and Stoicism see Babut (1969), Hershbell (1992). See also SVF II.1136 (= Gal. *UP* V.4). On Galen's attitude, strongly influenced by the Stoics, see *infra*.
[49] Pohlenz (1948), p. 100
[50] See Pohlenz II.175, G. Reale, A. P. Bos, *Monografia introduttiva*, in Reale, Bos (1995, 2a ed.), pp. 23–171, and Festugière (1949–54), II.460–518, who underlines the ambivalent relationship of the text with the Stoic doctrines.
[51] SVF I.85 (= D.L. VII.134). See also Posidon. 5 and 100.
[52] See again Ar. Did. (= Stob. I.13.1) and Duhot (1989).
[53] See Isnardi-Parente (1999), p. 21.
[54] Pohlenz (1948), p. 67.

whereby the dialectic between active and passive takes place entirely *within* the material element itself.

The first consequence is that the Stoic body is the conjunction of matter and quality: without the latter, the former would only be a dead ὕλη.⁵⁵ The second consequence is that the aggregate of matter and quality should be conceived as a dynamic being, always in motion. It is an aggregate moved by a particular kind of motion, originally conceived, once again, against the Aristotelian idea of a movement of actualisation of the form as well as the uncaused random movement of Epicureans.

Stoics place a tensional movement (τονικὴ κίνησις), caused by the πνεῦμα, *within* matter itself. Following Sambursky, Rist underlines that Stoics use the verb διήκω, 'pervade', implying 'vibration, such as is produced by the twanging of a taut string' and specifically distinguished, e.g. by Philo, from movement from one place to another.⁵⁶ As Galen reports, it has to be intended as a '"simultaneous movement in opposite directions", or as neither inwards alone nor outwards alone, but as a continual variation between the two, or as continually backwards and forwards'.⁵⁷

Pohlenz suggests that the tensional motion gives coherence and cohesion to the cosmos, and makes it an artwork of perfect beauty.⁵⁸ Clearly, the κίνεσις that the Stoics have in mind is opposed to the uncaused or spontaneous movement of Epicureans. Produced by the πνεῦμα, the tensional movement brings with it the spirit's rationality and reveals the design on which every individual thing depends. In this sense, the τονικὴ κίνεσις is the antidote to the παρέγκλισις.⁵⁹

Now, if one thinks about the Aristotelian notion of monstrosity as the failure of the informative movement, one can legitimately wonder whether the Stoic notion of monstrosity can be seen as a failure of, and within, the tensional movement with which the active πνεῦμα pervades and informs the passive matter. Several indications suggest this conclusion. In the physical world in the first place: without the πνεῦμα, the passive element would disintegrate, because it lacks the cohesive force (συνεκτικὴ δύναμις) that keeps things together.⁶⁰ Within human himself: the πνεῦμα's tone *falls* (καταπίπτω) when one has a passion, thus disintegrating, in some way, the spirit's consistency.⁶¹

---

⁵⁵ Pohlenz correctly argues that this position is developed by Neoplatonism. See Pohlenz (1948), p. 66, and Reale (1975–80), III, p. 355. This does not imply, however, that matter does not have a proper existence in itself, as Weil (1970) argues.
⁵⁶ Rist (1969), p. 86.
⁵⁷ Rist (1969), p. 86, and SVF II.446 (= Gal. *De tremore, palpitatione, convulsione*, VI).
⁵⁸ Pohlenz (1948), p. 76: 'ein Kunstwerk von vollkommener Schönheit'.
⁵⁹ Sambursky (1959), p. 57.
⁶⁰ Sambursky (1959), p. 31.
⁶¹ SVF II.877 (= Gal. *De locis affectis* IV.3).

Sambursky argues that the tone recalls Empedocles' forces acting in the universe. One could also wonder whether it is reminiscent of the Empedoclean conflictual nature of these forces and, as a consequence, of monstrosity as a result of the long and complex process of their stabilisation, slowly taking the appearance of what can eventually be observed and recognised as the currently normal structure of the universe. Does the Stoic tensional motion imply monstrosity as one of the possible outcomes of material vibration?

In Stoic literature, the strongest demotion of matter appears perhaps in Epictetus, whose tone is reminiscent of the Platonic hierarchies, and anticipates the Neoplatonist and Christian ontological grading. The body is, for Epictetus, frail: no more than earth, mud (πηλός) and almost a corpse: 'This body is not thine own, but only clay cunningly compounded.'[62] This principle is fundamentally important to him, in order to establish a solid ground for the freedom of moral choice: whereas the body can be impeded, the moral choice is free and in our power.[63]

No wonder, thus, that late Stoicism tends to emphasise the contrast, rather than the cooperation, between the active and the passive principles. Matter steadily becomes an element that resists God's formative action. Seneca is confident in answering what appears already an inconvenient question:

> How powerful is God? Does he form matter for himself or does he merely make use of what is already there? Which comes first: Does function determine matter, or does matter determine function? Does God do whatever he wishes? Or in many cases do the things he treats fail him just as many things are poorly shaped by a great artist not because his art fails him but because the material in which he works often resists his art?[64]

The response is explicitly directed against the Epicurean theory of chance. Stoics intend not only to explain nature according to a divine principle, but also to justify this principle for everything that happens in the universe. The core of Christian theodicy lies in the Stoic religious attitude toward evil and

---

[62] Arr. *Epict.* I.1.11. See also III.22.41: 'how can that which is naturally lifeless, earth, or clay, be great or precious?'

[63] Epict. *Ench.* 9. Materialism is the main obstacle to a Christian reception of Stoicism. Epictetus's attitude is the most important point that makes possible this reception, overcoming the 'scandal' represented by Stoics' materialism in the eyes of Christian thinkers. See for example Clem. Al. *Prot.* V.58P: 'the Stoics [...] say that the divine nature permeates all matter, even in its lowest forms; these men simply cover philosophy with shame'. See Pohlenz (1948), p. 409.

[64] Sen. *Nat.* I praef. 15. See also *Ep.* 58.27: matter prevents god from creating everything immortal, and to overcome the body's imperfections.

good as a result of the dialectic between the active and the passive principles in the universe. Marcus Aurelius makes it clear that

> the nature of the Whole would not have winked at [ill] things either out of ignorance or because (though it knew of them) it had not the power or skill, as to permit good and ill to befall indifferently, both good and bad men equally. Now death, and life, good report and evil report, pain and pleasure, wealth and poverty, these all befall men, good and bad alike, equally, and are themselves neither right nor wrong: they are therefore neither good nor ill.[65]

One the one hand, thus, we have the demotion of passive matter vis-à-vis the active divine principle. Evil and imperfection lie in matter's resistance to the πνεῦμα's action. On the other hand, we have the idea that matter and spirit, the passive and the active principles, are harmoniously integrated, and find their place, in the same universe, whose nature is accomplished and in which good and evil are in fact only *names* for things and events that reflect the same perfect nature. The inconsistency is only apparent. It is rather an ambivalence, depending on the immanence of goodness within materiality itself. This is why Christian thinkers, although ruling out the unacceptable materiality of the divine principle,[66] understand that Stoic philosophy offers a powerful tool for theodicy. This tool is a strong explanation of imperfection and monstrosities within the universe, whose providentially organised nature must be recognised beyond its only apparent imperfection.[67]

Tertullian is among the first Christian thinkers to recognise the paramount importance of the problem of natural evil. The mistake, he claims, is to assign a benevolent or malevolent character to nature. In fact, for God, nature is only a tool used to reward or punish human actions. Even the intervention of Satan has been explicitly allowed by God, and devils only operate through God's permission. Their monstrous nature emerges from their origin, as Tertullian explains: 'certain angels corrupted themselves and [. . .] from them was produced a brood of demons yet more corrupt, condemned by God with the authors of their race and that prince whom we have named'.[68] The devils

---

[65] M.Ant. II.11. See Farquharson in Marcus Aurelius (1944), II, pp. 520–1.
[66] See for example Tatian and Clement Alexandrinus, SVF I.159. A notable exception, as we have seen above, is Tertullian.
[67] See for example M.Ant. IV.29 and Farquharson in Marcus Aurelius (1944), II, pp. 319, as well as M.Ant. VIII.49–50 and Farquharson in Marcus Aurelius (1944), II, pp. 374. See also Pohlenz (1948), p. 348.
[68] Tert. Apol. XII.

are a veritable monstrous race: they are the descendants of angels who were attracted to women and revolted against God to satisfy their lust.[69] The result of these unnatural unions is a race whose function is to pervert and corrupt humanity.[70] They pass on to humans knowledge that makes them fall and condemns them to perdition. Satan's technique is precisely to use the beauty and attractiveness of creation to accomplish his purposes: beauty may have a monstrous use, just as monstrosity and evil, intended as a divine punishment, perform a function within God's plan.[71]

Lactantius also stresses the powerful malignant nature of the feminine in corrupting angels and transforming them into demons.[72] Lactantius develops his theodicy – which eventually has a dramatic impact on philosophy – in line with the philosophical ground offered by Stoicism, showing how good and evil, merit and vice, in the hands of God, always work together:

> I ask whether virtue is a good or an evil. It cannot be denied that it is a good. If virtue is a good, vice, on the contrary, is an evil. If vice is an evil on this account, because it opposes virtue, and virtue is on this account a good, because it overthrows vice, it follows that virtue cannot exist without vice; and if you take away vice, the merits of virtue will be taken away. For there can be no victory without an enemy. Thus it comes to pass, that good cannot exist without an evil. Chrysippus, a man of active mind, saw this when discussing the subject of providence, and charges those with folly who think that good is caused by God, but say that evil is not thus caused. [. . .] good and evil are so connected with one another, that the one cannot exist without the other.[73]

We know how bitter Lactantius can be against the Stoics. His approval of Chrysippus's ethics is thus even more significant, revealing how crucial Stoic inclusive ethics and the Stoic theory of the good use of evil are for early

---

[69] See e.g. Tert. *De virginibus velandi*, I.12.
[70] For this whole argument, see Zimmerman (1984), pp. 289 ff.
[71] See Tert. *Apol.* XII–XXIV. Evil also performs a plan according to Minucius, yet not as a punishment but rather as a test and a training through discipline. See Minucius Felix 36: 'For fortitude is braced by weaknesses, and calamity is frequently the school of virtue; strength, both of mind and body, grows slack without hard training. [. . .] in adversities [God] tries and tests us every one; weighs each man's disposition in the scales of peril; proves man's will even to the last extreme of death, with the assurance that in his sight nothing can perish. As gold is tried by fire so are we by ordeals.'
[72] Lact. *Epit.* XXII.10–2.
[73] Lact. *Epit.* XXIV.2–10 (= XXIX in AA. VV. (1970), vol. VII).

Christian thinkers.⁷⁴ Evil and vice are necessary, both to know good and virtue and to allow God's plan to unfold as He has ordered.

The powerful ambivalence of Stoic philosophy also appears in another important domain, namely the origin of human evil and imperfection, when humans do not follow their own nature and choose vice instead of virtue. Stoicism is adamant in claiming that evil comes upon humans from outside and does not belong to their nature. Rational souls have not been made evil by nature. They rather become evil because of a wrong education, or because they are diverted from virtue, or because they are confused to the point that vice becomes for them a second nature.⁷⁵ There is also a different perspective, though, within the Stoic movement itself, developed in particular by Posidonius, one that excludes the original purity and goodness of human souls. The ambivalence and ambiguity lie in human nature itself, which participates in both good and evil:

> Posidonius doesn't think [...] that vice [evil: κακία] comes in afterwards to human beings from outside, without a root of its own in our minds, starting from which it sprouts and grows big, but the very opposite. Yes, there is a seed even of evil in our own selves; and we all need not so much to avoid the wicked as to pursue those who will prune away and prevent the growth of our evil. For it is not the case, as the Stoics say, that the whole source of evil comes into our minds from outside us; no, in wicked men the greater part of it is internal, and only a very minor influence has an external source.⁷⁶

Posidonius is consciously countering Chrysippus's orthodoxy on this point, opening up to the idea of a *duality* of forces, rational and irrational, both operating within us.⁷⁷ This is a crucial point for Stoics' anthropology and, more widely, for their very conception of good and evil. Challenged by this contention, Christian anthropology eventually develops in a different and opposed direction, either stressing the Platonic transcendence of good vis-à-vis evil, including the goodness of humans, created in the image of God,

---

⁷⁴ See also Lact. *De opificio Dei* IV.1 on the meaning and reason of fragility and why God has given it to humans. See also *De ira dei* V.8 on the necessary coexistence of love and hate, XIII.23–4 on the necessity of evil, XV.3 on the necessary existence of things in the opposite, and XX.1 ff. on why evil strikes good people.

⁷⁵ *SVF* III.233 (= Origenes *Cels.* III.69).

⁷⁶ Posidon. 35 C (= Gal. *De Sequela* 819–20).

⁷⁷ Rist (1969), p. 213.

or underlining the immanence and thus the misery of humans, sinners forever lost without God's help. Whereas the former attitude tends to isolate the perfection of humans vis-à-vis the monstrosity of original sin, the latter approach brings the monster within human nature itself.[78]

No surprise, thus, that the monster-within powerfully and ominously surfaces from the dark landscapes of Lucan's *Pharsalia*. Nature as a whole, in Lucan's view, shows its horrible face, especially in his Africa, 'a region so fertile of monsters'.[79] A region, though, that is not to blame for what it is, since the Romans are the 'trespassers in a land of serpents' and somehow deserve the misery that they suffer. Africa's human inhabitants, on the contrary, are far from monstrous. Hardened by the harshness of the land and physically accustomed to its monstrosity, they even feel pity for the Romans' misery, and promptly provide relief to them.[80]

Not all the natives are kind and humane, though. In book VI Lucan gives one of the most astonishing portraits of monstrosity in classical literature, that of the Thessalian witch Erichto. Visited at night by Sextus Pompeius, younger son of Gnaeus Pompeius, Erichto performs her sacrilegious rite, waking up the corpse of a dead soldier and making him speak the future with hell's voice. Erichto embodies the obscure force that haunts Roman mentality in an age of awful and crucial transformation. Erichto's monstrosity plays a strategic function in the poem, and reveals aspects of the Stoic mentality – and its crisis – in Lucan's age. The witch is as powerful as she is hideous and frightful. She challenges the infernal power that hesitates one moment to respond to her call. '*Paretis?*' ('Do ye obey?') is her war cry, daring to threaten hell's power itself with an even higher and more monstrous force.[81] Erichto is not only the expression of chaotic disorder. She is the messenger of a monstrous counter-order that rises and opposes itself to the benign normality in which men delusionally believe.[82]

---

[78] Origen's, Basilius's and Ambrogius's anthropological thought are consistent with this version of Stoicism. See Pohlenz (1948), pp. 424 ff.

[79] Lucan. IX.700 ff.

[80] Lucan. IX.893–9. See Aumont (1968). On Africa's snakes see also Solin. 27.28 ff.

[81] Lucan. VI.744–9.

[82] Johnson (1987), p. 19. H. Le Bonniec, 'Lucain et la religion', in Durry éd. (1970), pp. 159–200 and *passim*, argues that Lucan himself speaks with Erichto's voice, but that the poet is only doubting because of tragic events, and has not lost his faith in the cosmic and human order. One can hardly recognise, however, the same *order* that Panaetius or Posidonius praise. Şerban (1973), p. 32 and *passim*, compares Lucan's anti-classicism to Romanticism, and contrasts it with Virgil's use of imaginary. The encounter with Erichto has traditionally been associated with, and opposed to, Aeneas's descent into Hades. Şerban interestingly remarks, however, that while Virgil's hero travels to the underworld, it is the hell itself that, in Lucan, comes to the surface.

Because of the absolute and fully natural character of goodness and beauty, Stoics postulate that ugliness and imperfection are, as a consequence, relative and derivative. This means that physical and moral ugliness, as well as monstrosity, are conceived as the privation and diminution of the perfection of goodness and beauty. It also means that their character is relative *within* the world itself. The consequence is a significant degree of relativism and openness in the judgement and treatment of alterity. In his *Discourses* III.I.1–9 Epictetus develops very clearly the idea of relativity:

> Tell me if you do not think that some dogs are beautiful, and some horses, and so every other creature. [...] Is not the same true also of men, some of them are handsome, and some ugly? [...] Do we, then, on the same ground pronounce each of these creatures in its own kind beautiful, or do we pronounce each beautiful on special grounds? [...] Since we see that a dog is born to do one thing, and a horse another, [...] in general it would not be unreasonable for one to declare that each of them was beautiful precisely when it achieved supreme excellence in terms of its own nature; and, since each has a different nature, each one of them, I think, is beautiful in a different fashion.[83]

Beauty and ugliness are relative and make sense only within a specific genus, that of the dog for dogs, that of the horse for horses. Within it, however, the criterion of excellence becomes absolute, and humans themselves must pursue their own virtue to the highest degree to be καλός. Every compromise makes them αἰσχρός or *turpis*. III.1 is also the only dissertation in which Epictetus makes use of the term τέρας, otherwise very rare in the Stoic vocabulary overall. Monstrous is, for Epictetus, the appearance of those whose nature or behaviour make them different precisely from the genus to which they belong: if a woman has hairs or a man depilates, they become monstrous and, to some extent, they make themselves monsters.

Monstrosity's relativism and imperfection helps the Stoics to build the idea of hierarchy within nature and, in particular, human nature. Nature's diversity stems from matter. It is a sign of richness, Manilius explains, and yet nature's different manifestations can be ordered according to degrees of perfection. Within human races, for example, 'nations are fashioned with their own particular complexions; and each stamp with a character of its own the like nature and anatomy of the human body which all share'. Whereas the Romans have 'the features of Mars, and Venus', and thus 'well-proportioned

---

[83] Arr. *Epict.* III.1.1–9.

limbs', the Ethiopians, Manilius adds, 'stain the world and depict a race of men steeped in darkness'.[84]

Stoics largely and generally prefer the term διάστροφος, deformis, to the monstrous (τεράστιος or τερατόμορφος), but also to the διάστροφος, pravus, twisted or distorted.[85] The choice of language is utterly important. Monteil explains that whereas the αισχρότης (deformitas) only implies the shape's alteration, without any presupposition of an ideal prototype, the διαστροφή (pravitas), on the contrary, involves a judgement of blame related to the violation of a norm. Whereas the αἰσχρός, preferred by Stoics, is absence of a form, the διάστροφος, significatively absent in Stoicism, refers to the abuse and violation of a pre-existing form.[86] Although the meaning varies, of course, depending on the cultural milieu and the epoch, this conclusion is consistent within the general framework of Stoicism. Lucan's vision of the world, as expected, plays the role of an exception. Lucan does not make a large use of informis, deformis and prauus. The monstrosity of the civil war and, as a consequence, of men's condition becomes evident through the frequent use of uultus and foedus, underlining respectively the idea of monstrous mutilation, sickness, indecency and dirtiness, as well as that of pestilential morality, pathologically altered physicality, exceptionality and sacrilegious debauchery.[87]

As a result, Stoics imagine that every single individual, animate and inanimate, has its own place in the universe. The universe can be ordered according to a hierarchy, but this necessarily includes, as one of its own parts, every single thing, no matter its degree of perfection or rationality. For Posidonius, this sensibility becomes intellectual curiosity with regard to anomalous, borderline and monstrous phenomena, within which the investigator of nature must recognise the same universal concept of life.[88] Even what is αἰσχρός and deformis, thus, has a place and a function to perform within nature. The order of nature and the place that things have in it is clear. When it is not clear, it will become so in due time. History shows, in fact, that utility and necessity have helped humans discover many things previously unknown, as Lactantius explains.[89]

---

[84] Manil. IV.715 ff. On Manilius's Stoicism see Salemme (1983), Abry (1983), Colish (1985) and R. Radice, M. Manilio, L'astronomia, in Radice (1998), pp. 1–687, especially the rich introductory essay and commentary. On the Ethiopians see infra.
[85] See Radice et al. a cura di (2007).
[86] Monteil (1964), p. 258 and passim.
[87] See Wacht (1992), ad. loc. and Monteil (1964).
[88] See Pohlenz (1948), p. 224.
[89] SVF II.1172 (= Lact. De ira dei XIII).

The Stoics try to give a solid theological and philosophical foundation to the explanation of imperfection, evil and thus monstrosity in the world. The theological argument is rooted in Heraclitus's logic of the necessary coexistence of contraries and is strongly defended by Chrysippus in his Περὶ προνοίας:

> There is absolutely nothing more foolish than those men who think that good could exist, if there were at the same time no evil. For since good is the opposite of evil, it necessarily follows that both must exist in opposition to each other, supported as it were by mutual adverse forces: since as a matter of fact no opposite is conceivable without something to oppose it.[90]

Evil is necessary, not only to the comprehension, but also to the existence of good. They exist only *together*, and almost support each other.[91] Pohlenz connects this passage to Pl. *Phd.* 60 b–c, but Chrysippus also has in mind the Platonic theory of natural catastrophes.[92] The philosophical argument developed by Chrysippus is rooted in nature's unity and universal identity, within which change and mutation must necessarily happen:

> For even if *the nature of the universe is one and the same*, the origin of evils is not by any means always the same. Although the nature of some particular individual man is one and the same, things are not always the same where his mind, his reason, and actions are concerned. [. . .] also even more may this be said of the universe, that, even if it remains one and the same generically, yet the events which happen to the universe are not always the same nor of the same kind. For there are not periods of productivity or of famine all the time, nor always of heavy rain or drought. In this way neither are there determined periods of fertility or famine in the life of good souls; and the flood of bad souls increases or decreases. In fact, for those who want to have the most accurate knowledge of everything that they can, it is an unavoidable doctrine that evils do not always remain the same in number on account of the providence which either watches over earthly affairs or cleanses them by floods and conflagrations, and probably not only earthly things but also those of the whole universe which is in need of purification whenever the evil in it becomes extensive.[93]

---

[90] SVF II.1169 (= Gell. VII.1.2–4).
[91] Pohlenz (1948), pp. 99–100.
[92] Pl. *Criti.* 109 d, *Ti.* 22 b–25 d, *Lg.* 677 b ff. See *supra*. This theory was much older. Already presented by Xenophanes, *Vorsokr.* 21 A 33 (= LM [8] XEN. P7, D22, R20 = Hippol. *Haer.* I.14), it was also developed by Aristotle. See also Bollack (1971).
[93] SVF II.1174 (= Origenes *Cels.* IV.64).

It is the whole, thus, that must be considered, and not only the single parts of the universe or the single events of a causal chain, historically developing according to the world's destiny and rationality. The pre-eminence of the whole over its parts is one of the most important arguments presented by Stoics to undermine the critique of nature as imperfect and disordered. It is also a pivotal argument for the reading of monstrosities within it. As Balbus explains:

> As in vines or in cattle we see that, unless obstructed by some force, nature progresses on a certain path of her own to her goal of full development, and as in painting, architecture and the other arts and crafts there is an ideal of perfect workmanship, even so and far more in the world of nature as a whole there must be a process towards completeness and perfection. The various limited modes of being may encounter many external obstacles to hinder their perfect realisation, but there can be nothing that can frustrate nature as a whole, since she embraces and contains within herself all modes of being.[94]

Different degrees of perfection establish differences among things and events.[95] As the Attic philosophy teaches, the heavenly region is indeed more perfect than the earthly one.[96] Observing the latter, thus, one might be induced to even doubt about the presence of a divine intelligence guiding the whole universe.[97] Yet the whole is precisely what wipes away any doubt, if one learns to look at it. On a global scale everything, including monstrosity and evil, has its own utility in this ontology:

> Vice is peculiarly distinguished from dreadful accidents, for even taken in itself it does in a sense come about in accordance with the reason of nature

---

[94] Cic. *ND* II.35. On Cicero's exposition of Stoic physics through Balbus see Festugière (1949–54), II, pp. 375–425, Dragona-Monachou (1976), Lévy (1992), and B. Besnier, 'La nature dans le livre II du *De natura deorum* de Cicéron', in Lévy éd. (1996), pp. 127–75.

[95] Posidon. 21, explains that 'the universe is governed according to intelligence and providence, as Chrysippus says in Bk V of *On Providence*, and Posidonius in Bk III of *On Gods*, since intelligence pervades every part of it as soul pervades us; but actually through some parts it is more, through some less. For through some parts it has come in cohesion, as through bones and sinews; through others as intelligence, as through governing principle.'

[96] Cic. *ND* II.56: 'In the heavens therefore there is nothing of chance or hazard, no error, no frustration, but absolute order, accuracy, calculation, and regularity. Whatever lacks these qualities, whatever is false and spurious and full of error, belongs to the region between the earth and the moon (the last of all heavenly bodies), and to the surface of the earth.'

[97] *SVF* II.1185 (= Origenes *Princip.* III).

and, if I may put it so, its genesis is not useless in relation to the universe as a whole, since otherwise the good would not exist either.[98]

Following Chrysippus, but beyond him, middle Stoicism is able to recognise order and beauty not only in the superior universe, as it was for early Stoicism,[99] but also and consistently in the earthly realm, with its diversity and multiplicity of landscapes, plants and animals. When Cicero's Balbus sketches the wonders of nature, the earth comes first, followed by celestial bodies:

> First let us behold the whole earth, situated in the centre of the world, a solid spherical mass gathered into a globe by the natural gravitation of all its parts, clothed with flowers and grass and trees and corn, forms of vegetation all of them incredibly numerous and inexhaustibly varied and diverse. [. . .] Think of all the various species of animals, both tame and wild! think of the flights and songs of birds! of the pastures filled with cattle, and the teeming life of the woodlands! Then why need I speak of the race of men? who are as it were the appointed tillers of the soil, and who suffer it not to become a savage haunt of monstrous beasts of prey nor a barren waste of thickets and brambles, and whose industry diversifies and adorns the lands and islands and coasts with houses and cities. Could we behold these things with our eyes as we can picture them in our minds, no one taking in the whole earth at one view could doubt the divine reason.[100]

Even more important than the beauty of the earthly realm is the perfection of the human body. Early Stoicism, once again, does not recognise the physical perfection of humans as intensely as middle Stoicism does. Panaetius in particular is able to create a new aesthetic of the human body, which is very far from the ideal perfection of the Greek canon, and much closer to the practical idea of an ontological adaptation and perfect adjustment of humans to the world. The human body is the most appropriate tool to accomplish the λόγος's action. Rather than naively celebrating anthropocentrism, Panetius recognises the human power of adaptation to the world.[101]

---

[98] SVF II.1181 (= Plu. *Moralia. De Stoicorum repugnantiis*] 1050 F. See also SVF II.935 (=1056 D): '[Chrysippus] has written that to particular natural entities and motions many obstacles and impediments present themselves but none at all to that of the universe as a whole;' See Sambursky (1959), p. 114, and Isnardi-Parente (1999), p. 29.
[99] See again SVF II.1185 (= Origenes *Princip.* III).
[100] Cic. *ND* II.98–9. See also Pohlenz (1948), p. 196, and Isnardi-Parente (1999), p. 136.
[101] Pohlenz (1948), p. 197.

One of the most powerful ancient celebrations of nature's diversity is Pliny the Elder's encyclopaedic enterprise. Pliny discusses monstrosity and *mirabilia* in a way that is influential for centuries in science, philosophy and the arts.[102] In his *Natural History*, he gladly accepts Aristotle's invitation to see the gods even in the kitchen, and to treat every aspect of nature's diversity as deserving the scientist's attention: 'The nature of [the world's] animals is as worthy of study as almost any other part thereof, if in fact the human mind is capable of exploring everything.'[103] The accent is on both nature's richness and the mind's capacity to grasp its meaning. Yet the opening of book VII immediately takes the argument in a direction of ambivalence and ignorance, one deriving from the paradoxical human position in which they are the greatest but also the weakest of all creatures: 'The first place will rightly be assigned to man, for whose benefit great nature seems to have created everything else. However, for her considerable gifts she exacts a cruel fee; so that it is difficult to decide whether she is more of a kind parent or a harsh stepmother to man.'[104] Pliny's argument reveals a well-meditated Stoic sensibility toward nature that nonetheless responds with astonishment to nature's disconcerting power.

One can clearly see the unifying principle of Stoic reasoning in the background of the prodigious quantity of materials collected, catalogued and explained in Pliny's encyclopaedic enterprise.[105] It is Stoicism's conception of the divine that gives consistency and coherency to overabundant nature, with its immense variety of beings and phenomena. Beyond the apparent proliferation of rules and exceptions that characterise different geographical regions and different ontological domains, Stoic teleology and providentialism give unity to the world as a whole. In fact, nature must be apprehended as a whole, or comprehension would be lost in the labyrinth of facts and their puzzling variety,

> [...] facts which will, I am sure, seem extraordinary and unbelievable to many readers. Who, after all, believed in the Ethyopians before actually seeing them? And what is not regarded as wondrous when it first gains public attention? How many things are judged impossible before they actually happen? Indeed, the power and might of nature lacks credibility at every point unless we comprehend her as a whole rather than piecemeal[106]

---

[102] See Stahl (1962), pp. 101–19, Beagon (1992), Healy (1999), pp. 63–70, Naas (2002), pp. 243–393, Beagon (2007) and Gibson, Morello eds. (2011).

[103] Plin. *HN* VII.1. On Aristotle's mention of Heraclitus's gods in the kitchen see *supra*. See also Beagon (1992), p. 129 and *passim*.

[104] Plin. *HN* VII.1–2.

[105] See e.g. E. Paparazzo, 'Philosophy and Science in the Elder Pliny's *Naturalis Historia*', in Gibson, Morello eds. (2011), p. 110, who underlines Pliny's debt towards Posidonius.

[106] Plin. *HN* VII.6–7.

Monstrosity is thus framed as a part of nature's rationality; otherness must be seen as variety within unity. The monstrous races, for example, which eventually have an enormous impact on medieval and early modern literature and art, are interesting because they reveal not only the blurred boundaries of humanity, but also because such a thing, i.e. humanity, reveals its thousand faces as yet another powerful manifestation of nature.[107] Although monstrous, these races are interesting precisely because they reveal their participation in and resemblance to humanity:

> India and the territory of the Ethiopians are particularly abundant in marvels. The largest animals are produced in India; [. . .] On a mountain called Nulus, according to Megasthenes, there are people with feet turned backwards and eight toes on each; while on many mountains there is a race of dog-headed men who dress in animal skins, bark rather than talk and live on animals and birds which they hunt armed only with their nails. He says there were more than 150,000 of them at the time he was writing. Ctesias also writes that in a certain Indian tribe the women give birth once in a lifetime and the hair of their children starts turning grey from the moment of birth. He also says that there is a race of men called the Monocolo ('One-legged men') by virtue of their single leg which enables them to jump with amazing agility. They are also called Sciapodae ('Shady-feet') because when it gets too hot they lie down on their backs on the ground and protect themselves with the shadow of their foot.[108]

Located in a remote and mysterious East and South, the monstrous races reveal yet another aspect of the world. They illustrate the principle that guides

---

[107] See Bianchi (1981). See also Garland (1995), pp. 159 ff.

[108] Plin. *NH* VII.21–3. Pliny enumerates many other races, including the satyrs, the Choromandae, 'who do not talk but emit harsh shrieks', the Struthopodes, the Sciratae, 'who only have holes where their nostrils should be and snake-like strap feet', the Astomi, 'a people with no mouths', the Trispithami ('Three-span men') and the Pygmies, the Cyrni who live for 140 years, and the Indians who 'copulate with animals and the offspring are human-animal hybrids'. Herodotus has already mentioned India's fecundity and, in it, the proliferation of species not so much as the violation of an ontological order, but rather as nature's force expressed through its playfulness. Revolving around strange and unusual customs, his account is much less focused on monstrosity. In this respect, Herodotus's influence on the genealogy of the idea of Indian monstrosities appears weaker than Pliny's. See Hdt. III.97–106 and *supra*, as well as Pohlenz (1937), Immerwahr (1966), Hartog (1991) and Munson (2001). On Pliny's India see Sedlar (1980). Ctesias (*FGH* 688) and Megasthenes (*FGH* 715) were the major sources for the Indian monstrous races who, through Pliny, also reach Solin. 51. 27–8. See also the texts in André and Filliozat (1986), as well as Mund-Dopchie (1992) and F. Nieto in Solino (2001).

the Stoic scientific attitude and interprets monstrosity as an aspect of normality, a part of the whole in which – though the full rationality of nature's design is not wholly clear – the unity of divine action is still recognisable. Within the material nature of the divine principle, Pliny looks for physical explanations for the diversity of shapes as well as the variety of customs and practices that work to build the concept of monstrous otherness.

Beagon stresses the attitude that distinguishes Pliny's astonished approach from Aristotle's colder and more rational explanation.[109] Aristotle speaks about the teratogenic environment created by the scarcity of water in Africa and the way it forces animals to gather in a limited space, thus inducing inter-species copulations, and their resulting monstrous offspring. Differently, Pliny focuses on India's and Africa's climate, its excessive heat and the stronger capacity of the mobile element of fire to mould bodies and carve their outlines.[110] Thus a natural element creates the monstrous offsprings more autonomously, indeed even without the willingness of animals to engage in cross-boundary intercourse. I believe, however, that Beagon exaggerates the difference between the two authors. Both Aristotle and Pliny are interested in the causal and physical explanation of monstrous phenomena, and Pliny's approach is no less rational than Aristotle's. It is more accurate to say that it is based on a different kind of rationality, one in which the individual behaviour of animal specimens is less important than nature's necessary unfolding. Pliny's worldview is the Stoic one, and thus based on the idea of an autonomous and necessary actualisation of the intervention of the divine in the world, regardless of the behaviour of individuals.

Now, if monstrous races, monsters and *mirabilia* belong to the order of nature and reveal the divine reason and its providential purpose, it is all the more difficult to grasp and fully explain such a purpose. Pliny attempts an explanation that reveals something less than a full commitment to Stoic providentialism:

> Nature has cleverly contrived these and similar species of the human race to amuse herself and to amaze us. As for the individual creations she produces every day, and almost every hour, who could possibly reckon them up? Let it be a sufficient revelation of her power to have placed entire races among her miracles.[111]

Nature does not do anything in vain. So be it. Yet for for the sake of what does it do such monstrous things? To amaze us, Pliny states. Here we see anthropocentrism resurfacing, with humans taking centre stage and bending the whole

---

[109] M. Beagon in [Pliny the Elder] (2005), p. 150.
[110] Plin. *NH* VI.187. See Dasen (1993), p. 178.
[111] Plin. *NH* VII.32.

of nature's purpose, even its deviations, to what is useful, meaningful or merely wonderful for them. Nature, Pliny adds, also produces monstrosity to amuse herself.[112] Nature's playfulness, in this context, seems like an aleatory exception to the principle of strict necessity that characterises the Stoic understanding of providential nature. Not only does it appear to respond more to the question 'why not' than the question 'why', it resembles more the atomist idea of potentially infinite compositions of matter that equally (and unprovidentially) exhaust nature's possibilities, than it does the necessitarianism of the Stoics. Let us listen to Pliny on the hereditary transmission of genetic character:

> [...] sound parents may produce deformed children and deformed parents may produce sound children with the same deformity as themselves. Birthmarks, moles, and even scars can reappear in descendants, a tattoo sometimes recurring up to the fourth generation among the Dacians. [...] Other children, again, may resemble their grandfather, and, in the case of twins, one may resemble the father, the other the mother.[113]

He seems amazed at the inconsistent and yet foreseeable behaviour of nature, at the regularity of irregularities for which there seems to be no causal explanation. Yet he does not respond to this seeming absence of explanation with the generic call for Stoic providentialism that we might expect.[114]

If monstrosity reveals the absolute and ultimate power of nature, such power remains unexplained. Nature seems to be more playful and less consistently rational and teleological than a Stoic attitude would imply. I believe that without renouncing the Stoic framework Pliny struggles to contain the wonderful diversity of nature within the monolithic principle of Stoic Providence. Something similar happens to Lucan. Whereas Lucan's Stoicism is challenged by the appalling misery that characterises humanity in his own time, Pliny's Stoicism is confronted with the astonishing diversity of nature, by

---

[112] M. Beagon in [Pliny the Elder] (2005), p. 162, points to the frequency of the theme of nature at play in *NH*.

[113] Plin. *NH* VII.50.

[114] If Pliny's explanation of genetic transmission of genetic character must be placed within a Stoic framework, it is certainly a heterodox framework, within which Pliny feels compelled to make room for the aleatory as much as for necessity. See Plin. *NH* VII.52: 'Resemblances offer considerable food for thought. They are believed to be influenced by many chance occurrences, including sight, hearing, memory, and images absorbed at the very moment of conception. Even a chance thought which briefly crosses the mind of one or other parent may form or confuse the resemblance. This is the reason why there are more variations within the human race than there are among all the other animals; the swiftness of man's thoughts, his mental agility and the versatility of his intelligence produce a wide variety of features; whereas the minds of other creatures are sluggish and exhibit a uniformity in keeping with their particular species.'

its incomprehensible and apparently inexplicable tendency to produce monsters and *mirabilia*. Pliny's response can be read as a sincere recognition of the limits of human understanding facing the immensity of nature and its divine character. It can also be read, though, as the recognition of nature's flexibility and inconsistency, an entity whose playfulness sometimes reveals aleatory physical behaviour rather than an inflexibly providential intervention.

There is a long tradition of connecting providence to nature's diversity and its marvellous character within Stoicism. It arises from the gap between sympathy as a general principle of explanation and the mystery of specific phenomena that cannot be explained by the science of the time. While everything reveals sympathy, not everything can be explained by it. Differently from Pliny's approach, a number of authors developed an interpretation of the world that tried to grasp its divine character through the supernatural and the teratological manifestations of nature rather than through rationalised enquiry. The Egyptian thinker Bolus of Mendes, for example, plays a paramount role in the second century BCE in connecting Stoic providence with the literary genre of paradoxography of which he is a recognised authority.[115] Following the work of Max Wellmann, Festugière underlines Bolus's break with Aristotle's scientific approach and early Hellenistic science more broadly.[116] Yet one should not forget that the modern meaning of scientific enquiry recognisable in Aristotle or Pliny's did not pre-exist, but was shaped by works interested in the *mirabilia*, the curious and the monstrous commonly found in nature, and that in his day, Bolus was not necessarily read *against* Aristotle, but with him.

The idea of sympathy is also emphasised in the work of a later author strongly interested in nature's curiosities, Claudius Aelianus. The intertwining of Stoicism and naturalism resurfaces in the second century and characterises Aelianus's encyclopaedism, which is very concerned with topics typically developed in paradoxographical literature. Like Pliny, Aelianus sees nature as a source of marvels. In his work, his scientific effort reveals a taste for the amazing and astonishing aspects of prolific nature. Such a taste, however, does not mean that he is credulous. When confronted in the dialogue between Silenus and King Midas with Teopompus's account of a monstrously giant race, or when describing the way that Ausones' forefathers are represented as centaurs, Aelianus makes his disbelief clear.[117] After indulging in the exploration of literary materials for stylistic purposes, Aelianus's final comment brings the argument back to a more rational explanation, one close

---

[115] See Giannini (1963), p. 262, and Payón Leyra (2011), pp. 118 ff.
[116] Festugière (1949–54), II, pp. 197–200.
[117] Ael. *VH* III.18 and IX.16.

to that of the Stoics. The Stoics' contention is mainly employed against the materialist theory of the pre-existence of the organ to the function. Although the praise of the human body can be generally referred to Platonic teleology, it is Stoicism that specifically develops this argument, with a particular attention to the central role played by the hand. Balbus sings a veritable hymn to the perfection of the body,[118] which culminates with the apology of the hand, whose perfect anatomy is recognised as the material ground of the development of the arts and, more in general, of civilisation.[119]

This argument eventually plays a central role in early Christian philosophy. Christian thinkers follow the Stoics' praise for the perfection of God's creatures, their beauty and clever engineering that lets the body achieve all its functions. Minucius Felix, for example, claims that the erect posture testifies to human nobility.[120] More generally, the creature's perfection reveals that of the creator. Against the Epicurean argument of chance, nothing could be more evident to those with intellect to understand and eyes to see than the gifts of the divine Artificer. Without His continual action, the whole universe would be in danger: 'How easily would confusion overtake the order, were it not held together by sovereign reason! [. . .] Above all, beauty of form declares the handiwork of God: our poise erect, our look upward, our eyes stationed in the watch-tower of the head, and the other senses all posted in the citadel.'[121]

The apology of the hand in particular, already discussed by Aristotle against Anaxagoras, becomes the apology of humanity as such.[122] It plays

---

[118] Cic. ND II.134 ff.
[119] Cic. ND II.150–2: 'What clever servants for a great variety of arts are the hands which nature has bestowed on man! The flexibility of the joints enables the fingers to close and open with equal ease, and to perform every motion without difficulty. Thus by the manipulation of the fingers the hand is enabled to paint, to model, to carve, and to draw forth the notes of the lyre and of the flute. And beside these arts of recreation there are those of utility, I mean agriculture and building, the weaving and stitching of garments, and the various modes of working bronze and iron; hence we realize that it was by applying the hand of the artificer to the discoveries of thought and observations of the senses that all our conveniences were attained, and we were enabled to have shelter, clothing, and protection, and possessed cities, fortifications, houses, and temples. [. . .] by means of our hands we essay to create as it were a second world within the world of nature.'
[120] Minucius Felix 17: '[. . .] our distinction from the beasts is this, that their downward earth-bound gaze is fixed only on their food: we, with countenance erect and heavenward gaze, endowed with speech and reason, enabling us to recognize, perceive and imitate God, neither may nor can ignore the heavenly sheen which thrusts itself upon our eyes and senses [. . .].'
[121] Ivi. Cf. Moreschini (2004), p. 543.
[122] Renehan (1992).

an important role in Galen and it soon becomes a classic topos in Christian apology.[123] Lactantius profusely illustrates the hand's virtues and how it epitomises God's wisdom and care for His beloved human creature:

> What shall I say of the hands, those ministers of reason and wisdom? The Master Artificer fashioned these with a plain and moderately concave surface so that whatever must be grasped can fitly occupy this surface. He terminated them in the fingers in which it is difficult to settle whether appearance or utility is the greater. For their number is perfect and complete; their order and gradation most appropriate; the curvature of matching joints is flexible; the form of the nails, rounded and tightly grasping the ends of the fingers with curved protection lest the softness of the flesh falter in the function of holding, furnishes great ornament.[124]

The Stoic teleological principle finds a perfect accomplishment in Lactantius's Christian apology of God's wisdom. The adaptation of the organs, and of the hand in particular, is perfect because the project of the divine artificer is perfect. Animals, and humans in particular, could not be more perfect than they are, because they have been engineered by the Almighty Himself. The idea of imperfection, along with that of spontaneous adaptation, disappears from the picture. Better: imperfection and the monstrous, or *turpis*, are assigned to anything that our imagination might forge that would be different from the existing reality which testifies to God's perfect plan:

> How marvellously the very things which are given to brutes and denied to man are ordered unto the beauty of man defies expression. For if He had added to man the teeth of wild beasts, or horns, or claws, or hoofs, or a tail, or hair of varied hues, who does not realise how unsightly [*turpe*] an animal he would be? [. . .] But since God made man an eternal and immortal animal, He armed him not exteriorly as He did the other animals, but interiorly; and He placed his defense not in his body but in his soul. For it would have been superfluous, since He had bestowed what was greatest on him, to have covered him with bodily defenses, especially since these would mar the beauty of the human body.[125]

---

[123] See Arist. PA IV.10, 687 a 3–b 25. See *infra* for Galen, and Grant (1952), pp. 12–13: 'Galen rejects the opinion of Anaxagoras that man's wisdom is due to the fact of his having hands, and defends the view of Aristotle that because he was wise he was given hands.' See also Hankinson (1989) and Hankinson (1998).

[124] Lact. *De opificio Dei* X.22–4.

[125] Lact. *De opificio Dei* II.7–9. See also *De ira Dei* VII.3 and X.22, in which the beauty of creation works as an antidote to the atomist's hypothesis.

Even from an ethical point of view, were humans not what they are, crushed by their fears, they would become monsters, and society itself would collapse:

> What mutual respect would there be? What order? What plan? What humanity? Or what would be more disgraceful [*tetrius*] than man? What more savage [*efferatius*]? What more cruel [*immanius*]? But since he is weak, and is not able by himself to live apart from man, he seeks society, so that life in common may be both more attractive and more secure.[126]

Lactantius is aware of the danger involved in claiming that, because everything *is* perfect, then God could have not done anything different from what he did. After all, is not God almighty? Could he not have produced more monsters, had He wanted to? Lactantius tries to preserve both God's omnipotent freedom and the necessity of His plan's perfection, but his answer poses inconvenient questions, and creates rather than solves problems: 'For considering the condition of things, I understand that nothing ought to be done otherwise. I do not say that nothing could be done otherwise, for God is all powerful, but it is of necessity that that Most Provident Majesty did what was better and more right.'[127]

Only the Christian, according to Lactantius, can grasp nature's perfection – pagans, including Stoics, blinded by their own ignorance, wander vainly trying to understand nature. Such blindness reveals the monstrosity of pagan philosophy itself, which is like a twisted and dislocated body whose members 'are at variance with one another, and are not united together by any connecting link, but as it were, dispersed and scattered, appear to palpitate rather than to live'.[128]

Stoicism also reworks the Aristotelian idea of the gods in the kitchen and the beauty of the universe as a whole, in each and every one of its parts. Marcus Aurelius perfectly summarises this idea, making a large use of Chrysippus's concept of attendant circumstances (ἐπακολούθησις):

> We must also observe [...] that even the secondary effects of Nature's processes possess a sort of grace and attraction. [Many] characteristics that are far from beautiful if we look at them in isolation, do nevertheless because they follow from Nature's processes lend those a further ornament and a fascination. And so, if a man has a feeling for, and a deeper insight into the processes of the Universe, there is hardly one but will

---

[126] Lact. *De opificio Dei* IV.20–1.
[127] Lact. *De opificio Dei* III.4.
[128] Lact. *Inst.* III.2.2. See also Pichon (1901), p. 93.

> somehow appear to present itself pleasantly to him, even among mere attendant circumstances [κατ' ἐπακολούθησιν]. Such a man also will feel no less pleasure in looking at the actual jaws of wild beasts than at the imitations which painters and sculptors exhibit, and he will be enabled to see in an old woman or an old man a kind of freshness and bloom, and to look upon the charms of his own boy slaves with sober eyes. And many such experiences there will be, not convincing to every one but occurring to him and to him alone who has become genuinely familiar with Nature and her works.[129]

Pohlenz suggests that Christian theodicy, so important for the early modern concept and interpretation of monstrosity, is rooted in this Stoic argument. He also claims that Marcus Aurelius's mediation is epitomised by the author who will be more easily Christianised, namely Epictetus, for whom Stoic fate easily becomes God's will.

Monstrosity explicitly appears in Epictetus's powerful example: 'What do you think Heracles would have amounted to, if there had not been a lion like the one which he encountered, and a hydra, and a stag, and a boar, and wicked and brutal men, whom he made it his business to drive out and clear away?'[130]

This argument also leads to a redefinition of the concept of παρὰ φύσιν, employed by Zeno and other Stoics. I believe that it should be read as *preternatural* rather than *against* nature. In Epictetus's words:

> How, then, can it be said that some externals are natural, and others unnatural [παρὰ φύσιν]? it is just as if we were detached from them. For I will assert of the foot as such that it is natural for it to be clear, but if you take it as a foot, and not as a thing detached, it will be appropriate for it to step into mud and trample on thorns and sometimes to be cut off for the sake of the whole body; otherwise it will no longer be a foot. We ought to hold some such view also about ourselves. What are you? A man. Now if you regard yourself as a thing detached, it is natural for you to live to old age, to be rich, to enjoy health. But if you regard yourself as a man and as a part of some whole, on account of that whole it is fitting for you now to

---

[129] M.Ant. III.2. See also IX.28 and the several passages quoted by Pohlenz (1948), p. 348 and n.

[130] Arr. *Epict.* I.6.32. See also Epict. *Ench.* 27: 'Just as a mark is not set up in order to be missed, so neither does the nature of evil arise in the universe.' Although the text is plain and straightforward, G. Boter in Epictetus (1999) *ad loc.* feels compelled to clarify: 'That is, it is inconceivable that the universe should exist in order that some things may go wrong; hence, nothing natural is evil, and nothing that is by nature evil can arise.' See also Pohlenz (1948), p. 339, and, on Epictetus and Christianity, Bonhöffer (1911) and Jagu (1989).

be sick, and now to make a voyage and run risks, and now to be in want, and on occasion to die before your time. Why, then, are you vexed? do you not know that as the foot, if detached, will no longer be a foot, so you too, if detached, will no longer be a man? for what is a man? A part of a state; first of that state which is made up of gods and men, and then of that which is said to be very close to the other, the state that is a small copy of the universal state.[131]

A genuine opposition is thus established between the general and the particular. Although men might perceive things only at their individual level, it is the whole that makes sense. Reason acts through general and not through particular ways. Whereas Epicureans maintain that gods' perfection consists in a complete indifference to the human world, Stoics deem that gods are indifferent only to *minora*, and when insignificant things are damaged, it is certainly not their fault, since they are superior to them, and indifferent to minor details, such as a king in his own kingdom.[132] 'De minimis non curat praetor,' says the Latin expression. This concept eventually has a major role in the Judeo-Hellenistic reception of Stoicism, such as in Philo's theodicy.[133] Fully material and yet spiritual, immanent and yet normative, impersonal and yet creator: this philosophical system requires a new and original definition of God, the divine and its providential intervention in the world.

Providence, God and Teleology

The Stoic conception of a providential divine intervention in the world, and thus nature's teleological character, is the strongest theoretical tool left by classic Stoicism to natural philosophy. The image of God in Stoicism, however, has a long and complex history, that goes from the early opposition to the Attic principle of transcendence of the divine, to its progressive anthropomorphisation and separation from the world, coherent with Christian theology. In this sense, the concept of providence also has various meanings within Stoicism. Initially relying upon a materialist ontology, providence steadily transforms itself into God's personal intervention in the world. Stoicism thus provides a versatile conceptual tool for understanding natural monstrosities by finding a place for evil and imperfection within a universe framed theologically.

The impersonal and immanent idea of God is typical of early Stoicism. Nonetheless, the tendency is toward a personal and transcendental conception of the divine, accentuated in later Stoicism, when the school comes in

[131] Arr. *Epict*. II.5. 24–6.
[132] *SVF* II.1179 (= Cic. *ND* III.86). See also *SVF* II.1180 (= Cic. *ND* III.90).
[133] See *infra*.

touch with Judaism and early Christianity.[134] These, I believe, should be seen as two different attitudes rather than two different stages. Both attitudes, in fact, appear across the centuries and characterise the different periods of the school's development. The early Stoics' conception of God is firmly rooted in the school's postulate of material monism. God's corporeality is its most important feature. God is the cause of all things because it is first and foremost the purest nature and cause:[135] purest and yet corporeal.[136] Causality and materiality cannot be disjointed; thus God is merely the highest peak of material reality, which is the only existing ontological reality within the Stoic universe, elaborated against Attic idealism.[137]

Nature thus has a divine character that immanently produces all its effects. The accent is put, in this perspective, on the unity of God and nature, on their correspondence and common existence. Pantheism is the short name for this indissoluble unity between the heaven and the earth, which share one and the same substance. Diogenes Laertius explains that

> Cosmos is the individually qualified being of the substance of the whole, or, as Posidonius says in the *Meteorology* (the elementary treatise), a systematic compound composed from heaven and earth and the natural constitutions in them, or a systematic compound composed from gods and men and what has come into being for their sake.[138]

Τό σύστημα is the orderly whole. Edelstein-Kidd translates it as 'systematic compound'. The term is consciously employed by Posidonius to underline the idea of a whole formed by several parts. The term has a long philosophical tradition. It is used by Plato to stress the strong unity of vital phenomena and its

---

[134] See Dragona-Monachou (1976) and Ewing (2008).
[135] Such is the πνεῦμα's nature. See Sambursky (1959), pp. 36–7.
[136] SVF I.153 (= Hippol. *Haer.* XXI.1). Seen Duncan (1952), pp. 128–9.
[137] SVF I.153 (= Gal. *Phil. Hist.* XVI) registers the Stoics' sharp opposition to Platonic idealism, and Plotinus, SVF II.315 (= Plot. VI.1.26), protests against it. See also the beautiful theological *incipit* of Sen. *Nat.* I praef. 13–4: 'What is god? The mind of the universe. What is god? All that you see, all that you do not see. In short, only if he alone is all things, if he maintains his own work both from within and without, is he given due credit for his magnitude that *that* can be contemplated. What, then, is the difference between our nature and the nature of god? In ourselves the better part is the mind, in god there is no part other than the mind. He is entirely reason.' Seneca is keen on underlying both the immanence and superiority of god: *et intra et extra opus suum tenet*. See *contra* Pohlenz (1948), p. 320, who perceives a strong sense of transcendency in *Nat.* A different atmosphere reigns in Seneca's tragedies in which, on the contrary, a powerful tension between divine goodness and human evil monstrosity emerges. See Dupont (1995).
[138] Posidon. 14. See also Posidon. 15: 'Zeno says that the substance of god is the whole universe and in particular, heaven [SVF I.163]; a similar version is given by Chrysippus, *On Gods* Bk I, and by Posidonius, *On Gods*, Bk I.'

comprehension as the highest form of wisdom,[139] by Aristotle as a synonym of animal organism,[140] and by Epicurus to describe the material aggregate of body and soul.[141] God and the world form an immanently organised system and a compound, whose laws express the highest form of rationality.

The laws of this immanent compound, divine and natural at the same time, should be conceived through the idea of rationality and perfection rather than that of normativity.[142] God and nature represent the laws that guide and inform the whole universe because the universe itself is rational and perfect.[143] The law and the right reason (the ὀρθός λόγος) *are* God itself, according to Chrysippus.[144] The difference between divine and human reason, Cicero's Balbus explains, is solely one of degree and not of nature.[145]

The idea of a community of reason between men and gods contrasts, of course, with the indifferent Epicurean gods as well as with the Attic transcendence of the divine, both in the form of the Platonic demiurge and the Aristotelian νοῦς. As Pohlenz suggests, the Stoic λόγος replaces the νοῦς, whose thinking activity is independent and separate from the physical and visible sphere.[146] Moreover, because God is φύσις *and* λόγος at the same time,[147] one possible consequence of this materialist pantheism is polytheism: another aspect of Stoicism that early Christianity rules out and fights against.[148]

In Stoic philosophy, however, there is a strong ambiguity that makes possible both a significant degree of transcendence in the concept of God as well as an

---

[139] Pl. *Epin.* 991 e.

[140] Arist. GA II.4, 740 a 20.

[141] Epicur. *Ep.* [2] 66. One could expand the analysis to the theological and political meaning of the term.

[142] Significantly, for men, normativity takes the form of the concrete necessity to follow a rational life, exempt from passions, namely a life according to the divine that is in us. See for example Posidon. 187.

[143] SVF II.1009 (*Placit.* I.6).

[144] SVF I.162 (= D.L. VII.88).

[145] SVF II.1127 (Cic. *ND* II.78): 'From the fact of the gods' existence (assuming that they exist, as they certainly do) it necessarily follows that they are animate beings, and not only animate but possessed of reason and united together in a sort of social community or fellowship, ruling the one world as a united commonwealth or state. It follows that they possess the same faculty of reason as the human race, and that both have the same apprehension of truth and the same law enjoining what is right and rejecting what is wrong.'

[146] Pohlenz (1948), pp. 34–5.

[147] Koester (1968), pp. 521–8, underlines the interchangeability of god and nature in Stoicism.

[148] See Reale (1975–80), III, p. 365 and, *contra*, Isnardi-Parente (1999), pp. 22–3. See also Solmsen (1963), p. 463. With regard to providence, Tertullian has one of the most interesting positions. He denounces the Stoic divinisation of providence because he feels that it challenges God himself: God, not providence, rules the universe. See Moreschini (2004), pp. 483 ff.

anthropomorphic view of the divine. Let's begin from the *end*, namely the universe's final conflagration. Although everything dies and is reborn in the same way, immanently transformed by and through a new beginning, Chrysippus suggests that the divine somehow survives *outside* nature and *above* the conflagration itself, alone and imperturbable. As Seneca puts it: '[The wise man's] life will be like that of Jupiter, who, amid the dissolution of the world, when the gods are confounded together and Nature rests for a space from her work, can retire into himself and give himself over to his own thoughts.'[149] When nature *cessat*, thus, God still *cogitat* in a separate state.

The most important testimony of a personal and transcendental conception of God in early Stoicism is, however, Cleanthes' hymn to Zeus.[150] In contrast with early Stoics' general lack of interest for the transcentental world,[151] a deep religiosity arises from Cleanthes' prayer. The conflagration becomes for him a sacred and cosmic ceremony that inaugurates the order beyond chaos. God is the lawgiver who rules the λόγος and the supreme king, the ὕπατος βασιλεύς. This expression is an unmistakable homage to the tradition of the Homeric Zeus.[152]

The hymn also addresses the problem of evil as a resistance of the earthly realm to the ordering principle of God's wisdom. Cleanthes offers a synthetic and yet elaborate picture of God's relationship to the creation that anticipates the core of subsequent theodicies. The πνεῦμα permeates nature, but in different ways and to different degrees. Not only, thus, does the world become anthropocentric, but every imperfection and monstrosity finds its place in it, within an ordered hierarchy of beings.[153]

No matter how strongly the early Stoic postulate of material monism resists the religious development toward a personal god, Cleanthes' position is extremely influential and constitutes the ground for the Hellenistic Judaist and Christian reworking of Stoicism into a theodicy.[154] With few

---

[149] SVF II.1065 (= Sen. *Ep.* 9.16).

[150] SVF I.537 (= Stob. I.1.12). On Cleanthes' hymn see Festugière (1949–54), II, pp. 310–32, James (1972), and K. Sier, *Zum Zeushymnos des Kleanthes*, in Steinmetz hrsg. (1990), pp. 93–108.

[151] Pohlenz (1948), p. 93.

[152] See Hom. *Od.* I.45: ὕπατε κρειόντων and Il. XIX.258: θεῶν ὕπατος.

[153] Pohlenz (1948), p. 82. This religious anthropocentrism, Pohlenz suggests, is the major obstacle to the understanding and acceptance of Aristarchus's heliocentrism. See also Aujac (1989). Anthopocentrism is also the major difference with Platonic providence, whereby Stoics think that god makes humans a creature of primary importance. See also Renehan (1992).

[154] See Clem.Al. *Prot.* VI.61P–62P: 'Cleanthes of Pedasis, the Stoic philosopher, sets forth no genealogy of the gods, after the manner of poets, but a true theology. [. . .] he teaches clearly, I think, what is the nature of God [. . .].'

exceptions,[155] Stoic philosophers tend to accept this personalisation of God. Cleanthes' idea that God is the father (πατήρ) of humanity is shared by Epictetus[156] and by Manilius.[157] Epictetus transforms the universal rationality of the divine principle into an individual relation between humans and God.[158] Aratus's Stoic moment is deeply rooted in Zeus's anthropomorphic character:

> Let us begin with Zeus, whom we men never leave unspoken. Filled with Zeus are all highways and all meeting-places of people, filled are the sea and harbours; in all circumstances we are all dependent on Zeus. For we are also his children, and he benignly gives helpful signs to men, and rouses people to work, reminding them of their livelihood, tells when the soil is best for oxen and mattocks, and tells when the seasons are right both for planting trees and for sowing every kind of seed. For it was Zeus himself who fixed the signs in the sky, making them into distinct constellations, and organised stars for the year to give the most clearly defined signs of the seasonal round to men, so that everything may grow without fail. That is why men always pay homage to him first and last. Hail, Father, great wonder, great boon to men, yourself and the earlier race! And hail, Muses, all most gracious! In answer to my prayer to tell of the stars insofar as I may, guide all my singing.[159]

The tendency to make God a personal entity, by the time Cicero composes his *De natura deorum*, is well established within Stoicism. Developing the older

---

[155] The most notable and important one being Lucan who, vis-à-vis the monstrosity of the human world, prefers to exclude the gods from his poem, or to include them only to criticise them because they have supported Caesar's victory and the loss of Roman freedom. See Tremoli (1968).

[156] Arr. *Epict.* I.6.40, I.9.6. See Radice (1982), K. Algra, *Epictetus and Stoic Theology*, in Scaltsas, Mason eds. (2007), pp. 32–3. Algra (p. 55) underlines, however, the wide limitations to Epictetus's theism, which set it apart from the Christian anthropomorphic conception of divinity.

[157] Manil. IV.883–93: 'We perceive our creator, of whom we are part, and rise to the stars, whose children we are. Can one doubt that a divinity dwells within our breasts and that our souls return to the heaven whence they came? Can one doubt that, just as the world, composed of the elements of air and fire on high and earth and water, houses an intelligence which, spread throughout it, directs the whole, so too with us the bodies of our earthly condition and our life-blood house a mind which directs every part and animates the man?'

[158] Pohlenz (1948), p. 339. Even more special is the relationship with the philosopher, who becomes god's ἄγγελος. See K. Ierodiakonou, *The Philosopher as God's Messenger*, in Scaltsas, Mason eds. (2007), pp. 56–70.

[159] Arat. I.1–18. See Kidd in Aratus (1997), p. 12 and p. 162. See also James (1972).

idea of God as an administrator of his household,[160] Cicero contributes to develop an influential metaphor, namely the image of God consciously acting upon nature in a fashion similar to that of the artisan crafting his own work. Cicero already reads this tendency in Zeno's concept of nature which is, he explains,

> 'a craftsmanlike fire [*ignis artificiosus*], proceeding methodically to the work of generation'. For he holds that the special function of an art or craft is to create and generate, and that what in the processes of our arts is done by the hand is done with far more skilful craftsmanship by nature, that is, as I said, by that 'craftsmanlike' fire which is the teacher of the other arts. And on this theory, while each department of nature is 'craftsmanlike', in the sense of having a method or path [*uia* and *secta*] marked out for it to follow, the nature of the world itself, which encloses and contains all things in its embrace, is styled by Zeno not merely 'craftsmanlike' but actually 'a craftsman [*natura non artificiosa solum sed plane artifex dicitur*]', whose foresight plans out the work to serve its use and purpose in every detail.[161]

In later Stoicism, Marcus Aurelius accomplishes the task of building an anthropomorphic image of God by revisiting the early idea of the divine λόγος and its opposition with the Aristotelian νοῦς. The philosopher-emperor thoroughly reverts to the concept of νοῦς in order to better isolate God *above* the corporeal sphere in which evil is concentrated in the form of a passional psychic life that hinders an ethical life.[162] Although Marcus Aurelius consciously avoids filling the gap between Stoicism and Christianity, the convergence is achieved.

The same pattern had been followed by Stoic philosophers in developing the idea of providence and finalism, another instrument in the theoretical toolbox necessary to understand and make sense of the concept of monstrosity. Scholars have suggested that because of its universal and general character, as well as the impersonal nature of God, the providence of the Stoics tends towards immanence rather than transcendence.[163] Yet Stoic providence is characterised by the same ambivalence that one may discern in the development of the idea

---

[160] SVF II.1127–31: *Mundum esse urbem (uel domum) bene administratam*.
[161] Cic. *ND* II.57–8.
[162] Pohlenz (1948), pp. 342 and 344.
[163] See Pohlenz (1948), p. 98 and Reale (1975–80), pp. 370–1. On Seneca and Christianity see Momigliano (1950), Colish (1985), Martina a cura di (2001). On Stoics' finalism, see Rieth (1934) and Dragona-Monachou (1976), specifically on Epictetus, pp. 227–9, and on Marcus Aurelius, pp. 252–3.

of divinity. Chrysippus, for example, speaks about providence as both God and the universe itself. Providence appears as the very same rational organisation of the material universe according to divine laws, namely to right reason itself.[164]

Cleanthes, however, realises that the mere correspondence between the universe and the divine principle is not enough to express the beauty and goodness of the universe. Thus, although God does not create matter but merely organises it, like Plato's demiurge, it acts teleologically and providentially.[165] The teleological character of the divine intervention is linked to the superiority and transcendence of God, signposted once again by the reference to the νοῦς: providence, Cicero explains by interpreting Zeno, enters the universe in the form of *mens mundi*, or the world's intellect.[166]

The whole of book II of *De natura deorum* is concerned with the providential and teleological character of nature, powerfully developed against the mechanical and antifinalist conception of Epicureans. Against the 'extraordinary democracy' of atoms,[167] self-organising without any external direction, Stoics claim the necessity of a guiding principle, reworking and developing Attic finalism. Cicero's Balbus clarifies the connection with the Socratic matrix: 'Man's intelligence must lead us to infer the existence of a mind [in the universe], and that a mind of surpassing ability, and in fact divine. Otherwise, whence did man "pick up" (as Socrates says in Xenophon)[168] the intelligence he possesses?' It is the regularity, beauty and order of nature that wipes away any doubt and reinforces the certitude that it has been created by a superior intelligence.

The main exception to this attitude within Stoicism is, once again, Lucan, who sees only an evil fate acting in human history and, specifically, in the wicked fate that brings Rome's freedom to an end.[169] In Lucan, fate does not express the world's rationality anymore, but it rather becomes the name of reason's death.[170] Gods do not exist or, if they do, they do not care about human miseries.[171] It is not the Epicurean divine imperturbability that Lucan

---

[164] SVF II.528 (= Ar. Did. apud Eusebium praep. Evang. XV.15). See also SVF II.1106–26: *De providentia et natura artefice*. See Simon and Simon (1956), p. 111.
[165] SVF I.509 (= Ph. *Prou.* II.48).
[166] Cic. *ND* II.58. See *contra* Goldschmidt (1953), pp. 91–2.
[167] This is the powerful concept used – and criticised – by the third-century Christian writer Dionysius of Alexandria in his *On Nature*. See Dion.Alex. and Grant (1952), p. 16.
[168] See X. *Mem.* I.4.8 and *supra*.
[169] See Pohlenz (1948), p. 284, and Narducci (1979).
[170] O. Steen Due, 'Lucain et la philosophie', in Durry éd. (1970), pp. 201–32.
[171] Lucan. VII.444–55: 'In very truth there are no gods who govern mankind: though we say falsely that Jupiter reigns, blind chance sweeps the world along. [...] Man's destiny has never been watched over by any god.'

suggests, but rather a malignant indifference, enriched by its ironical powerless presence in the human mind: what do gods do instead of directing the world or helping men in their pain? They send prodigies, so that even any remote hope for the future is pitilessly wiped away.[172] The Stoic spectacle of the universe's harmony has given way to the horrendous portrait of human solitude. Whereas the atheist or even the Epicurean feels reassured by this solitude, and grounds her materialism on it, Lucan becomes incapable of defending even the core of his Stoicism:

> Either this universe strays for ever governed by no law, and the stars move to and fro with course unfixed; or else, if they are guided by destiny, speedy destruction is preparing for Rome and for mankind. Will the earth gape and cities be swallowed up? Or will burning heat destroy our temperate clime? Will the soil break faith and deny its produce? Or will water everywhere be tainted with streams of poison? What kind of disaster are the gods preparing? What form of ruin will their anger assume?[173]

Not even the alternative between Epicurean chance and Stoic fate survives in this infernal landscape. Narducci has analysed Lucan's attitude toward providence, and the debate surrounding the poet's feelings on this pillar of the Stoic system. He correctly suggests that Lucan's invective goes much beyond pure rhetoric, and thus that the poem represents both a strong reaction against poetical classicism, soon triumphant in Virgil's masterpiece, and a serious blow to the Stoic claim to best interpret the tensions of this period.[174] In Narducci's view, however, Lucan remains to some extent faithful to Stoicism, making his tensions and ambiguities just more evident. Lucan's pessimism and anti-providentialism, Narducci argues, are not put forward against Stoicism, but rather derive from it.[175]

I believe that the crisis of Stoicism, in Lucan's poem, is more serious than Narducci claims. An orthodox Stoic vision of humanity's historical misery, facing the monstrosity of civil war, would not allow *any* pessimism at all, if this was the *necessary* course that the universe had to follow. No alternative, and no regret: this would be the orthodox conclusion, or else Stoicism would

---

[172] Lucan. I.522–25: '[. . .] that no hope even for the future might relieve anxiety, clear proof was given of worse to come, and the menacing gods filled earth, sky, and sea with portents.'
[173] Lucan. I.639–50. See also Steen Due, 'Lucain et la philosophie', pp. 211–12.
[174] Narducci (1979), p. 37. See also S. Casali, 'The *Bellum Civile* as an Anti-Aeneid', in Asso (2011), pp. 81–109.
[175] Narducci (1979), pp. 68–71: Lucan's would only be a particularly pessimistic view of the world's natural movement after the ἀκμή, tending relentlessly toward the final conflagration. In line with Stoicism, Lucan's pessimism abandons history, and becomes cosmic. On Lucan's physics see Schotes (1969).

renounce any ethical function and any aspiration to reach ἀπάθεια, or the absence of passions and suffering, which is anything but what Lucan asks the reader to experience through the painful lines of his poem.

Despite Lucan's exception, though, the faith in the regularity and beauty of the universe prevails within Stoicism, and it establishes itself as a dogma beyond and against human and natural weakness, imperfection and monstrosity. More importantly, teleology is employed as an argument to make sense of monstrosities and assign them a place in the universe. Clarifying the religious nature of early Stoicism, Balbus explains that

> lightning, storms, rain, snow, hail, floods, pestilences, earthquakes and occasionally subterranean rumblings, showers of stones and raindrops the colour of blood, also landslides and chasms suddenly opening in the ground, also unnatural monstrosities [*portenta*] human and animal, [. . .] [are] alarming portents [that] have suggested to mankind the idea of the existence of some celestial and divine power.[176]

Later Stoicism develops this vision and connects it with the anthropomorphic character of God. Nature, Epictetus explains, drags humans to follow its own will.[177] Learning nature's will is part of human morality.[178] Τὸ βούλημα τῆς φύσεως: it is not an end or τέλος that Epictetus has in mind anymore, but a genuine will or βούλησις.[179] With the verb βούλομαι, Epictetus stresses the personal will or wish of gods beyond the simple τέλος, following an ancient tradition already established by Homer and continuing up to the early Christian thinkers.[180] Before showing how this doctrine is connected with the belief in a universe hierarchically characterised by different degrees of perfection, let us first see Lactantius's position, one of the most important Christian thinkers, and deeply marked by pagan philosophy.

Lactantius has a strategic importance in the early Christian reworking of the Stoic providential divinity. Before his more direct condemnation of Stoic optimism in *De ira dei*, Lactantius's providentialism is built upon Stoic elements

---

[176] Cic. *ND* II.14.
[177] Arr. *Epict*. II.20. 15. See also I.6.1 ff., III.15.14 and III.17.1 ff.
[178] Epict. *Ench*. 26.
[179] This βούλησις eventually becomes the will of god and, in particular, his positive will for good which is not incompatible with his permission of evil. See DGE and Lampe *sub voce* and, in particular, Clem.Al. *Prot*. IV and *Strom*. IV.12.
[180] LSJ *sub voce*: 'Hom. uses βούλομαι for ἐθέλω in the case of the gods, for with them *wish* is *will*.' See also M.Ant. II.3: 'The work of the gods is full of Providence: the work of Fortune is not divorced from Nature or the spinning and winding of the threads ordained by Providence.' See also Farquharson in Marcus Aurelius (1944), II, pp. 284–5. See also TGL *sub voce* and Hijmans (1959).

and constitutes one of the most influential early visions of Christian providence. As we have seen, Lactantius's polemical argument is directed first and foremost against the 'folly' of Epicureans, who deny providence and 'assign the origin of things to inseparable and solid bodies from the chance combinations of which all things come to be and have arisen'. As with the Stoics, his condemnation is sharp and unambiguous: 'they are mad, even to the point of ridicule'.[181] Providence is in fact evidence that cannot be missed by the wise observer of nature:

> [. . .] who can doubt respecting a providence, when he sees that the heavens and the earth have been so arranged, and that all things have been so regulated, that they might be most befittingly adapted, not only to wonderful beauty and adornment, but also to the use of men, and the convenience of the other living creatures? That, therefore, which exists in accordance with a plan, cannot have had its beginning without a plan: thus it is certain that there is a providence.[182]

Lactantius uses providence as a weapon against the Epicurean theory of chance. In this part of the *Opificio*, which eventually proves very influential in building rising resistance against materialism, he directly tackles the argument of monstrosity:

> When Lucretius was showing that animals were produced, not by some fashioning of a divine mind, but as he put it, 'fortuitously', he said that, in the beginning of the world, there had been in existence innumerable other living creatures of wondrous form and size [*miranda specie ac magnitudine*], but that they could not continue because either the power of getting food or the means of coming together and reproducing had failed them. Of course, to make place for those atoms of his, flitting in the infinite and the emptiness, he had to rule out Divine Providence. But when he saw that there is a marvellous system of providence existing within all things that breathe, what emptiness for that scoundrel to say that there had existed monsters [*animalia prodigiosa*] in which this system ceased![183]

Aware that the concept of monstrosity, ontologically speaking, could destabilise the idea of an Almighty God just as it destroyed that of a caring demiurge, Lactantius addresses the core of the Epicurean theory of monstrosity. He conveniently leaves aside Lucretius's Empedoclean argument about the stabilisation

---

[181] Lact. *De opificio Dei* II.10–1.
[182] Lact. *Epit.* I.1 (= I in AA. VV. (1970), vol. VII, p. 224).
[183] Lact. *De opificio Dei* VI.1–14.

and regularisation of shapes out of nature's innumerable attempts, saying that if monsters existed once, which is absurd, then they would still exist today:

> if all things come to be, not by Providence, but by the chance of comings together of atoms, why does it never happen by chance that those principles come together in such a way as to effect an animal of such a kind that would hear with its nostrils, smell with its eyes, and see with its ears? If those 'first bodies' [*primordia*] leave no kind of position untried, monsters ought to have been produced daily of a sort in which a preposterous arrangement of members and widely different uses would prevail. But since all the kinds and all the parts in each observe their own laws and arrangement and guard the uses attributed to them [*leges, ordines et usus*], it is evident that nothing was made by chance, since the perpetual disposition of the divine plan is preserved.[184]

Let's leave aside the absurd Epicurean hypothesis, Lactantius suggests, and embrace instead the self-evident truth of the Christian God. His plan comes first, before everything else, so all things are therefore accomplished according to a perfect project. Lactantius uses the metaphor of the architect who, before constructing a building, considers carefully his problems, takes measurements, finds the best position for columns and conduits, light and heavy weights, etc. And if this is true for a modest but skilful builder, why should it not be so for the most sublime of the architects, God Almighty? Since everything has been done *cum ratione*, 'why should anyone think that God, in making the animals, did not provide all that would be necessary for living before He gave the life itself? The life surely could not exist unless there were first the means by which it exists.'[185]

Now that we have explored Lactantius's thought, let us return to pagan Stoicism. Its point of view is consistent with both the Platonic and the Aristotelian idea of different degrees of perfection in the universe. Stoics rework in their own guise the concept of accidental necessity, or necessity κατὰ συμβεβηκός, that Aristotle introduces to explain monstrosity. Chrysippus claims that perfect and imperfect beings are both necessary, and yet *not equally* so:

> [Chrysippus] does not think that it was nature's original intention to make men subject to disease; for that would never have been consistent with nature as the source and mother of all things good. 'But,' said he, 'when

---

[184] Lact. *De opificio Dei* VI.1–14. See M. Perrin in Lactance (1974), pp. 290–1.
[185] Lact. *De opificio Dei* VI.1–14. On the metaphor of the architect, see M. Perrin in Lactance (1974), pp. 290–1. See also *De ira Dei* IX.1 ff. and XIII.1 on the argument of teleology strongly influenced by Stoicism.

she was creating and bringing forth many great things which were highly suitable and useful, there were also produced at the same time troubles closely connected with those good things that she was creating'; and he declared that these were not due to nature, but to certain inevitable consequences, a process that he himself calls κατὰ παρακολούθησις. '[. . .] In the same way diseases too and illness were created at the same time with health. Exactly, by Heaven!' said he, 'as vices, through their relationship to the opposite quality, are produced at the same time that virtue is created for mankind by nature's design.'[186]

Per sequellas, Gellius says, hesitating on what looks like a subaltern necessity, 'quod ipse [sc. Chrysippus] appellat "κατὰ παρακολούθησις"'. Imperfection presents itself as a consequence of perfection. In Aristotle, παρακολουθέω – the Latin *consequi* – has the meaning of a necessary consequence, of an effect that goes hand in hand with its cause, always and logically following it.[187] Beyond this logical necessity, coordinating cause and effect, Chrysippus consciously subordinates the *accidental* result to its cause, and make it a mere by-product. Following, but somehow reworking, the Aristotelian explanation of monstrosity as necessary by accident, Chrysippus thinks of imperfection as the subaltern circumstance of perfection.

Evil and good necessarily coexist within providence's plan. Nonetheless, monstrosity and imperfection are not there intentionally and originally (προηγουμένως), but rather concomitantly (κατ' ἐπακολούθησιν).[188] Ἐπακολουθέω is also close to the Latin *subsequor*. This concept has a strong relevance for the interpretation of the role and function of monstrosity within the creation, especially in and through the Hellenistic Judaist and Christian theodicy, for example in both Philo's[189] and Origen's theodicies.[190]

Moving away from Cleanthes' reduction of evil to humanity's deviation from its ethical end, Chrysippus expands the place and role that evil and imperfection play in the universe. A much stronger theodicy, thus, is needed to save the image of a benevolent divinity. Imperfection and monstrosity need to be justified, and Chrysippus makes use of the τύχη, interpreting it as the result of concomitant, related and 'confatal' causes, whose complex outcome cannot be precisely foreseen but can still be conceived within God's providential action.[191]

---

[186] SVF II.1170 (= Gel. VII.1.7–13).
[187] Arist. *Top.* 131 b 9, 125 b 28, *Cat.* 8 a 33, *Metaph.* 1054 a 14.
[188] Pohlenz (1948), p. 100.
[189] See Ph. *Prou.* II.100 and *infra*. See also Barth (1906), p. 26.
[190] Pohlenz (1948), p. 426 n.
[191] On the *confatalia* or ἀργός λόγος see SVF II.956–64.

Monsters and monstrosities, thus, do not break with universal necessity. They find their place within nature and, as much as normal and normally beautiful events, they confirm the existence of the divine.[192] If it is true that individual beings are hierarchically ordered according to different degrees of perfection, it is also true that lower beings, including the most abnormal and exceptional ones, can sometimes reveal the divine, and even more conspicuously than the higher and more perfect beings. The relation between perfection and imperfection is here developed in a different direction, toward the concept of portent and prodigy.[193] It is through portents, prodigies and monstrosities that Stoics are able to assign a large weight to the concept of εἱμαρμένη or *fatum*.[194] It is also portents that illustrate the importance of divination – the tool that, once again, God grants to men so that they may find their way in the world.[195]

Firmly grounded on the physical dogma of continuity and the negation of the void, the Stoic concept of fate embraces the universe as a single unity, within which all events are necessarily connected to each other, no matter their degree of perfection or rationality. Stoics call this concept συμπάθεια, expressing the rigidity and inalterability of all cosmic events.[196] Because of universal sympathy, individual beings must be conceived as parts of a bigger individual, such as organs of the same organism.[197]

This organicism explains the inclusive nature of Stoic philosophy, whose outcome is a cosmopolitan conception of humanity, extended to barbarians and, in some cases and exceptionally, to animals as well.[198] Monstrosities cannot be condemned in this framework, and find their place within nature as an outcome

---

[192] This is the sense of the Stoics' interest in early paradoxography. See Giannini (1963).
[193] Prodigies are, in this sense, the real ancestors of the Christian miracle. Cic. ND II.7: 'Prophecies and premonitions of future events cannot but be taken as proofs that the future may appear or be foretold as a warning or portended or predicted to mankind – hence the very words "apparition", "warning", "portent", "prodigy." Even if we think that the stories of Mopsus, Tiresias, Amphiaraus, Calchas, and Helenus are mere baseless fictions of romance (though their powers of divination would not even have been incorporated in the legends had they been entirely repugnant to fact), shall not even the instances from our own native history teach us to acknowledge the divine power?' See Martinazzoli (1951) and, more recently, Cotter (1999).
[194] See Chase Green (1944), M. E. Reesor, *Necessity and Fate in Stoic Philosophy*, in Rist (1978), pp. 187–202, and Magris (1984).
[195] See Bouche-Leclercq (1879–82) and M. Schofield, 'Théologie et divination', in Brunschwig, Lloyd eds (1996), pp. 527–40.
[196] See Sambursky (1959), p. 41, for whom, at least initially, sympathy is an evolution of the Aristotelian idea of cosmic order.
[197] Pohlenz (1948), p. 216.
[198] See for example Chroust (1963).

of nature's power to produce diversity. As Seneca explains, summarising the inspiring principle of his *Natural Questions*:

> Nature does not present her work in only one form but prides herself on her variety. She has made some things larger, some swifter than others, some stronger, some more moderate; she has separated some from the crowd, so that they might move as unique and conspicuous things [*singula et conspicua*]; some she has consigned to the herd. Anyone who thinks that nature is not occasionally able to do something she has not done frequently, simply does not understand the power of nature [*naturae potentia*].[199]

On this ground, the philosopher must have the same attitude toward each and every natural phenomenon, including anomalies and monstrosities. Anything deserves the attention of the scientist, who knows that everything is connected in nature, and necessarily so. Sorabji has argued that this attitude is the original attempt made by Stoics to redefine the concept of normativity, in order to include all phenomena within natural laws.[200] This exceptionless regularity manifests itself in the idea of a repetition of the same circumstances over the endless cosmic cycle. It also manifests itself in the importance that prodigies and monstrosities have in revealing the key to understanding apparently unrelated events and offering a guide to those who are able to read them through divination. Monsters, in this sense, might not make sense in themselves, and yet they necessarily do within the global comprehension of nature. This is why, Seneca explains, divination becomes possible:

> You make God too unoccupied and the administrator of trivia if he arranges dreams for some people, entrails for others. Nevertheless, such things are carried out by divine agency, even if the wings of birds are not actually guided by God nor the viscera of cattle shaped under the very axe. The roll of fate is unfolded on a different principle, sending ahead everywhere indications of what is to come, some familiar to us, others unknown. Whatever happens, it is a sign of something that will happen. Chance and random occurrences, and without a principle, do not permit divination. Whatever has a series of occurrences is also predictable.[201]

---

[199] Sen. *Nat.* VII.27.3.

[200] R. Sorabji, 'Causation, Laws, and Necessity', in Schofield, Burnyeat, Barnes eds. (1980), pp. 250–82.

[201] Sen. *Nat.* II.32.3–4. In this sense, on Seneca's *Dialogues*, see A. Wilcox, 'Nature's Monster: Caligula as *Exemplum* in Seneca's *Dialogues*', in Sluiter, Rosen eds. (2008), pp. 451–75.

In this sense everything also deserves our astonishment, both the common and the unusual, both the normal and the abnormal. Against superstition, the scientific attitude educates men to the wonders of nature: a conclusion that resonates throughout the centuries and, in particular, in Augustine.[202]

A notable exception to the belief in divination is Panaetius's scepticism toward this practice.[203] Even more significant, however, is Diogenianus's criticism of this practice. Diogenianus's argument reveals what is at stake in the attempt to use monstrosities as an epistemological tool. Diogenianus contrasts science and chance, adopting the Aristotelian point of view that there is no science of the accidental. By definition, he claims, monsters are accidental, and thus cannot offer any real comprehension of nature's laws. Aristotelian teleology allows the understanding of monstrosity, but rules out its epistemological use.[204] Stoic determinism, on the contrary, makes everything necessary in the same way, including monsters, whose precise origin we might not know, but whose teleological harmony with nature can be granted as a postulate.[205]

Once again, Lucan also represents a notable exception to the orthodox Stoic stance on divination, and one that is much more radical than that of Panaetius. Given the radically negative view of the course of history, he asks, would it not be better to ignore future events? This remark confirms the Stoic belief in the possibility of divination. It turns upside down, though, the positive use that Stoics claim for divination itself. And no matter, for Lucan, the ontological ground that makes divination possible. Whether Stoic or Epicurean, nature can reveal only evil and misdeeds:

> And now heaven's wrath was revealed; the universe gave clear signs of battle; and Nature, conscious of the future, reversed the laws and ordinances of life, and, while the hurly-burly bred monsters, proclaimed civil war. Why didst thou, Ruler of Olympus, see fit to lay on suffering mortals this additional burden, that they should learn the approach of calamity by awful portents? Whether the author of the universe, when the fire gave way and he first took in hand the shapeless realm of raw matter, established the chain of causes for all eternity, and bound himself as well by universal law, and portioned out the universe, which endures the ages prescribed for it, by a fixed line of destiny; or whether nothing is ordained and Fortune, moving at random, brings round the cycle of events, and chance is master

---

[202] Sen. *Nat.* VII.1.1–2.
[203] See [Panaetius] (1952, 2nd ed.), 68 and 71. See also Grant (1952), p. 51, and Sambursky (1959), pp. 68 ff. Panaetius's attitude might be the Stoic source of Philo's denial of divination.
[204] Sambursky (1959), pp. 70–1. See also Ioppolo (1986).
[205] On Stoic determinism see Bobzien (1998).

of mankind – in either case, let thy purpose, whatever it be, be sudden; let the mind of man be blind to coming doom; he fears, but leave him hope.[206]

The argumentative force of Stoicism lies in its capacity to successfully join together religious faith in the teleological and providential character of divine intervention with scientific approach to the study of nature. Juvenal elegantly warns against the danger of making a vulgar use of divination.[207] Cicero's *De divinatione* is largely devoted to this problem, and presents, in a balanced manner, a direct response to the scepticism based on Peripatetic arguments.[208] Seneca explains that the knowledge of nature is the highest value. It is a value in itself, but also because it chases away fear and superstition:

> Since the cause of fear is ignorance, is it not worth a great deal to have knowledge in order not to fear? It is much better to investigate the causes and, in fact, to be intent on this study with the entire mind. [. . .] An earthquake produces a thousand strange things [*mille miracula*] and changes the appearances of places and carries away mountains, elevates plains, pushes valleys up, raises new islands in the sea. What causes these things to happen is a subject worth investigating.[209]

Anomalous and portentous phenomena, once again, help the philosopher continue such a difficult task. The more scientifically oriented authors agree on this. Balancing the religious and mystical attitude with a genuine belief in the epistemological value of divination, they frame monstrosities within the whole to which they belong. Gods cannot be directly responsible for every single

---

[206] Lucan. II.1–15. See Johnson (1987), p. 9.
[207] Iuu. XIII.
[208] Cic. *Div*. I.54: '[. . .] it is enough for me to find, not many, but even a few instances of divinely inspired prevision and prophecy. Nay, if even one such instance is found and the agreement between the prediction and the thing predicted is so close as to exclude every semblance of chance or of accident, I should not hesitate to say in such a case, that divination undoubtedly exists and that everybody should admit its existence.'
[209] Sen. *Nat*. VI.3.4–VI.4.1. See also Grant (1952), p. 167. Epictetus beautifully advises welcoming both the auspicious and the ominous response, and warns against the use of divination to avoid what must be done in any case. Epict. *Ench*. 32: 'Do not [. . .] bring to the diviner desire or aversion, and do not approach him with trembling, but having first made up your mind that every issue is indifferent and nothing to you, but that, whatever it may be, it will be possible for you to turn it to good use, and that no one will prevent this. [. . .] when it is your duty to share the danger of a friend or of your country, do not ask of the diviner whether you ought to share that danger. [. . .] reason requires that even at this risk [*sc*. Death] you are to stand by your friend, and share the danger with your country.'

detail, as the universe is too complex. Yet in the beginning, Cicero explains, the universe was made so that effects necessarily follow their causes, and can be foreseen by recognising their anticipatory symptoms.[210] The monsters that appear right before Caesar's death belong to such a category of symptoms:

> While [Caesar] was offering sacrifices on the day when he sat for the first time on a golden throne and first appeared in public in a purple robe, no heart was found in the vitals of the votive ox. Now do you think it possible for any animal that has blood to exist without a heart? [. . .] On the following day there was no head to the liver of the sacrifice. These portents were sent by the immortal gods to Caesar that he might foresee his death, not that he might prevent it.[211]

Signs, wonders and monstrosity are sent by the gods to instruct men: this idea is eventually developed in early Christianity and has a strong influence during the medieval and early modern periods. More generally, the ideas of both God and providence elaborated within Stoicism as a development and a reworking of Attic philosophy and as a polemical response against Epicureanism contribute to the philosophical framework left as a heritage to future centuries.

In this chapter we looked at the Stoic approach to monstrosity, paying attention to both the system's internal articulation and the way the school's ideas unfolded from the early Hellenistic period through the Imperial age. Stoics contribute to the debate on monstrosity by forging original intellectual tools to explain imperfection and evil in the framework of a rational cosmos providentially built and guided by a divine principle. I have argued that the original position developed by the Stoics rests on a nominalism that treats all generalisation and universalisation as the illusory abstractions of a weak human imagination. Through nominalism, Stoics obliterate the idea of transcendency and understand the material world's multiplicity, with all its imperfections, via the development of a divine rational principle. Comparing the two previous chapters lets us see that such immanency is different from the atomists' version. Stoics order the universe according to degrees of perfection, and instead of ruling out qualitative differences (e.g. between good and evil, normal and abnormal, beauty and ugliness), as the Epicureans do, they reintroduce them in a divinely providential, teleologically oriented structure.

---

[210] Cic. *Div*. I.52.

[211] Cic. *Div*. I.52. The argument also includes an attempt at explanation: 'Therefore, when those organs, without which the victim could not have lived, are found wanting in the vitals, we should understand that the absent organs disappeared at the very moment of immolation.'

Monstrosities are thus explained with original and powerful ideas such as the panspermia (i.e. the origin of the seed from the whole body and the whole genus), the vital forces informing matter, the *semina rerum* and, more generally, the uniqueness of every being, which Christian thought eventually transforms into God's omnipotent creation of wonders. I have highlighted in this chapter the ambivalent contrast between the immanency of the divine material principle throughout matter itself and the transcendent order that allows the distribution of beings of varying degrees of perfection. This can be seen, for example, in Manilius's thought, in which there exists a tension between the idea of relativity of beauty and ugliness on the one hand, for which nothing is absolutely superior to anything else, and the superiority of Western races to Ethiopians on the other, which undermines relativism. Stoics, I have argued, deem evil and monstrosity necessary to conceive and comprehend nature's diversity and its providential order. Imperfection and monstrosity become the subaltern circumstances of perfection. Moreover, these attitudes allow them to elaborate foundational arguments for teleological and providential philosophies such as the perfection of the human body. Scepticism, the third great system – in fact, the anti-system – of the Hellenistic age, will take an entirely different approach, as we willsee in the next chapter.

7

Scepticism

In 155 BCE, three philosophers travel to Rome from Greece with the task of obtaining the cancellation of the 500 talents fine imposed on the Athenians for the destruction of the city of Oropus. The mission is successful for the three ambassadors, Diogenes the Stoic, Critolaus the Peripatetic and Carneades the Academic. The political success, though, is accompanied by a cultural disaster. Waiting to be received by the Senate, they entertain the curious and inquisitive Romans with a series of philosophical lectures. Carneades opts for a very sensitive topic, namely the nature of justice.[1] Against a substantialist conception of justice, he argues for its problematic character, its being grounded on force, and ultimately he maintains relativism and the inexistence of natural right. More than a realistic and pessimistic position, Carneades intends to illustrate the powerful rhetorical and theoretical dimension of his philosophy, namely Scepticism.

Greek culture shows its monstrous face to Rome, the rising political power in the Mediterranean, after the battle of Pydna and the extinction of the Antigonid dynasty. Roman culture, at this time, is still relatively untouched by philosophical ideas. Cato the Elder is among the most shocked of his fellow citizens, and successfully pleads for the rapid expulsion of the three philosophers from Rome. The vain hope is to keep philosophy outside of the city, and to protect youth from its corruptive character. This ban is unsuccessful. What do Romans find abhorrent in Carneades' thought? What is so unbearable in his rhetoric and philosophy?

Romans certainly did not need to meet and greet the Greek ambassadors to be aware, in practice if not in theory, of the harsh character of justice. What was outrageous was rather the Sceptic belief that not only the idea of justice, but every philosophical and – as a consequence – scientific, theological and

---

[1] Cic. *Resp.* III.8–11.

moral idea does not and cannot have a solid and unquestionable ground. Men ordinarily claim truths, anchoring them, through a process of reasoning, on what they believe is a solid ground. The counter-truth argued by Carneades is that this very process is ungrounded, and thus all the past and, arguably, future philosophical theories must be doubted.

The definition, conception and treatment of monstrosity has been developed within the ontological, physical and metaphysical framework of previous schools of thought, notably atomism, Platonism, Peripateticism, Stoicism. The Sceptics call all of these schools dogmatic.[2] If Sceptics claim the ability to undo the latter's grounding frameworks, what remains of monstrosity? And also what remains, more worryngly, of the related concept of normality? If every theory and even every definition is ungrounded, how can anyone or anything be defined as normal or monstrous? Ancient Scepticism provides powerful tools to respond to these questions, tools that enjoy a long life being received and reworked in the following centuries.

In this chapter, I will focus mainly on the aspects of Scepticism that pertain to the interpretation of the concepts of normality and monstrosity. Although it is necessary to distinguish clearly between Pyrrhonism, Neo-Pyrrhonism and the new Academy,[3] these aspects reveal a certain consistency of treatment across the main stages of the development of Scepticism. I will reconstruct these aspects through authors whose doctrines are sometimes very diverse, although they contribute to developing a consistent set of tools against a strong concept of normality, tools that offer an original perspective on the idea of monstrosity.

The ground of Sceptic philosophy is the necessity of the suspension of every positive discourse (the ἀφασία) on the determinate nature of things, thus on good or evil, right or wrong, beauty or ugliness. Similarly to Stoicism and Epicureanism, the immediate τέλος of this philosophical attitude is an ethical concern, the ἀταραξία or imperturbability of the mind. The Neosceptic Sextus Empiricus, going back to Pyrrho and the ancient sources of his movement in search of the root of Scepticism, puts it plainly in his Πυρρώνειοι ὑποτυπώσεις by way of definition:

> Scepticism is an ability, or mental attitude, which opposes appearances to judgements in any way whatsoever, with the result that, owing to the equipollence of the objects and reasons thus opposed, we are brought firstly to

---

[2] See D.L. IX.74.
[3] On the New Academy see C. Lévy, 'Cicero and the New Academy', in Gerson (2010), pp. 39–62.

a state of mental suspense [ἐποχή] and next to a state of 'unperturbedness' or quietude [ἀταραξία].[4]

According to the Suda, Pyrrho was the first to introduce the ἐποχή, the suspension of judgement that generates the unperturbedness.[5] The conflicting appearances of things are the object of undecided or undetermined (ἀνεπίκριτος) disputes. It is interesting to note that while for Peripatetics such as Simplicius the undecidability comes from the fact that arguments are 'unexamined',[6] Sceptics rather insist on their *undecidable* character. Disputes *cannot* be decided, because knowledge lacks a solid ground for any decision whatsoever, even after careful examination of the problem. Whereas this might be seen as generating inquietude and painful uncertainty, Sceptics counterintuitively argue that undecidability helps men to recognise that nothing is good or evil, right or wrong, beautiful or ugly, normal or monstrous in itself. It helps them to be worried only for inevitable things and, even in this case, to be worried less than anyone else.[7]

Objections to this system, however, begin to be raised precisely on moral and ethical grounds, that is to say on the core of the doctrine itself. The Sceptic is portrayed as an antisocial individual. Diogenes Laertius tells that

---

[4] S.E. *P.* I.8. See also *P.* I.27–8: 'For the man who opines that anything is by nature good or bad is for ever being disquieted [. . .]. On the other hand, the man who determines nothing as to what is naturally good or bad neither shuns nor pursues anything eagerly; and, in consequence, he is unperturbed [ἀτάρακτος].' Robin (1944), p. 9, suggests that ethics and practical life are always the major concern in Scepticism, vis-à-vis ontological speculations and scientific knowledge.

[5] S.E. *P.* I.25–30.

[6] Simp. *In Ph.* 1148.29.

[7] S.E. *P.* I.30 and Aenesidemus of Cnossus (2014), B1 (=Phot. *Bibl.* 212 169 b 18–31). Pyrrho himself was indeed unworried, if one believes Antigonus of Carystus's testimony in D.L. IX.62: 'He led a life consistent with this doctrine, going out of his way for nothing, taking no precaution, but facing all risks as they came, whether carts, precipices, dogs or what not, and, generally, leaving nothing to the arbitrament of the senses; but he was kept out of harm's way by his friends who, as Antigonus of Carystus tells us, used to follow close after him. But Aenesidemus says that it was only his philosophy that was based upon suspension of judgement, and that he did not lack foresight in his everyday acts. He lived to be nearly ninety.' Besides the irony of this passage (but also the effectiveness of his friends' care, if he managed to live up to ninety years old!), this statement explains Pyrrho's dismissal of phenomena, which has a strategic importance in Sceptic philosophy (see *infra*). Reale interprets this image of Pyrrho as a direct attack on Aristotelian ontology based on the Law of Non-Contradiction. See G. Reale, 'Ipotesi per una rilettura della filosofia di Pirrone di Elide', in Giannantoni a cura di (1980), pp. 243–336, esp. p. 318. See *contra*, Bett (2000), pp. 123–31.

Pyrrho is reproached for ignoring his friend Anaxarchus fallen into a slough.[8] It is certainly madness, and it leads to contradiction, to deem all things equal, claims Eusebius of Caesarea, who bitterly asks: 'What sort of citizen, or judge, or counsellor, or friend, or, in a word, what sort of man would such an one be? Or what evil deeds would not he dare, who held that nothing is really evil, or disgraceful, or just or unjust? For one could not say even this, that such men are afraid of the laws and their penalties; for how should they, seeing that, as they themselves say, they are incapable of feeling or of trouble?'[9]

Both ethical and ontological objections were quite frequent in the Hellenistic philosophical school. Despite these objections, though, ancient Scepticism has solid philosophical roots and its exponents have sharp tools to counter any dogmatic claim, including the categorisation of normality, abnormality and indeed monstrosity. It is particularly relevant for the present enquiry that the main philosophical source of Scepticism, according to an established tradition, is Democritean atomism. Eusebius claims that Sceptics and Cyrenaics should be joined in the study of atomists.[10] As Dal Pra suggests, the major influence of atomism on Scepticism can be seen in the disjunction and opposition between reality and perception, or between how things are and how they are necessarily perceived by men.[11] This is how Galen describes Democritus's philosophy:

> 'For by convention colour, by convention sweet, by convention bitter, but in reality atoms and the voids' says Democritus, who thinks that all the perceptible qualities are brought into being, relative to us who perceive them, by the combination of atoms, but by nature nothing is white or black or yellow or red or bitter or sweet. By the expression 'by convention' he means 'conventionally' and 'relative to us', not according to the nature of things themselves, which he calls by contrast 'reality', forming the term from 'real' which means 'true'. The whole substance of this theory is as follows. People think of things as being white and black and sweet and bitter and all other qualities of that kind, but in truth 'thing' and 'nothing' is all there is. That too is something he himself said, 'thing' being his name for the atoms and 'nothing' for the void.[12]

---

[8] D.L. IX.63. Ironically, on this unfortunate occasion, only Anaxarcus himself 'praised [Pyrrho's] indifference and *sang-froid*'.

[9] Eus. *PE* XIV.18 (= Pirrone (1981), pp. 106–7).

[10] Eus. *PE* XIV.19 (= Pirrone (1981), p. 91).

[11] Dal Pra (1975, 2a ed.), p. 47. On Democritus and Scepticism see also F. Decleva Caizzi, 'Democrito in Sesto Empirico', in Romano a cura di (1980), pp. 393–410, and Gigante (1981).

[12] Gal. *De clementis secundum Hippocratem* I.2, *Vorsokr.* 68 A 49 (= LM [27] ATOM. D23b, D43, D63 = Taylor (1999) 179 d).

Galen clearly realises that atomic theory raises the question of essential or intrinsic properties: are secondary qualities intrinsic to things, or are they relative to the observer, engaged in the observation in a specific time and place?[13] Atomists propose two important principles in response to this question: 1) the knowledge of secondary qualities is necessarily relative to the encounter with the observer's organs of perception, and 2) it is precisely this theoretical and non-experimental conclusion that allows us to grasp the reality of nature's material structure.

Democritus's position, as regards the sensorial appearance of reality, leads to the conclusion that even when men agree on the appearance of things, it does not mean that the latter's inherent nature *is* in fact as it appears. Things' properties are rather νόμοι, by convention. In this ontological hypothesis, knowledge is threatened by the loss of any fixed and stable ground, and is exposed to the relativity and uncertainty of sensual perceptions. Pyrrho appears to be the first to draw such a conclusion from Democritus's attitude. Although Pyrrho is not mainly or directly interested in a deep immersion into physics or the study of nature's physical details, it is clear why he might have been attracted by an ontology that exposes the feebleness of every epistemological enterprise *because of*, and not *despite*, the nature of physical reality itself.

The Sceptic and relativist tendency of atomist physics is already developed by Democritus's pupil Metrodorus of Chios. Metrodorus insists on the clear distinction between knowledge through reason and knowledge through sensation. We do not know much, if anything, with the senses, and this makes knowledge impossible. The only legitimate knowledge is the rational kind, and the criticism of knowledge through sensation, upon which Scepticism is grounded, has thus a Democritean origin.[14] The convergence of Scepticism and atomism is, however, limited to perception. Whereas the two schools are very close on the ethical goals of the εὐθυμία (cheerfulness or contentment) and ἀταραξία (calmness or impassiveness), they diverge on the possibility of gaining rational knowledge *beyond* sense perception.[15] The atomic hypothesis, for Democritus and his followers, is indeed able to offer an explanation and provide knowledge of nature. It also provides an interpretation of the weakness of perception itself and of the reasons for which the senses deceive us.[16] Atomism, in this sense, is dogmatic because it claims positive knowledge and certainly does not pursue the suspension of judgement.

---

[13] See Taylor's commentary, pp. 176–7.
[14] Robin (1944), pp. 5, 16 and *passim*.
[15] Stough (1969), p. 32.
[16] See Bett (2000), p. 153 and Appendix C, p. 187.

The Tropes and the Critique of Essentialism

The richness of Scepticism, for the present enquiry, lies in turning doubt and ἐποχή into the ends and not only the means of philosophy. The boundary between normality and monstrosity can thus be challenged through Sceptic arguments. Let us follow this kind of contention in what is perhaps the most systematic development of Sceptic philosophy, namely the tropes. Ascribed to Aenesidemus in the number of ten, the tropes are the fundamental modes through which Sceptics defend undecidability and the suspension of judgement concerning how things are in their real nature.[17] The tropes, a real anti-dogmatic war machine,[18] contain strong conceptual tools for challenging and rethinking monstrosity. Three of them are particularly relevant in this sense: the first and second ones, on the diversity of phenomenological reality, sub-human and human alike, and the ninth one, on rare events.

The first trope concerns the relativity of affections that generate disharmony, unbalance and conflict in the animal world. Natural differences cause the same thing to produce different impressions and affections.[19] Sense-affection strongly implies a 'divergent, discordant, and conflicting character'.[20] Humans are thus confronted with a multiplicity of changing phenomena and dragged into the unstable and conflictual experience of reality. Stability and unshakeable certitude are illusions, because of the nature of reality, characterised by diversity and contradiction. Humans are able to tell how things appear, but certainly not how they are, or how they should be judged, or what their nature is: 'Although I shall be able to say what the nature of the underlying objects appears to me to be, I shall be compelled, for the reasons stated above, to suspend judgement as to its real nature.'[21]

Knowledge is thus exposed to the confusing nature of phenomenal reality. The phenomenon confronts the perceiver by taking centre stage and imposing on him a confusing experience. The phenomenon is from φαίνεσθαι, come to light, appear to be in a certain way, in sense experience or in mental reality, and also bring to light and cause to appear.[22] Both Plato and Aristotle use the

---

[17] On the tropes, see G. Striker, 'The Ten Tropes of Aenesidemus', in Burnyeat (1983), pp. 95–115, Flückiger (1990), pp. 78–89, Gaukroger (1995). See also Brochard (1923), Polito (2004) and Polito's commentary to the *testimonia* in Aenesidemus of Cnossus (2014).
[18] Conche (1973), esp. ch. XI.
[19] S.E. *P.* I.40.
[20] S.E. *P.* I.43.
[21] S.E. *P.* I.78.
[22] Cassin (2014), p. 777: 'We find the same Indo-European root *bh(e)ə2– (illumine, shine) in *phôs* [φῶς] (light), in *phantasia* [φαντασία] (imagination, representation), and also in *phêmi* [φημί] (to say).'

term phenomenon for what is, and appears to be, evident in itself. The epistemological fight concerning this concept becomes apparent early on, with the Sceptics using the term, especially against Stoics, for what appears to the senses and forbids rational evidence. Pyrrho evokes this idea with a powerful statement, preserved by Diogenes Laertius, Sextus and Galen: 'The phenomenon prevails on every side, wherever it may go' [ἀλλὰ τὸ φαινόμενον πάντη σθένει, οὗπερ ἂν ἔσθη].[23]

Scholars have underlined the different and plausible interpretations of Pyrrho's ambivalent statement: What does 'prevail' mean in this context? The ambivalence of this passage also depends on the meaning of the phenomenon itself, in a threatening and monstrous manner. The phenomenon reveals something about Being that, at the same time, makes its knowledge difficult and even impossible.[24] Being and phenomenon appear as mutually threatening and mutually dependent on each other, as Aristotle explains, suggesting that, without corresponding to Being but only to its appearance, the phenomenon nonetheless guides thought in its movement toward truth. By defining this relationship, Attic philosophy attempts a double move: establishing the agreement of thought and Being through a phenomenality, and perhaps a phenomenology, of truth (i.e. the essence manifesting itself in its visible form), while at the same time laying the ground for the distinction between visible and intelligible, as well as the subordination of the former to the latter. The phenomenon brings the philosopher to the heart of the ontological problem, i.e. the problem of Being and its truth.

Sceptic philosophers choose their target well. They understand that dogmatism can be undermined by attacking the legitimacy of the agreement between the phenomenon and the essence and the subordination of the one to the other. Sceptics ground their criticism, I believe, on another ambiguity implied in the concept of phenomenon. Modern languages still carry the memory of such an ambiguity in the double sense of the phenomenal, namely what appears to the senses, but also what is exceptional, extraordinary, remarkable or marvellous and ultimately amazing. Latins already have the *res*

---

[23] I follow Stough's translation of this passage, see *infra*. See Pirrone (1981), 63 A–C (Decleva in Pirrone (1981): 'L'apparenza totalmente domina, là dove giunga'); D.L. IX.105; Hicks in Diogenes Laertius (1950), p. 517: 'But the apparent is omnipotent wherever it goes'; Polito in Aenesidemus (2014), p. 138: 'But that which appears is all-powerful wherever it goes'; S.E. M. VII.30 (Bury in Sextus Empiricus (1953–61) II, p. 17: 'Yea, the Appearance is ev'rywhere strong, where'er it approacheth'), and Gal. *De dign. puls*, in Galeni, Claudii (1821–33), VIII.776.

[24] See Polito's elaborate comment of the articulation between different conceptions of the φαινόμενον within Scepticism in Aenesidemus (2014), pp. 139–52. See also Auroux éd. (1990) II, 1928–30.

mirabilis for the φαινόμενον: the Sceptics imperceptibly bring us to the heart of the discourse on monstrosity. The conflictuality comes forward: Being and essence claim stability; the phenomenon is supposed to reveal this stability, to make it apparent and bring it to light. Contrarywise, it disturbs the picture and confuses that claim. It has the *phenomenal* power of shaking the nature of beings[25] and making everything appear loose.

In the same way that the *simulacrum* claims its own autonomy vis-à-vis the symbiotic balance between original and copy,[26] the phenomenon claims *its own* reality vis-à-vis the intelligible reality itself. By doing so, the phenomenon exposes philosophy to the threat of the monstrous and phenomenal character of appearances.[27] Its strength, against the subtleties of dogmatism, lies in the plain and evident nature of everyone's experience. Common sense, as Sextus explains, cries out against the dogmatist's claim.[28]

'The phenomenon prevails on every side, wherever it may go': three interpretations of this statement, and of the status of the phenomenon in Scepticism, become possible. Sceptic philosophy has been criticised for leading to inaction, passivity and indolence, for the lack of criteria for judging life's conduct. What if, however, the phenomenon itself becomes a candidate for the role of criterion to be followed? This is the first sense that one can give to Pyrrho's statement, namely a normative meaning whereby the phenomenon is able to prevail only because nothing else can. The phenomenon becomes the mover, whose outcome is not inaction, as common sense seems to suggest, but rather *phenomenal* action. The criterion of such an action bars intellect and thought (διάνοια and λόγος), denying them any right whatsoever to draw any conclusion as to the nature of things, on the ground of the exclusive validity of the phenomenon.[29] Without

---

[25] Stough (1969), p. 23, underlines that 'Timon's use of φύειν (n. 3) suggests that φαινόμενον was contrasted with φύσις by the early Pyrrhonists.'

[26] See Deleuze (1969).

[27] Cassin éd. (2004), p. 777: '*Phainomenon* retains a certain ambiguity. Sometimes the term designates that which "appears" or seems to appear as this or that, without really or truly being so (thus a *phainomenos sullogismos* [φαινόμενος συλλογισμός] is one that "merely seems to reason" [Aristotle, *Top.* I, 100 b 25]); other times, it designates what we call, properly, "phenomena," that is, obvious and constraining events, such as natural phenomena, that are sometimes remarkable and for which we have to account (*apodounai ta phainomena* [ἀποδοῦναι τὰ φαινόμενα] [Aristotle, *Metaph.* Λ, 1073 a 36–7]).'

[28] S.E. P I.210: '[. . .] the view about the same thing having opposite appearances is not a dogma of the Sceptics but a fact which is experienced not by the Sceptics alone but also by the rest of philosophers and by all mankind.' See Flückiger (1990), p. 52.

[29] See Dumont (1972), p. 8 and *passim*. Dumont calls this attitude *phenomenism* and, reaching beyond its atomist origin, he gives the highest degree of consistency to the φαινόμενον: 'Le phénomène est une réalité matérielle ou, si l'on préfère, un corps.'

ruling out the ambiguity, Stough attributes this first possible interpretation to Timon, who 'may also mean, however, that the phenomenon prevails by commanding acceptance. That is, though we do not claim that honey really is sweet, we do (cannot help but) grant that it appears (tastes) sweet.'[30]

A second interpretation, more widely shared among scholars, suggests that the phenomenon negatively imposes its presence and exclusive reality, ruining the possibility of knowledge. By barring intellect and thought, it puts the perceiver in a passive position and subjugates her to the mere phenomenality of things. In this sense, the phenomenon produces a real psychological constriction, evoked by Sextus in P. I.19 and 22. In this interpretation, such constriction merely has a negative value and cannot be intended in any normative sense. Pyrrho's statement, following this argument, leads to the mere acknowledgement of human's misery and his intellectual weakness. Human life is dominated by what manifests itself, becoming his lord and master.[31]

Expanding on the phenomenal and monstrous character of the φαινόμενον, however, a third reading becomes possible for what, in Pyrrho's view, 'prevails on every side': ἀλλὰ τὸ φαινόμενον πάντῃ σθένει. Σθένω means, after all, to have strength or might, to have power and be able to do something, close to the Latin *valeo*. Sceptics are well aware of the relationship of force that exists between concepts. The mind is a real *Kampfplatz* upon which arguments confront each other, destroy each other, acquire hegemony and obtain the final victory. The overall Sceptic strategy is precisely to reveal that no victory is ever final. They obliterate the conditions of this fight by claiming that the belief in the superiority of one argument over the other is an illusion and that, in fact, arguments have always the same force, an ἰσοσθένεια that inevitably compels the suspension of judgement.[32]

The phenomenon autonomously appears, strong and mighty, in front of us. Like a *simulacrum*, it brings its polemical presence to the foreground. The appearance claims autonomy more than omnipotence, thus destroying every and any claim of the essences' power.[33] Sceptic phenomenalism reconnects with the conflictual incipit of Greek philosophy, in the Parmenidean clash between λόγος and experience (ἐμπειρία). In their phenomenal and conflictual diversity, things that appear (τὰ δοκοῦντα) claim their specific truth and being.[34]

[30] Stough (1969), p. 24. See also Brochard (1923), pp. 77–91, and Long (1978).
[31] See Decleva Caizzi in Pirrone (1981) who suggests the translation of φαινόμενον with appearance, esp. pp. 262–5.
[32] See S.E. M. IX.59.
[33] See Conche (1973), p. 56.
[34] *Vorsokr.* 28 B 1 (= LM [19] PARM. D4, R8, R16, R39, R52 = S.E. M. VII.111 ff.)

Plato, for example, is well aware of the danger represented by the δοκοῦντα,[35] and his strategy is to reduce the phenomena to mere φαντάσματα.[36] Yet the phenomenon resists this appropriation and reduction. Beyond the alternative between a criterion to be followed in the absence of any better ground, and the psychological constriction that imposes itself, the first trope's phenomenon embodies the monstrous nature of the anti-dogmatic principle *par excellence*. Autonomous and independent, the phenomenon grounds the diversity of the natural world on an open and flat ontology that questions the meaning of boundaries, the strength of definitions and the lines of distinction, and, ultimately, ruins hierarchies and divisions.

Aenesidemus's second trope is also relevant for the present enquiry. Connected to the first one by the idea of diversity and relativity, it explains that human customs and beliefs are necessarily different and a universal criterion of judgement is once again ruled out. The argument is directed against not only dogmatists in general, but also all partisans of the superiority and excellence of human reason over the irrational, thus Stoics in particular. Not only animal diversity, but also human differences lead inevitably to the suspension of judgement. Humans build standards of judgement, but illegitimately so. Standards cannot be generalised and they prove to be false and wrong in many cases. Affections and impressions vary as much as possible on earth, and thus the only logical and coherent position to avoid contradiction and illusion is, once again, the ἐποχή.

Sextus's argumentation is constructed quite effectively. First comes the mere acknowledgement of the universal diversity among humans, who differ in their shape (μορφή) and temperament, or body's habit (ἰδιοσυγκρασία): '[...] in respect of choice and avoidance of external objects men exhibit great differences [...] and the enjoyment of different things is an indication that we receive varying impressions from the underlying objects'.[37] Meat, wine or fish affect individuals in different ways and no universal norm can be established for subjects who are supposedly similar (e.g. humans), but in fact very different in all respects.

Although Sextus refers to a common knowledge that can be experienced by everyone, he brings into the picture extreme cases and exceptional examples to reinforce his argument and strike the reader. Human diversity not only abolishes normative and universal claims, but also makes room for what is close to the monstrous, namely the exceptional, the wonderful and

---

[35] See R. 505 d 5–9.
[36] R. 516 b 3–4.
[37] S.E. P. I.80.

the astonishing φαινόμενα: an old woman swallows thirty drams of hemlock; someone suffers no harm from scorpions' or poisonous spiders' stings; someone else is able to cross a desert without drinking a drop of water.[38] More importantly, Sextus fully addresses the question of otherness, generalising the peculiarities of those exceptions by bringing entire populations into the picture. The world is big: Sceptics know it, and denounce the dogmatist claims, throwing light on their ignorant provincialism: 'The body of an Indian differs in shape from that of a Scythian [. . .] thus Indians enjoy some things, our people other things [. . .]'. Sextus is unsystematic, but also very specific, naming the Psyllaeans of North Africa, the Tentyritae of Egypt, the Ethiopians of Lake Meroë.[39]

Humans are as multiple and diverse as animals and material things. Bodily diversity, moreover, impacts, or at least reflects, mental diversity. Thus, taste depends on judgement and reflects the lack of universality. There is nothing wrong or blamable in how the human body and mind work. What is wrong, however, is the dogmatist's claim to draw norms from their functioning, for example pointing to the superior knowledge and nature of the wise (the Stoics, once again, are particularly targeted by Sextus). The wise human will necessarily be Plato for the Platonist or Epicurus for the Epicurean. The paradox here is that in order to build a universal norm, dogmatists lean on their particular beliefs.

The final part of Sextus's argumentation concerning the second trope rules out even a possible compromise, based on a light form of dogmatism: what if one took the average as a rule, and the currently established norm for a guide, without attempting to dogmatise further? This argument recalls the traditional image of Scepticism following accepted customs and beliefs. Yet, if this resulted in anything different from ἐποχή, it would still be a mistake. The average exists, but it does not explain or justify precisely what it is supposed to explain, namely the unknowable diversity and richness of nature and men:

> He who maintains that we ought to assent to the majority is making a childish proposal, since no one is able to visit the whole of mankind and determine what pleases the majority of them; for there may possibly be races of whom we know nothing amongst whom conditions rare with

---

[38] S.E. P. I.81–4. For an opposite attitude towards the Ethiopians, e.g. in Manil., see *supra*, but also, a few years later, Solin. 30.1 ff. who recognises the Ethiopians' perverted customs but doubts their physical monstrosity. Further East, though, the *monstruosa facies gentium* makes its appearance (Solin. 30.12).

[39] S.E. P. I.81–4.

us are common, and conditions common with us rare [...] Necessarily, therefore, the differences in men afford a further reason for bringing in suspension of judgement.[40]

Sextus reaffirms the exigency of widening one's experience and bringing otherness into the picture, beyond and against any supposedly universal and dogmatic rule. Others can be wonderful and astonishing, but they are not marginal, or peripheral, or even rarer with us more than we are rare with them. In this respect, Scepticism connects once again with its Democritean source. Together with early atomists, Democritus had been attracted by the vastness of the world and the relativist and anti-dogmatic consequences that one can draw from it.[41]

Let us see now the ninth trope, which deals with the specific cause of humans' weakness and misuse of judgements, namely the rarity of events. This argument has a strong influence on discourses concerning abnormality and monstrosity in every domain. The trope, Sextus explains, is based on the frequency and rarity of events. Humans draw conclusions on the essence and nature of things, once again illegitimately grounding judgements on how things affect them. What is rare and uncommon (σπανός), however, says something only about the perceiver's relation with the event or thing, and nothing about its nature. Sextus employs the example of the comet, whose superstitious use was certainly familiar to the reader. The sun, he says, is certainly 'more amazing' than the comet, more beautiful and more useful. Humans are, nonetheless, accustomed to it, and thus judge it with no astonishment. The comet, on the contrary, that only rarely appears in the sky, is regarded with amazement, awe, and like a portent or a sign of Zeus (a διοσημία): 'rare things [...] we count as precious, but not what is familiar to us and easily got'.[42]

The ninth trope is clearly directed against the Stoic, whose rationalism does not imply abandoning the superstitious practice of divination. The comet, real monster of the sky, is a well-chosen example in this respect. Sextus knows that dogmatic knowledge has not only ontological but also practical consequences and, in a fashion similar to that of Epicureans, intends to dismantle their ground based on astonishment and ignorance. Notwithstanding the differences between the new Academy and Sextus's Neo-Pyrrhonism, Cicero develops a similar argument against divination and superstition.[43] In *Div.*, he recognises that wonders come from the unusual and portentous, explaining that this refers only to

---

[40] S.E. P. I.88–9.
[41] Robin (1944), p. 26, stresses the importance of Hecataeus of Abdera in this respect (p. 26).
[42] S.E. P. I.141–3.
[43] On Cicero's Scepticism, see Gigon (1973), Goerler (1974), pp. 185–97, and Lévy (1992).

our ignorance and certainly not to the nature or essence of the portent itself.[44] In *ND*, Cicero adds that, on this ground, the idea of ordering things according to their perfection, i.e. one of the core ideas of Stoicism, is flawed, because 'no definition is given of the meaning of "superior" and "more excellent"'.[45]

Once again, relativity overcomes every dogmatic claim. The conclusion flows in the same way and leads, following a logical and inevitable consequence, toward the ἐποχή. In Sextus's words:

> Since then, owing to the frequency or rarity of their occurrence, the same things seem at one time to be amazing or precious and at another time nothing of the sort, we infer that though we shall be able perhaps to say what nature appears to belong to each of these things in virtue of its frequent or rare occurrence, we are not able to state what nature absolutely belongs to each of the external objects. So because of this Mode [i.e. trope] also we suspend judgement regarding them.[46]

The tropes thus summarise the Sceptics' reasons for the suspension of judgement. Yet they should not be considered as a counter-dogmatics, presented as a consistent theory, but rather as the tool for the obliteration and demolition of every possible dogmatism. The consequences are great for the traditional ontological systems and, in particular, for every discourse concerning taxonomies, normativity and monstrosity.

Another strong argument, in this sense, is in Timon's early liquidation of determination, related to the explanation of Pyrrho's argument about the οὐδὲν μᾶλλον. In his Πυθών, Timon declares that

> the Sceptics even refute the statement 'Not more (one thing than another).' For, as forethought is no more existent than non-existent, so 'Not more

---

[44] Cic. *Div.* II.22: 'You spoke of a mule bearing a colt. Such an event excites wonder because it seldom occurs; but if it had been impossible it would not have occurred. And it may be urged with effect against all portents that the impossible never has happened and that the possible need not excite any wonder. Now, in case of some new occurrence, ignorance of its cause is what excites our wonder; whereas, the same ignorance as to things of frequent occurrence does not. For the man who marvels that a mule has foaled does not understand how a mare foals and is ignorant of animal parturition in general. What he sees frequently causes him no astonishment even though he does not know how it happened. If something happens which he never saw before he considers it a portent. Then, which is the portent – the mule's conception or its parturition? The conception, it may be, is contrary to the usual course of nature, but the parturition follows as a necessary sequel of conception.' See also *Div.* II.28.
[45] *ND* III.26. See Dal Pra (1975, 2a ed.), p. 193.
[46] S.E. *P* I.144.

(one thing than another)' is no more existent than not. Thus, as Timon says in the *Pytho*, the statement means just absence of all determination and withholding of assent [τὸ μηδὲν ὁρίζειν, ἀλλὰ ἀπροσθετεῖν].[47]

Timon prohibits every determination, in view of the suspension of judgement, not only on the inner nature of things, but also for what concerns their essence in relation to, and as distinguished from, that of other things. The verb ὁρίζειν means define, determine, ordain, lay down, but also delimit or limit, part or divide, and separate from, with a border or a boundary. Decleva correctly underlines the difference between 'determine' and 'define', suggesting the former reading in Timon's work.[48] The semantic distinction, though, does not obliterate the similarity of ontological effects produced by determination and definition alike. This similarity consists in the operation of *partage* that not only produces dogmatic conclusions, but also constructs essential differences on the mutually exclusive relation between sameness and otherness, identity and alterity and, from here, between normality and abnormality. Following Pyrrho, Timon appears to intend determination not only in the sense of ascertaining something, but also of setting boundaries, fixing positions, limiting and distinguishing something from something else. And this is precisely what Scepticism proscribes. Carneades means the same thing when he denies the possibility of knowing inherent and intrinsic features of things. At stake is the very concept of essence, whose consistency depends on a definition, which in turn depends on the construction and perception of 'essence'.[49]

Sceptics also forbid a different approach to the *partage* between normality and abnormality, an approach that is not definitional (i.e. based on the definition of their essence), but rather derivative, i.e. that obtains abnormality and monstrosity *from* normality by way of quantitative or qualitative transformation. A human can be said monstrously tall, or a cow monstrously fat. However: how tall, or how fat, is *monstrously* such? When is tall or fat *too much*, so much so that quantity becomes quality, and normality is transformed into monstrosity? Surely one can add a small quantity to a normal height or weight, and still be within normality. Supposedly, this operation cannot be repeated without, at

---

[47] D.L. IX.76 (= Pirrone (1981), fr. 54.).

[48] Decleva, in Pirrone (1981), p. 234: 'ὁρίζειν means «determine» and not, as it is often said of this text, "define" (cfr. LSJ. III 1; Bonitz, *Index Aristotelicus*, s. v. ὁρίζειν, p. 524: "forma activa ὁρίζειν logica definiendi significatione non videtur usurpari"). Von Fritz, *Pyrrhon* [in *RE* XXIV (1963), coll. 89–106], 100 is correct ("wir setzen nichts fest . . . wir grenzen nichts als wahr gegen etwas Falsches ab, wir sagen nichts bestimmtes aus") [my translation].' See also TGL *sub voce* and Dal Pra (1975, 2a ed.), p. 94.

[49] See Sextus, M. VII.411–15. See also Dal Pra (1975, 2a ed.) and Gigante (1980), p. 138 n.

some point, normality slowly fading, or abruptly transforming, into something abnormal and monstrous. Yet, Sceptics intend to deny this transformation and forbid precisely this passage. For them, abnormality or monstrosity cannot be derived or obtained from normality: it is the famous argument of the sorites.

'Sorites' comes from σωρός, the heap, a collection of objects piled up on each other. The metaphor is used to deny the possibility of attributing a predicate to a subject. Consider a heap of wheat grains: surely I can remove one grain, without the heap being transformed in something else or, more specifically, into a non-heap. What happens if I keep repeating the operation? Will the second-last grain, or the very last one, still be the same heap? And if not, when did it become a non-heap? Which grain was *the one* that changed the quantity into quality? The argument underlines the paradox of a threshold that supposedly transforms the nature and essence of the object – the heap or the tall human or the fat cow – into something else, i.e. a non-heap, or a monstrously tall being or a monstrously fat animal. Sceptics employ the sorites to argue against the consistency of determinations. Cicero describes the sorites fallacy as irrefutable:

> No faculty of knowing absolute limits has been bestowed upon us by the nature of things to enable us to fix exactly how far to go in any matter; and this is so not only in the case of a heap of wheat from which the name is derived, but in no matter whatsoever – if we are asked by gradual stages, is such and such a person a rich man or a poor man, famous or undistinguished, are yonder objects many or few, great or small, long or short, broad or narrow, we do not know at what point in the addition or subtraction to give a definite answer. [. . .] you admit my point, that you cannot specify in your answers either the place where 'a few' stops or that where 'many' begins; and this class of error spreads so widely that I don't see where it may not get to [. . .]. Consequently that science of yours gives you no assistance against a sorites, as it does not teach you either the first point or the last in the process of increasing or diminishing.[50]

Sceptics also use the argument to underline the changing and fluid nature of reality, which prevents universal conclusions and rigid definitions that would establish boundaries and fix identities in a certain and stable manner. Carneades' argument highlights the problem of the psychological threshold that makes us

---

[50] Cic. *Acad.* II.92–5, also for Carneades' response to Chrysippus's attempt to solve the sorites's paradox by remaining silent on the critical threshold. On the sorites see Auroux, p. 2427, Lalande, pp. 1011–13, Ritter, Gründer hrsg. (1971–2007), IX, cc. 1090–9. See also S.E. M. VII.416 ff., Dal Pra (1975, 2a ed.), p. 104 and *passim*, and Wiggins (1980).

able to grant or deny a certain status to something in virtue of the quantity of its components or its features. Such a status is always problematic, since the threshold depends on the infinite divisibility of that quantity and the infinitesimal quantity that, supposedly, makes or unmakes the thing's identity: whereas a continuity exists, the mind illegitimately perceives a discontinuity.[51]

Sorites-like arguments were not the exclusive monopoly of Sceptics. On the contrary, Stoics had made powerful use of them exploring the efficacy of ascending from the less to the most perfect, which in turn is based on the conception of degrees of perfection that, although in different ways, they share with Plato and Aristotle. Cleanthes' attempt to prove God's existence in this way is faithfully reported by Sextus.[52] Cleanthes' argumentation, nevertheless, is not entirely convincing, as it does not appear to fully exploit the potentiality of transitivity from one element to the other of the ascending chain. With Carneades, Cicero clearly understands the dogmatist's weakness. He declares that Stoic arguments are nothing less than *monstra* and plays the sorites argument against them:

> [. . .] if Zeus is a God, Poseidon also, being his brother, will be a God. And if Poseidon is a God, Achelous, too, will be a God; and if Achelous, Neilos; and if Neilos, every river as well; and if every river, the streams also will be Gods; and if the streams, the torrents; but the streams are not Gods; neither, then, is Zeus a God. But if there had been Gods, Zeus would have been a God. Therefore there are no Gods.[53]

If ontological dogmas do not resist the fluidity of thought, if everything is relative and *becomes* instead of *being*, if boundaries and essential distinctions are only fictional or delusional, not much room is left for the definition of normality

---

[51] Robin (1944), p. 83. See also Dumont (1972), p. 236, who connects this argument to the Sceptic's conception of sense knowledge.
[52] S.E. M. IX.88–91.
[53] S.E. M. IX.182–3. See also Cic. *ND* III.43: 'If I adopt your doctrines, tell me what answer I am to make to one who questions me thus: "If gods exist, are the nymphs also goddesses? if the nymphs are, the Pans and Satyrs also are gods; but they are not gods; therefore the nymphs also are not. Yet they possess temples vowed and dedicated to them by the nation; are the other gods also therefore who have had temples dedicated to them not gods either? Come tell me further: you reckon Jupiter and Neptune gods, therefore their brother Orcus is also a god; and the fabled streams of the lower world, Acheron, Cocytus and Pyriphlegethon, and also Charon and also Cerberus are to be deemed gods. No, you say, we must draw the line at that; well then, Orcus is not a god either; what are you to say about his brothers then?" These arguments were advanced by Carneades, not with the object of establishing atheism (for what could less befit a philosopher?) but in order to prove the Stoic theology worthless [. . .].' See also Cic. *ND* III.44.

and its opposition to abnormality and monstrosity. No space is left, moreover, for the traditional and orthodox conception regarding the entity that supposedly provides the stability and the meaning of the universe, namely God.

To What Purpose?

In a passage of the *Icaromenippus*, Lucian tells that, seated on a golden throne, Zeus listens to men's prayers. Grave difficulties loom when two men make contrary prayers and promise equal sacrifices: 'He was really in a dilemma [...] he didn't know which one of them to give assent to; so that he was in the same plight as the Academicians and could not make any affirmation at all, but suspended judgement for a while and thought it over, like Pyrrho.'[54] The Lucianic irony in this passage is not directed against Pyrrhonism, but rather against the orthodox believers in the divine's intervention in the world and, as a consequence, the possibility for humans to either influence or foresee it through divination.

In M. IX, Sextus develops a long and verbose analysis of several beliefs on the nature of gods, claimed by different philosophers and schools. The aim is not to praise atheism, but rather to juxtapose and contrast different opinions, producing the diaphony of many philosophical voices that inevitably leads to the suspension of judgement.[55] Because atheism can be as dogmatic as theism, Sextus's and the other Sceptics' intention is certainly to expose the inconsistency of a single belief, when several contrasting theories have been advanced by so many wise philosophers. I believe, however, that rather than a diaphony, it would be more appropriate to talk about the *cacophony* of the philosophers' opinions, i.e. a plurality that is so confusingly contradictory that it ruins entirely the belief in a rational and providential divinity. The coherent outcome of the strongest Sceptic argument leads inevitably to atheism, at least as a consequence, if not as a systematic theoretical position.[56]

The Sceptic critique of religion is directed first and foremost against Stoics, and only secondarily against Epicureans and other dogmatists.[57] Although Sceptics do not necessarily prefer Epicurean arguments to Stoic ones,[58] an effective Scepticism destroys the foundation of Stoicism on the nature of God as a lord and

---

[54] Luc. *Icar.* 25.
[55] Hankinson (1995), p. 240. See also Ley (1966–89), I, pp. 493–505, and G. Reale, 'Ipotesi per una rilettura della filosofia di Pirrone di Elide', in Giannantoni a cura di (1982), p. 309 ff., who follows Brehier (1967) and focuses on Pyrrho's religiosity, speaking about his concept of wisdom as an 'experience of the absolute' (p. 334). See also Dal Pra (1975, 2a ed.), pp. 210–13 and *passim*.
[56] See Conche (1973), esp. p. 182 and p. 197.
[57] Hankinson (1995), p. 238.
[58] Not infrequently, it is the opposite, as Cic. *ND* clearly demonstrates.

rational ruler of the universe. Scepticism unmakes, in other words, the ontological framework within which the concepts of monstrosities and anomalies have been systematised by Stoic dogmatism. When Sceptics claim their devotion, because of a prudent adoption of shared customs and beliefs, the irony implicit in this position should not be overestimated.[59] The intent of avoiding the accusation of impiety seems a reasonable justification for this prudent attitude, and a convergence between Scepticism and Stoicism on this point could be recognised.[60] However, although Stoics and Epicureans might have a common concern regarding the accusation of impiety, I rather believe that Sceptics directly target the pillars of the Stoics' conception of rational divinity and its providential role in nature, something they could not find in Epicureans.[61]

Moreover, when Sextus discusses the nature of God, he acquiesces in, and makes use of, the Epicurean argument on the presence of evil in the world and against providence. Sextus converges with the Epicureans on this point, and his argument eventually becomes classic, informing subsequent criticism of providentialism based on the presence of evil, imperfections and monstrosities in nature. Had God forethought (προνοέω) everything in the world, there would not be any badness (κακία) in it. If he forethinks only something and not everything, why this rather than that, especially since he surely has the will (βούλευμα, a term cherished by Stoics) and the power (δυναστεία) to take care of everything?[62] Sextus goes as far as to imagine the concept of an evil genius: 'And if, again, he has the power but not the will to have forethought for all, he will be held to be malignant; while if he has neither the will nor the power, he is both malignant and weak – an impious thing to say about God.' The conclusion is strikingly clear and has the force of a demonstration: 'God has no forethought for the things in the universe.'[63]

---

[59] See S.E. P. III.2: 'Since [. . .] the majority have declared that God is a most efficient Cause, let us begin by inquiring about God, first promising that although, following the ordinary view, we affirm undogmatically that Gods exist and reverence Gods and ascribe to them foreknowledge, yet as against the rashness of the Dogmatists we argue as follow [. . .].' Sounding like an *excusatio non petita*, Sextus's statement puts forward the two necessary elements that any dogmatist would expect to be there: the existence and the providence of god. See *contra* Chiesara (2003), p. 186 and *passim*, who argues that Sextus does not oppose the divine as the main efficient causality of everything, although more from the point of view of sentiment than like a proof or a demonstration.

[60] Dumont (1972), p. 39.

[61] See Flückiger (1990), p. 118.

[62] S.E. P. III.9–10.

[63] S.E. P. III.9–10. Sextus also makes use of this argument to introduce and explain the meaning of the tropes in P. I.32: 'We oppose [. . .] thoughts to thoughts, when in answer to him who argues the existence of Providence from the order of the heavenly bodies we oppose the fact that often the good fare ill and the bad fare well, and draw from this the inference that Providence does not exist.'

To revere God and to accept at the same time that the world is as we see it, full of evils and imperfections, is contradictory and shamefully impious. With the due differences, Cicero puts a similar argument into Velleius's mouth:

> I am not going to expound to you doctrines that are mere baseless figments of the imagination, such as the artisan deity and world-builder of Plato's Timaeus, or that old hag of a fortune-teller, the Pronoia (which we may render 'Providence') of the Stoics; nor yet a world endowed with a mind and senses of its own, a spherical, rotatory god of burning fire; these are the marvels and monstrosities of philosophers who do not reason but dream. [...] Those [...] who said that the world is itself endowed with life and with wisdom, failed entirely to discern what shape the nature of an intelligent living being could conceivably possess. [...] We see that vast portions of the earth's surface are uninhabitable deserts, being either scorched by the sun's proximity, or frost-bound and covered with snow owing to its extreme remoteness. But if the world is God, these, being parts of the world, must be regarded as limbs of God, undergoing the extremes of heat and cold respectively.[64]

The believers – this is the Sceptic conclusion – are in fact the more blasphemous.[65] Stoics, in particular, praise the rational nature of the world, and reason as the most divine principle, spread throughout nature. Yet, Sceptics contend, reason is also capable of the worst misdeeds, as the infamous case of Medea proves, as well as the infinite number of monstrosities that one finds in the human and the natural realm alike.[66]

Teleology, both Stoic and Aristotelian, is also targeted and in this, again, Sceptics converge with Epicureans. Cicero's Chrysippus considers teleology as a direct consequence of the unshakeable belief in God's existence.[67] The very

---

[64] Cic. ND I.18–24. See also Div. II.120: 'I ask for what reason did the deity, when making the universe for our sakes (for that is the view of your school), create so vast a supply of water-snakes and vipers, and why did he scatter so many death-bringing and destructive creatures over land and sea?' Also important is the striking absence of a theodicy in Balbus's exposition of the Stoic argument on divinity in the world, one that the reader would have expected, knowing that it was part of the classic Stoic argumentation. See B. Besnier, 'La nature dans le livre II du De natura deorum de Cicéron', in Lévy éd. (1996), p. 138.

[65] Robin (1944), p. 211.

[66] Cic. ND III.68: 'This gift of reason forsooth, which according to your school divine beneficence has bestowed on man alone, the beasts do not possess; do you see then how great a boon the gods have vouchsafed to us? [...] Medea was criminal, but also she was perfectly rational. Again, does not the hero plotting the direful banquet for his brother turn the design this way and that in his thoughts?' See Robin (1944), p. 110.

[67] Cic. ND III.26: 'If we saw a handsome mansion, we should infer that it was built for its masters and not for mice; so therefore we must deem the world to be the mansion of the gods. Assuredly I should so deem it if I thought it had been built like a house, and not constructed by nature, as I shall show that it was.'

ground of this evidence, however, has already been destroyed by Scepticism. Thus, one only has to draw the consequences of it, vis-à-vis the supposedly teleological character of nature:

> But then you tell me that Socrates in Xenophon asks the question, if the world contains no rational soul, where did we pick up ours? And I too ask the question, where did we get the faculty of speech, the knowledge of numbers, the art of music? unless indeed we suppose that the sun holds conversation with the moon when their courses approximate, or that the world makes a harmonious music, as Pythagoras believes. These faculties, Balbus, are the gifts of nature – not nature 'walking in craftsmanlike manner' as Zeno says [...], but nature by its own motions and mutations imparting motion and activity to all things [*omnia cientis et agitantis motibus et mutationibus suis*]. And so I fully agreed with the part of your discourse that dealt with nature's punctual regularity, and what you termed its concordant interconnexion and correlation; but I could not accept your assertion that this could not have come about were it not held together by a single divine breath. On the contrary, the system's coherence and persistence is due to nature's forces and not to divine power; she does possess that 'concord' (the Greek term *sympatheia*) of which you spoke, but the greater this is as a spontaneous [*sua sponte*] growth, the less possible is it to suppose that it was created by divine reason.[68]

The reference to Socrates in the opening lines, as well as to the world's harmonious music, highlights that the critique is not directed exclusively against Stoic teleology, but against finalism in general. The Sceptic strategy is twofold. First, like the Epicureans, they criticise the consistency of the concepts of, and the distinction between, order and confusion, beauty and ugliness, perfection and imperfection. Then, they attack the Stoics' concept of order from a different angle: even if one could say that order exists in nature, one could not conclude that it is the benevolent effect of a caring divinity, whose artificial intervention has teleologically moulded nature for men's sake. The order of nature is not an *order* at all if, by it, one intends the idea of a divinity acting as a craftsman with a τέλος in mind.

An Epicurean tone of a sort clearly resonates in this argument. Interestingly, this synergy between Scepticism and Epicureanism eventually finds an echo in one of the most interesting and less canonic Christian thinkers, Arnobius of Sicca. Between the third and fourth centuries, Arnobius makes

---

[68] Cic. *ND* III.27–8.

use of this eclectic approach to defend Christianity against the pagans who unjustly accused it of having brought all sort of evils and perturbations.[69] According to Arnobius, philosophers – and this shows how weak pagan knowledge is – do not know the laws that govern nature. For example, they cannot explain the causes of monstrosities, which nonetheless belong to natural phenomena: 'For what purpose have such limitless and countless kinds of monsters and snakes been fashioned or brought forth?'[70] In the same way, humans cannot understand why their nature is so limited and why so many evils plague their life and appear in nature.

Such ignorance suggests a Sceptic attitude (quite uncommon in Christian apologists), infused with Stoic elements of a passive acceptance of reality as it is given to us:

> Would you venture to say that this and that thing in the world, the origin and final cause of which you cannot explain or analyse, is bad, and because winter possibly hinders you from enjoying delights and pleasures, would you say that it is a pernicious, austere thing? [. . .] Hellebore is a poison to men: ought it for this reason not grow? The wolf lies in wait at sheepfolds: is nature at all to blame because it has created a beast most dangerous to the woolbearer? By its bite the serpent takes away life: would you really condemn the foundation of things because it added to living creatures monsters so fierce ?[71]

Nature behaves spontaneously, independent of any anthropocentrism or teleology. Evils happen for reasons unrelated to the effects they might have on men. That in no way means, however, that they happen for no reason. Nature's behaviour is autonomous and unknown and unknowable by humans:

> If anything occurs which fosters us and our affairs with but little happy success, it is not therefore an evil and to be regarded as pernicious. The world either rains or does not rain; it is for itself that it rains or does not rain, and though perhaps you do not know it, it either evaporates excessive moisture with drying heat or it moderates a long spell of dryness by shower of rain. It produces pestilences, diseases, famines, and other deadly forms of evil.

---

[69] On Arnobius's eclecticism, see Moreschini (2004), pp. 278 ff. On his Scepticism, see Pichon (1901), pp. 49 ff.
[70] Arnob. *Nat.* II.59.
[71] Arnob. *Nat.* I.11. See also I.8: 'What if – and this is nearest the truth – what seems adverse to us is not really evil to the world itself, and that judging all things in term of our own advantage, we blame the results of nature because of unproved opinions?'

> How can you tell whether it does not remove what exists in excess, to this end that by forcing things to take losses, it may set moderation upon their tendency to develop riotously?[72]

The causes of so much evil remain unknown. What is certain, however, is that God cannot be their author. This reveals how useless pagan knowledge and science is, and why only God, not nature, deserves our attention, because only He can be known through faith. Philosophers have failed utterly; Christ is the only master of truth.[73]

Again, such eclecticism, marked by a Sceptic tone, is uncommon in early Christian thinkers. This makes Arnobius's strategy even more interesting for us. He discusses the presence of evil and monstrosity in nature not to justify or explain God's actions, but to separate God from nature and its miseries. He also uses monstrosity to denounce humans' claim to every and any sort of primacy in the universe, both ontologically and – even more surprising for a Christian – morally. Arnobius plays with ontological boundaries to undermine humanity's claim to any special status. Precisely when other Christian thinkers praise the beauty and order of the universe and elevate humans above other creatures in the name of God's providence, Arnobius, using Sceptic irony, denies any order and providence. In his famous monologue on the ox, he gives animals the power of speech to denounce human monstrosity:

> O Jupiter, or whatever other god thou art, is this [*scil.* the sacrifice], then, humane or right, or is it to be regarded as fair at all, that when someone else has sinned, I should be killed and from my blood thou shouldst allow satisfaction to be given thee – [. . .] Ask Piety whether it is more just that I be slain, done away with, or that man should be pardoned and be free from punishment for what he has done. [. . .] Is not this [*scil.* human actions] bestial, monstrous, savage, does it not seem to thee, O Jupiter, unjust and barbarous for me to be killed, for me to be slain, that thou mightest be appeased and that acquittal rest on the guilty?[74]

Arnobius's attitude is rooted in the early history of pagan Scepticism, which converges with the Epicureans in their critique of teleology. The conceptual weapons they use, however, cannot be the same. The *spontaneous* character of order that Cicero recognises in nature is worthy to note. *Sua sponte*, Cicero says, obliterating the idea of a design from the Stoic συμπάθεια and thus

---

[72] Arnob. *Nat.* I.10.
[73] See B. Amata, *La polemica anticreazionista e antiscientifica di Arnobio di Sicca*, in AA. VV. (2007), pp. 317–29.
[74] Arnob. *Nat.* VII.9.

bereaving it of any teleological consistency. Even the Epicurean atoms work spontaneously, and chance has no other meaning for atomists. In interpreting Scepticism, nevertheless, Cicero carefully suggests avoiding the confusion. Although αὐτόματος is precisely *sua sponte*, Cicero makes an effort to distinguish the Sceptics' hypothetical character of nature's spontaneity from atomists' chance. He finds a suitable source for this in Strato of Lampsacus. We have seen *supra* Strato's approach to the problem of teleology. Cicero plays Strato against Democritus, rescuing the idea of spontaneity from the monopoly of atomism. Strato's point, as it is read and endorsed by Scepticism, is that there can be a spontaneous order that is neither the result of blind chance, nor the end of a providential divinity. Both dogmatisms are thus ruled out.[75] Ruled out together with this, moreover, is the ground for superstition and for the use of dogmatic authority for devotional purposes, namely the belief in divination.

Whatever knowledge can be gained from the observation of the order of nature, it comes from natural science, and certainly not from divination. Partisans of divination, such as the Stoics, respond to criticism by saying that everything is connected in nature, and thus phenomena that we can observe can be interpreted as signs of things that we do not know yet, but are still knowable with the use of the proper divinatory art. This argument eventually resonates through the centuries, to some extent resembling the specifically modern concept of symptom: is the fever not a clinical sign of a pathological process, or the wind a meteorological sign of a movement of air between areas of different atmospheric pressures? And is it not legitimate to use such signs and symptoms to foresee events, as in the case of meteorological conditions, and sometimes to influence them, as when we choose the appropriate treatment for a specific sickness?

This is quite a strong argument, and Sceptics need to provide an equally strong response. It is true that there are signs in nature, they grant. Yet even if these signs were knowable, Sceptics argue, this would be science's domain, and not a matter of divination:

> I am impressed with the force of the questions with which Carneades used to begin his discussions: 'What are the things within the scope of divination? Are they things that are perceived by the senses? But those are things that we see, hear, taste, smell, and touch. Is there, then, in such objects some quality that we can better perceive with the aid of prophecy and inspiration than we can with the aid of the senses alone?

---

[75] See Credaro (1889), pp. 224 ff., Dal Pra (1975, 2a ed.), pp. 191–2, Robin (1944), p. 104, Chiesara (2003), p. 82.

And is there any diviner, anywhere, who, if blind, like Tiresias, could tell the difference between white and black? Or, who, if deaf, could distinguish between different voices and different tones? Now you must admit that divination is not applicable in any case where knowledge is gained through the senses.'[76]

In other words, divination and science both foresee, and yet the former does it illegitimately. No matter that Scepticism does not intend to dogmatise, but only to demolish dogmatic arguments. In this case, converging with the Epicurean critique of divination, Scepticism leads to a profound attack on superstition in the form of divination. This argument is extremely relevant to the discourse of monstrosity, since it relies upon the nature of the thing or the event to be scrutinised, for example a monster or a portent. Does such a thing depend on chance and fortune, or is it the necessary outcome of material and mechanical conditions? If the latter, then it is science's business, and divination does not have any place or role to play in it. If the former, than both science and divinatory art have no power to grasp the portent's meaning. Because it is completely random – this is Carneades' conclusion – not only humans, but even a god would be unable to know it. If God were able to know it, and thus to produce it for the sake of men's knowledge, then it would be something necessary, and thus again an object of science and not of divination.[77]

Denunciation of knowledge's illusion, relativisation of judgement, obliteration of every determination in thought and in action, cast a sombre shadow on the idea of divinity and providence, and ridicule divination and, as a consequence, religious devotion: a rich haul for a movement of philosophers whose major claim is that they know only that they know not! The discourse on monstrosity comes out of the Sceptic experience enriched by arguments that challenge the traditional attitude vis-à-vis normality and abnormality.

Stoicism in particular comes under attack. Stoics recognise the danger and are scared by this movement, as much as they are by Epicurean materialism. Like the Romans in front of Carneades, they see the outrageous nature of their enemy, and the effectiveness of its attack. Zeno's orthodox disciple Aristo of Chio forges a powerful metaphor for his Sceptic adversary Arcesilaus, a metaphor of hybridity and monstrosity: 'Plato the head of him, Pyrrho the tail,

---

[76] Cic. *Div.* II.9. See Dal Pra (1975, 2a ed.), pp. 256–61. See also *ND* II.12–14 and *passim*. For Sextus, see M. V *passim*.

[77] Dal Pra (1975, 2a ed.), p. 217 and Robin (1944), p. 114 . On the Sceptic critique of divination see also Credaro (1889), pp. 243 ff., Barnes (1990), pp. 74–5, and Hankinson (1995), pp. 256–61.

in the midst Diodorus.'⁷⁸ Sceptics themselves are aware of the monstrosity of their philosophy, or rather of the monstrous force that is needed to eradicate the opposite monstrosity of dogmatism. In Cicero's words: 'I agree with Clitomachus when he writes that Carneades really did accomplish an almost Herculean labour in ridding our minds of that fierce wild beast [*fera et immanis belua*], the act of assent, that is of mere opinion and hasty thinking [. .].'⁷⁹

---

⁷⁸ S.E. P. I.234. Sextus refers to Diodorus Cronos the Megaric philosopher. See R. G. Bury in Sextus Empiricus (1953–61), I, p. 145: 'The verse is a parody of Homer, *Il.* VI.181 (cf. Hesiod, *Th.* 323), who thus describes the Chimaera: πρόσθε λέων, ὄπιθεν δὲ δράκων, μέσση δὲ χίμαιρα ("Lion the head of her, Dragon the tail of her, trunk of a She-goat").'
⁷⁹ Cic. Ac. II.108.

8
Middle and Neoplatonism

We have arrived at the last chapter of this enquiry, Middle and Neoplatonism. It is not that they should be considered the conclusion of antiquity or, somehow, the most mature, accomplished and harmonic evolution of ancient philosophy. On the contrary, as we will see, Platonism is possibly the most troubled philosophical movement of this period. It will be challenged to adapt in dramatic, sometimes ambiguous, always innovative ways. It changes tremendously to respond to the Hellenistic crisis. Rather than a peaceful and harmonic evolution, we will see a dazzling struggle to survive the tensions that characterise the end of the ancient world. I conclude this enquiry with Middle and Neoplatonism because, along with Stoicism, it is the philosophical movement that most naturally converges with Christianity, thus opening up original perspectives for the coming ages. This is why I have included here several early Christian thinkers – Augustine among them – whose philosophical background and inspiration are largely Platonic.

After the sceptical turn of the second century BCE, the Platonic Academy searched for a way to revitalise its prestige by turning back to its ancient dogmas. Some of the most fundamental points of Platonism, which had been successfully challenged by the Hellenistic schools, found new strength in the cultural environment and climate that steadily emerged in the early Imperial age. Platonism not only looked back at its own history and tradition; it also found strength in the encounter with ideas and doctrines originated beyond the boundaries of Greek and Latin culture, chiefly Judaism, Hermetism and Christianism. Platonism convergences with these cultures and reinvigorates its lost status. This effort, however, came at a price. The impact of Hellenistic philosophy on the mentality of the late Republican age had been too strong to simply revert back to Attic dogmatism. Platonism was thus forced to evolve and integrate concepts and ideas derived in particular from Stoicism, Peripateticism and Neo-Pythagoreanism, with all of which it finds common ground. This is the most substantial heritage that Middle and Neoplatonism, beyond occasional conflicts and incomprehensions, leave to the following centuries.

The convergence of these philosophical traditions under the common name of Platonism should not hide the fact that Middle and Neoplatonism, as well as Christian Platonism, are very diverse and eclectic phenomena.[1] Plato's heritage is constantly renegotiated with different philosophical influences, following the impulse of original individual philosophers who have very different attitudes toward the tradition. They offer diverging interpretations of both Plato's thought and of the whole history of Greek philosophy, back to the pre-Platonic thinkers. Many of the philosophers whose importance for Middle and Neoplatonism is unquestioned are indebted to different traditions. Philo of Alexandria to Judaism, for example, Alcinous to Peripateticism, Numenius of Apamea to Pythagoreanism, Antiochus of Ascalon, Maximus of Tyrus and Galen to Stoicism, which also influences Christian Platonists such as Justin Martyr, Origen and Augustine, without forgetting, of course, the great importance of the *Chaldean Oracles* and Hermetism.[2]

All these schools, in fact, had developed strong arguments rearding the main philosophical and theological problems at the heart of Platonism – problems, moreover, that Plato himself had left at least partially unanswered or not consistently developed, such as the role and status of demons and intermediate creatures or the creation of matter. Alongside Platonism, those schools have also fought their battle against the common enemy, namely materialism and Epicureanism. Thus, the movements that fall under the name of Middle and Neoplatonism develop original solutions for many points of philosophical and theological interest that are relevant to the interpretation of monstrosity. These are the conception of God, and in particular God's degree of immanence in or transcendence of the world; the question of the universe's order, creation and maintenance; the notion of ideal and material reality and their mutual relationship; the concept of providence and theodicy. Monstrosity plays a function in all these metaphysical, physical and theological areas, and it consistently surfaces in the thought and writings of this age, threatening the effectiveness and strength of their solutions.

The Material World and the Rediscovery of Transcendence

Middle and Neoplatonism rediscover God's transcendence. Whereas in the dualistic form openly maintained by several Middle Platonists and directly inspired by Plato's *Timaeus*, or in a monistic form more typical of Neoplatonism, the philosophy of this period reworks the ancient problem of the principle by

---

[1] Vimercati in Medioplatonici (2015), p. 52, speaks about the 'ecumenical' character of Platonism in this age.
[2] Influences that should recall for us all the limits of philosophical labels, when they are taken out of context and without confronting the primary sources.

stressing its transcendence toward the material universe.³ This is undoubtedly the main point of conflict with both Stoicism and, sometimes, Peripateticism. When it is interpreted by Platonists as a form of materialism, Peripateticism is as shocking and horrifying as atheism or Epicureanism.⁴ On this ground, the Eastern influence plays a major role and it is not a coincidence that one of the main pillars of the Platonist renaissance – Philo – lived and wrote in Alexandria of Egypt, one of the most lively cities of the Mediterranean and one of the most influenced by the cultural exchange with the East.⁵ Judaism, Hermetism, but also a genuine Platonic core of doctrines converge against the philosophical monstrosity represented by Stoic and atomist materialism, and in particular by Epicurus himself.

Maximus of Tyrus defiantly speaks about the monstrosity of materialism, naming the atomists Leucippus, Democritus and Epicurus alongside the atheist Diagoras of Melos and the Peripatetic Strato.⁶ The reference to Strato shows that even Peripateticism is seen as an enemy for the true transcendental and theologically oriented vision of the universe. Although Middle and Neoplatonist philosophers like Ammonius, Alcinous and Plotinus are strongly influenced by Aristotle, others like Philo and Atticus oppose the reconciliation with Peripateticism, openly rejecting its immanentist view of the first principle.

In different degrees, Middle and Neoplatonists' God is transcendent and ineffable. Source of all perfection, God is king and father of all people.⁷ He also creates nature – clearly an anti-Stoic opinion – as well as the law that governs it.⁸ In the *Opificio mundi*, Philo of Alexandria underlines the different ontological statuses of God and its creation. Only God *is*, in the full sense of the term, and its Being is opposed to the lesser non-Being of the world. The world is created, but its existence is a kind of non-Being vis-à-vis the absolute and true Being, which is untouched and unaffected by the process of generation and corruption. Philo, however, feels with astonishing clarity the problem that Middle and Neoplatonic philosophers experience, especially when they

---

³ See H. Dörrie, 'Die Frage nach dem Transzendenten im Mittelplatonismus', in AA. VV. (1957), pp. 191–241.

⁴ On Platonism and Stoicism, see W. Theiler, 'Plotin zwischen Plato un Stoa', in AA. VV. (1957), pp. 63–103. On Peripateticism see Atticus (1977). 3.49–65.

⁵ On Alexandria in the Imperial and Ptolemaic age see RE I.1, cc. 1376–88, Andresen et al. (1965), I, cc. 112–13, RAC I, cc. 271–83, BNP I, cc. 496–99, Jaeger (1961), and Fraser (1972).

⁶ Max.Tyr. XVII.5.

⁷ Ph. *Prou.* II.15. For the abbreviation of Philo's works, I follow Philon d'Alexandrie (1961–), pp. 15–16.

⁸ See Martens (2003), pp. 75 ff. and *passim*.

later have to face Gnosticism. The problem is to balance God's transcendence with its role in creating and maintaining the universe, as well as with the necessity of praising God's providence for the beauty and perfection of its creation. Philo thus invites the reader to join him in the glorification of the world, yet not above the creator itself. This would be impious. The world is indeed created, and thus its beauty and perfection are below those of its creator, as much as the world's Being is inferior to the creator's fullest Being.[9]

Philo makes use of the concept of monstrosity to stress the subordination of the creation to its creator. He denounces the materialist and Epicurean system as a monstrosity. This was already a widespread topos in his time and culture, but Philo originally contributes to establishing the equation of Epicurus's name with the horrifying position of atheism.[10] Philo focuses on the allegory of the snake, 'an animal without feet sunk prone upon his belly; [. . .] he takes clods of earth as food; [. . .] he carries in his teeth the venom with which it is his nature to destroy those whom he has bitten'.[11] The man subject to passions is similar to the snake, and falls into temptation because of the female's wicked influence. Through this allegory, Philo denounces in the *Opificio mundi* not only Epicurus's ethics based on pleasure, but also his physics and cosmology, based on the immanent pluralism of atoms generating the universe without any unifying and transcendent principle.[12] The allegory of the fall epitomises the transcendent unity of the divine principle, developed all along the *Opificio*. Philo's monotheist sensibility rises against the plurality and multiplicity of Epicurus's materialism, the worst of all ontological monstrosities.[13]

Philo's attack against philosophical materialism is conducted through theological conceptions inspired by Judaic monotheism as well as with philosophical weapons borrowed from different sources, but mainly from Platonism. Suffice to say that Philo finds the concept of the incorporeal, so deeply strategic for his theological philosophy, in Alexandrian Platonism and not in the Bible, from which it is absent.[14] Thus God's nature is ambiguously twofold: on the one hand, a pure transcendence and incorporeality, which makes him

---

[9] Ph. *Opif.* 8–9.
[10] M. Hadas-Lebel, 'Introduction', in Philon d'Alexandrie (1961–), XXXV, pp. 58–63.
[11] Ph. *Opif.* 157. On Clement's use of the same allegory see *infra*.
[12] A. Le Boulluec, 'La réflexion de Philon sur le plaisir', in Lévy, Besnier éds (1998), pp. 129–52, esp. pp. 140–3.
[13] See C. Lévy, 'Philon d'Alexandrie et l'épicurisme', in Erler, Bees hrsg. (2000), pp. 122–36.
[14] See ThWNT *sub* πνοή which, in the LXX, is used for the Hebrew נֶפֶשׁ or נְשָׁמָה. Philo contests its use instead of the more canonic πνεῦμα, the soul (*Leg.* I.33). He argues for the material consistency of the light breathing (πνεῦμα), while the πνοή is the spirit created in the divine image. More generally, on the hellenisation of Judaism see Jaeger (1961).

not only utterly perfect, but also absolutely absolved of whatever imperfection one might find in the world. On the other hand, God is the king, father and architect of the world, thus intimately connected with its creation.[15]

It does not come as a surprise, thus, that Philo develops a negative theology, testifying to an early use of attributes like unnamable (ἀκατονόμαστος) and unutterable (ἄρρητος), and whose roots are in early and Middle Platonism. This negative theology does not contribute to clarifying God's relation with its work, and remains ambiguous on points such as the actual meaning of creation.[16] These points are open to interpretation in Plato himself, and do not find a precise philosophical solution in Philo either, who tries to clarify the issue by accepting the concept of creation,[17] yet as an event that happens *outside* of time. The relation between the creature and the creator is thus one of complete dependence and ontological subordination, with the spirit and the intelligible element having sway over the sensible and material one.[18]

Philo reworks the Platonic theory of ideas to describe the creative act of God as a realisation of a work of art inspired by a model and a paradigm.[19] Whereas ideas were uncreated in Plato, in Philo's view God creates the paradigms first, from which he eventually builds the sensible reality.[20] The paradigms are an expression of God's total perfection.[21] Yet they are different and absolutely other from him, since God is absolute simplicity, no composite, and absolute Being, while ideas already possess parts, are composite and become something else.[22] God's perfection, for this reason, does not entirely survive in the copy, not even in the first one of Adam and Eve. Because the copy lives in the domain of Becoming, it is negatively affected because of feminine nature and sinful desire.[23] Becoming, thus, assaults Being and undermines its paradigmatic perfection. The connection with monstrosity is made clear by Philo, for example when he interprets the giants as an image of the sons of the earth, in other words the carnal men, defeated by passion.[24]

---

[15] Ph. *Opif.* 17–18. See also M. Hadas-Label, 'Introduction', p. 98, and Runia (2003a) on the philosophical image of God as king and architect.
[16] See Dillon (1977), pp. 145 ff.
[17] Ph. *Opif.* 7–9.
[18] Ph. *Aet.* 1.
[19] The theory of ideas is the ground of Philo's philosophy and makes him the founder of Middle Platonism, according to Wolfson (1948) I, p. 200. See also Dillon (1977), p. 159 and *passim*, Belletti (1987). For Plato's idea as a model, see *Grg.* 503 d–e; *Cra.* 389 a–c; and above.
[20] Ph. *Opif.* 19.
[21] Ph. *Opif.* 134 ff.
[22] Ph. *Leg.* II.1–3.
[23] Ph. *Opif.* 139–40.
[24] Ph. *Gig.* 62 ff., with reference to *Gen.* 6.4. See Winston, Dillon (1983).

Pleasures and desire are also at the heart of a suggestive passage of *De agricultura* in which Philo discusses humans' status vis-à-vis his passions through the allegorical interpretation of Moses's prayer in *Gen.* 49.17 ff. and, more generally, of the 'prodigies and marvels' of the biblical figure of the snake.[25] Moses compares the judging faculty of the soul to the snake, 'a creature tortuous in its movements, of great intelligence, ready to shew fight, and most capable of defending itself against wrongful aggression'. When passions take over the human, though, the snake becomes 'a crawling thing with many a twist, powerless to raise itself upright, always prone, creeping after the good things of earth alone, making for the hiding-places afforded to it by the body, making its lair in each of the senses as in cavities or dug-outs, giving advice to a human being, athirst for the blood of anything better than itself, delighting to cause death by poisonous and painless bites'.[26] Opposed to Moses's, this is Eve's serpent, representing feminine pleasure and subjection to the earthly passions of flesh, those of an 'evil kind'.[27]

Other texts of Philo suggest that the sensible and material dimension is not good or evil in itself, but rather absolutely passive, and a receptacle that can become everything. This probably depends on the fact that the material used for the cosmos is not created by God. As absolute unformed matter, it is available to him. The creative power of God thus finds a substrate which is unable to fully and completely reflect the creator's goodness.[28] When left alone, for its part, matter tends to chaos, and would fall to ruin, were not for the great architect's organisation.[29] Thus the world reveals at once its beauty and the sublime skills of its maker, since all things are, in their beauty and regularity, precisely what they ought to be.[30]

To describe the dependency of the world from the creator, Philo makes use of the Platonic concept of the Monad and the Dyad. Monad and Dyad belong to the ancient conceptual tools of Greek philosophy, and have been employed to explain the multiplicity and changeability of things as a function

---

[25] Ph. *Agric.* 95 ff.

[26] Ph. *Agric.* 95 ff. On this passage, see Calabi (2003).

[27] Philo insists on the origin of evil in the body and the lower animal part of the human being. Leaving the physical body with death is thus a relief and a liberation, since one abandons the corpse to which the true self is bound (νεκρὸς σύνδετος). This image, as Courcelle (1966), p. 104 and *passim*, has underlined, is close to that of the Etruscan torment in which the victim is attached to a corpse and left to die. The body becomes a veritable figure of monstrosity which threatens the real life. For the body as a tomb in Plato see *Grg.* 493 a, 525 a; *Cra.* 400 b–c; and *supra*. See also Buffière (1956), pp. 460–6.

[28] See Runia (2003b), p. 590.

[29] Ph. *Opif.* 22. See M. Hadas-Lebel, 'Introduction', p. 70.

[30] Ph. *Prov.* I.70.

of an individual and unique principle (μονάς). Plato had maintained the existence of a Dyad as an intelligible matter upon which the One acts and to which it establishes limits.[31] The doctrine of the Dyad is further developed by Neo-Pythagoreanism and is connected with Middle and Neoplatonic thought. The main problem, in the Imperial age, becomes the mutual relation of Monad and Dyad, and the origin of the latter vis-à-vis the former. The Neo-Pythagorean concept of Dyad stresses its passive character, opposed to the activity of the Monad. Immanent and transcendent solutions are confronted in the attempt to explain how God and creation can be connected, by both saving God's transcendence and claiming its more or less direct intervention in creating and maintaining order.

According to Aetius, Xenocrates borrows Plato's concept of Monad and Dyad.[32] He envisages the One as father of the universe, and the Dyad as mother of the gods. This testimony stresses the collaborative and harmonious character of the two divine beings, underlining the fact that godly forces inhabit the corporeal world. Although connected to the material world, however, the divine cause's transcendence is discussed and differently interpreted. For example, Antiochus of Ascalon, possibly with a Stoic accent, insists on the immanence of the primal cause to the universe, and its necessarily material character.[33] On the contrary, strongly influenced by Neo-Pythagoreanism, Eudorus of Alexandria claims the existence of two main and opposed principles, one ordered, definite, knowable, male, numerically odd, right and light, the other disordered, undetermined, unknowable, female, numerically even, left and dark.[34] The relation between Monad and Dyad is thus dialectically interpreted by different authors. The strongest philosophical interpretation of the two principles yet is in Plutarch's *Moralia*, in which one can see monstrosity emerging at the heart of Middle Platonist metaphysics.

Plutarch's work has a strong religious connotation. Some of his major texts from the *Moralia* describe the nature of the divine as highly transcendent vis-à-vis the world. Far from being marked by a harmonious development, though,

---

[31] See Pl. *Phlb.* 26 e–30 e. See also Dillon (1977), 126 ff., on the Platonic origin of the doctrine of the Monad and Dyad in Middle and Neoplatonism.

[32] Xenocrates 213, in Senocrate e Ermodoro (2012), p. 237 (= *Placit.* I.7.30)

[33] Similarly to the Stoics, the concept of an immaterial cause is for him unintelligible. This aspect is crucial for Antiochus's metaphysics, and in my view it prevents him being considered a Middle Platonist. See also Dillon (1977), 81 ff. For Antiochus's physics see Cic. *Acad.* I.27 ff. and *Fin.* IV.36.

[34] Eudor.Acad. (= Mazzarelli [1985], 5, pp. 201–2 = Medioplatonici [2015], p. 81 ff.). Even Eudorus, though, can barely be considered a Platonist, as suggested by Dillon in Goulet, éd. (1989–) *ad loc.*

the relation between the worldly and the divine is ambiguously and threateningly conflictual, revealing a tension in which monstrosity plays a great part. Cosmogony is, in Plutarch's view, a passage from chaos to order rather than a proper act of creation, as it was for Philo. The demiurge, in this sense, has initially confronted a recalcitrant matter that pre-existed its formative action. The resistance of matter is never definitely overcome and becomes the ground for the perennial clash between good and evil.[35]

In *De E apud Delphos*, a theological treatise on the nature of the divine, Plutarch describes the ambiguous status of the divine: when it is Apollo it is incorruptible and immutable by nature, and yet when it is Dionysus it endures a diversification that transforms it into the world's Being. Apollo is the purest divinity and Dionysus is divinity's other face. God's unity is thus torn apart and dismembered, not only in an ontological duality, but also in a physical multiplicity that manifests itself in the world.[36] Plutarch clearly contrasts God's unity with the world's multiplicity by underlining the atemporal nature of the former, as well the purity of its being vis-à-vis the heteroclite nature of becoming, a real otherness (ἑτερότης).[37] Now, in the *De defectu oracolorum*, alterity is also said to be a principle of dissolution (διαιρετικόν), and thus opens up to a dangerous and ambiguous dialectic of generation and corruption that inhabits the very movement of the divine toward the world.[38]

This movement of generation and dissolution is far from harmonic and peaceful in Plutarch's view. Thus, it immediately becomes important, to him, to clarify that not only is God not responsible for it, but also that God himself prevents the total destruction into which the non-Being, by its nature, would irreparably collapse:

> [. . .] as for [God's] vagaries and transformations when he sends forth fire that sweeps his own self along with it, as they say, and again when he forces it down here and directs it upon the earth and sea and winds and living creatures, and, besides, the terrible things done both to living creatures and to growing vegetation – to such tales it is irreverent even to listen; [. . .] For, on the contrary, so far as he is in some way present in the world, by this his presence does he bind together its substance and prevail over its corporeal weakness, which tends toward dissolution.[39]

---

[35] On the conflictual nature of Plutarch's cosmogony see Babut (1969), p. 286 and *passim*.
[36] Plu. *Moralia. De E apud Delphos* 388 E–F. For the titles of Plutarch's *Moralia* I follow the list given in Plutarch (1927–2004), I, pp. xxxiv–xxxvii.
[37] Plu. *Moralia. De E apud Delphos* 393 A–C.
[38] Plu. *Moralia. De defectu oracolorum* 429 B–D.
[39] Plu. *Moralia. De E apud Delphos* 393 E.

The opposition between Being and non-Being is thus clearly claimed, as well as the innocent character of God, to transcend the lower life of the world. The solution that Plutarch and several other Platonists find to maintain both the active character of God and its lack of responsibility for the changeable mundane reality is to imagine intermediate creatures that operate on its behalf and directly intervene in nature. I will explore later how the theory of intermediate entities is affected by the idea of monstrosity. Suffice to say, here, that Plutarch's intermediate entities entertain a twofold activity with nature itself. Whereas God is never responsible for destruction, its agents definitely are, since their 'office is concerned with Nature in dissolution and generation [περὶ τὴν ἐν φθορᾷ καὶ γενέσει φύσιν]'.[40] Because the 'other' gods or demigods necessarily belong to the realm of multiplicity, one must assume that such a realm, even if only at its highest point, is indeed capable of generating and producing some reality, and not only of destroying it. At conceptual level, thus, the realm of multiplicity reveals the existence of a poietic faculty which is threateningly autonomous from God himself.

Such a poietic faculty of multiplicity surfaces in the *De defectu oracolorum*, when Plutarch openly makes use of the older theory of the Monad and the Dyad. The former gives ontological consistency to the latter. This is clear through the theory of numbers, for which the multiple exists, i.e. acquires an ontological consistency, only through the One and when it is grasped through unity; otherwise it collapses into chaos, indetermination and ultimately non-Being.[41] Multiplicity definitely shows a riotous nature, tending to subtract itself from the normative nature and ordering faculty of the One. Its resistance to being delimited by Unity 'throws all into confusion, and makes it to be without rhythm, bounds, or measure'.[42] Yet it makes it something, and not nothing. Plutarch's struggle is against the autonomous power of multiplicity, whose ontological consistency he intends to reduce to nothing, but which resists its own annihilation by showing the autonomous power to produce a world, however monstrously confused and chaotic.

Matter is moved by the evil cosmic soul.[43] The demiurge, according to Plato, pervades the world with justice. It is however a geometrical and not an arithmetical justice (i.e. not proportional to the thing's position in the scale of beings), which alludes not only to the diversity within the universe but also to the role and function that forms exert over matter.[44] Geometrical forms become, in Plutarch's reading of Plato's myth, the limit imposed upon unformed and unharmonious matter. From it, ordered forms were able to emerge, guided by a

---

[40] Plu. *Moralia. De E apud Delphos* 394 A.
[41] Plu. *Moralia. De defectu oraculorum* 429 A–B.
[42] Plu. *Moralia. De defectu oraculorum* 429 A–B.
[43] Plu. *Moralia. De animae procreatione in Timaeus* 1014 D–E, 1015 E.
[44] The argument of a geometrical justice appears also in Plot. III.3.5. See *infra*.

superior principle of reason. Matter, however, spontaneously fights to resist this process and to return to the initial indistinction, the primordial ἄπειρον, with monstrosity as a weapon against its geometrical shaping and regularisation.[45]

Plutarch is aware of the monstrous nature of matter's autonomous poietic power, and he explicitly deals with this idea in a topical passage of *De Iside et Osiride* in which the threat is embodied by the allegory of Typhoeus:

> [...] they have a legend that the soul of Osiris is everlasting and imperishable, but that his body Typhon oftentimes dismembers and causes to disappear, and that Isis wanders hither and yon in her search for it, and fits it together again; for that which really is and is perceptible and good is superior to destruction and change. The images from it with which the sensible and corporeal is impressed, and the relations, forms, and likeness which this takes upon itself, like impressions of seals in wax, are not permanently lasting, but disorder and disturbance overtakes them, being driven hither from the upper reaches, and fighting against Horus, whom Isis brings forth, beholden of all, as the image of the perceptible world. Therefore it is said that he is brought to trial by Typhon on the charge of illegitimacy, as not being pure nor uncontaminated like his father, reason unalloyed and unaffected of itself, but contaminated in his substance because of the corporeal element. He prevails, however, and wins the case when Hermes, that is to say Reason, testifies and points out that Nature, by undergoing changes of form with reference to the perceptible, duly brings about the creation of the world.[46]

Of extraordinary force and size, Typhoeus shows strength and determination in contending with the Olympians, and succeeds in temporarily subjugating Zeus himself. Such a strength, hyperbolically underlined by the literary sources, does not find an equivalent in the surviving visual documents, to the point that the iconography sometimes suggests a creature whose monstrosity is definitely not impressive, and which dangerously reflects the divinity that is about to strike him. Typhoeus is not absolute chaos, but rather a viable counterpart to Zeus himself.[47]

---

[45] Plu. *Moralia. Quaestiones convivales* VIII.2.
[46] Plu. *Moralia. De Iside et Osiride* 373 A–C.
[47] See O. Touchefeu-Meynier in LIMC, VIII.1, *sub voce*: 'En fait, notre T. n'est pas très impressionnant. Sans doute a-t-il des traits, somme tout habituels, de la monstruosité: l'hybridité, avec partois la présence de quelques serpents annexes [...], la duplication [...], et parfois la grand taille suggérée par la position verticale dressée [...] ou par la présence d'un Zeus plus petit [...]. Certes, les images ne pouvaient prétendre rivaliser avec les portraits hyperboliques de la litérature. On s'étonne cependant de ne pas retrouver pour notre anguipède des procédés dont le langage iconographique est, d'habitude, habile à tirer parti pour suggérer la sauvagerie, la force, l'agressivité: T. est le plus souvent soigneusement coiffé et vêtu [...] bien loin d'être agressif [...].'

This attitude seems reflected in Plutarch's use of the myth, in which the monster brings Horus to trial 'on the charge of illegitimacy'. The material and inferior principle defies the higher god on the ground of an illegitimate claim to perfection, and is defeated only by the intervention of Hermes, who claims the reasonable character of creation. Plutarch's compelling argument succeeds in bringing the myth to the level of a theologico-philosophical cosmogony, borrowed from, and rooted in, Platonism. This also emerges when Plutarch subsequently merges the myth of Typhoeus with that of Apollo's birth:

> The birth of Apollo from Isis and Osiris, while these gods were still in the womb of Rhea, has the allegorical meaning that before this world was made visible and its rough material was completely formed by Reason, it was put to the test by Nature and brought forth of itself the first creation imperfect. This is the reason why they say that this god was born in the darkness a cripple [ἀνάπηρος], and they call him the elder Horus; for there was then no world, but only an image and outline of a world to be. But this Horus is himself perfected and complete; but he has not done away completely with Typhon, but has taken away his activity and strength. Hence they say that at Kopto the statue of Horos holds in one hand the privy members of Typhon, and they relate a legend that Hermes cut out the sinews of Typhon, and used them as strings for his lyre, thereby instructing us that Reason adjusts the Universe and creates concord out of discordant elements, and that it does not destroy but only cripples the destructive force. Hence this is weak and inactive here, and combines with the susceptible and changeable elements and attaches itself to them, becoming the artificer of quakes and tremblings in the earth, and of droughts and tempestuous winds in the air, and of lightning-flashes and thunderbolts.[48]

Following the tradition, Horus itself is presented as twofold. The older one, as being spontaneously generated without waiting for the informing principle of Reason to properly act upon matter, and the newer one, as the accomplished and perfect creature, finally responding to the rational character transmitted to it from above. A strongly dualist interpretation of Platonism appears to inform this text, with the sharp opposition between the rational soul taming and informing the material substratum.[49] The world self-generated depends only on matter's activity. It is a misshapen attempt, a crippled being and a monstrous abortion. The echo of ancient cosmogonies, and of Empedocles' in particular, clearly resonates.

[48] Plu. *Moralia. De Iside et Osiride* 373 A–C.
[49] See Dillon (1977), pp. 26 and 207.

The destructive activity of Typhoeus and the reconstructive activity of Isis does not resemble a dialectic, but rather a proper and open conflict between two opposing gods. Compared to the dissolution brought about by multiplicity in *De E apud Delphos*, the material monster of *De Iside et Osiride* shows a more threatening capacity of building an alternative order, or at least a configuration of Being: crippled and chaotic, but an order nonetheless. Its ontological illegitimacy is decided only through force and deception in the myth, and its philosophical meaning is the sharp conflict between the principle of transcendence, embodied by reason, and that of immanence, embodied by monstrosity.[50]

Plutarch aims at a philosophical victory of transcendence and of the Platonic demiurgic principle over immanence and the exclusively material nature of the cause, shared by atomists and Stoics: Zeus comes out victorious over Typhoeus after all.[51] Yet, as in the myth, monstrosity is far from being defeated once and for all. Typhoeus is weak and emasculated, and yet the poietic faculty of reason comes into being only through ordering, from above, the monstrous creation, and not through its destruction. The reasonable world, in its perfection, is described as harmony created out of discordant elements, and Typhoeus's destructive force is not annihilated, but only crippled. This is the reason why tumultuous and tempestuous phenomena still happen on earth. Normality is full of residual monstrosity and, even worse in Plutarch's perspective, normality is nothing but the crippling of the destructive force, and indeed the monstrification of monstrosity itself.

Plutarch's dualist conception has a great influence on several Middle Platonists, such as Maximus of Tyrus. The material realm is, for Maximus, sharply opposed to the intelligible one. The latter, however, is also the origin and cause of everything beautiful and good one can find in the former.[52] Matter is however what binds humans to passionality, ruining the soul's freedom.

---

[50] See *contra* C. Froidefond in Plutarque (1972–93), V.2, p. 303, and Froidefond (1972), p. 66. In my view the powerful use of the myth testifies less to an Aristotelian attitude toward the rehabilitation of matter, as Froidefond claims, and more to a specifically Middle Platonic anxiety toward matter's claimed activity, at the same time autonomous and monstrous. Appropriately, Donini (1992b), p. 105 and *passim*, underlines that the 'rebel necessity' of matter surfaces more vividly in the texts of Plutarch in which, like in the *Quaestionum convivialium*, the physical explanation of phenomena becomes predominant and the rhetorical appeal to theocentrism does not offer any protective ground against the spontaneous manifestation of the material reality.

[51] On Plutarch's hostility to Stoic's immanentism see Babut (1969), pp. 462–3 and *passim*. See also Hershbell (1992a). On the importance of Plutarch's attitude for Neoplatonism see Zambon (2002).

[52] See Goulet, éd. (1989–) IV, pp. 324–48 and Soury (1942a).

Maximus makes use of monstrosity to explain this idea, and in particular of the old monstrous races, which he interprets allegorically:

> Poets tell us that there was once a Thessalian race that lived on Pelion and had strange bodies, with the rear quarters of horses, from the navel down. In such an uncouth conjunction as this it is surely entirely inevitable that human and bestial nature should pasture together: that such creatures should speak like men but feed like beasts, see like men but mate like beasts. Well done, poets and sons of poets, progenitors of an ancient and noble poetry; what a clear allegory you have given us of the bond that binds us to the pleasures! When bestial desires overwhelm the soul, they do not alter the external human appearance, but in the actions he performs they reveal their victim as a beast not a man. This is what is meant by the Centaurs, the Gorgons, the Chimaeras, Geryon, and Cecrops. Remove the desires of the belly, and you have removed the beast from man; remove the desires of the privy parts, and you have cut the beast in two! But as long as these desires live in a man and are nourished in him, and he defers to them and tends them, it is inevitable that it should be their impulses that dominate, and that his soul should speak with their accents.[53]

Maximus is undoubtedly echoing the influential image of the tripartite soul of R. IX, 588 c ff.[54] Even more interesting, I believe, is the radical form of monstrosity that Maximus conjures up. Whereas Plato's image has the function of explaining how the beast can and must be tamed, Maximus more drastically suggests that the only cure is to cut it in two pieces. No mediation is envisageable and no taming is possible for humans when passions take over the soul.

On this ground, Middle Platonism appears to converge with Pythagoreanism, and in particular with Numenius, who also claims the primacy of the incorporeal over the material and the causal dependency of the latter from the former. Like Plutarch and Philo, Numenius insists on the opposition between divine Being on the one hand and terrestrial Becoming, or non-Being, on the other. Together with Plutarch and Philo, Numenius embodies the highly religious approach to the Platonic discourse on divinity, and his thought comes close to Philo's Hellenic Judaism, explicitly claiming that Plato is Moses speaking Greek.[55]

Numenius, however, originally reworks the Pythagorean position about the negativity of matter and adapts it to the Platonic dialectic between

---

[53] Max. Tyr. XXXIII.8.
[54] See Puiggali (1978), pp. 429 ff, and *supra*.
[55] Numen. 8 (= Eus. PE XI.10.12–14).

the demiurge and its work. Along with its negative character, according to Chalcidius, Numenius insists on its necessary presence and on the benefic intervention of divinity:

> [. . .] God adorned matter with a magnificent strength and corrected her defects in every way, while not destroying them lest material nature perish entirely, nor permitting her to spread and expand in every direction. But, while nature stood fast and could thus be called away from a troublesome state to a favorable one and be transformed, by conjoining order to disordered confusion, limit to immoderation, and cultivation to filth, he converted her total state, illuminating and embellishing it. In short, Numenius denies and denies correctly that any condition of generated objects can be found anywhere exempt from defect: not in the arts of man, not in nature, not in the bodies of animals, nor indeed in trees and plants; not in fruits, not in the flow of air or in an expanse of water, nor even in the heaven itself. For everywhere it mingles itself with providence as if it were some stain of an inferior nature.[56]

God tames matter. He is also careful not to destroy it entirely, but keeps it in check, so to speak, by infusing order, measure and beauty where they are lacking.

The exigency of establishing a comfortable separation between God and the world returns, like a footprint, in all the major Middle and Neoplatonist philosophers. An interesting interpretation is offered, for example by Galen's teacher Alcinous (or Albinus).[57] Strongly influenced by Stoicism, and contrary to Atticus's attitude, Alcinous is open to the reconciliation of Aristotle's and Plato's thought. Although conceived as a handbook of Platonism, Alcinous's *Didaskalikos* is far from being a mere repetition of Plato's doctrine. It is probably the most coherent text of Middle Platonism on the nature of God. It nonetheless reveals the exigency of negotiating between transcendence and the presence of the divine in the world.

In book X, Alcinous develops a coherent treatise on the nature of God. He eminently ascribes goodness, beauty and perfection to God, thus claiming its separateness from the world which it inhabits and providentially rules.[58] The ambiguity that we have seen in Plutarch's writings, though, also emerges

---

[56] Numen. 52 (= Chalcid. *In Timaeum* 299). See also Dragona-Monachou (1994), pp. 44–76.
[57] On the difficult identification of this Middle Platonic author see in particular Goulet, éd. (1989–), *ad loc.*, Moraux (1973–84), II, pp. 441 ff., Dillon (1977), pp. 267–304, and Dillon, *Introduction*, in Alcinous (1993).
[58] Alcinous (1993), X.

in Alcinous. Notwithstanding his horror toward materialism, and thus his opposition to every physical interpretation of the divine inspired by Stoicism, Alcinous is in fact brought to recognise that matter is indeed necessary to the cosmos. Although it is the principle of everything that is chaotic, matter is still a principle, together with God and ideas.[59]

In Latin Middle Platonism, the principle of transcendence is more clearly argued, such as in Apuleius of Madauros.[60] In his *De deo Socratis*, Apuleius strongly claims the separation of the gods from the world[61] as well as their ineffable character.[62] Like Plutarch, but with an even stronger accent, he also claims, in the *De Platone*, the opposition between two essences, one eternal and truly existent, and the other created and mortal. The latter is entangled in Becoming, and thus like a shadow of the former.[63] Beaujeu has pointed out that the separation between God's substance and power is the truly original character of Apuleius's *De mundo*, the translation of the Pseudo-Aristotle's Περὶ κόσμου, in which God is father and saviour of the universe, and yet is not engaged in its production.[64] The transcendence of the divine is argued with an even stronger emphasis than in the original Greek text.[65]

Apuleius reworks the concept of archetypal ideas, from among which God selects his models to shape individual and concrete things.[66] Everything originates in matter, and yet initially in a chaotic form, which is eventually ordered by the demiurge.[67] The ambiguities that one can read in Plutarch surface again in Apuleius. Everything is composed from different elements, well balanced and harmonised to best imitate the model.[68] This resemblance, however, somehow threatens the model itself, questioning the purity and transcendence of the idea. The ability of the lower being to imitate the higher one indirectly implies the necessity for the higher one to somehow be *assimilated*. The original purity and transcendence of the paradigm is lost, vis-à-vis every concrete realisation. Apuleius gives an initial definition of ideas in *Plat.* 190, where one reads that

---

[59] See G. Invernizzi, 'Introduzione', in Invernizzi (1976).
[60] On Apuleius's philosophy see in particular Dillon (1977), pp. 312–27, and Gersh (1986), pp. 215–325.
[61] Apul. *Soc.* 123 and 128.
[62] Apul. *Soc.* 124.
[63] Apul. *Plat.* 193.
[64] Apul. *Mund.* 343. On the Περὶ κόσμου see *infra*.
[65] Published in Aristotle (1955). See also Moreschini (1978), p. 69, and Gersh (1986), pp. 273–9. This strong contrast, as Dragona-Monachou has underlined, intends to recover the original Platonic inspiration, following in particular *Lg.* X.
[66] Apul. *Plat.* 192–3.
[67] Apul. *Plat.* 194.
[68] Apul. *Mund.* 334.

they are *nulla specie nex qualitatis significatione distinctae* ('distinguished by no mark of species or quality'). As Beaujeu and many others have suggested, this is probably only a mistake of the copyist, since Apuleius cannot have assigned matter's characteristics to ideas.[69] Yet Apuleius does not think about ideas as God's thought, like Alcinous. Even if he cannot be such a poor Platonic philosopher, something emerges in his thought that reveals the ambivalence of the threatening relation between material things and their models.

Notwithstanding the strong claim for transcendence, and thus for God's purity, the ambiguity of the divine nature surfaces in one of the most philosophically inspired texts of Apuleius, namely the tale of Cupid and Psyche in the *Metamorphoses*.[70] The tale is inspired by Plato's theory of Love in *Phaedrus* 248 c–252 c. Although the allegorical reading of the tale is not philosophically straightforward, Eros fully maintains the traditional ambiguity of his character in Apuleius, according to a genealogy that can be traced back to archaic theogonies. Here, Eros is often born together with the Earth, and straight out of Chaos.[71] His paternity is uncertain, and he can be cunning, unmanageable and even cruel,[72] sublimely epitomised by Sappho's image of the bittersweet creature (γλυκύπικρον ὄρπετον).[73] Euripides' Phaedra considers Eros her master in the first Hippolytus.[74] The divine principle, in this philosophically complex text of the *Metamorphoses*, is far from pure. It is on the contrary exposed to the ambiguity that derives from its erotic contact with the earthly world of passion and desire.[75]

Middle Platonism develops an increasingly negative view of matter. This will appear as a problem to which Neoplatonism tries to find a solution. It is worthy to mention, here, that also the *Chaldean Oracles* and the *Corpus Hermeticum* contribute to this negative conception. The former explicilty talks about evil matter (κακῆς ὕλης), seen as an aggressive and demonic force, from which only the higher sphere of the Ethereal World is spared,[76] and opposed to '[. . .]

---

[69] Beaujeu in Apulée (1973), *commentaire, ad loc*. See also Moreschini (1978) who is more prudent.

[70] See O'Brien (2002) and Fletcher (2014).

[71] Hes. *Th.* 120 ff. and Hyg. *Fab.* prologue. See also F. I. Zeitlin, *Eros*, in Settis a cura di (1996–2002), I, pp. 369–430, and Brisson (2008, 2e ed.), p. 76. Plato, *Smp.* 178 b, believes the opposite.

[72] See Hornblower and Spaworth (2012, 4th ed), Roscher (1884–90), Grimal (1951), Grimal (1965), Gantz (1993) and LIMC, *sub voce*.

[73] Sapph. (= *PLF* fr. 130).

[74] Euripide (1927–2003), VIII.2, pp. 221–48.

[75] See Janoušek (2006), p. 33. For the tragic roots of the ambivalence within the divine, see Untersteiner (1955, 2a ed.), *passim*.

[76] *Orac.Chald.* 88.

the light-hating world, boisterous of matter, where there is murder, discord, foul odours, squalid illnesses, corruptions, and fluctuating works'.[77] The *Asclepius* simply states the inferiority of the concrete individuals to their model and form,[78] since only the latter is stable and pure, while the former are necessarily different from each other and constantly changing. The *Corpus Hermeticum* makes a direct connection with the idea of monstrosity: 'The vice of soul is ignorance. For the soul, when it is blind and discerns none of the things that are nor their nature nor the good, is shaken by the bodily passions, and the wretched thing becomes – in ignorance of itself – a slave to vile and monstrous bodies [ἀλλόκοτος and μοχθηρός], bearing the body like a burden, not ruling but being ruled. This is the vice of soul.'[79]

These ideas are also explored in the early Christian thought influenced by Platonism, often in contrast to Stoic Christianity, but sometimes with a sincretic and eclectic approach. Clement of Alexandria is a good representative of Christian Platonism. Although we do not possess his cosmogony, Clement closely follows Philo and considers the sensible world to be only a copy of the intellectual world, which serves as a model.[80]

Humans, Clement claims, are composed of a rational and irrational element. The soul and the body, whose distinction becomes so important for early Christian thinkers, are rooted in the basic elements of the Platonic analysis. The body is linked to the earth, while the soul stretches out toward God:

> [Man] is like, it appears to me, the Centaur, a Thessalian figment, compounded of a rational and irrational part, of soul and body. Well, the body tills the ground, and hastes to it; but the soul is raised to God: trained in the true philosophy, it speeds to its kindred above, turning away from the lusts of the body, and besides these, from toil and fear [. . .][81]

Along with the centaur, Clement also follows Philo's allegorical argument about the snake, which represents the blameful turn toward matter, i.e. pleasure and sin. However, the corporeal must not be condemned, Clement adds, drawing his material straight from the *Timaeus*, and explicitly writing against

---

[77] *Orac.Chald.* 134.
[78] Ps.Apul. *Ascl.* 35.
[79] *Corp.Herm.* X.8. Scott, in [Corpus Hermeticum] (1924–36), I, p. 193, has it as 'uncouth and noxious bodies'. Ἀλλόκοτος means of unusual nature, or form, strange, portentous (Pl. *Euthd.* 306 e), but also horrible and monstrous. Μοχθηρός is closer to wretched (Pl. *Phdr.* 268 e *Grg.* 504 e, *R.* 343 e), in a moral sense, knavish, rascally.
[80] Clem.Al. *Strom.* V.93.4 (= AA. VV. (1970), II, p. 467). Cf. Lilla (1971). See also the collection of excerpts known as the eighth *Stromateus* in Havrda (2016).
[81] Clem.Al. *Strom.* IV.3.9 (= AA. VV. (1970), II, p. 410).

the Gnostics. Instead, if we want to grasp the double constitution of humans, best understood through the metaphor of the centaur, one of the more complex ancient mythological monsters, we must understand the corporeal terms of human nature and its features.[82]

One of the most interesting questions raised by Christians vis-à-vis pagan Platonism is the problem of the negative in considering the development from the merely organising role of the demiurge to the creative role of God. We have seen how pagan middle Platonism interprets evil and monstrosity in relation to the inferior world and matter's behaviour in the hands of the powerful demiurge. What happens, however, when Christian Platonism abandons the idea of demiurgic activity in favour of the creation *ex-nihilo*? In the first half of the second century, Origen plays a fundamental role in clarifying the new dogma, thus opening up a new and problematic domain for the role and status of monstrosity. If God creates the universe, rather than merely organising its pre-existing matter, he becomes even more directly responsible for the presence of evil and, in particular, of monstrosity. What role does monstrosity have in a world created out of nothing according to the project and plan of an almighty crafter?

In his *On First Principles*, Origen explains that everything was always contained and comprised, forever, in the Wisdom of the Almighty:

> Since within [the] very subsistence of Wisdom was every capacity and form of the creation that would come to be – both of those things which exist primarily and of those which occur in consequence, having been formed beforehand and arranged by the power of foreknowledge regarding these very created things, which had been as it were outlined and prefigured in Wisdom herself – Wisdom herself says through Solomon that she was *created the beginning of the ways* of God, that is, containing within herself the beginning and the reasons and the species of the entire creation.[83]

Everything has already been formed, forever, in God's pre-science, and this includes monstrosity. In this case, every argument that explained monstrosity through a resistance of the lower reality to the higher informative principle or through a necessary corruption due to the dynamic involved in the process of actualisation of forms loses its validity. Monstrosity, like normality, has a role written since ever and forever in the original plan of creation. This argument, through several mediations and transformations, eventually constitutes

---

[82] See Henne (2016), pp. 205–7. On the fight against Gnosticism see Monfrinotti (2014), pp. 162 ff.
[83] Origenes *Princ.* I.2.2. See also I.4.4, II.3.6.

the foundation of preformationist explanation, whose theoretical core is thus Platonic and based on the new Christian vision of creation.

Let's go back to pagan Platonism and the question of love and desire, which is at the heart of the relation between the divine and the world.[84] When one moves from Middle to Neoplatonism, one sees a similar analysis, but also an interesting evolution. Love is an essential part of Plato's theory of the soul, and its function is to grasp Truth. Plotinus grants a much wider role to Love, making the erotic movement the ground of the procession of the One toward the intelligible world. Love is life's power, and yet it does not lose, for Plotinus, the ambiguous status that derives from its origin. The erotic desire is originally corporeal and a demon that lacks something and desires what it has not. Although its lack is only partial, since there would be no desire of goodness in the complete absence of goodness, it refers to matter and thus to the absolute evil and privation.[85]

Matter can be thus contrasted to the One (Ἕν), in which no duality can be found since it precedes the Dyad,[86] and about which one can hardly speak, given its ineffable nature beyond Being and essence. The One is the principle of everything, and yet it is nothing in particular, because of its absolute transcendence and anteriority.[87] However, through the ἕνωσις or oneness, Plotinus also intends the One as present, in a certain manner, in things.[88] With Philonic accent, Plotinus calls the world God's son, and a supremely beautiful one.[89] This relationship is even stronger than in Philo. The One is absolute Goodness and it functions as a model for every individual being. Beings derive their own consistency and unity from their conversion toward the One, following their own erotic desire for it.

No conflict or duality, thus, attains the ineffable and transcendent One from which everything else derives. Beyond the One, on the contrary, everything seems threatened by such a dependency of its ontological consistency from its desire. The desire reveals things' lack of and *thirst* for Being rather than the peaceful plenitude of a harmonic cosmos. It is a monstrous desire that things have for what they are not, and for their otherness.[90] This is the source of Plotinus's theory of evil:

> Is matter, then, also evil because it participates in good? Rather, because it lacks it; for this means that it does not have it. Anything which lacks

---

[84] On Plotinus see Wolters (1985). More broadly, on Eros in Plato and Neoplatonism, see Cornford (1952), pp. 80 ff., and Rist (1967b).
[85] Plot. III.5.9. See Laurent (1999), p. 93 and *infra*.
[86] Plot. V.1.5.
[87] Both positively, e.g. in V.6.3 and VI.9.3, and negatively, e.g. in III.8.10 and VI.8.8.
[88] Plot. VI.9 and V.4.1. On the One, see Meijer (1992).
[89] Plot. V.8.12. See Brehier (1928) and Guyot (1906).
[90] Laurent (1992), p. 92.

something, but has something else, might perhaps hold a middle position between good and evil, if there is more or less of a balance between its lack and its having; but that which has nothing because it is in want, or rather is want, must necessarily be evil. For this thing is not want of wealth but want of thought, want of virtue, of beauty, strength, shape, form, quality. Must it not then be ugly? Must it not be utterly vile, utterly evil?[91]

Evil does not have a proper autonomy and ontological consistency. It is a by-product of the good and a necessary outcome of its relative distance from the principle. It is privation (στέρεσις), whose function is to establish a monist metaphysics against the dualist tendency.[92]

As Plotinus makes clear, evil must be conceived in connection with the material element. Plotinus builds a new philosophical meaning for the term ἀπόστασις, previously used to talk about the distance between the earth and the stars[93] or about death as the abandonment of life.[94] Yet the ἀπόστασις is also the rebellion and the defection. Monstrosity thus has, for Plotinus, the diminishing character of a degradation, that of matter because of its distance from the One. It is also a threatening and rebellious abandonment that establishes the gap with being as an opposition based on absolute otherness.

Plotinus, however, makes an interesting attempt not to present the relation between matter and form in terms of an open conflict. This is the ground of one of the most original and difficult passages of the Enneads, strongly influenced by Stoicism. It is treatise 18, Ennnead V.7.7, in which Plotinus denies Plato's conclusion that ideas of individual things do not exist. They do exist, Plotinus argues, or else concrete individuals would be completely cut off from the intelligible world, with evidently deleterious ethical consequences. The treatise is the occasion, for Plotinus, to accept the Stoic theory of ἰδίως ποιόν, for which individual differences are essential and not accidental, and they depend on the form and not on matter or, in other words, on the individual's essence and not on its actual embodiment in the material and sensible world.[95]

---

[91] Plot. II.4.16, translation modified.
[92] See Kalligas (2014), pp. 223 ff. On Plotin's theory of evil see also Schröder (1916) and D. O'Meara's commentaire, in Plotin (1999).
[93] Archim. Aren. I.5, Xenoph., Vorsokr. 21 A 41a (= LM [8] XEN. D31, D35), Anaximen., Vorsokr. 13 A 7(6) (= LM [7] ANAXIMEN. P2, D3), X. Mem. IV.7.5, Arist. Cael. 291 b 8.
[94] E. Hipp 277.
[95] Although Brehier in Plotin (1991) underlines Plotinus's tendency toward Stoicism on this point, one should not forget that the quality is, for Stoics, strictly immanent to matter, while Neoplatonism intends it in an idealistic manner, with matter as subordinate and derived from form. See Reale (1975–80), IV, p. 571.

The distinction is important, and Plotinus makes use of the concept of monstrosity to denounce as absurd the hypothesis that he condemns, as well as to avoid the direct confrontation between form and matter:

> [...] how does it come about that children conceived in different seasons are different? Is it then the matter which makes the difference since it is not dominated in the same way [in the different seasons?] If that were so, then all the children but one would be contrary to nature. But if the difference is a great diversity of beauty, the form is not one. Only ugliness is to be attributed to the influence of matter, and even there the perfect forming principles are present, hidden but given as wholes.[96]

Plotinus faces an alternative: either matter alone is responsible for the actual individual characteristics, or they rather depend on forms and essences, which are specific in themselves to individual beings. According to the former hypothesis, all individuals but one would be monstrous. By denying this absurd hypothesis, Plotinus must admit that matter and forms are unequally responsible for those differences, and they are, so to speak, heterogeneous in their effects: matter alone is responsible for ugliness, while forms alone are responsible for beauty, in all its degrees and individual differences. Plotinus thus adapts the Stoic theory of individual qualities to his own theory of the powerless character of forms. The consequence is that, to avoid the absurd consequence of calling only one child normal and all other children παρὰ φύσιν, one would have to suspend judgement on individual features, which would paradoxically have to be considered beautiful vis-à-vis the form, but also ugly vis-à-vis matter.

Elsewhere, however, Plotinus presents forms and matter as directly confronting each other, within the homogeneous domain of the concrete and informed material reality.[97] Matter now has the character of an active and threatening resistance against the form:

> [...] evil is not in any sort of deficiency but in absolute deficiency; a thing which is only slightly deficient in good is not evil, for it can even be perfect on the level of its own nature. But when something is absolutely deficient – and this is matter – this is essential evil without any share in good [...]. But if one considers that things external to the soul are evils, illness or poverty for instance, how will one trace them back to the nature

---

[96] Plot. V.7.2. On the interpretation of this treatise and its difficult character see É. Brehier in Plotin (1999), V. pp. 119–22, L. Brisson et al. in Plotin (2003), pp. 405–7.

[97] On Plotinus's ambivalence regarding the active malignant character of matter see also Brehier (1928), p. 205.

of matter? Illness is defect and excess of material bodies which do not keep order and measure; ugliness is matter not mastered by form; poverty is lack and deprivation of things which we need because of the matter with which we are coupled, whose very nature is to be need.[98]

Plotinus's attempt is to relegate evil and monstrosity to the absolute non-Being. The language of participation is employed to explain the relative degrees of imperfection of actual things. Negativity, thus, is always relative insofar as it is embodied, and it is absolute only when taken in itself. In itself, however, it does not have ontological consistency. Indeed, evil is *something* precisely and only *because* of its embodiment and of the form's incapacity to dominate matter.[99] One is able to partially represent ugliness as a defect and an imperfect actualisation of the form. How does one, however, represent what is completely formless? Such a complete lack of form, I would call absolute monstrosity, which can only be thought through a complete negation, a void of forms that leaves space for matter's unchained power:

> [. . .] when for instance we see an ugly face in matter, because the formative principle in it has not got the better of the matter so as to hide its ugliness, we picture it to ourselves as ugly because it falls short of the form. But how do we know what has absolutely no part in form? By absolutely taking away all form, we call that in which there is no form matter; in the process of taking away all form we apprehend formlessness in ourselves, if we propose to look at matter.[100]

As we have seen above, Plato himself suggests that matter, uncreated by the demiurge, resists its information. I think, however, that Plotinus's attempt to frame this concept within a strict monism reveals the deep influence of the Aristotelian concept of matter's resistance to its formal and final cause, which is precisely the ground of his theory of monstrosity as something's failure to realise its own teleology.[101]

---

[98] Plot. I.8.5. See Kalligas (2014), *ad loc.*
[99] See also Plot. VI.1.9 and Laurent (1992), pp. 94 ff.
[100] Plot. I.8.9. See also Rist (1967a), pp. 127–8 and Plot. II.4.16: 'Is matter, then, the same thing as otherness? No, rather it is the same thing as the part of otherness which is opposed to the things which in the full and proper sense exist, that is to say rational and formative principles. [. . .] that which is has nothing because it is in want, or rather is want, must necessarily be evil. For this thing is not want of wealth but want of thought, want of virtue, of beauty, strength, shape, form, quality. Must it not be ugly? Must it not be utterly vile, utterly evil?'
[101] See above. On Plotinus's theory of matter's resistance see also IV.4.38.

The active threat represented by matter in Plotinus's universe surfaces in the treatise on evil. Matter undoubtedly has some power. It is not only a negative power of resistance, though. It is now a destructive power, or rather a contaminating and polluting one, namely the capacity to affect the forms from which it receives its ontological consistency. Forms are thus justified or absolved, that is to say they are not responsible for misshapes and monstrosities. Yet they are also incapable, in Aristotelian terms, of fully accomplishing their informative task. Forms necessarily and consistently lose in their struggle with matter:

> The forms in matter are not the same as they would be if they were by themselves; they are formative forces immanent in matter, corrupted in matter and infected with its nature. [. . .] For matter masters what is imaged in it and corrupts and destroys it by applying its own nature which is contrary to form, not bringing cold to hot but putting its own formlessness to the form of heat and its shapelessness to the shape and its excess and defect to that which is measured, till it has made the form belong to matter and no longer to itself [. . .].[102]

This is the price that Plotinus has to pay for his strict monism. If it is true that evil is always touched by goodness in a certain manner, and thus made relative and subordinate, the contrary is also true: goodness is necessarily touched and contaminated by evil. In defining evil as lacking measure (ἄμετρος), unlimited (ἄπειρος) and formless (ἀνείδεος), the measure, the limit and the form themselves are touched and polluted by such a power of negativity. By limiting evil, form and goodness are also reciprocally limited.[103]

Evil, as Whittaker has argued, comes from matter when it has reached its ultimate term, ἔσχατος, and it cannot produce anything good or beautiful any more. Matter thus drags the form far from its origin and its purity. And yet this is the ambiguous and ambivalent conclusion that affects Plotinus's Neoplatonism: matter is also necessary, because without it, there would not be any goodness in general, nor anything good in particular.[104] Evil and monstrosity, as in Aristotle, become threateningly necessary to goodness and normality.

---

[102] Plot. I.8.8. Kalligas (2014), p. 235, also reads this passage as the confirmation that matter could not be completely passive, without being at the same time the origin of evil. See also Plot. I.8.14, and Laurent (1992), pp. 89–90, who correctly speaks about the 'danger que la radicale impuissance représente'.

[103] See the clear explanation of De Capitani (1985), with specific reference to Plot. I.8.7.

[104] Whittaker (1928, 2nd ed.), p. 81. See also Kalligas (2014), with specific reference to the ἔσχατον and to Plot. I.7.7.

This is the source of chaos, but also of life, and without this source, there would be only the solitude and silence of the One.[105]

Although ambivalent and sometimes ambiguous, Plotinus's monism is the attempt to overcome the ambiguities implicitly conveyed by a dualism of Neo-Pythagorean inspiration, which eventually develops in Gnosticism, one of the strongest adversaries of Platonism.[106] Plotinus's monism is of paramount importance both in the development of Platonism in the Imperial age, and its relationship with Christianity. Two fundamental dogmas of Christianity, namely creationism and the resurrection of the flesh, are unacceptable for those who, like several Middle Platonist philosophers, assign autonomy to the principle of Evil. This is one of the main causes of the conflict between Middle Platonists like Porphyry and Celsus, and Christians like Origen. Overcoming dualism, Plotinus makes monism the ground for a possible reconciliation of Platonism and Christianity, which is eventually accomplished by Eusebius and Augustine.[107]

Plotinus's pupil, Porphyry, also reveals in his thought the tension between monism and dualism, and makes monstrosity play an interesting role in the analysis of the divine. Porphyry refers to the Hebrew God as αὐτογένετος, self-generated.[108] Only an apophatic description of it can be given, since human words cannot explain its complete autonomy and oneness, at the origin of everything.[109] For Porphyry, however, ineffable is far from also meaning almighty, as in the Judeo-Christian tradition. In his criticism, Porphyry makes use of the concept of monstrosity to denounce Christian lies, and in particular the concept of a god that would be able to make anything, for example that the past did not happen or that two plus two could make anything different from four.[110]

---

[105] See J. M. Rist, 'The Problem of Otherness in the Enneads', in AA. VV. (1971), p. 81: 'The metaphysical explanation which Plotinus offers of the otherness present in the intelligible world, and at all subsequent levels of the cosmos, is in terms of motion. Motion is defined by Aristotle as an incomplete activity, and it is incomplete in so far as it has not attained its end. Thus it is natural for Plotinus to associate motion closely with some kind of desire or striving; and it is of course a mark of all levels of reality below the One that they are striving to return to their source. If there was no otherness present in things, Plotinus argues, we should have the stillness and silence of the One [V.1.4.38–9]. Without otherness there is no motion. And motion involves lacking.'

[106] See Rist (1965), Barra (1972), De Capitani (1985). *Contra* Dillon (1977), p. 45 and *passim*.

[107] Like Origen, Plotinus was a disciple of Ammonius Saccas in Alexandria. See Gilson (1969, 2e ed.).

[108] Porph. *De philosophia ex oraculis haurienda* 324 F (= Eus. PE IX.10.3–5; XIV.10.5).

[109] Porph. *De philosophia ex oraculis haurienda* 325 F (= *Theos.* 173.17–174.22).

[110] Porph. *Chr.* 89 and 90 a (= Mac.Magn. IV.6–7) on the monstrous falsity of the idea that the heavens will be subject to the final judgement. See also *Chr.* 94 (= Mac.Magn. IV.24), against god's omnipotence.

From Plotinus's henology, Porphyry draws the idea of a duality that proceeds from, and is absorbed by, the unity. This idea is common to Indian philosophy, and reveals an explicit syncretism in Porphyry's interest in Eastern thought. In a fragment on his work on the River Styx preserved by Stobaeus, Porphyry introduces the image of a statue that represents Shiva as lord of the universe.[111] Quoting the Syriac Gnostic Bardaisan, Porphyry describes the statue as an androgyne being, on which a complete cosmology would be written. Through the intermingling of the opposites, one can grasp the complex relation between unity and duality.[112] The opposites coincide in the divine totality, one and undifferentiated. It is the monstrous androgyne that sublimely conveys this idea. The hermaphrodite becomes in Porphyry the paradigm of an undifferentiated state that precedes the individual classifications of beings that we experience in the visible world. The divine represented by the statue is total and monstrous, possibly total *because* monstrous. If this is the case, not only does monstrosity precede normality; it becomes in some sense its origin and its destiny, in an indistinction that does not frighten anymore, but rather seduces for its potentiality.[113]

Porphyry also joins the Neoplatonic denunciation of matter as evil. In the *Sentences*, he poetically tries to provide the full range of ambiguous characterisation of matter vis-à-vis forms:

> According to the ancient sages such are the properties of matter. Matter is incorporeal because it differs from bodies. Matter is not lifeless, because it is neither intelligence, nor soul, nor anything that lives by itself. It is formless, variable, infinite, impotent; consequently, matter cannot be existence, but

---

[111] Porph. *De Styge* 376 F (= Stob. I.3.56 = Porfirio (2006), fr. 7.25–77).

[112] See C. Castelletti, 'Introduzione', in Porfirio (2006), pp. 69 ff., and Brisson (1997). For the Platonic origin of the theme of androgyny see *Smp.* 189 d–193 d, and *supra*. See also O'Flaherty (1980).

[113] The ambivalence of the androgyne in Middle Platonism is already present in Philo, for whom sexuality represents both the moment of creation and the origin of sin. See Baer (1970). Paradoxographers are also interested in the androgyne and its ambivalent nature. The androgyne, along with the ghost, is the subject of one of the most famous tales of Phlegon of Tralles, a paradoxographer with an acutely neoplatonist sensibility. At the beginning of his *Book of Marvels*, Phlegon reports a child born in strange circumstances among the Aitolians. The child exhibits male and female genitals 'that differed amazingly in their nature'. The amazingly discordant nature of the creature reflects itself in the ambivalent role she plays in this intricate story: first she is claimed by the ghost of Polykritos, her deceased father, whose apparent intent is to save her from being burned by the community. The ghost, however, devours the child, sparing only her head, which prophesies a bloody war between the Aitolians and the Akarnanians. A monstrous androgyne and a ghost violently break socially accepted rules and impose an obscure outcome, which is ultimately beneficial for the community, as the prophecy allows it to prepare for the coming war. See Phleg. *Book of Marvels* II (= FGH 257 F 36.II).

nonentity. Of course it is not nonentity in the same way that movement is nonentity; matter is nonentity really. It is an image and a phantom of extension, because it is the primary substrate of extension. It is impotence, and the desire for existence. The only reason that it persists is not rest [but change]; it always seems to contain contraries, the great and small, the less and more, lack and excess. It is always 'becoming', without ever persisting in its condition, or being able to come out of it. Matter is the lack of all existence and, consequently, what matter seems to be is a deception. If, for instance, matter seems to be large, it really is small; like a mere phantom, it escapes and dissipates into nonentity, not by any change of place, but by its lack of reality. Consequently, the substrate of the images in matter consists of a lower image. That in which objects present appearances that differ according to their positions is a mirror, a mirror that seems crowded, though it possesses nothing, and which yet seems to be everything.[114]

Porphyry closely follows his teacher here, underlining however the dualist conception of the universe, whose beings exist between the One, above, and matter, below.

In Augustine, we find a similar degree of complexity regarding the concept and role of matter and the causal relation between God and the created universe. In the *Confessions*, Augustine explains how, initially, he thought of matter and its imperfection vis-à-vis the perfection of other forms. Matter, for Augustine, embodied the horrible status of an absolute monstrosity:

I used to think of [matter] as having countless and varied shapes, and therefore I was not thinking about matter at all. My mind envisaged foul and horrible forms nevertheless. I used to use the word formless not for that which lacked form but for that which had a form such that, if it had appeared, my mind would have experienced revulsion from its extraordinary and bizarre shape, and my human weakness would have been plunged into confusion. But the picture I had in my mind was not the privation of all form, but that which is relatively formless by comparison with more beautiful shapes. True reasoning convinced me that I should wholly subtract all remnants of every kind of form if I wished to conceive the absolutely formless. I could not achieve this. I found it easier to suppose something deprived of all form and nothingness, neither endowed with form nor nothing, but formless and so almost nothing.[115]

---

[114] Porh. *Sent.* 20 (= 10. (7) in [Porphyry] (1988), pp. 36–7).
[115] Aug. *Confessiones* XII.6.6. Chadwick mentions, in the footnote, a reference to Simp. in *Epict.* 34 for which Mani's prince of darkness has five shapes: lion's head, eagle's shoulder, serpent's stomach, fish's tail, demon's feet.

In the retrospective struggle to conceptualise matter and overcome the illusions of Gnosticism, Augustine conveys a complex idea of a threatening monstrosity. Such an idea, however, is soon encompassed by an inclusive approach that extends God's power and generosity to the whole creation, including its lowest and most monstrous beings. Formed and unformed beings, in Augustine's language, reveal God's work across the spectrum, from high to low, according to an idea of Platonic gradation, process, and emanation.[116] Forms are located above us, as explained in *On the Trinity*, because they are immutable, and offered to us so we can judge the sensible reality.[117] The ideal forms are the ground of our knowledge and, in particular, the form of goodness is what lets us us judge whether an individual thing is also good.[118] God, in this theological framework, is goodness itself, and all other creatures are good only by participation.[119]

God is also the only and unique creator. Any and every other creature, even when it produces something, can do so only by the will of the Almighty. Inferior creatures thus produce other individuals, more or less good, more or less normal or monstrous, by developing seeds that already exist, visible or hidden, in nature itself.[120] Demons also make use of seeds to produce and act. These seminal reasons have been implanted by God in nature. The origin of everything is in them, and production occurs when all the necessary conditions are present. There is an interesting resemblance, in this passage, to creatures that are born from hidden seeds and are unable to develop completely. Augustine is keen to avoid any Aristotelian tone that might suggest a spontaneous failure of the production process: God is and remains the creator. Even when Jacob artificially produces his sheep, it is God who is responsible for the outcome.[121]

Nature is not the cause, Augustine repeats, no matter what Pliny and Cicero claim.[122] God is the supreme cause, and this idea is so important that it makes the whole Aristotelian theory of causality an oddity to be forgotten: 'every cause is efficient, everything efficient is greater than that which is produced, and nothing is greater than God's will. Therefore [God's will] has no cause to be sought after.' *Omnis causa efficiens est* is thus the only divine causality a Christian need contemplate.[123]

---

[116] See e.g. Aug. *Confessiones* XIII.2.2.
[117] Aug. *De trinitate* XII.2.2.
[118] Aug. *De trinitate* VIII.3.4.
[119] Aug. *De trinitate* VIII.3.4–5.
[120] Cf. Aug. *De trinitate* III.8.13 and III.9.18.
[121] Aug. *De trinitate* III.8.15.
[122] Aug. *De trinitate* III.2 as well as *Ciu.* XXI.
[123] Aug. *Diuersis quaestionibus* 28.

Seminal reasons are in nature, as they were for the Stoics, but they are also directly in God. As we have seen, Stoicism already bends toward a certain transcendence of the divine principle, but Augustine exploits the conceptual tools offered by Neoplatonism to push divine transcendence much further. As for the Stoics, Augustine's seminal reasons function as legal boundaries and as normative principles of individual phenomena.[124] In *De Genesis ad litteram*, Augustine explains:

> All the normal course of nature is subject to its own natural laws. According to these all living creatures have their particular, determinate inclinations . . . and also the elements of non-living material things have their determinate qualities and forces, in virtue of which they function as they do and develop as they do, and not in some other way. From these primordial principles everything that comes about emerges in its own time in the due course of events, and having come to its end passes away, each according to its nature.[125]

Against the Stoics, however, one must recognise that efficient causes are not just material. God, Augustine explains, does not act as a material cause, but as a will.[126] Transcendence is thus preserved, allowing the explanation not only of ordinary and normal phenomena, but also of rare and unique events, including miracles and the birth of monstrosities. Because of their direct origin in God, seminal reasons ambiguously explain both normality and exceptions, encompassing everything under nature, all of which is the direct creation of the almighty God. God's power is absolute, and revealed not by inconstancy, but by the wisdom that characterises his work: *Neque enim potentia temeraria, sed sapientiae uirtute omnipotens est.*[127]

Transcendence is also at the heart of Proclus's consideration of the divine, together with several other attributes such as immutability, self-sufficiency, imperturbability, simplicity, truth, wisdom, and beauty, that makes gods' nature of the utmost perfection.[128] Time and Being are posterior to, and dependent on, the divine. Proclus's philosophy also revolves around the One and the concept of henology, with the main preoccupation of absolving the divine from evil and denying evil's existence, certainly in the higher spheres, but in

---

[124] Not, however, as Lucretian *foedera naturae*. See, *contra*, Bouton-Toubolic (2004), pp. 192 ff.
[125] Aug. *Gen.ad Litt* IX.17.32.
[126] See *Causa*, in Mayer (1986–), I.
[127] Aug. *Gen.ad Litt* IX.17.32. See also *Creatio, creator, creatura*, in Mayer (1986–), I, and, again, Bouton-Toubolic (2004), pp. 192 ff. See also Morgan (1984), pp. 295 ff.
[128] Procl. *Theol.Plat.* I.19–24; II.2 and *passim*.

a certain manner in the sensible world as well.[129] Proclus's major concern is in fact to avoid dualism. He thus connects with the Plotinian effort to establish a solid monism, going however much beyond Plotinus, whom he criticises precisely for having granted a too broad space to negativity as a principle. In *De malorum subsistentia*, Proclus's attempt is to deny any consistency to the dualist hypothesis, and yet he also rejects the idea that evil comes, in any conceivable form, from the divine.[130] The divine and the mundane thus entertain a hierarchical relation, in which evil is not only subordinated to, but also functional to, and tamed by, the higher goodness:

> [...] blessed and truly happy are those who say that evil things, too, are adorned by the gods, and that the unlimitedness of evil things is measured and their darkness bounded by them, insofar as evils, too, receive a portion of the good and are allotted the power to exist. These people have called this cause by which evils, too, are adorned and ordered the fount of evils, not in that it were the mother that gives birth to them – for it is inconceivable that the first causes of beings would be the principle[s] of the generation of evils – but as providing them with the limit and end, and as illuminating their darkness by its own light. Indeed, for evils, too, the unlimited is due to partial causes, and limit to universal causes.[131]

Good is not the mother of evil, but its keeper, insofar as evil is tamed and bounded by the divine, which provides it with a limit and a reason for existence in the whole economy of the universe. The whole treatise *De malorum subsistentia* is a critique of Plotinus *Ennead* I.8. Against it, Proclus argues that no absolute evil exists, symmetrical to the absolute good, as Plotinus claims. Not one Evil, but only evils exist, as the title's plural already indicates. Evils do not collectively form anything consistent or positive in themselves. They are scattered throughout the existence as a plural heterogeneity, whose explanation can only be given for each individual case. The concept of monstrosity itself could not have any consistency in Proclus's system, since every monster would be a singular and individual case with no link to other monsters and no connection with anything but itself:

> By no means should we posit one cause that is a unique, *per se* cause of evils. For if there is one cause of good things, there are many causes of evils, and not one single cause. If all good things are commensurate with,

---

[129] See Procl. *De malorum subsistentia* 11.
[130] Procl. *De malorum subsistentia* 31.8–20.
[131] Procl. *De malorum subsistentia* 41.17–24.

similar to, and friendly with one another, with evils it is the complete opposite: neither among themselves nor in relation to good beings do they have a common measure. [. . .] we have to posit not one cause of evils, but a multitude of causes, some for souls, others for bodies, and examine evil from these causes and in these causes. [. . .] For what monad or what boundary or what eternal principle could there be for evils, the very being of which, down to the level of individual beings, is naturally defined by dissimilitude and indefiniteness? The whole, on the contrary, is everywhere without badness.[132]

Proclus's powerful strategy is to demote evil and deprive it of any ontological consistency. Evil and monstrous individuals have only an individual consistency and a singular explanation that prevents them from representing any threat to the only Monad from which all goodness comes.[133]

On this basis, Proclus is also able to move beyond Plotinus and, somehow, beyond Plato and much of the Middle and Neoplatonic views, on the negative status assigned to matter. In *De malorum subsistentia* 27.7–14 a dualist and conflictual vision of matter seems to arise, whereby it is good when the rational principle is in control of matter, and it is contrariwise bad when the latter gains control and autonomy: darkness, deformity, powerlessness and lack of order are the outcomes of such a situation.[134] This confrontation, though, is undermined in the rest of the treatise, and especially in 36, in which matter remains a dysteleological principle, and yet its necessity acquires the status of a third principle, next to good and evil. Whereas for Plotinus matter is negative *and yet* necessary, Proclus argues against him that matter is necessary *and thus* not negative:

[. . .] there is another, a third nature, that is neither simply good nor evil, but necessary. Indeed, evil leads away from the good and flees from its nature; but the necessary is everything it is for the sake of the good, and it has a relation to the good. And any generation that befalls the necessary, happens because of the good. If then matter exists for the sake of generation, and if

---

[132] Procl. *De malorum subsistentia* 47.1–18. See also 37.7–25: 'And in general, it is not true that evil exists on its own anywhere, for there is no unmixed evil, no primary evil. For if evil were contrary to the good in all respects, then, given the fact that the good that is on its own and primary precedes the good in other things, evil, too, has to be twofold: evil itself, and evil in something else. [. . .] nothing is contrary to the primary good, and neither to all things that participate in it, but there is only contrariety to things whose participation is not immutable.'
[133] See also O'Meara, *Introduction*, in Plotin (1999), p. 32.
[134] Procl. *De malorum subsistentia* 27.

no other nature exists for the sake of matter in such a way that we could call it the goal or the good, then we must say that matter is necessary to generation, that it is not evil and that it is produced by divinity as necessary, and that it is necessary for the forms that are incapable of being established in themselves.[135]

Matter's neutrality is thus the solution to overcome dualism, but also the consequence of a too rigid monism, that is to say to hold the Monad responsible for, and name it as the source of, evil and monstrosities. Proclus's thought is the attempt, within Platonism, to tame abnormalities and monstrosities by individualising them and, as such, reintroducing them within a harmonious vision of the emanative being as well as of providence.

The world, however, is objectively full of evils and monstrosities. Their origin and function become a major preoccupation in the development of Middle and Neoplatonism. The questions of the nature of the divine and the ontology of evil are thus coupled with the search for an explanation of how the divine actually communicates with and ultimately takes care of the material world. Early Platonism had offered an explanation based on the theory of demons as intermediate agents. This solution is thoroughly explored, and originally reworked, by Middle and Neoplatonist philosophers as well as early Christian thinkers.

Demons

The rediscovery of divine transcendence poses the question of God's nature and its relation with the world. The Stoics offer the solution of a divinity intended as an acting logos, material and wholly immanent to the world. God permeates the world in the Stoic system, without any mediation. Moving away from, and radically condemning, Stoic immanentism, Middle and Neoplatonism have thus a major problem to solve. They have to explain how a transcendent God communicates with the world. The more God is conceived as transcendental, the more it needs an intermediate reality that allows communication between the divine and the earthly domain. A further question emerges from this problematic. Middle and Neoplatonism intends to maintain God's direct and benevolent intervention in the world, and yet discharge it of any responsibility for creating evil and even for being in contact, in whatever manner, with the lower nature.

---

[135] Procl. *De malorum subsistentia* 36.15–23. See also 33 and 37.1–7, as well as Whittaker (1928, 2nd ed.), p. 234.

The ancient idea of demons as intermediate creatures between the divine and the earthly domain responds to this twofold problematic.[136] The discourse on demons testifies to a dynamic circulation of ideas between philosophy and popular culture that is far from being unidirectional. Greek philosophy is certainly influenced, especially during the Imperial age, by Eastern philosophical and religious doctrines. It also receives, however, ideas rooted in popular religion and superstition, concerning the existence of immaterial creatures above humans. The Orphic origin of the theme of demons attests to the eternal conflict between good and evil. The monstrous nature of demons emerges from one of the oldest feminine mythological characters, the Κῆρες.[137] Sometimes a goddess, sometimes the immanent power of an individual, the Κήρ has an ambiguous status. Daughter of the Night in Hesiod's *Theogony*,[138] the lurid creature flies over the Homeric battlefield, with its black wings, sharp teeth and long nails, tearing apart corpses, drinking their blood and transporting the dead to Hades.[139] Plato has it as a literary reminiscence, close to the Harpies, plaguing and deadly spirits of corruption.[140]

Homer speaks of δαίμονες for the divine characters, while in Hesiod 'demon' already has the specific meaning of 'divine spirit'.[141] The idea of a protecting soul develops into the more specific personal demon, like the one that inspires Socrates according to Plato's account. The εὐδαίμον and κακοδαίμων introduce the idea of being guided by a benign creature or, conversely, tormented by an evil genius.

Plato distinguishes three kind of demons: the guardian (*Phd.* 107 d–8 c), the demon-soul (*Ti.* 40 d–41) and the semi-god (*Smp.* 202 ff.). This last text is possibly the most influential, and the starting point of every following version on the role of demons.[142] Stoics too grant the existence of demons, as beings linked to humans by συμπάθεια and superior to them. Stoics, however, are less interested in the intermediate role that demons can play between humans and the higher divine sphere. This explains the limited space devoted to demonology

---

[136] On the δαίμων see above and Hild (1881), Buffière (1956), pp. 521–31, Untersteiner (1972, 2a ed.), pp. 110 ff., Winkler-Horaček (2015).

[137] See Daremberg, Saglio éds. (1877–1919), *sub voce*, Roscher (1884–90), Rohde (1894), Grimal (1951), Grimal (1965), Chantraine (1968–80) and LIMC, *sub voce*, Gantz (1993) and Shapiro (1993), *passim*.

[138] Hes. *Th.* 211, and *Sc.* 156–60, 248–57.

[139] *Il.* I.228 and *passim*, *Od.* XVII.547. See Pârvulescu (1968).

[140] Pl. *Lg.* XI, 937 d. See also Beaujeu, *Commentaire*, in Apulée (1973).

[141] Hes. *Th.* 991.

[142] See also *Cra.* 397 e–398 c for the etymology of the name. On demons in Plato, see also F. Solmsen, *Hesiodic Motifs in Plato*, in AA. VV. (1962), pp. 173–211. A wider analysis in Béchec (2013).

in Latin culture dominated by Stoicism, until the Middle and Neoplatonic renaissance of the Imperial age. Furthermore, Stoics conceive demons mainly as entities charged by gods to punish wicked and unjust humans.[143]

What is relevant about demons for our research on monstrosity is not only their function of a bond (σύνδεσμος) between the divine and the human, i.e. what keeps God's transcendence intact, but also the explanation of their intervention in the world. It is more specifically their nature and action, the role they perform and the impact that they have, especially on humans, in terms of good and evil. Very early on, in fact, their status has been questioned, and philosophers have asked whether demons are always and necessarily good, or whether they can also be wicked and evil. Euripides already hesitates on the ambiguous nature of divine intervention, about which doubts legitimately arise when justice fails to establish itself. 'If gods do anything shameful, they are not gods,' says Bellerophon.[144] What then are demons?[145] Plato's demons seem to be unambiguously positive and yet, when Plutarch speaks about malignant demons, he quotes *Lg.* X, 896–8, an influential text for those who believe in their evil nature: 'Must we [. . .] necessarily agree,' asks the Athenian stranger, 'that soul is the cause of good and bad, beautiful and ugly [αἰσχρός], just and unjust, and all the opposites, if we are to assume it to be the cause of all things?' And this, the Athenian continues, is due to several souls, 'no less than two – the beneficent soul and that which is capable of effecting results of the opposite kind'.[146] Middle and Neoplatonism are caught in this tension, between a benevolent origin – at least philosophically speaking – of demons, and their evolution in the sense of wicked geniuses that torment men and are responsible for evil in the world.

The demon becomes sometimes a real figure of monstrosity, whose function is nonetheless strategic in explaining the metaphysical structure of the world and its dependence on the divine. Philo of Alexandria recognises the exigency of a mediating reality between God and the world.[147] He attributes this function to the mediating logos. Without it, in Philo's view, God would immediately be responsible for everything happening in the earthly region, as it is for the Stoics. The logos's mediating function, thus, is to be the cause of natural reality, less perfect than God itself, and thus at the origin of evil. Evil exists because everything depends on God, and yet not without the logos's mediation.[148] The

---

[143] *SVF* II.1101–5.
[144] E. *Bellerophon* (= Euripides (1995) Fr. 282).
[145] See also *Hec.* 489–91, and Magris (1986), p. 624.
[146] *Lg.* X.896 e. On this passage see Cherniss (1954).
[147] Ph. *Opif.* 25.
[148] See Brehier (1950), p. 130.

term logos is explicitly borrowed from Stoicism, but the meaning is different because Philo intends to claim divine transcendence, while at the same time granting God's benevolent intervention in its creation. Philo's logos, thus, operates in a Platonic way like a τομεύς, a divider or a carver, but also in an Aristotelian way, as a δύναμις which needs to be actualised.[149] This is precisely the notion that Aristotle employs to speak about monstrosity and imperfection in nature. Philo makes use of this genealogy to explain the presence of evil in nature, at the same time preserving God's absolute perfection and separateness. It would be unworthy, for God, to wander around in the world, but it is perfectly understandable for its δύναμις to accomplish the necessary and benevolent task of exercising sovereignity (ἐξουσία) and spreading goodness (ἀγαθότης).[150]

Philo presents the genesis of evil in a twofold way. On the one hand, originating in the logos's intermediate nature, evil is the implicit and consequent outcome of the creative act. On the other hand, and more interestingly for the present enquiry, evil is also the sudden irruption of an essential deformity in human creation.[151] It is thus a rupture, a break of the homogeneity of the divine emanation into the world. It is thus understandable that demons also respond to a twofold categorisation. They are positive and benevolent helpers of God, not subject to any evil,[152] but they are also malignant creatures that execute God's punishment.[153]

Without neglecting Chrysippus's influence, the genealogy of Philo's dualism can be traced back to *Lg.* X and the hypothetically dual structure of the soul in Plato. Middle Platonism develops in precisely this direction. A strategic role, in this sense, is played by Xenocrates, whose originality consists in the introduction of the twofold characterisation of demons in Middle Platonism, according to Plutarch's testimony.[154] Plutarch himself, however, is the author who more strongly insists on the evil and monstrous character of demons, giving prominence to their malefic function and the religious aspects connected with it.

---

[149] Dillon (1977), pp. 160–1.
[150] A term employed also by Plot. IV.8.6.
[151] Mazzanti (1988).
[152] Ph. *Gig.* 7.
[153] Ph. *Quaest. Ex.* I.23: 'Into every soul at its very birth their enter two powers, the salutary and the destructive. If the salutary one is victorious and prevails, the opposite one is too weak to see. And if the latter prevails, no profit at all or little is obtained from the salutary one. Through these powers the world too was created. People call them by other names: the salutary (power) they call powerful and beneficent, and the opposite one (they call) unbounded and destructive.' See Dillon (1977), p. 173.
[154] Xenocrates 222, in Senocrate e Ermodoro (2012), pp. 239–40.

Plutarch's early reflection develops a balanced view on the opposite positions of materialist atheism and fanatical superstition. The comparison between atheists and the superstitious is already found in *Lg.* X, but Plutarch emphasises how much worse the outcome of a monstrous religion is. While the atheist, although wrong, at least lives a quiet life, the superstitious person is constantly tormented and assailed by monstrous apparitions (τεράστια φάσματα).[155] The rites and sacrifices of the superstitious are worthy of a monstrous world in which Typhoeus or the giants would have won against the gods.[156] *De genio Socratis* also puts forward a rational argument, through Galaxidorus's excursus on the political connotation of religion as a tool to check the multitude. Socrates' genius, Galaxidorus argues, did not partake of anything supernatural. In fact, it was the divinatory spirit common to everybody, only a stronger one, and perhaps nothing more than a sneeze.[157]

Plutarch's later work develops a much more detailed theory of demonology, which occupies a prominent place in Middle Platonism. In *De Iside et Osiride* and *Defectu oracolorum*, Plutarch traces the theory of evil demons back to a Stoic origin.[158] Although some similarity emerges, Plutarch departs from the Stoic doctrine, both because demons are essential to a Platonically inspired transcendent notion of the divine, and because he disagrees with the Stoics' claim of the material nature of all beings. Demons, for Plutarch, are wicked precisely because they are closer to the material nature and they possess the bodily characteristic that brings them toward evil. Were they not evil, judiciously asks Plutarch, what would be the difference between them and the gods?[159]

Demons can be affected by passions, precisely because God, in its purity and transcendence, cannot. In thus being affected, they act between the human and the divine sphere on behalf of God and as its ministers.[160] Typhoeus and giants can also be seen as demons rather than gods, and in particular as fallen souls, punished and imprisoned in bodies.[161] Typhoeus and giants thus enjoy this ambiguous status of semi-divine beings, casting shade on the role of divinity, whose nature is by definition pure, and yet to some extent connected to the evil that its ministers bestow on the world. This tension, once

---

[155] Plu. *Moralia. De superstitione* 165 E.
[156] Plu. *Moralia. De superstitione* 171 D.
[157] Plu. *Moralia. De genio Socratis* 579 F ff. See also Soury (1942b) and J. Hani, *Introduction*, in Plutarque (1980).
[158] See Babut (1969), especially pp. 388 ff. See also Buffière (1956), pp. 521 ff.
[159] Plu. *Moralia. De defectu oracolorum* 418 F – 419 A.
[160] Plu. *Moralia. De defectu oracolorum* 416 E – 417 B. See also Dillon (1977), p. 216.
[161] Plu. *Moralia. De facie quae in orbe lunae apparet* 945.

again, derives from Plutarch's interpretation of Plato's theory of the maleficent soul in *Lg.* X. Although the quotation of Plato's authority could suggest a distance from the strict dualism typical of further Gnosticism,[162] the opposite can legitimately be argued: Plutarch's Platonism gives consistency to a sharp split between good and benevolent creatures on the one hand, and monstrously malevolent demons on the other. This interpretation of Plato's theory of the evil soul also underlines the active and conscious character of the maleficent force ominously threatening humanity from above, rather than a simple principle of chaos that unconsciously escapes the demiurgical ordering action.[163]

Plutarch's attitude makes a different articulation within Middle Platonism emerge. Middle Platonist philosophers treat God's relation with the world both from a more rationalist standpoint and, conversely, with a deeper religious preoccupation. Alcinous is a typical upholder of the former approach. Demons are only briefly mentioned in chapter XV of his *Handbook of Platonism*, as 'created gods', with no mention of their nature as evil.[164] On the contrary, a religiously inspired approach, full of preoccupation with the supernatural, characterises Apuleius's work, whose *De deo Socratis* is the longest explanation of demonology in classical antiquity.[165]

Apuleius seems to admit evil creatures acting above men, especially in the allegorical dimension of his literary masterpiece, the *Metamorphoses*.[166] His more philosophical works, however, grant less space to the morally evil nature of demons and focus on their ontological status. In *De genio Socratis*, Apuleius is more interested in explaining their character of 'intermediate' beings, whose nature is to be μεταξύ, 'in between' God and nature, and neither good nor bad in terms of qualities. They are thus *medioximi* (intermediate spirits), the spirits of humans whose disharmony with themselves condemns them to restlessly wander after death, with the effect of scaring the living.[167]

Apuleius's ambiguous definition refers to a doctrine that lacks consistency within Platonism. Demons can represent otherness, sometimes divinely

---

[162] See e.g. Dillon (1977), pp. 202–4.
[163] Plu. *Moralia. De Iside et Osiride* 361 B: '[Xenocrates] believes that there exists in the space about us certain great and powerful natures, obdurate, however, and morose, which take pleasure in such things as these [sc. festivals with beatings, lamentations, fastings, or scurrilous language or ribald jests], and, if they succeed in obtaining them, resort to nothing worse.'
[164] Alcin. XV.
[165] See J. Beaujeu, *Introduction*, in Apulée (1973). Apuleius also devotes much space to demonology in his *Mund*. See Goulet, éd. (1989–) *ad loc.*
[166] See e.g. *Met.* 9.29.
[167] See Hijmans (1987), esp. p. 468 ff.

inspired, sometimes wickedly threatening. They can also be reduced to human souls, that is to say, to our inner self wandering around (and above) after death, depending once again on the moral quality of humans themselves. The monstrous threat, thus, has also a fluid status, referring to causes that can be interior or exterior to ourselves, dependent on or independent of our behaviour, testifying to the evil outside or inside us.

The conflict between souls and demons is at the heart of Numenius's interpretation, as reported by Proclus and referred to in Plato's myth of Atlantis. Wicked demons struggle against the souls during their descent into bodies. They are of 'corrupt kind' and 'soul polluters'. Echoing Plutarch, Numenius evokes the monstrous background, arguing that 'the ancient theologians ascribed such conflicts to Osiris and Typhon, or Dionysius and the titans, while Plato refers these matters back to the Athenians and Atlanteans through piety'.[168]

Maximus of Tyrus's demonology also reflects the ambiguity of the demons' status. 'Alongside gods, men, and beasts,' Maximus writes, a 'race of δαιμόνια' exists.[169] Closer to Plutarch's demons than Alcinous's or Apuleius's, such beings are nevertheless immortal, unlike Plutarch's. Unlike many Middle Platonist philosophers, moreover, Maximus does not make use of them to solve the problem of evil vis-à-vis God.[170] He rather employs them to explain that, as in the human realm in which different kinds of humans exist, so in heaven different kinds of demons find their place, 'some terrifying, some benevolent'.[171] More important to him is that without such an intermediate realm, in which benevolent and malevolent beings find their place, the relation between God and the world could not be explained.[172]

The monstrous dimension of demonology prominently surfaces in the *Chaldean Oracles*, whose authority is as great as that of Plato himself for Middle and especially Neoplatonists.[173] Demons are here described as a 'race of evil demons [that] draws down souls, (a race) which is also called "... bestial and shameless" since it is turned towards Nature'.[174] The *Oracles* clearly evokes the conflictual dimension that characterises inferior nature. Chaos and confusion irreparably invade the world, from which God seems to have retired.

---

[168] Numen. 37 (= Procl. *in Ti.* I.76.30–77).
[169] Max.Tyr. VIII.4.
[170] See Puiggali (1978), esp. pp. 191–240.
[171] Max.Tyr. VIII.8.
[172] Max.Tyr. XV.2. See also Goulet, éd. (1989–) *ad loc.*
[173] See Dillon (1977), p. 384.
[174] *Orac.Chald.* 89.

The Latin *Asclepius* reproduces this gloomy conception, through the influential image of the *nocentes angeli*:

> How mournful when the gods withdraw from mankind! Only the baleful angels remain to mingle with humans, seizing the wretches and driving them to every outrageous crime – war, looting, trickery, and all that is contrary to the nature of souls. Then neither will the earth stand firm nor the sea be sailable; stars will not cross heaven nor will the course of the stars stand firm in heaven. Every divine voice will grow mute in enforced silence. The fruits of the earth will rot; the soil will no more be fertile; and the very air will droop in gloomy lethargy.[175]

Like the *Oracles*, the *Asclepius* also stresses that God has retired from the world, an idea whose genealogy can be traced to Plato's age of Kronos in the *Statesman*.[176]

Although demonology already has religious connotations in pagan philosophy, it is in Christianity, particularly when influenced by Neoplatonism, that demons catalyse theologians' attention. Clement of Alexandria offers a vivid representation of Satan's role, function and operation. Rebel and slanderer, Satan is able to corrupt humans' behaviour and drag men and women into sin.[177] Following the terminology used by the LXX to translate names of biblical monsters like Leviathan or crocodile, the devil is a dragon or snake.[178] Influenced by Philo, Clement explores Satan's work, for example, in corrupting women via their efforts to embellish their bodies through jewels and makeup. Embellishment, Clement suggests, is a perversion of the creation of God that prolongs the perversion of Eve's original sin. Women thus become similar to beasts, and the image of God they once bore disappears.

For Origen, the devil's function is tied to lifting the responsibility for the existence of sin and evil from God. Creatures are all endowed with free will, including the demons – rational beings who chose to abandon God. They cannot, in Origen's view, be evil by nature, as that would make God directly responsible for their wickedness and, in some sense, for evil itself. Devils mediate between God's goodness and sin via the free will that makes them capable of choosing, just as humans can either resist or surrender to sin and evil.[179]

---

[175] Ps.Apul. *Ascl.* XXV. See also Scott in [*Corpus Hermeticum*] (1924–36), III, 175–6.
[176] See *supra*.
[177] See e.g. Clem.Al. *Paed.* III.5.4. See also Monfrinotti (2014), pp. 259 ff.
[178] On the dragon, see Ciccarese (2002), pp. 379–92 and Ciccarese (2007), 253–83.
[179] Origenes *Princ.* I.5.3.

Their freedom does not imply God's powerlessness to stop them from committing evil. On the contrary, these mediators work in accordance with God's plan: they are here to test humans and their resistance to sin.[180]

It follows that their nature, as well as their appearance, is monstrous, as vividly explained by Methodius of Olympus:

> Do not lose heart at *the deceits* and the slanders of the Beast, but equip yourselves sturdily for the battle, arming yourselves with *the helmet* of salvation, your *breastplate* and your greaves. For if you attack with great advantage and with stout heart you will cause him consternation; and when he sees you arrayed in battle against him by Him who is his superior, he will certainly not stand his ground. Straightaway will the hydra-headed, many-faced Beast retreat and let you carry off the prize for the seven contests. *Lion in front, serpent behind, in the midst chimaera,/Belching forth dread might of flaming fire./And He slew it, relying on His Father's omens,/Christ the King. Many indeed had it destroyed, not could any endure/The deadly foam that spilled from its jaws,* had not Christ weakened and crushed it, making it completely impotent and contemptible in our eyes.[181]

The demons, with a striking resonance with classical ideas, become here a veritable chimera, powerfully testifying to the transformation of pagan ideas into Christian rhetoric.[182] Demons have an inherently double status. They represent a challenge to and rebellion against God's rule, but at the same time, they act in accordance with his will, and perform a function under his absolute rule. To successfully combat Manichaeism, in fact, every idea of the autonomy of evil and its actors must be ruled out. This preoccupation, of course, characterises pagan Platonism as well.

Although Plato's mythical tale refers more to the complementarity of Kronos's and Zeus's ages than to their opposition and conflictuality, the presence or absence of God in the cosmos takes a threatening form in the gloomier version of Middle Platonism. It is for this reason that Neoplatonism, like Christianity, seeks to rule out such a threat by establishing a strong monism and, with regard to demons, subsume them under the unique benevolent principle of the universe.

---

[180] Augustine eventually takes a completely different track. Devils are not mediators because God does not need any mediator to act and intervene directly in the world. Contrary to many other Fathers of the Church, Augustine sees the doctrine of devil-mediators developed by Middle Platonists like Apuleius as more of an obstacle than a solution for the Christian.

[181] Meth. *Symp.* VIII.12.

[182] See e.g. Moreschini (2013), p. 464.

Plotinus explores the topic of demons in III.4. Demons are not evil for him, they are souls, and like every soul they travel and transmigrate from one body to another. Although it is true that the divine Being is opposed to the demonic Becoming of the inferior world, souls regularly reflect the behaviour of past lives, and they thus enjoy different degrees of nobility. Plotinus explicitly criticises the gloomy conception of Plutarch, and makes the demon reflect the highest part of the soul.[183] This is also due to Plotinus's scepticism toward the monopoly of a religious and mythical interpretation of psychology. He thus tends to consider demons as an allegory for the soul's most rational part.[184]

Such a scepticism is not shared by Porphyry, who grants a broad space to magic and, in particular, γοητεία, witchcraft and the magic of nature, which, according to *Abst.* II.41.5, is made through evil demons. Demons are also connected with rationality and the soul and yet, contrary to Plotinus's enlightened reading, also with the soul's dark side.[185] Rationality at least partially controls demons, thus making them good. There are also evil demons, though, κακουργοὶ or φαυλοὶ, which are overcome by irrationality.[186]

Demons are thus a constant in Middle and Neoplatonism. Their peaceful or wicked nature plays the strategic function of determining the kind of relationship that the divine entertains with the mundane. Monstrosity is thus, once again, at centre stage, and works as the characterising factor of either optimistic and positive views or pessimistic and gloomy conceptions of nature. The effort, however, is always to give an explanation of the world's order and disorder, framed within a more or less explicit vision of divine providence. Middle and Neoplatonism, in this sense, are in dialogue with earlier schools, and contribute to the last pagan systematisation of theology before the radical innovation brought into the Mediterranean culture first by Judaism, and eventually by Christianity.

The World Order

Like the Stoics, Middle and Neoplatonist philosophers do not develop a coherent theory of monstrosity. Yet they are widely concerned by the problem of order in nature and by the correlative domain within which monstrosity

---

[183] See Cilento (1973).
[184] See Kalligas (2014), p. 486, and Rist (1963).
[185] Whereas demons can be interpreted as a mere allegory in Plotinus, they are a dark reality in Porphyry. This shift is due, according to Cilento (1973), mainly to the change in the cultural climate and the new harsh struggle against Christianity. On allegory in Middle and Neoplatonism see Pépin (1958), pp. 176–214.
[186] Porph. *Abst.* II.36–45. See Whittaker (1928, 2nd ed.), p. 116.

ordinarily takes place, i.e. that of disorder and evil. The question becomes to know how the transcendent God creates, organises and maintains order in nature, and what kind of normativity it imposes on the earthly domain. The problem of norms and normativity concerns at once the physical question about God's creation and organisation of matter, and the ethical question of how humans should behave if they aim at their salvation. Facing and experiencing physical and moral evil, Middle and Neoplatonists look for a way to define and clarify their concept of nature's perfection.

Middle and Neoplatonism pursue the discussion on the world's order and perfection that is at the core of all major philosophical schools, since at least Diogenes of Apollonia. Philosophy and theology go hand in hand in search of a solution to the apparent and threatening chaos of the world. Even when it exists, chaos must be apparent and subsumed under a divine plan for the whole. Because of its transcendence, the divine might be unseen (ἀφανής) and its causality not immediately apparent (ἄδηλος), and yet an effort will reveal it to the acute observer, for example in the harmony of the body and its organs, with which humans are able to satisfy all their needs.[187]

The idea of caring divine intervention is transmitted by Diogenes of Apollonia to Plato and becomes a pillar of the demiurgical theory. Plato's starting point is the opposition between the intelligible and the sensible which precedes the appearance of life. Life is in fact the merging of the two domains through the active work of the demiurgic craftsman, who forces and binds them together. Intelligence, thus, moulds matter and its necessity. This process, however, remains marked by the latent presence of chaos, evil and monstrosity as a threatening possibility. As we have seen *supra*, the major Platonic texts on evil, i.e. *Tht.* 176 ff., *Ti.* 48 a, *Plt.* 273 a ff., and *Lg.* 904 a 6–e 3, do not offer a sharply defined or exhaustive solution. *Lg.* X even explicitly suggests that the soul can choose evil, which exists as such and must be conceived as a polemic adversary (ὑπεναντίος) against goodness. The dark side of Middle and Neoplatonism thus has its origin in Plato himself and, through Platonism, it eventually reaches Gnosticism.[188]

Middle and Neoplatonism put an enormous effort into averting this possibility, by integrating and developing the Stoic idea of finalism in the universe, in more or less anthropocentric versions. Middle and Neoplatonists largely agree with Chrysippus, who argues that apparent evil has a function in the world, and is a παρακολούθημα, something which follows, an attendant circumstance. It is,

---

[187] X. *Mem.* I.4.5–6 and IV.3.3. See also *infra* and Magris (1985), p. 626 and *passim*.

[188] See *supra*. See also Magris (1985), pp. 673–4 and *passim*, De Capitani (1985), and Festugière (1949–54), II, on the ambivalence inherent to Plato himself (pp. 110 ff.) and to Platonism (p. 93).

however, not sufficient to claim the existence of order. Like Stoics, Platonic philosophers try to explain why the current order is also the best one. As Magris has nicely put it, moral and physical order converge within anthropocentric finalism, as a result of what Plato had already developed with his view of providence.[189] Plato projects human values onto his concept of nature, in order to eventually justify those same values from nature itself: the authoritarian state of the *Republic* and the providential cosmos of the *Timaeus* are intimately connected.[190] These are the hypotheses or, better, the unshakeable dogmas within which the same question keeps being asked in different forms: If God exists, where do evil and monstrosity come from?

Philo of Alexandria follows Plato, as well as Aristotle's theory of natural place, on the idea of forced composition of different elements within the compound. He calls it a state against nature (παρὰ φύσιν), violently brought into being by God's laws. Philo has a paramount importance in the Middle Platonist discourse about the world's order and its dependence on God. Philo is probably the first author to coherently develop the idea of laws of nature in Greek thought.[191] His use of the concept is surely wider than any philosopher before him, and contributes to the justification of an idea that was perceived as a paradoxical contradiction for many authors before him. As might be expected, Philo connects this concept with the Jewish idea of God as legislator, and draws the conclusion of an order that reflects the sovereign's will. He thus argues against the materialist and Epicurean idea of a spontaneous origin and configuration of the cosmos, whether ordered or not. Philo regards the materialist hypothesis as monstrous, since it is grounded on chaos and ruinous confusion (σύγχυσις), prompting the absurd hypothesis not only of an origin from chaos, but also of a total dissolution of the cosmos back into its originating parallel rain of atoms.[192] Epicureans thus preach the opposite of order, and are themselves compared to the monstrous eunuch that has lost his substance and has become unshapen matter.[193]

The Epicurean monstrosity is also reflected, as a threat, by the human tendency to indulge in abnormal behaviours, at once physically and morally blameable, such as illicit sexuality. In *De specialibus legibus*, Philo discusses the sixth commandment. Adultery destroys families and the legitimate descent.[194]

---

[189] See Pl. *Phd.* 46–7 and *supra*.
[190] Magris (1985), p. 642.
[191] Koester (1968), *passim*.
[192] Ph. *Aet.* 5–6: nothing comes from nothing and nothing falls back into nothing, according to Philo's interpretation of Empedocles.
[193] Ph. *Spec.* I.328–9.
[194] Ph. *Spec.* III.45.

Several forms of violation are identified, from the less serious, such as marrying a stranger, to the more serious, like the union between brother and sister, that Philo has defined as a monstrous or disharmonic agreement (ἁρμονίαν ἀνάρμοστον).[195] Homosexuality is also a particularly serious violation in Philo's view, and the transgressors should be ruthlessly eliminated, since the pleasure they are after is παρὰ φύσιν.[196]

The monstrosity of unruled sexuality is not a tangential thought. It comes to the forefront of Philo's argumentation through the character of Pasiphae, king Minos's wife, and her sin of zoophilia. Interestingly, Philo makes use of this example not only to condemn the ultimate degree of infamy that humanity has reached, but also to alert the reader about a major threat to the entire order of nature, if passions are left unbridled. Abominable monsters (τέρατα παλίμφημα) will be born, beings that do not appear to be from this world, non-existent (ἀνύπαρκτος) and unreal, like hippocentaurs, chimeras and other creatures of the same stock.[197] It is worth underlying the originality of Philo's use of the argument of mythical and monstrous animals.[198] Whereas in Empedocles' cosmogony they are at the beginning of the creative process, and in Lucretius's they are denied any possibility of existence, mythical monsters are now projected in an apocalyptic and catastrophic future by Philo, as a real threat to an undisciplined humanity lusting after beasts. Monstrosity is not the archaic premise of normality, but rather its potential threat, when sexual desire takes over the regular regime of physical unions.[199] The total dissolution of elements, seen as the impossible and absurd hypothesis claimed by Epicureans, now becomes real and concrete, as the baleful destiny of humanity that challenges God's laws and throws itself into the arms of monstrosity: 'His ornament has been removed, everything appears as a gloomy deformity, matter hurries to leave its form (*ablatum decus est: tristi deformitate universa affecta sunt: materia formam exuere properat*).'[200]

Such a confusion, though, has a double meaning in Philo, since God himself can make use of it against human evil, as in the punishment of humanity in *De confusione linguarum*.[201] Confusion and disorder thus become God's tools and the necessary means to the final triumph of goodness. God makes use of evil as well as of monstrous prodigies to communicate with humans and, beyond that,

---

[195] Ph. *Spec.* III.23.
[196] On pursuing pleasure against nature see also Pl. *Phdr.* 251 a.
[197] Ph. *Spec.* III.45.
[198] See A. Moses, in Philo (1961–), XXV, p. 86.
[199] On human violations of natural laws, see also Martens (2013), p. 77.
[200] Ph. *Prou.* I.90.
[201] Ph. *Confus.* 187–9. See also Scarpat (1991).

to actively intervene in his creation. Supernatural and prodigious facts are at the heart of God's relation with his people, sometimes directly, sometimes through the mediation of Moses.²⁰² The world itself is, for Philo, a prodigious creation.²⁰³

However, Philo is keen in taming the prodigious manifestations of nature and keeping them strictly under God's pattern and providence. In a sense, the *abnormal* and the prodigious are tools that God *normally* employs. Philo does underline that the only reasonable conception of nature is the one that springs out of the biblical message, while alternative visions must only be considered mythical and ultimately impossible. This is the case, for example, of the ancient cosmogonies that speak about beings born from the earth. To this monstrous conception, Philo opposes the amazing regularity of nature, astonishing and divine (τεράστιον καὶ θεῖον), whose action is grounded on the laws of God.²⁰⁴

Admiration can also be a tool for humans to reach God, when they realise that the harmony and beauty of creation has been established for his purpose. Humans thus make themselves into the final cause of God, through the admiration of his work, which must however remain subordinate to the admiration for the creator itself. The opposite would mean to misunderstand the divine order of nature and turn the world upside down. This is why revelation becomes the favoured way towards God, while knowledge of God through knowledge of nature remains subordinate in Philo's view.²⁰⁵

The laws of nature, i.e. divine laws, must thus be deemed good and fair not in themselves, but precisely because they are created by God and remain subordinate to his will. God can in fact change them whenever and however he desires. The door is thus open to the rational explanation of miracles, anomalies and the formation of natural monstrosities. Wolfson has claimed that Philo's God is indeed very close to Plato's demiurge. A fundamental difference, however, remains, at least on this ground: whereas Plato's demiurge is immutable and his laws unbreakable, Philo's God remains absolute master of the universe and the omnipotent source of its normativity.²⁰⁶ Natural things, Philo stresses, 'through the power of God, admit of change and transition, so

---

²⁰² See e.g. *Aet.* 2, *Mos.* I.80, 90–1, 95, 165, II.71, 257, 266, *Spec.* II.218, IV.129, *Prob.* 5, *Abr.* 118, *Congr.* 173.
²⁰³ Ph. *Plant.* 4.
²⁰⁴ Ph. *Aet.* 55 ff.
²⁰⁵ See M. G. Crepaldi, 'Admiration philosophique et admiration théologique: la valeur du θαυμάζειν dans la pensée de Philon d'Alexandrie', in Lévy, Besnier éds (1998), pp. 77–86.
²⁰⁶ God's power, as Wolfson underlines, is autocratic (αὐτοκράτωρ). See Wolfson (1948), pp. 355 and *passim*.

as often to produce effects quite the reverse of the ordinary'.[207] The paradox is only apparent: the law of nature as well as its breaking are not contrasted to each other. On the contrary, they both reveal God's superiority in establishing laws and derogating from them whenever he wishes.[208]

This is how Philo reinterprets Plato's demiurgic cosmogony through Jewish creationism. The *Timaeus* is thus mediated with, and read through, the Bible. God brings things from non-Being into Being through a veritable poietic activity, within which any anomaly and any monstrosity finds its place.[209] Monstrosity, like evil, also loses its abnormal character and becomes part of God's plan since the beginning. The divine informs matter, and thus descends into the lower realm, in which intelligence comes in contact with sensibility. Like the Platonic demiurge, God produces models of perfection, which eventually are plunged into the realm of matter and generate the imperfect reality that we all experience. Act and perfection, in this sense, precede power and imperfection, and yet they are necessarily bound to each other.

Philo claims the absolute perfection of creation.[210] In that case, however, imperfect and sometimes monstrous Becoming must not only have its origin in the perfect and normal Being, but also be its inevitable outcome. In *De opificio mundi*, for example, Philo describes the actual creation of all species, by God, at once. All plants and trees are generated at the same time, fully grown and mature, for eventually breeding themselves through the normal process of reproduction by seeds.[211] The perfect act, like a model, precedes the necessarily imperfect power. Philo reads the biblical account along these lines, claiming that God creates animals from the earth, all perfect but according to ontological degrees of relative perfection, since they occupy different levels in the scale of beings. The act of God is thus present both in the creation of ideal forms and in their subsequent movement of natural reproduction through seeds and sperm.[212] By making God the source and origin of both moments, Philo indirectly subordinates physical monstrosity, as well as any kind of evil, to the initial plan of the omnipotent maker of the universe.[213]

---

[207] Ph. *Deus* 87–8. See also Bockmuehl (1995), pp. 39–42 and *passim*.

[208] On Philo's concept of law, see also Myre (1976), Decharneaux (1991) and Martens (2003). Thus, Philo does not distinguish between natural law and eternal law. Augustine's distinction is a development of Philo's position. See Girardet (1995), pp. 292–8.

[209] On the conflict and the mediation between Platonism and Judaism see Weiss (1966). On Philo's creationism see Tobin (1992) and Nikiprowetzky (1996).

[210] See e.g. *Prov.* II.46.

[211] Ph. *Opif.* 40 ff.

[212] Ph. *Opif.* 62–8.

[213] Brehier (1950), p. 171 and *passim*, has underlined the Stoic tone of such a conception of order and harmony within the divine design. See also Spitzer (1963), n. 14, pp. 146–7.

The world's order implies divine providence, which comes very close, in Philo's thought, to the regularity of Stoic destiny (εἱμαρμένη).[214] Providence, however, does not contrast with free will.[215] In this sense, it has first and foremost a demonstrative function, whereby men are alerted by things they cannot explain, e.g. natural monstrosities or terrible phenomena such as lights and thunders.[216] When such events strike and harm us individually, one has to think that suffering also has a pedagogic function, in order to remove what is shameful, as physical monstrosities need to be healed or removed, as if they were *ossa superflua*, bony excrescences.[217] Moreover, what harms someone in particular can be of general utility, according again to the Stoic idea of secondary effects of necessary and providential causes.[218] Providence deploys itself on the allegorical battlefield between normality and monstrosity. While pious humans struggle to survive, for example, the impious and monstrous race of Kyklopes enjoys the plenitude of natural resources: what would appear more unfair and unjust? Yet, Philo remarks, this must be a necessary consequence of God's providential plan.[219] Providence can be thus qualified as something good which successfully imitates something evil for the sake of a greater good.[220] This becomes possible, in Philo's theology, because he contrasts it with monstrosity, i.e. an evil that unsuccessfully imitates the good, without being able to harm it in the least.

The excellence of the cosmos is thus at the heart of Philo's influential attempt to merge Platonism and Judaism. This excellence is also the core of other Middle Platonic works, such as the anonymous Περὶ κόσμου.[221] Strongly influenced by Aristotelianism and Stoicism, this text faithfully represents the transformation that Platonism has been subjected to in the Imperial age without losing its character, and thus maintaining the recognisable traits that make it a fundamental source for Middle Platonism.[222] Similar to what Philo stresses

---

[214] Ph. *Prou.* I.33. On the centrality of providence for Philo's theology, see Frick (1999), chs 4 and 5 in particular. The older Wendland (1892) is still interesting.
[215] See Dragona-Monachou (1975–6) and M. Hadas-Lebel, *Introduction*, in Philo (1961–), XXXV, p. 53, Ewing (2008). See *contra* Dillon (1977), p. 166, for whom Philo's providence inclines toward a kind of determinism inspired by Stoicism.
[216] Ph. *Prou.* I.37–9.
[217] Ph. *Prou.* I.46.
[218] Ph. *Prou.* II.99–100. See also Runia (2003b), p. 587.
[219] Ph. *Prou.* II.94–5.
[220] See Hadas-Lebel, *Introduction*, p. 107.
[221] On this text and its history see in particular Festugière (1949–54), II, pp. 460–520, Moraux (1973–84), II, pp. 5–82, and G. Reale and A. P. Bos, 'Monografia introduttiva', in Reale, Bos (1995, 2a ed.), pp. 23–171.
[222] Festugière (1949–54), *passim*, and Moreschini (1978), p. 130, rather stress the hermetic character of the Περὶ κόσμου.

about the necessity of keeping a clear distinction between the creator and the creature, the text has a strong theological dimension. In chapters V-VII, the author praises the cosmos's excellency because of its harmony. Quoting Heraclitus, the text intends harmony as the outcome of diversity and even irregularity.[223] Harmony, however, is more in the creative force than in the creation itself. Diversity and irregularity are indeed present in the world, and yet subordinated by the creator to a perfection teleologically built in view of the whole.[224] Everything has its function and utility, even phenomena that appear absurd or monstrous. Like Plato and Philo after him, the Περὶ κόσμου underlines the forced constraint that elements have endured, under the action of the creative force, for order to be created in the universe.

This position is also shared by Plutarch, who interprets in this sense the meaning of παρὰ φύσιν. Somehow unnaturally, elements have been moved and forced together to produce the cosmos. The character of this movement, however, does not cause the universe to be against nature, nor does it cause anything *within* the universe to be abnormal or unnatural. Plutarch thus contrasts the position of those who claim that some movements or positions of celestial bodies are against nature.[225] Being natural is related not to the essence of a thing, but rather to its function, role and position in the universe vis-à-vis the whole of which it is a part:

> [. . .] no part of a whole all by itself seems to have any order, position, or motion of its own which could be called unconditionally 'natural'. On the contrary, each and every such part, whenever its motion is usefully and properly accommodated to that for the sake of which the part has come to be and which is the purpose of its growth or production, and whenever it acts or is affected or disposed so that it contributes to the preservation or beauty or function of that thing, then, I believe, it has its 'natural' position and motion and disposition.[226]

---

[223] Ps.Arist. (= Reale, Bos (1995, 2a ed.), 396 b 20). Apuleius echoes such praise for the cosmos's excellency in his translation, see esp. *Mund.* 337. See also Apul. *Mund.* 333.

[224] Meteorological events, for example, can be locally disastrous, *regionaliter pestifera*, for Apuleius, and yet healthy for the general state of the world: Apul. *Mund.* 340. God's help and support is general and not individual or particular, precisely as the the king's action is in his own realm: Apul. *Mund.* 344 ff. It is worth asking whether Apuleius is conscious of the tension between this idea and the several mechanical metaphors he uses to describe the top–bottom action of god on the world, such as the stringed puppet (*Mund.* 351–2) or the army as a war machine (*Mund.* 357).

[225] Plu. *Moralia. De facie quae in orbe lunae apparet* 926 C ff.

[226] Plu. *Moralia. De facie quae in orbe lunae apparet* 927 D.

Individual natures are subordinated to their constituent role as parts of a whole. Everything becomes perfect when it is viewed in its proper context, namely the context of the whole perfection.

One can observe, in Plutarch, the development of a principle of paramount importance for the explanation of nature in general and the understanding of the role and function of monstrosity in particular. According to this principle, monstrosity, like evil and imperfection, has to be framed within the general and the whole of which it necessarily is a part. I believe that although already present in other philosophical schools, and especially in Stoicism, as well as in Philo, this principle receives a strongly coherent systematisation in Middle Platonism and, eventually, in Neoplatonism. In fact, contrary to Stoics, Middle Platonists are particularly concerned by the necessity of claiming God's direct action in the world, maintaining at the same time its transcendence of and purity from the world's evil and imperfection. It does offer a strong account of the necessity and perfection of God's laws together with the explanation and justification of every phenomenon in the world.

In *De fato*, for example, Plutarch claims the inviolable, unalterable, infallible, permanent and perpetual (ἀπαράβατος) character of divine rules, intended as fate. These rules, in fact, emanate from a cause that, by definition, cannot be hindered (ἀνεμπόδιστος).[227] Although everything happens *within* fate, however, not everything happens *according to* it. Plutarch explains this difference, apparently minor and yet of paramount importance, through the analogy with the civil law, which *generally* covers all aspects of the citizens' life, and yet does not determine each *particular* and individual behaviour.[228] Room is thus made for the contingent, and Plutarch grounds his argument on an Aristotelian idea that had been cardinal to explaining how monstrosities and imperfections happen in nature, namely the distinction between act and power.

Plutarch quite openly recognises Aristotle's influence, twisting however his argument through the distinction between potency, the potent and the possible: the potent pre-exists power, which in its turn pre-exists the possible. The latter, thus, comes into existence only when nothing hinders its existence from the outside.[229] Monsters, Aristotle wrote, come into existence precisely when something hinders their normal formation from the outside. Plutarch reworks the Aristotelian concept of chance, thinking about abnormal and

---

[227] Plu. *Moralia. De fato* 568 C–D.
[228] Plu. *Moralia. De fato* 569 A–E. See also J. Hani, *Notice*, in Plutarch (1972–93), VIII.
[229] Plu. *Moralia. De fato* 571 A. See Arist. GC 317 b 16 and Alex.Aphr. *Fat.* 176. See also *Moralia. De fato* 570 B on the definition of the necessary as the possible whose contrary is impossible, and the contingent as the possible whose contrary is also possible.

anomalous events, namely events that should have happened in one way (i.e. normally), but happened in another way (e.g. monstrously) and somehow inconsistently with their context and isolated from it.[230]

Plutarch's *De fato* is directed against the Stoics with the aim of liberating both human action and divine providence from a rigid conception of destiny. By announcing the existence of contingency, possibility, fortune and chance, Plutarch intends to maintain the existence of a sphere of events that is not determined in advance. He also intends to maintain God's transcendence vis-à-vis this sphere, and God's control of it. Plutarch thus makes use of monstrosity through the same conceptual tools that Aristotle had used to explain it, but gives them a transcendent turn. Plutarch's position has two outcomes. First, he claims that miracles and prodigies are indeed possible, if God wants them to happen. Natural causes do not explain the whole reality, and although prodigies and monstrosities rarely happen, they are indeed possible, without being against nature.[231] Second, slightly moving away from Plato himself, Plutarch argues that the divine acts in the world only at a general level, and not on base details, which are thus open to the possibility of monstrous and chance deviations from what ordinarily happens.[232]

The consequences of this attitude toward the ordinary and the exceptional create an interesting sense of relativism in Plutarch's thought. The concepts of beauty and ugliness acquire a relative status, for example, when one carefully considers aesthetic judgement. Seen from the earth, Lucius argues in *De facie in orbe lunae*, the moon is beautiful, 'but as a star or luminary or a divine and heavenly body she is, I am afraid, misshapen, ugly (ἄμορφος and ἀπρεπὴς), and a disgrace to the noble title [. . .]'.[233] Maybe it is true that the moon is not inhabited, Plutarch writes, by monstrous races, similar to those discussed by Megasthenes in his *Indika*.[234] Other races, Plutarch unironically declares, might however exist, whose practices and habits humans cannot understand. What would happen if one saw only the sea surface? Would anyone be able to imagine the richness of the sea creatures? Would not a selenite, in the same manner, think about the earth as a miserable place, and deem her moon as the only 'earth?'[235]

These arguments also offer Plutarch the occasion to undermine the mechanist explanation of both individual things and the universe as a whole, in favour of an explanation that ultimately relies on the transcendent rational

---

[230] Plu. *Moralia. De fato* 572 D.
[231] See Babut (1969), pp. 478 ff.
[232] Moraux (1973–84), II, pp. 495–505.
[233] Plu. *Moralia. De facie quae in orbe lunae apparet* 929 A.
[234] Megasth. XXIX (= Str. 15.1.57 = FGH n. 715). See *supra* on Magasthenes as a source for Pliny.
[235] Plu. *Moralia. De facie quae in orbe lunae apparet* 940 D.

and divine principle, a principle that has the primacy over its parts and components. Different causalities exist in the universe, and different events and beings can be related to natural causes as well as to intelligible ones. Philosophers of nature have the tendency to grasp only the former, while poets and theologians to consider exclusively the latter. Both causes, however, exist in the universe and must be considered at once, as Plato has sublimely done.[236]

Although everything can be attributed to God, Plutarch does not deny the necessary action of matter. Monstrosity shows clearly that a double explanation is necessary, through the monstrous example of Pericles' one-horned ram.[237] Anaxagoras the philosopher explains the physical causes, also called necessary ones, by an anatomical dissection and a mechanical explanation of the anomaly. Lampon the seer, though, explains the meaning of this extraordinary event, which is that the mastery of the city will finally be devolved to one man. He reveals the link between the superior causality and the divine. No doubt, in fact, that the monstrous is due to God's causal intervention, as Plutarch clarifies.

In my view, however, Plutarch not only establishes a double level of causality. He also puts the higher level in control of the lower, to maintain the order and consistency of the universe. Without divine intervention, Lamprias explains in *De facie orbis*, natural laws would not suffice to preserve order, and the universe would be doomed to chaos and anarchy.[238] This is why '[. . .] in everything the better has the control of the necessary',[239] with a thesis that runs against Stoic materialism. Plutarch reduces the physical explanation to Stoic necessitarianism, in order to claim the primacy of a divine providence that acts above and beyond the material causes, otherwise 'I cannot make out what use there is of providence or of what Zeus, "the master-craftsman", is maker and father-creator.'[240] In his polemic, Plutarch fails to admit that his conclusion about God bringing everything toward the best is indeed of Stoic origin.[241] However, whereas natural and divine order coincide in Stoicism, they are different and even opposed for Plutarch, and this makes possible miracles and monstrosities in nature.[242]

---

[236] Plu. *Moralia. De defectu oracolorum* 435 E–436 A.

[237] Plu. *Per.* 6.

[238] Plu. *Moralia. De facie quae in orbe lunae apparet* 926 F, which refers to Pl. *Ti.* 53 b. See P. L. Donini, *I fondamenti della fisica e la teoria delle cause in Plutarco*, in Gallo a cura di (1992), pp. 99–120.

[239] Plu. *Moralia. De facie quae in orbe lunae apparet* 928 C.

[240] Plu. *Moralia. De facie quae in orbe lunae apparet* 927 A–B.

[241] See P. Donini, 'Introduzione', in Plutarco (2011). See also Plu. *Moralia. De fato* 572 F and 573 C.

[242] See Babut (1969), pp. 331, 473 and *passim*.

Philosophers must also learn to recognise intelligible and final causes even when they do not immediately or evidently appear. Once again, every phenomenon and being has its role in the global economy of the creation, as the example of the moon once again confirms. Lamprias and Theon discuss its function: similarly to what is asked for monsters, if the moon is not inhabited, Theon demands, than why does it even exist? What would its final cause be? Lamprias's answer is clear: even if the moon is a desert, it does not mean that it came to be 'in vain and to no purpose'. The moon can indeed have an end and a function, like the parts of our heart that are equally a desert.[243]

The ontological priority of teleology is thus confirmed, by Plutarch, in view of claiming the perfection of God's creation and the universe. With Aristotelian accents, Plutarch maintains the ontological priority of act over power. This equates to the priority of perfection over imperfection or, rather, of Being over Becoming, whereby the former serves as a model for the latter. Plutarch discusses this aspect through the apparently simple and classic question of which comes first, the chicken or the egg. In the *Table-Talk*, Firmus offers a wholly mechanist explanation, for which the egg must precede, since what is less perfect produces what is more perfect, contributing to the evolution of life as well as its diversity. Senecio responds that, on the contrary, perfection must indeed precede imperfection, as the entire comes before the mutilated, and the whole before the parts. On this ground, Senecio's argument re-establishes the priority of the normal over the abnormal and the monstrous, which are exceptions and perfect only insofar as they contribute to the perfection of the whole.[244]

Plutarch also makes use of the ancient cosmogonic argument of generation from the earth. Because what is perfect and complete must precede what is imperfect and incomplete, living beings have initially been generated from the earth in their accomplished form, as one can still observe today with the mice of Egypt, snakes, frogs and cicadas. It is not the earth that imitates the woman, but the woman that imitates the earth, as Plato also claims.[245] Interestingly, Plutarch forgets that the Empedoclean and materialist generation from the earth implies the earth's attempt to reach viable forms by producing innumerable monsters, a few of which survive only because they are able to reproduce themselves.[246] Plutarch might have in mind the spontaneous generation discussed by Diodorus Siculus. As for Empedocles, though, Plutarch seems to forget that these creatures were only half normal, and in fact monstrous in their lower part, which remained unshaped and muddy, like the matter

---

[243] Plu. *Moralia. De facie quae in orbe lunae apparet* 938 ff.
[244] Plu. *Moralia. Quaestiones convivales* 637 B.
[245] Plu. *Moralia. Quaestiones convivales* 637 B.
[246] See *supra*.

from which they were made.[247] Monstrosity is now left behind, in Plutarch's attempt to firmly establish the priority of perfection over imperfection, and of the divine, stable and rational cause over the natural, unstable and mechanistic explanation of the universe.

A similar position is carried forward by Galen of Pergamon, one of the most important figures of classical medicine and science. Although his thought reveals a strong autonomy and independence, and a distinct capacity of borrowing from different philosophical schools and sources, I believe that for what concerns monstrosity and the conceptual area surrounding it, Galen deliberately develops a Platonic approach. The result of his enterprise remains one of the most influential attempts in classical culture to claim, in a scientific way, the caring presence of the divine in the world and frame anomalies and monstrosities within this providential conception. The scientific approach is not claimed against the theological one, as is the case with materialist philosophers. Rather, Galen aims at reconciling science and theology, by first criticising the materialists for their ignorance. Their conclusions on the structure of bodies, for example, are vitiated by a poor knowledge of anatomy,[248] and this criticism also includes Aristotle.[249] Thus Galen argues for a scientific approach whose backbone is supported by the recognition of the divine in the world.[250]

Galen sings a veritable 'hymn of praise' to nature and its creator in *De usu partium* III.10. This text, which inspires several ancient and modern authors, develops the equation between reality and perfection. Galen interprets this perfection first and foremost in terms of 'usefulness of the actions' that the parts and organs of a body, for example, are expected to perform. The configuration of bodies is admirable and it is absurd to ask why things are not different or better, as several philosophers (like Epicurus, Anaxagoras and the atheist Diagoras) have asked, unjustly and absurdly condemning nature.[251] By simply asking this question, in fact, materialist philosophers make the divine itself monstrous, 'crippling and blinding the godlike faculty by which alone

---

[247] D.S. I.10.2: 'As proof that animal life appeared first of all in their land [Egyptians] would offer the fact that even at the present day the soil of the Thebaid at certain times generates mice in such numbers and of such sizes to astonish all who have witnessed the phenomenon; for some of them are fully formed as far as the breast and front feet and are able to move, while the rest of the body is unformed (ἀδιατύπωτος), the clod of earth still retaining its natural character.' See also F. Fuhrmann, 'Notes complémentaires', in Plutarch (1972–93), IX.1, p. 182, and Guthrie (1957), p. 39.

[248] Gal. UP VI.20.

[249] Gal. UP VII.14.

[250] Galen's teleological theology, as Donini (1992) explains, is however polemically opposed to the Mosaic and mystery religions. See also Temkin (1973) and J. Boulogne, L'«Épode» de Galien. Une célébration du merveilleux, in Bianchi, Thévenez eds (2004), pp. 307–20.

[251] Gal. UP XII.6.

Nature enables a man to behold the truth [. . .]'.[252] Nothing could be better or be improved in animal bodies, whose perfection reflects that of the heavens and of the whole universe. Thus Galen moves away from the idea of degrees of perfection, and recognises the same mark of the divine in the arrangement of animal and celestial bodies,[253] according to nature's behaviour, which is, as also Hippocrates claims, more just than justice itself.[254]

Should anything in nature be different from what it currently is, it would inevitably transform reality into something monstrous. Monstrosity is thus used by Galen as the hypothetical *otherness* to respond to Epicurus's and Asclepiades's followers, who claim that individuals evolve depending on their activities and the exercise of certain parts of their bodies, and further that this could not only be considered as an improvement, but could also undermine the idea of a general nature or essence of a class of beings. What would a human or a horse be, if humans and horses changed and developed their bodies depending on their activity? Galen's response is that such an alleged improvement would only be monstrous:

> [. . .] perhaps you think that in individuals who take exercise, parts somehow become double, and that in those who are lazy, parts are diminished by half. If this is so, then hard workers will doubtless have four feet and four hands, and those who take their ease will have only one leg and one hand![255]

Galen also attempts a mechanical explanation of such an impossibility, thinking about similar arguments put forward by Aristotle on the contradiction represented by centaurs. No such powerful monster as a centaur can exist. A monster is a monster, and thus outside of nature, in the sense of being contradictory and logically impossible:

> But why, then was [man] not given four legs and hands as well, like the centaur? The reason is that, in the first place, a commingling of such widely different bodies was impossible for Nature. For it was not merely their shapes and colours that she would have had to combine, as sculptors and painters do; she would also have been obliged to blend their very substances, which are absolute and will not mingle. Indeed, if man and horse should ever mate, the uterus would not bring the seed to perfection. If Pindar as a poet accepts the myth of the centaurs, we should be indulgent, but if he speaks as an intelligent man, pretending to understand what is beyond the grasp of ordinary

---

[252] Gal. *UP* III.10.

[253] Gal. *UP* III.10. Galen's rejection of Epicureanism and materialism is mainly inspired by the biological ideas of Plato's *Timeus*. See Moraux (1973–84), II. pp. 685–808, Goulet, éd. (1989–) *sub voce*. Dillon (1977) does not include Galen in his analytical survey.

[254] Gal. *UP* V.9.

[255] Gal. *UP* I.21.

mortals, we must censure his claims to wisdom [...] And even if we should grant that this animal, so strange and monstrous, could be conceived and perfected, nothing could be found to nourish the creature. Would the lower, horselike parts be nourished with grass and raw barley, and the upper parts on cooked barley and food fit for men?[256] In that case the animal should be given two mouths, one human and the other that of a horse, and if we must judge from the presence of two breasts, it seems likely that it would also have two hearts. [...] a man is better able than that monstrosity, the centaur, to leap over an obstacle [...] perhaps it would be better for us to have four legs if they were human legs and not those of a horse. Such an arrangement, however, would be of no help to us in any action, and we should lose our natural swiftness as well.[257]

Nothing can be more perfect that what it is. Galen's position is interesting because it faces two very different enemies: Epicureans and materialists, as we have seen, but also theologians who claim that God could have indeed made things more perfect if only he had wanted to. We have seen this argument running through several versions of Platonism, following Philo's argument in favour of God's omnipotence or Plutarch's anti-Stoic critique. For Galen, on the contrary, if nature and God do not do anything different, it is because it is impossible to indiscriminately gather all the advantages of different animal species, such as human and horse, together. Nature must choose and give to different species the advantages that make them perfect not absolutely, but in themselves.[258] Galen thus embraces the critique of the almighty God, arguing for a limit and a boundary to what nature can achieve. Nature's plenitude, in this sense, looks closer to Stoics' necessity than to Plutarch's and Philo's higher and unbound power.[259]

---

[256] See Arist. HA VIII.28, 607 a 1–8 and GA II.7, 746 a 29–35.

[257] Gal. *UP* III.1. Daremberg, in Galien (1854–6), I, *ad loc.* suggests the reference to Lucr. V.878. See *supra* for both Aristotle and Lucretius on centaurs and chimaeras.

[258] Gal. *UP* III.4.

[259] Gal. *UP* XI.14: 'Is this the way in which Moses reasons about Nature (and it is a better way that Epicurus')? Yet it is best for us to adopt neither, but, continuing to derive the principle of generation from the Creator in all things generable, as Moses does, to add to this the material principle. For our Creator has made these hairs feel the necessity of preserving always an even length for the reason that this was the better thing. [...] Now it was not enough merely to will that they should be so; for even if he wished to make a rock into a man all of a sudden, it would be impossible. And this is the point at which my teaching and that of Plato and the other Greeks who have treated correctly of natural principles differs from that of Moses. For him it suffices for God to have willed material to be arranged and straightaway it was arranged, because Moses believed everything to be possible to God, even if he should wish to make a horse or a beef out of ashes. We, however, do not feel this to be true, saying rather that some things are naturally impossible and that God does not attempt these at all but chooses from among the possible what is best to be done.' See also Pichot, 'Introduction', in Galien (1994).

This boundary, according to a Platonic reading of the demiurgic action, but also to the Aristotelian idea of resistance to the form, is due to matter. Galen's God is not almighty, because he does not create from nothing, and encounters a pre-existing matter that is and remains an obstacle.[260] Degrees of perfection, however, exist *within* mundane nature, and different beings can be deemed less valuable and inferior. An example that Galen repeatedly brings forth is that of the ape: '[. . .] because the ape has a ridiculous soul and is a poor mimic, the body Nature has bestowed on it is correspondingly ridiculous [and] uses its legs in the same way as a man who is playing the clown and making fun of the way a cripple stands, and limps as he walks and runs'. Galen does not deny that the ape's body makes this animal more apt to perform its proper functions than, let's say, a human. Apes, for example, are perfectly fit to climb on trees. This relativism, however, is subordinated to a scale of degrees of perfection that has humans at its top. The ape's amusing and ludicrous nature depends on its comparison with human functions.[261]

Galen's argument on apes is intended to firmly establish the distinction between human and animal. The recognition of the former's priority is established by making the latter monstrous. It is however a curious monstrosity, since the ape's character, although laughable, is to be *monstrously perfect*. In fact, by giving to this being, whose soul is inferior, an inferior body, nature has acted according to justice and perfection:

> Tell me, O noble sophists and clever accuser of Nature, have you ever seen in the ape this finger that is commonly called the antihand [. . .]? And if you have not seen the ape's thumb, will you have the effrontery to say that it is just like the human thumb? If you have indeed seen one, I suppose you saw that it is short, slender, distorted and altogether ridiculous, just as the ape's whole body is. [. . .] Nature would say to you that an animal with a ridiculous soul should be given a body with a ridiculous structure. Accordingly, as my discourse proceeds, it will show how the ape's whole body is a caricature of the human body. You will see how true this is of the hands when you reflect with me that if an artist or sculptor intended to produce a caricature of the human hand, the result would be exactly like what we see in the ape. For we are most inclined to laugh at those imitations which carefully preserve the likeness in most of their parts but go entirely astray in the most important ones. Then what advantage is there in having four fingers well formed if the thumb is so poorly arranged that it cannot even be called the great finger?[262]

---

[260] See Gal. UP III.1. See also Moraux (1973–84), II, p. 766, and Hankinson (1989), p. 218.
[261] See e.g. Gal. UP III.8. See *contra* Hankinson (1989), p. 217.
[262] Gal. UP I.22.

It is remarkable that Galen claims ape's monstrosity vis-à-vis human perfection and through the recognition of a certain proximity between the good model and an inferior imitation. The ape is not ludicrous because it represents the human's *otherness*, but rather because it resembles and imitates humanity, without reaching its degree of beauty. One can think about Plato's theory of the *simulacrum*. The ape becomes the human's simulacrum and threatens the boundary between human and animal, since it reclaims, with its resemblance, the gap that Galen intends to preserve.[263]

Despite the claim for the equation between reality and perfection, the ape's argument reveals a priority and superiority of essence over existence in Galen's thought. What one thing *should* be becomes prominent over what it actually is. Galen develops this point, once again contrasting the mechanistic explanation of anatomy, in this case by quoting Anaxagoras on the human hand, veritable 'instrument for instruments'. Galen, however, turns upside down Anaxagoras's mechanist explanation. Human intelligence, Galen argues, is not the outcome of development due to humans' use of hands. Rather, intelligence derives from the essence of the intelligent being himself:

> It is not because he has hands that he is the most intelligent, as Anaxagoras says, but because he is the most intelligent that he has hands, as Aristotle says,[264] judging correctly. Indeed, not by his hands, but by his reason has man been instructed in the arts.[265]

The human is thus not the result of a mechanical development, but rather the actualisation of a perfect model or essence, to which having hands is appropriate and suitable, and whose organs have the best possible disposition. Galen of course follows Aristotle on this argument and explains that the disposition is determined by the end and the scope of such a being, and its perfection means a structure that ensures its accomplishment.[266] The act has thus, once again, the priority over the power, since it is what guides and

---

[263] On the *simulacrum*, see below. Galen is probably recalling here Socrates's search for the beautiful in itself and absolutely. See Pl. *Hp.Ma.* 289 a–c, and esp b 2 ff.: '[. . .] does not Heraclitus, whom you cite, mean just this, that the wisest of men, if compared with a god, will appear a monkey, both in wisdom and in beauty and in everything else?' See also Daremberg, in Galien (1854–6), I, p. 162, n. 3.

[264] See Arist. *PA* IV.10, 687 a 7–18.

[265] Gal. *UP* I.3.

[266] Gal. *UP* I.9. For Aristotle on the hand see *PA* IV.10, 687 a 3–b 25 and above, as well as Temkin (1973), p. 179 and *passim*, and Hankinson (1989), who stresses the difference between the genuine teleology defended by Galen and the immanent teleology of the form argued by Aristotle. Galen's Platonism would thus be syncretistic. See also Hankinson (1998). *Contra* De Lacy (1972) who argues for Galen's genuine Platonism.

controls the individual's movement toward its τέλος: the function should be the point of departure of every enquiry, as well as the criterion for each discovery.[267]

Teleology occupies a central position in Galen's philosophy. In *De usu partium* VI.12 he elaborates a theory of causality that slightly modifies Aristotle's taxonomy, building on five different kinds of causes. The primacy of the cause for the sake of which, the 'first and most important', is argued through the reference to Plato's criticism of Anaxagoras's limited use of finalism in *Phaedo* 97 d–99 b.[268] Galen extends the critique to materialists, and in particular to Asclepiades, expanding once again on the notion of monstrosity:

> Asclepiades passes by two causes, that derived from the providence of the Creator, which I have called the first cause, and the second, called the material cause, so to speak, and arrives at a sort of cause which is the most insignificant of all [. . .]. It would be a fine thing if we had more fingers on our hands in good health and fewer when we are ill! So too, it would be a sight worthy of the wisdom of Asclepiades to see Thersites with perhaps three fingers, Ajax with seven, Achilles with still more, and Orion and Talos with more fingers, I suppose, than an *iulus* has feet! Oh, most noble Asclepiades, a man using unsound bases for his teachings cannot escape making himself ridiculous at every turn. There is an Intelligence ordering and arranging all these things, not merely corpuscles combining with one another spontaneously.[269]

Galen is probably intending to use a good scientific approach against the bad materialism of Epicureans. For example, he sees in the order that universally characterises nature the mark of a design. If order were only in one species, he argues again in *De usu partium* XI.8, we might even believe that chance exists, as Epicurus and Asclepiades claim. But because order is in every and any species, than prudence and reason are definitely required, and one cannot believe in the monstrous and ridiculous[270] hypothesis of material chance. The Platonic activity of a wise God is thus claimed as the source of nature's perfection and regularity.[271]

---

[267] Gal. *UP* I.10.

[268] Daremberg (in Galien [1854–6], I, pp. 420–2) clarifies what is at stake in Galen's reworking of Aristotle's theory of causality.

[269] Gal. *UP* VI.13. On Galen's theory of causality see also Hankinson (1994).

[270] Gal. *UP* XI.9 and *passim*.

[271] See *contra* P. Moraux, 'Galien comme philosophe: la philosophie de la nature', in Nutton (1982), pp. 87–116, who argues for an immanent principle of regularity, deriving from Aristotle rather than from Plato.

Providence, in this sense, is openly admitted, as an inner faculty that regulates and maintains the otherwise too complex structure of animal bodies:

> For, if there was not *an inborn faculty* given by Nature to each one of the organs at the very beginning, then animals could not continue to live even for a few days, far less for the number of years which they actually do. For let us suppose they were under no guardianship, lacking in creative ingenuity and forethought; let us suppose they were steered only by material forces, and not by any special *faculties* (the one attracting what is proper to it, another rejecting what is foreign, and yet another causing alteration and adhesion of the matter destined to nourish it); if we suppose this, I am sure it would be ridiculous for us to discuss natural, or, still more, physical, activities – or, in fact, life as a whole. For there is not a single animal which could live or endure for the shortest time if, possessing within itself so many different parts, it did not employ faculties which were attractive of what is appropriate, eliminative of what is foreign, and alterative of what is destined for nutrition.[272]

What are then, in this framework, anomalies? Besides the relative differentiation of degrees of perfection that Galen the philosopher, for example, claims between human and ape, Galen the anatomist must be well aware of the existence not only of differences, but also of abnormalities within a single species. Even in this case, Galen thinks that nature cannot be accused of anything. The similitude with art helps build the argument. The great sculptor Polycletus may make a mistake. He remains Polycletus and nobody will dare to accuse him of being unskilled if, among so many perfect works, one or a few of them contain a small error.[273] The relatively small frequency of monstrosities in nature prevents the possibility of accusing such a skilled craftsman. When imperfection becomes more frequent, Galen suggests, then one has to look for its meaning within the whole. The female, for example, is indeed less perfect than the male, as also Aristotle had claimed. As Aristotle recognises, though, she is necessary to procreation and the reproduction of the whole species.[274]

The *Corpus Hermeticum* can be considered a text of transition between Middle and Neoplatonism. The *Corpus* describes the fixed and immutable order of the cosmos, which depends on stable laws of nature.[275] The divine

---

[272] Gal. *Nat. Fac.* II.3.
[273] Gal. UP XVII.1.
[274] Gal. UP XIV.6. See above for Aristotle on the imperfection of females. On the difference between Galen's and Aristotle's teleology see Pichot, 'Introduction', in Galien (1994) and Hankinson (1989).
[275] *Corp.Herm.* XIX and XX.

manifests itself through the beauty and order (τάξις) of the world, which contrasts with its disorder (ἀταξία):[276]

> Everything that is an order <has been made; only> something placeless (ἄτακτος) and measureless (ἄμετρος)[277] can be not made. But even this does not lack a master, my child. Even if the unordered is deficient {– deficient, that is, in that it does not retain the character of order –} it is still subject to a master who has not yet imposed order on it.[278]

The interesting point of this contrast is that the text considers disorder and lack of measure provisional, only a residue of the ancient chaos which has not yet been subjugated and ordered by the master of the universe. It is the material element of it that survives and reveals the original conflict from which everything comes. Order is thus not an essence but a promise, to be reached through a conflictual process which is still in the making.[279]

Corruption is at the heart of this conception, and must be constantly tamed by God, bringing back things to their principle:

> There is nothing evil or shameful about the maker himself; such conditions [sc. evil and disorder] are immediate consequences of generation, like corrosion on bronze or dirt on the body. The bronzesmith did not make the corrosion; the parents did not make the dirt; nor did God make evil. But the persistence of generation makes evil bloom like a sore, which is why God has made change, to repurify generation.[280]

There is a tendency of each thing to decline and move toward imperfection, as if the lapse of time would resolve itself only in an inevitable becoming-monstrous of reality. Only divine intervention can stop this process of corruption, defeating the otherwise unavoidable negativity of terrestrial things, and re-establish order.[281]

---

[276] Corp.Herm. V.3 and VIII.3–4. W. Scott in [Corpus Hermeticum] (1924–36), II.156 ff., suggests the Stoic origin of the argument of contemplation of the world order.

[277] See also Nock and Festugière in [Corpus Hermeticum] (1991, 7e ed.) ad loc.: 'l'absence de lieu et d'ordre', followed by Ramelli in [Corpus Hermeticum] (2005): 'l'assenza di luogo e di misura', and Scarpi in [Corpus Hermeticum] (2009–11): 'mancanza di luogo e di misura'.

[278] Corp.Herm. V.4.

[279] All the terminology employed especially refers to military order and organisation in the army. See W. Scott in [Corpus Hermeticum] (1924–36), II, p. 162.

[280] Corp.Herm. XIV.7.

[281] See also W. Scott, in [Corpus Hermeticum] (1924–36), II, pp. 426–7.

A completely different approach to the problem of order is taken by early Christian Platonists, who face a wide range of theological and philosophical problems in their attempt to explain the order God creates and maintains in the universe, and what role evil, the exception, the abnormality and monstrosity play in it. Christian Platonists often stress God's will and the fact that the order God builds has a teleological and anthropocentric meaning. The concept of a good order is at the heart of the ideas of Justin Martyr, possibly the first Christian apologist to make explicit use of Platonism, in particular the *Timaeus*, mediated by Philo. At the heart of his writings lies the idea of God's plan of creation and salvation, or the οἰκονομία. Clement of Alexandria also makes the εὐταξία, the good order, which is fully dependent on God's will (βούλευμα), one of the central elements of his theology. While humans are at the centre of creation and everything is created for them, Clement is keen to recognise the supreme author and underscore the praise He deserves. There must be no confusion: it is the creator, not the creation, that must be worshipped.[282]

Origen also develops the concept of οἰκονομία, which points to God's activity for the sake of humans: '[. . .] the providence of God justly governs all things and rules immortal souls with the most equitable economy according to the merits and motives of each'.[283] A good administrator, God manages and arranges things in favour of humans – this is the real meaning of providence or πρόνοια. Origen follows Platonism in order to deny the Stoic concept of providence. Providence does not pervade the world as a material πνεῦμα, but as an immaterial soul and informative power that acts from above and gives unity, coherency and consistency to a world that would otherwise be left in chaos.

Origen's position opens up the problem of the interpretation of things and events that seem at odds with the harmony of the world. Monstrosity is among them:

> [. . .] with respect to the works of that providence which embraces the whole world, some appear most clearly to be works of providence, while others are concealed in such a way as to seem to furnish ground for disbelief in that God who orders all things with unspeakable skills and power.[284]

This is especially true for realities on the earth, in contrast with what happens in the sky, where providence's action is more regular and gives less occasion for doubt. The supposed unity and harmony, at least in the earthly world, is

---

[282] See e.g. Clem.Al. *Paed.* I.6.5–6. See also Monfrinotti (2014), pp. 196 ff.
[283] Origenes, *Princ.* III.1.17. See also III.1.13–4, IV.2.2.
[284] Origenes, *Princ.* IV.1.7. See also *Provvidenza*, in Monaci Castagno (2000).

stained by a capricious diversity that might confuse the believer. It is thus of paramount importance for Origen to explain its origin and status. One reads in *On the First Principles*:

> When, *in the beginning*, [God] created those beings that he desired to create, that is, rational beings, he had no other reason for creating them other than himself, that is, his own goodness. As, then, he himself, in whom was neither variation nor change nor inability, was the cause of all those things which were to be created, he created all whom he created equal and alike, since there was in himself no ground for variety and diversity. But since these rational creatures [...] were endowed with the faculty of free will, this freedom of will either incited each one to progress by the imitation of God or drew him to defection through negligence. And this [...] is the cause of the diversity among rational creatures, drawings its origin not from the will or judgement of the Creator, but from the freedom of the individual will. [...] these are the causes, in my opinion, why this world has assumed its diversity, while divine providence arranges each individual according to the variety of their movements or of their intellects and purposes.

God is not interested in, and does not aim at, diversity. The unity and regularity of the world initially reflect God's perfection and depend on His absolute and perfect power. The free will of His creatures, however, makes them diverse, and over time this gives the world the irregular face one can now observe. God's providence keeps directing everything, but not as Stoic fate does. Providence leaves room for imperfection, sin and monstrosity, as much as it allows perfection and purity, which are not ontological features, but are acquired by creatures in the dynamic activity that follows creation. Evil, for this reason, lacks ontological consistency. In the *Commentary on the Gospel according to John*, Origen explains in detail the nature of evil:

> [...] evil or wickedness is opposite to the good, and 'not being' is opposite to 'being'. It follows that wickedness and evil are 'not being'. Perhaps it is this that deceived those who said the devil is not a creation of God. For insofar as he is the devil, he is not a creation of God, but to the extent that it falls to the devil 'to be', being made, since there is no creator except our God; he is a creation of God. It is as if we should say also that a murderer is not a creation of God, while we do not annul the fact that *qua* man, he has been made by God. [...] we said before that 'not being' and 'nothing' are synonyms, and for this reason those 'who are not' are 'nothing', and all evil is 'nothing', since it too is 'not being'.[285]

---

[285] Origenes, *Io.* II.96–9.

Origen's solution is extremely important and influential for how Christian thinkers eventually use the Platonic theory of evil. The idea comes from Platonism, yet Origen modifies it substantially by denying any concrete existence to evil, which is not, as it is in Platonism, the form of the non-being. Evil or imperfection or monstrosity are nothing in themselves, although they are something, insofar that evil, imperfect or monstrous things exist *qua* things. And existing, they can only have been created by God.[286]

Going back to Pagan philosophy, Neoplatonists expand on the main explanations offered by Middle Platonist authors for the sense and meaning of order. What becomes particularly relevant is the question of the autonomy of evil vis-à-vis the divine, and the alternative between dualist and monist readings of their relationship. Plotinus, for example, carries on the critique of materialism and Epicureanism, denouncing the ridiculous hypothesis of an immanent and self-producing order in nature. The atomist cosmogony, based on the παρέγκλισις, means nothing more than absence of causality.[287] Creation, on the contrary, has its own causality, and it is clearly vertical; that is to say, it descends from the higher and divine sphere to the lower realm, making disorder ontologically subordinate and inferior to, and ultimately dependent on, order:

> [. . .] order does not exist because of disorder or law because of lawlessness, as someone [sc. Epicurus] thinks, that these good things may exist and be manifested because of the worse ones; but disorder and lawlessness exist because of order, which is imposed from outside. It is because there is order that disorder exists, and on account of the law and formative reason, just because it is reason, that there is transgression of the law and folly; not that the better things produce the worse, but the things which ought to receive the better are unable to do so because of their own nature or because of some chance circumstance or hindrance from others. For when something has its order from outside it may fail to correspond to it either of its own accord and from itself or because of and impelled by something else; and many things are affected by others when those which act on them do not intend to do so and are aiming at something else.[288]

Plotinus thus establishes a hierarchical relationship that includes particular evil and imperfections under the general presupposition of divine goodness. The world speaks for itself and puts beauty and perfection in front of the acute

---

[286] See *Male*, in Monaci Castagno (2000), as well as Moreschini (2013), pp. 415 ff.
[287] Plot. III.1.1.
[288] Plot. III.2.4. See Boot (1984).

observer's eyes, regardless of the few imperfections and monstrosities that come into existence. Similarly to Galen's argument on Polycletus's hypothetically imperfect statue, Plotinus names the crippled and monstrous Thersites, who certainly does not represent the entirety of the human race. Blaming the whole on account of a rare imperfection is thus simply unreasonable.[289]

Evil assumes interesting features in Plotinus's reading, whose argument on this point will eventually be extremely influential in the following centuries. Plotinus develops the idea that evil is both necessary to goodness and subordinate to it, insofar as it is nothing more than privation or lack (ἔλλειψις) of goodness itself.[290] Using an argument reminiscent of Aristotle's recognition of the necessity of the unaccomplished for the existence of successful accomplishments, Plotinus asks what the divine would be different from, if everything simply were divine and perfect,[291] and what providence would be providential for, if there were nothing to be taken care of.[292] The divine, thus, is placed at centre stage, and its contrary is defined as absence of goodness, the necessary absence that makes its presence possible elsewhere, namely in the highest sphere.[293]

This brings forth a certain relativism in Plotinus's argument, since one ought not to ask whether something is more or less than something else, 'but whether it is, as itself, sufficient; for all things ought not to have been equal. [...] it was according to nature for things to come about so'.[294] Plotinus means here the spontaneous order that emanates from above and descends below, even with its diverse degree of accomplishment. This order is spontaneous and necessary rather than depending on a personal deity, such as for Philo and the Christians.[295] Magris interprets this spontaneous character of the emanation of goodness as a Stoic argument.[296] However, I believe that Stoic immanentism implies the necessary presence of goodness across the creation in equal measure and in every corner of the reality. Plotinus cannot commit to this principle of indistinction and to this *materialisation* of goodness at every level. For him, matter is the imperfect principle that has an inferior degree of goodness's presence.

---

[289] Plot. III.2.3.

[290] See Whittaker (1928, 2nd ed.), p. 78.

[291] Plot. III.2.9. Dragona-Monachou (1994), pp. 4479–80, reads here an echo of the Aristotelian critique of the excessive unity of the universe of Socrates and Plato.

[292] Plot. III.3.7.

[293] Plot. III.2.5 and I.8.6.

[294] Plot. III.3.3 and III.3.5 on the relativity of the aesthetic judgement.

[295] Plot. III.2.14. See Brehier (1928), p. 192, who argues that Plotinus also goes beyond the Platonic image of the anthropomorphic demiurge, too close to the personal god of the Christians.

[296] Magris (1985), pp. 662 ff.

This dynamic relation between perfection and imperfection is framed within a theory of providence. Providence's plan is not to overcome but rather to reflect the diversity that characterises the whole vertical emanation. Its justice, as in Plutarch, is geometrical and not arithmetical: every individual thing has everything it is owed, by having nothing more that it receives:

> Providence, then, which in its descent from above reaches from the beginning to the end, is not equal as in a numerical distribution but differs in different places according to a law of correspondence, just as in a single living creature, which is dependent on its principle down to its last and lowest part, each part having its own, the better part having the better part of the activity, and that which is at the lower limit still active in its own way and undergoing the experiences which are proper to it as regards its own nature and its co-ordination with anything else. [. . .] one thing results from all, and there is one providence; [. . .][297]

Plotinus's providence, however, is far from being the absolute and unconditional guarantee that, as a dogma, it represents for Judeo-Christian thinkers. The treatise on evil reveals, maybe unexpectedly and as an ultimate hesitation, the unstable and conditional character of beauty and harmony in the universe:

> [. . .] because of the power and nature of good, evil is not only evil; since it must necessarily appear, it is bound by a sort of beautiful fetters, as some prisoners are in chains of gold, and hidden by them, so that it may not appear to the gods, although being present, and men may be able not always to look at evil, but even when they do look at it, may be in company with images of beauty to remind them.[298]

Evil must be chained and hidden. It is defeated and thus rendered less ugly, covered up by golden chains, but its makeup is also the ambivalent mark of its rebel character, which always threatens to surface, as a rebel slave, against the order imposed upon him.[299]

Similarly to Plotinus, Porphyry insists on the necessity of a recognisable order in nature. His argument takes the form of the anti-Christian polemic against the almighty God that, as we have seen, also finds its place within Middle Platonism. Porphyry, on the contrary, believes that such a conception

---

[297] Plot. III.3.5. See also Spitzer (1963), pp. 168–9.
[298] Plot. I.8.15. On the text's emendation see Kalligas (2014), p. 241.
[299] Laurent (1992), p. 99.

of God is purely monstrous. Were God to break the good order of the universe, the world would be disfigured and made unnatural:

> Even if such a thing were possible, it is monstrous [τερατώδης] and removed from all that is sensible. For Nature, which created all things from the beginning, appointed places befitting things brought into being, and said each should have its proper sphere [...]. The divine and active Logos [...] does not do and will what he is able to do according to his own ability. Rather according to its suitability he preserves things, watching over things according to the law of order [τὸν τῆς εὐταξίας φυλάττει νόμον]. [...] Nor does he change a man into a winged creature. Nor does he place the stars below and the earth above.[300]

It is within this cultural and intellectual environment that Augustine elaborates one of the most powerful philosophical systems of late Antiquity. It stands at the crossroads of Platonism and Christianism, and is also influenced by Stoicism and Peripateticism. We have already seen the Bishop of Hippo's eclectic reception of Platonism in the question of God's relation to His creation. It is, however, around the question of natural order and the role and status of monstrosity within it that Augustine offers the most interesting and original ideas. Monstrosity becomes for him an explicit domain of enquiry and a theoretical object that deserves philosophical attention. His reflections are spread across his body of work, but it is in *On Order*, the *Confessions* and *On Trinity* that we find the most interesting analyses of the problem.

In his youth, Augustine was haunted by the problem of evil and disorder, especially because of the powerful presence Gnosticism had in his cultural and intellectual formation. When, through Neoplatonism and Plotinus in particular, Augustine embraces Christianity, the problem of evil finds a clear and unambiguous solution, succinctly illustrated through his mother Monica's words in *De ordine*: 'I reject the notion that nothing at all can happen outside God's order. The very evil that began did not do so from within God's order, but God's justice did not allow it to stay out of that order, but reduced and compelled it to become part of it.'[301] The problem of evil is thus the question of its origin, whether it starts inside or outside order. Moving away from the anthropocentrism of several earlier Church Fathers, Augustine insists that the best vantage point from which to frame the problem is the global order, not the limited perspective of an individual. Only from that point of view, as both the Stoics and Plotinus had explained, although differently, can one understand how the universal order encompasses everything, including evil and monstrosity:

---

[300] Cels. 35 (= Mac.Magn. IV.2).
[301] Aug. *De ordine* II.7.23.

A. [. . .] what do you think might be contrary to order? L. Nothing. How can anything be contrary to a whole encompassing everything? Anything contrary to order, strictly speaking, ought to be outside it. But I see nothing outside order, therefore there must be nothing contrary to it. T. Ah, but isn't error contrary to order? L. Not at all. I cannot see anyone making a mistake without a cause. Any series of causes must be included in order. Even error as such is not only due to a cause, but itself becomes the cause of something else as well. then what is not outside order cannot be contrary to it.[302]

Thus everything is within order, *bona et mala in ordine sunt*. This has important consequences for the attitude the good Christian should assume toward all things that happen both in nature and to her. Wonder, for example, which had such an important role in pagan philosophy, is here denounced by Augustine as a vice generated by something that appears to be outside the order. As he explains, this is only the 'obvious' order, the expected order, not the whole encompassing order that contains every and any event. There is nothing in that order that should cause wonder in the mind of those who recognise God's authority and the way He operates upon nature.[303] Foolishness, for example, might disgust those who approach it from the wrong perspective:

> [. . .] the whole life of a fool, though running in fits and starts and in perennial disorder, is nevertheless inserted into the order of things by divine providence. God's ineffable and everlasting law has set aside a definite place for it, not allowing it to operate outside it. Should anyone then limit one's attention to the narrow reality of that life, he would feel utterly disgusted by it. But on raising the eyes of the mind to such heights as to survey the whole universe, he would find nothing out of order, each thing perfectly fitting in its own assigned place.

Once again Augustine invites the reader not to focus on the individual and the particular, to resist the hypnotic force of 'narrow reality' and embrace instead the global perspective of nature as a whole. Once this is done, wonder can be rediscovered, directed, however, not toward the rare and astonishing, but the common and the normal, since normality, the direct expression of God's work, is what truly deserves our wonder.[304]

This attitude makes space for Augustine's attention, unprecedented in early Christian thought, to the topic of monstrous races. We have seen how

---

[302] Aug. *De ordine* I.6.15. See also Plot. III.2.14, III.2.17 and *supra*. Grandgeorge (1896) is still useful for a rapid survey of connected texts of the two authors.
[303] Aug. *De ordine* I.3.8.
[304] See e.g. Aug. *De uera religione* XLIX.94 and *Ciu.* XXI.8. On this idea see Marrou (1958, 2e ed.), pp. 136–57.

monstrous races, for instance in Pliny, were thematised by pagan philosophy. Augustine considers this a typically pagan problem, but one of great importance for the Christian: 'The histories of the nations tell of certain monstrous races of men. If these tales are to be believed, it may be asked whether such monsters are descended from the sons of Noah, or rather from that one man from whom the sons of Noah themselves have come.'[305] He believes prudence is required here. It is the history *of* and *by* pagans that claims the existence of monstrous peoples in remote lands. These tales must thus be accepted only conditionally. If, however, they are true, then their existence is of paramount importance for the theologian, because of problem concerning the origin of these nations in the sacred history.

Augustine then moves forward and speaks *as if* their existence was confirmed, relating and summarising the ancient pagan knowledge, mainly from Pliny, about these peoples:

> Some of these are said to have only one eye, in the middle of their forehead. Others have feet which point backwards, behind their legs. Others combine in themselves the nature of both sexes, having the right breast of a man and the left of a woman, and, when they mate, they take it in turn to beget and conceive. Others have no mouths, and live only by breathing through their nostrils. Othes again are only a cubit high, and these are called Pygmies by the Greeks, after their word for a cubit, *pygme*. Elsewhere, we come across females who conceive at the age of five and who do no live to be more than eight years old. Again, there is a race whose feet are attached to a single leg which does not bend at the knee, yet they move with marvellous speed. These are called 'Shadow-feet' because in hot weather they lie on their backs on the ground and take shelter in the shade of their feet. There are some men without necks, who have eyes in their shoulders; and other men, or men-like cretures, are depicted in mosaic on the marie parade at Carthage, taken from books as examples of the curious things to be found in natural history. And what am I to say of those dog-headed men whose dogs' heads and actual barking show that they are more beasts than men?[306]

Through the accumulation of monstrous features, Augustine seems to seek to produce an effect of astonishment and wonder in his reader. The last race, the Cynocephalies, is presented through a rhetorical question that highlights the list's oddest features and thus seems intended to produce the highest amazement in the reader. Yet as we already know, Augustine wants to undermine

---

[305] Aug. *Ciu.* XVI.8.
[306] Aug. *Ciu.* XVI.8.

amazement and neutralise wonder under the umbrella of an encompassing logic that makes every and any phenomenon, no matter how strange or unbelievable, the production of the unique God. Thus Augustine continues,

> It is not, of course, necessary to believe in all the kinds of men which are said to exist. But anyone who is born anywhere as a man (that is, as a rational and mortal animal), no matter how unusual he may be to our bodily senses in shape, colour, motion, sound, or in any natural power or part or quality, derives from the original and first-created man; and no believer will doubt this. It is, however, clear what constitutes the natural norm in the majority of cases and what, in itself, is a marvellous rarity.[307]

The inclusive logic Augustine develops both magnifies monstrosity and undermines its exceptionality and oddity. Nothing must be left outside of the sacred history, because nothing is outside of the only existing reality, that created by God according to his plan.

This is also true of a less exotic form of monstrosity, namely the physical anomaly, or human monstrosity, which Augustine and his contemporaries might have seen close up. *On Trinity* introduces a new argument that is eventually very influential for Christian writers. After having confirmed that God's will is the cause of everything, and that our amazement about some event has to do with its rarity, as in the case of monstrous births,[308] Augustine links these strange phenomena to miracles. They become both a sort of exceptional language and a language of exceptions, one used by God to signify something to men. Monsters become signs through which the divine communicates with the lower world:

> [...] just as it was not impossible for God to create whatever natures He chose, so it is not impossible for Him to change those natures which He has created in whatever way He chooses. This is why there has sprung up so great a multitude of those marvels which are called 'monsters', 'signs', 'portents' or prodigies'. If I chose to recall and mention them all, would this work ever come to an end? The word 'monster', we are told, clearly comes from 'to demonstrate' [*monstrare*], because monsters are signs by which something is demonstrated. 'Sign' [*ostentum*] comes from 'to show' [*ostendere*]; 'portent' from 'to portend', that is 'to show in advance' [*praeostendere*]; and 'prodigy' from 'to speak of what is far away' [*porro dicere*], that is, to foretell the future.[309]

---

[307] Aug. *Ciu.* XVI.8. See also *Ciu.* XXI.8.
[308] Aug. *De trinitate* III.2.7.
[309] Aug. *Ciu.* XXI.8. See also *De trinitate* III.10.19.

Human monstrosities thus prolong the argument about monstrous races, only to confirm and, if possible, reinforce the inclusive and normalising logic that Augustine intends to develop. Augustine is aware, of course, that this logic does not add anything to the actual knowledge and aetiological understanding of monstrosity. Yet this is not a difficulty for him. On the contrary, he reintroduces here the argument of God's ineffability and incomprehensibility, in line with his transcendentalism. Only God perfectly knows himself, and humans should not even dare to attempt a similar understanding. Monstrosity thus also serves to remind us of the finitude of human intellect:

> He Himself knows where and when anything should be, or should have been, created; and He knows how to weave the beauty of the whole out of the similarity and diversity of its parts. The man who cannot view the whole is offended by what he takes to be the deformity of a part; but this is because he does not know how it is adapted or related to the whole. We know of men who were born with more than five fingers or five toes. This is a trivial thing and not any great divergence from the norm. God forbid, however, that someone who does not know why the Creator has done what He has done should be foolish enough to suppose that God has in such cases erred in allotting the number of human fingers. So, then, even if a greater divergence should occur, He Whose work no one may justly condemn knows what He has done.[310]

No ambiguity is possible for Augustine. Using his Platonic theoretical arsenal, revised and strengthened by Christian theology, Augustine takes on the Aristotelian and Peripatetic theory that sees monstrosity as a result of a failed actualisation of forms. Unlike Aristotle's nature, God never errs. As the Stoics understood, we must embrace the whole with our limited intellect, not to fully understand it, but to fully accept it in all its manifestations, even monstrous ones.[311]

At the end of this chapter of *The City of God*, Augustine pushes his interpretation one step further. His argument seems to fall back on anthropocentrism of a sort:

> If, however, the creatures of which these wondrous things are written are indeed men, why was it God's will to create some races in this way? Perhaps it was so that, when monsters are born of men among us, as they must be, we should not think them the work of an imperfect craftsman: perhaps it was so that we should not suppose that, despite the wisdom with which

---

[310] Aug. *Ciu.* XXI.8.
[311] See Bouton-Toubolic (2004), pp. 200–1.

He fashions the nature of human beings, God has on this occasion erred. In which case, it ought not to seem absurd to us that, just as some monsters occur within the various races of mankind, so there should be certain monstrous races within the human race as a whole. I shall, then, conclude my discussion of this question with a tentative and cautious answer. Either the written accounts which we have of some of these races are completely worthless; or, if such creatures exist, they are not men; or, if they are men, they are descended from Adam.[312]

This conclusion is notable more for its prudence than for its philosophical power. Besides the fact that it does not explain why or how God would make a monster to be born among us (unless, indirectly, to signify something to humans, as a miracle or a sign), the hypothesis is at least disproportionate. God created entire races of monsters so that, when one of them is born among us, we will not be amazed. But we should probably stop looking for the argument of a scientist or a Platonist philosopher here, and see what Augustine wants his reader to see, that is, the logic that inflexibly includes everything under the positive power of God. Monsters do not exist or, if they exist, they are not humans or, if they are humans, then they are no different from us, i.e. sons and daughters of the same man created by the only God.

For Augustine, it is really a matter of seeing. Better, it is a matter of training our vision through faith so it can discern what is in fact already under our eyes, namely the beauty of creation. Augustine's Platonism, here, converges with the Stoic praise for the universe's beauty that Cicero, Galen and Lactantius, among others, had so profoundly expressed. Our situation, Augustine explains in *De Ordine*,

> is akin to that of one who, confined to surveying a single section of a mosaic floor, looked at it too closely, and then blamed the artisan [*artifex*] for being ignorant of order and composition, In reality it is he himself who, in concentrating on an apparently disordered variety of small coloured cubes, failed to notice the larger mosaic work. The apparent disorder of the elements really comes together onto the unity of a beautiful portrait. The same can be said of the feeble-minded ignoramus. Unable to grasp the harmony and interaction of the universe as a whole [*universam rerum coaptationem atque concentum*], and hurt by what is beyond their ken, such people rashly conclude that things are inherently ugly and disorderly.[313]

---

[312] Aug. *Ciu.* XXI.8.
[313] Aug. *De ordine* I.1.2. See *infra*, Cic. *Diu.* II.33 and *ND* II.119. See also *SVF* II.534, 546, 1013, and 1211.

This passage reveals Stoicism's great influence on the idea of harmony. Cicero translates the Stoic συμπάθεια with *concentus naturae*, which is the argument that Stoics and Middle Platonists used to oppose the Atomist hypothesis, precisely as Augustine does, by denouncing the absurdity of chance and playing *ratio* against *casus*.[314]

It is however Platonism, particularly Plotinus, that most inspires Augustine in his concluding argument on the ontological consistency of evil. Against Gnosticism and Manichaeism, Augustine explains that evil must not be thought of as some sort of negative substance, but rather as lack and privation of substance,[315] as privation and non-being:

> It was obvious to me that things which are liable to corruption are good. If they were the supreme goods, or if they were not good at all, they could not be corrupted. For if they were supreme goods, they would be incorruptible. If there were no good in them, there would be nothing capable of being corrupted. [...] whatever things exist are good, and the evil into whose origins I was inquiring is not a substance, for if it were a substance, it would be good. Either it would be an incorruptible substance, a great good indeed, or a corruptible substance, which could be corrupted only if it were good. Hence I saw and it was made clear to me that you made all things good, and there are absolutely no substances which you did not make.[316]

There is no substantial evil in the world, just as there is no real monstrosity. The reality of evil and monstrosity around us, however, demands an explanation, a theodicy, and Augustine uses arguments from Neoplatonism to explain that evil is not the opposite of goodness, but only a lack, a minor imperfection characterising things that nonetheless originate in God. Moreover, Augustine adds, once again revealing not only the Stoic accents of his philosophy, but also elements of Aristotelianism, filtered through Plotinus, evil is the condition of goodness. It is something that makes the world move in the right direction and that contributes, indirectly and idiosyncratically, but nonetheless necessarily, to the global perfection of the universe:

> God does not love evil. It would not be in order for Him to do so. He loves order so much that for its sake He does not love evil. Since God does not love evil, does it mean that there can be any evil outside order? This is precisely the order of evil things, that God should not love them. Do you

---

[314] On this passage, see Solignac (1957), p. 451 and Trelenberg (2009).
[315] Aug. *Confessiones* V.10.19–20.
[316] Aug. *Confessiones* VII.12.18.

think it is a mean order that God should love good things and not evil ones? Evil things are not outside order because God does not love them. He in fact loves to love good things, and also loves not to love evil things. This is the greater order of divine disposition. Both order and disposition keep the universe together by this very distinction, rendering the existence of evil somewhat necessary. This clashing of contraries, which we love so much in rhetoric, gives body to the overall beauty of the universe.[317]

The nonbeing of evil is one of the theories in which Augustine comes closer to his Neoplatonic sources. It is also the metaphysical ground of his theory of monstrosity, both of which were eventually extremely influential for Christian thinkers. The debate, however, also continues in pagan Neoplatonism, in particular in Proclus. Augustine's theory, especially his metaphysics, helps us understand this further development of Neoplatonism and its consequences for late Antiquity's comprehension of the problem of monstrosity.

Proclus maintains the sufficiency and perfection of natural order, to which nothing could be added that would make it better than it actually is. Everything is in agreement with the whole, and particular imperfections are subordinated to the universal perfection.[318] Even for Proclus, thus, evil's existence is quasi-paradoxical: inferior and yet necessary. Its Being is not absolute but relative, because evil exists as mixed and subordinated to the good.[319] The consequence of this relative existence, though, is that evil's necessity must be accepted, with everything that is corrupted, deformed and even monstrous, because the whole needs it for its internal articulation.[320]

The typical Neoplatonic conception of a hierarchical order is the attempted solution to such a paradox. The relative ontological consistency of different things translates into a layered conception of the universe, structured according to different levels of perfection.[321] Monstrosity is thus not an absolute concept, but only the specific charateristic of individual things that can only be said monstrous in themselves. Nothing, in fact, is against nature, since nature's order encompasses everything. This solution, however, rather than limiting and circumscribing monstrosity, spreads it over the entirety of nature itself. In some sense, if nothing is monstrous and imperfect for nature in its entirety, *everything* becomes in a certain manner monstrous for any particular nature, when it is considered in itself. No matter, in fact, how high or low

---

[317] Aug. *De ordine* I.7.18. See also II.1.2 and *Evil and Theodicy*, in Pollman et al. (2013).
[318] Procl. *Opusc. De providentia et fato* 34.
[319] Procl. *Opusc. De malorum subsistentia* 7 and 9.
[320] Procl. *Opusc. De malorum subsistentia* 5.
[321] Procl. *Opusc. De malorum subsistentia* 10.

something is in the scale of Being, it is always marked by its imperfection.[322] Proof of it is that a certain disorder, although different from the material one, can be found even in the higher sphere, since order, at every ontological level, must fight with disorder to establish itself.[323]

Providence, in any case, takes care of the single parts as much as of the entire whole, of beings against nature, as much as of beings according to nature, of the individual without a species (*sine specie*), as much as of entire species.[324] As in Plutarch and Plotinus, though, providence's justice is geometrical and not arithmetical. The providential design is one, but it is not the same for everything.[325] Things themselves are determined to receive more or less from providence, depending on their degree of perfection: 'tantum capere quantum potest recipere'.[326]

Proclus's energies are also devoted to building a strong theodicy. Evil must not be thought of in contrast with providence. On the contrary, it exists to allow the perfection of the whole *qua* whole and to distinguish the first from the last things. Evil can thus be said to exist *because of* providence and certainly according to it, for the sake of the higher good. Evil things can, for example, be the cause of the generation of other things, whose goodness might not be immediately clear to humans. What exists *for* the good cannot be entirely evil. This explains the strongly teleological nature of the universe's structure. The goodness of the ultimate effect casts its shadow backward on the antecedent cause, rendering it functional to the highest *end*, no matter what the nature of the *means* is, either good, or evil.[327]

The language of teleology insinuates itself into Proclus's argument with unparalleled strength. Finalism keeps evil in check, building a special concept of ontological consistency for it:

> Certainly one must not put the final cause of all among the causes of evil. Indeed, it would not be suitable that the good were the goal of evils. But since souls pursue what is in every way good and do everything, including

---

[322] Procl. *Opusc. De malorum subsistentia* 27. Sorabji ed. (2004), p. 58, underlines the presence of this idea in Chrysippus and Philoponos.
[323] Procl. *Opusc. De malorum subsistentia* 29.
[324] Procl. *Opusc. De malorum subsistentia* 4. *De malorum* only survives in William of Moerbeke's thirteenth-century Latin translation and in a summary by the eleventh-century Byzantine prince Isaak Sebastokrator. *Sine specie* translates ἀνείδεος, often coupled with ἄπλαστος, thus formless in the same sense that evil is vis-à-vis goodness. See DGA *sub voce* and also Plotin's use of the term in I.8.3. On providence's range see also *Opusc. De decem dubitationibus circa providentia* II.6 and *Theol. Plat.* I.12–17.
[325] Procl. *Opusc. De malorum subsistentia* 17–8.
[326] Procl. *Opusc. De malorum subsistentia* 20.
[327] Procl. *Opusc. De decem dubitationibus* 29.

evil things, for its sake, someone might perhaps think that for evils, too, the good is the final cause. For all things are for the sake of this good, all the good and all the contrary things alike. [...] perhaps it would be better to make neither the efficient cause, nor the natural paradigm, nor the *per se* final cause the principal cause of evils. For the form of evils, their nature, is a kind of defect, an indeterminateness and a privation; their [mode of existence, or] *hupostasis*, is, as it is usually said, more like a kind of [parasitic existence, or] *parupostasis*.[328]

Evil takes its power from the good within which, like a parasite, it insinuates itself.[329] It has a quasi-existence, a παρά-ὑπόστασις, in the sense that it does not exist *properly* (κυρίως). It has however the power to actively absorb something from its contrary. It is not only the negation of good. It is its negation by virtue of its participation in it, which is in fact a violation of the good's purity and integrity. Sharing one of the classic attributes of monsters, evil is also incapable of generation (ἄγονος). Being deprived of the fount of good things, unlimited, weak, incommensurate, false, ugly, unfounded in its own nature, unstable, bearing only privation and lifelessness, it embodies one of the strongest figures of monstrosity of late ancient philosophy. Because the highest cause is the final cause, and because evil is not produced from a principal cause, nor has it an end, nor does it belong to any order of which it would be a positive means, evil is deprived of consistency and reduced to a parasitic existence: 'Everything that is produced, is produced for the sake of the good; but evil, coming from outside and being adventitious, consists in the non-attainment of that which is the appropriate goal of each thing.'[330]

Proclus also establishes a connection between the external and non-teleological character of evil and the idea of multiplicity, as opposed to the One. It is a dangerous pattern, since everything below the One incurs the risk of becoming evil in a certain manner, precisely because of its essential alterity:

> The non-attainment is due to the weakness of the agent, since the agent has received a nature of such a kind that a part of it is better, a part worse, each part being separate from the other. For where the One is, there at the same time is the good. But evil is – and the One is not – present in a split nature. For incommensurability, disharmony and contrariety are in multitude; and from these weakness and indigence proceed. Indeed, in the gods, too, are to be found the 'winged nature' and 'both horses'; but there 'these are all good, consist of good things' and not 'of contrary things'. But

---

[328] Procl. *Opusc. De malorum subsistentia* 49.
[329] Procl. *Opusc. De malorum subsistentia* 52–4. See also Procl. *Theol. Plat.* I.18.
[330] Procl. *Opusc. De malorum subsistentia* 50.

in other beings these are mixed; in them there is multitude and diversity of powers, and each [of these powers] pulls towards different things. In the superior realm multitude looks at the One and is determined according to one kind of life. But where multitude and diversity appear because of a decrease in union, there lack of power appears – for all power is what it is by the One and from the One –, as well as disharmony and dissidence of one thing from another, each being drawn by its own desires.[331]

The opposition built by Proclus seems to weaken the concept of παρυποστᾶσις, since besides the One, what would not be engulfed by alterity and multiplicity? A closer scrutiny of the concept can perhaps clarify the ambivalent existence of evil. Sorabji explores the παρυπόστασις within the framework of the commentaries.[332] Following Opsomer and Steel, Sorabji locates its origin in Aristotle's thought, and in particular in the account of coincidences and chance events that are not due to nature's intention.[333] While Sorabji mainly sees a link with Aristotle's *Metaphysics*,[334] Opsomer and Steel also relate the παρυπόστασις to the Aristotelian texts in which monstrosity is explained, i.e. *Ph*. II.4–5.[335]

In an influential article, A. C. Lloyd had suggested interpreting the παρυπόστασις as a parasitic existence rather than a quasi-existence.[336] His analysis is based not only on *De malorum subsistentia*, but also on Proclus's commentaries and the *Platonic Theology*. Lloyd underlines the weak existence of evil, which is something next to nothing and yet capable of attaining, and sometimes even overcoming, the unity of being. It is a perversion of a preceding and perfect form of existence 'combining the notions of incidental and from outside.' It is a parasite, insofar as it is dependent on the host to ensure its survival.[337] Lloyd thus criticises D. Isaac's interpretation, based on a more conflictual and threatening idea. The παρυπόστασις, in Isaac's view, is the original and inspired solution given by Proclus to the problem of naming what is at the same time contrary, complementary, symmetrical and subordinated, 'that is to say a counter existence, an inverted replica of the Good, a shade of the Real,

---

[331] Procl. *Opusc. De malorum subsistentia* 50.
[332] Sorabji ed. (2004), pp. 95 ff.
[333] Sorabji ed. (2004), p. 100.
[334] Arist. *Metaph*. VI.3.
[335] J. Opsomer, C. Steel, Introduction, in Proclus (2003), p. 26: 'The basis of Proclus' argument is certainly Aristotle's distinction between a causality *per se* and a causality *per accidens*. The accidental is not necessary, but indeterminate (*aoriston*); and of such a thing the causes are unordered (*atakta*) and indefinite (*apeira*).' See Arist. *Ph*. II.4–6 and *supra*.
[336] A. C. Lloyd, *Parhypostasis in Proclus*, in Boss, Seel éds. (1987), pp. 145–57.
[337] A. C. Lloyd, *Parhypostasis in Proclus*, in Boss, Seel éds. (1987), p. 157.

something secondary and relative implying degrees, vis-a-vis the primary absolute without them. [...] With Proclus, the [παρυπόστασις] takes definitively the sense of opposition, deviation, diminution, and dependance.'[338] Isaac thus accepts the parasitic character of evil, but he also underlines its non-osmotic nature, that is to say the character of the malignant guest that openly threats its host by its parasitic activity.

In my view, the παρυπόστασις brings to mind the existence of the Platonic *simulacrum*. I believe that Lloyd's characterisation excessively neutralises the threatening nature of evil *qua* monstrous other.[339] Isaac grasps something In Proclus's struggle to set the divine free from any responsibility vis-à-vis evil, while maintaining a strictly monistic approach, like Plotinus before him. Evil has a counter-existence, which is indeed parasitic, not only in the sense of being subordinate, but also disturbingly malignant and threateningly alien.

The danger of characterising all nature as evil through the παρυπόστασις is great. Proclus makes use of monstrosity to clarify, at the end of the treatise, the way in which evil can be said to be subordinated, functional and parasitically part of the good. The parasitic and adventitious dimension of evil is explicitly connected with many of the characteristics of monstrosity: disharmony, formlessness, deformity of the body and the mind.[340] Evil is assimilated to the *monstra naturae* (τέρατα φύσεος), the monsters that haunt all of nature and yet belong to it:

> The evil inherent in bodies [...] is twofold, one kind existing as foulness, the other as disease – I call foul all things contrary to nature that are not diseases, for monsters, too, are foulnesses of nature. Of these two kinds, [let us consider] foulness. Foulness is in accordance with universal nature, as reason and form are to be found in it, <yet not in accordance with particular nature.> indeed, in a particular nature there is one rational principle, and what is contrary to it is for this thing against nature, but in universal nature all the rational principles and forms exist naturally. And sometimes one thing only is generated out of one form [...] sometimes many things are generated out of one thing [...] sometimes one thing is generated out of many, as in the case of mixtures of matter-related forms – these mixtures

---

[338] D. Isaac, *Introduction*, in Proclus (1977–82), III, pp. 13 and 15.
[339] A. C. Lloyd, *Parhypostasis in Proclus*, in Boss, Seel éds. (1987), p. 155: 'In M. Isaac's case I can certainly find no good reason to translate "parhypostasis" as "contre-existence." If Proclus has understood it on the analogy of παρὰ φύσιν he would, I think, have made this clearer than he has, to judge by Moerbeke's translation and Sebastokrator's résumé of *De mal. subsist.* 50.'
[340] Procl. *Opusc. De malorum subsistentia* 56–7.

seem to be monsters with respect to the individual nature, which desires to be dominated by and exist according to a single form; sometimes many things are generated from many things [...].[341]

The spectre of multiplicity is haunting nature. Proclus's attempt is to follow the traditional pattern of many and different parts of a single whole. Yet the one single form to which everything naturally aspires is doomed to be only partially attained. Every *real* existence, beyond the perfectly formal one, is a parasitic existence that spreads monstrosity throughout nature.

The discourse on monstrosity progresses and develops through several transformations in Middle and Neoplatonism. Platonist philosophers make a great effort in discussing, interacting with and appropriating theories and doctrines from the principal Hellenistic systems, in order to recover the ancient Platonic message without losing its original character. Their attempt is directed mainly at integrating evil and monstrosity in the world, explaining them, making sense of their apparently irrational and threatening character. The aim is to save the divine from evil: an apparently paradoxical enterprise, since evil is by definition inferior, for Platonists, to the divine. And yet, without this attempt, God himself, the God of the philosophers, would be weakened, facing the multifarious manifestations of a threatening nature: the Zeus of Platonism has yet to overcome Typhoeus.

For reasons of consistency, I have explored Middle and Neoplatonism, a complex and long-lived philosophical movement, through the same categories used in previous chapters, namely the conflict between immanence and transcendence, the questions of nature's hierarchies, teleology and providence, and the origin of evil. However, I introduced new elements because of the peculiar reworking of these ideas within the new monotheism of the Judeo-Christian early tradition, as well as their importance for the later medieval and early modern philosophy. The reflection on monstrosity, however, plays a central role in the task of elaborating a systematic response to many if not all of the problems explored in the previous chapters.

Middle and Neoplatonism try to introduce evil and monstrosity in a scale of being, through a hierarchy that emanates from above and receives, in different degrees, the unique perfection of the One. Yet the solutions are different, because so are the problems and the philosophical threats that these thinkers consider, addressed to them by philosophers of different schools. Monstrosity is normalised. It is normalised, though, by spreading it across the hierarchy of beings, all the more intensely the more one moves away from the One and the higher reality. Evil and monstrosity are assigned a paradoxical role in this

---

[341] Procl. *Opusc. De malorum subsistentia* 60.

ontological structure: an inferior and yet a necessary one. Not only, thus, are Being and the divine not saved from monstrosity; they are, on the contrary, attacked by it at every level of being. The Platonic discourse on monstrosity culminates in the concept of parasitic existence. Far from being the solution, this is, for ancient philosophy, only the beginning of the philosophical problem. As the parasite cannot live without its host, the host, in this case, cannot *exist*, beyond its *essence*, without *hosting* the parasite. Only a fully theological decision is now able to prevent philosophy from succumbing to the problem of monstrosity. Christian theology takes Platonism, together with other metaphysical solutions, with the only exception of the mechanist and Epicuren one, as its ground to develop a new perspective.

Bibliography

Reference Works

Adrados, F. R. (dir.) (1989–). *Diccionario griego-español*. Madrid: Consejo Superior de Investigaciones Científicas.

Andresen, C. et al. (1965). *Lexicon der alten Welt*. Zürich: Artemis Verlag.

Auroux, S. (éd.) (1990). *Les notions philosophiques. Dictionnaire*. Paris: Presses Universitaires de France. [Abbreviated: Auroux]

Bailly, A. (1961). *Dictionnaire grec-français*. Ed. revue par L. Séchan et P. Chantraine. Paris: Hachette.

Bell, R. E. (1982). *Dictionary of Classical Mythology: Symbols, Attributes and Associations*. Santa Barbara: ABC-CLIO.

Bell, R. E. (1991). *Women of Classical Mythology: A Biographical Dictionary*. Santa Barbara: ABC-CLIO.

Betz, H. D. et al. (hrsg.) (1988–2005). *Religion in Geschichte und Gegenwart. Handwörterbuch für Theologie und Religionswissenschaften. Vierte, völlig neu bearbeitete Auflage*. Tübingen: Mohr Siebeck.

Betz, H. D. et al. (eds) (2007). *Religion Past and Present: Encyclopedia of Theology and Religion*. Leiden, Boston, Cologne: E. J. Brill.

Blaise, A. (1954). *Dictionnaire latin-français des auteurs chrétiens*. Turnout: Brepols.

Boardman, J. et al. (eds) (1981–2009). *Lexicon Iconographicum Mythologiae Classicae*. Zürich: Artemis Verlag. [Abbreviated: LIMC]

Bodoh, J. J. (1970). *An Index of Greek Verb Forms*. Hildesheim, Zürich and New York: Olms-Weidmann.

Boisacq, E. (1938). *Dictionnaire étymologique de la langue grecque*. 3e ed. Paris: Klincksieck, and Heidelberg: Winter.

Botterweck, G. J. et al. (hrsg.) (1970–93). *Theologisches Wörterbuch zum alten Testament*. Stuttgart: Kohlhammer.

Brodersen, K., and B. Zimmermann (2000). *Metzler Lexikon Antike*. Stuttgart: Metzler.

Brunner, H., K. Fessel, F. Hiller et al. (hrsg.) (1990–93). *Lexikon Alte Kulturen.* Mannheim: Meyers Lexikonverlag.

Brunner, O., W. Conze and R. Koselleck (eds) (2004). *Geschichtliche Grundbegriffe.* 2 ed. Stuttgart: Klett-Cotta.

Brunotte, H., and O. Weber (hrsg.) (1956–61). *Evangelisches Kirkenlexicon. Kirchlich-theologisches Handwörterbuch.* Göttingen: Vandenhoeck & Ruprecht.

Cancik, H., and H. Schneider (hrsg.) (1996–2003). *Der Neue Pauly. Enzyklopädie der Antike.* Stuttgart: J. T. Metzler.

Cassin, B. (éd.) (2004). *Vocabulaire européen des philosophies: Dictionnaire des intraduisibles.* Paris: Seuil.

Cassin, B. (ed.) (2014). *Dictionary of Untranslatables: A Philosophical Lexicon.* Princeton and Oxford: Princeton University Press.

Chantraine, P. (1968–80). *Dictionnaire étymologique de la langue grecque. Histoire des mots.* Paris: Editions Klincksieck. [Abbreviated: Chantraine]

Chevalier, J. (éd.) (1969). *Dictionnaire des symboles.* Paris: Robert Laffont.

Craig, E. (ed.) (1998). *Routledge Encyclopedia of Philosophy.* London: Routledge and Kegan Paul.

Danker, F. W. (2000). *A Greek-English Lexicon of the New Testament and Other Early Christian Literature.* 3rd ed. Chicago and London: University of Chicago Press.

Daremberg, C., and E. Saglio (éds.) (1877–1919). *Dictionnaire des antiquités grecques et romaines d'après les textes et les monuments.* Paris: Hachette.

Della Corte, F. (1987). *Dizionario degli scrittori greci e latini.* Milan: Marzorati.

Di Berardino, A. (a cura di) (1983). *Dizionario patristico e di antichità cristiane.* Genoa: Marietti.

Ernout, A., and A. Meillet (1959). *Dictionnaire étymologique de la langue latine. Histoire des mots.* Paris: Editions Klincksieck.

Estienne, H. (2008). *Thesaurus graecae linguae.* Naples: La scuola di Pitagora editrice. [Abbreviated: TGL]

Fahlbusch, E. et al. (eds) (1999). *Encyclopedia of Christianity.* Leiden, Boston and Cologne: E. J. Brill.

Fontanier, J.-M. (2012). *Le lexicon. Dictionnaire trilingue français, latin, grec.* Rennes: Presses universitaires de Rennes.

Forcellini, A. (1831). *Lexicon totius latinitatis.* Schneebergae: Sumptibus et typis G. Schumanni.

Frisk, H. (1973). *Griechisches etymologisches Wörterbuch.* 2. ed. Heidelberg: C. Winter.

Gantz, T. (1993). *Early Greek Myths: A Guide to Literary and Artistic Sources.* Baltimore and London: The Johns Hopkins University Press.

Glare, P. G. W. (1968–). *Oxford Latin Dictionary.* Oxford: Clarendon Press. [Abbreviated: OLD]

Goulet, R. (ed.) (1989–). *Dictionnaire des philosophes antiques.* Paris: CNRS Editions.

Grimal, P. (1951). *Dictionnaire de la mythologie grecque et romaine.* Paris: Presses Universitaires de France.

Hornblower, S., and A. Spaworth (2012). *Oxford Classical Dictionary.* 4th ed. Oxford: Oxford University Press.

Klauser, T. (1941–). *Reallexikon für Antike und Christentum.* Stuttgart: A. Hiersemann.

Krause, G., and G. Müller (hrsg.) (1977–2004). *Theologische Realenzyklopädie.* Berlin and New York: Walter de Gruyter.

Lacoste, J.-Y. (1998). *Dictionnaire Critique de Théologie.* Paris: Presses Universitaires de France.

Lalande, A. (1956). *Vocabulaire technique et critique de la philosophie.* 7e ed. Paris: Presses Universitaires de France. [Abbreviated: Lalande]

Lampe, G. W. H. (1961). *A Patristic Greek Lexicon.* Oxford: Clarendon Press.

Landfester, M., H. Cancik and H. Schneider (eds) (2006–11). *Brill's New Pauly.* Leiden, Boston and Cologne: E. J. Brill. [Abbreviated: BNP]

Leclant, J. (éd.) (2000). *Dictionnaire de l'antiquité.* Paris: Presses Universitaires de France.

Liddell, H. G., and R. Scott (eds) (1940). *A Greek-English Lexicon.* 9th ed. Oxford: Clarendon Press. [Abbreviated: LSJ]

Pauly, A., G. Wissowa et al. (hrsg.) (1893–; 1972–). *Pauly's Real- Encyclopädie der Classischen Altertumswissenschaft, neue Bearbeitung begonnen von G. Wissowa.* Munich: Alfred Druckenmüller Verlag. [Abbreviated: RE]

Pizzardo, G., and P. Paschini (éds.) (1948–54). *Enciclopedia cattolica.* Vatican City: Ente per l'enciclopedia cattolica.

Reid, J. D. (1993). *The Oxford Guide to Classical Mythology in the Arts, 1300–1900s.* Oxford: Oxford University Press.

Ritter, J., and K. Gründer (hrsg.) (1971–2007). *Historische Wörterbuch der Philosophie.* Basel and Stuttgart: Schwabe & Co.

Roberts, H. E. (ed.) (1998). *Encyclopedia of Comparative Iconography: Themes Depicted in Works of Art.* Chicago and London: Fitzroy Dearborn.

Romano, R. (a cura di) (1977–84). *Enciclopedia Einaudi.* Turin: Einaudi.

Roscher, W. H. (hrsg.) (1884–90). *Ausführliches Lexikon der griechischen und römischen Mythologie.* Leipzig: Teubner.

Roth, C., and G. Wigoder (eds) (1971–2). *Encyclopaedia Judaica.* Jerusalem: Keter Publishing House.

Schmitt, H. H. (hrsg.) (1993). *Kleines Wörterbuch des Hellenismus.* 2. ed. Wiesbaden: O. Harrassowitz.

Souriau, E. (éd.) (1990). *Vocabulaire d'esthétique.* Paris: Presses Universitaires de France.

Souter, A. (ed.) (1957). *A Glossary of Later Latin to 600 ad*. 2nd ed. Oxford: Clarendon Press.
Thesaurus linguae latinae (1900–6). Leipzig: Teubner. [Abbreviated: TLL]
Ueding, G. (hrsg.) (1992–2014). *Historische Wörterbuch der Rhetorik*. Tübingen: Max Niemeyer Verlag. [Abbreviated: HRW]
Vacant, P. et alii. (éds.) (1903–50). *Dictionnaire de théologie catholique*. Paris: Letouzey & Ané.
Vigouroux, F. (éd.) (1881–). *Dictionnaire de la Bible*. Paris: Letouzey & Ané.
Walde, A. (1938). *Lateinisches etymologisches Wörterbuch*. 3 neubearbeitete Auflage von J. B. Hofmann. Heidelberg: C. Winter.
Woodhouse, S. C. (1932). *English-Greek Dictionary: A Vocabulary of the Attic Language*. 2nd ed. London: Routledge and Kegan Paul.
Wuellner, B. (1956). *Dictionary of Scholastic Philosophy*. Milwaukee: Bruce Publishing Company.
Zeyl, D. J. (ed.) (1997). *Encyclopedia of Classical Philosophy*. London and Chicago: Fitzroy Dearborn.

Electronic Resources

Ancient Commentators on Aristotle Project. General editor, R. Sorabji. <http://www.kcl.ac.uk/artshums/depts/philosophy/research/commentators/index.aspx> (last accessed 13 April 2019).
Bibliothèque numérique Medic@. <http://www.biusante.parisdescartes.fr/histoire/medica/index.php> (last accessed 13 April 2019).
Corpus Medicorum Graecorum. <http://cmg.bbaw.de/epubl/online/editionen.html> (last accessed 13 April 2019).
Corpus Thomisticum. Subsidia Studii ab E. Alarcón collecta et edita: <http://www.corpusthomisticum.org/> (last accessed 13 April 2019).
Diccionario griego-español. Editor-in-chief, F. R. Adrados. <http://dge.cchs.csic.es/> (last accessed 13 April 2019).
Le Dictionnaire des Antiquités Grecques et Romaines de Daremberg et Saglio. <http://dagr.univ-tlse2.fr/sdx/dagr/index.xsp> (last accessed 13 April 2019).
Iconclass. <www.iconclass.nl/home> (last accessed 13 April 2019).
LSJ, wiki implementation. <https://lsj.translatum.gr/wiki/Main_Page> (last accessed 13 April 2019).
Stanford Encyclopedia of Philosophy. Principal editor, E. N. Zalta. <http://plato.stanford.edu/index.html> (last accessed 13 April 2019).
The Suda on Line: Byzantine Lexicography. Senior editor, D. Whitehead. <www.stoa.org/sol> (last accessed 13 April 2019).
Thesaurus Linguae Graecae: A Digital Library of Greek Literature. Project director, M. Pantelia. <http://stephanus.tlg.uci.edu/index.php> (last accessed 13 April 2019).

Primary Sources

[A.]

Eschyle (1920–5). [*Tragédies*]. Texte établi et traduit par P. Mazon. Paris: Les Belles Lettres.

Aeschylus (1926). [*Tragedies*]. With an English translation by H. Lloyd-Jones. Cambridge, MA: Harvard University Press.

Eschilo (2003). *Le tragedie*. A cura di M. Centanni. Milan: Mondadori.

Aeschylus (2008). [*Tragedies*]. Edited and translated by A. H. Sommerstein. Cambridge, MA: Harvard University Press.

Aeschylus (2008). *Fragments*. Edited and translated by A. H. Sommerstein. Cambridge, MA: Harvard University Press.

[A.R.]

Apollonios de Rhodes (1974–81). *Argonautique*. Texte établi et commenté par F. Vian et traduit par E. Delage. Paris: Les Belles Lettres.

Apollonius Rhodius (1988). *Argonautica*. With an English translation by R. C. Seaton. Cambridge, MA: Harvard University Press.

AA.VV. (1970). *The Ante-Nicene Fathers*. Translations of *The Writings of the Fathers down to ad 325*. Edited by A. Roberts and J. Donaldson. Revised and chronologically arranged, with brief prefaces and occasional notes by A. C. Coxe. Grand Rapids, MI: Wm. B. Eerdmans Publishing Company.

AA.VV. (1982). *Greek Lyric*. Edited and translated by D. A. Campbell. Cambridge, MA: Harvard University Press.

AA.VV. (1989–2008). *Corpus dei papiri filosofici greci e latini*. Florence: Olschki.

[Ael.]

Aelian (1958–9). *On the Characteristics of Animals*. With an English translation by A. F. Scholfield. Cambridge, MA: Harvard University Press.

Aelian (1997). *Historical Miscellany*. With an English translation by N. G. Wilson. Cambridge, MA: Harvard University Press.

[Aenesidemus Cnossius philosophus]

Aenesidemus of Cnossus (2014). *Testimonia*. Edited with introduction and commentary by R. Polito. Cambridge: Cambridge University Press.

[Alcin.]

Invernizzi, G. (1976). *Il Didaskalikos di Albino e il medioplatonismo. Saggio di interpretazione storico-filosofica con traduzione e commento*. Rome: Abete.

Alcinoos (1990). *Enseignement des doctrines de Platon*. Introduction, texte établi et commenté par J. Whittaker, et traduit par P. Louis. Paris: Les Belles Lettres.

Alcinous (1993). *The Handbook of Platonism*. Translated with an introduction and commentary by J. M. Dillon. Oxford: Clarendon Press.

[Alex.Aphr.]
  Alexander of Aphrodisias (1983). *Alexander of Aphrodisias On Fate*. Text, trans. and commentary R. W. Sharples. London: Duckworth.
  Alexandre d'Aphrodise (1984). *Traité du destin*. Texte établi et traduit par P. Thiller. Paris: Les Belles Lettres.
[Anaxag.]
  Sider, D. (2005). *The Fragments of Anaxagoras*. 2nd ed. St Augustin: Academia Verlag.
  Anaxagoras of Clazomenae (2007). *Fragments* and *Testimonia*. A text and translation with notes and essays by P. Curd. Toronto, Buffalo and London: University of Toronto Press.
  André, J., and J. Filliozat. (1986). *L'Inde vue de Rome. Textes Latin de l'antiquité relatifs à l'Inde*. Paris: Les Belles Lettres.
[Ant.Lib.]
  Antoninus Liberalis (1968). *Les Métamorphoses*. Texte établi, traduit et commenté par M. Papathomopoulos. Paris: Les Belles Lettres.
  Antoninus Liberalis (1992). *The Metamorphoses*. A translation with a commentary by F. Celoria. London: Routledge.
[Antisth.]
  [Antisthenes of Athens] (2015). *Texts, Translation and Commentary*. Edited by S. H. Prince. Ann Arbor: University of Michigan Press.
[Apollod.]
  Apollodorus (1921). *The Library*. With an English translation by J. G. Frazer. London: W. Heinemann.
  Apollodoro (1996). *I miti greci*. A cura di P. Scarpi. Traduzione di M. G. Ciani. Milan: Mondadori.
  Apollodorus (2007). *The Library of Greek Mythology*. A new translation by R. Hard. Oxford: Oxford University Press.
[Apul.]
  Apuleius (1822). *The Metamorphosis, or Golden Ass, and Philosophical Works of Apuleius*. Translated from the original Latin by T. Taylor. London: R. Triphook, T. Rodd.
  Apulée (1973). *Opuscules et fragments philosophiques*. Texte établi, traduit et commenté par J. Beaujeu. Paris: Les Belles Lettres.
  Apuleio (1980). *Metamorfosi o asino d'oro*. A cura di G. Augello. Turin: UTET.
  Apuleius (1993). *The God of Socrates*. Foreword by D. Driscoll. Gillette, NJ: Heptangle Books.
  Apuleius (1996). *Metamorphoses*. Edited and translated by J. Arthur Hanson. Cambridge, MA: Harvard University Press.
  Apuleius (2001). *Apuleius' Rhetorical Works*. Translated and annotated by S. J. Harrison, J. L. Hilton and V. J. C. Hunink. Oxford: Oxford University Press.

[Ar.]
    Aristophane (1923–30). *[Oeuvres]*. Texte établi par V. Coulon et traduit par H. Van Daele. Paris: Les Belles Lettres.
    Aristophanes (1998–2007). *[Comedies and Fragments]*. Edited and translated by J. Henderson. Cambridge, MA: Harvard University Press.

[Ar.Did.] see [Placit.].

[Arat.]
    Aratus (1997). *Phaenomena*. Edited with introduction, translation and commentary by D. Kidd. Cambridge: Cambridge University Press.
    Aratos (1998). *Phénomènes*. Texte établi, traduit et commenté par J. Martin. Paris: Les Belles Lettres.

[Archim.]
    Archimède (1971). *De l'équilibre des figures planes: L'arénaire*. Texte établi et traduit par C. Mugler. Paris: Les Belles Lettres.

[Arist.]
    Aristotle (1935). *Metaphysics*. Translated by H. Tredennick. Cambridge, MA: Harvard University Press.
    Aristotle (1942). *Generation of Animals*. With an English translation by A. L. Peck. Cambridge, MA: Harvard University Press.
    Aristotle (1955). *On Sophistical Refutations. On Coming-To-Be and Passing-Away. On the Cosmos*. Translated by E. S. Forster and D. J. Furley. Cambridge, MA: Harvard University Press.
    Aristotle (1970). *Physics: Books I and II*. Translated with introduction, commentary, note on recent work, and revised bibliography by W. Charleton. Oxford: Clarendon Press.
    Aristotele (1975). *Il 'De Ideis' di Aristotele e la teoria platonica delle idee*. Ed. W. Leszl, edizione critica del testo a cura di D. Harlfinger. Florence: Leo S. Olschki.
    Aristotle (1980). *The Physics*. With an English translation by Philip H. Wicksteed and Francis M. Cornford. Cambridge, MA: Harvard University Press.
    Aristotle (1983). *Parts of Animals*. With an English translation by A. L. Peck. Cambridge, MA: Harvard University Press.
    [Aristotle] (1995). *Aristoteles latine*. Interpretibus variis edidit Academia Regia Borussica Berlin 1831. Nachdruck herausgegeben und eingeleitet von E. Keßler. Munich: Fink.
    Reale, G., and A. P. Bos (1995). *Il trattato Sul cosmo per Alessandro attribuito ad Aristotele*. Monografia introduttiva, testo greco con traduzione a fronte, commentario, bibliografia ragionata e indici [a cura di] G. Reale e A. P. Bos. Indici generali a cura di G. Girgenti e F. Sarri. 2a ed. Milan: Vita e Pensiero.

[Arnob.]
> Arnobius of Sicca (1949). *The Case Against the Pagans.* Newly translated and annotated by G. E. McCracken. Westminster, MD: Newman Press.
> Arnobe (1982–). *Contre les Gentils.* Texte établi, traduit et commenté par H. Le Bonniec et al. Paris: Les Belles Lettres.

[Arr.]
> See Epictetus (1925–8).

[Ath.]
> Athénée de Naucratis (1956). *Les Deipnosophistes.* Livres I et II. Texte établi et traduit par A. M. Desrousseaux. Paris: Les Belles Lettres.

[Attic.]
> Atticus (1977). *Fragments.* Texte établi et traduit par E. des Places. Paris: Les Belles Lettres.

[Aug.]
> Augustine (1991a). *Confessions.* Translated with an introduction and notes by H. Chadwick. Oxford: Oxford University Press.
> Augustine (1991b). *On Genesis: Two Books on Genesis: Against the Manichees and On the Literal Interpretation of the Genesis: An Unifinished Book.* Edited by R. J. Teske. Washington, DC: Catholic University of America Press.
> Augustine (1991c). *The Works of Saint Augustine: A Translation for the 21st Century.* Edited by J. E. Rotelle, trans. and notes E. Hill. Brooklyn, NY: New City Press.
> Augustine (1992). *Confessions.* Introduction, text and commentary by J. J. O'Donnell. Oxford: Clarendon Press.
> Augustine (1998). *The City of God gainst the Pagans.* Edited and translated by R. W. Dyson. Cambridge: Cambridge University Press.
> Augustine (2002). *Eighty-three Different Questions.* Translated by D. L. Mosher. Washington, DC: Catholic University of America Press.
> St Augustine (2007). *On Order [De Ordine].* Translation and introduction by S. Borruso. South Bend, IN: St Augustine's Press.
> Augustine (2010). *On the Free Choice of the Will, On Grace and Free Choice, and Other Writings.* Edited and translated by P. King. Cambridge: Cambridge University Press.

[Call.]
> Pfeiffer, R. (ed.) (1949–53). *Callimachus.* Oxford: Clarendon Press.
> Callimachus (1955). *Hymns and Epigrams.* With an English translation by A. W. Mair. 2nd ed. Cambridge, MA: Harvard University Press.
> Callimaco (1996–2010). *Aitia.* Introduzione, testo critico, traduzione e commento di G. Massimilla. Pisa: F. Serra.

[Carn.]
> Karneades (1970). *Fragmente*. Text und Kommentar von B. Wiśniewski. Wrocław: Zakład Narodowy im. Ossolińskich.
>
> Mette, H. J. (1985). *Weitere Akademiker heute (Fortsetzung von Lustr. 26, 7–94): von Lakydes bis zu Kleitomachos*. 'Lustrum' 27: 39–148.

[Cels.]
> Celsus (1987). *On the True Doctrine. A Discourse Against the Christians*. Translated and introduced by R. J. Hoffmann. Oxford: Oxford University Press.
>
> Celso (1989). *Il discorso della verità: Contro i cristiani*. Introduzione di G. Baget-Bozzo, traduzione, premessa al testo e note di S. Rizzo. Milan: Rizzoli.

[Chal.]
> Chalcidius (2016). *On Plato's* Timaeus. Edited and Translated by J. Magee. Cambridge MA: Harvard University Press.

[Chrys.]
> Jean Chrysostome (1961). *Sur la providence de Dieu*. Introduction, texte critique, traduction et notes de A.-M. Malingrey. Paris: Les Éditions du Cerf.
>
> John Chrysostom (1986-92). *Homilies on Genesis*. Translated by C. R. Hill. Edited by T. P. Halton. Washington, DC: Catholic University of America.
>
> John Chrysostom (2015). *On the Providence of God*. Ed. by St Herman of Alaska Brotherhood. Platina, CA: St. Herman of Alaska Brotherhood.

[Chrysipp.] see *SVF*.

[CIAG]
> AA.VV. (1882–). *Commentaria in Aristotelem Graeca*. Edita consilio et auctoritate Academiae Litterarum Borussicae. Berlin: G. Reimeri.

[Cic.]
> Cicero, Marcus Tullius (1920–3). *De divinatione. Libri duo*. Edited (with commentary) by A. S. Pease. Urbana: University of Illinois Studies.
>
> Cicero (1923). *On Old Age. On Friendship. On Divination*. With an English translation by W. A. Falconer. Cambridge, MA: Harvard University Press.
>
> Cicero, Marcus Tullius (1928). *De re publica. De legibus*. With an English translation by C. W. Keyes. Cambridge, MA: Harvard University Press.
>
> Cicero, Marcus Tullius (1931a). *Orations*. With an English translation by N. H. Watts. Cambridge, MA: Harvard University Press.
>
> Cicero, Marcus Tullius (1931b). *On Ends*. With an English translation by H. Rackam. Cambridge, MA: Harvard University Press.
>
> Cicero, Marcus Tullius (1933). *Nature of the Gods. Academics*. With an English translation by H. Rackam. Cambridge, MA: Harvard University Press.

Cicero, Marcus Tullius (1942). *De oratore Book III. On Fate. Stoic Paradoxes. Divisions of Oratory*. With an English translation by H. Rackam. Cambridge, MA: Harvard University Press.

Cicero, Marcus Tullius (1945). *Tusculan Disputations*. With an English translation by E. J. Kings. Cambridge, MA: Harvard University Press.

Cicero, Marcus Tullius (1955). *De natura deorum*. Edited by A. S. Pease. Cambridge, MA: Harvard University Press.

[Cleanth.]
Pearson, A. C. (ed.) (1891). *The Fragments of Zeno and Cleanthes*. Cambridge: Cambridge University Press.

[Clem.Al.]
Clément d'Alexandrie (1948–81). [*Oeuvres*]. Introduction, traduction et notes de C. Mondésert. Paris: Les Éditions du Cerf.

Clement of Alexandria (1953). [*Works*]. With an English translation by G. W. Butterworth. Cambridge, MA: Harvard University Press.

[Colum.]
Columella, Lucius Junius Moderatus (1941). *On Agriculture*. With an English translation by H. B. Ash. Cambridge, MA: Harvard University Press.

[Corn.]
See Ramelli, I. (ed.) (2008).
See Kasteel, H. van (2012).
L. Anneus Cornutus (2016). *Greek Theology*. Draft translation by G. Boys-Stones, <https://www.academia.edu/6394535/Cornutus_On_Greek_Theology> (last accessed 13 April 2019).

[Corp.Herm.]
[AA. VV] (1924–36). *Hermetica: The Ancient Greek and Latin Writings Which Contain Religious or Philosophic Teachings Ascribed to Hermes Trismegistus*. Edited with English translation by W. Scott. Oxford: Clarendon Press.

Hermès Trismégiste (1991). *Corpus Hermeticum*. Texte établi et traduit par A. D. Nock et A.-J. Festugière. 7e ed. Paris: Les Belles Lettres.

Copenhaver, B. (ed.) (1992). *Hermetica: The Greek* Corpus Hermeticum *and the Latin Asclepius in New English Translation*. Cambridge: Cambridge University Press.

[AA. VV] (2005). *Corpus Hermeticum*. Edizione e commento di A. D. Nock e A.-J. Festugière. Edizione dei testi ermetici e copti e commenti di I. Ramelli. A cura di I. Ramelli. Milan: Bompiani.

[AA. VV] (2009–11). *La rivelazione segreta di Ermete Trismegisto*. A cura di P. Scarpi. Milan and Rome: Mondadori-Fondazione Lorenzo Valla.

[Cratin.] see *PCG*.
[Ctes.] see *FGH*.

[D.L.]
> Diogenes Laertius (1925). *Lives of the Eminent Philosophers*. With an English translation by R. D. Hicks. Cambridge, MA: Harvard University Press.
>
> Diogenes Laertius (2013). *Lives of Eminent Philosophers*. Edited with an introduction by T. Dorandi. Cambridge: Cambridge University Press.

[D.S.]
> Diodorus of Sicily (1960–7). With an English translation by C. H. Olfather et al. Cambridge, MA: Harvard University Press.
>
> Diodore de Sicile (1993–2014). *Bibliothèque historique. Fragments*. Texte établi par B. Bertrac et alii et traduit par Y. Vernière et alii. Paris: Les Belles Lettres.

[Democr.]
> Lur'e, S. E. (1970). *Democritea*. Collegit Emendavit Interpretatus est Salomo Luria. Leninopoli: Nauka.
>
> Taylor, C. C. W. (ed.) (1999). *The Atomists: Leucippus and Democritus*. Toronto, Buffalo and London: University of Toronto Press.
>
> Leszl, W. (2009). *I primi atomisti. Raccolta dei testi che riguardano Leucippo e Democrito*. Florence: Leo S. Olschki.

[Diog.Apoll.]
> Laks, A. (1983). *Diogène d'Apollonie. La dernière cosmologie présocratique*. Edition, traduction, et commentaire des fragments et des témoignages. Lille: Presses Universitaires de Lille.

[Dion.Alex.]
> Dionysios von Alexandria (2016). *De Natura (περὶ φύσεως)*. Übersetzung, Kommentar und Würdigung K. J. Fleischer. Turnhout: Brepols.
>
> Dörrie, H. et al. (hrsg.) (1987–2008). *Der Platonismus in der Antike*. Stuttgart, Bad, Cannstatt: Frommann-Holzbog.

[E.]
> Euripide (1927–2003). [*Oeuvres*]. Texte établi et traduit par L. Méridier et alii. Paris: Les Belles Lettres.
>
> Euripides (1994–2008). [*Plays and Fragments*]. With an English translation by D. Kovacs et al. Cambridge, MA: Harvard University Press.

[Emp.]
> Empedocle (1975). *Poema fisico e lustrale*. Edited by C. Gallavotti. Milan and Rome: Mondadori-Fondazione Lorenzo Valla.
>
> Empedocles (1981). *The Extant Fragments*. Edited, with an introduction, commentary, and concordances by M. R. Wright. New Haven and London: Yale University Press.
>
> Empedocles (1992). *The Poem of Empedocles*. Text and translation with an introduction, edited by B. Inwood. Toronto, Buffalo and London: University of Toronto Press. [Abbreviated: Inwood]

[Epict.]
  Epictetus (1925–8). *The Discourses as reported by Arrian, The Manual, and Fragments*. With an English translation by W. A. Oldfather. Cambridge, MA: Harvard University Press.
  Epictetus (1999). *The Encheiridion of Epictetus and its three Christian adaptations. Transmission and critical editions*. Edited by G. Boter. Leiden, Boston and Cologne: E. J. Brill.
  Epitteto (2009). *Tutte le opere*. A cura di G. Reale e C. Cassanmagnago. Milan: Bompiani.
[Epicur.]
  Usener, H. (hrsg.) (1887). *Epicurea*. Leipzig: Teubner. [Abbreviated: Usener]
  Epicurus (1926). *The Extant Remains*. With short critical apparatus, translation and notes by C. Bailey. Oxford: Clarendon Press.
  Epicuro (1973). *Opere*. A cura di G. Arrighetti. 2a ed. Turin: Einaudi.
  Ramelli, I. (a cura di) (2002). *Epicurea. Testi di Epicuro e testimonianze epicuree nella raccolta di Hermann Usener*. Milan: Bompiani.
  Epicuro (2012). *Sulla natura. Libro II*. Edizione, traduzione e commento a cura di G. Leone. Naples: Bibliopolis.
[Eudor.Acad.]
  Mazzarelli, C. (1985). 'Raccolta e interpretazione delle testimonianze e dei frammenti del medioplatonico Eudoro di Alessandria. Parte prima: Testo e traduzione delle testimonianze e dei frammenti sicuri'. *Rivista di Filosofia Neoscolastica* 77: 197–205, and 'Parte seconda: Testo e traduzione delle testimonianze non sicure'. *Rivista di Filosofia Neoscolatica* 77: 535–55.
[Eus.]
  Eusebius of Caesarea (1903). *Eusebii pamphilii evangelicae praeparationis*. Edited by E. H. Gifford. Oxford: Oxford University Press.
  Eusèbe de Césarée (1974–91). *La préparation évangélique*. Introduction, texte grec, traduction et commentaire par J. Sirinelli, E. des Places et alii. Paris: Les Éditions du Cerf.
  Eusebius (1980). *The Ecclesiastical History*. With an English translation by K. Lake and J. E. L. Oulton. Cambridge, MA: Harvard University Press.
[Eust.]
  Eustathius Thessalonicensis (1825–6). *Commentarii ad Homeri Odysseam ad fidem exempli Romani editi*. Leipzig: J. A. G. Weigel.
  Eustathius Thessalonicensis (1971–87). *Commentarii ad Homeri Iliadem Pertinentes*. Curavit M. Van der Valk. Leiden, Boston and Cologne: E. J. Brill.
  See Kasteel, H. van (2012).
Festa, N. et al. (hrsg.) (1894–1902). *Mytographi Graeci*. Leipzig: Teubner.

[FGH]
: Jacoby, F. (1929–58). *Die Fragmente der griechischen Historiker*. Leiden, Boston and Cologne: E. J. Brill.

: Fowler, R. L. (ed.) (2000–13). *Early Greek Mythography*. Volume 1: Text and Introduction. Volume 2: Commentary. Oxford: Oxford University Press.

[Gal.]
: Galeni, Claudii (1821–3). *Claudii Galeni Opera omnia*. Editionem curavit C. G. Kühn, Leipzig, C. Cnobloch [= Hildesheim, Zürich and New York: Olms-Weidmann, 1964–5].

: Galien (1854–6), *Œuvres anatomiques, physiologiques et médicales de Galien*. Edited by C. Daremberg. Paris: Baillière.

: [Galen] (1907). *Galeni de Usu partium libri XVII*. Ad codicum fidem recensuit G. Helmreich. Leipzig: Teubner.

: Galenus (1968). *On the usefulness of the parts of the body*. Edited by M. Tallmadge May. Ithaca, NY: Cornell University Press.

: Galenus (1969). *On the Natural Faculties*. With an English translation by A. J. Brock. Cambridge, MA: Harvard University Press.

: Larrain, C. J. (1992). *Galens Kommentar zu Platons Timaios*. Leipzig: Teubner.

: Galien (1994). *Oeuvres médicales choisies*. Traduction de C. Daremberg, choix, présentation et notes par A. Pichot. Paris: Gallimard.

: Galenus (1997). *Selected Works*. Translated with an introduction and notes by P. N. Singer. Oxford: Oxford University Press.

[Gell.]
: Aulus Gellius (1946–52). *The Attic Nights*. With an English translation by J. C. Rolfe. Cambridge, MA: Harvard University Press.

: Graham, D. W. (2010). *The Texts of Early Greek Philosophy: The Complete Fragments and Selected Testimonies of the Major Presocratics*. Cambridge: Cambridge University Press.

[Hdt.]
: Herodotus (1922–38). With an English translation by A. D. Godley. Cambridge, MA: Harvard University Press.

: Erodoto (1988–2006). *Le storie*. A cura di D. Asheri et alii. Milan: Mondadori.

: Hérodote (1993). *Histoires*. Texte établi et traduit par Ph.-E. Legrand. 6e ed. Paris: Les Belles Lettres.

[Hellanic.]
: See *FGH* n. 4.

[Heraclit. (= Heraclitus allegorista)]
: Héraclite (1962). *Allégories d'Homère*. Texte établi et traduit par F. Buffière. Paris: Les Belles Lettres.

Heraclitus (2005). *Homeric Problems*. Edited and translated by D. A. Russell and D. Konstan. Atlanta, GA: Society of Biblical Literature.

See Kasteel, H. van (2012).

[Heraclit. (= Heraclitus philosophus)]

Heraclitus (1954). *The Cosmic Fragments*. Edited with an introduction and commentary by G. S. Kirk. Cambridge: Cambridge University Press.

Héraclite (1986). *Fragments*. Texte établi, traduit, commenté par M. Conche. Paris: Presses Universitaires de France.

Eraclito (2007). *Testimonianze, imitazioni e frammenti*. A cura di M. Marcovich, R. Mondolfo e L. Tarán. Introduzione di G. Reale. Milan: Bompiani.

[Hes.]

Hesiod (1914). *The Homeric Hymns and Homerica*. With an English translation by H. G. Evelyn-White. Cambridge, MA: Harvard University Press.

Hésiode (1928). *Théogonie. Les Travaux et les Jours. Le Bouclier*. Texte établi et traduit par P. Mazon. Paris: Les Belles Lettres.

[Hesiod] (1965). *Hesiodi Scutum*. Introduzione, testo critico e commento con traduzione e indici a cura di C. F. Russo. 2a ed. Florence: La Nuova Italia.

Hesiod (1966). *Theogony*. Edited with prolegomena and commentary by M. L. West. Oxford: Clarendon Press.

Hesiod (2006). [*Works*]. Edited and translated by G. W. Most. Cambridge, MA: Harvard University Press.

Esiodo (2009). *Tutte le opere e i frammenti, con la prima traduzione degli scolii*. Introduzione, traduzione, note e apparati di C. Cassanmagnago. Milan: Bompiani.

[Hippol.]

Hippolytus (1921). *Philosophumena, or the Refutation of All Heresies*. Translated by F. Legge. London: Society for Promoting Christian Knowledge.

Hülser, K. H. (1987–8). *Die Fragmente zur Dialektik der Stoiker: neue Sammlung der Texte mit deutscher Übersetzung und Kommentaren*. Stuttgart, Bad Cannstatt: Frommann-Holzboog.

[h.Hom.]

Allen, T. W. et al. (1936). *The Homeric Hymns*. 2nd ed. Oxford: Clarendon Press.

Càssola, F. (a cura di) (1975). *Inni omerici*. Milan: Mondadori.

Rayor, D. J. (ed.) (2004). *The Homeric Hymns*. A translation, with introduction and notes. Berkeley: University of California Press.

[Hom.]

Omero (1981–6). *Odissea*. Introduzione generale di A. Heubeck et alii. Testo e commento a cura di S. West et alii. Traduzione di G. A. Privitera. Milan: Mondadori.

Homer (1988). *The Iliad*. With an English translation by A. T. Murray; revised by G. E. Dimock. Cambridge, MA: Harvard University Press.

Homer (1995). *The Odyssey*. With an English translation by A. T. Murray. Cambridge, MA: Harvard University Press.

[Hor.]

[Horace] (1914–26). *Satires, Epistles, and Ars Poetica*. With an English translation by H. R. Fairclough. Cambridge, MA: Harvard University Press.

[Horace] (2004). *Odes and Epodes*. Edited and translated by N. Rudd. Cambridge, MA: Harvard University Press.

[Hp.]

Hippocrates of Cos (2012). *Generation. Nature of the Child. Diseases 4. Nature of Women and Barrenness*. Edited and translated by P. Potter. Cambridge, MA: Harvard University Press.

[Hyg.]

Hyginus (1960). *The Myths of Hyginus*. Translated and edited by M. Grant. Lawrence: University of Kansas Publications.

Hygin (1983). *L'astronomie*. Texte établi et traduit par A. Le Bœuffle. Paris: Les Belles Lettres.

Hygin (1993). *Fabulae*. Edidit P. H. Marshall. Leipzig: Teubner.

Hygin (1997). *Fables*. Texte établi et traduit par J.-Y. Boriaud. Paris: Les Belles Lettres.

Igino (2000). *Miti*. A cura di G. Guidorizzi. Milan: Adelphi Edizioni.

[I.]

Thackeray, H. S. J. et al. (1943). *Josephus*. Cambridge, MA: Harvard University Press.

[Iust.Phil.]

Justin (1995). *Apologie pour les Chretiens*. Ed. et trad. C. Mounier. Fribourg: Editions Universitaires.

Justin Martyr (1997). *The First and Second Apologies*. Translated with introduction and notes by L. W. Barnard. New York: Paulist Press.

Justin (2003a). *Dialogue avec Tryphon*. Edited by P. Bobichon. Fribourg: Editions Universitaires.

Justin (2003b). *Dialogue with Trypho*. Translated by T. B. Falls. Revised and with a new introduction by T. P. Halton. Edited by M. Slusser. Washington, DC: Catholic University of America Press.

Justin, Philosopher and Martyr (2009). *Apologies*. Edited with a commentary on the text by D. Minns and P. Parvis. Oxford: Oxford University Press.

[Iuu.]

Juvenal and Persius (2014). Edited and translated by S. Morton Braund. Cambridge, MA: Harvard University Press.

Kasteel, H. van (2012). *Questions Homériques. Physique et métaphysique chez Homer*. Grez-Doiceau: Beya.

Keller, O. (recensuit) (1877). *Rerum Naturalium Scriptores Graeci Minores*. Vol. 1. Leipzig: Teubner.

Kirk, G. S., and J. E. Raven (1960). *The Presocratic Philosophers*. 2nd ed. Cambridge: Cambridge University Press.

[Lact.]
- [Lactantius] (1890). *L. Caelii Firmiani Lactantii Opera omnia*, Accedunt Carmina ejus quae feruntur et L. Caecilii qui inscriputs est de Mortibus presecutorum liber. Recensuerunt Samuel Brandt et Georgius Laubmann. Vienna: F. Tempsky.
- Lactantius (1965a). *The Divine Institutes*. Translated by M. F. McDonald. Washington, DC: Catholic University of America Press.
- Lactantius (1965b). *The Minor Works*. Translated by M. F. McDonald. Washington, DC: Catholic University of America Press.
- Lactance (1974). *L'ouvrage du Dieu créateur*. Introduction, texte critique, traduction par M. Perrin. Paris: Les Éditions du Cerf.
- Lactance (1982). *La colère de Dieu*. Introduction, texte critique, traduction, commentaire et index par C. Ingremeau. Paris: Les Éditions du Cerf.
- Lactance (1987). *Épitomé des Institutions Divines*. Introduction, texte critique, traduction et notes par M. Perrin. Paris: Les Éditions du Cerf.
- Lattanzio (2008). *La collera di Dio*. A cura di L. Gasparri. Postfazione di G. Girgenti. Milan: Bompiani.

Laks, A., Most, G. W. eds. (2016). *Early Greek Philosophy*. Cambridge, MA: Harvard University Press. [Abbreviated: LM]

[Leucipp.]
- See [Democr.] Taylor (1999).
- See [Democr.] Leszl (2009).

Long, A. A., and D. N. Sedley (eds) (1987). *The Hellenistic Philosophers*. Cambridge: Cambridge University Press.

[Luc.]
- Lucian (1913–67). With an English translation by A. M. Harmon et al. Cambridge, MA: Harvard University Press.
- Lucien (1993–2008). *Oeuvres*. Texte établi et traduit par J. Bompaire. Paris: Les Belles Lettres.

[Lucan.]
- Lucan (1943). *The Civil War*. With an English translation by J. D. Duff. Cambridge, MA: Harvard University Press.

[Lucr.]
- Lucretius (1891). *T. Lucreti Cari De rerum natura libri sex*. With notes by H. A. J. Munro. 4th ed. Cambridge: Deighton Bell and Co.

[Lucretius] (1896–98). *T. Lucreti Cari De rerum natura libri sex*. Revisione del testo, commento e studi introduttivi di C. Giussani. Turin: E. Loescher.

Lucretius (1924). *De la nature*. Texte établi et traduit pas A. Ernout. Paris: Les Belles Lettres.

[Lucretius] (1942). *T. Lucreti Cari De rerum natura libri sex*. Edited with an introduction and commentary by W. E. Leonard and S. B. Smith. Madison: The University of Wisconsin Press.

Lucretius (1947). *De rerum natura: libri sex*. Edited with prolegomena, critical apparatus, translation and commentary by C. Bailey. Oxford: Clarendon Press.

Lucretius (1975). *De rerum natura*. With an English translation by W. H. D. Rouse, revised by M. F. Smith. Cambridge, MA: Harvard University Press.

Lucretius (1984). *De rerum natura V*. Edited, with introduction and commentary by C. D. N. Costa. Oxford: Clarendon Press.

Lucretius (2002–09). *De rerum natura*. Edizione critica con introduzione e versione a cura di E. Flores. Naples: Bibliopolis.

[M.Ant.]

Marcus Aurelius (1944). *The Meditations of the Emperor Marcus Antoninus*. Edited with translation and commentary by A. S. L. Farquharson. Oxford: Oxford University Press.

Marcus Aurelius (2008). *The Meditations of the Emperor Marcus Aurelius Antoninus*. Edited and with an introduction by J. Moore and M. Silverthorne. Translated by F. Hutcheson and J. Moor. Indianapolis: Liberty Fund.

[Mac.Magn.]

Crafer, T. W. (1919). *The 'Apocriticus' of Macarius Magnes*. London: Society for Promoting Christian Knowledge.

Macarios de Magnésie (2003). *Le Monogénès*. Introduction générale, édition critique, traduction française et commentaire par R. Goulet. Paris: Librairie Philosophique J. Vrin.

[Manil.]

Manilius (1977). *Astronomica*. Cambridge, MA: Harvard University Press.

[Max.Tyr.]

Maximus of Tyre (1997). *The Philosophical Orations*. Translated, with an introduction and notes by M. B. Trapp. Oxford: Clarendon Press.

Medioplatonici (2015). *Opere, testimonianze, frammenti*. Introduzione, traduzione, note e apparati di commento a cura di E. Vimercati. Milan: Bompiani.

[Megasth.]

See *FGH*.

McCrindle, J. W. (1877). *Ancient India as described by Megasthênes and Arrian; being a translation of the Indika of Megasthênes collected by Dr. Schwanbeck, and of the first part of the Indika of Arrian*. London: Trübner & Co.

[Meth.]
    St Methodius (1958). *The Symposium: A Treatise on Chastity*. Translated and annotated by H. Musurillo. New York, NY and Ramsey, NJ: Newman Press.
    Méthode d'Olympe (1963). *Le banquet*. Introduction et texte critique par H. Musurillo. Traduction et notes par V.-H. Debidour. Paris: Les Éditions du Cerf.
    Minucius Felix (2003). [*Octavius*]. With an English translation by T. R. Glover. Cambridge, MA: Harvard University Press.

[Myrsil.]
    See *FGH* n. 477.

[Numen.]
    Numenius of Apamea (1917). *Fragments*. Translation and commentary by R. Petty. Dilton Marsh, Westbury: The Prometheus Trust.
    Numénius (1973). *Fragments*. Texte établi et traduit par E. des Places. Paris: Les Belles Lettres.

[Orac.Chald.]
    Lewy, H. (1978). *Chaldean Oracles and Theurgy: Mysticism, Magic and Platonism in the Later Roman Empire*. Nouvelle édition par M. Tardieu avec une contribution de P. Hadot. Paris: Études augustiniennes.
    The Chaldean Oracles (1989). Text, translation and commentary by R. Majercik. Leiden, Boston and Cologne: E. J. Brill.
    Oracles Chaldaïques (1989). Texte établi et traduit par E. des Places. 2e ed. Paris: Les Belles Lettres.

[Origenes]
    Origen (1965). *Contra Celsum*. Translated with an introduction and notes by E. Chadwick. 2nd ed. Cambridge: Cambridge University Press.
    Origenes (1967–76). *Contre Celse*. Introduction, texte critique, traduction et notes par M. Borret. Paris: Les Belles Lettres.
    Origène (1976). *Traité des principes (Peri Archôn)*. Introduction et traduction par M. Harl, G. Dorival, A. Le Boulluec. Paris: Études augustiniennes.
    Origène (1978–80). *Traités des principes*. Texte établi et traduit par H. Crouzel et M. Simonetti. Paris: Les Éditions du Cerf.
    Origen (1993). *Commentary on the Gospel according to John*. Translated by R. E. Heine. Washington, DC: Catholic University of America Press.
    Origenes (2001). *Contra Celsum: libri VIII*. Edidit M. Marcovich. Leiden, Boston and Cologne: E. J. Brill.
    Origen (2017). *On First Principles*. Edited and translated by J. Behr. Oxford: Oxford University Press.

[Ou.]
    Ovid (1977–89). [*Works*]. With an English translation by G. P. Goold et al. Cambridge, MA: Harvard University Press.

Ovide (1991–9). *Les Métamorphoses.* Texte établi et traduit par G. Lafaye. Paris: Les Belles Lettres.

Ovidio (2005–15). *Le metamorfosi.* A cura di A. Barchiesi et alii. Traduzione di L. Koch et alii. Milan: Mondadori.

[Palaeph.]

See Festa, N. et al. (hrsg.) (1894–1902). III. II.

Palaephatus (1996). *On unbelievable tales.* Translation, introduction and commentary by J. Stern. With notes and Greek text from the 1902 G. G. Teubner edition. Wauconda, IL: Bolchazy-Carducci Publishers.

Palefato (2000). *Storie incredibili.* A cura di A. Santoni. Pisa: ETS.

[Panaet.]

[Panaetius] (1952). *Panaaetii Rhodii Fragmenta, collegit iterumque edidit Modestus Van Straaten.* 2nd ed. Leiden, Boston and Cologne: E. J. Brill.

Panezio (2002). *Testimonianze e frammenti.* Introduzione, edizione, traduzione, note e apparati a cura di E. Vimercati. Milan: Bompiani.

[Paus.]

Pausanias (1977–88). *Description of Greece.* With an English translation by W. H. S. Jones. Cambridge, MA: Harvard University Press.

[PCG]

Pelagius (1922–31). *Pelagius's Expositions of Thirteen Epistles of St Paul.* Edited by A. Souter. Cambridge: Cambridge University Press.

Kassel, R., and C. Austin (ediderunt) (1983–2000). *Poetae Comici Graeci.* Berlin and New York: W. de Gruyter.

[Pelagius] (1993). *Pelagius's Commentary on St Paul's Epistle to the Romans.* Translated with introduction and notes T. de Bruyn. Oxford: Clarendon Press.

Pelagio (2012). *Commento all'epistola ai Romani. Commento alle epistole ai Corinzi.* Introduzione, traduzione e note a cura di S. Matteoli. Rome: Città Nuova.

[PGR]

[AA.VV.] (1967). *Paradoxographorum graecorum reliquiae.* Recognovit, brevi adnotatione critica instruxit, latine reddidit, A. Giannini. Milan: Istituto Editoriale Italiano.

[Ph.]

[Philo] (1896–1930). *Philonis Alexandrini opera quae supersunt.* Edidit P. Wendland, L. Cohn et S. Reiter [vols I–VI], *Indices ad Philonis Alexandrini opera,* composuit I. Leisegang. Berlin: G. Reimeri.

Philo (1929–62). With an English translation by F. H. Colson and G. H. Whitaker. Supplement translated by M. Ralph. Cambridge, MA: Harvard University Press.

Philon d'Alexandrie (1961–). *Les œuvres [. . .].* Publiées sour le patronage de l'Université de Lyon par R. Arnaldez, C. Mondésert, J. Pouillous. Introduction, traduction et notes par R. Arnaldez et alii. Paris: Les Éditions du Cerf.

Radice, R. (a cura di) (2005). *Filone di Alessandria. Tutti I trattati del Commento Allegorico alla Bibbia.* Milan: Bompiani.

[Pherecyd.]
See *FGH* n. 3 and 333.

[Phld.]
Philodemus (1978). *On methods of inference.* Edited, with translation and commentary by P. H. de Lacy and E. A. de Lacy. Revised edition. Naples: Bibliopolis.

[Phleg.]
Phlegon of Tralles (1996). *Book of Marvels.* Translated with an introduction and commentary by W. Hansen. Exeter: University of Exeter Press.

Phlegon Trallianus (2011). *Opuscula de rebus mirabilibus. De longaevis.* Edidit. A. Stramaglia. Berlin and New York: De Gruyter.

Flegonte di Tralle (2013). *Il libro delle meraviglie e tutti i frammenti.* A cura di T. Braccini e M. Scorsone. Turin: Einaudi.

[Phlp.]
Philoponus (1993). *On Aristotle's Physics 2.* Translated by A. R. Lacey. London: Duckworth.

[Phot.]
Photius (1959–91). *Bibliothèque.* Texte établi et traduit par R. Henry. Paris: Les Belles Lettres.

[Pi.]
Pindar (1997). [*Odes and Fragments*]. Edited and translated by W. H. Race. Cambridge, MA: Harvard University Press.

Pirrone (1981). *Testimonianze.* A cura di F. Decleva Caizzi. Naples: Bibliopolis.

[Pl.]
Plato (1925). *Philebus.* With translation by H. N. Fowler. Cambridge, MA: Harvard University Press.

Cornford, F. M. (1937). *Plato's Cosmology: The Timaus of Plato Translated with a Running Commentary.* London: Routledge and Kegan Paul.

Plato (1963). *The Republic of Plato.* Edited with critical notes, commentary and appendices by James Adams, with an introduction by D. A. Rees. 2nd ed. Cambridge: Cambridge University Press.

Plato (1976). *The 'Laws' of Plato.* With introduction and notes by E. B. England. New York: Arno Press, 1976.

Plato (2013). *Republic.* Edited and translated by C. Emlyn-Jones and W. Preddy. Cambridge, MA: Harvard University Press.

[*Placit.*]
    Diels, H. (1879). *Doxographi graeci*. Berlin: G. Reimer.
    Diels, H. (1961). *I dossografi greci*. Tradotti da L. Torraca. Padua: Cedam.
[*PLF*]
    Lobel, E., and D. Page (eds) (1955). *Poetarum lesbiorum fragmenta*. Oxford: Clarendon Press.
[Plin.]
    Plinius (1938–62). *Natural History*. With an English translation by H. Rackam et al. Cambridge, MA: Harvard University Press.
    [Pliny the Elder] (2005). *The Elder Pliny on the Human Animal: Natural History Book 7*. Translated with introduction and historical commentary by M. Beagon. Oxford: Clarendon Press.
[Plot.]
    Plotinus (1966–88). With an English translation by A. H. Armstrong. Cambridge, MA: Harvard University Press.
    Plotin (1989). *Ennéades*. Texte établi et traduit par É. Brehier. Paris: Les Belles Lettres.
    Plotin (1999). *Traité 51. I, 8*. Introduction, traduction, commentaires et notes par D. O'Meara. Paris: Les Éditions du Cerf.
    Plotin (2003). *Traités 7–21*. Traductions sous la direction de L. Brisson et J.-F. Pradeau. Paris: Flammarion.
[Plu.]
    Plutarch (1927–2004a). *Plutarch's Lives*. With an English translation by B. Perrin et al. Cambridge, MA: Harvard University Press.
    Plutarch (1927–2004b). *Plutarch's Moralia*. With an English translation by H. Cherniss et al. Cambridge, MA: Harvard University Press.
    Plutarque (1972–93). *Œuvres morales*. Texte établi et traduit par J. Sirinelli et alii. Paris: Les Belles Lettres.
    Kindstrand, J. F. (hrsg.) (1990). *Plvtarchi 'De Homero'*. Leipzig: Teubner.
    Plutarco (1997). *L'E di Delfi*. Introduzione, testo critico, traduzione e commento di C. Moreschini. Naples: M. D'Auria editore.
    Plutarco (2006). *Cause dei fenomeni naturali*. Introduzione, testo critico e commento a cura di L. Senzasono. Naples: M. D'Auria editore.
    Plutarco (2011). *Il volto della luna*. Introduzione, testo critico, traduzione e commento di P. Donini. Naples: M. D'Auria editore.
[*PMG*]
    Page, D. L. (edidit) (1962). *Poetae Melici Graeci*. Oxford: Clarendon Press.
[Polystr.]
    [Polystratus] (1905). *Polystrati epicurei Peri alogou kataphroneseos libellus*. Hrsg. C. Wilke. Leipzig: Teubner.

[Porph.]
- [Porphyre] (1956). *L'antre des nymphes de l'Odyssée*, in Buffière (1956), *Les mythes d'Homère et la pensée grecque*. Paris: Les Belles Lettres, pp. 597–616.
- [Porphyry] (1983). *Porphyry on the Cave of the Nymphs*. Translated by R. Lamberton. Barrytown, NY: Midpoint Trade Books Inc.
- Porfirio (1986). *L'antro delle ninfe*. A cura di L. Simonini. Milan: Adelphi Edizioni.
- [Porphyry (1988)] *Porphyry's Launching-Points to the Realm of Mind: An Introduction to the Neoplatonic Philosophy of Plotinus*. Translated from the Greek by K. S. Guthrie. With an Introduction by M. Hornum. Grand Rapids, MI: Phanes Press.
- Porphyrius (1993). *Porphyrii Philosophi Fragmenta*. Edidit A. Smith. Fragmenta arabica D. Wasserstein interpretante. Stuttgart and Leipzig: In aedibus B. G. Tevbneri.
- Porphyre (2005). *Sentences. Études d'introduction, texte grec et traduction française, commentaire*, par l'Unité propre de Recherche n° 76 du C.N.R.S. avec une traduction anglaise de J. M. Dillon. Travaux édités sour la responsabilité de L. Brisson. Paris: Librairie Philosophique J. Vrin.
- Berchman, R. M. (2005). *Against the Christians*. Leiden, Boston and Cologne: E. J. Brill.
- Porfirio (2006). *Sullo Stige*. Introduzione, traduzione, note e apparati di C. Castelletti. Presentazione di T. Dorandi. Milan: Bompiani.
- Porfirio (2011). *La filosofia rivelata dagli oracoli. Con tutti i frammenti di magia, stregoneria, teosofia e teurgia*. Monografia introduttiva di G. Girgenti. Saggio Interpretativo, traduzione, note e apparati di G. Muscolino. Milan: Bompiani.

[Posidon.]
- Posidonius (1989). *The Fragments. Vol. I: The Fragments, vol. II: The Commentary, vol. III: The Translation of the Fragments*. Edited by L. Edelstein and I. G. Kidd. Cambridge: Cambridge University Press.
- Posidonio (2004). *Testimonianze e frammenti*. Introduzione, traduzione, commentario e apparati di E. Vimercati. Milan: Bompiani.

[PPF]
- Diels, H. (1901). *Poetarum Philosophorum Fragmenta*. Edidit H. Diels. Berlin: apud Weidmannos.

[Procl.]
- Proclus (1933). *The Elements of Theology*. A revised text with translation and commentary by E. R. Dodds. Oxford: Clarendon Press.
- Proclus (1977–82). *Trois études sur la Providence*. Texte établi et traduit par D. Isaac. Paris: Les Belles Lettres.

Proclus (1987). *Proclus' Commentary on Plato's Parmenides*. Translated by G. R. Morrow and J. M. Dillon with introduction and notes by J. M. Dillon. Princeton: Princeton University Press.

Opsomer, J., and C. Steel (2003). *Proclus: On the Existence of Evils*. London: Duckworth.

Proclus (2004). *Tria opuscola. Provvidenza, libertà, male*. Testo latino e greco. Introduzione, traduzione, note e apparati di F. D. Paparella. Milan: Bompiani.

Steel, C. (2007). *Proclus: On Providence*. London: Duckworth.

Proclus (2007–13). *Commentary on Plato's Timaeus*. Translated with an introduction and notes by H. Tarrant et al. Cambridge: Cambridge University Press.

Marzillo, P. (2010). *Des Kommentar des Proklos zu Hesiods 'Werken und Tagen'*. Edition, Übersetzung und Erläuterun der Fragmente. Tübingen: Narr Verlag.

Opsomer, J., and C. Steel (2012). *Proclus: Ten Doubts Concerning Providence*. London: Duckworth.

Strobel, B. (2014). *Proklos, Tria opuscula. Textkritish kommentierte Retroversion der Übersetzung Wilhelms von Moerbeke*. Berlin and New York: De Gruyter.

[Ptol.]

Ptolemaeus (1940). *Tetrabiblos*. With an English translation by F. E. Robbins. Cambridge, MA: Harvard University Press.

Ptolemaeus (1985). *Claudio Tolomeo. Le previsioni astrologiche (Tetrabiblos)*. Edited by S. Feraboli. Milan and Rome: Mondadori-Fondazione Lorenzo Valla.

Ramelli, I. (a cura di) (2007). *Allegoristi dell'età classica. Opere e frammenti*. Milan: Bompiani.

Ramelli, I. (a cura di) (2008). *Stoici romani minori*. Milan: Bompiani.

[S.]

Sophocle (1989–90). Texte établi par A. Dain et traduit par P. Mazon et J. Irigoin. Paris: Les Belles Lettres.

Sophocles (1994–6) [*Plays and Fragments*]. Edited and translated by H. Lloyd-Jones. Cambridge, MA: Harvard University Press.

[S.E.]

Sextus Empiricus (1914–62). *Sexti Empirici Opera*. Recensuerunt H. Mutschmann und J. Mau. Leipzig: Teubner.

Sextus Empiricus (1953–61). *Sextus Empiricus: in four volumes*. With an English Translation by R. G. Bury. Cambridge, MA: Harvard University Press.

[Sapph.]
  See Lobel, E., and D. Page (eds) (1955).
  See AA.VV. (1982a).
[Sen.]
  Seneca (1917–20). *Epistulae morales*. With an English translation by R. M. Gummere. Cambridge, MA: Harvard University Press.
  Seneca (1971). *Natural Questions*. With an English translation by T. H. Corcoran. Cambridge, MA: Harvard University Press.
[Simp.]
  Simplicius (1997). *On Aristotle Physics 2*. Translated by B. Fleet. London: Duckworth.
  Simplicius (2002). *On Epictetus Handbook*. Translated by C. Brittain and B. Trennan. London, Duckworth.
[Solin.]
  C. Ivlii Solini (1864). *Collectanea rervm memorabilivm*. Recognovit Th. Mommsen. Berlin: in aedibus Friderici Nicolai.
  Solino (2001). *Colleción de hechos memorables o El Erudito*. Introducción, traducción y notas de F. J. F. Nieto. Madrid: Editorial Gredos.
Sorabji, R. (ed.) (2003). *The Philosophy of the Commentators, 200–600 ad. A Sourcebook*. Vol. 1. Psychology. London: Duckworth.
Sorabji, R. (ed.) (2004). *The Philosophy of the Commentators, 200–600 ad. A Sourcebook*. Vol. 2. Physics. London: Duckworth.
Sorabji, R. (ed.) (2005). *The Philosophy of the Commentators, 200–600 ad. A Sourcebook*. Vol. 3. Logic and Metaphysics. London: Duckworth.
[SSR]
  Giannantoni, G. [a cura di] (1990). *Socratis et socraticorum reliquiae*. Collegit, disposuit, apparatibus notisque G. Giannantoni. Naples: Bibliopolis.
[Stob.]
  Stobaeus (1884–1912). *Ioannis Stobaei Anthologium*. Libri duo priores (t. I et II) recensuit C. Wachsmuth, libri duo posteriores (t. III et IV) recensuit O. Hense. Berlin: apud Weidmannus.
[Str.]
  Strabo (1983). *The Geography of Strabo*. With an English translation by H. L. Jones. Cambridge, MA: Harvard University Press.
[Strato Lamps.]
  Desclos, M.-L., and W. W. Fortenbaugh (eds) (2011). *Strato of Lampsacus: Text, Translation and Discussion*. New Brunswick and London: Transaction Publishers.
[Sud.]
  Adler, A. (ed.) (1928–38). *Su(i)dae Lexicon*. Leipzig: Teubner.

[SVF]
　Arnim, H. von (hrsg.) (1903–05). *Stoicorum Veterum Fragmenta*. Leipzig: Teubner.
　Radice, R. (ed.) (1998). *Stoici antichi. Tutti i frammenti raccolti da Hans von Arnim*. Milan: Rusconi.
[Tert.]
　Tertullian (1931). *Apology. De Spectaculis*. With an English translation by T. R. Glove. Minucius Felix. *Octavius*. With an English translation by G. H. Rendall. Cambridge, MA: Harvard University Press.
　Tertullien (1997). *Le voile des vierges. De virginibus velandi*. Introduction, commentaire et texte critique par E. Schulz-Flügel, traduit par P. Mattei. Paris: Les Éditions du Cerf.
　De virginibus velandi, in G. D. Dunn (2004), *Tertullian*. London: Routledge and Kegan Paul.
[Theoc.]
　Theocritus (1952). [*Works*]. Edited with a translation and commentary by A. S. F. Gow. Cambridge: Cambridge University Press.
[Theos.]
　Erbse, H. (hrsg.) (1941). *Fragmente der Griechischer Theosophien*. Hamburg: Hansischer Gildenverlag.
[Thphr.]
　Theophrastus (1929). *Metaphysics*. With translation, commentary and introduction by W. D. Ross and F. H. Forbes. Oxford: Clarendon Press.
　Theophrastus (1976–90). *De causis plantarum*. With an English translation by B. Einarson and G. K. K. Link. Cambridge, MA: Harvard University Press.
　Fortenbaugh, W. W. et al. (eds) (1985). *Theophrastus of Eresus. On His Life and Work*. New Brunswick and London: Transaction Publishers.
　Theophrastus (1990–). *Enquiry into Plants and Minor Works on Odours and Weather Signs*. With an English translation by A. Hort. Cambridge, MA: Harvard University Press.
　Fortenbaugh, W. W., and D. Gutas (eds) (1992). *Theophrastus: His Psychological Doxographical and Scientific Writings*. New Brunswick and London: Transaction Publishers.
　Theophrastus (1993). *Metaphysics*. With an introduction, translation and commentary by M. van Raalte. Leiden, Boston and Cologne: E. J. Brill.
　Théophraste (1993). *Métaphysique*. Texte édité, traduit et anoté par A. Laks et G. Most et alii. Paris: Les Belles Lettres.
　Theophrastus of Eresus (1993). *Sources for His Life, Writings, Thought and Influence*. Edited and translated by W. W. Fortenbaugh et al. Leiden, Boston and Cologne: E. J. Brill.

Theophrastus of Eresus (1998). *Sources for His Life, Writings, Thought and Influence.* Commentary volume 3.1. Sources on Physics (Texts 137–223). By R. W. Sharples et al. Leiden, Boston and Cologne: E. J. Brill.

Théophraste (2012–7). *Les causes des phénomènes végétaux.* Texte établi et traduit par S. Amigues. Paris: Les Belles Lettres.

[Timo]
Lloyd-Jones, H., and P. Parsons (ediderunt) (1983). *Supplementum Hellenisticum.* Berlin and New York: Walter de Gruyter, pp. 368–95.

Timone di Fliunte (1989). *Silli.* Introduzione, edizione critica, traduzione e commento di M. Di Marco. Rome: Edizioni dell'Ateneo.

[TrGF]
Snell, B. et al. (ed.) (1971–2004). *Tragicorum Graecorum Fragmenta.* Editio correctior et addendis aucta curavit R. Kannicht. Göttingen: Vandenhoeck & Ruprecht.

Untersteiner, M. (a cura di) (2009). *Sofisti. Testimonianze e frammenti.* Con la collaborazione per *Crizia* di A. Battegazzore. Introduzione di G. Reale. Indici di V. Cicero. Milan: Bompiani.

[Var.]
Varro, M. Terentius (1976). *Antiquitates Rerum Divinarum.* Hrsg. B. Cardauns. Mainz: Akademie der Wissenschaften und der Literatur.

[Verg.]
Virgilio (1978–83). *Eneide.* A cura di E. Paratore. Traduzione di L. Canali. Milan: Mondadori.

Virgil (1999–2000). *Eclogues, Georgics, Aeneid, Appendix Vergiliana.* With an English translation by H. Rushton Fairclough, revised by G. P. Goold. Cambridge, MA: Harvard University Press.

Vimercati, E. (a cura di) (2015). *Medioplatonici. Opere, frammenti, testimonianze.* Introduzione, traduzione, note e apparati di commento a cura di E. Vimercati. Milan: Bompiani.

[Vitr.]
[Vitruvius] (1931–4). *On Architecture.* With an English translation by F. Granger et al. Cambridge, MA: Harvard University Press.

[Vitruvius] (1964). *De architectura libri decem.* Übersetzt und mit Anmerkungen versehen von C. Fensterbusch. Darmstadt: Wissenschaftliche Buchgesellschaft.

[Vorsokr.]
Diels, H., and W. Kranz (hrsg.) (1951–4). *Die Fragmente der Vorsokratiker.* 7. ed. Berlin: Weidmannsche Verlagsbuchhandlung.

Wehrli, F. (hrsg.) (1967–9). *Die Schule des Aristoteles. Texte und Kommentar.* 2. ed. Basel and Stuttgart: Schwabe & Co.

Winkler, J. J. (1995). *Ancient Greek Novels: The Fragments*. Introduction, text, translation and commentary by S. A. Stephens and J. J. Winkler. Princeton: Princeton University Press.

[X.]
    Xenophon (2013). *Memorabilia*. With an English translation by E. C. Marchant. Cambridge, MA: Harvard University Press.

[Xenocrates philosophus]
    Senocrate e Ermodoro (2012). *Testimonianze e frammenti*. Edizione, traduzione e commento a cura di M. Isnardi-Parente. Edizione rivista e aggiornata a cura di T. Dorandi. Pisa: Edizioni della Normale.

[Zeno Eleat.]
    See [Cleanth.] Pearson (1891).

Secondary Sources

AA.VV. (1936). *Mélanges Franz Cumont*. Annuaire de l'Institut de philologie et d'histoire orientales et slave. Vol. IV. Brussels: Sécretariat de l'Institut.

AA.VV. (1957). *Les sources de Plotin. Dix exposés et discussions*. Vandœuvres-Genève: Fondation Hardt.

AA.VV. (1960). *Eléments orientaux dans la religion grecque ancienne: Colloque de Strasbourg, 22–24 mai 1958*. Paris: Presses Universitaires de France.

AA.VV. (1962). *Hésiode et son influence*. Vandœuvres-Genève: Fondation Hardt.

AA.VV. (1971). *Le Néoplatonisme. Actes du Colloque de Royaumont, 9–13 Juin 1969*. Paris: Éditions du CNRS.

AA.VV. (1974). *Atti del Convegno Internazionale sul tema: Plotino e il Neoplatonismo in Oriente e Occidente (Roma 5–9 ottobre 1970)*. Rome: Accademia Nazionale dei Lincei.

AA.VV. (1978). *Lucrèce. Huit exposés suivis de discussions*. Vandœuvres-Genève: Fondation Hardt.

AA.VV. (1983). *Lalies 2 (Actes des Sessions de Linguistique et de littérature: Thessalonique, 24 Août–6 Septembre 1980)*. Paris: Publications de la Sorbonne Nouvelle.

AA.VV. (1993). *Aristophane*. Vandœuvres-Genève: Fondation Hardt.

AA.VV. (2003). *Galien et la philosophie*. Vandœuvres-Genève: Fondation Hardt [R. J. Hankinson, 'Causation in Galen', pp. 31–72; M. Frede, 'Galen's Theology', pp. 73–129; J. Jouanna, 'La notion de nature chez Galien', pp. 229–68].

AA.VV. (2007). *La cultura scientifico-naturalistica nei padri della chiesa (I–V sec.). XXV incontro di studiosi dell'antichità cristiana, 4–6 maggio 2006*. Rome: Institutum Patristicum Augustinianum.

Abel, G. (1978). *Stoizismus und frühe Neuzeit*. Berlin and New York: Walter de Gruyter.

Abry, J. H. (1983). 'Les *Astronomiques* de Manilius'. *Pallas* 19: 49–61.
Ackermann, E. (1979). *Lukrez und der Mythos*. Wiesbaden: Steiner.
Adam, A. (1948–62). *Histoire de la littérature française au XVIIe siècle*. Paris: Domat Montchrestien.
Adorno, F. (1983). 'Fisica epicurea, fisica platonica e fisica aristotelica'. *Elenchos* 4: 207–33.
Agamben, G. (1995). *Homo sacer. I, Il potere sovrano e la nuda vita*. Turin: Einaudi.
Albrecht, M. von (1981). 'Mythos und römische Realität in Ovids "Metamorphosen"', in W. Haase (hrsg.), *Aufstieg und Niedergand der römischen Welt (ANRW): Geschichte und Kultur Roms im Spiegel der Neuereun Forschung*, II.31.4. Berlin and New York: Walter de Gruyter, pp. 2328–42.
Alfieri, V. (1953). *Atomos Idea. L'origine del concetto dell'atomo nel pensiero greco*. Florence: Le Monnier.
Algra, K., M. H. Koenen and P. H. Schrijvers (eds) (1997). *Lucretius and His Intellectual Background*. Amsterdam: Royal Netherland Academy of Arts and Sciences.
Algra, K. et al. (eds) (1999). *Hellenistic Philosophy*. Cambridge: Cambridge University Press.
Allan, W. (2006). 'Divine Justice and Cosmic Order in Early Greek Epic'. *Journal of Hellenic Studies* 126: 1–35.
Allen, J. (1990). 'The Skepticism of Sextus Empiricus', in W. Haase (hrsg.), *Aufstieg und Niedergand der römischen Welt (ANRW): Geschichte und Kultur Roms im Spiegel der Neuereun Forschung*, II.36.4. Berlin and New York: Walter de Gruyter, pp. 2582–607.
Allen, J. (1993). 'Pyrrhonism and Medical Empiricism: Sextus Empiricus on Evidence and Inference', in W. Haase (hrsg.), *Aufstieg und Niedergand der römischen Welt (ANRW): Geschichte und Kultur Roms im Spiegel der Neuereun Forschung*, II.37.1. Berlin and New York: Walter de Gruyter, pp. 646–90.
Althusser, L. (1994). 'Le courant souterrain du matérialisme de la rencontre', in *Ecrits philosophiques et politiques*. Paris: Stock/Imec.
Anderson, G. (1976). 'Lucian: Theme and Variation in the Second Sophistic'. *Mnemosyne*, Suppl. 41. Leiden, Boston and Cologne: E. J. Brill.
Anderson, G. (1982). 'Lucian: A Sophist's Sophist'. *Yale Classical Studies* 27: 61–92.
Andreae, B. (1982). *Odysseus. Archäologie des europäischen Menschenbildes*. Frankfurt: Societäts Verlag.
Annas, J. (1981). *An Introduction to Plato's 'Republic'*. Oxford: Oxford University Press.
Annas, J., and J. Barnes (1985). *The Modes of Scepticism: Ancient Texts and Modern Intepretations*. Cambridge: Cambridge University Press.

Arrighetti, G. (1993). 'La stirpe funesta delle donne (Esiodo, Teog. vv. 590–591)', in M. Bandini and F. G. Pericoli (a cura di), *Scritti in memoria di Dino Pieraccioni*. Florence: Istituto Papirologico G. Vitelli, pp. 35–7.

Arruzza, C. (2011). *Les mésaventures de la théodicée. Plotin, Origène, Grégoire de Nysse*. Turnhout: Brepols.

Asso, P. (ed.) (2011). *Brill's Companion to Lucan*. Leiden, Boston and Cologne: E. J. Brill.

Ast, F. (1835–8). *Lexicon Platonicum siue uocum Platonicarum index*. Leipzig: Libraria Weidmanniana.

Atherton, C. (ed.) (2002). *Monsters and Monstrosity in Greek and Roman Culture*. Bari: Levante.

Aubenque, P. (1962). *Le problème de l'être chez Aristote*. Paris: Presses Universitaires de France.

Aubenque, P. (1980). 'La loi selon Aristote'. *Archives de Philosphie du Droit* 25: 147–57.

Aujac, G. (1989). 'Stoïcisme et hypothèse géocentrique', in H. Temporini (hrsg.), *Aufstieg und Niedergand der römischen Welt (ANRW): Geschichte und Kultur Roms im Spiegel der Neuereun Forschung*, II.36.3. Berlin and New York: Walter de Gruyter, pp. 1430–53.

Aumont, J. (1968). 'Sur "l'épisode des reptiles" dans la Pharsale de Lucain (IX, 587–937'. *Bulletin de l'association Guillaume Budé*. I. pp. 103–19.

Axelos, K. (1962). *Héraclite et la philosophie. La première saisie de l'être en devenir de la totalité*. Paris: Editions de Minuit.

Babut, D. (1969). *Plutarque et le stoïcisme*. Paris: Presses Universitaires de France.

Babut, D. (1974). *La religion des philosophes grecs*. Paris: Presses Universitaires de France.

Babut, D. (1978). 'Anaxagore jugé par Socrate et Platon'. *Revue des Études Grecques* 91: 44–76.

Bacci, M. (1976). *L'opera completa di Piero di Cosimo*. Milan: Rizzoli.

Bachelard, G. (1933). *Les intuitions atomistiques (Essai de classification)*. Paris: Boivin & Cie.

Bachofen, J. J. (1861). *Das Mutterrecht. Eine Untersuchung über die Gynaikokratie der alten Welt, nach ihrer religiösen und rechtlichen Natur*. Stuttgart: Krais und Hoffmann.

Baer, R. A. (1970). *Philo's Use of the Categories Male and Female*. Leiden, Boston and Cologne: E. J. Brill.

Bailey, C. (1928). *The Greek Atomists and Epicurus*. Oxford: Clarendon Press.

Bajon, M. G. (1992). 'Apuleio filosofo platonico: 1940–1990'. *Lustrum* 34: 339–90.

Baldwin, B. (1973). *Studies in Lucian*. Toronto: Hakkert.

Ballabriga, A. (1990). 'Le dernier adversaire de Zeus. Le mythe de Typhon dans l'épopée grecque archaique'. *Revue de l'Histoire des Religions* 207: 3–30.

Balme, D. M. (1939). 'Greek Science and Mechanism, I: Aristotle on Nature and Chance'. *The Classical Quarterly* 33: 129–38.

Balme, D. M. (1941). 'Greek Science and Mechanism, II: The Atomists'. *The Classical Quarterly* 35: 23–8.

Barchiesi, A. (2005). *Centre and Periphery*, in S. Harrison (ed.), *A Companion to Latin Literature*. Oxford: Blackwell, pp. 394–405.

Barnes, J. (1979). *The Presocratic Philosophers*. London: Routledge and Kegan Paul.

Barnes, J. (1990). *The Toils of Scepticism*. Cambridge: Cambridge University Press.

Barnes, J., M. Schofield and R. Sorabji (eds) (1975). *Articles on Aristotle: vol 1: Science*. London: Duckworth.

Barnes, T. D. (1971). *Tertullian: A Historical and Literary Study*. Oxford: Clarendon Press.

Barra, G. (1972). 'Apuleio e il problema dell'origine del male'. *Vichiana* 1 N.S.: 102–13.

Barth, P. (1906). 'Die Stoische Theodizee bei Philo', in *Philosophische Abhandlungen. Max Heinze zum 70. Geburtstage gewidmet von Freunden und schüler*. Berlin: Ernst Siegfried Mittler und Sohn.

Battegazzore, A. M., and F. Decleva Caizzi (a cura di) (1989). *L'etica della ragione. Ricordo di Mario Untersteiner*. Milan: Cisalpino – Istituto Editoriale Universitario.

Baudry, G. H. (1996). 'La responsibilité d'Eve dans la chute: analyse d'une tradition'. *Mélanges de Science Religieuse* 53: 293–20.

Beagon, P. (1992). *Roman Nature: The Thought of Pliny the Elder*. Oxford: Clarendon Press.

Beagon, P. (2007). 'Situating Nature's Wonders in Pliny's *Natural History*'. *Bulletin of the Institute of Classical Studies* 50: 19–40.

Beazley, J. D. (1963). *Attic Red-Figure Vase Painters*. 2nd ed. Oxford: Clarendon Press.

Béchec, C. (2013). *La vie surnaturelle dans le monde gréco-romain*. Rennes: Presses Universitaires de Rennes.

Belletti, B. (1987). 'Idea e creazionismo in Filone di Alessandria'. *Sapienza* 40: 277–304.

Benoit, A., and M. Simon (1968). *Le judaïsme et le christianisme antique, d'Antioque d'Epiphane à Constantin*. Paris: Presses Universitaires de France.

Benveniste, E. (1949). 'La légende des Danaïdes'. *Revue de l'Histoire des Religions* 136: 129–38.

Benveniste, E. (1969). *Le vocabulaire des institutions indo-européennes*. Paris: Editions de Minuit.

Beretta, M., and F. Citti (a cura di) (2008). *Lucrezio. La natura e la scienza*. Florence: Leo S. Olschki.

Bernhardt, J. (1971). *Platon et le matérialisme ancien. La théorie de l'âme-harmonie dans la philosophie de Platon*. Paris: Payot.
Berryman, S. (2009). *The Mechanical Hypothesis in Ancient Greek Natural Philosophy*. Cambridge: Cambridge University Press.
Berti, E. (1989–90). 'La finalità in Aristotele'. *Fondamenti* 14–16: 7–44.
Berve, H. (1967). *Die Tyrannis bei den Griechen*. Munich: C. H. Beck.
Bett, R. A. (2000). *Pyrrho: His Antecedents and his Legacy*. Oxford: Oxford University Press.
Bett, R. A. (2010). *The Cambridge Companion to Ancient Scepticism*. Cambridge: Cambridge University Press.
Bianchi, E. (1981). 'Teratologia e geografia. L'homo monstruosus in autori dell'antichità classica'. *Acme* 34: 227–49.
Bianchi, O., and O. Thévenez (eds) (2004). *Mirabilia. Conceptions et représentations de l'extraordinaire dans le monde antique*. Volume édité sous la direction de P. Mudry. Bern: Peter Lang.
Bianchi, U. (1960). *Teogonie e cosmogonie*. Rome: Editrice Studium.
Bignone, E. (1916). *Empedocle*. Turin: Fratelli Bocca.
Bignone, E. (1936). *L'Aristotele perduto e la formazione filosofica di Epicuro*. Florence: La Nuova Italia.
Bloch, R. (1963). *Les prodiges dans l'antiquité classique*. Paris: Presses Universitaires de France.
Blok, J. H. (1995). *The Early Amazons: Modern and Ancient Perspectives on a Persistent Myth*. Leiden, New York and Cologne: E. J. Brill.
Blumenberg, H. (1979). *Schiffbruch mit Zuschauer. Paradigma einer Daseinmetapher*. Frankfurt: Suhrkamp.
Boas, M. (1952). 'The Establishment of Mechanical Philosophy'. *Osiris* 10: 412–541.
Bobzien, S. (1998). *Determinism and Freedom in Stoic Philosophy*. Oxford: Clarendon Press.
Bockmuehl, M. (1995). 'Natural Law in Second Temple Judaism'. *Vetus Testamentum* 45: 17–44.
Bodin, J. (1581). *De la démonomanie des sorciers*. Paris: Jacques Du Puys.
Bodin, J. (1995). *On the Demon-Mania of Witches*. Translated by R. A. Scott. Toronto: Victoria University Press.
Bodin, J. (2006). *Demonomania de gli stregoni*. Edited by A. Suggi, translated by E. Cato. Rome: Storia e letteratura.
Bolgar, R. R. (ed.) (1971). *Classical Influences on European Culture* AD *500–1500*. Cambridge: Cambridge University Press.
Bolgar, R. R. (ed.) (1976). *Classical Influences on European Culture* AD *1500–1700*. Cambridge: Cambridge University Press.
Bollack, J. (1959). 'Lukrez und Empedokles'. *Die Neue Rundschau* 70: 656–86.
Bollack, J. (1965–69). *Empédocle*. Paris: Editions de Minuit.

Bollack, J. (1971). 'Mytische Deutung und Deutung des Mythos', in M. Fuhrmann (hrsg.), *Terror und Spiel. Probleme der Mythenrezeption*. Munich: W. Fink, pp. 67–119.
Bollack, J. (1980). 'La cosmogonie des anciens atomistes'. *Siculorum gymnasium: Rassegna della Facoltà di lettere e filosofia dell'Università di Catania* 33: 11–59.
Bollack, J. (1990). *L'Oedipe roi de Sophocle*. Lille: Presses Universitaires de Lille.
Bollack, J. (1995). *La naissance d'Oedipe. Traduction et commentaires d'Oedipe roi*. Paris: Gallimard.
Bollack, M. (1978). *La raison de Lucrèce. Constitution d'une poétique philosophique avec un essai d'interprétation de la critique lucrétienne*. Paris: Editions de Minuit.
Bonhöffer, A. (1911). *Epiktet und das Neue Testament*. Giessen: A. Töpelmann.
Bonitz, H. (1870). *Index aristotelicus. Aristotelis Opera. V.* Edidit Academia Regia Borussica. Berlin: G. Reimerum. [Abbreviated: Bonitz]
Boot, P. (1984). *Plotinus over Voorzienigheid: Enneade III 2–3*. Amsterdam: V. U. Boekhandel.
Booth, A. P. (1994). 'The Voice of the Serpent: Philo's Epicureanism', in W. Welleman (ed.), *Hellenization Revisited: Shaping a Christian Response within the Greco-Roman World*. Lanham, MD: University Press of America, pp. 159–72.
Borgen, P., K. Fuglseth and R. Skarsten (2000). *The Philo Index: A Complete Greek Word Index to the Writings of Philo of Alexandria*. Grand Rapids, MI, and Cambridge: W. B. Eerdmans; Leiden, Boston and Cologne: E. J. Brill.
Boss, G., and G. Seel (éds.) (1987). *Proclus et son influence. Actes du Colloque de Neuchâtel, juin 1985*. Zürich: Editions du Grand Midi.
Bossina, L. (2012). *Stoa, ellenismo e catastrofe tedesca*. Bari: Edizioni di pagina.
Bottici, C. (2007). *A Philosophy of Political Myth*. Cambridge: Cambridge University Press.
Bouche-Leclercq, A. (1879–82). *Histoire de la divination dans l'antiquité*. Paris: E. Leroux.
Bouche-Leclercq, A. (1899). *L'astrologie grecque*. Paris: E. Leroux.
Bourgery, A. (1928). 'Lucain et la magie'. *Revue des Études Latines* 6: 299–313.
Bourgey, L. (1955). *Observation et expérience chez Aristote*. Paris: Librairie Philosophique J. Vrin.
Bouton-Touboulic, A.-I. (2004). *L'ordre caché. La notion d'ordre chez saint Augustin*. Paris: Institut d'études augustiniennes.
Boyancé, P. (1963). *Lucrèce et l'épicurisme*. Paris: Presses Universitaires de France.
Boys-Stone, G. (2001). *Post-Hellenistic Philosophy: A Study of its Development from the Stoics to Origen*. Oxford: Oxford University Press.
Brague, R., and J.-F. Courtine (éds.) (1990). *Herméneutique et ontologie. Mélanges en hommage à Pierre Aubenque*. Paris: Presses Universitaires de France.
Brandwood, L. (1974). *A Word Index to Plato*. Leeds: W. S. Maney and Son.

Brehier, É. (1907). *Les idées philosophiques et religieuses de Philon d'Alexandrie.* Paris: Librairie Alphonse Picard & Fils.

Brehier, É. (1910). *Chrysippe et l'ancien stoïcisme.* Paris: Félix Alcan.

Brehier, É. (1928). *La philosophie de Plotin.* Paris: Boivin et Cie.

Brehier, É. (1967). *Histoire de la philosophie.* Revised and updated edition by P.-M. Schuhl and M. de Gandillac. Paris: Presses Universitaires de France.

Brien, P. (1968). 'La génération des êtres vivants dans la philosophie épicurienne'. *Revue de Synthèse* 89: 311–25.

Brisson, L. (2008). *Le sexe incertain. Androgynie et hermaphroditisme dans l'Antiquité gréco-romaine.* 2e ed. Paris: Les Belles Lettres.

Brochard, V. (1923). *Les sceptiques grecs.* Paris: Librairie Philosophique J. Vrin.

Brochard, V. (1926). *Études de philosophie ancienne et de philosophie moderne.* Collected and introduced by V. Delbos. 2e ed. Paris: Librairie Philosophique J. Vrin.

Brown, A. L. (1983). 'The Erinyes in the Oresteia: Real Life, the Supernatural, and the Stage'. *Journal of Hellenic Studies* 103: 13–34.

Brown, C. G. (1996). 'In the Cyclop's Cave: Revenge and Justice in *Odyssey* 9'. *Mnemosyne* 49: 1–29.

Brunschwig, J., and G. E. R. Lloyd (1996). *Le savoir grec: dictionnaire critique.* Paris: Flammarion.

Buffière, F. (1956). *Les mythes d'Homère et la pensée grecque.* Paris: Les Belles Lettres.

Burkert, W. (1984). *Die orientalisierende Epoche in der griechischen Religion und Literatur.* Berlin: C. Winter.

Burnyeat, M. (ed.) (1983). *The Skeptical Tradition.* Berkeley: University of California Press.

Busa, R. (ed.) (1974–80). *Index Thomisticus: Sancti Thomae Aquinatis Operum Omnium Indices et Concordantiae.* Stuttgart and Bad Cannstatt: Frohmann-Holzboog.

Busa, R., and A. Zampolli (1975). *Concordantiae senecanae.* Hildesheim, Zürich, New York: Olms-Weidmann.

Calabi, F. (2003). 'Il serpente e il cavaliere: piacere e sophrosyne in Filone d'Alessandria'. *Annali di scienze religiose* 8: 199–215.

Calame, C. (1985). 'Les figures grecques du gigantesque'. *Communications* 42: 147–72.

Calderone, S. (1972). 'Superstitio', in H. Temporini (hrsg.), *Aufstieg und Niedergand der römischen Welt (ANRW): Geschichte und Kultur Roms im Spiegel der Neuereun Forschung*, I.2. Berlin and New York: Walter de Gruyter, pp. 377–96.

Calogero, G. (1967). *Storia della logica antica. vol. I: L'età arcaica.* Bari and Rome: Laterza.

Cambiano, G. (1992). 'Le filosofie tra l'impero e il cielo', in A. Schiavone (a cura di), *Storia di Roma*. Turin: Einaudi, III: 321–60.

Campbell, A. Y. (1935). 'Aeschylus *Agamemnon* 1223–38 and treacherous monsters'. *The Classical Quarterly* 29: 25–36.

Campbell, G. L. (2003). *Lucretius on Creation and Evolution: A Commentary on De Rerum Natura, Book Five, Lines 772–1104*. Oxford: Oxford University Press.

Campbell, G. L. (2006). *Strange Creatures: Anthropology in Antiquity*. London: Duckworth.

Canfora, L. (1979). *Intellettuali in Germania tra reazione e rivoluzione*. Bari: De Donato.

Canfora, L. (1980). *Ideologie del classicismo*. Turin: Einaudi.

Canguilhem, G. (1966). *Le normal et le pathologique*. Paris: Presses Universitaires de France.

Canguilhem, G. (1981). *Idéologie et rationalité dans l'histoire des sciences de la vie. Nouvelles études d'histoire et de philosophie*. Paris: Librairie Philosophique J. Vrin.

Caratelli, G. P. (a cura di) (1983). Συζήτησισ. *Studi sull'epicureismo greco e romano offerti a M. Gigante*. Naples: Macchiaroli.

Casini, P. (1963). 'Zoogonia e trasformismo nella fisica epicurea'. *Giornale critico della filosofia italiana* 42: 178–207.

Cassin, B. (1995). *L'effet sophistique*. Paris: Gallimard.

Cassirer, E. (1923–77). *Philosophie des symbolische Formen*. Berlin: B. Cassirer [vols 1–3] and Darmstadt: Wissenschaftliche Buchgesellschaft [vol. 4].

Cassirer, E. (1925). *Sprache und Mythos. Ein Beitrag zum Problem der Götternamen*. Leipzig: Teubner.

Caster, M. (1937). *Lucien et la pensée religieuse de son temps*. Paris: Les Belles Lettres.

Catapano, G. (2001). *Il concetto di filosofia nei primi scritti di Agostino: analisi dei passi metafilosofici dal 'Contra Academicos' al 'De uera religione'*. Rome: Institutum Patristicum Augustinianum.

Caye, P. et al. (a cura di) (2011). *L'Harmonie entre philosophie, science et arts, de l'antiquité à l'âge moderne*. Naples: Giannini.

Céard, J. (1977). *La Nature et les prodiges. L'insolite au XVIe siècle en France*. Geneva: Droz.

Charlton, W. (1970). *Aristotle's Physics Books I and II*. Oxford: Clarendon Press.

Chase Green, W. (1944). *Moira, Fate, Good and Evil in Greek Thought*. Cambridge, MA: Harvard University Press.

Cherniss, H. (1935). *Aristotle's Criticism of Presocratic Philosophy*. Baltimore: The Johns Hopkins Press.

Cherniss, H. (1944). *Aristotle's Criticism of Plato and the Academy*. Baltimore: The Johns Hopkins Press.
Cherniss, H. (1954). 'The Sources of Evil According to Plato'. *Proceedings of the American Philosophical Society* 98: 23–30.
Chevallier, R., and R. Poignault (éds.) (1991). *Présence de Senèque*. Paris: J. Touzot.
Chiabò, M., and L. Roberti (eds) (2001). *Hygini fabularum index verborum*. Hildesheim, Zürich and New York: Olms-Weidmann.
Chiesara, M. L. (2003). *Storia dello scetticismo greco*. Turin: Einaudi.
Chroust, A. H. (1963). 'Some Historical Observations on Natural Law and "According to Nature"'. *Emerita* 31: 285–98.
Ciccarese, M. P. (a cura di) (2002–7). *Animali simbolici. Alle origini del pensiero cristiano*. Bologna: EDB.
Cilento, V. (1973). *Saggi su Plotino*. Milan: Mursia.
Claesson, G. (1974). *Index tertullianeus*. Paris: Études augustiniennes.
Clair, J. (1989). *Méduse*. Paris: Gallimard.
Codino, F. (1963). 'Recensione a Max Pohlenz, "L'uomo Greco", traduzione di Beniamino Proto, Florence, La Nuova Italia Editrice'. *Critica Marxista* 1: 197–202.
Cole, T. (1967). *Democritus and the Sources of Greek Anthropology*. Cleveland, OH: Press of Western Reserve University for the American Philological Association.
Colish, M. (1985). *The Stoic Tradition from Antiquity to the Early Middle Ages*. Leiden, Boston and Cologne: E. J. Brill.
Colli, G. (1949). *Lezioni di storia della filosofia antica: Empedocle*. Pisa: Libreria goliardica.
Colli, G. (1975). *La nascita della filosofia*. Milan: Adelphi.
Colli, G. (2010). *Apollineo e dionisiaco*. Milan: Adelphi.
Collobert, C., P. Destrée and F. J. Gonzalez (eds) (2012). *Plato and Myth: Studies on the Use and Status of Platonic Myths*. Leiden, New York and Cologne: E. J. Brill.
Conacher, D. J. (1967). *Euripidean Drama: Myth, Theme and Structure*. Toronto, Buffalo and London: University of Toronto Press.
Conche, M. (1973). *Pyrrhon ou l'apparence*. Villers-sur-Mer: Editions de Mégare.
Conrad, L. I. (ed.) (1995). *The Western Medical Tradition: 800 bc–1800 ad*. Cambridge: Cambridge University Press.
Cornford, F. M. (1934). 'Innumerable Worlds in Presocratic Philosophy'. *The Classical Quarterly* 28: 1–16.
Cornford, F. M. (1952). *Principium Sapientiae: The Origins of Greek Philosophical Thought*. Cambridge: Cambridge University Press.

Cornford, F. M. (1957). *From Religion to Philosophy: A Study in the Origins of Western Speculation*. 2nd ed. New York: Harper.
Cotter, W. (1999). *Miracles in Greco-Roman Antiquity*. London: Routledge and Kegan Paul.
Courcelle, P. (1966). 'Le corps-tombeau. (Platon, Gorgias, 493 a, Cratyle, 400 c, Phèdre, 250 c)'. *Revue des Études Anciennes* 68: 101–22.
Courtès, J.-M. (1968). 'La dialectique du réel et du possible dans le *De rerum natura* de Lucrèce'. *Revue des Études Latines* 46: 170–9.
Coussin, P. (1929). 'L'origine et l'evolution de l'ΕΠΟΧΗ'. *Revue des Études Grecques* 42: 373–97.
Coussin, P. (1937). 'Carnéade et Descartes', in R. Bayer (ed.), *Travaux du IXe congrès international de philosophie: congrès Descartes. IIIeme partie, Études cartésiennes*. Paris: Hermann, pp. 9–16.
Credaro, L. (1889). *Lo scetticismo degli accademici*. Rome: Tipografia alle terme diocleziane di Giovanni Balbi.
Crouzel, H. (1962). *Origène et la philosophie*. Paris: Aubier.
Crouzel, H. (1994). 'Diables et démons dans les homélies d'Origène'. *Bulletin de Littérature Ecclésiastique* 95: 303–31.
Cuny-Le Callet, B. (2005). *Rome et ses monstres. Naissance d'un concept philosophique et rhétorique*. Paris: Jérôme Million.
Curi, U. (2000). *Pólemos. Filosofia come guerra*. Turin: Bollati Boringhieri.
D'Agostino, F. (1979). *Per un'archeologia del diritto. Miti giuridici greci*. Milan: Giuffrè.
Dal Pra, M. (1975). *Lo scetticismo greco*. 2a ed. Bari and Rome: Laterza.
Dante Alighieri (1996). *The Divine Comedy*. Edited and translated by Robert M. Durling. Oxford: Oxford University Press.
Darwin, C. (1887). *The Life and Letters*. Edited by F. Darwin. London: John Murray.
Darwin, C. (1986–9). *The Works of Charles Darwin*. Edited by P. H. Barrett and R. B. Freeman. London: William Pickering.
Dasen, V. (1993). *Dwarfs in Ancient Egypt and Greece*. Oxford: Clarendon Press.
Daston, L., and K. Park (1998). *Wonders and the Order of Nature, 1150–1750*. New York: Zone Books.
Daston, L., and M. Stolleis (eds) (2008). *Natural Laws and Laws of Nature in Early Modern Europe*. Burlington, VT: Ashgate.
De Capitani, F. (1985). 'Il problema del male nell'VIII trattato della prima Enneade di Plotino', in AA.VV., *Sapienza antica: studi in onore di D. Pesce*. Milan: Franco Angeli, pp. 68–98.
De Lacy, P. (1948). 'Lucretius and the History of Epicureanism'. *Transactions and Proceedings of the American Philological Association* 79: 12–23.

De Lacy, P. (1969). 'Limits and Variation in the Epicurean Philosophy'. *Phoenix* 23: 104–13.

De Lacy, P. H. (1972). 'Galen's Platonism'. *American Journal of Philology* 93: 27–39.

De Ley, H. (1980). '3: Democritean notes on Aristotle's *Generation of Animals*'. *Hermes* 108: 129–53.

De Witt, N. W. (1954). *Epicurus and His Philosophy*. Minneapolis: University of Minnesota Press.

Decharme, P. (1904). *La critique des traditions religieuses chez les Grecs*. Paris: A. Picard.

Decharneaux, B. (1991). 'Apparitions et miracles des anges et démons chez Philon d'Alexandrie et Plutarque', in A. Dierkens (ed.), *Apparitions et miracles*. Brussels: Editions de l'Université de Bruxelles, pp. 61–8.

Deferrari, R. J., M. Inviolata Berry and M. R. P. McGuire (1939). *A Concordance of Ovid*. Washington, DC: The Catholic University of America Press.

Deforge, B. (1986). *Eschyle, poète cosmique*. Paris: Les Belles Lettres.

Deitz, L. (1987). 'Bibliographie du platonisme impérial antérieur à Plotin: 1926–1986', in W. Haase (hrsg.), *Aufstieg und Niedergand der römischen Welt (ANRW): Geschichte und Kultur Roms im Spiegel der Neuereun Forschung*, II.36.1. Berlin and New York: Walter de Gruyter, pp. 124–82.

Del Lucchese, F. (2011). 'Monstrosity and the limits of the intellect: philosophy as teratomachy in Descartes'. *Journal of French and Francophone Philosophy – Revue de la philosophie française et de langue français* 19: 107–34.

Del Real Francia, P. J. (1998). *Lexicon Manilianum*. Hildesheim, Zürich and New York: Olms-Weidmann.

Delatte, L., J. Denooz and S. Govaerts (a cura di) (1977). *Index du Corpus Hermeticum*. Rome: Edizioni dell'Ateneo e Bizzarri.

Delcourt, M. (1957). *Héphaistos ou la légende du magicien*. Paris: Les Belles Lettres.

Deleuze, G. (1969). *Logique du sens*. Paris: Editions de Minuit.

Della Torre, A. (1902). *Storia dell'accademia platonica di Firenze*. Florence: Tipografia G. Carnesecchi e figli.

Delumeau, J. (1978). *La peur en Occident: XIVe–XVIIIe siècles*. Paris: Fayard.

des Places, E. (éd.) (1989). *Platon Œuvres Complètres, tome XIV: Lexique*. Paris: Les Belles Lettres.

Destrée, P., and R. G. Edmonds III (eds) (2017). *Plato and the Power of Images*. Leiden, New York and Cologne: E. J. Brill.

Detienne, M. (1962). *Homère, Hésiode et Pythagore. Poésie et philosophie dans le Pythagorisme ancien*. Brussels: Berchem.

Devereux, D., and P. Pellegrin (éds.) (1990). *Biologie, logique et métaphysique chez Aristote. Actes du Séminaire CNRS-NSF, Oléron 28 juin – 3 juillet 1987*. Paris: Editions du Centre National de la Recherche Scientifique.

d'Hoine, P. et al. (2002). *Proclus: Fifteen Years of Research.* Göttingen: Vandenhoeck & Ruprecht.

Di Benedetto, V. (1978). *L'ideologia del potere e la tragedia greca.* Turin: Einaudi.

Diano, C. A. (1952). *Forma ed evento. Principii per una interpretazione del mondo greco.* Venice: Neri Pozza.

Diller, H. (1946). 'Hesiod und die Anfänge der griechischen Philosophie'. *Antike und Abendland* 2: 140–51.

Dillon, J. M. (1977). *The Middle Platonists: 80 BC to AD 220.* Ithaca, NY: Cornell University Press.

D'Ippolito, G. (1980). 'La narrativa scientifica nel mondo grecolatino', in L. Russo (a cura di), *La fantascienza e la critica.* Milan: Feltrinelli, pp. 151–65.

Dodd, C. H. (1954). *The Bible and the Greeks.* 2nd ed. London: Hodder & Stoughton.

Dodds, E. R. (1951). *The Greeks and the Irrational.* Berkeley: University of California Press.

Donini, P. (1992). 'Galeno e la filosofia', in W. Haase (hrsg.), *Aufstieg und Niedergand der römischen Welt (ANRW): Geschichte und Kultur Roms im Spiegel der Neuereun Forschung,* II.36.5. Berlin and New York: Walter de Gruyter, pp. 3484–504.

Doody, A. (2010). *Pliny's Encyclopedia: The Reception of the 'Natural History',* Cambridge: Cambridge University Press.

Drachmann, A. B. (1922). *Atheism in Pagan Antiquity.* London and Copenhaghen: Gyldendal.

Dragona-Monachou, M. (1975–6). 'Το πρόβλημα του κακού στο Φίλωνα τον Αλεξανδρέα με ειδική αναφορά στο 'Περί προνοίας'. *Φιλοσοφία* 5–6: 306–53.

Dragona-Monachou, M. (1976). *The Stoic Arguments for the Existence and Providence of the Gods.* Athens: National and Capodistrian University of Athens.

Dragona-Monachou, M. (1994). 'Divine Providence in the Philosophy of the Empire', in W. Haase (hrsg.), *Aufstieg und Niedergand der römischen Welt (ANRW): Geschichte und Kultur Roms im Spiegel der Neuereun Forschung,* II.36.7. Berlin and New York: Walter de Gruyter, pp. 4417–90.

DuBois, P. (1982). *Centaurs and Amazons: Women and the Pre-History of the Great Chain of Being.* Ann Arbor: University of Michigan Press.

Duchemin, J. (1967). 'Le personnage de Lyssa dans l'Héracles furieux d'Euripide'. *Revue des Études Grècques* 80: 130–9.

Dudley, J. (2012). *Aristotle's Concept of Chance: Accidents, Cause, Necessity, and Determinism.* New York: SUNY Press.

Dufour, R. (2002). *Plotinus: A Bibliography (1950–2000).* Leiden, Boston and Cologne: E. J. Brill.

Duhot, J.-J. (1989). *La conception stoïcienne de la causalité.* Paris: Librairie Philosophique J. Vrin.

Dumézil, G. (1924). *Le crime des Lemniennes. Rites et légendes du monde égéen*. Paris: Librairie Orientaliste Paul Geuthner.

Dumont, J. P. (1972). *Le scepticisme et le phénomène. Essai sur la signification et les origines du pyrrhonisme*. Paris: Librairie Philosophique J. Vrin.

Dumortier, J. (1975). *Les images dans la poésie d'Eschyle*. 2e ed. Paris: Les Belles Lettres.

Duncan, A. R. C. (1952). 'The Stoic View of Life'. *Phoenix* 6: 123–38.

Dupont, F. (1995). *Les monstres de Sénèque*. Paris: Belin.

Durry, M. (éd.) (1970). *Lucain: Sept exposés suivis de discussion*. Vandœuvres-Genève: Fondation Hardt.

Ebeling, H. (edidit) (1885). *Lexicon homericum*. Composerunt F. Albracht et alii. Leipzig: Teubner.

Edinger, H. G. (éd.) (1981). *Index Analyticus Graecitatis Aeschyleae*. Hildesheim, Zürich and New York: Olms-Weidmann.

Ellendt, F. (1872). *Lexicon sophoclevm*. Editio altera emendata. Cvravit H. Genthe. Berlin: Svmptibus Fratrvm Borntraeger.

Erler, M., and R. Bees (hrsg.) (2000). *Epikureismus in der späten Republik und der Kaiserzeit. Akten der 2. Tagung der Karl- und Gertrud-Abel-Stiftung vom 30. September – 3 Oktober 1998 in Würzburg*. Stuttgart: Steiner.

Ernout, A., and L. Robin (1925–8). *Lucrèce. De rerum natura. Commentaire exégétique et critique*. Paris: Les Belles Lettres.

Evans, G. R. (1982). *Augustine on Evil*. Cambridge: Cambridge University Press.

Ewing, J. D. (2008). *Clement of Alexandria's Reinterpretation of Divine Providence: The Christianization of the Hellenistic Idea of* Pronoia. Lewiston, Queenston and Lampeter: The Edwin Mellen Press.

Fahr, W. (1969). *«Theous nomizein». Zum Problem der Anfänge des Atheismus bei den Griechen*. Hildesheim, Zürich and New York: Olms-Weidmann.

Fantuzzi, M., Papanghelis, T. eds. (2006). *Brill's Companion to Greek and Latin Pastorals*. Leiden-Boston-Köln: E. J. Brill.

Farkas, A. E., O. Harper and E. B. Harrison (eds) (1987). *Monsters and Demons in the Ancient and Medieval World: Papers Presented in Honor of Edith Porada*. Mainz on Rhine: Verlag Philipp von Zabern.

Farrar, C. (1988). *The Origins of Democratic Thinking: The Invention of Politics in Classical Athens*. Cambridge: Cambridge University Press.

Farrington, B. (1947). *Head and Hand in Ancient Greece*. London: Watts.

Ferguson, J. (1965). 'On the Date of Democritus'. *Symbolae Osloenses* 40: 17–26.

Festugière, A.-J. (1949–54), *La révélation d'Hermès Trismégiste*. Paris: Les Belles Lettres.

Festugière, A.-J. (1971). *Études de philosophie grecque*. Paris: Librairie Philosophique J. Vrin.

Festugière, A.-J. (1975). *Études d'histoire et de philologie*. Paris: Librairie Philosophique J. Vrin.

Finazzo, G. (1971). *La realtà del mondo nella visione cosmogonica esiodea*. Rome: Edizioni dell'Ateneo.
Finley, M. I. (1954). *The World of Odysseus*. New York: Viking Books.
Fletcher, R. (2014). *Apuleius' Platonism: The Impersonation of Philosophy*. Cambridge: Cambridge University Press.
Floyd, W. E. G. (1971). *Clement of Alexandria's Treatment of the Problem of Evil*. Oxford: Oxford University Press.
Flückiger, H. (1990). *Sextus Empiricus: Grundriss der pyrrhonischen Skepsis. Buch I – Selektiver Kommentar*. Bern: P. Haupt.
Foley, M. P. (1999). 'Cicero, Augustine, and the Philosophical Roots of the Cassiciacum Dialogues'. *Revue des Études Augustiniennes* 45: 51–77.
Forbes Irving, P. M. C. (1990). *Metamorphosis in Greek Myths*. Oxford: Clarendon Press.
Foucault, M. (1999). *Les anormaux. Cours au Collège de France. 1974–1975. Édition établie sous la direction de F. Ewald et A. Fontana, par V. Marchetti et A. Salomoni*. Paris: Gallimard-Seuil.
Fowden, G. (1986). *The Egyptian Hermes: A Historical Approach to the Late Pagan Mind*. Cambridge: Cambridge University Press.
Fowler, D. (2002). *Lucretius on Atomic Motion: A Commentary on Lucretius* De rerum natura *2.1–332*. Oxford: Oxford University Press.
Fränkel, H. (1962). *Dichtung und Philosophie des frühen Griechentums. Eine Geschichte der griechischen Epik, Lyrik und Prosa bis zur Mitte des fünften Jahrhunderts*. 2. ed. Munich: C. H. Beck'sche Verlagsbuchhandlung.
Fraser, P. M. (1972). *Ptolemaic Alexandria*. Oxford: Clarendon Press.
Fredouille, J.-C. (1972). *Tertullien et la conversion de la culture antique*. Paris: Études augustiniennes.
Freeman, K. (1959). *The Pre-Socratic Philosophers: A Companion to Diels, Fragmente der Vorsokratiker*. Oxford: Blackwell.
French, R. K., and F. Greenaway (eds) (1986). *Science in the Early Roman Empire: Pliny the Elder, His Sources and Influence*. London: Croom Helm.
Frick, P. (1999). *Divine Providence in Philo of Alexandria*. Tübingen: Mohr-Siebeck.
Froidefond, L. (1972). 'Sur quelques passages du *De Iside et Osiride* de Plutarque'. *Revue des Études Grecques* 85: 63–71.
Frontisi-Ducroux, F. (1995). *Du masque au visage*. Paris: Flammarion.
Frutiger, P. (1930). *Les mythes de Platon, étude philosophique et littéraire*. Paris: F. Alcan.
Fuller, B. A. G. (1912). *The Problem of Evil in Plotinus*. Cambridge: Cambridge University Press.
Furley, D. (1967). *Two Studies in the Greek Atomists*. Princeton: Princeton University Press.
Furley, D., and R. E. Allen (eds) (1970–5). *Studies in Presocratic Philosophy*. London: Routledge and Kegan Paul.

Furtwängler, A., and K. Reichhold (hrsg.) (1904–32). *Griechische Vasenmalerai. Auswahl hervorragender Vasenbilder.* Munich: F. Brickmann.

Gagarin, M. (1973). 'Dikē in the Works and Days'. *The Classical Quarterly* 68: 81–94.

Gagarin, M. (1974). 'Dikē in archaic Greek thought'. *The Classical Quarterly* 69: 186–97.

Gale, M. (1994). *Myth and Poetry in Lucretius.* Cambridge: Cambridge University Press.

Gale, M. (ed.) (2007). *Oxford Readings in Classical Studies: Lucretius.* Oxford: Oxford University Press.

Gall, D., and A. Wolkenhauer (hrsg.) (2009). *Laokoon in Literatur und Kunst. Schriften des Symposions «Laokoon in Literatur und Kunst» vom 30.11.2006 Universität Bonn.* Berlin and New York: Walter de Gruyter.

Gallo, I. (a cura di) (1992). *Plutarco e le scienze. Atti del IV convegno plutarcheo. Genova – Bocca di Magra, 22–25 aprile 1991.* Genoa: Sagep editrice.

Garin, E. (1952). *L'umanesimo italiano.* Bari: Laterza.

Garland, R. (1995). *The Eye of the Beholder: Deformity and Disability in the Graeco-Roman World.* Ithaca, NY: Cornell University Press.

Gatzemeier, M. (1970). *Die Naturphilosophie des Straton von Lampsakos. Zur Geschichte des Problems der Bewegung im Bereich des frühen Peripatos.* Meisenheim a. Glan: Anton Hain.

Gaukroger, S. (1995). 'The Ten Modes of Aenesidemus and the Myth of Ancient Scepticism'. *British Journal for the History of Philosophy* 3: 371–87.

Gersh, S. (1986). *Middle Platonism and Neoplatonism: The Latin Tradition.* Notre Dame, IN: University of Notre Dame Press.

Gerson, L. P. (2010). *The Cambridge History of Philosophy in Late Antiquity.* Cambridge: Cambridge University Press.

Gerson, L. P. (2013). *From Plato to Platonism.* Ithaca, NY: Cornell University Press.

Geymonat, L. (1970). *Storia del pensiero filosofico e scientifico.* Milan: Garzanti.

Giannantoni, G. (a cura di) (1982). *Lo scetticismo antico. Atti del Convegno organizzato dal centro di studio del pensiero antico del C.N.R., Roma, 5–8 nov. 1980.* Naples: Bibliopolis.

Giannantoni, G., and M. Gigante (a cura di) (1984). *Epicureismo greco e romano. Atti del Congresso Internazionale, Naples 19–26 maggio 1993.* Naples: Bibliopolis.

Giannantoni, G. et al. (1995). *La tradizione socratica.* Naples: Bibliopolis.

Giannantoni, G. (2005). *Dialogo socratico e nascita della dialettica nella filosofia di Platone.* Naples: Bibliopolis.

Giannini, A. (1963). 'Studi sulla paradossografia greca. I. Da Omero a Callimaco: motivi e forme del meraviglioso'. *Rendiconti dell'Istituto Lombardo* 97: 247–60.

Giannini, A. (1964). 'Studi sulla paradossografia greca. II. Da Callimaco all'età imperiale: la letteratura paradossografica'. *Acmé* 17: 99–140.

Gibson, R. K., and R. Morello (eds) (2011). *Pliny the Elder: Themes and Context*. Leiden, Boston and Cologne: E. J. Brill.

Gigandet, A. (1998). *Fama deum: Lucrèce et les raisons du mythe*. Paris: Librairie Philosophique J. Vrin.

Gigandet, A., and P. M. Morel (2007). *Lire Épicure et les épicuriens*. Paris: Presses Universitaires de France.

Gigante, M. (1956). *Nomos basileus*. Naples: Edizioni Glaux.

Gigante, M. (1981). *Scetticismo e epicureismo: per l'avviamento di un discorso storiografico*. Naples: Bibliopolis.

Gigon, O. (1945). *Der Ursprung der griechischen Philosophie, von Hesiod bis Parmenides*. Basel and Stuttgart: Schwabe & Co.

Gigon, O. (1973). 'Cicero und die griechische Philosophie', in H. Temporini (hrsg.), *Aufstieg und Niedergand der römischen Welt (ANRW): Geschichte und Kultur Roms im Spiegel der Neuereun Forschung*, I.4. Berlin and New York: Walter de Gruyter: 226–61.

Gilson, E. (1969). *L'esprit de la philosophie médiévale*. 2e ed. Paris: Librairie Philosophique J. Vrin.

Gilson, E. (1971). *D'Aristote à Darwin et retour. Essai sur quelques constantes de la biophilosophie*. Paris: Librairie Philosophique J. Vrin.

Girard, R. (1972). *La violence et le sacré*. Paris: B. Grasset.

Girardet, K. M. (1995). 'Naturrecht und Naturgesetz: eine gerade Linie von Cicero zu Augustinus?' *Rheinisches Museum* 138: 266–98.

Girgenti, G. (1996). *Il pensiero forte di Porfirio. Mediazione fra henologia platonica e ontologia aristotelica*. Milan: Vita e Pensiero.

Glenn, J. (1978). 'The Polyphemus Myth: Its Origin and Interpretation'. *Greece and Rome* 25: 141–55.

Goerler, W. (1974). *Untersuchungen zu Ciceros Philosophie*. Heidelberg: Carl Winter.

Goldschmidt, V. (1949). *La religion de Platon*. Paris: Presses Universitaires de France.

Goldschmidt, V. (1953). *Le système stoïcien et l'idée de temps*. Paris: Librairie Philosophique J. Vrin.

Gombrich, E. H. (1972). 'Raphael's *Stanza della Segnatura* and the Nature of its Symbolism', in *Symbolic Images: Studies in the Art of the Renaissance*. London: Phaidon, pp. 85–101.

Goodenough, E. R. (1940). *Introduction to Philo Judaeus*. New Haven: Yale University Press.

Gordon, C. A. (1963). *A Bibliography of Lucretius*. London: R. Hart-Davis.

Goslin, O. (2010). 'Hesiod's Typhonomachy and the Ordering of Sound'. *Transactions of the American Philological Association* 140: 351–73.

Gotthelf, A. (1976–7). 'Aristotle's Conception of Final Causality'. *Review of Metaphysics* 30: 226–54.

Gotthelf, A. (ed.) (1985). *Aristotle on Nature and Living Things: Philosophical and Historical Studies Presented to David M. Balme on his Seventieth Birthday*. Pittsburgh: Mathesis Publications.

Gotthelf, A. (1989). 'Teleology and Spontaneous Generation in Aristotle: A Discussion'. *Apeiron* 22: 181–93.

Gotthelf, A., and J. G. Lennox (eds) (1987). *Philosophical Issues in Aristotle's Biology*. Cambridge: Cambridge University Press.

Gould, J. B. (1974). 'The Stoic Conception of Fate'. *Journal of the History of Ideas* 56: 1–32.

Grabmann, M. (1909–11). *Die Geschichte der scholastischen Methode*. Freiburg im Bresgau: Herder.

Grandgeorge, L. (1896). *Saint Augustin et le néo-platonisme*. Paris: E. Leroux.

Grant, R. M. (1952). *Miracle and Natural Law in Graeco-Roman and Early Christian Thought*. Amsterdam: North-Holland.

Grant, R. M. (1967). *After the New Testament*. Philadelphia: Fortress Press.

Graves, R. (1958). *Greek Myths*. London: Cassell.

Grimal, P. (1965). *La mythologie grècque*. Paris: Presses Universitaires de France.

Grimal, P. (1989). 'Sénèque et le Stoïcisme Romain', in W. Haase (hrsg.), *Aufstieg und Niedergand der römischen Welt (ANRW): Geschichte und Kultur Roms im Spiegel der Neuereun Forschung*. II.36.3. Berlin and New York: Walter de Gruyter, pp. 1962–92.

Grmek, M. D. (1972). 'A Survey of the Mechanical Interpretations of Life from Greek Atomists to the followers of Descartes', in A. D. Breck and W. Yourgrau (eds), *Biology, History, and Natural Philosophy*. New York: Plenum Press, pp. 181–96.

Grosew, D. (1958). 'Der Materialismus des Demokrit'. *Das Altertum* 4: 215–21.

Grumack, E. (1932). *Physis und Agathon in der alten Stoa*. Berlin: Weidmannsche Buchhandlund.

Guadalupe Masi, F., and S. Maso (a cura di) (2015). *Epicurus on Eidola:* Peri Phuseos *Book II. Update, Proposals, and Discussions*. Amsterdam: A. M. Hakkert.

Guthrie, W. K. C. (1935). *Orpheus and Greek Religion: A Study of the Orphic Movement*. London: Methuen.

Guthrie, W. K. C. (1950). *The Greeks and their Gods*. London: Methuen.

Guthrie, W. K. C. (1957). *In the Beginning: Some Greek Views on the Origins of Life and the Early State of Man*. London: Methuen.

Guthrie, W. K. C. (1962–81). *History of Greek Philosophy*. Cambridge: Cambridge University Press.

Guyau, M. (1927). *La morale d'Epicure et ses rapports avec les doctrines contemporaines*. 7e ed. Paris: Félix Alcan.
Guyot, H. (1906). *Les réminiscences de Philon le Juif chez Plotin*. Paris: Félix Alcan.
Hadot, P. (1963). *Plotin ou la simplicité du regard*. Paris: Plon.
Hadot, P. (1968). *Porphyre et Victorinus*. Paris: Librairie Philosophique J. Vrin.
Hadot, P. (2002). *Exercices spirituels et philosophie antique*. 2e ed. Paris: A. Michel.
Hadot, P. (2004). *Le voile d'Isis. Essai sur l'histoire de l'idée de nature*. Paris: Gallimard.
Hadzsits, G. D. (1963). *Lucretius and His Influence*. New York: Cooper Square Publishers.
Hagendahl, H. (1958). *Latin Fathers and the Classics*. Gothenburg: Elander.
Hager, F. P. (1962). 'Die Materie und das Böse im antiken Platonismus'. *Museum Helveticum* 19: 73–103.
Hahm, D. E. (1977). *The Origin of Stoic Cosmology*. Columbus: Ohio State University Press.
Hankins, J. (1990). *Plato in the Italian Renaissance*. Leiden, Boston and Cologne: E. J. Brill.
Hankinson, R. J. (1988). 'Galen Explains the Elephant'. *Canadian Journal of Philosophy* supp. vol. 14: 135–57.
Hankinson, R. J. (1989). 'Galen and the Best of all Possible Worlds'. *The Classical Quarterly* 39: 206–27.
Hankinson, R. J. (1992). 'Galen's Philosophical Eclecticism', in W. Haase (hrsg.), *Aufstieg und Niedergand der römischen Welt (ANRW): Geschichte und Kultur Roms im Spiegel der Neuereun Forschung*, II.36.5. Berlin and New York: Walter de Gruyter, pp. 3505–22.
Hankinson, R. J. (1994). 'Galen's Theory of Causation', in W. Haase (hrsg.), *Aufstieg und Niedergand der römischen Welt (ANRW): Geschichte und Kultur Roms im Spiegel der Neuereun Forschung*, II.37.2. Berlin and New York: Walter de Gruyter, pp. 1757–74.
Hankinson, R. J. (1995). *The Sceptics*. London: Routledge and Kegan Paul.
Hankinson, R. J. (1998). *Cause and Explanation in Ancient Greek Thought*. Oxford: Clarendon Press.
Happ, H. (1971). *Hyle. Studien zum Aristotelischen Materie-Begriff*. Berlin and New York: Walter de Gruyter.
Hardie, P. (ed.) (2009). *Paradox and the Marvellous in Augustan Literature and Culture*. Oxford: Oxford University Press.
Hartog, F. (1991). *Le miroir d'Hérodote: essai sur la représentation de l'autre*. 2e ed. Paris: Gallimard.

Havrda, M. (2016). *The So-Called Eighth* Stromateus *by Clement of Alexandria*. Leiden, Boston and Cologne: E. J. Brill.

Hawes, G. (2014). *Rationalizing Myth in Antiquity*. Oxford: Oxford University Press.

Healy, J. F. (1999). *Pliny the Elder on Science and Technology*. Oxford: Oxford University Press.

Hegel, G. W. F. (1969–71). *Werke in zwanzig Bänden*. Frankfurt: Suhrkamp Verlag.

Hegel, G. W. F. (1989). *Vorlesungen über die Geschichte der Philosophie. Teil 2. Griechische Philosophie. I. Thales bis Kyniker*. Hrsg. P. Garniron und W. Jaeschke. Hamburg: Felix Meiner Verlag.

Heidegger, M. (1975–). *Gesamtausgabe*. Frankfurt: Vittorio Klostermann.

Heidel, W. A. (1911). 'Antecedents of Greek Corpuscular Theories'. *Harvard Studies in Classical Philosophy* 22: 11–172.

Heinimann, F. (1945). *Nomos und Physis. Herkunft und Bedeutung einer Antithese im griechischen Denken des 5. Jahrhunderts*. Basel: F. Reinhardt.

Helm, N. J. (1902). 'Lukian und die Philosophenschulen'. *Neue Jahrbücher für das klassische Altertum* 9: 188–213, 351–69.

Henne, P. (2016). *Clément d'Alexandrie*. Paris: Les Éditions du Cerf.

Hensellek, W., and P. Schilling (1973). *Vorarbeiten zu einem Augustinus-Lexikon. A3 = De Ordine. Werksindex*. Vienna: Der Österreichischen Akademie der Wissenschaft.

Herescu, N. I. (éd.) (1958). *Ovidiana, recherches sur Ovide, publiées à l'occasion du bimillénaire de la naissance du poète*. Paris: Les Belles Lettres.

Hershbell, J. P. (1970). 'Hesiod and Empedocles'. *The Classical Journal* 65: 145–61.

Hershbell, J. P. (1992a). 'Plutarch and Stoicism', in W. Haase (hrsg.), *Aufstieg und Niedergand der römischen Welt (ANRW): Geschichte und Kultur Roms im Spiegel der Neuereun Forschung*, II.36.5. Berlin and New York: Walter de Gruyter, pp. 3336–52.

Hershbell, J. P. (1992b). 'Plutarch and Epicureanism', in W. Haase (hrsg.), *Aufstieg und Niedergand der römischen Welt (ANRW): Geschichte und Kultur Roms im Spiegel der Neuereun Forschung*, II.36.5. Berlin and New York: Walter de Gruyter, pp. 3353–83.

Heubeck, A. (1986). '"Erinys" in der archaischen Epik'. *Glotta* 64: 143–65.

Heubeck, A. et al. (1988). *A Commentary on Homer's Odyssey*. Oxford: Clarendon Press (= Omero (1981–6)).

Highet, G. (1949). *The Classical Tradition: Greek and Roman Influences on Western Literature*. Oxford: Oxford University Press.

Hijmans, B. L. (1959). 'Epictetus and the teleological explanation of nature'. *Proceedings of the African Classical Association* 2: 15–21.

Hijmans, B. L. (1987). 'Apuleius, Philosophus Platonicus', in W. Haase (hrsg.), *Aufstieg und Niedergand der römischen Welt (ANRW): Geschichte und Kultur Roms im Spiegel der Neuereun Forschung,* II.36.1. Berlin and New York: Walter de Gruyter, pp. 395–475.

Hild, J. A. (1881). *Étude sur les démons dans la littérature et la religion des Grecs.* Paris: Hachette.

Himmelmann, N. (1983). *Realistic Art in Alexandria.* Proceedings of the British Academy, London, volume LXVII (1981). Oxford: Oxford University Press.

Höffe, O. (2005). *Aristoteles-Lexikon.* Stuttgart: Alfred Kröner.

How, W. W., and J. Well (1912). *A Commentary on Herodotus.* Oxford: Clarendon Press.

Huffman, C. A. (ed.) (2014). *A History of Pythagoreanism.* Cambridge: Cambridge University Press.

Ibrahim, A. (ed.) (2005). *Qu'est-ce qu'un monstre?* Paris: Presses Universitaires de France.

Immerwahr, H. R. (1966). *Form and Thought in Herodotus.* Cleveland, OH: Press of Western Reserve University.

Ioppolo, A. M. (1980). *Aristone di Chio e lo stoicismo antico.* Naples: Bibliopolis.

Ioppolo, A. M. (1986). *Opinione e scienza. Il dibattito tra Stoici e Accademici nel III e II secolo a. C.* Naples: Bibliopolis.

Isnardi-Parente, M. (1966). *Techne. Momenti del pensiero greco da Platone ad Epicuro.* Florence: La Nuova Italia.

Isnardi-Parente, M. (1977). 'Le obiezioni di Stratone al Fedone e l'epistemologia peripatetica nel primo ellenismo'. *Rivista di filologia classica* 105: 285–306.

Isnardi-Parente, M. (1991). *Filosofia e scienza nel pensiero ellenistico.* Naples: Morano.

Isnardi-Parente, M. (1999). *Introduzione allo stoicismo ellenistico.* Bari and Rome: Laterza.

Italie, G. (1964). *Index Aeschyleus.* Editio altera correcta et aucta curavit S. L. Radt. Leiden, Boston and Cologne: E. J. Brill.

Jaeger, W. (1923). *Aristoteles, Grundlegung einer Geschichte seiner Entwicklung.* Berlin: Weidmann.

Jaeger, W. (1934–47). *Paideia. Die Formung der griechischen Menschen.* Berlin and Leipzig: W. de Gruyter.

Jaeger, W. (1947). *The Theology of the Early Greek Philosophers.* Oxford: Clarendon Press.

Jaeger, W. (1961). *Early Christianity and Greek Paideia.* Cambridge, MA: The Belknap Press of Harvard University Press.

Jagu, A. (1989). *La morale d'Epictète et le christianisme. Aufstieg und Niedergand der römischen Welt (ANRW): Geschichte und Kultur Roms im Spiegel* der Neuereun Forschung, II.36.3. Berlin and New York: Walter de Gruyter, pp. 2164–99.

James, A. W. (1972). 'The Zeus Hymns of Cleanthes and Aratus'. *Antichton* 6: 28–38.

Janáček, K. (2000). *Sexti empirici indices*. Florence: Leo S. Olschki.

Janka, M., and C. Schäfer (hrsg.) (2014). *Platon als Mythologe: Interpretationen zu den Mythen in Platons Dialogen*. Darmstadt: Wissenschaftliche Buchgesellschaft.

Janet, P. (1865). *La crise philosophique*. Paris: G. Baillière.

Janet, P. (1876). *Les causes finales*. Paris: G. Baillière.

Janko, R. (1986). 'The *Shield of Heracles* and the Legend of Cycnus'. *Classical Quarterly* 36: 38–56.

Janoušek, J. (2006). 'Le *Metamorfosi* di Apuleio alla luce delle sue opinioni filosofiche'. *Sborník prací filozofické fakulty brněnské univerzity. Řada klasická* 11: 27–35.

Jaulin, A., and D. Lefebvre (éds.) (2015). *La Métaphysique de Théophraste. Principes et apories*. Leuven, Paris, and Bristol, CT: Peeters.

Jellamo, A. (2005). *Il cammino di Dike. L'idea di giustizia da Omero a Eschilo*. Rome: Donzelli.

Jenkyns, R. (ed.) (1992). *The Legacy of Rome*. Oxford: Oxford University Press.

Johnson, M. R. (2005). *Aristotle on Teleology*. Oxford: Clarendon Press.

Johnson, M. R. (2009). 'Spontaneity, Democritean Causality and Freedom'. *Elenchos: Rivista di studi sul pensiero antico* 30: 5–52.

Johnson, W. R. (1987). *Momentary Monsters: Lucan and His Heroes*. Ithaca, NY: Cornell University Press.

Jones, H. (1992). *The Epicurean Tradition*. London: Routledge and Kegan Paul.

Jones, H. (1993). 'Lucretius and nature's monsters'. *Helmantica* 44: 199–203.

Jones, J. W. (1956). *The Law and the Legal Theory of the Greeks*. Oxford: Clarendon Press.

Jouan, F. (éd.) (1986). *Mort et fécondité dans les mythologies. Actes du Colloque de Poitiers, 13–14 mai 1983*. Paris: Les Belles Lettres.

Jouan, F., and B. Deforge (éds.) (1988). *Peuples et pays mythique. Actes du Ve colloque du centre de recherches mythologiques de l'Université de Paris X, Chantilly, 18–20 septembre 1986*. Paris: Les Belles Lettres.

Jouanna, J. (2007). *Sophocle*. Paris: Fayard.

Joubaud, C. (1991). *Le corps humain dans la philosophie platonicienne. Étude à partir du 'Timée'*. Paris: Librairie Philosophique J. Vrin.

Judson, L. (ed.) (1991). *Aristotle's Physics: A Collection of Essays*. Oxford: Clarendon Press.

Junge, M. (1983). *Untersuchungen zur Ikonographie der Erinys in der griechischen Kunst*. Kiel: Universität.

Kalligas, P. (2014). *The Enneads of Plotinus: A Commentary*. Volume I. Princeton and Oxford: Princeton University Press.
Kelsen, H. (1943). *Society and Nature*. Chicago: The University of Chicago Press.
Kerényi, K. (1966–88). *Werke in Einzelausgaben*. Hrsg. M. Kerény. Munich and Vienna: A. Langen-G. Müller.
Kingsley, P. (2005). *Ancient Philosophy, Mystery, and Magic: Empedocles and Pythagorean Tradition*. Oxford: Clarendon Press.
Kitto, H. D. F. (1958). *Sophocles: Dramatist and Philosopher*. London: Oxford University Press.
Klibansky, R. (1939). *The Continuity of the Platonic Tradition during the Middle Ages*. London: The Warburg Institute.
Klowski, J. (1966). 'Der historischer Ursprung des Kausalprinzips'. *Archiv für Geschichte der Philosophie* 48: 225–66.
Koester, G. (1968). 'ΝΟΜΟΣ ΦΨΣΕΩΣ: The Concept of Natural Law in Greek Thought', in J. Neusner (ed.), *Religions in Antiquity: Essays in Memory of E. R. Goodenough*. Leiden, Boston and Cologne: E. J. Brill, pp. 521–41.
Kollesch, J., and D. Nickel (1994). *Bibliographia Galeniana: Die Beiträge des 20. Jahrhunderts zur Galenforschung*, in W. Haase (hrsg.), *Aufstieg und Niedergand der römischen Welt (ANRW): Geschichte und Kultur Roms im Spiegel der Neuereun Forschung*, II.37.2. Berlin and New York: Walter de Gruyter, pp. 1351–420.
Kors, A. C. (1997). 'Monsters and the Problem of Naturalism in French Thought'. *Eighteenth-Century Life* 21: 23–47.
Krafft, F. (1971). 'Anaximandros und Hesiodos. Die Ursprünge rationaler griechischer Naturbetrachtung'. *Archiv für Geschichte der Medizin (= Südhoffs Archiv)* 51: 152–79.
Krappe, A. H. (1932). 'Ἐρινύς'. *Rheinisches Museum* 81: 305–20.
Kranz, W. (1912). 'Empedokles und die Atomistik'. *Hermes. Zeitschrift für classische Philologie* 47: 18–42.
Kranz, W. (1944). 'Lukrez und Empedokles'. *Philologus. Zeitschrift für das klassische Altertum* 96: 68–107.
Krings, H. (1982). *Ordo. Philosophisch-historische Grundlegung einer abendländischen Idee*. 2. ed. Hamburg: Felix Meiner Verlag.
Kucharski, P. (1964). 'Anaxagore et les idées biologiques de son siècle'. *Revue Philosophique de la France et de l'Étranger* 154: 137–66.
Küster, E. (1913). *Die Schlange in the griechischen Kunst und Religion*. Gießen: Töpelmann.
Kullmann, W. (1979). *Die Teleologie in der aristotelischen Biologie: Aristoteles als Zoologe, Embryologe und Genetiker*. Heidelberg: Carl Winter.
Lachenaud, G. (1978). *Mythologie, religion et philosophie de l'histoire dans Hérodote*. Thèse présentée devant l'Université de Paris IV. Lille: Atelier reproduction des theses, Université de Lille III.

Lachmann, C. (1866). *In T. Lucretii Cari de rerum natura libros commentarius.* Berlin: Typis et impensis Georgii Reimeri.
Lämmli, F. (1962). *Vom Chaos zum Kosmos. Zur Geschichte einer Idee.* Basel: Verlag Friedrich Reinhardt.
Lange, F. A. (1873–5). *Geschichte des Materialismus und Kritik seinen Bedeutung in der Gegenwart.* Iserlon: J. Baedeker.
Lanza, D., and O. Longo (a cura di) (1989). *Il meraviglioso e il verosimile tra antichità e medioevo.* Florence: Leo S. Olschki.
Lanzi, S. (2000). *Theos Anaitios. Storia della teodicea da Omero ad Agostino.* Rome: Il Calamo.
Lasswitz, K. (1890). *Geschichte der Atomistik vom Mittelalter bis Newton.* Hamburg: Leopold Voss.
Laurent, J. (1992). *Les fondements de la nature dans la pensée de Plotin. Procession et participation.* Paris: Librairie Philosophique J. Vrin.
Leitner, H. (1973). *Bibliography to the Ancient Medical Authors.* Bern, Stuttgart and Vienna: H. Huber.
Lenoble, R. (1969). *Histoire de l'idée de nature.* Paris: Albin Michel.
Lerner, M.-P. (1969). *La notion de finalité chez Aristote.* Paris: Presses Universitaires de France.
Lévècque, P. (1988). 'Pandora ou la terrifiante fémininité'. *Kernos* 1: 49–62.
Lévy, C. (1992). *Cicero Academicus: recherches sur les Académiques et sur la philosophie cicéronienne.* Rome: Collection de l'École française de Rome.
Lévy, C. (éd.) (1996). *Le concept de nature à Rome. La physique.* Paris: Rue d'Ulm.
Lévy, C., and B. Besnier (éds.) (1998). *Philon d'Alexandrie et le langage de la philosophie. Actes du colloque international organisé par le Centre d'études sur la philosophie hellénistique et romaine de l'Université de Paris XII-Val de Marne (Créteil, Fontenay, Paris, 26–28 octobre 1995).* Turnhout: Brepols.
Ley, H. (1966–89). *Geschichte der Aufklärung und des Atheismus.* Berlin: Deutscher Verlag der Wissenschaften.
Lilla, S. R. C. (1971). *Clement of Alexandria: A Study in Christian Platonism and Gnosticism.* Oxford: Oxford University Press.
Lloyd, G. E. R. (1979). *Magic, Reason, and Experience: Studies in the Origins and Development of Greek Science.* Cambridge: Cambridge University Press.
Lloyd, G. E. R. (1996). *Aristotelian Explorations.* Cambridge: Cambridge University Press.
Lloyd-Jones, H. (1983). *The Justice of Zeus.* 2nd ed. Berkeley: University of California Press.
Lloyd-Jones, H. (1989). 'Les Erinyes dans la tragédie grècque'. *Revue des Études Grecques* 102: 1–9.
Lo Schiavo, A. (1983). *Omero filosofo.* Florence: Le Monnier.

Lo Schiavo, A. (1997). *Themis e la sapienza dell'ordine cosmico*. Naples: Bibliopolis.
Long, A. A. (1967). 'Carneades and the Stoic telos. *Phronesis* 12: 59–90.
Long, A. A. (1971). *Problems in Stoicism*. London: The Athlone Press of the University of London.
Long, A. A. (1974). *Hellenistic Philosophy: Stoics, Epicureans, Sceptics*. London: Duckworth.
Long, A. A. (1977). 'Chance and Natural Law in Epicureanism'. *Phronesis* 22: 63–88.
Long, A. A. (1978). 'Timon of Phlius: Pyrrhonist and Satirist'. *Proceedings of the Cambridge Philological Society* 204 (new series, 24): 68–91.
Longo, O. (forthcoming). 'La biologia animale in età ellenistico-romana. Da Aristotele al Physiologus', in W. Haase and G. Temporini (hrsg.), *Aufstieg und Niedergand der römischen Welt: Geschichte und Kultur Roms im Spiegel der Neuereun Forschung*, II.37.4. Berlin and New York: Walter de Gruyter.
Loraux, N. (1978). 'Sur la race des femmes et quelques-unes de ses tribus'. *Aretusa* 9: 43–87.
Loraux, N. (1993). *L'invention d'Athènes. Histoire de l'oration funèbre dans la 'cité classique'*. 2e ed. Paris: Payot.
Loraux, N. (1996). *Né de la terre. Mythe et politique à Athene*. Paris: Seuil.
Louis, P. (1945). *Les métaphores de Platon*. Rennes: Imprimeries Réunies.
Louis, P. (1967). 'Les animaux fabuleux chez Aristote'. *Revue des études grecques* 80: 242–6.
Louis, P. (1975). 'Monstres et monstruosités dans la biologie d'Aristote, in J. Bingen, G. Cambier and G. Nachtergael (eds), *Le Mond grec. Pensée, littérature, histoire, documents. Hommage à Claire Préaux*. Brussels: Editions de l'Université Libre de Bruxelles, pp. 277–84.
Lovejoy, A. O. (1909). 'The Meaning of φύσις in the Greek Physiologers'. *Philosophical Review* 18: 369–83.
Lovejoy, A. O. (1942). *The Great Chain of Being: A Study of the History of an Idea*. Cambridge, MA: Harvard University Press.
Lovejoy, A. O., and G. Boas (eds) (1935). *Primitivism and Related Ideas in Antiquity*. Baltimore: Johns Hopkins University Press.
Lur'e [Luria], S. E. (1964). *Zur Frage der materialistischen Begrundung der Ethik bei Demokrit*. Berlin: Akademie Verlag.
Lynch, J. P. (1972). *Aristotle's School*. Berkeley and Los Angeles: University of California Press.
McClure, L. (1999). *Spoken Like a Woman: Speech and Gender in Athenian Drama*. Princeton: Princeton University Press.
McGinty, P. (1978). *Interpretation and Dyonisos' Method in the Study of a God*. The Hague: Mouton Publishers.

Magris, A. (1984). *L'idea di destino nel pensiero antico.* Udine: Del Bianco Editore.

Mansfeld, J. (1992). 'A Theophrastean Excursus on God and Nature and its Aftermath in Hellenistic Thought'. *Phronesis* 37: 314–35.

Mariën, B. (1949). 'Bibliografia critica degli studi plotiniani', in Plotino, *Enneadi. Prima versione integra e commentario critico di V. Cilento.* Bari: Laterza, III, pp. 389–622.

Marignac, A. de (1951). *Imagination et dialectique. Essai sur l'expression du spirituel par l'image dans les dialogues de Platon.* Paris: Les Belles Lettres.

Marrou, H.-I. (1958). *Saint Augustin et la fin de la culture antique.* 2e ed. Paris: E. de Boccard.

Martano, G. (1950). 'Il concetto di materia nelle ἀφορμαί porfiriane'. *Rivista critica di storia della filosofia* 5: 277–80.

Martens, J. W. (2003). *One God, One Law: Philo of Alexandria on the Mosaic and Greco-Roman Law.* Leiden, Boston and Cologne: E. J. Brill.

Martin, A., and O. Primavesi (1999). *L'Empédocle de Strasbourg.* Berlin and New York: Walter de Gruyter.

Martin, J. P. (1982). *Providentia deorum: Recherches sur certains aspects du pouvoir impérial romain.* Rome: Ecole française de Rome.

Martin, R. (1987). 'Fire on the Mountain: *Lysistrata* and the Lemnian Women'. *Classical Antiquity* 6: 77–105.

Martina, A. (a cura di) (2001). *Seneca e i cristiani. Atti del convegno internazionale. Università Cattolica del S. Cuore, Biblioteca Ambrosiana, Milan, 13–14 ottobre 1999.* Milan: Vita e Pensiero.

Martinazzoli, F. (1951). 'Le testimonianze stoiche sul cristianesimo e la concezione del miracolo'. *Annali della Facoltà di Lettere e Filosofia dell'Università di Cagliari* 18: 221–74.

Marx, K., and F. Engels (1956–2015). *Werke.* Berlin: Dietz. [Abbreviated: MEW]

Marzot, G. (1944). 'Seneca scrittore nel Seicento', in *L'ingegno e il genio del Seicento.* Florence: La Nuova Italia, pp. 133–69.

Matteoli, S. (2011). *Alle origini della teologia di Pelagio. Tematiche e fonti delle* Expositiones XIII Epistularum Pauli. Pisa and Rome: Fabrizio Serra Editore.

Maurach, G. (hrsg.) (1975). *Seneca als Philosoph.* Darmstadt: Wissenschaftliche Buchgesellschaft.

Mayer, C. P. (hrsg.) (1986–). *Augustinus-Lexikon.* Basel and Stuttgart: Schwabe & Co.

Mayer, G. (1974). *Index Philoneus.* Berlin and New York: Walter de Gruyter.

Mayer, M. (1887). *Die Giganten und Titanen in der antiken Sage und Kunst.* Berlin: Weidmannsche Buchhandlung.

Mayor, A. (2001). *The First Fossil Hunters: Paleontology in Greek and Roman Times*. Princeton: Princeton University Press.

Mayor, A. (2014). *The Amazons: Lives and Legends of Warrior Women Across the Ancient World*. Princeton: Princeton University Press.

Mazzanti, A. M. (1988). 'Antropologia e radici del male in Filone d'Alessandria: due possibili opzioni'. *Augustinianum* 28: 187–201.

Mazzocchini, P. (2003). 'Centimani ed Olimpi: per una rilettura della *Titanomachia* esiodea (*Th.* 617–721)'. *Giornale italiano di filologia* 55: 3–42.

Mehring, F. (1923). *Karl Marx. Geschichte seines Lebens*. Leipzig: Leipzieger Buchdruckerei Aktiengesellschaft.

Meijer, P. A. (1992). *Plotinus on the Good or the One (Enneads VI, 9)*. Amsterdam: Gieben.

Melsen, A. G. (1952). *From Atomos to Atom: The History of the Concept of Atom*. Pittsburgh: Duquesne University Press.

Merguet, H. (1877–84). *Lexikon zu den Reden des Cicero mit Angabe sämmtlicher Stellen*. Jena: Verlag von Hermann Dufft.

Merguet, H. (1887–94). *Lexikon zu den philosophischen Schriften Ciceros mit Angabe sämmtlicher Stellen*. Jena: Fischer.

Merguet, H. (1912). *Lexikon zu Vergilius*. Leipzig: R. Schmidt.

Merlan, P. (1960). *From Platonism to Neoplatonism*. 2nd ed. The Hague: Martinus Nijhoff.

Mesnard, P. (1947). 'Antifinalisme et finalité chez Lucrèce'. *Revue des Sciences Humaines* 46: 97–116.

Michel, A. (1973). 'Rhétorique et philosophie dans les traités de Cicéron', in H. Temporini (hrsg.), *Aufstieg und Niedergand der römischen Welt (ANRW): Geschichte und Kultur Roms im Spiegel der Neuereun Forschung*, I.3. Berlin and New York: Walter de Gruyter, pp. 139–208.

Milton, J. R. (1981). 'The Origin and Development of the Concept of the "Laws of Nature"'. *Archives européennes de Sociologie* 22: 173–95.

Momigliano, A. (1950). 'Note sulla leggenda del cristianesimo di Seneca'. *Rivista Storica Italiana* 62: 325–44.

Momigliano, A. (1968). 'Prospettiva 1967 della storia greca'. *Rivista Storica Italiana* 80: 5–18.

Monaci Castagno, A. (a cura di) (2000). *Origene. Dizionario. La cultura, il pensiero, le opere*. Rome: Città Nuova.

Mondésert, C. (1944). *Clément d'Alexandrie. Introduction à l'étude de sa pensée religieuse à partir de l'écriture*. Paris: Aubier.

Mondi, R. (1983). 'The Homeric Cyclopes: Folktale, Tradition, and Theme'. *Transaction of the American Philological Association* 113: 17–38.

Mondolfo, R. (1956). *L'infinito nel pensiero dell'antichità classica*. Florence: La Nuova Italia.

Mondolfo, R. (1963). 'L'uomo greco secondo Pohlenz'. *Il Ponte* 19: 205–19 and 363–77.
Monfrinotti, M. (2014). *Creatore e creazione, il pensiero di Clemente Alessandrino*. Rome: Città Nuova.
Monteil, P. (1964). *Beau et laid en latin. Étude de vocabulaire*. Paris: Klincksieck.
Montoneri, L. (1985). 'Plotino *Enn*. I 8 e la trasformazione della dottrina platonica del male', in C. Giuffrida and M. Mazza (a cura di), *Le trasformazioni della cultura nella tarda antichità. Atti del Convegno tenuto a Catania, Università degli Studi, 27 sett. – 2 ott. 1982*. Rome: Jouvence, vol. I: 247–63.
Moraux, P. (1973–84). *Der Aristotelismus bei den Griechen*. Berlin and New York: Walter de Gruyter.
Moreau, A. (1976–7). 'L'oeil maléfique dans l'oeuvre d'Eschyle'. *Revue des Études Anciennes* 78–9: 50–64.
Moreau, A. (1985). *Eschyle: la violence et le chaos*. Paris: Les Belles Lettres.
Moreau, A. (2006). *La fabrique des mythes*. Paris: Les Belles Lettres.
Moreau, J. (1975). 'Le mécanisme épicurien et l'ordre de la nature'. *Les Études Philosophiques* 29: 467–86.
Morel, P.-M. (1996). *Démocrite et la recherche des causes*. Paris: Klincksieck.
Morel, P.-M. (2000). *Atome et nécessité: Démocrite, Epicure, Lucrèce*. Paris: Presses Universitaires de France.
Morel, P.-M. (2007). *De la matière à l'action. Aristote et le problème du vivant*. Paris: Librairie Philosophique J. Vrin.
Moreno, P. (1994). *Scultura ellenistica*. Rome: Istituto Poligrafico e Zecca dello Stato.
Moreschini, C. (1978). *Apuleio e il platonismo*. Florence: Leo S. Olschki.
Moreschini, C. (2004). *Storia della filosofia patristica*. Brescia: Morcelliana.
Moreschini, C. (2013). *Storia del pensiero cristiano tardo-antico*. Milan: Bompiani.
Morfino, V. (2013). 'Lucrèce et les monstres: entre Bergson et Canguilhem', in A. Gigandet (ed.), *Lucrèce et la modernité: le vingtième siècle*. Paris: Armand Colin, pp. 55–76.
Morgan, K. A. (2000). *Myth and Philosophy from the Presocratics to Plato*. Cambridge: Cambridge University Press.
Morgan, W. R. (1984). *Constructing the Monster: Notions of the Monstrous in Classical Antiquity*. Unpublished PhD thesis, School of Humanities, Deakin University.
Mossé, C. (1969). *La tyrannie dans la Grèce antique*. Paris: Presses Universitaires de France.
Motto, A. L. (1970). *Seneca Sourcebook: Guide to the Thought of Lucius Aanneus Seneca*. Amsterdam: A. M. Hakkert.
Moussy, C. (1977). 'Esquisse de l'histoire de monstrum'. *Revue des Études Latines* 55: 345–69.

Moutsopoulos, E., and M. Protopapas-Marneli (eds) (2007). *Necessity – Chance – Freedom in Ancient Philosophy*. Athens: Academy of Athens.

Mugler, C. (1970). 'Méditations cosmologiques chez Sophocle'. *Annales de la Faculté de Lettres et Sciences Humaines de Nice* 11: 19–26.

Mund-Dopchie, M. (1992). 'Autour des Sciapodes et des Cynocéphales: la périphérie dans l'imaginaire antique'. *Analele Universitatii Bucaresti, Istorie* 41: 31–9.

Muñoz Valle, I. (1969). 'Evolución del concepto de nomos desde Hesiodo a la Estoa'. *Miscelanea Comillas. Revista semestral de estudios historicos* 51: 5–31.

Munson, R. V. (2001). *Telling Wonders: Ethnographic and Political Discourse in Herodotus*. Ann Arbor: University of Michigan Press.

Myers, K. S. (1994). *Ovid's Causes: Cosmogony and Aetiology in the Metamorphoses*. Ann Arbor: University of MIchigan Press.

Myre, A. (1972). 'La loi dans l'ordre cosmique et politique selon Philon d'Alexandrie'. *Science et Esprit* 24: 217–47.

Myre, A. (1976). 'La loi de la nature et la loi mosaïque selon Philon d'Alexandrie'. *Science et Esprit* 28: 163–81.

Naas, V. (2002). *Le projet encyclopédique de Pline l'ancien*. Paris and Rome: Ecole française de Rome.

Naddaf, G. (1992). *L'origine et l'évolution du concept grec de phusis*. Lewiston, Queenston and Lampeter: The Edwin Mellen Press.

Narducci, E. (1979). *La provvidenza crudele. Lucano e la distruzione dei miti augustei*. Pisa: Giardini.

Natali, C., and S. Maso (a cura di) (2005). *La catena delle cause. Determinismo e antideterminismo nel pensiero antico e in quello contemporaneo*. Amsterdam: Adolf M. Hakkert Editore.

Navia, L. E. (1993). *The Presocratic Philosophers: An Annotated Bibliography*. New York and London : Garland Publishing.

Nestle, W. (1901). *Euripides, der Dichter der griechischen Aufklärung*. Stuttgart: W. Kohlhammer.

Nestle, W. (1930–4). *Die griechische Religiosität in ihren Grundzügen und Hauptvertretern von Homer bis Proklos*. Berlin and Leipzig: Walter de Gruyter.

Nestle, W. (1934). *Menschliche Existenz und politische Erziehung in der Tragödie des Aischylos*. Stuttgart and Berlin: W. Kohlhammer.

Nestle, W. (1942). *Von Mythos zum Logos. Die Selbstentfaltung des griechischen Denkens von Homer bis auf die Sophistik und Sokrates*. 2. ed. Stuttgart: A. Kröner.

Nieppel, W. (1990). *Griechen, Barbaren, und 'Wilde'. Alte Geschichte un Sozialanthropologie*. Frankfurt: Fisher.

Nietzsche, F. (1967–). *Werke. Kritische Gesaumtausgabe*. Begründet von G. Colli und M. Montinari. Berlin and New York: Walter de Gruyter.

Nikiprowetzky, V. (1996). *Études philoniennes*. Paris: Les Éditions du Cerf.

Nilsson, M. P. (1950). *Geschichte der griechischen Religion*. 2. ed. Munich: C. H. Beck.

Nutton, V. (ed.) (1982). *Galen: Problems and Prospects. A collection of papers submitted at the 1979 Cambridge conference*. London: Wellcome Institute for the History of Medicine.

O'Brien, C. S. (2015). *The Demiurge in Ancient Thought: Secondary Gods and Divine Mediators*. Cambridge: Cambridge University Press.

O'Brien, D. (1969). *Empedocles' Cosmic Cycle*. Cambridge: Cambridge University Press.

O'Brien, D. (1984). *Theories of Weight in the Ancient World*. Leiden, Boston and Cologne: E. J. Brill, and Paris: Les Belles Lettres.

O'Brien, D. (1993). *Théodicée plotinienne, théodicée gnostique*. Leiden, Boston and Cologne: E. J. Brill.

O'Brien, M. C. (2002). *Apuleius' Debt to Plato in the* Metamorphoses. Lewiston, NY: Mellen Press.

O'Flaherty, W. D. (1980). *Women, Androgynes, and Other Mythical Beasts*. Chicago and London: The University of Chicago Press.

Oldfather, W. A., H. V. Canter and P. E. Perry (1934). *Index Apuleianus*. Middletown, CT: American Philological Association.

Oriol-Boyer, C. (1975). 'Les monstres de la mythologie grecque: réflexion sur la dynamique de l'ambigu'. *Circé: Cahiers du centre de recherches sur l'imaginaire* 4: 25–50.

Otis, B. (1981). *Cosmos and Tragedy: An Essay on the Meaning of Aeschylus*. Chapel Hill: University of North Carolina Press.

Otto, W. F. (1933). *Dionysos. Mythus und Kultus*. Frankfurt: Vittorio Klostermann.

Pacchi, A. (1976). *Materia*. Milan: Istituto Editoriale Internazionale.

Paduano, G. (1975). 'In margine al "Sophokles" di Karl Reinhardt'. *Annali della Scuola Normale Superiore di Pisa. Classe di Lettere e Filosofia*. Serie III.5: 1373–1407.

Pagel, W. (1953). 'The Reaction to Aristotle in Seventeenth-Century Biological Thought', in E. Ashworth Underwood (ed.), *Science, Medicine and History: Essays in Honour of Charles Singer*. Oxford: Oxford University Press, vol. I, pp. 489–509.

Panaccio, C. (éd.) (2012). *Textes clés du nominalisme. Ontologie, language, connaissance*. Paris: Librairie Philosophique J. Vrin.

Panofsky, E. (1939). *Studies in Iconology*. New York: Oxford University Press.

Papathomopoulos, M. (ed.) (2006). *Concordantia Sophoclea*. Hildesheim, Zürich and New York: Olms-Weidmann.

Paquet, L., M. Roussel and Y. Lafrance (1988–95). *Les présocratiques: bibliographie analytique*. Paris and Montréal: Les Belles Lettres-Bellarmin.

Paratore, E. (1973). 'La problematica sull'Epicureismo a Roma', in H. Temporini (hrsg.), *Aufstieg und Niedergand der römischen Welt (ANRW): Geschichte und Kultur Roms im Spiegel der Neuereun Forschung*, I.4. Berlin and New York: Walter de Gruyter, pp. 116–204.

Pârvulescu, A. (1968). 'L'homérique κήρ. Étude sémantique'. *Helikon. Rivista di tradizione e cultura classica dell'Università di Messina* 8: 277–310.

Passannante, G. (2012). *The Renaissance of Lucretius: Philology and the Afterlife of Tradition*. Chicago: University of Chicago Press.

Patera, M. (2015). *Figures grecques de l'épouvante de l'antiquité au présent. Peurs enfantines et adultes*. Leiden, Boston and Cologne: E. J. Brill.

Paulson, J. (1911). *Index Lucretianus*. Gothenburg: Typis expresserunt Zachrisson et socii.

Paulson, J., confecit (1890). *Index Hesiodeus*. Lund: H. Müller.

Payón Leyra, I. (2011). *Entre ciencia y maravilla. El género literario de la paradoxografía griega*. Zaragoza: Prensas Universitarias de Zaragoza.

Pellegrin, P. (1982). *La classification des animaux chez Aristote: Statut de la biologie et unité de l'Aristotélisme*. Paris: Les Belles Lettres.

Pellegrin, P. (2007). *Dictionnaire Aristote*. Paris: Ellipses.

Pepe, L. (1996). *La misura e l'equivalenza. La fisica di Anassagora*. Naples: Loffredo.

Pépin, J. (1957). *Mythe et allégorie. Les origines grecques et le contestations judéo-chrétiennes*. Paris: Aubier.

Perutelli, A. (2006). *Ulisse nella cultura romana*. Florence: Felice Le Monnier.

Philippart, H. (1930). 'Iconographie des «Bacchantes» d'Euripide'. *Revue belge de philologie et d'histoire* 9: 1–72.

Pichard-Cambridge, A. (1968). *The Dramatic Festivals of Athens*. 2nd ed. Oxford: Clarendon Press.

Pichon, R. (1901). *Lactance. Étude sur les mouvements philosophiques et religieux sous le règne de Constantin*. Paris: Hachette.

Pierris, A. L. (ed.) (2005). *The Empedoclean Κόσμος: Structure, Process and the Question of Cyclicity*. Proceedings of the Symposium Philosophiae Antiquae Tertium Myconense. 6–13 July 2003. Patras: Institute for Philosophical Research.

Pievani, T. (2013). *Anatomia di una rivoluzione. La logica della scoperta scientifica di Darwin*. Milan: Mimesis.

Pigead, J. (1980). 'La physiologie de Lucrèce'. *Revue des Études Latines* 58: 176–200.

Pigeaud, J. (1988). 'La greffe du monstre'. *Revue des Études Latines* 66: 197–218.

Pittet, A. (1937). *Vocabulaire philosophique de Sénèque*. Paris: Les Belles Lettres.

Pohlenz, M. (1933). 'Laokoon'. *Die Antike. Zeitschrift für Kunst und Kultur des klassischen Altertums* 9: 54–71.

Pohlenz, M. (1937). *Herodot, der erste Geschichtschreiber des Abendlandes.* Leipzig: Teubner.
Pohlenz, M. (1947). *Der hellenische Mensch.* Göttingen: Vandenhoeck & Ruprecht.
Pohlenz, M. (1948). *Die Stoa. Geschichte einer geistigen Bewegung.* Göttingen: Vandenhoeck & Ruprecht.
Pohlenz, M. (1954). *Die griechische Tragödie.* 2. ed. Göttingen: Vandenhoeck & Ruprecht.
Pohlenz, M. (1964). *Paulus und die Stoa.* Darmstadt: Wissenschaftliche Buchgesellschaft.
Polito, R. (2004). *The Sceptical Road: Aenesidemus' Appropriation of Heraclitus.* Leiden, Boston and Cologne: E. J. Brill.
Polito, R. (2007). 'Was Skepticism a Philosophy ? Reception, Self-definition, Internal Conflicts'. *Classical Philology* 102: 333–62.
Pollmann, K. et al. (2013). *The Oxford Guide to the Historical Reception of Augustine.* Oxford: Oxford University Press.
Powell, J. E. (1938). *A Lexicon to Herodotus.* Cambridge: Cambridge University Press.
Powell, J. G. F. (ed.) (2005). *Cicero the Philosopher: Twelve Papers.* Oxford: Clarendon Press.
Preus, A. (1975). *Science and Philosophy in Aristotle's Biological Works.* Hildesheim, Zürich and New York: Olms-Weidmann.
Preus, A. (ed.) (2001). *Before Plato.* New York: State University of New York Press.
Puiggali, J. (1978). *Étude sur les Dialexeis de Maxime de Tyr, conférencier platonicien du IIème siècle.* Lille: Atelier national de reproduction des thèses, Université de Lille III.
Quarantotto, D. (2001). 'Ontologia della causa finale aristotelica', *Elenchos* 21: 329–65.
Quarantotto, D. (2005). *Causa finale, sostanza, essenza in Aristotele. Saggio sulla struttura dei processi teleologici naturali e sulla funzione del telos.* Naples: Bibliopolis.
Radice, R. (1982). *La concezione di Dio e del divino in Epitteto.* Milan: Cusl.
Radice, R. (1983). *Filone di Alessandria. Bibliografia generale. 1937–1982.* Naples: Bibliopolis.
Radice, R. (1989). *Platonismo e creazionismo in Filone di Alessandria.* Milan: Vita e Pensiero.
Radice, R. et al. (a cura di) (2003). *Lexicon I: Plato.* Milan: Biblia.
Radice, R. et al. (a cura di) (2004). *Lexicon II: Plotinus.* Milan: Biblia.
Radice, R. et al. (a cura di) (2005). *Lexicon III: Aristotle.* Milan: Biblia.

Radice, R. et al. (a cura di) (2007). *Lexicon IV: Stoics.* Milan: Biblia.
Reale, G. (1975–80). *Storia della filosofia antica.* Milan: Vita e Pensiero.
Reeve, C. D. C. (1980–1). 'Anaxagorean Panspermism'. *Ancient Philosophy* 1: 89–108.
Reich, K. (1958). 'Der historische Ursprung des Naturgesetzbegriffs', in *Festschrift Ernst Kapp zum 70. Geburtstag am 21. Januar 1958.* Hamburg: Marion von Schröder Verlag, pp. 121–34.
Reinhardt, K. (1926). *Kosmos und Sympathie. Neue Untersuchungen über Poseidonios.* Munich: C. H. Beck.
Reinhardt, K. (1927). *Platons Mythen.* Bonn: F. Cohen.
Reinhardt, K. (1933). *Sophokles.* Frankfurt: Vittorio Klostermann.
Reinhardt, K. (1949). *Aischylos als Regisseur und Theologe.* Bern: A. Francke.
Reinhardt, K. (1960). *Tradition und Geist. Gesammelte Essays zur Dichtung.* Hrsg. C. Becker. Göttingen: Vandenhoeck & Ruprecht.
Renehan, R. (1992). 'The Greek Anthropocentric View of Nature'. *Harvard Studies in Classical Philology* 85: 239–59.
Repici, L. (1988). *La natura e l'anima. Saggi su Stratone di Lampsaco.* Turin: Tirrenia Stampatori.
Repici, L. (1991). 'Limits of Teleology in Theophrastus' Metaphysics?'. *Archiv für Geschichte der Philosophie* 72: 182–213.
Rey, A. (1930–48). *La science dans l'antiquité.* Paris: La Renaissance du livre.
Reydams-Schils, G. J. (1999). *Demiurge and Providence: Stoic and Platonist Readings of Plato's* Timaeus. Turnhout: Brepols.
Rief, J. (1962). *Der Ordobegriff des jungen Augustinus.* Paderborn: F. Schöningh.
Riese, W. (1963). 'La pensée morale de Galien'. *Revue philosophique de la France et de l'étranger* 153: 331–46.
Rieth, O. (1934). 'Über das telos der Stoiker'. *Hermes* 69: 13–45.
Rist, J. M. (1961). 'Plotinus, on Matter and Evil'. *Phronesis* 6: 154–66.
Rist, J. M. (1963). 'Plotinus and the *Daimonion* of Socrates'. *Phoenix* 17: 13–24.
Rist, J. M. (1965). 'Monism. Plotinus and Some Predecessors'. *Harvard Studies in Classical Philology* 69: 329–44.
Rist, J. M. (1967a). *Plotinus: The Road to Reality.* Cambridge: Cambridge University Press.
Rist, J. M. (1967b). *Eros and Psyche: Studies in Plato, Plotinus, and Origen.* Toronto, Buffalo and London: University of Toronto Press.
Rist, J. M. (1969). *Stoic Philosophy.* Cambridge: Cambridge University Press.
Rist, J. M. (ed.) (1978). *The Stoics.* Berkeley, Los Angeles and London: University of California Press.
Rist, J. M. (1994). *Augustine: Ancient Thought Baptized.* Cambridge: Cambridge University Press.

Robin, L. (1923). *La pensée grecque et les origines de l'esprit scientifique.* Paris: Renaissance du Livre.

Robin, L. (1935). *Platon.* Paris: Félix Alcan.

Robin, L. (1944). *Pyrrhon et le scepticisme grec.* Paris: Presses Universitaires de France.

Robinson, C. (1979). *Lucian and His Influence in Europe.* London: Duckworth.

Rocca, J. (2017). *Teleology in the Ancient World: Philosophical and Medical Approaches.* Cambridge: Cambridge University Press.

Rodier, G. (1890). *La physique de Straton de Lampsaque.* Paris: Félix Alcan.

Rodis-Lewis (1975). *Epicure et son école.* Paris: Gallimard.

Roger, J. (1963). *Les sciences de la vie dans la pensée française du XVIIIe siècle. La génération des animaux de Descartes à l'Encyclopedie.* Paris: Armand Colin.

Rohde, E. (1894). *Psyche. Seelencult und Unsterblichkeitsglaube der Griechen.* Freiburg im Bresgau: P. Siebeck.

Roisman, H. M. (ed.) (2014). *The Encyclopedia of Greek Tragedy.* Oxford: Wiley-Blackwell.

Rolland, R. (1918). *Empedocle d'Agrigente et l'Age de la Haine.* Paris: La maison française.

Romano, F. (a cura di) (1980). *Democrito e l'atomismo antico. Atti del convegno internazionale di Catania (18–21 aprile 1979). Siculorum Gymnasium*, 33.

Romm, J. S. (1992). *The Edges of the World in Ancient Thought: Geography, Exploration and Fiction.* Princeton: Princeton University Press.

Rosen, S. (2005). *Plato's Republic: A Study.* New Haven and London: Yale University Press.

Ross, D. O., Jr (1987). *Virgil's Elements: Physics and Poetry in the* Georgics. Princeton: Princeton University Press.

Ross, W. D. (1923). *Aristotle.* London: Methuen & Co.

Rossetti, L. (1928). 'Il *De opificio Dei* di Lattanzio e le sue fonti'. *Didaskaleion* 6: 115–200.

Rössler, W. (1970). *Reflexe vorsokratischen Denkens bein Aischylos.* Meisenheim am Glan: Hain.

Rostand, J. (1930). *La formation de l'être.* Paris: Hachette.

Rostand, J. (1956). *L'atomisme en biologie.* Paris: Gallimard.

Rudberg, G. (1952). 'Empedokles und Evolution'. *Eranos* 50: 23–30.

Runia, D. T. (1986). *Philo of Alexandria and the* Timaeus *of Plato.* Leiden, Boston and Cologne: E. J. Brill.

Runia, D. T. (1992). 'The Language of Excellence in Plato's *Timaeus* and Later Platonism', in S. Gersh and C. Kannengiesser (eds), *Platonism in Late Antiquity.* Notre Dame, IN: University of Notre Dame Press, pp. 11–37.

Runia, D. T. (2001). *Philo on the Creation of the Cosmos according to Moses.* Leiden, Boston and Cologne: E. J. Brill.

Runia, D. T. (2003a). 'The King, the Architect, and the Craftsman: a Philosophical Image in Philo of Alexandria', in R. W. Sharples and A. Sheppard (eds), *Ancient Approaches to Plato's Timaeus*. London: Institute of Classical Studies, pp. 89–106.

Runia, D. T. (2003b). 'Theodicy in Philo of Alexandria', in A. Laato and J. C. de Moor (eds), *Theodicy in the World of the Bible*. Leiden, Boston and Cologne: E. J. Brill, pp. 576–604.

Runia, D. T. (2012). *Philo of Alexandria: An Annotated Bibliography 1997–2006 with Addenda for 1987–1996*. Leiden, Boston and Cologne: E. J. Brill.

Salem, J. (1990). *Lucrèce et l'ethique: la mort n'est rien pour nous*. Paris: Librairie Philosophique J. Vrin.

Salem, J. (1993). *Commentaire de la lettre d'Epicure à Hérodote*. Brussels: Ousia.

Salem, J. (1994). *Tel un dieu parmi les hommes. L'éthique d'Epicure*. Paris: Librairie Philosophique J. Vrin.

Salem, J. (1996a). *Démocrite: grains de poussière dans un rayon de soleil*. Paris: Librairie Philosophique J. Vrin.

Salem, J. (1996b). *La légende de Démocrite*. Paris: Kimé.

Salem, J. (1996c). 'La fortune de Démocrite'. *Revue philosophique* 1: 55–74.

Salem, J. (1997). *L'atomisme antique: Démocrite, Epicure, Lucrèce*. Paris: Librairie générale française.

Salemme, C. (1983). *Introduzione agli* Astronomica *di Manilio*. Naples: Società Editrice Napoletana.

Sambursky, S. (1956). *The Physical World of the Greeks*. London: Routledge and Kegan Paul.

Sambursky, S. (1959). *Physics of the Stoics*. London: Routledge and Kegan Paul.

Sambursky, S. (1962). *The Physical World of Late Antiquity*. London: Routledge and Kegan Paul.

Sancassano, M. L. (1997). *Il serpente e le sue immagini. Il motivo del serpente nella poesia greca dall'*Iliade *all'*Odissea. Como: Edizioni New Press.

Sasso, G. (1987). *Il progresso e la morte. Saggi su Lucrezio*. Bologna: Il Mulino.

Sauron, G. (1979). 'Les monstres au coeur des conflits esthétiques à Rome au Ier siècle avant J.-C.' *Revue de l'art* 90: 35–45.

Scaltsas, T., and A. S. Mason (eds) (2007). *The Philosophy of Epictetus*. Oxford: Oxford University Press.

Scarpat, G. (1991). 'La Torre di Babele in Filone e nelle Sapienze (Sap. 10, 5)'. *Rivista Biblica* 39: 167–73.

Schadewaldt, W. (1978). *Die Anfänge der Philosophie bei den Griechen*. Frankfurt: Suhrkamp.

Schäfer, C. (hrsg.) (2013). *Platon-Lexikon. Begriffswörterbuch zu Platon und der platonischen Tradition*. 2. ed. Darmstadt: Wissenschaftliche Buchsgesellschaft.

Schofield, M., M. Burnyeat and J. Barnes (eds) (1980). *Doubt and Dogmatism: Studies in Hellenistic Epistemology*. Oxford: Clarendon Press.

Scholl, A., and G. Platz-Horster (hrsg.) (2007). *Die Antikensammlung: Altes Museum. Pergamonmuseum*. Mainz: Zabern.

Schotes, H. A. (1969). *Stoische Physik, Psychologie und Theologie bei Lucan*. Bonn: R. Habelt.

Schneider, C. (1954). *Geistesgeschichte des Antiken Christentums*. Münich: C. H. Beck.

Schrader, C. (ed.) (1996). *Concordantia Herodotea*. Hildesheim, Zürich and New York: Olms-Weidmann.

Schrijvers, P. H. (1970). 'Horror ac diuina voluptas'. *Études sur la poétique et la poésie de Lucrèce*. Amsterdam: Hakkert.

Schrijvers, P. H. (1974). 'La pensée de Lucrèce sur l'origine de la vie, V, 780–820'. *Mnemosyne* 27: 245–59.

Schrijvers, P. H. (1999). *Lucrèce et les sciences de la vie*. Leiden, Boston and Cologne: E. J. Brill.

Schröder, E. (1916). *Plotins Abhandlung ΠΟΘΕΝ ΤΑ ΚΑΚΑ (Enn. I, 8)*. Borna-Leipzig: Druck von Robert Noske.

Schuhl, P.-M. (1947a). *Études sur la fabulation platonicienne*. Paris: Presses Universitaires de France.

Schuhl, P.-M. (1947b). *Essai sur la formation de la pensée grecque. Introduction historique à une étude de la pensée platonicienne*. 2e ed. Paris: Presses Universitaires de France.

Scotti Muth, N. (1993). *Proclo negli ultimi quarant'anni. Bibliografia ragionata della letteratura primaria e secondaria riguardante il pensiero procliano e i suoi influssi storici (anni 1949–2004)*. Milan: Vita e Pensiero.

Sedlar, J. W. (1980). *India and the Greek World: A Study in the Transmission of Culture*. Totowa, NJ: Rowman & Littlefield.

Sedley, D. (1982). 'The Stoic Criterion of Identity'. *Phronesis* 27: 255–75.

Sedley, D. (1989). 'The Proems of Empedocles and Lucretius'. *Greek, Roman, and Byzantine Studies* 30: 269–96.

Sedley, D. (1998). *Lucretius and the Transformation of Greek Wisdom*. Cambridge: Cambridge University Press.

Seippel, G. (1939). *Der Typhonmythos*. Greifswald: Adler.

Şerban, G. (1973). *Les fonctions du fantastique dans la Pharsale*. Bucharest: Centrul de multiplicare al universităţii din Bucureşti.

Serres, M. (1977). *La naissance de la physique dans le texte de Lucrèce. Fleuves et turbulences*. Paris: Editions de Minuit.

Settis, S. (a cura di) (1996–2002). *I greci*. Turin: Einaudi.

Severino, E. (2015). *Dike*. Milan: Adelphi Edizioni.

Shapiro, A. H. (1993). *Personifications in Greek Art: The Representation of Abstract Concepts, 600–400 bc*. Zürich: Akhantus.
Sharples, R. W. (1994). 'Plato, Plotinus, and Evil'. *Bulletin of the Institute of Classical Studies* 39: 171–81.
Šijaković, B. (2001). *Bibliographia praesocratica. A Bibliographical Guide to the Studies of Early Greek Philosophy in its Religious and Scientific Contexts with an Introductory Bibliography on the Historiography of Philosophy*. Paris: Les Belles Lettres.
Sillitti, G. (1980). *Tragelaphos. Storia di una metafora e di un problema*. Naples: Bibliopolis.
Simon, H., and M. Simon (1956). *Die alte Stoa und ihr Naturbegriff. Ein Beitrag zur Philosophiegeschichte des Hellenismus*. Berlin: Aufbau Verlag.
Slater, W. J. (1969). *Lexicon to Pindar*. Berlin: Walter de Gruyter.
Sleeman, J. H., and G. Pollet (1980). *Lexicon Plotinianum*. Leiden, Boston and Cologne: E. J. Brill.
Sluiter, I., and R. R. Rosen (eds) (2008). *Kakos: Badness and Anti-Value in Classical Antiquity*. Leiden, New York and Cologne: E. J. Brill.
Solignac, A. (1957). 'Réminiscences plotiniennes et porphyriennes dans le début du De ordine de saint Augustin'. *Archives de Philosophie* 20: 446–65.
Solmsen, F. (1937). 'The Erinys in Aischylos' Septem'. *Transactions and Proceedings of the American Philological Association* 68: 197–211.
Solmsen, F. (1949). *Hesiod and Aeschylus*. Ithaca, NY: Cornell University Press.
Solmsen, F. (1950). 'Chaos and apeiron'. *Studi Italiani di Filologia Classica* N.S. 24: 235–48.
Solmsen, F. (1960). *Aristotle's System of the Physical World: A Comparison with His Predecessors*. Ithaca, NY: Cornell University Press.
Solmsen, F. (1961). *Cleanthes or Posidonius? The Basis of Stoic Physics*, 'Mededelingen der koninklijke Nederlandse Akademie der Wetenschappen, afd. Letterkunde', *Nieuwe Reeks* 24: 265–89.
Solmsen, F. (1963). 'Nature as Craftsman in Greek Thought'. *Journal of the History of Ideas* 24: 473–96.
Sorabji, R. (1980). *Necessity, Cause and Blame: Perspectives on Aristotle's Theory*. London: Duckworth.
Soury, G. (1942a). *Aperçus de philosophie religieuse chez Maxime de Tyr, platonicien éclectique*. Paris: Les Belles Lettres.
Soury, G. (1942b). *La démonologie de Plutarque. Essai sur les idées religieuses et les mythes d'un platonicien éclectique*. Paris: Les Belles Lettres.
Spanneut, M. (1957). *Le stoicisme des pères de l'Eglise*. Paris: Seuil.
Spanneut, M. (1970). 'La notion de nature des stoïcien aux pères de l'Eglise'. *Recherches de theologie ancienne et médiévale* 37: 165–73.

Spitzer, L. (1963). *Classical and Christian ideas of World Harmony. Prolegomena to an Interpretation of the Word «Stimmung»*. Baltimore: The Johns Hopkins Press.

Spoerri, W. (1959). *Späthellenistische Berichte über Welt, Kultur und Götte. Untersuchingen zur Diodoro von Sizilien*. Basel: Reinhardt.

Spoerri, W. (1997). '"Crescebant uteri terram radicibus apti": A propos de la zoogonie de Lucrèce (DRN, V, 791. sqq.)', in D. Knoepfler et al. (eds), *Nomen latinum*. Neuchâtel/Geneva: Faculté de Lettres/Droz, pp. 55–82.

Stahl, W. H. (1962). *Roman Science: Origin, Development, and Influences to the Later Middle Ages*. Madison: University of Wisconsin Press.

Stählin, O. (hrsg.) (1936). *Clemens Alexandrinus. Vierter Band. Register*. Leipzig: J. C. Hinrichs'sche Buchhandlung.

Stanford, W. B. (1939). *Ambiguity in Greek Literature: Studies in Theory and Practice*. Oxford: Blackwell.

Steidle, W. (1939). *Studien zur Ars poetica des Horaz*. Würzburg and Aumühle: Triltsch.

Stein, P. (1909). *ΤΕΡΑΣ*. Marburg: Typis expressit Gustavus Shade (Otto Franck).

Steiner, G. (1955). 'The Scepticism of the Elder Pliny'. *Classical Weekly* 48: 137–43.

Steinmetz, P. (hrsg.) (1990). *Beiträge zur hellenistischen Literatur und ihrer Rezeption in Rom*. Stuttgart: F. Steiner.

Stokes, M. C. (1962). 'Hesiodic and Milesian cosmogonies I'. *Phronesis* 7: 1–37.

Stokes, M. C. (1963). 'Hesiodic and Milesian cosmogonies II'. *Phronesis* 8: 1–34.

Stough, C. L. (1969). *Greek Skepticism: A Study in Epistemology*. Berkeley: University of California Press.

Stramaglia, A. (1999). *«Res inauditae, incredulae». Storie di fantasmi nel mondo greco-latino*. Bari: Levante.

Strauss-Clay, J. (2003). *Hesiod's Cosmos*. Cambridge: Cambridge University Press.

Stückelberger, A. (1972). 'Lucretius reviviscens, Von der antiken zur neuzeitlichen Atomphysik'. *Archiv für Kulturgeschichte* 54: 1–25.

Sturz, F. W. (1964). *Lexicon Xenophonteum*. Hildesheim, Zürich and New York: Olms-Weidmann.

Tackaberry, W. H. (1930). *Lucian's Relation to Plato and the post-Aristotelian Philosophers*. Toronto, Buffalo and London: University of Toronto Press.

Tannery, P. (1898–9). 'Le concept de chaos'. *Annales de philosophie chrétienne*. Nouvelle série 39: 512–26.

Tannery, P. (1930). *Pour l'histoire de la science hellène. De Thalès à Empédocle*. 2e ed. Paris: Gauthier-Villars.

Taylor, A. E. (1928). *A Commentary on Plato's Timaeus*. Oxford: Oxford University Press.

Tebben, J. R. (1977). *Hesiod-Konkordanz: A Computer Concordance to Hesiod*. Hildesheim, Zürich and New York: Olms-Weidmann.

Temkin, O. (1973). *Galenism: Rise and Decline of a Medical Philosophy*. Ithaca, NY and London: Cornell University Press.

Timpanaro Cardini, M. (1960). 'La zoogonia di Empedocle e la critica aristotelica'. *Physis* 2: 5–13.

Theiler, W. (1924). *Zur Geschichte der teleologischen Naturbetrachtung bis auf Aristoteles*. Zürich: K. Hoenn.

[Sancti] Thomae Aquinatis (1954). *In octo libros Physicorum Aristotelis expositio*. Cura et studio P. M. Maggiolo. Turin and Rome: Marietti.

Thomas Aquinas (1963). *Commentary on Aristotle's Physics*. Translated by R. J. Blackwell, R. J. Spath and W. E. Thirkell. London: Routledge and Kegan Paul.

Thomas, R. (2000). *Herodotus in Context: Ethnography, Science and the Art of Persuasion*. Cambridge: Cambridge University Press.

Thomson, G. D. (1941). *Aeschylus and Athens: A Study in the Social Origin of Drama*. London: Lawrence & Wishart.

Thorndike, L. (1922). 'Galen: The Man and His Time'. *The Scientific Monthly* 14: 83–93.

Thorndike, L. (1923–58). *A History of Magic and Experimental Science*. New York: Columbia University Press.

Timothy, H. B. (1973). *The Tenets of Stoicism, Assembled and Systematized from the Work of L. A. Seneca*. Amsterdam: A. M. Hakkert.

Tobin, T. H. (1992). 'Interpretations of the Création of the World in Philo of Alexandria', in R. J. Clifford and J. J. Collins (eds), *Creation in the Biblical Tradition*. Washington, DC: The Catholic Biblical Association of America, pp. 108–28.

Tocanne, B. (1978). *L'idée de nature en France dans la seconde moitié du XVIIème siècle*. Paris: Klincksieck.

Tralau, J. (2015). *Monstret i mig: Myter om gränser och vilddjur*. Stockholm: Atlantis.

Tralau, J. (2016). 'The Justice of the Chimaira: Goat, Snake, Lion, and Almost the Entire *Oresteia* in a Little Monstrous Image'. *Arion: A Journal of Humanities and the Classics* 24: 41–68.

Trelenberg, J. (2009). *Augustins Schrift De ordine. Einführung, Kommentar, Ergebnisse*. Tübingen: Mohr Siebeck.

Tremoli, P. (1968). *Religiosità e irreligiosità nel «Bellum Civile» di Lucano*. Udine: Del Bianco.
Trousson, R. (1964). *Le thème de Prométhée dans la littérature européenne*. Geneva: Droz.
Tsagdis, G. (2016). 'From the Soul: Theriopolitics in the *Republic*'. *Philosophy Today* 60: 7–24.
Untersteiner, M. (1949). *I sofisti*. Turin: Einaudi.
Untersteiner, M. (1955). *Le origini della tragedia e del tragico*. 2a ed. Turin: Einaudi.
Untersteiner, M. (1971). *Scritti minori. Studi di letteratura e filosofia greca*. Brescia: Paideia.
Untersteiner, M. (1972). *La fisiologia del mito*. 2a ed. Florence: La Nuova Italia.
Untersteiner, M. (1974). *Sofocle. Studio critico*. Milan: Lampugnani Nigri editore.
Usener, H. (1977). *Glossarium Epicureum*. Rome: Edizioni dell'Ateneo.
Valero, J. B. (1980). *Las bases antropologicas de Pelagio en su tratado de las Expositiones*. Madrid: Publicaciones de la Universidad Pontificia Comillas.
Valero, J. B. (1982). 'El estoicismo de Pelagio'. *Estudios Eclesiasticos* 57: 39–63.
Vallance, J. (1993). 'The Medical System of Asclepiades of Bithynia', in W. Haase and G. Temporini (hrsg.), *Aufstieg und Niedergang der römischen Welt (ANRW): Geschichte und Kultur Roms im Spiegel der Neuereun Forschung*, II.37.1. Berlin and New York: Walter de Gruyter, pp. 693–727.
Van den Berg, R. M. (2014). 'Proclus on Hesiod's *Works and Days* and 'Didactic Poetry'. *The Classical Quarterly* 64: 383–97.
Van Dijck, J. G. M. (1997). *ΑΙΝΟΙ, ΛΟΓΟΙ, ΜΥΘΟΙ: Fables in Archaic, Classical, and Hellenistic Greek Literature*. Leiden, New York and Cologne: E. J. Brill.
Vecchiotti, I. (1970). *La filosofia di Tertulliano*. Urbino: Argalìa.
Vegetti, M. (1998–2007). *Platone. La Repubblica. Traduzione e commento*. Naples: Bibliopolis.
Verbeke, G. (1945). *L'évolution de la doctrine du Pneuma du Stoïcisme à St. Augustine*. Paris: Desclée de Brouwer.
Verde, F. (2013). *Elachista. La dottrina dei minimi nell'epicureismo*. Leuven: Leuven University Press.
Verdenius, W. J. (1983). 'Hylozoism in Aristotle', in L. P. Gerson (ed.), *Graceful Reason: Essays in Ancient and Medieval Philosophy Presented to Joseph Owens CSSR*. Toronto: Pontifical Institute of Mediaeval Studies, pp. 101–14.
Vernant, J.-P. (1965). *Mythe et pensée ches les Grecs*. Paris: François Maspéro.
Vernant, J.-P. (1985). *La mort dans les yeux. Figures de l'autre en Grèce ancienne*. Paris: Hachette.
Vernant, J.-P. (1999). *L'univers, les dieux, les hommes. Récits grecs des origines*. Paris: Seuil.
Vernant, J.-P., and P. Vidal-Naquet (1972). *Mythe et tragédie en Grèce ancienne*. Paris: Maspero.

Vernière, Y. (1977). *Symbole et mythe dans la pensée de Plutarque: essai d'interprétation philosophique et religieuse des 'Moralia'*. Paris: Les Belles Lettres.
Veyne, P. (1983). *Les Grecs ont-ils cru à leur mythes? Essai sur l'imagination constituante*. Paris: Seuil.
Vian, F. (1945). 'Le combat d'Héraklès et de Kyknos'. *Revue des Études Anciennes* 47: 5–32.
Vian, F. (1952). *La guerre des Géants. Le mythe avant l'époque hellénistique*. Paris: Klincksieck.
Vian, F. (1963). *Les origines de Thèbes. Cadmos et les Spartes*. Paris: Klincksieck.
Viarre, S. (1964). *L'image et la pensée dans les Métamorphoses d'Ovide*. Paris: Presses Universitaires de France.
Vlastos, G. (1945–6). 'Ethics and Physics in Democritus'. *Philosophical Review* 54: 578–92 and 55: 53–64.
Vlastos, G. (1950). 'The physical theory of Anaxagoras'. *Philosophical Review* 59: 31–57.
Vlastos, G. (1991). *Socrates: Ironist and Moral Philosopher*. Cambridge: Cambridge University Press.
Von Campenhausen, H. F. (1955). *Griechische Kirkenväter*. Stuttgart: W. Kohlhammer.
Von Campenhausen, H. F. (1960). *Lateinische Kirkenväter*. Stuttgart: W. Kohlhammer.
Von Wilamowitz-Moellendorff, U. (1931–2). *Der Glaube der Hellenen*. Berlin: Weidmann.
Wacht, M. (1990). *Concordantia in Lucretium*. Hildesheim, Zürich and New York: Olms-Weidmann.
Wacht, M. (1992). *Concordantia in Lucanum*. Hildesheim, Zürich and New York: Olms-Weidmann.
Wakeman, M. K. (1973). *God's Battle with the Monster: A Study in Biblical Imagery*. Leiden, Boston and Cologne: E. J. Brill.
Waltzing, J.-P. (1984). *Apologétique. Commentaire analytique, grammatical & historique*. Paris: Les Belles Lettres.
Warden, J. R. (1971). 'The Mind of Zeus'. *Journal of the History of Ideas* 32: 3–14.
Wartelle, A. (1978). *Bibliographie historique et critique d'Eschyle et de la tragédie grecque. 1518–1974*. Paris: Les Belles Lettres.
Waszink, J. H. (1954). 'Lucretius and Poetry'. *Mededelingen der Koninklijke Nederlandse Akademie van Wetenschappen* 17: 243–57.
Waszink, J. H. (1964). 'La création des animaux dans Lucrèce'. *Revue Belge de Philologie et d'Histoire* 42: 48–56.
Weil, E. (1970). 'Le "matérialisme" des Stoïciens', in *Essais et Conférences*, I, Paris: Librairie Philosophique J. Vrin, pp. 106–23.

Weiss, H. F. (1966). *Untersuchungen zur Kosmologie des hellenistischen un palästinischen Judentums*. Berlin: Akademie Verlag.

Wendland, P. (1892). *Philos Schrift über die Vorsehung: ein Beitrag zur Geschichte der nacharistotelischen Philosophie*. Berlin: R. Gaertner.

Wenley, R. M. (1924). *Stoicism and its Influence*. London: G. Harrap & Co.

Whistler, C., and D. Bomford (1999). *The Forest Fire by Piero di Cosimo*. Oxford: Ashmolean Museum.

Whittaker, T. (1928). *The Neo-Platonists: A Study in the History of Hellenism*. 2nd ed. Cambridge: Cambridge University Press.

Wieland, W. (1962). *Die aristotelische Physik: Untersuchungen über die Grundlegung der Naturwissenschaft und die sprachlichen Bedingungen der Prinzipienforschung bei Aristoteles*. Göttingen: Vandenhoeck & Ruprecht.

Wiersma, W. (1937). 'Telos und Kathekon in der alten Stoa'. *Mnemosyne* 3: 219–28.

Wiggins, D. (1980). *Sameness and Substance*. London: Blackwell.

Winiarczyk, M. (hrsg.) (1994). *Bibliographien zum antiken Atheismus: 17 Jahrhundert–1990*. Bonn: Habelt.

Winiarczyk, M. (2011). *Die hellenistische Utopie*. Berlin and New York: Walter de Gruyter.

Winiarczyk, M. (2013). *Diagoras of Melos: A Contribution to the History of Ancient Atheism*. Berlin and New York: Walter de Gruyter.

Winiarczyk, M. (2013). *The Sacred History of Euhemerus of Messene*. Berlin and New York: Walter de Gruyter.

Winkler-Horaček, L. (2015). *Monster in der frühgriechischen Kunst. Die Überwindung des Unfassbaren*. Berlin and New York: Walter de Gruyter.

Winston, D., and J. M. Dillon (1983). *Two Treatises of Philo of Alexandria: A Commentary on* De gigantibus *and* Quod Deus sit immutabilis. Chico, CA: Scholars Press.

Wiśniewski, B. (1973). 'Le problème du dualisme chez Démocrite et Epicure'. *ΘΠ: A Journal for Greek and Early Christian Philosophy* 2: 114–125.

Wlosok, A. (1960). *Laktanz und die philosophische Gnosis. Untersuchungen zur Geschichte und Terminologie der gnostischen Erlösungsvorstellung*. Heidelberg: Carl Winter.

Wolfson, H. A. (1948). *Philo: Foundations of Religious Philosophy in Judaism, Christianity, and Islam*. Cambridge, MA: Harvard University Press.

Wolfson, H. A. (1956). *The Philosophy of the Church Fathers*. Cambridge, MA: Harvard University Press.

Wolters, A. M. (1984). *Plotinus 'On Eros': A Detailed Exegetical Study of* Enneads *III.5*. Toronto: Wedge Pub. Foundation.

Woltjer, J. (1877). *Lucretii philosophia cum fontibus comparata*. Groningen: P. Noordhoff.

Wyttenbach, D. (1962). *Lexicon Plutarcheum [Plutarchi moralia operum tomus VIII. Index graecitatis]*. 2. ed. Hildesheim, Zürich and New York: Olms-Weidmann.
Yartz, F. J. (1997). 'Aristotle on Monsters'. *The Ancient World* 28: 67–72.
Zambon, M. (2002). *Porphyre et le Moyen-Platonisme*. Paris: Librairie Philosophique J. Vrin.
Zafiropulo, J. (1948). *Anaxagore de Clazomène*. Paris: Les Belles Lettres.
Zafiropulo, J. (1956). *Diogène d'Apollonie*. Paris: Les Belles Lettres.
Zeitlin, F. I. (1996). *Playing the Other: Gender and Society in Classical Greek Literature*. Chicago: University of Chicago Press.
Zeller, E. (1856). *Die Philosophie der Griechen in ihrer geschichtlichen Entwicklung*. Tübingen: L. F. Fues.
Zerhoch, S. (2015). *Erinys in Epos, Tragödie und Kult: Fluchbegriff und personale Fluchmacht*. Berlin: De Gruyter.
Zimmerman, C. E. (1984). *Trampling the Serpent's Head: Discipline and Theodicy in Tertullian's Use of* Indulgentia Dei. PhD dissertation, Emory University

Index Locorum

Aeschylus
A.
  996–7   16
  1228–39   51

Ch.
  461   44

Eu.
  46–59   42
  490 ff.   46
  640–3   34
  696–703   45
  990–1   45

Fr.
  38   16

Pers.
  65–86   31
  406   32

Pr.
  12–81   40
  195 ff.   39
  219–21   19
  224–5   39
  350–76   39
  354–62   30
  449–50   16
  516–19   35

Supp.
  9–11   48
  141–4   48
  277–88   48

Th.
  423–36   25
  489–99   32
  504–20   33

Apollonius Rhodius
  730 ff.   20

Aelian
VH
  II.13   87
  III.18   200
  V.21   53
  IX.16   200

Aenesidamus Cnossius philosophus
  B1   225

Alcinous
  XV   283

Alexander of Aphrodisias
de An.   172

Fat.
  176   295

Anaxagoras of Clazomenae
  A1   59
  A16   60
  A19   59
  A43   59
  A44   61
  A45   58, 61
  A46   61
  A47   59
  A48   58
  A56   58
  A57   62
  A61   63
  B4a   56
  B4b   56–7
  B12   61

Antoninus Liberalis
  28.2   28

Apollodorus
  I.1.4   41
  I.2.1   21
  I.6.1–2   25
  I.6.3   28, 31

INDEX LOCORUM

II.4.3	17
II.7.7 (155)	15

Apuleius
Met.

9.29	283

Mund.

333	294
334	262
337	294
340	294
343	262
344 ff.	294
351–52	294
357	294

Plat.

190	262
192–3	262
193	262
194	262

Soc.

123	262
124	262
128	262

Apuleius (Pseudo–)
Ascl.

25	285
35	264

Aratus

I.1–18	209

Archimedes of Syracuse
Aren.

I.5	267

Aristophanes
Nu.

828 ff.	73

Aristotle
Cael.

291 b 8	267
302 a 28	59
306 b 17–19	78

Cat.

8 a 33	216

de An.

434 a 31–32	111

GA

I.1	111
740 a 20	207
746 a 29–35	301
762 a 24–7	111
767 b, 10–13	119, 158
767 b, 13–15	118
769 a 10–771 a 14	125
769 b 11 ff.	112
769 b 30	113
769 b 30–6	76
770 b 10	113–14
772 b 26–31	128

GC

315 a 23	64
317 b 16	295

HA

607 a 1–8	301

Metaph.

982 a 4	9
982 b 11–983 a 25	95
983 a 23	9
983 a 24 ff.	99
985 a 18	59
1000 b 12	154
1017 a 35 ff.	107
1026 a 32 ff.	119
1054 a 14	216
1069 b 15 ff.	63
1070 b 22	99
1073 a 36–7	230
VI.3	322

PA

640 a 12 ff.	108
640 a 20 ff.	109
640 b 24–9:110	
640 b 28–9	110
645 a 7 ff.	94
645 a 19–23	95
663 b 22	107
670 a 30	120
687 a 3–b 25	202
687 a 7–18	203

Ph.

194 a 20 ff.	98
194 a 28	98
194 b 11	98
194 b 24–7	99
194 b 27–9	99
194 b 29–33	99
194 b 33–5	100
195 a 23–6	100
195 b 30 ff.	105
196 b 10 ff	105
198 a 7–10	107
198 b 3 ff.	107
198 b 10–32	115
198 b 33–199 a 7	115
199 a 8–21	117
199 a 32–3	117
199 a 33–b 9	117
199 b 15–32	117
199 b 23–6	121
203 a 19	58
203 b 20 ff.	77

Ph. (cont.)
209 b 11–12	78	
256 b 24	58	
II.2	97	
II.4–5	322	
II.4–6	322	
II.5	106	
II.6	106	
II.7	107	
IV.8	72	

Po.
1451 a 1–2	164

Top.
100 b 25	230
125 b 28	216
131 b 9	216

Aristotle (Pseudo–)
Mu. 294

Arius Didymus
Posidon. 184

Arnobius of Sicca
Nat.
I.8	243
I.10	244
I.11	243
II.59	243
VII.9	244

Arrianus
Epict.
I.1.11	186
I.6.1 ff.	213
I.6.32	204
I.6.40	209
I.9.6	209
II.5.24–6	205
II.20.15	213
III.1.1–9	191
III.15.14	213
III.17.1	213
III.22.41	186

Athenaeus of Naucratis
Deipnosophistae
XI.462 C   13

Athenagoras of Athens
Leg.
6   175

Atticus
3.49–65   250

Augustine
Ciu.
XVI.8	314–5
XXI	274
XXI.8	313, 315–7

Confessiones
V.10.19–20	318
VII.12.18	318
XII.6.6	273
XIII.2.2	274

De ordine
I.1.2	317
I.3.8	313
I.6.15	313
I.7.18	319
II.1.2	319
II.7.23	312

De trinitate
III.2	274
III.2.7	315
III.8.13	274
III.8.15	274
III.9.18	274
III.10.19	315
VIII.3.4	274
VIII.3.4–5	274
XII.2.2	274

De uera religione
XLIX.94   313

Diuersis quaestionibus
28   274

Gen.ad Litt
IX.17.32   275

Biblia
Gen.
6.4	252
49.17	253

Callimachus
Dian.
72–9   24

Chalcidius
In Timaeum
299   261

Celsus
35   312

Chaldean Oracles
88	261
89	284
134	264

Chrysippus
On Gods
I   206

Cicero
Acad.
I.27 ff.	254
I.41	180

II.92–5	237
II.108	247
II.121	127

Div.
I.13	149
I.23	149
I.52	221
I.54	220
II.9	246
II.21	149
II.22	235
II.28	235
II.33	313
II.120	241

Fin.
I.19	136
IV.14	183
IV.36	254

ND
I.11	58
I.18–24	241
I.35	126
II.7	217
II.12–14	246
II.14	213
II.35	194
II.56	194
II.57–8	210
II.58	211
II.78	207
II.86–7	176
II.98–9	195
II.119	317
II.134 ff.	201
II.150–2	201
III.26	235, 241
III.27–8	242
III.43	238
III.44	15, 238
III.68	241
III.86	205
III.90	205

Resp.
III.8–11	223

Scaur.
5	159

Clement of Alexandria
Paed.
I.6.5–6	307
III.5.4	285

Prot.
V.58P	186
VI.59P	72
VI.61P–62P	208

Strom.
II.14	62
IV.3.9	264
IV.12	213
V.8.48	183
V.93.4	264

Columella
De re rustica	146

Cornutus
ND
17	34
32	183

Corpus Hermeticum
V.3	306
V.4	306
VIII.3–4	306
X.8	264
XIV.7	306
XIX	305
XX	305

Ascl. see Pseudo–Apuleius.

Cratinus
171–9	39

Democritus
D164	75
D165	75
D168	76

Diodorus of Sicily
I.10.2	299

Diogenes Laërtius
II.9	59
II.9.40	71
VII.53	173
VII.88	207
VII.94	182
VII.100	183
VII.134	184
VII.135–7	174
IX.62	225
IX.63	226
IX.74	224
IX.76	236
IX.105	229
X.26	130

Dionysius of Alexandria
On Nature	211

Empedocles
D10	154
D11	54
D57	63
D58b	69
D62	69
D64	69

Empedocles (cont.)
D71	69
D72	69
D73	64
D75	64, 141
D77a	69
D94	154
D152	65
D154	65
D156	65
D177	109
D199	67, 69
D200	67, 69
D213	67
D214	67, 69
D259	69
R20	109
R48	154
R50	154
R68	67, 69
R70	64, 67, 69, 141
R74	154
R75	65
R89	154
R93	69

Epictetus
Ench.
9	186
26	213
27	204
32	220

Epicurus
Ep. [2]
38–9	131
39	156
40	132
45.4–11	136
50	133
60	135
66	207
68–73	134
73–6	161
76–7	139
77	139

Ep.[3]
85	138
114	130

Ep. [4]
134	135

Fr.
76	137
281	135
307	138
333	130
368	139
377	139

Eudorus of Alexandria
5	254

Euripides
Ba.
395	49
536–44	27
538–44	25
685 ff	49
1109–13	49

Bellerophon:
282	280

Cyc.
625	23
670	23

Hec.
489–91	280
1151–81	90

HF
345–7	34

Hipp
277	267

Io
987–97	17

IT
969–75	45

Med.
44	52
230	52
248–51	52
264	52
395 ff.	52
574	52
1244	52
1358	52
1389	43

Or.
256	173

Ph. | 27 |

Eusebius of Caesarea
PE
IX.10.3–5	271
XI.10.12–14	260
XIV.10.5	271
XIV.18	226
XIV.19	226
XV.15	211
XV.816 d	170

INDEX LOCORUM

Die Fragmente der Griechischen Historiker [FGH]

IV F 88	21
257 F 36.II	272
257 F 36.XV	140
688	197
715	197, 296

Galenus

d. defin med.

439	75

De dign. puls

	229

De elementis secundum Hippocratem

I.2	226

De locis affectis

IV.3	185

De sequela

819–20	189

De tremore, palpitatione, convulsione

VI	185

Nat. Fac.

II.3	305

UP

I.3	303
I.9	303
I.10	304
I.21	300
I.22	302
III.1	301–2
III.4	301
III.8	202
III.10	300
V.4	184
V.9	300
VI.12	304
VI.13	304
VI.20	299
VII.14	299
XI.8	304
XI.9	304
XI.14	301
XII.6	299
XIV.6	305
XVII.1	305

Phil. Hist.

XVI	206

Gellius

VII.1.2–4	193
VII.1.7–13	216

Hellanikos of Lesbos

IV F 88	21

Heraclitus allegorista

All.

21 ff.	34
70	22

Herodotus

II.156	9
III.97–106	197
III.107–9	10
III.116	9
IV.23	9
IV.29–30	10
IV.105	9

Hesiod

Op.

55 ff.	53

Sc.

144–67	14
156–60	279
248–57	279
249–69	15

Th.

120 ff.	263
139–46	21
211	279
217	42
321–2	84
323	247
390 ff.	35
501–6	20
507 ff.	38
571 ff.	53
588–602	54
652–3	20
820–35	29
844–52	28
855–80	30
991	279
1055	42

Hippolytus

Haer.

I.14	193
I.8.12	59
VII.29	154
XXI.1	206

Homer

Il.

I.228	279
I.396–406	33
VI.180–3	84
VI.181	247
XVIII.535	14
XIX.258	208
XX.144–8	140

Od.
  I.45   208
  IX.411–2   22
  XVII.547   279

Homeric Hymns
  h.Ap.   29
  h.Cer.   41
  h.Ven.   41

Horatius
Ars poetica
  1–13   163

C.
  II.20   163

Hyginus
Fab.
  Prologue   15
  152   28, 30

John Chrysostom
Homilies on Genesis
  VII.12   178

Josephus
Ap.
  II.265   59

Juvenal
  XIII   220

Lactantius
De ira dei
  V.8   189
  VII.3   202
  IX.1 ff.   215
  X.1   125
  X.22   202
  XIII   192
  XIII.1   215
  XIII.23–4   189
  XV.3   189
  XX.1 ff.   189

De opificio Dei
  II.7–9   202
  II.10–11   214
  III.4   203
  IV.1   189
  IV.20–1   203
  VI.1   131
  VI.1–14   214–5
  X.22–4   202

Epit.
  I.1   214
  XXI   178
  XXII.10–12   188
  XXIV.2–10   188

Inst.
  III.2.2   203

Lucian
Icar.
  25   239

Lucan
  I.72–83   175
  I.522–5   212
  I.589   179
  I.639–50   212
  II.2   157
  II.1–15   220
  II.289–91   175
  VI.744–9   190
  VII.444–55   211
  IX.700 ff.   190
  IX.893–9   190

Lucretius
  I.62–79   138
  I.150   132
  I.159–60   132
  I.215–16   132
  I.265 ff.   132
  I.418 ff.   132
  I.449–50   134
  I.584–98   133
  I.586   154–5
  I.830 ff.   61
  I.958 ff.   137
  I.1021–7   137, 139
  II.62 ff.   132
  II.216–24   135
  II.244   158
  II.294–309   155
  II.302   154
  II.333 ff.   132
  II.700–29   149
  II.718–20   157
  II.719   157
  II.1048 ff.   137
  III.87–93   138
  III.416   154
  III.687   157
  IV.825–42   161
  IV.1209–17   157
  V.55   156
  V.57   154
  V.146   139
  V.222–34   182
  V.310   154, 158
  V.419–31   139
  V.772–836   140
  V.828–36   142
  V.833–900   151
  V.834–6   151
  V.837–54   142
  V.845–6   148
  V.849   159

INDEX LOCORUM

V.850	145		*Oracles see Chaldean Oracles*	
V.855–70	143			
V.855–77	146		**Origenes**	
V.871–7	143		*Cels.*	
V.876	144		I.37	175
V.878	301		III.69	189
V.878–82	151		IV.64	193
V.878 ff.	150			
V.881	151		*Io.*	
V.907–24	152, 158		II.96–9	308
V.924	154			
VI.906	154–5		*Princ.*	
			I.2.2	265
Macarius Magnes			I.4.4	265
IV.2	312		I.5.3	285
IV.6–7	271		II.3.6	265
IV.24	271		III	194–5
			III.1.13–14	307
Manilius			III.1.17	307
I.149–70	171		IV.1.7	307
I.247–54	183		IV.2.2	307
I.492–3	159			
II.62	159		**Ovid**	
IV.715 ff.	192		*Met.*	
IV.883–93	209		I.5–9	15
			I.416–37	167
Marcus Aurelius			I.438–44	168
II.3	213		III.511 ff	27
II.11	187		IV.794–803	17
III.2	204		V.532	159
IV.20	182		VII.20–1	53
IV.29	187		XIII.760–2	23
VIII.49–50	187		XIII.840–53	24
IX.28	204		XV.153–9	166
Maximus of Tyre			**Palaephatos**	
VIII.4	284		*Introduction*	11
VIII.8	284		1	151
XI.5	126		3	27
XV.2	284		19	34
XVII.5	250		32	46
XXXIII.8	260			
			Pausanias	
Megasthenes			I.24.5–7	1
XXIX	296			
			Poetae Comici Graeci [PCG]	
Methodius of Olympus			IV, fr. 171–9	39
Symp.				
VIII.12	286		**Pelagius**	
			Exp. Rom.	
Minucius Felix			1.19	179
17	201		1.20	179
17.7–9	154			
19.8	126		**Philo of Alexandria**	
20	177		*Abr.*	
34.2–3	154		118	291
36	188			
			Aet.	
Numenius of Apamea			1	252
8	260		2	291
37	284		5–6	289
52	261		55 ff.	291

Agric.	
95 ff.	253
Confus.	
187–9	290
Congr.	
173	291
Deus	
87–8	292
Gen.	
49.17 ff.	253
Gig.	
7	281
62 ff.	252
Leg.	
I.33	251
II.1–3	252
Mos.	
I.80	291
I.90–1	291
I.95	291
I.165	291
II.71	291
II.257	291
II.266	291
Opif.	
7–9	252
8–9	251
17–18	252
19	252
22	253
25	280
40 ff.	292
62–8	252
134 ff.	252
139–40	252
157	251
Plant.	
4	291
Prob.	
5	291
Prou.	
I.33	293
I.37–9	293
I.46	293
I.70	253
I.90	290
II.15	250
II.46	292
II.48	211
II.94–5	293

II.99–100	293
II.100	216
Quaest. Ex.	
I.23	281
Spec.	
I.328–9	289
II.218	291
III.23	290
III.45	289–90
IV.129	291
Philodemus of Gadara	
Sign.	157
Philoponus	
in Ph.	
235.18–20	110
261.26–262.2	105
Philoxenus of Cythera	
2–11	23
Phlegon of Tralles	
Book of Marvels	
II	272
XIV	140
XV.2	140
Photios	
Bibl.	
212 169 b 18–31	225
Pindar	
P.	
I.18–26	30
Placita philosophorum	
I.3.5	61
I.5.4	77
I.6	207
I.7.30	254
I.7.33	175
V.3.6	75
V.8.2, 905 F–906 A	126
Plato	
Cra.	
389 a–c	252
397 e–398 c	279
399 d	81
400 b–c	253
400 c 1	81
Criti.	
109 d	193
Epin.	
991 e	207

INDEX LOCORUM

Euthd.
297 c	83
306 e	264

Grg.
493 a	81
503 d–e	252
504 e	264
525 a	81

Hp.Ma.
289 a–c	303

Lg.
677 b ff.	193
889 b–d	80
892 b	81
896–8	280
896 d 3–897 b 4	82
896 e	280
900 d 2–3	89
903 b	80
904 a 6–e 3	288
937 d	279
X	262, 281–2

Phd.
46–7	289
60 b–c	193
74 b–c	97
97 b–98 c	59
97 c	102
97 d–99 b	304
107 d–8 c	279

Phdr.
229 d	85
245 c	81
247 c–e	155
248 c–252 c	263
251 a	290
268	264

Phlb.
54 a–c	109

Plt.
270 e	90
273 a ff.	288

Prm.
130 b 2–3	97

R.
343 e	264
376 e–377 c	84
378 e ff.	88
379 b–c	89
505 d 5–9	232
507 e 5–508 a 2	87
516 b 3–4	232
588 b–c	86
588 c	83
588 c ff.	269
588 d–e	84
588 e–589 a	85
595 a–608 b	

Smp.
178 b	263
189 d–190 c	90
189 d–193 d	272
191 d	91
202 ff.	279

Sph.
227 d 5–228 d 2	83
235 a 10–236 b 3	88

Tht.
176 ff.	288

Ti.
22 b–25 d	193
29 c–d	89
29 e 1–30 c 1	89
34 d–35 a	81
35 a	
40 d–41	89
41 a ff.	80
46 d 5–e 2	81
47 e–48 a	79
48 a	288
49 a	78
51 a	78
52 a–c	81
52 b	79
53 b	297
68 e–69 a	79
69 a	78

Pliny the Elder
NH
VI.187	198
VII.1	196
VII.1–2	196
VII.6–7	196
VII.9	22
VII.21–3	196
VII.32	198
VII.50	199
VII.52	199

Plotinus
I.7.7	270
I.8	276
I.8.5	269
I.8.6	310
I.8.7	270
I.8.8	270
I.8.9	269
I.8.14	270

Plotinus (cont.)
I.8.15	311
II.4.16	267, 269
III.1.1	309
III.2.3	310
III.2.4	309
III.2.5	310
III.2.9	310
III.2.14	310, 313
III.2.17	313
III.3.3	310
III.3.5	256, 310–11
III.3.7	310
III.4	287
III.5.9	266
III.8.10	266
IV.4.38	269
IV.8.6	281
V.1.4	271
V.1.5	266
V.4.1	266
V.6.3	266
V.7.2	268
V.7.7	267
V.8.12	266
VI.1.9	269
VI.1.26	206
VI.8.8	266
VI.9	266
VI.9.3	266

Plutarch
Adversus Colotem
14.1114 F–1115 B	126
16.1116C	132

De animae procreatione in Timaeus
1014 D–E	256
1015 E	256

De communibus notitiis adversus Stoicos
34.1076 C	184

De defectu oraculorum
416 E–417 B	282
418 F–419 A	282
429 A–B	256
429 B–D	255
435 E–436 A	297

De E apud Delphos
388 E–F	255
393 A–C	255
393 E	255
394 A	256

De exilio
604 A	43

De facie quae in orbe lunae apparet
926 C ff.	294
926 F	297
927 A–B	297
927 D	294
928 C	297
929 A	296
938 ff.	298
940 D	296
945	282

De fato
568 C–D	295
569 A–E	295
570 B	295
571 A	295
572 D	296
572 F	297
573 C	297

De genio Socratis
579 F ff.	282

De Iside et Osiride
361 B	283
373 A–C	257–8

De Stoicorum repugnantiis
1050 F	195
1056 D	195

De superstitione
165 E	282
171 D	282

Per.
6	297

Quaestiones convivales
VIII.2	257
637 B 298	

Poetae Melici Graeci [PMG]
207	14
815–24	23

Poetarum Lesbiorum Fragmenta [PLF]
130	263

Porphyry
Abst.
II.36–45	287
II.41.5	287

Chr.
89	271
90 a	271
94	271

De philosophia ex oraculis haurienda
324 F	271
325 F	271

De Styge
376 F	272

Sent.
  20   273

Posidonius
  5   184
  14   206
  15   206
  21   194
  35 C   189
  100   184
  187   207

Proclus
ad.Hes.Op.
  Prolegomena I.1   18
  60 ff.   54

De decem dubitationibus circa providentia
  II.6   320

De malorum subsistentia
  4   320
  5   319
  7   319
  9   319
  10   319
  11   276
  17–18   320
  20   320
  27   277, 320
  27.7–14   277
  29   320
  31.8–20   276
  33   278
  36.15 23   278
  37.1–7   278
  37.7–25   277
  41.17–24   276
  47.1–18   276
  49   321
  50   321–3
  52–4   321
  56–7   323
  60   324

De providentia et fato
  34   319

in Prm.
  V   174

in Ti.
  I.76.30–77   284

Theol.Plat.
  I.12–17   320
  I.18   321
  I.19–24   275
  II.2   275

Sappho see *Poetarum Lesbiorum Fragmenta*

Seneca
Ep.
  9.16   208
  58.15   174
  58.27   184
  106.2   183

Nat.
  I praef. 13–14   206
  I praef. 15   184
  II.32.3–4   218
  VI.3.4–VI.4.1   220
  VII.1.1–2   219
  VII.27.3   218

Sextus Empiricus
M.
  V   246
  VII.30   229
  VII.111 ff. 231
  VII.411–15   236
  VII.416 ff. 237
  VIII.56   173
  IX.59   231
  IX.88–91   238
  IX.182–3   238
  XI.99   182

P.
  I.8   225
  I.19   231
  I.22   231
  I.25–30   225
  I.27–8   225
  I.30   225
  I.32   240
  I.40   228
  I.43   228
  I.78   228
  I.80   232
  I.81–4   233
  I.88–9   234
  I.141–3   234
  I.144   235
  I.210   230
  I.234   247
  III.2   240
  III.9–10   240

Simplicius
in Cael.
  528.30   141

in Cat.   178

in Epict.
  34   273

in Ph.
  34.18–20   56
  34.20–7   56
  156.13   57, 61

in Ph. (cont.)
308.25–33	102
327.26	59
382.2–21	118
460.4	61
1148.29	225

Socratis et Socraticurum Reliquiae [SSR]
V A	22

Solinus
27.28 ff.	190
30.1 ff.	233
30.12	233
51.27–8	197

Sophocles
Ant.
125	27
332–3	51
376	50
1075	43

El.
480	43

Stesichorus
30	14

Stobaeus
I.1.12	208
I.3.56	272
I.13.1	184
I.136.21	178
II.77.16	181

Stoicorum Veterum Fragmenta [SVR]
I.60	180
I.65	172
I.85	184
I.98	170
I.153	206
I.159	187
I.162	207
I.163	206
I.502–3	183
I.509	211
I.537	208
II.87	173
II.88	173
II.278	172
II.315	206
II.332	174
II.357–68	172
II.394	172
II.446	185
II.528	211
II.534	317
II.546	317
II.580	174
II.717	174
II.739	175
II.877	185
II.935	195
II.956–64	216
II.1009	207
II.1013	317
II.1027	175
II.1065	208
II.1101–5	280
II.1106–26	211
II.1127	207
II.1127–31	210
II.1136	184
II.1168	184
II.1169	193
II.1170	216
II.1172	192
II.1174	193
II.1179	205
II.1180	205
II.1181	195
II.1185	194–5
II.1211	317
III.13	183
III.16	181
III.29–37	181
III.38	182
III.76	182
III.83	183
III.84	183
III.233	189

Strabo
15.1.57	296

Strato of Lampsacus
18	127
19A	126
19B	126
19C	125
20	126
21	126
74	126

Tertullian
Adu.Marc. — 176

Adu.Val. — 176

Apol.
XII	187
XII–XXIV	188

Cult.fem. — 176

De virginibus velandi
I.12	188

Theocritus
XI	23

Theophrastus
CP
  V.1.2 ff. — 124
  V.2.1. — 124
  V.4.7 — 125

Metaph.
  IX.10 a 22. — 121
  IX.10 a 22–8 — 122
  IX.10 a 26–7 — 124
  IX.10 b 24–11 a 1 — 123
  IX.11 b 25–7 — 122

Meteorology
  6 — 124

Theosophorum Graecorum Fragmenta [Theos.]
  173.17–174.22 — 271

Tragicorum Graecorum Fragmenta [TrGF]
  III.A1 30–2 — 43

Virgil
Aen.
  III.26 — 162
  VI.285–9 — 162
  VI.292–4 — 163
  VI.570–2 — 41
  VI.724 — 162
  VII.21 — 162
  VII.325–6 — 41

B.
  IV.37–48 — 162
  VI.31 ff. — 162

G.
  I.60 — 157

Vitruvius
  VII.V.3–4 — 164

Vorsokratiker [Vorsokr.]
  4 — 57
  13 A 7(6) — 267
  21 A 33 — 193
  21 A 41a — 267
  21 B 1 — 13
  22 B 94 — 43
  28 B 1 — 231
  31 B 6 — 63
  31 B 17 — 64
  31 B 19 — 69
  31 B 21 — 69
  31 B 30 — 154
  31 B 32–4 — 69
  31 B 35 — 65, 141
  31 B 57 — 65
  31 B 61 — 65
  31 B 73 — 67, 69
  31 B 75 — 67, 69
  31 B 86 — 67
  31 B 87 — 67, 69
  31 B 97 — 109
  31 B 115 — 154
  31 B 151 — 69
  68 A 49 — 226
  68 A 141 — 75
  68 A 146 — 113
  68 B 124 — 75
  70 A 6 — 77

Xenocrates philosophus
  213 — 254
  222 — 281

Xenophon of Athens
Mem.
  I.4.5–6 — 101, 288
  I.4.8 — 211
  IV.3.3 — 288
  IV.7.5 — 267

Index Verborum

Index of Greek words

ἀγαθός, 89, 181
ἀγαθότης, 281
ἀγαυός, 19
ἄγγελος, 209n
ἄγνωστος, 89
ἄγονος, 321
ἀγριωπός
   ἀ. τέρας, 27
ἄγριος, 21, 89
ἄδηλος, 288
ἀδιατύπωτος, 299.
ἀδίκημα, 117
ἀδικία, 36
ἀδύνατος, 11
ἀθέσμως, 39
ἀθέτως, 39
αἱρεῖν, 88
αἵρεσις, 88
αἴσθησις, 180
αἶσχος, 83
αἰσχρός, 23, 181, 191–2, 280
αἰτεῖν, 36
αἰτία, 36, 80, 99, 121
   πλανωμένη α., 79
αἰτιᾶσθαι, 36
αἴτιος, 36
ἀκατονόμαστος, 252
ἀκμή, 212n
ἀλήθεια, 171
ἀληθής, 10
ἀλλόκοτος, 264
ἄλογος, 52, 89
ἁμάρτημα, 117
ἀμετρία, 83
ἄμετρος, 270, 306
ἀμήχανος, 11
ἄμορφος, 296
ἀμύμων, 20
ἀναγκαῖος, 79
   ἀ. φύσεως, 107n
ἀνάγκη, 65–6, 74, 79–80, 88, 124
   ἀ. φύσεος, 107

ἐξ ἀ., 113
ὑλικὴ ἀ., 139
ἀνάπηρος, 112, 258
ἀνάρμοστος
   ἁρμονίαν ἀ., 290
ἀνατύπωμα, 173
ἀνδροφυής
   ἀ. βούκρανα, 151n
ἀνδρόγυνος, 90
ἀνείδεος, 270, 320
ἀνεμπόδιστος, 295
ἀνεπίκριτος, 225
ἄνθρωπος, 51, 86
   ἄγριοι ἀ., 21
ἄνοια, 79
ἀντιάνειρα, 46
ἀνύπαρκτος, 290
ἀπαράβατος, 295
ἄπειρον, 257
ἄπειρος, 57, 270
ἀπίθανος, 11
ἄπλαστος, 320n
ἄποιος, 184
ἀπόστασις, 267
ἀποστροφή, 17
ἀπρεπής, 296
ἀπροσθετεῖν
   τὸ μηδὲν ὁρίζειν, ἀλλὰ ἀ., 236
ἁπτός, 82
ἀργός
   ἀ. λόγος, 216n
Ἄρης, 44
ἄριστος
   εἰς τὸ ἄ., 122
ἁρμονία
   ἀ. ἀνάρμοστον, 290
ἄρρητος, 252
ἀρχή, 36
   ἀ. τῆς κινήσεως, 99
ἀσώματος, 172
ἄτακτος, 306
ἀταξία, 19, 306
ἀτάρακτος, 225
ἀταραξία, 138, 224–5, 227

INDEX VERBORUM 409

ἄτιμος, 94, 112
ἄτομος, 71
ἀτύχημα, 117
αὐτογένετος, 271
αὐτοκρατής, 57
αὐτοκράτωρ, 57, 291
αὐτόματον, 74, 123
αὐτόματος, 90, 104, 106–7, 115, 245
ἀφανής, 288
ἀφασία, 224

βάρος, 132
βασανίζειν, 88
βασιλεύς
   ὕπατος β., 208
βία, βίη, 21, 25, 40, 89
βιάζεσθαι, 88
βουγενής
   β. ἀνδρόπωρα, 65, 151n
βούλευμα, 213, 240, 307
βούλησις, 213

γένεσις, 108
γηγενής, 26
γιγαντικός, 24
γνώμη, 57, 101, 104
γοητεία, 287
γονή, 75

δαίμονες, 279
δαιμόνιος
   δ. τέρας, 50
δαίμων, 279, 284
δεινός, 13, 45, 49, 51–?
δείς, 71
διαθιγή, 71
διαιρεῖν, 88
διαιρετικός, 255
διάνοια, 230
διαστροφή, 192
διάστροφος, 192
διήκειν, 185
δίκη, 37, 40, 44, 46, 50
δῖος, 39
διοσημία, 234.
δισσός
   δ. λόγοι, 44n
δοκοῦν, 231–2
δράκων, 247n
δύναμις, 57, 107–8, 281
   συνεκτικὴ δ., 185
δυναστεία, 240
δυνατός, 157
δύσπιστος, 11
δωτήρ, 19

ἑαυτοῦ
   μόνος αὐτὸς ἐφ' ἑ. ἐστιν, 57
ἐθέλειν, 213
ἔθνος
   ἔ. μυρία θνητῶν, 141
εἶδος, 99, 172

εἰκός, 85
εἱμαρμένη, 74, 171, 293
εἶναι
   τί ἦν ε., 99
   τὸ μὴ ε., 108
εἷς, 266
ἐκπύρωσις, 174–5.
ἐλάχιστος, 134
ἔλλειψις, 310
ἐμπειρία, 231
ἐμπνευμάτωσις, 126
ἐμποδίζειν, 110
ἔμφρων
   ἔ. φύσις, 80
ἕνεκα, 74, 108
   Ἕ. Του, 121
   οὗ ἕ. καί τἀγαθόν, 99
   τοῦ πάνθ' ἕ. του καὶ μηδὲν μάτην, 121–2
ἐνέργεια, 107–8
ἐνύπαρκτος
   λόγος ἐ., 184
ἐνυπάρχω, 99
ἕνωσις, 266
ἕξις, 171
ἐξουσία, 281
ἐπακολουθεῖν, 216
ἐπακολούθησις, 203
   κατ' ἐ., 204, 216
ἐπανορθοῦν, 85
ἐπικράτεια, 75–7, 114
ἐπιμέλεια, 89
ἐπιστήμη, 119n
ἐποχή, 225, 232–3, 235
ἔργον, 104
ἔσχατον, 270
ἔσχατος, 270
ἑτερότης, 255
εὐδαίμων, 279
εὐεργετικός, 82
εὐθυμία, 227
εὐμενής, 40
εὐταξία, 307, 312

ζείδωρος
   ζ. ['Ἀφροδίτην], 69
ζῆν
   ζ. ὁμολογουμένως, 182
   κατὰ φύσιν ζ., 182
ζυγόν, 87
ζῷον
   ἀτιμοτέρων ζ., 94

ἦτορ
   ὑπέρβιος ἦ., 21

θαῦμα, 9
   θ. ἰδέσθαι, 14, 65, 141
θαυμάζειν, 95
θαυμαστός, 94
θεῖος, 79, 291
θεός, 80
θέσις, 71

θεωρία, 119n
θήρα, 88
θήρειος, 23
θηρίον, 87
θηριώδης, 89
θνητός
    ἔθνεα μυρία θ., 141
θυμός, 46

ἰδέα, 72, 86
ἰδιοσυγκρασία, 232
ἰσοσθένεια, 231
ἰσχύς, 21

κακοδαίμων, 279
κακός, 89, 181, 189, 240
κακουργός, 287
καλός, 89, 95, 181, 191
κατάληψις, 180
καταπίπτειν, 185
κενός, 71, 132
κῆτος, 140n
κίνησις
    τονικὴ κ., 185.
κρατεῖν, 114, 119
κράτος, 35, 40, 48
κρείων
    ὕπατε κ., 208n
κυρίως, 110, 321

λεκτός, 172–3
λεπτότης, 57
λέων, 247n
λογιστικόν, 86
λόγος, 171, 173–6, 180, 182, 195, 208, 210, 230–1
    ἀργός λ., 216n
    δισσοὶ λ., 44n
    λ. ἐνυπάρχων, 184n
    ὀρθὸς λ., 207
    σπερματικός λ., 171, 174–7

μάτην, 106, 121–2
μεγαλόσπλαγχνος, 52
μέγεθος, 132
μεσήρης, 247
μεταξύ, 283
μηδέν, 71, 121–2
μηχανή, 20–1
μιγνύναι, 16
μῖσος, 52
μονάς, 254
μόνος
    μ. αὐτὸς ἐφ᾽ ἑαυτοῦ ἐστιν, 57
μορφή, 232
    ἡ γὰρ κατὰ τὴν μ. φύσις κυριωτέρα τῆς ὑλικῆς
    φύσεως, 110
μοχθηρός, 264
μυριόκρανος, 83
μυρίος
    ἔθνεα μ. θνητῶν, 141

νεῖκος, 64
νηλεόποινος, 42
νόμος, 171, 227, 312
νοῦς, 57–8, 62, 80, 88, 105, 107, 207, 210

οἰκείωσις, 182n
οἰκονομία, 207
ὁμολογουμένως
    ζῆν ὁ., 182
ὄπιθεν
    ὁ. δὲ δράκων, 247
ὁρατός, 82
ὀρθός
    ὁ. λόγος, 207
ὁρίζειν, 236 and n
ὅρκος
    ὅ. πλατύς, 154
ὅρος, 122–3
ὅρπετον
    γλυκύπικρον ὅ., 263
οὐδέν
    ο. μᾶλλον, 235
οὐλοφυής, 66–7
οὐσία, 99, 108
    γένεσις ἕνεκα τῆς ο. ἐστίν, ἀλλ᾽οὐκ ἡ ο. ἕνεκα τῆς
    γενέσεως, 108

πάθος, 108
πανσπερμία, 75
παράδειγμα, 99
παρακολούθημα, 288.
παρακολουθεῖν, 216
παρακολούθησις
    κατὰ π., 216
παραλλαγή, 157
παρανομία, 26
παρέγκλισις, 135, 185, 309
παρυπόστασις, 321–3
πᾶσ, 132
πατήρ, 209
πηλός, 186
πήρωμα, 112
πλανητός
    π. αἰτία, 79
πλημμέλεια, 19
πλήρης, 71
πνεῦμα, 171, 176, 185, 187, 206, 208, 251n, 307
πνοή, 251n
ποιός
    ἰδίως π., 267
πολύς
    ὡς ἐπὶ τὸ π., 113
πονηρός, 89
προηγουμένως, 216,
προνοεῖν, 240
πρόνοια, 89, 101, 104, 307
πρόσθεν
    π. λέων, 247n
πρόσωπον, 45
πῦρ
    π. τεχνικόν, 170, 184

INDEX VERBORUM

ῥόθος, 32
ῥυσμός, 71

σῆμα, 81
σθένειν
   ἀλλὰ τὸ φαινόμενον πάντῃ σ., 229
σπανός, 234
Σπαρτοί, 26
σπέρμα, 57, 75, 171
σπερματικός
   σ. λόγος, 171, 174–7
στέρεσις, 267
στοιχεῖον, 70
   τὸ ἕν σ., 64n
σύγχυσις, 289
συλλογισμός
   φαινόμενος σ., 230n
συμβεβηκός, 108, 134
   ἡ γὰρ τύχη τῶν κατὰ σ. αἰτίων, 121 and n
   κατὰ σ., 106, 118, 119n, 121, 215
σύμβολον, 91
συμπάθεια, 244
σύμπτωμα, 134
συμπτωματικῶς, 124
σύνδεσμος, 280
συνεκτικός
   σ. δύναμις, 185
σύνοδος, 160
σύστημα, 206
σφάλλειν, 68n
σχῆμα, 71, 132, 172
σῶμα, 75, 81, 132
σωματοειδής, 82
σωρός, 237

τάξις, 71, 306
ταραχή, 79
τέλειος, 37, 112
τέλος, 18, 66, 68, 80, 88, 100, 106, 112n, 135–6, 150, 213, 224, 242
τέρας, 9, 76, 112, 120, 130, 191
   ἀγριωπός τ., 27
   δαιμόνιον τ., 50
   τ. παλίμφημα, 290
   τ. φύσεος, 323
τεράστιος, 192, 291
   τ. φάσματα, 282
τερατεία, 130
τερατόμορφος, 192.
τερατώδης, 312
τέχνη, 80
τίμιος, 112
τομεύς, 281
τόνος, 171
τόπος, 132
τραγέλαφος, 112n
τροπή, 71
τυγχάνειν, 68 and n
τυραννίς
   Διὸς τ., 39
τύχη, 65–6, 74, 101, 104, 106, 115, 216

ἡ γὰρ τ. τῶν κατὰ συμβεβεκός αἰτίων, 121
τὰ μόρια τῶν ζῴων ἀπὸ τ. γενέσθαι τὰ πλεῖστά φησιν, 105
τυχόντως, 114

ὕβρις, 25–6, 50, 79
ὕλη, 78, 82, 99, 184–5
   κακῆς ὕ., 263
ὑλικός
   ἡ γὰρ κατὰ τὴν μορφὴν φύσις κυριωτέρα τῆς ὑ. φύσεως, 110
   ὑ. ἀνάγκη, 139
ὕπατος
   ὕ. βασιλεύς, 208
ὑπεναντίος, 288
ὑπέρβιος
   ὑ. ἦτορ, 21
ὑποδοχή, 78
ὑποκείμενον, 99
ὑπόστασις, 321

φαίνεσθαι, 228
φαινόμενον, 229–30n, 231 and n, 233
   ἀλλὰ τὸ φ. πάντῃ σθένει, οὗπερ ἂν ἔσθῃ, 229–30
   ἀποδοῦναι τὰ φ., 230n
φαντασία, 228
φάντασμα, 172, 232
φάρμακον, 85
φάσμα
   τεράστια φ., 282
φαῦλος, 89, 287
φημίζειν, 228
φθορά
   περὶ τὴν ἐν φ. καὶ γενέσει φύσιν, 256
φιλότης, 64
φρόνησις, 79
φύειν, 16
φυλάττειν, 312.
φύσις, 43, 73, 95, 105, 107, 171, 207, 230n
   ἀναγκαίας φ., 107
   ἔμφρων φ., 80
   ἡ γὰρ κατὰ τὴν μορφὴν φ. κυριωτέρα τῆς ὑλικῆς φ., 110
   λόγον φ., 107
   παρὰ φ., 106, 113, 119, 182, 204, 289–90, 294, 323n
   τέρατα φ., 323
φῶς, 228

χίμαιρα, 247n
χώρα, 79

ψυχή, 81–2, 171

ὠφέλεια, 101

Index of Latin Words

absterrere
   natura a. auctum, 142

accidens
  per a., 118
administrare
  mundum esse urbem (uel domum) bene a., 210n
admirari
  nihil a., 164
adsequi, 68n
aequalis
  a. foedere, 159
aeternus
  continuo has leges a. foedera certis imposuit natura locis, 157
agitare
  omnia cientis et a. motibus et mutationibus suis, 242
angelus
  nocentes a., 285
animal, 214
animans
  mixtas a., 152
animus / anima, 154n
artifex
  natura non artificiosa solum sed plane a. dicitur, 210
artificiosus
  ignis a., 210
atomos, 136

bellum, 157
belua
  fera et immanis b., 247
bonum
  b. et mala in ordine sunt, 313

caecus
  c. foedere, 159
cadere, 106n
casus, 318
causa, 161
  c. efficiens, 99, 274
  c. finalis, 99
  c. formalis, 99
  c. materialis, 99
  omnis c. efficiens est, 274
cessare, 208
certus, 156
  c. discrimen, 152–3
  imagines c., 164
  seminibus c. certa generatrice creata, 149
clinamen, 135, 158
coaptatio
  uniuersam rerum c. atque concentum, 317
cogitare, 208
commutare
  si primordia rerum c. aliqua possent ratione reuicta, 133
complexus
  inter se c., 158
conari, 144, 146
concentus
  c. naturae, 318
  uniuersam rerum coaptationem atque c., 317
concordia
  discors c., 167

concurrere, 147
  multa uidemus enim rebus c. debere, 142, 146, 159
concursio
  turbulenta c., 136
concursus, 159
condicio, 156
confatalis, 216n
coniunctum, 134
consequi, 216
conspicuus, 218
corpus, 134, 155
  in sua c. rursum dissoluat natura neque ad nilum interemat res, 132
  sola c. esse, non esse ideas, 172
creare
  c. conatast, 142
  seminibus certis certa generatrice c., 149
creatio, 275n
creator, 275n
creatura, 275n
crescere
  haud igitur potuere utendi c. causa, 161
cura, 104n
curare
  de minimis non c. praetor, 205

decus
  ablatum d. est, 290
defectus, 87 and n
deformis, 192
deformitas, 192, 290
deterior
  uideo meliora proboque, d. sequor, 53
determinatio
  d. est negatio, 147
dicere
  natura non artificiosa solum sed plane artifex d., 210
  porro d., 315
discors
  d. concordia, 167
discrimen
  certum d., 152–3
dissoluere, 132
disterminare
  ratio d. omnia, 149
diuinitus
  nullam rem e nilo gigni d. umquam, 132
diuulsus
  totaque discors machina d. turbabit foedera mundi, 175
domus, 210n

efferatus, 203
efficiens
  causa e., 99
  omnis causa e. est, 274
elementum, 153
euentum, 134

facies
  monstruosa f. gentium, 233n
fatalis
  uincla f., 143–4
fatum, 158, 171

INDEX VERBORUM 413

fera
   f. et immanis belua, 247
figura, 157
finalis
   c. finalis, 99
finis, 160
   fati f., 158
finitus
   f. potestas, 133
foedus / foedera, 134, 154, 158–9
   aequali f., 159
   caeco f., 159
   continuo has leges aeternaque f. certis imposuit natura locis, 157
   f. mundi, 175
   f. naturae, 142, 148, 152, 154–6, 158–60, 168–9
   f. rerum, 157
   fati f., 156
   quantum cuique datum est per f. naturai, 156
foedus see *uultus*
forma
   materia f. exuere properat, 290
formalis
   causa f., 99

generatrix
   seminibus certis certa g. creata, 149
gens
   monstruosa facies g., 233n
genus, 143
gignere
   nullam rem e nilo g. diuinitus umquam, 132

iactus
   i. ueneris, 148
idea
   sola corpora esse, non esse i., 172
ignis
   i. artificiosus, 210
imago
   i. certae, 164
immanis
   fera et i. belua, 247
impossibilia, 150, 152, 162
impossibilis, 141
inane, 134
index
   pulchrum i. ueri, 97
infinitus, 137
Informis, 192
ira, 157

letum
   lex l., 157
lex, 149–50, 157, 159, 171, 215
   continuo has l. aeternaque foedera certis | imposuit natura locis, 157
   foedera rerum l., 157
   l. leti, 157
   l. naturalis, 154
   nec ualidas ualeant aeui rescindere l., 156
locus
   natura l., 157

machina
   totaque discors m. diuulsi turbabit foedera mundi, 175
magnitudo, 214
magnus
   m. mater, 141, 143
malum
   bona et m. in ordine sunt, 313
manifestus
   m. belli signa, 157
mater
   magna m., 141, 143
materia, 290
materialis
   causa m., 99
Medioximus, 283
melior
   uideo m. proboque, deteriora sequor, 53
membrum, 161
mens
   m. mundi, 211
minimum
   de m. non curat praetor, 205
minus, 205
mirabilis
   m. monstrum, 162
   res m., 230
mirabilia, 196, 198, 200
miraculum
   mille m., 220
mirari
   m. specie, 214
mixtus
   m. animantum, 152
modus
   multa m. multis mutata, 137
monstrare, 315
monstrifer, 157
monstrum, 142
   mirabile m., 162
   noua m., 167
monstruosus
   m. facies gentium, 233n
mundus
   m. esse urbem (uel domum) bene administratam, 210
   mens m., 211
   totaque discors machina diuulsi turbabit foedera m., 175
motus
   omnia cientis et agitantis m. et mutationibus suis, 242
mutare
   multa modis multis m., 137
mutatio

natura, 142
   concentus n., 318
   monstra n., 323
   n. potentia, 218
   n. species ratioque, 138n
   ordo n., 179
nefas, 157
negatio
   determinatio est n., 147
nequiquam, 142–3

nihil ultra, 137
nilum
   in sua corpora rursum dissoluat natura neque ad n. interemat res, 132
nocens
   n. angeli, 285
notitia
   n.utilitatis, 161
nouus
   n. monstra, 167
numen
   sanctum n., 158
numerus, 149

omnipotens, 275
opus, 206n
ordo, 154, 215
   bona et mala in o. sunt, 313
   o. naturae, 179
ornatus
   o. mundi, 136
ossum, 293
ostendere, 315
ostentum, 315

parere, 190
peruersus
   p. ratione, 161
pestifer
   [adluuiones et flammae] regionaliter p., 294
Physicus, 126
portentum, 142, 213
posse, 133, 145
possibilis, 141
potentia, 275
   p. naturae, 218
potestas
   finita p., 133
praeostendere, 315
praeposterus, 161
praescius, 157
praetor
   de minimis non curat p., 205
prauitas, 192
prauus, 192
primordium, 215
   p. rerum, 133, 137
procreare, 161
prodigiosus
   animalia p., 214
prouidentia, 104n
prouincia
   quasi p. atomis dare, 136
pulcher
   p. index ueri, 97

qualitas, 263

ratio, 133, 136, 138, 140, 149–50, 155–7, 161, 164, 318
reddere
   r. rationem, 179
res, 132, 137, 142, 146
   multa uidemus r. concurrere debere, 159
   semina r., 166, 174, 176–7, 222
rescindere, 156
reuincere, 133

sanctus
   s. numen, 158
sapientia, 275
secta, 210
semen, 179
   s. certis certa generatrice creata, 149
   s. rerum, 166, 174, 176–7, 222
sensus, 161
sequella, 216
seruare, 152
significatio, 263
signum, 152
similis, 156
simulacrum, 230–1, 303 and n, 323
singuli, 218
species, 263
   sine s., 320 and n
sponte, 74
   sua s., 242, 244–5
subsequi, 216
superfluum, 293

taeter, 203
temerarius, 275
tenere, 206
terminus, 142
   ratione atque alte t., 133
terra, 155
tumultus, 157
turbare, 175
turbulentus
   t. concursio, 136
turpis, 202n

ualere, 231
ualidus, 156
ueritas, 149, 171
uerum, 97
   pulchrum index u., 97
uia, 210
uinclum
   u. fatales, 143
   u. fatalia, 144
uirtus, 275
uniuersus, 317
urbs, 210
usus, 161, 215
utilitas, 161
uultus, 192

Index Rerum

Accidental, 106, 119
Amazons, 1, 46–8
Amphisbaena, 51
Angels see demons
Anomaly, 60
Anthropocentrism, 140–1, 143, 195, 198, 244, 316–17
Anthropomorphism, 25, 60, 62, 64, 73, 135, 139, 156, 208
Ape, 302–3
Areopagus, 44
Art, 116–17
Atheism, 60, 73
Atom, 71, 132–7, 211, 245
Atomism, 59, 63, 70–7
Autochthony, 27

Bacchae, 34 and n., 47
Barbarians, 22, 26, 31–2, 46–8
Being and becoming, 63–4, 68, 71, 252, 260, 273, 287, 292, 298
Body, 47, 49–50, 81, 185–6, 195, 201, 253n, 285

Cannibalism, 22n
Causality, 10–11, 35–55, 60, 79, 97–107, 111–12, 116, 136
Centaur, 1, 47, 145, 150–1, 158, 164, 173, 177, 260, 264–5, 301
Centimanes see Hecatoncheires
Chance, 65, 74–5, 104–7, 114–16, 123, 148–9, 159, 214–5, 218–9
Chaos, 1, 4, 13–19, 28, 32, 66, 150, 175
Chimera, 47, 84–5, 145, 149–51, 158, 163, 260, 301
Civilisation, 21–2, 27, 48
Cosmogony, 9, 12, 16, 25, 37, 58, 63, 171, 175, 255, 258

Danaids, 47–8
Deformity, 23, 50, 52, 83, 86, 112, 277
Demiurge, 82, 89, 134, 211
Demons, 41–2, 187, 278–87
Deviation, 135–7
Diversity, 59, 195–6, 199–200, 228, 233
Divination, 217–20, 234, 239, 245–6
Dragon, 26–7, 31, 173, 285 and n

Earth, 59, 66, 90, 140, 142, 167
Emanation, 174
Emptiness see void
Encounter, 68
End see teleology
Epigenesis, 75–6
Erynies, 34–5, 40n, 41–6
Essence, 99–100, 108, 236
Ethics, 138–9, 188, 225n, 251
Eumenides, 44
Evil, 18, 81–2, 176, 189, 193, 216, 267, 270–1, 276–7, 280–1, 288, 309–12, 318–21, 323

Fate, 26, 35, 40–1, 74, 144–5, 158–61, 171, 175, 204, 212
Fear, 45, 60
Femininity, 41, 46, 50–5
Fire, 30, 38, 49, 54, 61, 167, 170, 174, 184
Form, 98, 100, 174
Freak, 120
Furies see Erynies

Geography, 10
Giants, 1, 12, 17–18, 27–8
Gigantomachy, 24–6
Gnosticism, 82, 176, 251, 274, 283, 312
God and the divine, 9, 13, 20, 36–7, 39, 43–4, 67, 79, 95–6, 138–9, 171, 177, 184, 187, 189, 205–22, 239–40, 249–51, 261–6, 274–5, 301, 316
Gorgons, 15, 260

Hand, 201–2, 210, 302–3
Harmony, 64, 66, 68, 117, 167, 183n, 187, 259, 294, 317
Heat, 59
Hecatoncheires, 18–20, 33, 34n.
Hermaphrodite, 47, 90–1, 142, 151n, 272
Hibridity, 26–7, 30, 47
Historiography, 9–11
Homeomeries, 60
Homosexuality, 290

Idea, 72, 81, 172, 174, 180, 252, 262–3
Idealism, 4, 59–60, 97

Immanence, 59, 73
Infinite, 136–8
Intellect, 57–9, 62–3

Justice, 15, 35, 37–8, 40n, 41, 43–4, 46, 50, 87

Keres, 15, 42
Kyklopes, 18, 20–3, 293

Law, 11, 12n., 42, 45, 145, 147, 150, 153–61, 171, 175, 177, 180, 207, 289, 291–2, 295
Lemnian women, 47–8
Lestrygons, 22

Manichaeism, 286
Mask, 43, 47, 87n
Materialism, 4–5, 59–60, 72–3, 98, 171–2, 176, 183, 206
Matter, 61, 72, 78–9, 99, 101–2, 112, 114, 171, 185–7, 253–63, 266–70, 272–3, 275, 277–8, 292, 302
Mechanicism, 64, 67–8, 73, 76, 110–11, 114–16, 120, 127, 167
Miracle, 180–1, 198, 315–16
Moirai, 42–3
Mutiplicity, 71, 256, 259, 324
Myth, 8–9, 12–13, 78, 84–5, 258–9
Mythology, 8–55

Nature, 25, 43, 58, 96–7, 109, 113–14, 116–17, 119, 136, 138, 141, 166, 182, 185, 187, 199, 218
Necessity, 35, 43, 64–5, 73–5, 79, 104, 114, 118–21, 139, 141, 159, 217
Nominalism, 97, 172–81
Norm, 59, 62, 69
Normality and abnormality, 4, 25, 47, 50, 55, 58, 60–1

One, 64, 71
Order, 5, 12, 13–19, 20, 25, 28, 31–4, 37–8, 42, 48, 54, 62, 68, 74–5, 79, 89, 161, 171, 179, 194, 242, 259, 306, 312–13, 319
Organ, 201
Orphism, 64, 89 and n, 279

Pangenesis, 75 and n
Paradoxography, 10–11, 85n, 200, 272n
Parcae, 159
Parthenon, 25–6, 46–7
Perfection, 59, 67–8, 96, 100, 145, 189, 191, 194–5, 202–3, 217, 292, 299

Pergamon Altar, 17
Pneuma, 126, 128, 171, 174, 176, 185–7, 208, 251, 307
Power, 17, 19, 24, 28, 39–40, 42, 49, 51, 57–8, 64
Preformationism, 75
Prodigy, 212
Providence, 10, 18, 67, 74, 89, 104, 125, 143, 168, 175–6, 178, 196, 198–200, 205–21, 293, 305, 307–8, 311, 320

Race, 188, 197–8, 200, 296, 313–17
Reason, 52, 86, 241
Regularity, 105, 159
Relativism, 191, 225–7, 232, 234
Roots, 63–4, 102

Seeds, 56–7, 62, 75–6, 132, 149–50, 152, 157–8, 171, 174–5, 178, 274–5
Simulacrum, 54, 163, 230–1, 303 and n, 323
Snake, 10, 30, 41 and n., 49, 253, 264
Sophists, 44, 88
Soul, 81–8, 256, 260, 264, 266, 284, 287
Sphynx, 1, 164
Spontaneity *see* chance in atomism
Superstition, 139, 245
Swerve *see* deviation
Sympathy, 200

Teleology, 18–19, 58, 66–7, 70, 74, 76, 80, 88, 98–107, 111–12, 116–17, 121–4, 127–8, 135–6, 141, 144–5, 150, 158–60, 196, 201–2, 205–21, 241–3, 269, 288–9, 298, 304, 320–1
Teratology, 9
Theodicy, 35, 95, 172, 186–8, 208, 216, 320
Theogony, 9, 11, 13, 16, 18–19
Theomachy, 19, 28–33
Time, 151
Titans and titanomachy, 18–20, 25, 28–9, 33, 35, 38–9
Tragedy, 12, 16, 36–7, 44 and n, 46
Typhonomachy *see* teomachy

Violence, 15, 30, 37, 40 and n., 79
Void, 63, 71–2, 132, 134, 171–2

Witchcraft, 190
Wonder, 9, 95, 141, 166, 195, 200, 219, 221, 291, 313

Zoogony, 57, 59, 65–7, 140–52

Index Nominum

Abry, J. H., 192n
Achelous, 238
Achilles, 14, 33, 46, 304
Acis, 24
Ackermann, E., 144n
Adam, 252, 317
Adams, J., 84n
Aegaeon, 33
Aegipan, 31
Aegyptus, 48
Aelianus, 200n
Aeneas, 162–3, 190n
Aenesidemus of Cnossus, 225n, 228 and n, 229n, 232
Aeschylus, 12n, 16, 25–6, 29, 32 and n, 33–5, 37–41, 43, 44 and n, 47, 51, 87
Aetius, 65, 175n, 254
Agamben, G., 40n
Agamemnon, 16, 51
Agenor, 26
Aidoneus, 63
Ajax, 304
Akousilaos, 9
Albinus *see* Alcinous
Alcinous, 249–50, 261 and n, 262, 283 and n, 284
Alecto, 41
Alexander of Aphrodisia, 295
Alfieri, V., 135
Alfonsi, L., 165 and n
Algra, K., 161n, 209n
Allan, W., 37 and n, 41n
Allen, R. E., 58n
Allen, T. W., 29n
Amata, B., 244n
Ambrogius, 190n
Amigues, S., 125n
Ammonius Saccas, 250, 271n
Amphitryon, 34n
Anaxagoras of Clazomenae, 6, 12n, 52–63, 65, 72, 80, 131n, 201, 202n, 297, 299, 303–4
Anaxarcus, 226 and n
Anaximander, 12n, 36, 90
Anaximenes of Miletus, 267n
Anchises, 162

Andreae, B., 22n
Annas, J., 86n
André, J., 197n
Andresen, C., 250n
Antigone, 50–1
Antigonus of Carystus, 225n
Antiochus of Ascalon, 249, 254 and n
Antisthenes, 22–3
Aphrodite, 17, 48, 64, 67n, 69, 191
Apollo, 14, 34, 45–6, 91, 255, 258
Apollodorus, 15, 21, 25, 28, 30
Apuleius of Madauros, 262 and n, 263, 279 and n, 283 and n, 284, 286n, 294n
Aquinas, Thomas, 118n
Aratus, 209n
Arcesilaus, 246
Archimedes, 267n
Ares, 14–5, 26–7, 32–3, 64, 191
Arges, 21
Aristarchus, 208n
Aristo of Chio, 246
Aristodemus, 101, 104–5
Aristophanes, 49n, 73, 87n
Aristotle, 6, 9, 56, 58, 59n, 62, 65, 68, 70, 71 and n, 74 and n, 75–7, 92, 93–121, 122–9, 132, 137, 144–6, 150, 158, 164, 169, 172, 176, 178–9, 183, 193n, 196 and n, 198, 200–1, 202n, 207 and n, 216n, 228–9, 230n, 238, 250, 261, 267n, 270, 281, 289, 295–6, 299–300, 301n, 303–4 and n, 305, 310, 316, 322 and n
Aristotle (pseudo–), 294 and n
Aristoxenus, 71
Arius Dydimus, 211n
Arnobius of Sicca, 131n, 242, 243–4 and n
Arrian, 186n, 204–5n, 209n, 213n
Arrighetti, G., 130–1n
Artemis, 24
Asclepiades of Bithynia, 300, 304
Asso, P., 212n
Ast, F., 79n
Athamas, 31
Athena, 1, 17, 27–8, 33, 40, 45–6
Athenagoras, 175n

Atherton, C., 2, 22n
Atticus, 250 and n, 261
Aubenque, P., 95–6 and n, 109 and n, 119 and n
Augustine, 176, 219, 248–9, 271, 273–4 and n, 286n, 292n, *312–19*
Aujac, G., 208n
Aumont, J., 190n
Aurenty, I., 21n
Auroux, S., 64n, 79n, 104n, 107n, 229n, 237n
Axelos, K., 45n

Babut, D., 88n, 184n, 255n, 259n, 282n, 296–7n
Bacchus *see* Dionysos
Bacci, M., 65n
Bachofen, J. J., 46n, 49n
Baer, R. A., 272n
Bailey, C., 57n, 131–2n, 143–6n, 148 and n, 150 and n, 151n, 153–4n, 160n
Balbus, 194 and n, 195, 201, 207, 211, 213, 241n, 242
Ballabriga, A., 28n
Balme, D. M., 109n
Barchiesi, A., 166n
Bardaisan (Ibn Daisan), 272
Barnes, J., 246n
Barra, G., 271n
Barth, P., 216n
Basilius, 190n
Battegazzore, A. M., 44n
Beagon, M., 165–6 and n., 167
Beagon, P., 196n, 199n
Beaujou, J., 262, 263 and n, 279n, 283n
Beazley, J. D., 68n
Béchec, C., 279n
Bees, R., 251n
Bellerophon, 280
Belletti, B., 252n
Benveniste, E., 37, 38 and n
Beretta, M., 131n
Bernhardt, J., 87n, 89n
Berryman, S., 73n
Berti, E., 102n
Berve, H., 39n
Besnier, B., 194n, 241n, 251n, 291n
Bett, R. A., 227n
Betz, H. D., 104n
Bianchi, E., 10n, 197n
Bianchi, O., 21n, 299n
Bignone, E., 139 and n
Blok, J. H., 46n, 47 and n
Boas, G., 140–1n
Bobzien, S., 219n
Bockmuehl, M., 292n
Bollack, J., 8n, 63–5n, 67–8 and n, 72n, 85n, 131n, 134n, 153 and n, 193n
Bolus of Mendes, 200
Bomford, D. 65n
Bonhöffer, A., 181n, 204n
Bonitz, H., 107n, 236n
Boot, P., 309
Boreas, 85
Bos, A. P., 184n, 293–4n

Boss, G., 322–3
Bossina, L., 12n, 181n
Bottici, C., 8n
Bouche–Leclercq, A., 217n
Boulogne, J., 299
Bouton–Touboulic, A.–I., 275n, 316n
Boyancé, P., 131n, 154n, 160 and n
Brehier, É., 239n, 266–8n, 280n, 292n, 310n
Briareus, 33, 34 and n, 162
Brinker, W., 81n
Brisson, L., 263n, 268n, 272n
Brochard, V., 85n, 228n, 231n
Brontes, 21, 24
Brown, A. L., 22n, 42n
Brown, C. G., 22
Brunschwig, J., 12n, 16n, 217n
Buffière, F., 9n, 11–2n, 22n, 33n, 63–4n, 85n, 253n, 279n, 282n
Burkert, W., 31n
Burnyeat, M., 228n
Bury, R. G., 229n, 247n

Caesar, 209n, 221
Cairn, D., 87n
Calabi, F., 253n
Calame, C., 20–1n
Callimachus, 24
Campbell, G. L., 131n, 141 and n, 142n, 144–6n
Campenhausen, H. F., 181n
Canfora, L., 181n
Canguilhem, G., 114n
Capelle, W., 126n
Caratelli, G. P., 139n, 155n
Carneades, 223–4, 236–8, 245–7
Casali, S., 212n
Casini, P., 140n, 144 and n, 146n, 161n
Cassandra, 51
Cassin, B., 44n, 228n, 230n
Castelletti, C., 272n
Cato the Elder, 223
Caye, P., 64n, 183n
Céard, J., 7
Cecrops, 260
Celsus, 271
Censorinus, 130
Cerberus, 83, 238n
Chadwick, H., 273n
Chalcidius, 26 and n
Chantraine, P., 15n, 68n, 87 and n, 112n, 279n
Chaos, 15, 263
Chardin, T. de, 67 and n
Charles, D., 102n
Charlton, W., 97 and n, 120n
Charon, 238n
Chase Green, H., 2, 217n
Cherniss, H., 82–3n, 115–6 and n, 118n, 280n
Chevallier, R., 174n
Chiesara, M. L., 240n, 245n
Christ *see* Jesus of Nazareth
Chronos, 17–9, 28–9, 33, 37, 41, 89–90
Chroust, A. H., 153n, 182n, 217n

INDEX NOMINUM

Chrysippus, 170, 172–3, 179, 181, 188–9, 193, 194n, 195 and n, 206n, 207–8, 211, 215–16, 237n, 241, 288, 320n
Ciccarese, M. P., 285n
Cicero, 15, 58, 126, 127 and n, 136, 139, 149n, 159, 194n, 195 and n, 207n, 209, 210–11 and n, 220–1 and n, 223n, 234–5 and n, 237–8 and n, 240 and n, 244–5, 246n, 247 and n, 254n, 274, 317 and n, 318
Cilento, V., 287n
Circe, 162
Citroni, M., 164 and n
Citti, F., 131n
Clair, J., 15n, 17n
Clare, R. J., 22n
Cleanthes, 170, 183, 208 and n, 211, 216, 238
Clement of Alexandria, 62 and n, 72n, 186–7n, 208n, 213n, 264 and n, 285 and n, 307 and n
Clitomachus, 247n
Clytemnestra, 46–7, 51–3
Codino, F., 12n
Colish, M., 192n, 210n
Colli, G., 34n
Collobert, C., 85n, 87n
Columella, 146
Conche, M., 228n, 231n, 239n
Cornford, F. M., 8–9n, 19n, 63n, 99n, 266n
Cornutus, 33–4
Costa, C. D. N., 144 and n, 146n, 159n
Cotter, W., 3, 217n
Cottus see Kottos
Courcelle, P., 81n, 253n
Courtès, J.-M., 148n, 157n
Cratinus, 39
Credaro, L., 245–6n
Creon, 50–1
Crepaldi, M. G., 291n
Critolaus, 223
Cronos see Kronos
Ctesias, 197 and n
Cuny-Le Callet, B., 2, 67n
Cupid, 263
Curd, P., 57n
Curi, U., 88 and n
Cypris, 67n

D'Agostino, F., 38n
Daiber, H., 124n
Dal Pra, M., 226 and n, 235–6n, 239n, 245n, 246n
Danaus, 48
Dante Alighieri, 73n
Daremberg, C., 104n, 279n, 301n, 303–4n
Darwin, C., 10, 75n, 97n, 111n, 141n, 146
Dasen, V., 198n
Daston, L., 96n, 154n
De Capitani, F., 270n, 271n, 288n
De Lacy, P., 131n, 148n, 155 and n, 157–8 and n, 303n
De Ley, H., 75 and n

Decharneaux, B., 292n
Decleva Caizzi, F., 44n, 226n, 229n, 231n, 236 and n
Deforge, B., 21n
Del Lucchese, F., 174n
Delcourt, M., 47n, 53n
Deleuze, G., 230n
Delphyne, 31
Delumeau, J., 22n
Democritus, 6, 10, 56, 63, 70–7, 78, 91, 93, 98, 104, 105n, 106, 108, 110, 112–16, 127–8, 130–1, 135–6, 226–7, 234, 245, 250
Deremetz, A., 146n, 162 and n
Descartes, R., 7, 174n
Desclos, M.-L., 125–6n
Destrée, P., 85n, 87n
Detienne, M., 8n, 12n
Devereux, D., 95n
DeWitt, N. W., 135n
Di Benedetto, V., 39n, 42–3n
Di Berardino, A., 104n
Diagoras of Melos, 250, 299
Diels, H., 128n
Dijck, J. G. M. van, 8n
Diller, H., 12n
Dillon, J. M., 252n, 254n, 258n, 261–2n, 271n, 281n, 282–4n, 293n, 300n
Diodorus Cronos, 247 and n
Diodorus Siculus, 161n, 298
Diogenes Laertius, 59, 130, 173, 184 and n, 206, 224n, 225, 229 and n
Diogenes of Apollonia, 288
Diogenes of Babylon, 223
Diogenianus, 219
Dionysius of Alexandria, 211n
Dionysus, 13, 33, 34 and n, 37, 50, 255, 284
Dodds, E. R., 34n, 42n, 81n, 84n
Dörrie, H., 250n
Donini, P., 259n, 297n, 299n
Drachmann, A. B., 73n
Dragona-Monachou, M., 194n, 206n, 210n, 261–2n, 293n, 310n
Droz-Vincent, G., 154n, 160 and n
DuBois, P., 46n
Dudley, J., 114 and n, 120n
Duhot, J.-J., 184n
Dumézil, G., 49n
Dumont, J. P., 230n, 238n, 240n
Duncan, A. R. C., 181n, 206n
Dupont, F., 206n
Durry, M., 190n, 211n

Earth see Gaia
Echion, 27
Edelstein, L., 206
Edmonds III, R. G., 85n, 87n
Empedocles, 6, 10, 12–4, 25, 56–7, 59, 63–70, 71, 73, 75, 77, 90–1, 93, 96, 97n, 98, 104, 105n, 108–10, 112–13, 115 and n, 116–17, 118 and n, 131 and n, 141, 144–5, 146n, 151–2, 154, 166–8, 171, 175, 186, 258, 290, 298

Empousa, 41n
England, E. B., 80n, 82n
Epictetus, 186 and n, 191, 204 and n, 209 and n, 210n, 213 and n, 220n
Epicurus, 73, 93, 130–9, 156, 168–70, 180, 207 and n, 233, 250–1, 299, 300, 304
Epimetheus, 53
Erechtheus *see* Erichthonius
Erichthonius, 1, 40
Erichto, 190
Erler, M., 251n
Ernout, A., 153–4n, 156–7n, 161n
Eros, 263
Eteocles, 32–3, 36
Eudorus of Alexandria, 254
Euripides, 12n, 17, 22–3, 27, 45, 49–52, 263 and n, 267n, 280 and n
Europa, 26
Eusebius of Caesarea, 211n, 226 and n, 271 and n
Eusthatius, 14
Eve, 252–3, 285
Ewing, J., 206n, 293n

Fahlbusch, E. 104n
Fahr, W., 73n
Fantuzzi, M., 162n
Farquharson, A. S. L., 182n, 187n, 213n
Farrar, C., 71n
Ferguson, J., 71n
Festa, N., 27n, 46n, 151n
Festugière, A. J., 3, 35 and n, 74n, 79–82n, 184n, 194n, 200 and n, 288n, 293n, 306n
Filliozat, J., 197n
Finazzo, G., 17n
Finley, M. I., 8, 21n
Firmus, 298
Fletcher, R., 263n
Flores, E., 144 and n, 153n, 156n
Flückiger, H., 228n, 230n, 240n
Fontanier, J.-M., 68n
Fortenbaugh, W. W., 124–6n
Foucault, M., 2
Fowler, D., 141n
Fränkel, H., 8
Fraser, P. M., 250n
Frede, G., 79n
Frick, P., 293n
Fritz, K. von, 236n
Froidefond, C., 259n
Frontisi-Ducroux, F., 15n, 17n, 43n, 47n
Frutiger, P., 85n
Fuhrmann, F., 299n
Furley, D., 58n

Gagarin, M., 38n, 43n
Gaia, 16–20, 28–9, 37, 39–41, 43, 54, 263
Galatea, 23
Galaxidorus, 282
Gale, M., 131n
Galen, 139, 184n, 185 and n, 189, 202 and n, 206n, 226 and n, 227, 229 and n, 249, 261, 299–305, 310, 317

Gallo, I., 297n
Gantz, T., 11, 83n, 263n, 279n
Garland, R., 22n, 53n, 197n
Gastaldi, S., 86n
Gatzemeier, M., 126n, 128
Gaukroger, S., 228n
Gellius, 216
Gello, 41n
Gemelli Marciano, M. L., 65n
Gersh, S., 262n
Gerson, L. P., 224n
Geryon, 260
Giannantoni, G., 145n, 225n, 239n
Giannini, A., 9n, 85n, 200n, 217n
Gibson, R. K., 196n
Gigandet, A., 147–8 and n, 149–50n, 152n
Gigante, M., 35n, 40n, 145n, 226n, 236n
Gigon, O., 8n, 234n
Gilson, E., 97n, 117 and n, 271n
Ginzburg, C., 8n, 85n
Girard, R., 67n
Girardet, K. M., 292n
Glaucon, 83
Glaucus, 16
Glenn, J., 21n
Goerler, W., 234n
Goldschmidt, V., 211n
Gomperz, T., 102
Gonzalez, F. J., 85n, 87n
Gorgo, 17
Goslin, O., 29n
Gotthelf, A., 96 and n, 103 and n, 109n, 115 and n
Goulet, R., 71n, 259n, 283–4n, 300n
Gourinat, J.-B., 123n
Grandgeorge, L., 313n
Grant, R. M., 138n, 151n, 153–4n, 176, 177n, 181n, 202n, 211n, 219–20n
Grimal, P., 83n, 263n, 279n
Gründer, K., 64n, 79n, 104n, 107n, 237n
Guadalupe Masi, F., 130n
Guidorizzi, G., 15n, 31n
Gummere, R. M., 174n
Gutas, D., 124n
Guthrie, W. K. C., 12n, 21n, 26n, 34n, 68n, 140n, 146n, 299n
Guyot, H., 266n

Hadas–Lebel, M., 251–3n, 293n
Hades, 15, 21, 28, 279
Hager, F. P., 82n
Hahm, D. E., 171n
Hani, J., 282n, 295n
Hankinson, R. J., 202n, 239n, 246n, 302–5n
Happ, H., 114n
Hardie, P., 146n, 162n, 165n
Harmonia, 27
Hartmann, N., 103n
Hartog, F., 9 and n, 197n
Havrda, M., 264n
Hawes, G., 11, 151n
Healy, J. F., 196n
Hecataeus of Abdera, 234n

INDEX NOMINUM

Hecataeus of Miletus, 9
Hecate, 52
Hecuba, 49, 52
Hegel, G. W. F., 102 and n
Heidegger, M., 46n, 50, 51n, 87n
Hellanikos of Lesbos, 9
Helle, 31
Henne, P., 265n
Hephaestus, 21, 24, 30, 40, 53 and n, 54
Hera, 28–9, 33, 37, 63
Heracles, 14–5, 25, 38, 46, 140n, 204
Heraclitus allegorista, 14, 22, 33–4
Heraclitus philosophus, 36, 43, 45n, 80, 95–6, 170, 193, 196n, 294, 303n
Herescu, N. I., 165n
Hermes, 31–3, 257–8
Hermodorus, 281n
Herodotus, 9–10, 87, 197n
Hershbell, J. P., 12 and n, 63n, 184n, 259n
Hesiod, 9, 11, 12 and n, 13, 15–6, 18, 21, 28, 37–8, 84, 165, 247n, 263n, 279 and n
Hesione, 140n
Heubeck, A., 42n
Hicks, R. D., 229n
Hijmans, B. L., 213n, 283n
Hild, J. A., 279n
Hippocrates, 65, 300
Hippolytus, 59n, 263
Hippomedon, 32–3
Hirschmann, W., 183n
Homer, 8, 11, 12 and n, 14, 16, 21–2, 37, 63, 72, 84, 87, 165, 208n, 213n, 247n, 279 and n
Horace, 161, 163–4, 165, 169
Hornblower, S., 263n
Horus, 257–8
Hyginus, 15, 28, 30, 263n
Hyperbius, 32–3
Hypermnestra, 48
Hypsipyle, 49

Ibrahim, A., 96n
Icard–Gianolio, N., 65n
Ierodiakonou, K., 209n
Immerwahr, H. R., 197n
Invernizzi, G., 262n
Inwood, B., 64–5n, 69n
Ioppolo, A. M., 219n
Iphigenia, 51
Isaac, D., 322, 323n
Isis, 257–9
Isnardi–Parente, M., 172, 173n, 180n, 184n, 195n, 207n

Jackson, S., 49n
Jacob, C., 11n
Jaeger, W., 3, 8–9n, 36n, 63n, 85n, 250–1n
Jagu, A., 204n
James, A. W., 208–9n
Janet, P., 146n
Janka, M., 85n
Janko, R., 14n
Janoušek, J., 263n

Japetus, 25, 38
Jason, 52
Jaulin, A., 96n, 123n
Jellamo, A., 16n, 18n
Jerome, 138
Jesus of Nazareth, 244, 286
John Chrysostom, 178n
Johnson, M. R., 74n, 75 and n, 96n, 102–3 and n, 109n, 120 and n
Johnson, W. R., 2, 175n, 190n, 220n
Jones, H., 2, 141n
Jones, J. W., 38n
Josephus, 59n
Jouan, F., 17n, 21n
Jove see Zeus
Judson, L., 102n
Junge, M., 42n
Jupiter see Zeus
Justin Martyr, 249, 306
Juvenal, 220 and n

Kadmos, 26–7, 64n
Kalligas, P., 267n, 269n, 287n, 311n
Kant, I., 102n, 103
Kapaneus, 25
Kekrops, 27
Ker, 14, 279
Keto, 17
Kidd, D., 209n
Kidd, I. G., 206
Kirk, G. S., 35n, 90n
Klowski, J., 71n
Klymene, 38
Koenen, M. H., 161n
König, J., 65n
Koester, G., 153n, 207n, 289n
Koios, 25
Kottos, 20, 34n
Krafft, F., 12n
Kranz, W., 141n
Krappe, A. H., 42n
Krings, H., 12n
Krios, 25
Kronos, 26, 285–6
Kucharski, P., 59 and n
Küster, E., 41 and n
Kyknos, 14

Lachenaud, G., 9n
Lacoste, J.-Y., 104n
Lactantius, 125, 131n, 139, 177, 178 and n, 188 and n, 189n, 192 and n, 202–3 and n, 213–5 and n, 317
Lämmli, F., 8n, 68 and n
Laks, A., 122, 123 and n, 128
Lalande, A., 64n, 79n, 104n, 107n, 172n, 237n
Lamia, 41n
Lampe, G. W. H., 172n
Lampon, 60, 297
Lamprias, 297–8
Lange, F. A., 101 and n, 102
Lanza, D., 95n

Laurent, J., 266n, 269n, 311n
Le Bonniec, H., 190n
Le Boulluec, A., 251n
Lefebvre, D., 123n
Leibniz, G. W., 147
Lennox, J. G., 109n, 115n, 122n
Leone, G., 136n
Lerner, M.-P., 111n
Leszl, W., 83n
Leto, 24
Leucippus, 71 and n, 72, 104, 132, 135, 250
Leviathan, 285
Lévy, C., 154n, 160n, 194n, 224n, 234n, 241n, 251n, 291n
Ley, H., 239n
Lilla, S. R. C., 264n
Lloyd, A. C., 322-3 and n
Lloyd, G. E. R., 12n, 16n, 96 and n, 112n, 217n
Lloyd-Jones, H., 35n, 44n
Lo Schiavo, A., 19n
Long, A. A., 142n, 231n
Longo, O., 95n
López Ferez, J. A., 21n
Loraux, N., 27n, 40n, 49n
Louis, P., 2, 84n, 118n, 119
Lovejoy, A. O., 81n, 140-1n
Lucan, 157, 179, 190 and n, 191, 199, 209n, 211-2 and n, 213, 219
Lucian, 139, 239
Lucretius, 61-2, 65n, 67n, 70n 73, 130-61, 162-70, 175, 214, 290, 301n
Lur'e, S. E., 72n
Lynceus, 48

Macarius Magnes, 271n
McClure, L., 46n
McGinty, P., 34n
Magris, A., 3, 43n, 217n, 280n, 288n, 289 and n, 310n
Mani, 273n
Manilius, 159, 171n, 191-2, 209 and n, 222, 233n
Mansfeld, J., 124 and n
Marcus Aurelius, 182 and n, 187 and n, 203, 204 and n, 210 and n, 213n
Marignac, A. de, 84n
Marrou, H. I., 313n
Mars see Ares
Martens, J. W., 153n, 250n, 290n, 292n
Martin, R., 49n
Martina, A., 210n
Martinazzoli, F., 217n
Marx, K., 71n, 135-6n, 139n
Marzillo, P., 54n
Marzot, G., 174n
Maso, S., 130n
Mason, A. S., 209n
Matteoli, S., 179n
Maximus of Tyrus, 126, 249, 250 and n, 259, 260 and n, 284 and n
Mayer, C. P., 275n

Mayor, A., 46n, 140n
Mazon, P., 40n, 44n, 48n
Mazzanti, A. M., 281n
Mazzarelli, C., 254n
Mazzocchini, P., 20n
Medea, 47-8, 51-3, 241
Medusa, 1, 15, 17, 46
Megaera, 41
Megasthenes, 197 and n, 296 and n
Mehring, F., 71n
Meijer, P. A., 266n
Meliae, 17
Melissus, 63
Menander, 184n
Mesch, W., 89n
Mesnard, P., 160n
Methodius of Olympus, 286 and n
Metis, 19
Metrodorus of Chios, 77, 227
Midas, 200
Milton, J. R., 154n
Minerva see Athena
Minos, 290
Minucius Felix, 154n, 177 and n, 188n, 201 and n
Momigliano, A., 12n, 210n
Monaci Castagno, A., 307-8n
Mondi, R., 21n
Mondolfo, R., 12n, 77n, 137n
Monfrinotti, M., 265n, 285n, 307n
Monica of Hippo, 312
Monteil, P., 192 and n
Moraux, P., 261n, 293n, 296n, 300n, 302n, 304n
Moreau, A., 16 and n, 17n, 24-5n, 30n, 32n, 35n, 39n, 42n, 44-6n, 49n, 85n
Moreau, J., 130n, 137n, 150n, 153 and n, 159n
Morel, P.-M., 74n, 130n
Morello, R., 196n
Moreno, P., 17n, 25, 26 and n
Moreschini, C., 176n, 179n, 181n, 201n, 207n, 243n, 263n, 286n, 293n, 308n
Morfino, V., 2, 146, 153n
Morgan, K. A., 8-9n, 21n, 46n, 85n, 87n
Morgan, W. R., 2, 65n, 96n, 141n, 275n
Mormo, 41n
Moses, 253, 260, 291, 201
Moses, A., 290n
Mossé, C., 39n
Most, G., 122, 123 and n, 128
Müller, J., 80n
Mugler, C., 12n, 63n
Mund-Dopchie, M., 197n
Muñoz Valle, I., 12n
Munro, J., 138n, 144 and n, 151 and n, 153n
Munson, R. V., 197n
Myers, K. S., 165 and n
Myre, A., 292n
Myrsilys of Methymna, 49n

Naas, V., 196n
Naddaf, G., 3

Narducci, E., 211n, 212 and n
Neilos, 238
Nelis, D., 165, 166n, 167 and n
Neptune *see* Poseidon
Nestis, 63
Nestle, W., 8n, 19n, 41n, 85n
Nieto, F., 197n
Nietzsche, F. W., 35 and n, 59n, 64n, 86, 87 and n, 181n
Night *see* Nyx
Nikiprowetzky, V., 292n
Nock, A. D., 306n
Numenius of Apamea, 249, 260–1 and n, 284 and n
Nutton, V., 304n
Nyx, 279

O'Brien, C. S., 79n
O'Brien, D., 66–7 and n, 71n
O'Brien, M. C., 263n
O'Flaherty, W. D., 272n
O'Meara, D., 267n, 277n
Odysseus, 21–3
Ogle, W., 111n
Opsomer, J., 322 and n
Orcus, 238n
Oreithyia, 85
Orestes, 34, 42, 44–5
Origen, 189–90n, 193n, 195n, 216, 249, 265 and n, 271n, 285 and n, 307–8 and n, 309
Oriol-Boyer, C., 83n
Orion, 304
Osiris, 257–8, 284
Otto, W. F., 34n
Ouranos, 17–8, 24, 37, 41
Ovid, 15 and n, 17, 23–4, 53, 159 and n, 161, 165–8

Pacchi, A., 114n
Paduano, G., 51n
Palaephatus, 9–10, 11 and n, 46, 85n, 151–2 and n, 165–6
Palaimonius, 40
Panaccio, C., 172n
Panaetius, 171n, 195, 219 and n
Pandora, 47, 53
Panofsky, E., 65n
Papanghelis, T., 162n
Paparazzo, E., 196n
Parmenides, 57, 63, 70
Pârvulescu, A., 279n
Pasiphae, 290
Patera, M., 41n
Paulson, J., 144n
Payón Leyra, I., 11n, 140n, 200n
Pegasus, 17
Pelagius, 178, 179 and n
Pelasgus, 48
Pellegrin, P., 95n, 126n, 127
Pelops, 45
Pentheus, 25, 27 and n, 49

Pépin, J., 8n, 85n, 287n
Pericles, 60, 63, 297
Perrin, M., 215n
Perseus, 17
Perutelli, A., 22n
Phaedra, 263
Pherekydes of Athens, 45
Pherecydes of Syros, 9
Phidias, 1
Philippart, H., 34n
Philo of Alexandria, 170, 185, 205, 216, 219n, 249, 250–3 and n, 260, 264, 266, 272n, 280–1 and n, 285, 289–93 and n, 294, 301, 307
Philodemus, 157n
Philoponos, 105n, 320
Philoxenus of Cythera, 23
Phineus, 41
Phlegon of Tralles, 140n, 272n
Phoebus, 45
Phorcys, 17
Phytocles, 138
Piazzi, L., 131n
Pichon, R., 203n, 243n
Pichot, A., 301n, 305n
Piero di Cosimo, 65n
Pierris, A. L., 65n
Pievani, T., 141n
Pigeaud, J., 69 and n, 70, 145–6 and n, 152n
Pindar, 25, 30n
Pinotti, P., 95n
Places, E. des, 79n
Plato, 6, 43, 56, 58, 59n, 60, 71–3, 75, 77, 78–92, 93, 96–7, 100–1, 108–9, 123–9, 137, 141, 159, 163, 171 and n, 172, 182–3, 206, 211, 228, 232–3, 238, 241, 246, 249, 251 and n, 253n, 254 and n, 256, 260–1, 263 and n, 264n, 267, 269, 276, 279–80 and n, 281, 283–5, 288, 289 and n, 291, 294–5, 297 and n, 298, 300n, 303 and n, 304, 310n
Platt, W., 165n
Platz–Horster, G., 68n
Pliny, 22n, 196–200, 274, 296n, 314
Plotinus, 139, 206n, 250, 266–71 and n, 272, 276, 281n, 287, 309–11 and n, 312, 318, 320 and n, 323
Plutarch, 60, 126, 137, 139, 184, 254, 255–8 and n, 260–2, 280–1, 282–3 and n, 287, 294–8 and n, 299, 301, 311, 320
Pohlenz, M., 12 and n, 13n, 31n, 34–5n, 40n, 42n, 43 and n, 49n, 50 and n, 52 and n, 53n, 170n, 172–3n, 175–6n, 181n, 184–5 and n, 187n, 190n, 192n, 193 and n, 195n
Poignault, R., 174n
Polito, R., 228–9n
Pollman, K., 319n
Polybius, 11
Polycletus, 305
Polydorus, 49, 162
Polykritos, 272
Polymestor, 49

Polyphemus, 21–3
Polystratus the Epicurean, 157
Pompeius, Gnaeus, 190
Pompeius, Sextus, 190
Porphyry of Tyre, 217–2 and n, 287 and n, 311
Porter, J. J., 89n
Poseidon, 17, 21–2, 27, 33–4, 238
Posidonius, 165, 175, 184, 189 and n, 191, 194n, 196n, 206 and n
Preus, A., 66n, 102 and n, 108 and n, 116n, 120 and n
Proclus, 18, 275–6 and n, 284, 319–24
Prometheus, 19n, 35, 38–40, 41 and n, 53
Protagoras, 63
Protarchus, 108–9
Psyche, 263
Puiggali, J., 260n, 284n
Pyrrho of Elis, 224–5, 226n, 227, 229 and n, 230–1, 235–6, 239 and n, 246
Pythagoras, 159, 166, 168, 242
Python, 167–8

Quarantotto, D., 103n

Raalte, M. van, 123 and n
Radice, R., 192n, 209n
Ramelli, I., 306n
Raven, J. E., 90n
Reale, G., 8 and n, 9, 73n, 139n, 172n, 174n, 184–5n, 207n, 210n, 225n, 239n, 267n, 293–4n
Reesor, M. E., 217n
Reeve, C. D. C., 59n
Reich, K., 154n
Reid, J. D., 83n
Reinhardt, K., 39 and n, 42–3n, 45–6 and n, 51n, 85n
Renehan, R., 38n, 201n, 208n
Repici, L., 122 and n, 127, 128 and n
Reydams-Schils, G. J., 79n, 171n
Rhea, 258
Rieth, O., 210n
Rist, J. M., 171n, 185 and n, 189n, 217n, 266n, 269n, 271n
Ritter, J., 64n, 79n, 104n, 107n, 237n
Robin, L., 71n, 141n, 150 and n, 154n, 156–7 and n, 161n, 225n, 227n, 234n, 238n, 241n, 245–6n
Rodier, G., 126 and n, 127–8
Rössler, W., 12n
Roger, J., 7
Rohde, E., 34n, 42n, 279n
Romano, F., 72n, 226n
Romm, J. S., 10n
Rosati, G., 168 and n
Roscher, W. H., 83n, 263n, 279n
Rosen, R. R., 218n
Rosen, S., 86n, 89n
Ross, D. O. jr., 146n
Rouse, W. H. D., 138n, 144n, 153–4n, 156n
Runia, D. T., 252n, 293n
Russo, C. F., 14n

Saglio, E., 104n, 279n
Salem, J., 71–2n, 74 and n, 75–6n, 157 and n
Salemme, C., 192n
Sambursky, S., 82n, 185 and n, 186, 195n, 206n, 217n, 219n
Sancassano, M. L., 41n
Santoni, A., 11n
Sappho, 263 and n
Satan, 187–8, 285
Scaltsas, T., 209n
Scarpat, G., 290n
Scarpi, P., 306n
Schadewaldt, W., 67n
Schäfer, C., 79–81n, 85n, 89n
Schatkin, M. A., 178n
Schmitt, C., 46n
Schönberger, R., 89n
Schofield, M., 217n
Scholl, A., 68n
Schotes, H. A., 212n
Schrijvers, P. H., 140n, 145 and n, 151 and n, 152, 161n
Schröder, E., 267n
Schuhl, P. M., 63n, 85n, 90n
Scott, W., 285, 306n
Scylla *see* Skylla
Sebastokrator, 320, 323n
Sedlar, J. W., 197n
Sedley, D., 65n, 131n, 180n
Seel, G., 322–3n
Seippel, G., 28n
Seneca, 174, 183, 186 and n, 206n, 208, 210n, 218 and n, 220 and n
Senecio, 298
Şerban, G., 190n
Serres, M., 147 and n
Settis, S., 8n, 85n, 263n
Severino, E., 38n
Sextus Empiricus, 173, 224, 225n, 228n, 229–35 and n, 236–7n, 238–40 and n, 246–7n
Shapiro, A. H., 279n
Shiva, 272
Sier, K., 208n
Silenus, 23, 162, 200
Sillitti, G., 112n
Simon, H., 171n, 211n
Simon, M., 171n
Simplicius, 57, 61–2, 102n, 118n, 139 and n, 144n, 225 and n
Siron, 162
Skylla, 51–2, 83, 177
Sluiter, I., 89n, 218n
Smith, M. F., 144n, 153–4n, 156n
Socrates, 53, 56, 58, 60, 71, 78, 80–1, 83–7, 101, 104–5, 108–9, 123, 172, 211, 242, 282, 303n, 310n
Solignac, A., 318n
Solin, 197n, 233n
Solmsen, F., 15n, 18n, 20n, 39–40n, 44n, 53n, 79n, 100n, 101n, 207n, 279n
Solomon, 265

INDEX NOMINUM

Sommerstein, A. H., 32n
Sophocles, 12, 27
Sorabji, R., 218 and n, 320n, 322 and n
Soury, G., 259n, 282n
Spanneut, M., 179n, 181–3n
Spaworth, A., 263n
Spitzer, L., 64n, 183n, 292n, 311n
Spoerri, W., 130–1n, 141n, 144n, 146n, 161n
Stahl, W. H., 196n
Stanford, W. B., 37n
Steel, C., 322 and n
Steen Due, O., 211–2n
Steidle, W., 164 and n
Steinmetz, P., 208n
Stern, J., 11n
Steropes, 21
Stesichoros, 14
Stobaeus, 172n, 181n, 208n, 272 and n
Stokes, M. C., 12n
Stolleis, M., 96n, 154n
Stough, C. L., 227n, 229n, 230n, 231 and n
Strabo, 11
Strato of Lampsacus, 93, 121, *125–8*, 129, 245, 250
Strauss Clay, J., 13 and n, 18n
Striker, G., 228n
Sturz, F. W., 104n
Szabados, A.-V., 65n

Talos, 304
Tannery, P., 15n, 57n
Tartarus, 28–9
Tatian, 187n
Taylor, C. C. W., 76n, 78–81n, 108 and n, 226–7n
Temkin, O., 299n, 303n
Teopompus, 200
Tertullian, 176 and n, 187 and n, 188n, 207n
Theiler, W., 58n, 74n, 250n
Themis, 41
Themistius, 144n
Theocritus, 23
Theon, 298
Theophrastus of Eresos, 93, *121–5*, 128–9
Thersites, 304, 310
Theseus, 46
Thetis, 33–4
Thévenez, O., 21n, 299n
Thoas, 48
Thomas, R., 9–10n
Thomson, G. D., 46n
Thrasymacus, 83
Thucydides, 60
Timon of Phlius, 230n, 231, 235–6
Tiresias, 246
Tisiphone, 41
Tityos, 173
Tobin T. H., 292n
Tocanne, B., 7
Todd, R. B., 171n
Torraca, L., 128 and n

Touchefeu–Meynier, O., 30, 257n
Toutain, J., 42n
Trelenberg, J., 318n
Tremoli, P., 209n
Trousson, R., 41n
Tsagdis, G., 87n
Typhoeus, 25, 27, *29–33*, 39, 64n, 168, 257 and n, 258–9, 282, 284, 324
Typhon *see* Typhoeus.

Ueding, G., 64n
Untersteiner, M., 9n, 12 and n, 19n, 31n, 34–6n, 39n, 43n, 44 and n, 48n, 85n, 88n, 263n, 279n
Usener, H., 131–2n, 135n, 138–9

Valero, J. B., 179n
Van den Berg, R. M., 18n
Vegetti, M., 86n
Velleius, 241
Venus *see* Aphrodite
Verde, F., 134n
Vernant, J.-P., 13n, 37 and n, 44n, 48n
Veyne, P., 8n
Vian, F., 15n, 24n, 27n, 31 and n
Vidal-Naquet, P., 13n, 37 and n, 44n, 48n
Vimercati, E., 249n
Virgil, 146n, 157, 161, *162–3*, 165, 169, 190n, 212
Vitruvius, 161, *164–5*, 166, 169
Vlastos, G., 57 and n, 61, 62 and n

Wacht, M., 144n, 155–6n, 192n
Warden, J. R., 12n, 59n, 70n, 80n
Waszink, J. H., 141n
Wehrli, F., 71n, 126n, 127–8
Weil, E., 185n
Weiss, H. F., 292n
Wellmann, M., 200
Wendland, P., 293n
West, M. L., 20n
Whistler, C., 65n
Whittaker, T., 270 and n, 278n, 287n, 310n
Wieland, W., 102–3n, 108n
Wiersma, W., 182n
Wiggins, D., 237n
Wilcox, A., 218n
Wilcox, J., 66n
William of Moerbeke, 320n, 323n
Wilson, C., 96, 154 and n
Winiarczyk, M., 73n
Winkler-Horaček, L., 69n, 279n
Winston, D., 252n
Wismann, H., 72n
Wiśniewski, B., 72n
Wolfson, H. A., 252n, 291 and n
Wolters, A. M., 266n
Woltjer, W., 131n, 161n

Xenocrates, 254 and n, 281, 283n
Xenophanes, 13, 193n

Xenophon, 101 and n, 104 and n, 105, 211 and n, 242, 267n, 288n
Xerxes, 26, 31–2

Yartz, F. J., 2

Zagdoun, M.-A., 183n
Zambon, M., 259n
Zeitlin, F. I., 46n, 263n
Zeller, E., 67 and n, 74n, 103n
Zeno of Citium, 170, 172, 176, 180, 204, 206n, 210–11, 242, 246
Zeno of Elea, 132n
Zerhoch, S., 42n
Zeus, 13, 17–8, 19 and n, 21–3, 28–33, 34–5 and n, 37–42, 50, 53–4, 63–4, 73, 89, 91, 208–9, 234, 238–9, 244, 257 and n, 259, 286, 297, 324
Zimmer, G., 68n
Zimmerman, C. E., 188n

EU representative:
Easy Access System Europe
Mustamäe tee 50, 10621 Tallinn, Estonia
Gpsr.requests@easproject.com

www.ingramcontent.com/pod-product-compliance
Lightning Source LLC
Chambersburg PA
CBHW052054300426
44117CB00013B/2115